THE GENDER OF REPARATIONS
Unsettling Sexual Hierarchies While Redressing Human Rights Violations

Reparations programs seeking to provide for victims of gross and systematic human rights violations are becoming an increasingly frequent feature of transitional and post-conflict processes. Given that women represent a very large proportion of the victims of these conflicts and the authoritarianism generating them, and that women arguably experience conflicts in a distinct manner, it makes sense to examine whether reparations programs can be designed to redress women more fairly and efficiently and seek to subvert gender hierarchies that often antecede the conflict.

Focusing on themes such as reparations for victims of sexual and reproductive violence, reparations for children and other family members, as well as gendered understandings of monetary, symbolic, and collective reparations, *The Gender of Reparations* gathers information about how past or existing reparations projects dealt with gender issues, identifies best practices to the extent possible, and articulates innovative approaches and guidelines to the integration of a gender perspective in the design and implementation of reparations for victims of human rights violations.

Ruth Rubio-Marín is a Chair in Comparative Public Law at the European University Institute in Florence, Italy, and holds a tenured position in constitutional law at the Law School of Seville. She is author and editor of several books, including *Immigration as a Democratic Challenge* (Cambridge University Press, 2000), *The Gender of Constitutional Jurisprudence* (Cambridge University Press, 2004), and *What Happened to the Women? Gender and Reparations for Human Rights Violations* (2006).

The Gender of Reparations

UNSETTLING SEXUAL HIERARCHIES WHILE
REDRESSING HUMAN RIGHTS VIOLATIONS

Edited by
RUTH RUBIO-MARÍN
International Center for Transitional Justice

CAMBRIDGE UNIVERSITY PRESS
Cambridge, New York, Melbourne, Madrid, Cape Town, Singapore, São Paulo, Delhi

Cambridge University Press
32 Avenue of the Americas, New York, NY 10013-2473, USA

www.cambridge.org
Information on this title: www.cambridge.org/9780521517928

© Cambridge University Press 2009

This publication is in copyright. Subject to statutory exception
and to the provisions of relevant collective licensing agreements,
no reproduction of any part may take place without the written
permission of Cambridge University Press.

Chapter 8, "Gender and Collective Reparations, in the Aftermath of Conflict and
Political Repression," was first published in *The Politics of Reconciliation in
Multicultural Societies*, Will Kymlicka and Bashir Bashir eds. (Oxford: Oxford
University Press, 2008). It is reprinted with the kind permission of Oxford University
Press.

First published 2009

Printed in the United States of America

A catalog record for this publication is available from the British Library.

Library of Congress Cataloging in Publication data

The gender of reparations : unsettling sexual hierarchies while redressing human rights
violations / edited by Ruth Rubio-Marín.
    p.   cm.
Includes bibliographical references and index.
ISBN 978-0-521-51792-8 (hardback)
1. Crimes against humanity.   2. Reparation (Criminal justice)   3. Women – Crimes
against.   4. Feminist jurisprudence.   I. Rubio-Marín, Ruth.   II. Title.
K5301.G46   2009
341.6′6–dc22   2009012408

ISBN   978-0-521-51792-8 hardback

Cambridge University Press has no responsibility for the persistence or
accuracy of URLs for external or third-party Internet Web sites referred to in
this publication and does not guarantee that any content on such Web sites is,
or will remain, accurate or appropriate. Information regarding prices, travel
timetables, and other factual information given in this work are correct at
the time of first printing, but Cambridge University Press does not guarantee
the accuracy of such information thereafter.

Contents

Acknowledgments	page vii
Contributors	ix
Photo Credits: "Gender, Memorialization, and Symbolic Reparations," in The Gender of Reparations	xiv
International Center for Transitional Justice (ICTJ)	xv

Introduction: A Gender and Reparations Taxonomy — 1
Ruth Rubio-Marín

1. **Gender and Violence in Focus: A Background for Gender Justice in Reparations** — 18
   Margaret Urban Walker

2. **The Gender of Reparations in Transitional Societies** — 63
   Ruth Rubio-Marín

3. **Reparation of Sexual and Reproductive Violence: Moving from Codification to Implementation** — 121
   Colleen Duggan and Ruth Jacobson

4. **Reparations as a Means for Recognizing and Addressing Crimes and Grave Rights Violations against Girls and Boys during Situations of Armed Conflict and under Authoritarian and Dictatorial Regimes** — 162
   Dyan Mazurana and Khristopher Carlson

5. **Repairing Family Members: Gross Human Rights Violations and Communities of Harm** — 215
   Ruth Rubio-Marín, Clara Sandoval, and Catalina Díaz

6	Tort Theory, Microfinance, and Gender Equality Convergent in Pecuniary Reparations *Anita Bernstein*	291
7	Gender, Memorialization, and Symbolic Reparations *Brandon Hamber and Ingrid Palmary*	324
8	Gender and Collective Reparations in the Aftermath of Conflict and Political Repression *Ruth Rubio-Marín*	381

Index   403

Acknowledgments

This project has been a longer venture than expected, and I have incurred many debts in the time it has consumed. First and foremost, I want to express my immense gratitude to the International Center for Transitional Justice (ICTJ) for hosting the project and lending it unconditional support. The institution is in general an incredibly stimulating place, with extremely able and hard-working professionals. The research unit, committed as it is to research that combines both normative and empirical inquiries, is a wonderfully stimulating setting for those of us coming from the academic world but aspiring to make a concrete contribution to some of the most urgent themes on the contemporary international agenda. Special thanks go to Juan Méndez and Paul van Zyl, president and vice-president of ICTJ, for their support and trust. My greatest thanks go to Pablo de Greiff, director of the research unit, for the time he has devoted to supervise the project and carefully read and discuss each of the chapters, always providing useful insight yet always allowing for autonomous decision making and judgment. Also within the research unit, I would like to express my gratitude to Roger Duthie, who has provided invaluable assistance, meticulously editing all of the chapters. The help of Lizzie Goodfriend and Debbie Sharnak with the organization of the meetings to discuss the work in progress as well as with the administration of the project deserves special recognition. Finally, I would like to thank ICTJ's Colombia team, and in particular Catalina Díaz and Andrea Bolaños for their help in organizing a conference in Bogotá to explore the findings of the research.

The Gender of Reparations is a book that explores a subject that had never before received specific and in-depth scholarly attention. Two elements have made it possible. First, the courage of the authors who decided to venture into this new domain, many of whom confessed to being challenged and motivated by the opportunity to explore new ground and by the wide set of expertise that writing each of these chapters required. Thanks to all of them for their courage and their patience throughout the endless rounds of revisions that this process of reciprocal learning and ongoing discussions has entailed. The book was also facilitated by the empirical research provided in a previous volume (*What Happened to the Women? Gender and Reparations for Human Rights Violations*, Ruth Rubio-Marín, ed. [New York: Social Science Research Council, 2006]). My gratitude to the authors who participated in it and to the many victims and civil society organizations for the interviews and the data provided for the elaboration of the country studies.

This project was supported by a grant from the International Development Research Centre (IDRC). Within it, I would like to thank Colleen Duggan for her great support and her enthusiastic engagement with the project.

I would like to dedicate my share of the contribution to this book to my husband, Pablo, for all the personal and professional support he has lent me during the years this project has lasted, including during some especially rough times. I owe my opening to the transitional justice field to him and will never be able to thank him enough for the personal enrichment that this expansion has brought about.

Contributors

Anita Bernstein is the Anita and Stuart Subotnick Professor of Law at Brooklyn Law School. She writes primarily on tort law and on feminist jurisprudence, legal ethics, products liability, and comparative law. She has taught at Michigan, Iowa (where she was the Mason Ladd Distinguished Visiting Professor of Law), Chicago-Kent, Fordham, Seton Hall, San Diego (at Oxford), Emory, and Cornell law schools. Prior to her academic career, she was law clerk to Chief Judge Jack B. Weinstein of the Eastern District of New York, and she practiced with Debevoise & Plimpton. She holds a BA from Queens College (City University of New York) and a JD from Yale Law School.

Khristopher Carlson is a Senior Researcher at the Feinstein International Center at Tufts University. He specializes in international human rights and humanitarian law, with an emphasis on youth and armed conflict. He is a graduate of the International Human Rights Law LLM program at the University of Essex, UK. Carlson has written a number of publications regarding the experiences of youth during situations of armed conflict, and he has worked as a consultant and advisor for various governments on projects regarding youth in conflict and post-conflict situations in Angola, Burundi, the Democratic Republic of Congo, northern Uganda, Southern Sudan, and Sierra Leone. Carlson's current research investigates forced-marriage practices of abducted girls and young women by armed groups and the resulting implications on the lives of the girls and their children as they reenter civilian life.

Catalina Díaz is a Colombian lawyer with an LLM from New York University, where she was the recipient of a Global Public Service Law Scholarship. Díaz currently coordinates the reparations team at the Bogotá Office of the International Center for Transitional Justice (ICTJ), leading comparative and participatory field research and ICTJ's contribution to legislative and policy initiatives at the national and local levels, aiming at guaranteeing victims' rights. She has been involved also as a researcher with the comparative research project "Transitional Justice from Below" at Queens University Belfast. Her work "Challenging Impunity from Below: The Contested Ownership of Transitional Justice in Colombia" was published in the edited book *Transitional Justice from Below: Grassroots Activism and the Struggle for Change* (Kieran McEvoy and Lorna McGregor, eds. [Oxford, UK: Hart Publishing, 2008]). At the Colombian Commission of Jurists (CCJ) in Bogotá, she led legislative advocacy efforts in connection with victims' rights and civil liberties issues in antiterrorism legislation. For the CCJ, she also conducted a consultative process for Colombian human rights NGOs on human rights conditions tied to US military aid and advised rural Afro-Colombian communities on humanitarian law matters. She has also worked as a law clerk at the Constitutional Court of Colombia. Since August 2007 she has taught legal theory at the Rosario University in Bogotá.

Colleen Duggan is a Senior Program Specialist at the International Development Research Centre (IDRC). She has a Masters in International Human Rights and Humanitarian Law from Essex University and holds a graduate degree in International Development and Economic Cooperation from the Université d'Ottawa. Currently with the Evaluation Unit, she has also worked with IDRC's Peace, Conflict and Development Program and with its Women's Rights and Citizenship Program. Prior to joining IDRC, she spent ten years with the United Nations, with the UN High Commissioner for Human Rights in Colombia, with UNDP's Bureau for Crisis Prevention and Recovery in New York, and in the field with the UNDP in El Salvador, Guatemala, Honduras, and Haiti. Her research interests include human rights, transitional justice and reconciliation processes, conflict analysis and preventive action, and peacebuilding evaluation. She has published a number of works on peacebuilding and gender and transitional justice, most recently "Reparations for Sexual and Reproductive Violence: Challenges and Prospects for Achieving Gender Justice in Guatemala and Peru" (with J. Guillerot and C. Paz) in *International Journal of Transitional Justice* (2008) and "Reparation of Sexual Violence and Democratic Transition: In Search of Gender Justice" (with A. Abushsharaf) in P. de Greiff, ed. *The Handbook of Reparations* (New York: Oxford University Press, 2005).

Brandon Hamber is the Director of INCORE (International Conflict Research Institute), an associate center of the United Nations University, based at the University of Ulster. Prior to moving to Northern Ireland in 2001, he coordinated the Transition and Reconciliation Unit at the Centre for the Study of Violence and Reconciliation in Johannesburg, South Africa. He is Chairperson of the Healing Through Remembering Initiative – a cross-community membership organization focusing on ways of dealing with the past relating to the conflict in and about Northern Ireland. He has written extensively on the South African Truth and Reconciliation Commission, the psychological implications of political violence, transitional justice, trauma, and reconciliation in various contexts. He has published some 40 book chapters and scientific journal articles, and he edited *Past Imperfect: Dealing with the Past in Northern Ireland and Societies in Transition*, which was published by INCORE/University of Ulster. His next book, *Transforming Transitional Societies: Truth, Reconciliation, and Mental Health*, is to be published by Springer in 2009. In addition to his work in South Africa and Northern Ireland, he has participated in peace, transitional justice, and reconciliation initiatives and projects in Liberia, Mozambique, the Basque Country, and Sierra Leone, among others.

Ruth Jacobson has worked on issues of conflict since the 1980s. From 1983 to 1986, she lived in the town of Lichinga, Mozambique, while working for the Ministry of Education. During this period, she worked principally with the state women's organization, the Organizacao das Mulheres Mocambicanos (OMM). Jacobson campaigned in the UK and Europe about the impact of apartheid on the Southern African region. She completed a Masters degree in Gender and Development at the Institute of Development Studies and pursued a PhD at the Department of Peace Studies at Bradford University, where her topic was the conceptualization and operationalization of women's citizenship in Southern Africa. In 1994, Jacobson carried out a gender audit of the postwar elections in Mozambique. After completing her PhD in 1996, she stayed on at the Department of Peace Studies as a Lecturer. She continued to teach, research, and write on war in Southern Africa but also started looking at conflicts closer to home, in Northern Ireland. She contributed a chapter on this topic to the volume she coedited with Susie Jacobs and Jen Marchbank in 2000, *States of Conflict: Gender, Violence and Resistance*. She left full-time academic work in 2002 but remains an Honorary Visiting Research Fellow at the Department of Peace Studies. She has continued to make field trips to "post-conflict" Mozambique, including interviewing former female combatants and evaluating the gender aspects of civilian weapons collections programs. In 2007, she carried out an evaluation of women's peacebuilding organizations in the South Caucasus.

Dyan Mazurana directs the Gender, Youth and Community Program of the Feinstein International Famine Center at Tufts University. Her areas of specialty include women's human rights, war-affected children, armed conflict, and peacekeeping. She is a primary author of *Women, Peace and Security: Study of the United Nations Secretary-General as Pursuant Security Council Resolution 1325* (New York: United Nations, 2002) and has published more than 40 scholarly and policy books and essays in numerous languages. She works with a variety of governments, UN agencies, and human rights and child protection organizations working to improve efforts to assist girls associated with fighting forces. Mazurana has written and developed training materials regarding gender, human rights, armed conflict, and post-conflict periods for civilian, police, and military peacekeepers involved in UN and NATO operations. In conjunction with international human rights groups, she wrote materials now widely used to assist in documenting human rights abuses against women and girls during conflict and post-conflict reconstruction periods. Her research focuses on the experiences of armed conflict on youth combatants and civilian populations and their efforts for justice and peace. She has worked in Afghanistan, the Balkans, and southern, west, and east Africa.

Ingrid Palmary is Coordinator of the Gender, Violence, and Displacement Initiative of the Forced Migration Studies Programme at the University of Witwatersrand. She has a PhD in psychology from Manchester Metropolitan University and an MA in research psychology from the University of Natal, Pietermaritzburg. She was previously a Senior Researcher at the Centre for the Study of Violence and Reconciliation. Her work has focused on gender-based violence in times of conflict and gender and transitional justice.

Ruth Rubio-Marín is Professor of Comparative Public Law at the European University Institute in Florence, Italy. She also holds a tenured position at the Law School of Seville, Spain, and is part of the Hauser Global Law School Program at New York University. She is author of *Immigration as a Democratic Challenge* (New York: Cambridge University Press, 2000); coeditor of *The Gender of Constitutional Jurisprudence* (New York: Cambridge University Press, 2004); and editor of *What Happened to the Women? Gender and Reparations for Human Rights Violations* (New York: Social Science Research Council, 2006), among others. She has taught at different North American academic institutions, including Princeton University and Columbia Law School, and she has worked as a consultant in antidiscrimination theory and policy for the European Commission. She has worked as a consultant for the International Center for Transitional Justice for several years, managing a research project on Gender and Reparations in societies undergoing transition to democracy and advising Morocco's Instance d'Equité et Reconciliation.

Clara Sandoval is a lecturer in the School of Law, Co-Director of the LLM in International Human Rights Law, and member of the Human Rights Centre at the University of Essex. She teaches and researches on areas related to transitional justice, the inter-American system of human rights, legal theory, and business and human rights. Her more recent scholarship has been focused on reparations for gross human rights violations. As part of such research, she was a visiting professional at the International Criminal Court and advised it on the award of reparations for gross human rights violations by regional human rights courts. Besides her academic commitments, she also engages in human rights litigation, training, and capacity building with organizations such as the IBA and REDRESS. She has been part of different IBA missions to assess the implementation and protection of human rights in the administration of justice in countries such as Venezuela and Colombia. Her latest mission was in 2007 to Colombia, where she was a part of the IBA-FCO team that assessed the implementation of the justice and peace law/demobilization and prosecution process in the country and the role played by international cooperation.

Margaret Urban Walker is Lincoln Professor of Ethics in the Philosophy Department at Arizona State University. Professor Walker's research and teaching fields include Anglo-American moral and political theory, feminist ethics, and restorative justice and reparations. Her latest book is *Moral Repair: Reconstructing Moral Relations after Wrongdoing* (New York: Cambridge University Press, 2006), which examines the ethics and moral psychology of responding to wrongdoing in ways that restore trust and hope, the basis of moral relations. Her current research explores the logic of reparations and the moral and political dimensions of truth-telling. Walker received her PhD in philosophy from Northwestern University in 1975 and was on the faculty of Fordham University from 1974 to 2002. She was named to the Cardinal Mercier Chair in Philosophy at the Catholic University of Leuven in 2001, was a Laurance S. Rockefeller Visiting Fellow at Princeton University's Center for Human Values in 2003, and received Arizona State University's Award for Defining Edge Research in the Humanities in 2007.

Photo Credits: "Gender, Memorialization, and Symbolic Reparations," in *The Gender of Reparations*

South Africa Women's Memorial, 1913
Photograph by Gerrit Penning

World War II Women's Memorial in London
Photograph by Louis Bickford

Vietnam War Women's Memorial, Washington, DC
Photograph by George Cassutto, http://www.cyberlearning-world.com

Arthur Ashe Memorial in Richmond, VA
Photograph by Mary Ann Sullivan

Vietnam War Memorial, Washington, DC
Photograph by George Cassutto, http://www.cyberlearning-world.com

Yuri Gagarin Memorial in Moscow
Photograph by Andy House

International Center for Transitional Justice (ICTJ)

The International Center for Transitional Justice (ICTJ) assists countries pursuing accountability for past mass atrocity or human rights abuse. The Center works in societies emerging from repressive rule or armed conflict, as well as in established democracies where historical injustices or systemic abuse remains unresolved.

In order to promote justice, peace, and reconciliation, government officials and nongovernmental advocates are likely to consider a variety of transitional justice approaches including both judicial and nonjudicial responses to human rights crimes. The ICTJ assists in the development of integrated, comprehensive, and localized approaches to transitional justice comprising five key elements: prosecuting perpetrators, documenting and acknowledging violations through nonjudicial means such as truth commissions, reforming abusive institutions, providing reparations to victims, and facilitating reconciliation processes.

The field of transitional justice is varied and covers a range of disciplines, including law, public policy, forensics, economics, history, psychology, and the arts. The ICTJ works to develop a rich understanding of the field as a whole and to identify issues that merit more in-depth research and analysis. Collaborating with colleagues in transitional societies and often commissioning outside studies, the Center targets its research to address the complex issues confronting policymakers and activists. Identifying and addressing the most important gaps in scholarship, it provides the benefit of comparative analysis to its staff and to practitioners worldwide.

Introduction: A Gender and Reparations Taxonomy

Ruth Rubio-Marín

In recent years, work in a variety of disciplines has sought to illuminate and highlight women's experience of conflict and authoritarianism. UN Security Council Resolution 1325 on women, peace, and security[1] reflects this when addressing the need to recognize the impact of armed conflict on women and girls, the role of women in peacebuilding, and the gender dimensions of peace processes and conflict resolution. The serious and pervasive nature of gender-based violence in conflict, especially sexual and reproductive violence, has also been increasingly recognized under international criminal law.[2] Relevant discussions about how other transitional justice measures, including truth-telling mechanisms, can do better justice to women have followed.[3] It comes as no surprise, then, that the time is ripe to raise the question of how reparations programs for mass human rights violations can be designed in ways intended to redress women more fairly and efficiently.[4]

The fact that reparations programs are becoming an increasingly frequent feature of transitional and post-conflict processes renders the topic of this book

---

[1] United Nations Security Council, Resolution 1325, S/RES/1325 (2000), October 31, 2000.
[2] Proof of this is the Rome Statute of the International Criminal Court, which adopts "rape, sexual slavery, enforced prostitution, forced pregnancy, enforced sterilization, or any other form of sexual violence of comparable gravity" as part of its definition of crimes against humanity and war crimes. See the Rome Statute of the International Criminal Court, Arts. 7 and 8.
[3] Debra L. DeLaet, "Gender Justice: A Gendered Assessment of Truth-Telling Mechanisms," in *Telling the Truths: Truth Telling and Peace Building in Post-Conflict Societies*, ed. Tristan Anne Borer (Notre Dame, IN: University of Notre Dame Press, 2006), 151–181; World Bank, "Gender, Justice, and Truth Commissions," Washington, DC: World Bank, June 2006; Vasuki Nesiah et al., "Truth Commissions and Gender: Principle, Policies and Procedures," (New York: ICTJ, 2006); Fionnuala Ni Aoláin and Catherine Turner, "Gender, Truth and Transition," *UCLA Women's Law Journal* 16 (2007): 229–279.
[4] International civil society has started to echo this concern: in March 2007, the Nairobi Declaration on Women's and Girls' Right to a Remedy and Reparation was adopted. See http://www.womensrightscoalition.org/site/reparation/signature_en.php.

only more relevant and urgent. Indeed, there is a growing conviction that doing justice in transitional scenarios requires not only doing something against the perpetrators, but also doing something specifically for victims.[5] This trend is confirmed by the recommendations of several truth commissions, and by the jurisprudence of both national and international human rights bodies, including the European Court of Human Rights and the Inter-American Court of Human Rights. Nations as diverse as Argentina, Chile, Brazil, South Africa, Guatemala, Peru, and Morocco are examples of countries that have thought of reparations initiatives as an important component of their package of transitional justice measures. The UN has also supported this evolution toward enhancing the importance of the reparative venue and giving victims adequate recognition and redress: in 2005, the General Assembly approved the *Basic Principles and Guidelines on the Right to a Remedy and Reparation for Victims of Gross Violations of International Human Rights Law and Serious Violations of International Humanitarian Law*,[6] and just recently the High Commissioner for Human Rights has produced a tool on reparations programs as part of its series of *Rule-of-Law Tools for Post-Conflict States*.[7] The latter document is intended, among other things, to guide state practice on how to render the *Basic Principles* operative.

The moves toward "engendering transitional justice" and pushing forward the reparations agenda have thus far progressed in parallel and without meaningful encounters. For the most part, reparations initiatives around the world have to this day failed to raise systematically the question of how to incorporate women's specific needs and concerns. This is striking in view of the fact that a significant number of victims of authoritarianism and conflict are women who are known to experience both phenomena in distinct ways. Similarly, it is common knowledge that in most cases women play a crucial role in the follow-up of violence – searching for victims or their remains, trying to reconstitute families and communities, carrying on the tasks of memory, and

---

[5] See Pablo de Greiff, "Introduction," in *The Handbook of Reparations*, ed. Pablo de Greiff (Oxford: Oxford University Press, 2006), 1–18 [*The Handbook*, hereafter].

[6] *Basic Principles and Guidelines on the Right to a Remedy and Reparation for Victims of Gross Violations of International Human Rights Law and Serious Violations of International Humanitarian Law*, A/RES/60/147, March 21, 2006 [*Basic Principles*, hereafter]. See also the UN Secretary General's 2004 report, *The Rule of Law and Transitional Justice in Conflict and Post-Conflict Societies*, S/2004/616, August 23, 2004; *Updated Set of Principles for the Protection and Promotion of Human Rights through Action to Combat Impunity*, E/CN.4/2005/102/Add.1, February 8, 2005; Diane Orentlicher, *Independent Study on Best Practices, Including Recommendations, to Assist States in Strengthening Their Domestic Capacity to Combat All Aspects of Impunity*, E/CN.4/2004/88, February 27, 2004; and *Report of the Independent Expert to Update the Set of Principles to Combat Impunity*, E/CN.4/2005/102, February 18, 2005.

[7] Available at http://www.ohchr.org/Documents/Publications/ReparationsProgrammes.pdf.

demanding justice. Despite all of this, reparations programs have not been designed with an explicit gender dimension. And yet, there are few reasons to believe that so-called "gender-neutral" reparations programs equally facilitate the achievement of the underlying goals of reparations programs, including recognition, civic trust, and social solidarity for men and women.[8] True, the goals of a reparations program are to provide a measure of justice, albeit imperfect, to victims; but reparations are also intimately tied to building a just and peaceful foundation for a transitioning society. A program that fails to provide redress or justice to women in effect weakens the link between the goals of reparations and their contribution to the establishment of a democratic state.

This book seeks to lay the foundations for a gender-sensitive analysis of reparations programs that would increase their effectiveness as redress measures available to female victims and their families. The analysis is also intended to maximize the transformative potential of reparations programs and thus their capacity to help advance toward more inclusive and egalitarian democracies (potential and capacities that it is important not to overestimate). The book is the result of an ambitious three-year research project undertaken by the International Center for Transitional Justice (ICTJ). Besides learning what reparations programs to date *in fact* have done with respect to gender issues, the project took to heart the task of starting to articulate what future programs *ought to do* if they aspire to do justice to female victims in transitional or post-conflict situations, and thus of articulating the normative goals of reparations programs with respect to gender issues. This dual empirical and normative perspective characteristic of ICTJ research projects would, it was hoped, make it possible to identify best practices and, more importantly, to propose innovative approaches to the integration of a gender perspective into the design and implementation of reparations programs. It would ultimately also serve to test and to illustrate the project's underlying hypothesis, namely, that a gender perspective *would* make a difference in the field of reparations.

The first task was to make up for the dearth of factual information on the different needs of men and women vis-à-vis reparations. We tried to do this by compiling case studies that provided detailed accounts of how six countries – Peru, Guatemala, Sierra Leone, Rwanda, Timor-Leste, and South Africa – have dealt or failed to deal with gender issues in their discussions about how to repair victims.[9] Then came the challenge of thinking about the topic both

---

[8] These are some of the goals that are attributed to reparations programs by Pablo de Greiff in his "Justice and Reparations," in *The Handbook*, 451–477.

[9] See the six case studies in Ruth Rubio-Marín, ed., *What Happened to the Women? Gender and Reparations for Human Rights Violations* (New York: Social Science Research Council, 2006) [*What Happened*, hereafter].

thematically and normatively, which is what the present book attempts to do – benefiting from the empirical information gathered in the previous volume.

Before entering into a brief discussion of the contents and structure of this collection, two preliminary comments are called for. The first one has to do with the prevailing emphasis that the book places on women. Of course, "gender" need not refer to women alone. However, given present conditions, concerns about gender and gender sensitivity in this and most other contexts in which justice issues arise refer to the disparities and inequities in access, power, opportunities, and rights experienced by women across a wide spectrum of spheres. Although we have followed this well-established use of the term gender in this book, most authors have come up with insight on how patterns and notions of masculinity can interfere either with the assessment of the harms that men are subject to during times of repression and conflict, or with their possibilities for redress, thereby underscoring the need to conceptually broaden the gender and reparations agenda so as to include men and boys.

The second comment has to do with the overwhelming (if not exclusive) focus on reparations programs as opposed to other modalities such as judicial reparations procedures, which typically operate on a case-by-case basis and which individualize compensation measures, tailoring each of them so as to compensate in proportion to the harm suffered by each individual victim. There are general and gender-specific reasons for our focus on programs rather than court procedures. In general, international practice seems to suggest that more and more countries are coming to the realization that when reparations are owed to a large universe of victims resulting from widespread and systematic use of violence, administrative programs may be better suited to the task. In part, this choice is motivated by reasons of expediency. However, there may be another important reason to favor massive programs: in compensating everyone within the same category of violation in roughly the same way, rather than adjusting the payment in accordance with calculations of individual harms, the programs avoid a potentially inegalitarian message and consequent divisions among victims.[10] Also, in providing redress for the violation of *rights* rather than compensating the loss of wealth, the programs indicate their nature as rights-promoting and rights-enhancing measures.[11] Reparations then become mainly a form of recognizing victims as citizens and equal rights bearers.

[10] See de Greiff, "Justice and Reparations," 458.

[11] For an elaboration of the reasons why in transitional situations reparations programs may be a better response than individual case-by-case judicial procedures, see de Greiff, "Justice and Reparations"; Pablo de Greiff and Marieke Wierda, "The Trust Fund for Victims of the International Criminal Court: Between Possibilities and Constraints," in *Out of the Ashes: Reparation for Victims of Gross and Systematic Human Rights Violations*, ed. Marc Bossuyt, Paul Lemmens, Koen de Feyter, and Stephan Parmentier (Antwerp: Intersentia, 2005) [*Out of*

Introduction: A Gender and Reparations Taxonomy 5

If all of the above is true in general, I have argued elsewhere that there are also gender-specific reasons to favor large-scale reparations programs that place the emphasis on the recognition of victims as opposed to judicial reparations seeking compensation in proportion to harm.[12] Maybe the most important one is that reparations programs can obviate some of the difficulties and costs associated with litigation, including high expenses, the need to gather evidence (which in some cases may be unavailable), the pain associated with cross-examination, and the lack of confidence on the part of victims in judicial systems[13] – difficulties that may have a particularly strong disparate and negative effect on women. Overrepresented among the poor, the illiterate, those with little information, those facing language barriers, and those overburdened with family-related obligations that make traveling long distances a difficult task, women may find it particularly difficult to access the court system. Also, the large underreporting of gender crimes even in "normal times" speaks of the challenges women face in most societies in trying to make use of criminal processes that can so often result in their further victimization.

STRUCTURE AND CONTENTS OF THE BOOK

The first two chapters of the volume were conceived as the normative framework of the project. Margaret Walker's "Gender and Violence in Focus: A Background for Gender Justice in Reparations" provides an overview and analysis of the nature and varieties of violence and harms that are known to affect women in contexts of armed conflict and political repression. The chapter examines both the forms of violence that affect women and the gendered character of these forms of violence. Current research establishes that violence and harms suffered by women in these contexts are many and are often linked in complex ways. The links create destructive synergies of loss and suffering: violence inflicted on women harms women; some harms expose women to further violence and additional harms; and serious, even life-altering

---

the Ashes, hereafter]; Debra Satz, "Countering the Wrongs of the Past: The Role of Compensation," in *Reparations: Interdisciplinary Inquiries*, ed. Jon Miller and Rahul Kumar (New York: Oxford University Press, 2007); and Naomi Roht-Arriaza, "Reparations in the Aftermath of Repression and Mass Violence," in *My Neighbor, My Enemy: Justice and Community in the Aftermath of Mass Atrocity*, ed. Eric Stover and Harvey M. Weinstein (Cambridge: Cambridge University Press, 2004).

[12] See Ruth Rubio-Marín and Pablo de Greiff, "Women and Reparations," *International Journal of Transitional Justice* 1, no. 3 (2007): 317–337.

[13] See de Greiff, "Justice and Reparations," and Heidy Rombouts, Pietro Sardaro, and Stef Vandeginste, "The Right to Reparation for Victims of Gross and Systematic Violations of Human Rights," in *Out of the Ashes*, 488.

or life-threatening harms result from forms of violence and repression that do not target primarily women but that nevertheless affect them decisively. The chapter begins with the assumption that certain forms of coercion and violence against women are recurrent to a greater or lesser extent in many contemporary societies. It develops a critical and cautionary perspective, however, on the idea that violence in conflict is best seen as being "on a continuum" with everyday violence against women. Though a unifying explanation of violence against women serves important purposes for policy analysis and designing future-oriented preventive measures, it does not capture adequately the experience of catastrophic and life-changing violence many women experience in conflict situations. A victim-oriented perspective is crucial for understanding the meaning and consequences of violence with an eye to reparations. Walker articulates seven factors that emerge as salient in conceptualizing and understanding the violence and harm women suffer: (1) some of the forms of violence that target women are status-defining male exchanges; (2) violence is often used as a threat and punishment for women's gender transgression in political contexts; (3) many of the forms that violence against women takes target women's sexuality or reproductive capacity; (4) violence against women also takes the shape of women's property being appropriated or destroyed; (5) women's access to and their roles in creating social capital are frequently damaged by violence; (6) women are exposed to special and intense forms of shame and exclusion after they experience violence; and (7) women are frequently blocked from being, or insecure or socially discredited as, testifiers to violence to themselves. The chapter proposes the nonexclusive categories of *gender-normative violence, sex-, reproduction-, or care-specific violence, gender-skewed violence,* and *gender-multiplied violence* as constituting an analytic grid for tracking different ways in which harms befall women "because they are women," sexually, psychologically, socially, and politically. These categories are rooted in research on actual instances of conflict and repression, and the idea is that they can help us ask the right questions about how women are harmed.

The aim of Chapter 2, "The Gender of Reparations in Transitional Societies," is to flesh out the potential of large-scale reparations programs in transitional democracies for recognizing and redressing women victims of human rights abuses. It also provides insight about the transformative potential of reparations, namely, the potential to subvert, instead of reinforce, preexisting structural gender inequalities and thereby to contribute, however minimally, to the consolidation of more inclusive democratic regimes.[14] The chapter

---

[14] For the concept of transformative reparations, see Ruth Rubio-Marín, "Gender and Collective Reparations in the Aftermath of Conflict and Political Repression," in *The Politics of Reconciliation in Multicultural Societies*, ed. Will Kymlicka and Bashir Bashir (Oxford: Oxford University Press, 2008), reproduced at the end of this volume.

starts by developing a normative framework for conceptualizing reparations, one that sets the main aim of reparations to be to give victims due recognition *as citizens*, something which, I argue, requires all of the following: the recognition of the wrongful violations of victims' rights; the acknowledgment of state responsibility for such violations; the recognition of harms ensuing from the violations; and the attempt to help victims cope with the effects of harms in their lives and to subvert, however minimally, the structures of subordination that might have led to the violations of their rights in the first place. The chapter then spells out what "engendering reparations" might mean in the light of these requirements. In summary, it means: first, avoiding formal gender discrimination in the design and implementation of such programs; second, looking for ways of ensuring that patriarchal norms and sexist standards and systems of values do not leak into reparations; and, third, exploring ways to optimize the (admittedly modest) transformative potential of reparations programs so that they serve to advance toward the ideal of a society altogether free of gender subordination. I try to show that taking all of this into account has an impact on how reparations programs are designed and implemented. Specifically, it affects the selection of the crimes or violations for which there will be reparations, ensuring, for example, that crimes that affect predominantly women are not left out of the list of those that trigger access to reparations programs; the definition of the notion of "beneficiary," which should reflect that violations of rights may affect male and female victims disparately, and that generally these violations affect families and communities and not only individuals; and the design of the packet of possible benefits in favor of those that will best reach women and address the multifaceted harms they experience and, to the extent possible, help women move beyond the socioeconomic status they held before the violations.

Following these two chapters is a set focusing on specific topics that are of particular importance for the issue at hand. Chapter 3 is devoted to the reparation of sexual and reproductive violence. In spite of systematic underreporting, it is well documented that both under repressive regimes and in large-scale civil conflict women and girls are often subject to many forms of sexual and reproductive abuses, including rape (sometimes mass and multiple), sexual amputations, forced prostitution, sexual slavery, forced unions, forced impregnations, forced abortions and sterilization, and other forms of sexual denigration. Men and boys are sometimes subject to similar forms of abuse, although in view of widespread cultural prejudices that "feminize" male victims of sexual violence, the underreporting in such cases is even more severe. Recent (implemented or at least recommended) reparations programs and measures, such as those in Peru, Guatemala, Rwanda, Sierra Leone, Timor-Leste, and Morocco, have reacted to the widespread use of sexual and reproductive violence and explicitly include sexual violence among the violations that entitle victims to reparations. In this chapter, Colleen Duggan and Ruth Jacobson address the challenges and possibilities of repairing victims of the many forms of sexual and reproductive violence, providing the most comprehensive overview of the forms of reparations that have been either implemented or recommended in the past and identifying best practices and suggesting possible innovations in the field. The challenges of coming up with adequate reparations measures for victims of sexual and reproductive violence include taking into account the variety of harms that these violations can produce, such as loss of status, communal ostracism, material destitution, contraction of sexually transmitted diseases, other harms to victims' reproductive and mental health, and the bearing and raising of unwanted children. Special difficulties for reparation come from those harms that follow not directly from the violation itself but from the reaction to the violation on the part of the spouse, extended family, or community (such as harm to the person's social status, impossibility of remarrying, repudiation by the husband and other family and community members, etc.), all of which suggest the need to come up with innovative ways to deal with reparations targeting both the individual and her environment while being careful not to reinforce sexual stereotyping or entrench sexual bias. The fact that sexual violence is the only crime for which victims themselves are often blamed is only one of the reasons that repairing this kind of violation is a particularly daunting enterprise.

It is well documented that both boys and girls are subject to various forms of abuse, including illegal detention (together with their mothers), forced recruitment, abduction and forced removal from their families, sexual abuse, sexual and domestic labor, slavery, forced marriage, and amputations, among others. Children also bear some of the most serious consequences of violations committed against their parents, such as executions or illegal detention, which can result in upbringing in an orphanage or a single- or child-headed household. Gender seems to play a significant role in the type of abuse that girls and boys more commonly experience, with girls being more often subject to sexual violence, sexual and domestic labor, and forms of slavery, and boys to forceful recruitment for combat. Also, violations affect boys and girls in gender-specific ways. Finally, given that in many societies women are the main caretakers of minors, the differential impact on whether children become beneficiaries of reparations measures on women is undeniable. All of this explains the importance in a volume such as this one of Dyan Mazurana and Khristopher Carlson's Chapter 4, "Reparations as a Means for Recognizing and Addressing Crimes and Grave Rights Violations against Girls and Boys during Situations of Armed Conflict and under Authoritarian and Dictatorial

Regimes." Their study classifies the forms of violations and harms that children and youth experience most typically in times of political turmoil as a result of violent acts that target them or their parents. It then looks systematically at the experiences, possibilities, and challenges around repairing children for the harms they endure, placing the emphasis on the need to consult them and include their voices in reparations processes and to draft programs that enhance the visibility of children as rights bearers and not only dependent family members.

Whereas many of the forms of violence committed under dictatorial regimes and during large-scale ethnic and civil strife target men for their political activities, family members – particularly in societies predominantly organized around the family structure embracing the breadwinner model – are not only severely impacted by the violations committed against men, but also sometimes directly targeted for abuse because of their status, precisely as relatives of those who will become the "primary" victims. In either case, parents, partners, spouses, and children of the disappeared, executed, or detained persons are often left emotionally desolate and economically destitute. This is especially true of partners and spouses who are left with the entire burden of raising a family without a breadwinner, often in societies where women lack income-generating skills, have little education, and may even be stigmatized for their involvement in activities outside the home. Ironically, these are precisely the women who, in most experiences, lead the fight for justice and truth about their loved ones, frequently relegating reparations claims for their own suffering and hardship to the bottom of their list of claims. In Chapter 5, "Repairing Family Members: Gross Human Rights Violations and Communities of Harm," I, along with Clara Sandoval and Catalina Díaz, address the challenges, possibilities, and experiences of repairing the family members of victims of grave violations of human rights. The chapter is ambitious in its scope as it tries to provide a comprehensive account as well as a critical analysis of how the subject matter has been treated under the case law of the European Court of Human Rights and the Inter-American Court of Human Rights, and by national reparations programs. Among other things, the article underscores the importance of departing from a succession paradigm, according to which family members will receive reparations only if their loved ones have died or disappeared, in favor of one that recognizes the need to repair next of kin in their own right for the moral and material harm they experience as a result of the violations.

Chapters 6 and 7 shift the focus from forms of victimization and categories of victims and beneficiaries to forms or modalities of reparations. In Chapter 6, "Tort Theory, Microfinance, and Gender Equality Convergent in Pecuniary

Reparations," Anita Bernstein uses tort theory as a framework to underscore the importance of providing women material redress through reparations. Doing so is important for several reasons, including the fact that by law, custom, and religion women often do not enjoy control over property and wealth comparable to men of similar class position. Also, as is well known, violent upheavals that disrupt and transform traditional divisions of labor, power, and ownership, or that involve displacement and geographical relocation, often result in dramatic and inequitable economic losses for women, or in women being unable to assert rights to property. Official statistics used to define policies of reconstruction may ignore households run de facto by women when husbands are absent or missing. With the current long-delayed and still not fully effective focus on sexual violence toward women in political conflict, there is the possibility that women's losses of livelihood, land, wealth, and economic assets or the economic effects of violations on women's lives may be eclipsed. Hence, placing the question of women's material well-being to the fore when discussing reparations is important. More concretely, Bernstein's chapter explores the possibility of giving victims shares in microfinance institutions as a promising kind of material reparations benefit. It discusses how such an alternative might encourage development in regions that are too poor to be able to dispense large payments to victims of human rights abuses. It also analyzes how, by encouraging victims' agency and security, reparations through microfinance can be especially promising for women and help them improve their status.

Brandon Hamber and Ingrid Palmary's Chapter 7, "Gender, Memorialization, and Symbolic Reparations," takes us from the realm of the material to that of the symbolic. Whereas symbolic reparations measures are becoming an increasingly common feature in reparations programs (including memorialization activities, museums, naming of streets and public activities, monuments, official apologies, etc.), there has been virtually no discussion as to whether female and male victims have gained equal/proportional symbolic recognition through reparations schemes. Nor has it been discussed whether there may be good reasons to believe that male and female victims require different forms of symbolic redress, including modalities of apologies, or are differently engaged by memorialization attempts that are interactive in nature. This chapter explores the theoretical question of what engendering memorialization and symbolic reparations projects can entail. It argues that this venture requires including women in the traditional forms of representation and symbolic recognition while at the same time changing those traditional forms in ways that have the capacity to reach and be meaningful to women. More concretely, the chapter makes suggestions as to how symbolic reparations could make a more substantial contribution to promoting gender justice by incorporating sufficiently complex and rich notions of masculinity and femininity.

The book closes with a chapter on gender and collective reparations[15] that tries to shed some light on the multifaceted and increasingly popular notion of collective reparations and to address the possibilities that this notion opens to rendering reparations programs more gender sensitive. Because virtually everywhere women are indispensable to, and dependent on, the maintenance of the daily order of communal life, both materially and socially, the creation or reconstruction of social tissue, collective resources, and communal institutions that are often severely damaged during conflict and political repression may be essential to the normalization of their lives and the sustainability of their existence. The concept of collective reparations invites a geographical or regional approach to reparations and has clear synergies with the development and reconstruction agendas. The chapter explores ways in which collective reparations can also be linked with feminist agendas. Drawing from Walker's opening piece in this book, the chapter argues that much of the violence women experience under authoritarianism and during conflict affects them *collectively* by reinforcing gender meanings that are detrimental to women. More importantly, it examines whether collective reparations can stimulate reforms aimed at nonrepetition, that is, reforms that seek to guarantee not only that victims will not be victimized again, but also that no new victims will be generated. Although victims should definitely not feel under any obligation to become sacrificial lambs, some may draw a sense of satisfaction from knowing that with their lives and suffering they contributed, however modestly, to the better lives of future generations of women.

GENDER AND A TAXONOMY OF REPARATIONS PROGRAMS

Pablo de Greiff's groundbreaking book on reparations offers a taxonomy of reparations efforts organized around the basic challenges faced whenever such programs have been undertaken. Drawing from some of the lessons learned through our research, I now want to see how such a taxonomy can be assessed (in terms of the relevance and adequacy of the chosen categories) from a gender perspective. De Greiff's taxonomy refers to the following categories: scope, completeness, comprehensiveness, complexity, internal and external integrity or coherence, finality, and munificence.[16] Based on our work in this project, I would like to propose two additional categories, one to designate a reparations

---

[15] Rubio-Marín, "Gender and Collective Reparations," reproduced at the end of this volume.
[16] de Greiff, "Introduction," 6–13.

program's potential to transform social relations – "transformative potential" – and one to designate the degree to which a reparations program has been designed and implemented with the participation of relevant stakeholders, including, of course, women – "openness."

By the "scope" of a program, de Greiff refers to the total number of beneficiaries it covers. But, as he rightly argues, since that is an absolute number and its correlation with the total number of potential beneficiaries is not clear, there is not much that can be said in abstract about the virtues of a program having a greater or smaller scope.[17] The more relevant categories are those related to the ability of the program to cover, at the limit, the whole universe of potential beneficiaries ("completeness"), something that depends, crucially, on the selection of the crimes and harms that lead to reparations ("comprehensiveness"), to the evidentiary standards required for victims to qualify, and to the outreach efforts undertaken to publicize the existence of the program and render it accessible to victims.[18]

Much of the difference that a gender perspective can make when thinking about reparations has to do with these two categories, completeness and comprehensiveness. Leaving out of the program the worst forms of violence with a disparate impact on women and girls (such as sexual and reproductive violence) is a sure path to failure in terms of maximizing the contribution that reparations initiatives can make to reestablishing female victims' citizenship status. The same applies to endorsing a narrow definition of beneficiaries that does not take into account the harms caused by the violations to the family members of victims of political violence or the diminution of communal resources on which women disparately depend for their daily existence. The trend we observe in recent reparations initiatives toward embracing collective reparations together with individual reparations is therefore to be celebrated, as is the incipient (and still inconsistent) trend to recognize family members as victims in their own right and to include sexual and reproductive violence in the list of violations.

This said, probably the greatest obstacle for victimized women to access reparations has to do with procedural hurdles (closed lists, short application deadlines, territorially centralized procedures, high evidentiary standards, lack of confidentiality, inadequate payment mechanisms) as well as with weak outreach and dissemination policies. True, reparations programs usually fare well on these criteria compared to other reparations venues, especially courts. But this depends on explicit efforts to maximize this potential.

[17] Ibid., 6.
[18] Ibid., 6–10.

In this regard, certain recent and innovative approaches deserve to be highlighted. Among them are several initiatives of Timor-Leste's Commission for Reception, Truth and Reconciliation, which, in view of the severe impact of violence on women, decided to dedicate 50% of the funds allocated for reparations to women, in the hope that this would push the follow-up body in charge of implementing the recommendations to create strong gender policies.[19] The commission's reparations program (which, unfortunately, has not been implemented as of yet) would also allow women to qualify for benefits under multiple criteria, so that women who suffered sexual violence or had a child from rape could be seen as receiving reparations for other harms and in this way escape stigmatization. The program would also provide collective reparations to communities, making gender balance of beneficiaries a condition for supporting such programs. It would also link the distribution of benefits to qualifying children to the provision of services to their mothers as a way to encourage women to think about themselves, specifically offering services to women in the same place they have to visit to get the scholarship stipends for their children. Finally, Timor-Leste's commission recommended keeping its list open for two years after the closing of operations to ensure the completeness of its reparations policy.

The "complexity" of a reparations program refers to the diversity of benefits that it distributes.[20] Whereas very simple programs limit themselves to the distribution of payments, the evolution toward increasingly complex programs is shown by the fact that reparations programs now often incorporate – together with payments – health, education, and housing services and symbolic measures of redress, often addressed at both individuals and collectivities. Reparations programs best accomplish one of their main goals – to provide recognition to victims – if they reflect awareness of how the different types of violations affect victims, and if they craft their benefits accordingly, so as to help victims move forward with their lives in concrete ways. Given that the effects of violence are often gendered, complexity brings with it the possibility of targeting benefits flexibly so as to respond to women's specific needs more closely. For instance, sexual violence has multifaceted effects on women's lives, and it is not clear that the payment of compensation money, important as it may be, can *by itself* provide adequate reparation.[21] Hamber and Palmary's

---

[19] See Galuh Wandita, Karen Campbell-Nelson, and Manuela Leong Pereira, "Learning to Engender Reparations in Timor-Leste: Reaching Out to Female Victims," in *What Happened*, 284–334.

[20] de Greiff, "Introduction," 10.

[21] See Colleen Duggan and Adila Abusharaf, "Reparations of Sexual Violence in Democratic Transitions: In Search of Gender Justice," in *The Handbook*, and Duggan and Jacobson, in this volume.

chapter in this volume illustrates this point with the story of the so-called "comfort women," women who were exploited sexually by the Japanese army during the second world war and who have since always insisted on the importance of monetary payments being accompanied by the proper form of apology.[22] More generally, although including compensation payments in a reparations program may be essential to enhance women's economic independence, relying exclusively on monetary payments may prove inadequate reparation for a variety of reasons, including the possibility that the money will end up in men's hands and the fact that, when asked about reparations, women tend to prioritize the provision of services.[23] Mazurana and Carlson express similar skepticism in their chapter about relying on monetary compensation as the main reparation measure when the intended beneficiaries are boys and girls.

"Integrity" (or "coherence") is a category that has both an internal and an external dimension. Whereas "internal coherence" refers to the relationship between the different types of benefits a program distributes and is achieved when the different benefits support each other in the achievement of the underlying aims of the program, "external coherence" expresses the requirement that the reparations efforts be designed in such a way as to be closely connected with other transitional justice mechanisms such as criminal justice, truth-telling, and institutional reform measures. According to de Greiff, coherence increases the likelihood that the different transitional efforts will satisfy the expectations of citizens. As he rightly points out, reparations without truth or justice may be perceived as a state attempt to buy the silence of victims and their families.[24] In real-life scenarios, when we talk about families of victims, we are often talking about mothers and widows of the politically detained, executed, or disappeared. These women take it as their primordial task to vindicate their loved ones via truth and justice measures, and thus for many of them, compensation in the absence of other efforts to elucidate the fate and vindicate the lives of their loved ones simply will not be an option.

External coherence is also most relevant for women in another regard, especially when applied in a broad sense to include not only coherence between the measures of transitional justice, but also coherence between justice measures and all those that form the entire package of democratization measures. To see this, it is important to bear in mind that women are often subject to multiple and standard forms of abuse and exploitation before, during, and after the conflict, and that these abuses are usually committed with almost total

---

[22] See Hamber and Palmary, in this volume.
[23] See Ruth Rubio-Marín, "Introduction," in *What Happened*, 20–47, and Rubio-Marín, in this volume, Chapter 2.
[24] de Greiff, "Introduction," 10–11.

impunity. If the aim of a reparations program is to reassert the status of victims as equal citizens and rights holders, it is difficult to envision how this task can be achieved unless, at the same time and as part of the democratization process, structural reform measures are also undertaken to eradicate practices and transform institutions expressing women's subordinate status as second-class citizens. Thus, depending on the country at stake, ensuring the external coherence of a reparations program with the aim of reasserting women's and girls' equal citizenship status may be an essential but daunting task involving major legal and institutional reforms – reforms that obviously call for more interactions between victims' and women's groups (among others) than has been the norm in most transitions.[25]

The category of "finality" refers to whether receiving benefits from a program forecloses other avenues of civil redress.[26] Though there may be both advantages and disadvantages to rendering a program final, all I would like to add here is that if a program is made final in this sense, it can apply only to violations for which there has been reparations instead of referring, more generically, to past abuses. This will ensure that in the case of those reparations programs that systematically fail to include the worst forms of violence and abuse perpetrated and tolerated against women as "repairable crimes," the judicial path remains open. A sequence of successful cases may act as a trigger to motivate the state to undertake new programmatic reparations initiatives to ensure, at least over time, the comprehensiveness of its reparations policy. Hence, the importance of circumscribing carefully the reach of a program's finality.

The "munificence" of a reparations program relates to the magnitude of its benefits from the individual beneficiary's perspective.[27] Because so much of what has been said thus far would seem to indicate that "engendering reparations" will require multiplying the number of potential beneficiaries (mostly by enhancing the completeness and comprehensiveness of the program), it is worth thinking about how to respond to the likely criticism that this will either increase the costs of reparations (and maybe make governments more resistant to the idea of reparations) or reduce the amounts distributed to each beneficiary to such an extent that reparations become meaningless in practice. There are several concrete options for policymakers to explore here. These include, when talking about individual payments, the option of apportioning them among different family members, but also thinking about ways of distribution (of the same amounts) that may ensure that they reach women better (for instance, small pensions versus large one-time lump-sum payments). A possibility

[25] Rubio-Marín, "Introduction."
[26] de Greiff, "Introduction," 12.
[27] Ibid., 12–13.

explored in Timor-Leste and Sierra Leone includes prioritizing, when it comes to monetary reparations, the most vulnerable victims (something that is likely to have a positive impact on women).[28] More importantly, the complexity of a reparations program that combines small individual payments with other types of benefits (services, symbolic, collective) to ensure that reparations are truly meaningful to victims may be just as successful. After all, past experiences show that the complexity (especially a combination of material and symbolic) and the coherence (especially the delivering of reparations together with truth and/or justice) of a reparations program may be more important in determining victims' satisfaction than its overall munificence.

Although de Greiff ends his taxonomy here, I would like to propose adding two further categories for the assessment of reparations programs. The first one can be called "openness" and refers to the level of participation of victims, victims' groups, and other relevant actors in civil society in the design of a reparations program. There are both instrumental and intrinsic reasons to commend the openness of a reparations program. The main idea is that victims' adequate participation in the process can not only provide information needed for the proper design of programs, but can also, in itself, have a reparative effect by affirming the victims' status as active citizens buttressed by the state's willingness to engage with them as valid interlocutors.[29] Although this effect may obtain generally, regardless of the type of victim, it may be particularly important for sectors of the population that have been systematically marginalized and not only episodically oppressed. This usually includes women, but it also includes, depending on the case, other marginalized groups such as indigenous groups and other oppressed minorities.

In this regard, there is a promising trend. Until recently, women's groups have not been particularly engaged in discussing reparations. Rather, such discussions tended to be exclusively left to victims' groups and human rights groups. Thus, women's participation tended to be mostly conducted either through their involvement in victims' groups (in which they often participate as family members of the disappeared or killed) or through specific associations representing some partial interest (such as widows' associations, or associations focusing on the displaced). This is now changing. Indeed, in more recent reparations discussions, such as those that took place in Sierra Leone[30] and those now taking place in Colombia, there is some involvement of groups representing women's rights more broadly. This can have the important effect

---

[28] See Wandita, Campbell-Nelson, and Pereira, and Jamesina King, "Gender and Reparations in Sierra Leone: The Wounds of War Remain Open," in *What Happened*, 246–283.
[29] See Rubio-Marín and de Greiff, "Women and Reparations."
[30] See King.

of incorporating the views of victims of sexual violence who in many contexts and for obvious reasons are unlikely to organize and mobilize publicly as such. More generally, conceived as a space for the participation of victims, the design and implementation of an administrative reparations program can, in itself, be a project that offers women a reparative sense of recognition both as victims and as valuable agents of political and social transformation.

Finally, by "transformative potential" I mean the extent to which a reparations program has the capacity to subvert, instead of reinforce, preexisting structural inequalities. Although our concern here is with gender hierarchies of power, this concept may apply to other forms of structural inequalities. The challenge that this category responds to is that of understanding how a reparations project, whose aim is to give victims recognition as equal rights holders, can address the fact that some groups were not equal rights holders *before* the violent or authoritarian episode that triggered their access to the reparations benefits. This said, we must bear in mind that reparations can at best bring about very modest transformations, and that larger transformations will have to come from broader structural and legal reforms that ought to accompany the democratization process. Still, because of their symbolic meaning and the need for internal and external coherence, reparations programs should not miss out on whatever opportunities there are to contribute to the transformation. To illustrate, reparations programs need not conform to or contribute to the entrenchment of preexisting patterns of female land tenure, education, or employment. They may also challenge gender-biased inheritance rules. This was the case, for instance, in Morocco, where the recent Equity and Reconciliation Commission (2002–2003), departing from the prior precedent set by the Arbitration Commission (1999), decided to apportion benefits among family members of the deceased victims in a way that departs from the sharia-based law of inheritance, giving a larger share of those benefits to women (40% as opposed to 1/8 or 12.5%) rather than to the eldest son. Also, and as Bernstein's chapter in this volume shows, there is space to think about what modalities of reparation (including shares in microfinance institutions, education, and vocational training) can help women move beyond the baseline they departed from and help them achieve greater autonomy and independence during the reconstruction. Ideally, then, the process of designing a reparations program should provide an opportunity to discuss what it takes for a democratic regime to be truly inclusive of women.

1

Gender and Violence in Focus: A Background for Gender Justice in Reparations

Margaret Urban Walker

The ad hoc International Criminal Tribunal for the former Yugoslavia (ICTY), the International Criminal Tribunal for Rwanda (ICTR), and the International Criminal Court (ICC) have put sexual violence against women in contexts of conflict squarely on the map of international criminal law in the past decade.[1] Acts of sexual violence can now be charged as genocide, crimes against humanity, war crimes, and grave breaches of humanitarian standards. The 1994 genocide in Rwanda produced significant coverage of mass rapes that accompanied mass killings. The 1998 *Akayesu* judgment of the ICTR made the historically unprecedented connection between rape and genocide, and the statute and indictments of the ICTR incorporate rape as a crime against humanity. Yet a 2004 Human Rights Watch report reveals that neither the ICTR, local courts, nor the recently launched traditional gacaca hearings are dealing adequately with sexual violence.[2] The indictment and conviction of Bosnian Serb soldiers for sexual assaults and enslavement of women in Foca at the ICTY in 2001 was seen as a historic moment for the recognition of specifically sexual violence against women in the context of armed conflict. Even so, tribunal judges lamented the difficulty of getting sexual violence

---

[1] A detailed comparative summary of convergences and differences in the statutes and actions of the ICTY, ICTR, and ICC is provided by Angela M. Banks, "Sexual Violence and International Criminal Law: An Analysis of the Ad Hoc Tribunal's Jurisprudence and the International Criminal Court's Elements of Crimes," Women's Initiatives for Gender Justice, September 2005, http://www.iccwomen.org/publications/resources/index.php, accessed February 26, 2009. See also Kelly D. Askin and Dorean M. Koenig, eds., *Women and International Human Rights Law* (Ardsley, NY: Transnational, 1999).

[2] Human Rights Watch, "Rape Survivors Find No Justice," http://hrw.org/english/docs/2004/09/30/rwanda9391.htm, accessed February 26, 2009. See also Human Rights Watch on the lack of a consistent and comprehensive approach to rape at the ICTR in "We'll Kill You If You Cry: Sexual Violence in the Sierra Leone Conflict," *Human Rights Watch Report* 15, no. 1 (January 2003): 59.

against women on the agenda, and into the indictments, of the tribunal.³ In other recent conflicts on the African continent, widespread abduction, rape, sexual enslavement, and captivity of young women has been publicized, but it is unclear how, whether, and where this violence will be addressed. Despite deliberate attention to women's situations and activism by women's organizations in South Africa, the South African Truth and Reconciliation Commission (TRC) did not much succeed in inducing women, including politically active women, to talk about experiencing sexual violence. Women gave testimony to affirm grave crimes against their husbands and children, but not often those against themselves.⁴

Sexual violence is not, however, the only violence women suffer in situations of armed conflict and political repression.⁵ Rape and abusive sexual treatment are grave criminal acts, among the grossest violations of human rights and crimes against humanity when systemic in nature. Women's vulnerability to sexual violation, however, is but one of the threats and dangers women face as combatants and civilians in armed conflict or as citizens or political activists under repression. Women too are killed, wounded, tortured, mutilated, disabled, terrorized, forced to relocate or emigrate, and stranded in refugee camps. Women too lose homes, land, possessions, sources of income, local networks of material and emotional support, and family members or whole families. In some cases women's losses are the results of sexual violation;

---

[3] See interviews with Gabrielle Kirk McDonald, then president of the ICTY, and with Elizabether Odio Benito, then justice of the ICTY, in *Assault on the Soul: Women in the Former Yugoslavia*, ed. Sara Sharratt and Ellyn Kaschak (Binghamton, NY: Haworth Press, 1999). Human Rights Watch describes the tribunals' record as "lackluster and inconsistent on investigating and prosecuting crimes of sexual violence," in Human Rights Watch, "Bosnia: Landmark Verdicts for Rape, Torture, and Sexual Enslavement," http://www.hrw.org/en/news/list/40?page=398, accessed February 26, 2009.

[4] Beth Goldblatt and Sheila Meintjes report on varied dimensions of women's victimization and suffering in South Africa's struggle, including the "laconic and euphemistic" nature of women's reluctant admissions of their own victimization; Beth Goldblatt and Sheila Meintjes, "South African Women Demand the Truth," in *What Women Do in Wartime: Gender and Conflict in Africa*, ed. Meredeth Turshen and Clotilde Twagiramariya (New York and London: Zed Books, 1998), 65–66. See also Ashnie Padarath, "Woman and Violence in KwaZulu/Natal," in the same volume. Human Rights Watch reports, however, that in Sierra Leone rape was so widespread and public that there is less stigmatization of victims, and 65% of women (in a small group of 94 interviewees) reported their violation to a health care provider or healer. See Human Rights Watch, "We'll Kill You If You Cry," 52. Clearly, the perception and reality of shaming and stigmatization requires close investigation in context.

[5] See Judith Gardam and Hilary Charlesworth, "Protection of Women in Armed Conflict," *Human Rights Quarterly* 22 (2000): 148–149; yet see Anne Gallagher, "Ending the Marginalization: Strategies for Incorporating Women into the United Nations Human Rights System," *Human Rights Quarterly* 19 (1997): 317, note 111, on almost exclusive attention to sexual abuse in Myanmar and in Rwanda.

women are often stigmatized or abandoned because sexual violation renders them socially unacceptable or unmarriageable, or gross sexual abuse renders them sterile or incontinent. It also happens that some harms women suffer give rise to conditions that make sexual violation more probable, as women in refugee camps lose the protection of family and neighbors, or peacekeeping troops commit rapes or patronize brothels in post-conflict settings where women are struggling to survive. Not all violations and harms suffered by women are sexual in nature. Neither are the harms women suffer always the outcome of actions intended to harm them. Women also suffer grave and irreparable losses through consequences of conflict even where women are not the primary targets of violence. When men are absent or killed in conflict, for example, women may lose the male support that insures their social standing and economic survival. When men are injured, women may have to assume responsibilities for both the support of families and the care of disabled men. The disruption of local economies and food production or widespread violence may force women to move to areas where they hope food and security are available, a hope sometimes bitterly disappointed as displaced women may experience further exposure to violence and loss.

The violence and harms suffered by women in contexts of armed conflict and political repression are many and are often linked. The links create destructive synergies of loss and suffering: violence inflicted on women harms women; some harms expose women to further violence and additional harms; and serious, even life-altering or life-threatening harms result from forms of violence and repression in which women are not the primary targets of conflict yet are decisively affected by it. It is clearly a time of rising attention to the violence and harm that women suffer in conflict situations. United Nations Security Council Resolution 1325 in 2000 and the even more urgently worded Security Council Resolution 1820 in 2008 affirm active concern for both the impacts on women in armed conflict and commitment to women's participation in peace processes.[6] A study of women's repression in 57 countries published in 2004, however, can still say, "Violence against women has eluded the global human rights agenda for almost fifty years."[7] Certainly that has begun to change, and we may hope this change is decisive and irreversible. Still, the tasks of

---

[6] United Nations Security Council, Resolution 1325, October 31, 2000, S/RES/1325 (2000) and United Nations Security Council, Resolution 1820, June 19, 2008, S/RES/1820 (2008).

[7] Conway Henderson, "The Political Repression of Women," *Human Rights Quarterly* 26 (2004): 1029. For an uncompromising critique of the gaps between the theory and practice of acknowledging and defending women's rights, see Catharine A. MacKinnon, *Are Women Human? And Other International Dialogues* (Cambridge, MA: Belknap Press of Harvard University Press, 2006).

understanding the nature, dimensions, conditions, and consequences of violence and harm that are done to women under repression and conflict are large, varied, and relatively new.

Looking at women and violence under conditions of armed conflict or repression prompts many questions about men, women, and violence: In conditions of conflict or repression, is sexual violence the gravest violence intentionally done to women? If not, is there still good reason to put particular emphasis, in reporting and remedies, on sexual violence? Does sexual violation typically matter to women in a different way from other assault, harm, indignity, and loss that are inflicted on women by conflict? If sexual violation should not be specially emphasized, how should it be registered in assessing and repairing injuries to women, compared to other nonsexual injuries? What kinds of violence befall women as combatants and noncombatants in the same ways that they befall men? What nonsexual forms of violence or harm commonly happen to, or have particularly grave effects for, women? Are there nonsexual harms to women that are less likely to be taken seriously than comparable harms to men? Are there nonsexual kinds of violence and harm that are likely to affect women disproportionately in comparison to men?

Closely related questions arise about the *gendered* character of violence in conflict contexts: What are the different ways violence and harm suffered by women can be specifically linked to female gender? What gives forms of violence, including violence toward women, specifically gendered masculine meanings for male perpetrators? Are differences between gender-linked and gender-neutral violence important in identifying, acknowledging, and repairing what happens to women and men in conflict? Does it matter if gender-linked violence is consciously seen as such by the perpetrator rather than enacted without clear understanding of its gendered character? Do harms caused by violence, sexual and nonsexual, differ in meaning and impact for women and for men? Can responses to victims violated or harmed be gendered or sexualized even when the violence or harm that was done to them is not obviously sexual or gender-linked?

These questions describe a sweeping research program on gender and political violence beyond the scope of a single study. Perhaps some of these questions can be answered only by attending closely to given instances of violence in their political and social contexts. The topic is not yet deeply researched or even fully conceptualized. We need to remain open and alert to contextual and situational differences in addressing violence and harm to women in developing adequate conceptual frames, but it is urgent not to delay the task of recognizing and repairing violence toward women. In this essay, I try to organize parts of a general scheme for thinking through some questions about gender, violence, and harm to women in situations of conflict and repression, specifically with an eye to reparation.

Because of women's activism of the past several decades, there is now a large literature on women and violence, concerned mostly with domestic violence and rape, as well as sexual harassment and pornography.[8] There is also a significant and growing literature on women's standing in international law and women's exposure to violence as a part of inter-state or intra-state political conflict.[9] This essay, however, is informed by the ultimate goal of contributing to understanding violence and harm to women as a focus of *reparations* in the wake of repression and conflict. I ask: How do we conceptualize harms to women with an eye to the demands of reparative justice? How must we think about harms that come about in and because of conflict from the point of view of moral obligations to repair human lives, relationships, communities, and nations? The issue is wrongful harm, loss, and suffering that would not have befallen women but for the impact of armed conflict and state repression, and that might as a result be the object of reparative action as a matter of justice. We cannot be sure in advance whether or not the categories and assumptions currently available in legal or political practice adequately respond to this issue, and the very idea of "gender-sensitive," "gender-equitable," or "gender-just" repair of violation and loss is a novelty. The schematic structure I offer is tentative and entirely provisional. Any such scheme would ideally be open-ended and adaptable: a sensitizing, heuristic, and critical instrument for approaching specific cases flexibly in their distinct political and historical context, including their particular gender roles and relationships.

---

[8] Recent sources include the National Research Council, *Understanding Violence Against Women*, ed. Nancy A. Crowell and Ann W. Burgess (Washington, DC: National Academy Press, 1996); Claire Renzetti, Jeffrey L. Edleson, and Raquel Kennedy Bergen, eds. *The Sourcebook on Violence Against Women* (Thousand Oaks, CA: Sage Publications, 2001); and Michael L. Penn and Rahel Nardos, *Overcoming Violence Against Women and Girls: The International Campaign to Eradicate a Worldwide Problem* (Lanham, MD: Rowman and Littlefield, 2003).

[9] See Sheila Meintjes, Anu Pillay, and Meredeth Turshen, eds. *The Aftermath: Women in Post-Conflict Transformation* (London and New York: Zed Books, 2001); Turshen and Twagiramariya, *What Women Do In Wartime*; Caroline O. N. Moser and Fiona C. Clark, eds., *Victims, Perpetrators or Actors? Gender, Armed Coflict and Political Violence* (London: Zed Books, 2001); Susie Jacobs, Ruth Jacobson, and Jennifer Marchbank, eds., *States of Conflict: Gender, Violence, and Resistance* (London: Zed Books, 2000); Wenona Mary Giles and Jennifer Hyndman, eds. *Sites of Violence: Gender and Conflict Zones* (Berkeley and Los Angeles: University of California Press, 2004); Sally Engle Merry, *Human Rights and Gender Violence: Translating International Law into Local Justice* (Chicago: University of Chicago Press, 2006); and Marie Vlachovà and Lea Biason, eds., *Women in an Insecure World: Violence Against Women – Facts, Figures and Analysis*. (Geneva: Geneva Centre for Democratic Control of the Armed Forces, 2005).

First, I consider some very general features of violence and harm suffered by women. I base the discussion on what we know about the structural and social inequalities and symbolic associations of women in most societies, as well as what is known about the violence women suffer typically or systematically both in everyday life and in the extremities of conflict or severe repression. I begin from the assumption that *coercion of women and violence against women are normative* to a greater or lesser extent in many contemporary societies. Second, I take up the consequential and contested issue of whether we can best conceive what happens to women in conflict as "on a continuum" with the nature of everyday violence against women. I argue that emphasis on a continuum of violence has indispensable uses. It is a basis for predicting forms of violence and harm women are likely to suffer, and it is essential to understanding social, institutional, and legal reforms needed in the aftermath of violence in conflict. Even so, it does not adequately capture the experience of catastrophic and life-changing violence many women experience in these conflict situations. In the context of reparations, a focus on the victim's experience of harm and loss is essential. Third, I describe several key factors that are important in recognizing, understanding, and properly assessing harms against women in conflict, based on what is already known. Finally, I suggest that it is useful to have some general categories to keep track of the different ways in which harms befall women "because they are women," sexually, psychologically, socially, and politically; categories rooted in research on actual instances of conflict and repression help us ask the right questions. I propose four such categories: (1) *gender-normative violence*; (2) *sex-, reproduction-, or care-specific violence*; (3) *gender-skewed violence*; and (4) *gender-multiplied violence*. These categories emerge from attempting to capture the gendered dimensions of what happens to women in conflict. Yet significantly, and perhaps unsurprisingly, these categories also form the basis for a gender-comparative analysis, to which I will return.

A final word of caution: the idea of an obligation to undertake reparations, however symbolic and incomplete, for victims of political violence and repression is itself a still fairly novel idea honored mostly in the breach. The sad fact is that most victims of violence, whether male or female, adult or child, will suffer their losses – emotional, material, social, moral, and spiritual – without significant attention, much less redress. The fact that there has been, and will doubtless continue to be, massive unaddressed and unredressed suffering, however, does not diminish the importance of doing justice more fully and truly when the opportunity is there. To reckon women's losses and harms with due weight alongside men's where reparation is at issue is one case of pursuing available justice. Unless we deny that women are entitled to justice for wrongful harm, there is no reason to use the tragic incompleteness of justice in a violent and repressive world as an excuse not to give women their due. That women may not believe anything is due them in virtue of their violation, or may in any case be afraid or ashamed to claim it, is one of the problems to confront in conceiving violence and harm to women from the point of view of reparation.

GENDER AND NORMATIVE VIOLENCE AGAINST WOMEN

I use the terminology of *normative coercion, domination, violence,* and *silencing* of women to refer to the fact that men's domination of women and men's aspiration to control women's lives remain to a greater or lesser extent a reality in human societies. Control of women extends to women's productive, sexual, and reproductive activities and capacities and to women's speech and self-expression, from modes of dress to legal testimony to religious and political participation. The construction of gender is in this way a construction of unequal power among men and women, and of men's entitlement to power over and control of women in a variety of ways, some overt and some indirect. The claim that violence against women is "normative" draws on several decades of feminist research on gender, domination, and violence. Although the regimes of control and the methods of enforcement vary in diverse cultural and political contexts, and vary with social privilege within particular societies, men's authority over many aspects of women's lives, bodies, and social relations is the rule, not the exception. The rule of men over women is typically both expected and accepted in many or most domains of life. It is explained or legitimated through social, religious, and cultural norms. Social, moral, cultural, and religious understandings are typically intertwined in ways that justify and often naturalize male control of women. Male control is represented as proper, divinely ordained, socially functional, natural, inevitable, innate, or biologically determined or predisposed.[10]

Other forms of hierarchy that distribute power, authority, and opportunities in distinct and unequal ways, however, are as commonplace in human societies as is male domination. A given society's norms for acceptable and required

---

[10] Anne Fausto-Sterling, *Myths of Gender: Biological Theories about Women and Men*, 2nd ed. (New York: Basic Books, 1993) critically examines the biological arguments. On the cultural construction and reinforcement of masculinity in a number of contexts, see Lee H. Bowker, ed., *Masculinities and Violence* (Thousand Oaks, CA: Sage Publications, 1998). On men's moral complicity in rape of women as a social pattern and the idea of a "rape culture," see Larry May with Robert Strikwerda, "Rape and Collective Responsibility," in Larry May, *Masculinity and Morality* (Ithaca, NY: Cornell University Press, 1997). The classic theory of rape as the enforcement end of a general male regime of power remains (Susan Brownmiller, *Against Our Will: Men, Women, and Rape* [New York: Ballantine Books, 1993]).

conduct of men and women typically differ for different and unequally privileged social, ethnic, economic, or religious groups within that society. Gender norms for women and men relatively privileged by race, ethnicity, economic resources, religion, or other factors will often differ from those for individuals of lower-ranking class, caste, race, religious, or ethnic groups in the social hierarchy. What remains consistent is that gender norms in most societies constitute positions of women at any level of social power as unequal to the positions of men of similar or higher status. At the same time, gender norms constitute forms of domination, coercion, violence, and silencing of women *by* men at a given level as socially legitimate: either tolerated, permissible, or required. Put simply, it is both normal and in accordance with established social "rules" that women are both unequal to men and dominated by men socially, economically, and civilly, at least within social levels. Men's everyday control of and authority over women's lives – up to and including forms of coercion and violence – is at once an *expression* of women's subordination, a *means* of sustaining male control, and a *prerogative* permitted by maleness as a social standing.

Gender norms are differentiated both within and between social groups of unequal privilege.[11] Men of dominated or oppressed groups will not be able to enjoy positions of control over women of more privileged social groups in many contexts. Lower-class men or men of low-status or stigmatized racial, ethnic, or indigenous groups may be subject to the authority of better-educated or middle-class women in workplaces, government institutions, or legal systems. It can be a potent source of gendered humiliation or resentment that the masculinity of the lower-status man is socially neutralized by a woman's superior class status. Women of oppressed racial or economic groups may be perceived as economically or sexually more exploitable, or exploitable in different ways and with greater impunity, by more privileged men than are women of social status comparable to those men. This constitutes a heightened form of vulnerability for women who are also socially disempowered by class or race. When men compete, the ability to command the sexuality or services of women, including "other men's women," becomes a form of victory, and when the men already possess superior social power, it is a display of that superiority as a superior masculinity, as being "more of a man."

Whole groups of men and women oppressed by racial hierarchy, histories of colonization and genocide, or entrenched poverty face exposure to contempt, neglect, and abuse by official structures of power dominated by men (and

---

[11] On social groups and the complexities of interacting oppressions, see Iris Marion Young, *Justice and the Politics of Difference* (Princeton: Princeton University Press, 1990).

sometimes, to a limited extent, by women) of greater social power. Less privileged men may find that their abilities to exercise masculine prerogatives over women, at least in their own communities, are one of their most significant and valued forms of relative social power; in this regard, they can see themselves as empowered in ways comparable to men of higher social standing insofar as they retain control over "their" women. Women who belong to poor, racially stigmatized, or indigenous communities may find that solidarity with men in their communities and desires to protect these communities make it difficult to publicize or protest forms of gendered violence, coercion, and deprivation. They may see protesting domestic or sexual violence as exposing their men to powerful and hostile social authorities or betraying their men by publicly showing disrespect for men who already experience social devaluation and oppression. Sometimes women so situated see problems of domestic violence and sexual assault, though serious, as less urgent than the problems of poverty, marginalization, and political repression their communities endure. Sometimes, they may simply be afraid to face the reprisals of men in their own communities if they defy the authority of those men. At the same time, women with greater social privilege have significant social and economic interests in a status quo from which they benefit by their affiliation with and loyalty to socially privileged men and may be unwilling to jeopardize their status by reporting or condemning gender-based violence or domination. No spontaneous identification of women with each other, or solidarity among women to oppose gendered domination and violence, can be expected under these circumstances.

There are, in short, different "masculinities" and "femininities" that are not equally available to all within multiply stratified societies, and there are differing social locations created by class, race, ethnicity, indigeneity, and other factors that affect the reality and the perception of the relative power and opportunity of male and female individuals. Women's subjection in most societies to some or many forms of male control, and women's very common exposure across societies to domestic and sexual violence, are commonplace conditions, but these conditions play out in different ways and with distinct meanings and costs for women and men at different social places. The gendered meanings of power, authority, status, submission, respect – indeed, of violence itself as a display of power or right, an emblem of masculinity – emerge against this complex backdrop. Men's and women's unequal social positions are constantly measured in relation to women and men of their own and other social groups. Several implications of this complex backdrop are relevant for looking at violence against women in conflict.

First, because forms of violence against women and the domination of women, sexual and otherwise, *are* so widely normative, it has been difficult historically for many men and women to "see" violence toward women, much less subordination of women, as an intolerable moral outrage, or, in contemporary political-legal parlance, as a gross violation of human rights. Even now, it can appear simply as what (perhaps sadly but inevitably) "happens to women," one unchangeable aspect of the "way of the world." More privileged men and women may collude in ignoring gendered power and violence within their own social group, locating gender domination or violence as a class or cultural problem afflicting primarily groups who are poor, less educated, or marginalized by race, ethnicity, or religion.

Second, the imperative of male control, at its most crude, encourages men to see women as "for" the fulfillment of men's needs for sex, service, labor, and progeny. Even fairly extraordinary violence and coercion visited on women may be considered within the norms of masculinity from the point of view of individual male perpetrators or among men in groups who legitimize and reward each other's behavior. The unusual conditions of conflict, where the use of extreme force becomes legitimate, might seem to permit treating women in ways that are not usually acceptable and that ignore established social patterns through which women may enjoy some forms of control over male access to what they offer. Sex, service, and labor may be expected and claimed more indiscriminately or through threatening and violent means that go far outside of the social constraints through which societies limit and distribute the entitlement of particular men to control particular women.

Third, and of great importance in conflict, a good deal of violence that men do to women (and that women, too, sometimes engage in or assist men in, in largely male-directed organizations and groups) functions as a way of confirming something to or among *men*, and becomes part of a contest among men. The contest is driven by the equation of manliness or masculinity with greater power than women, more power over women, or power over more women than some other men. Demonstrating not only the power but also the willingness or sense of entitlement to use women instrumentally, and if necessary coercively, to satisfy their desires and needs, can prove manliness to men themselves, to women, and to other men (as can the power to protect and provide for women also prove manliness in traditional patriarchal terms). The desires and needs fulfilled by using women at will, however, are not necessarily desires and needs for (or only or primarily for) sex or service, but may in fact be desires and needs *to feel and appear manly* in their own and other men's and women's eyes. They may also be desires and needs to be safe from reprisal from other men who expect conformity and solidarity in their presumption of masculine dominance and of dominance of women as defining masculinity. In parallel, the ability of men to provide protection for and to shield "their own" women from harm or violation by other men is a measure of masculinity, making the violation of other men's women an objective of opposed groups in conflict.

When aggression, dominance, and even the power to subjugate and humiliate are seen as markers of masculinity, they function in multiple ways. Men reassure each other that they are men by acting in aggressive, dominating, or violent ways toward women, creating a solidarity, a "pact," of masculinity in contrast to women. When men turn their aggression, dominance, and violence on each other, they define an order within masculinity by relative manliness that is measured by who has power over whom. The hierarchy of manliness can be either a cooperative hierarchy or a battle for dominance. Thus, violence in conflict can express, confirm, and reinforce masculinity; violence toward both women and other men is freighted with meanings and messages of manliness; and the audience for the messages men send includes other men, women, and themselves. As feminists have told us for decades, maleness is a biological configuration, but masculinity is a *status* and has to be claimed and affirmed by others. There are elements of gender confirmation and affiliation at stake for men in contexts of violence, and there are corresponding vulnerabilities of women to being instruments of that confirmation and affiliation by and between men. These generalizations, however, are rough guides. Cultural and institutional environments may set terms for the demonstration of masculinity in diverse ways, and individuals can also express and interpret masculine behavior, within limits, in their own ways.

IS THERE A "CONTINUUM" OF VIOLENCE IN CONFLICT?

In the literature on violence against women in conflict, the trope of a "continuum" of violence is common. In the *Amnesty International Report 2005*, violence against women in conflicts and post-conflict situations is described as "an extreme manifestation of the discrimination and inequalities women experienced in peacetime."[12] Similarly, Cynthia Cockburn argues for a "connectedness between kinds and occasions of violence," which links personal to international, pre-conflict to conflict and post-conflict, and social to economic and political relations. Cockburn says "No wonder women often say, 'War? Don't speak to me of war. My daily life is battlefield enough.'"[13] In an introduction to the collection containing Cockburn's paper, editors Wenona Mary Giles and Jennifer Hyndman comment that Cockburn's continuum stretches

---

[12] *Amnesty International Report 2005*, Regional Overview 2004, Africa, http://www.amnesty.org/en/library/info/POL10/001/2005, accessed February 26, 2009.
[13] Cynthia Cockburn, "The Continuum of Violence: A Gendered Perspective on War and Peace," in *Sites of Violence*, Giles and Hyndman, 43.

from "the gender violence of everyday life, through the structural violence of economic systems that sustain inequalities and the repressive policing of dictatorial regimes, to the armed conflict of open warfare."[14]

It is certainly true that the accumulated sophistication of gender analysis of violence against women that feminists have developed since the 1960s provides a framework indispensable for understanding how gender structures and legitimates many forms of male violence against women. A unifying explanation of gender oppression, male domination, and violence against women at a high level of generality serves important purposes of pre-conflict prediction and prevention and of post-conflict policy analysis and reform. Even so, it does not fully capture the experience of women who suffer extreme forms of violence in conflict. A theoretical explanation that identifies patterns and similarities for purposes of analysis does not necessarily reflect the shattering experience of discontinuity, the sense of enormity and outrage, or the terror, despair, and social ruin of victims in many actual instances of violence in conflict. What theory reconstructs conceptually as a continuum may not correspond to victims' shocking and traumatizing experiences of violence in conflict and repression situations. This is the reported experience of many victims of public mass rape, domestic enslavement, or sexual mutilation, even where these women's ordinary lives embodied significant components of harsh male control, physical cruelty, coercion, sexual assault, and silencing. The startling Human Rights Watch report on sexual violence against women in Sierra Leone, "We'll Kill You If You Cry," reports the very low pre-conflict status of women as a background factor, yet details graphically the extraordinary pain, loss, physical damage, and despair that women violated in conflict experienced. In a perspective that looks at violence with an eye to *reparation* for victims, the individual victim's experience of catastrophic *discontinuity* needs to hold a central place.[15]

If there are typically forms or levels of violence that are normative against women in many societies, what makes cases of violation in conflict often

---

[14] Wenona Mary Giles and Jennifer Hyndman, "Introduction," in *Sites of Violence*, Giles and Hyndman, 19. For a more complex use of the continuum, see Caroline O. N. Moser, "The Gendered Continuum of Violence and Conflict: An Operational Framework," in *Victims, Perpetrators or Actors?* Moser and Clark.

[15] There is a corresponding danger here of overgeneralizing about victim perspectives. Individual cases call for close attention to victims' own reports and individual assessments in context, but there are also problems of voice that can make it difficult for victims to represent their experiences. I discuss briefly the uncertainties surrounding whether women's own preferences and understandings are completely "colonized" by oppressive circumstances in Margaret Urban Walker, "Truth and Voice in Women's Rights," in *Recognition, Responsibility, and Rights: Feminist Ethics and Social Theory*, ed. Hilde L. Nelson and Robin N. Fiore (Lanham, MD: Rowman and Littlefield, 2003).

catastrophic for individuals? The key is remembering that normative social behaviors and positions, by their nature, constitute an *order*, and that order is in many and profound ways suspended, deformed, or destroyed in conflict situations. If everyday life in many instances is a limiting, cruel, demeaning, or defeating order for women, it is nonetheless one around which women build their lives, make their choices and compromises, and determine their behaviors. So, the idea of normative coercion and violence does not imply that all forms of coercion and violence, no matter how extreme, are to a greater or lesser extent familiar to or expected by women. On the contrary, a woman who is bound to accept uncomplainingly her husband's beatings and marital rape is not thereby prepared for being beaten by strangers, raped repeatedly in public, being raped by a male child (perhaps her own, under threat of death), or being kidnapped, terrorized by physical abuse, and held captive as a sexual and domestic servant of an enemy military. Women who are accustomed to the harsh physical labor required to fulfill their everyday domestic and care-giving responsibilities are not thereby prepared for the threats and hardships of sustaining their families under conditions of displacement and in the absence of material resources and social networks. Even painful and mutilating practices of genital cutting widely practiced in some societies, creating grave forms of physical pain and disability, are socially ritualized and integrated into marriage and family practices that reproduce a cultural order (even if the order is in this respect a cruel one). This is very unlike rape and sexual mutilation intended to soil and ruin, producing social rejection.

The indignities, abuses, injuries, and violations increasingly documented in conflict are often not normal or normative from the victims' point of view. Some of the most intense shame and despair women report as a result of sexual violation by enemies and strangers in conflict is precisely the sense of having been irrevocably spoiled and damaged, thereby rendered unsuitable for the normal life these women previously lived, even if that was itself a life of significant or severe sexual, economic, and social restriction or subjugation. Women very often do not *experience* severe violations merely as more intense forms of what they are used to, and differences of economic class, race, ethnicity, or religious culture will likely affect women's perceptions of continuities and discontinuities of male dominance in peacetime and in conflict.[16] This

---

[16] Judy El-Bushra analyzes several African conflicts emphasizing the importance to women of "respect" even under conditions of domination and exploitation: "They are willing to pay for the public acknowledgment that they make important contributions to society, and for the removal of doubt about the security of their marital and other relationships"; Judy El-Bushra, "Transforming Conflict: Some Thoughts on a Gendered Understanding of Conflict Processes," in *States of Conflict*, Jacobs et al., 83.

is not only an aspect of women's experience, however; it is a fact about what can and does regularly happen in conflict. Just as in combat generally, where unnecessary violence, atrocity, and unjustified killing happen, male coercion and violence in conflict can become disengaged from the larger structure of social norms that limit and channel gender domination within normative boundaries. Women can then no longer rely on these limits and what protection they might offer, and they may find they are exposed to an extreme and nightmarish discontinuity. As United Nations relief official Jan Egeland recently said of rape as a weapon of war, "There has been such a deterioration in the social and moral fabric that sexual violence has become a method of war, and not just soldiers do it, many civilians do, too.... It's like there are no barriers anymore."[17] And it is part of the aim of violence toward women in conflict, used increasingly as a strategy of war, to disrupt and destroy a social order and leave isolation, defeat, and terror in its place.

The theoretical construct of a continuum of violence nonetheless has a central role to play in forecasting the exposure of women to particular forms of loss, coercion, and violence and in making good guarantees of nonrepetition in the wake of violent conflict and repression. Violence against women, so studies suggest, is primarily about control, where controlling women – either one's own or those of other men – is emblematic of masculine power.[18] This factor predicts features of pre-conflict, conflict, and post-conflict situations for women as targets of violence. The pre-conflict condition of militarization often includes a retrenchment and sharp reiteration of masculine and feminine roles, with men as leaders, and heightens a competitive but comradely masculinity, with emphasis on hardness and aggression. During conflict, some of the forms of coercion and violence that are normative in ordinary life are likely to be the ones that escalate beyond normative bounds: routine and extreme sexual abuse and in certain conditions domestic enslavement of women, although on a massive scale or with more gratuitous humiliation and physical harm, are depressingly predictable. Post-conflict, as is now increasingly reported, there is an increase in levels of domestic and social violence toward women.[19] Men

---

[17] Warren Hoge, "U.N. Relief Official Condemns Use of Rape in African Wars," *The New York Times*, June 22, 2005.

[18] See National Research Council, *Understanding Violence Against Women*. On a study in the Eastern Cape that finds it is not violence per se that constitutes masculinity but rather the leverage it gives in controlling women, see Tina Sideris, "Rape in War and Peace: Social Context, Gender, Power and Identity," in *The Aftermath*, Meintjes et al., 145.

[19] Colleen Duggan and Adila Abusharaf, "Reparation of Sexual Violence and Democratic Transition: In Search of Gender Justice," in *The Handbook of Reparations*, ed. Pablo de Greiff (New York: Oxford University Press, 2006).

after conflict need to reassert control over women (and, not incidentally, over themselves, after what may have been traumatizing experiences of violence both done and suffered). They also need to reestablish their place in masculine groups and hierarchies. Their stake in doing so may be enlarged if men are not fully able to enact other forms of masculine behavior, like economic provision and social leadership. Poor men, disenfranchised men, and jobless men may be tempted to control women as the principal expression of masculinity when their demobilization offers little in the way of masculine achievement or affirmation, perhaps not even decent employment. They might control and violate women because that is power and it might be the only power they can exercise. More powerful men, on the other hand, also need to exhibit their control of women, because that is a form of power that confirms and completes their other forms of social power, signifying heteronormative "manliness."

From the point of view of impending or existing conflict, enough is now known to predict women's gendered vulnerability to specific forms of loss and violence in conflict and women's lesser access to resources, limited mobility, inadequate political representation, and unequal access to legal mechanisms. From the point of view of comprehensive programs of reparations, for which the international standards include guarantees of nonrepetition for those violated, it is crucial to understand that women are very likely to face not only "ordinary" levels of violence in conflict and its aftermath, but also escalated everyday violence. Thus, the continuum identifies *areas for preventive and protective concern*, especially legal and social provision for women's rights and safety, that fall within the scope of some reparative measures. It cautions against reparation processes that might be undermined or exploited by continuing vulnerability of women to male control and violence. It helps us understand why, even at extremities, abuse of women can be so easily ignored.

The continuum of male violence toward and domination of women helps us think about necessary social, political, and legal changes that are needed to confront violence against women within conflict and everyday life, and the links between these. Focus on the experience of victims, however, foregrounds the terror of extreme violence in conflict that profoundly disrupts social controls that normally contain male dominance so that even a harsh gendered social order still has its limits and rules. Several specially commissioned reports in a recent study by the International Center for Transitional Justice note a pattern in post-conflict situations, where women's rights organizations were more concerned with forward-looking legal and social change to restructure women's daily lives, whereas victim organizations often did not focus specifically on women who suffered in conflict but rather on women as relatives and dependents of those harmed.[20] The forward-looking agenda of advocacy for women's rights can leave behind victims, just as a focus on men as primary victims and women as survivors can leave female victims of direct violence with no place to turn, or with inadequate acknowledgment of their terrible losses. As Ruth Rubio-Marín's contribution to this volume argues, reparations must express a commitment to a rights-respecting political order for all citizens while at the same time acknowledging and addressing wrongs and harms to individuals who are violated.

SIGNIFICANT DIMENSIONS OF VIOLENCE AGAINST WOMEN

What are some of the common patterns of violence that afflict women in armed conflict and repression? I explore a variety of factors involving gender that appear in research on conflict situations. These common patterns alert us to where and for what we should look in identifying violence toward women and harms women suffer.

Male Exchanges through Violence toward Women

Cockburn writes that "male-dominant systems involve a hierarchy between men, producing different and unequal masculinities, always defined in relation not only to each other but to women."[21] In this way men's normative control of women becomes a means of solidarity among men allied to each other and becomes a strategy of humiliating and expressing dominance over the male opposition in conflict. When men acknowledge and endorse each other's possession, protection, and control of women, they confirm each other's masculinity. The same principle of male control also accommodates and serves to express differences among men in a hierarchy of power and status.[22] When

---

[20] On the gap between advocacy for women generally and advocacy for women victims, see Beth Goldblatt, "Evaluating the Gender Content of Reparations: Lessons from South Africa," in *What Happened to the Women? Gender and Reparations for Human Rights Violations*, ed. Ruth Rubio-Marín (New York: Social Science Research Council, 2006), 56–57; also in the same volume, see Claudia Paz y Paz Bailey, "Guatemala: Gender and Reparations for Human Rights Violations," 131, note 78; Julie Guillerot, "Linking Gender and Reparations in Peru: A Failed Opportunity," 145–149; Heidy Rombouts, "Women and Reparations in Rwanda: A Long Path to Travel," 205–206; and Galuh Wandita, Karen Campbell-Nelson, and Manuela Leong Pereira, "Learning to Engender Reparations in Timor-Leste: Reaching Out to Female Victims," 292–296. Jamesina King, "Gender and Reparations in Sierra Leone: The Wounds of War Remain Open," in the same volume, 253–256, tells a somewhat different story.

[21] Cynthia Cockburn, "The Continuum of Violence," 29, citing Carol Pateman.

[22] A Human Rights Watch report on Sierra Leone describes the result of a rebel commander's attempt to spare an old woman from rape by troupes: "But the other rebels got annoyed and

men violently appropriate and violate women who are supposed to be within the possession, protection, and control of other men, they subordinate or challenge the other men's manliness, expressed in their ability to remain in control of their women. Women are thus a medium through which men transact exchanges signifying relative power, alliance, or opposition.

The pattern is unsettling in its simplicity and catastrophic for women where men enter into wholesale and violent conflict; there appropriation, violation, and abuse of women are at once practically effective in disrupting social life and its material maintenance but also expressively effective in signaling disrespect, disdain, and contempt for other men.[23] Though it is true that men are also raped or sexually abused by men in conflict or detention, the meaning of this abuse is clearly that the man sexually used becomes an unmanly (lesser) man or even "a woman," a meaning common in the rape of men in prison environments, but also in the rape and sexual abuse of men by men in armed conflict and repression.[24] Women, too, participate in these symbolic exchanges that take all too literal forms, where women may express the dominance of "their" men, and the higher social status they derive from it, by their ability to command or to evade the authority of other lowering-ranking men, or to participate in subjecting enemy men to sexual humiliation. When women abuse women, they may also enhance and exhibit their position as protected and inviolate by participating in rendering other women used and demeaned. In an implacable hierarchy enforced by coercion and violence, women too will claim places of *relative* power.[25] The common denominator is that in most human groups an exercise of power, especially sexual power, over women is a symbolically masculine and superordinate position, whereas being the object of sexual control and coercion is feminine and subordinate. The more benign aspect of this gendered symbolic order is the protective face of masculinity, with masculine obligations to support and protect; the uglier aspect is men's sense of entitlement to women's bodies and labor for "individual

---

started insulting the commander saying, 'Fine, you can fuck any women you want, anytime you want, but now that we have one we want, you say no.' The commander finally said that they could go ahead so all five rebels, including a small boy of fifteen years, raped her." Human Rights Watch, "We'll Kill You If You Cry," 37.

[23] Dorothy Q. Thomas and Regan E. Ralph, "Rape in War: Challenging the Tradition of Impunity," *SAIS Review* (1994): 82–99.

[24] For analysis of the meanings of men's rape and sexual mutilation of men in the former Yugoslavia, see Dubravka Zarkov, "The Body of the Other Man: Sexual Violence and Construction of Masculinity, Sexuality and Ethnicity in Croatian Media," in *Victims, Perpetrators or Actors?* Moser and Clark. See also Sandesh Sivakumaran, "Male/Male Rape and the 'Taint' of Homosexuality," *Human Rights Quarterly* 27 (2005): 1274–1306.

[25] On women's roles in domestic, caste, and religious violence, see Parita Mukta, "Gender, Community, Nation: The Myth of Innocence," in *States of Conflict*, Jacobs et al.

gratification or political ends."²⁶ Both aspects, however, are rooted in widespread beliefs that masculinity requires and is measured by control of and access to women.

The Symbolism of Gender and Punishment of Women's (and Men's) Gender Transgression

A symbolic dimension of gender invests women and men with culturally significant meanings. There are considerable similarities in the gendered meanings of womanhood that traverse cultural contexts, and these can be adapted to specific situations in which women become the medium for representing cultural identity or its transformations. Yuval-Davis says, "Women often become the symbolic bearers of modernity. Unveiling women in Ata Turk's revolution of 1917, which was aimed at constructing Turkey as a modern nation-state, was as important as veiling them has been to Muslim fundamentalists in the contemporary Middle East."²⁷ In another example, a society's admitting or inducting women into its armed forces is also a symbolically freighted move that can signify civic equality but also society-wide militarization. In a variety of ways women function as "iconic representations" of cultural, ethnic, or national identity.²⁸

Women are often vehicles for the representation of a nation's quest for independence and freedom from incursion or violation by an external power, or for an ethnic or religious group's reiteration of its defining "tradition." V. Spike Peterson and Anne Sisson Runyan call "gendered nationalism" the "manipulation of gender identities and symbols and gendered divisions of power, labor, and resources" that are recruited to the task of winning wars of national liberation and establishing independence.²⁹ Women's purity symbolizes the inviolability of a community and the power of its men to protect its boundaries, making sexual violence by outside men a humiliation of individual women, a violation of communal integrity, and a shaming defeat of men in their protective roles. Women also commonly symbolize "home and hearth," the stability and continuity of a community's daily life, making the killing and violation

---

[26] Amnesty International, "Violence Against Women: A Fact Sheet," http://www.amnestyusa.org/women/violence/index.html, accessed February 26, 2009.

[27] Niva Yuval-Davis, "Gender, the Nationalist Imagination, War, and Peace," in *Sites of Violence*, Giles and Hyndman, 172.

[28] Giles and Hyndman, "Introduction," in *Sites of Violence*, Giles and Hyndman, 9, quoting Amartya Sen.

[29] V. Spike Peterson and Anne Sisson Runyan, *Global Gender Issues* (Boulder, CO: Westview Press, 1993), 132–133. See also Cynthia Enloe, *Maneuvers: The International Politics of Militarizing Women's Lives* (Berkeley and Los Angeles: University of California Press, 2000).

of women an assault on the bases of social order.³⁰ Men, too, are bearers of symbolic meaning, for example, that of the warrior or protector. Like material resources, however, cultural symbolic resources are apt to be controlled in many social settings by powerful men rather than by women. The protection or the abuse of women, both in times of conflict and repression and in the aftermath, will invariably be seen as statements not only about women and men, but about society's moral, political, and cultural values and identity. So charged are the social and cultural meanings invested in both the violation and protection of women that the suffering and human rights of individual women may be overshadowed by social struggles over these meanings.

Transgression by women of their socially assigned meanings provokes forms of repression and violence that are anything but symbolic. Post-conflict reports from Peru, Guatemala, Timor-Leste, and South Africa include assassination, disappearance, rape, torture, harassment, and detention of women for daring to engage in political activity or community organization, or taking active roles in pursuing the mistreatment or disappearance of male relatives.³¹ Women's confinement to domestic or familial spheres and the definition of politics as a male domain, as well as the presumption that women will not contest or confront male authority, constitute these activities as intolerable transgressions of women's gendered places and their required subservience to male authorities. Women who show resilience under the hands of male torturers may provoke additional punishment. Furthermore, women fare no better when they are seen as mere extensions of their male relatives. They have been used as hostages, or are detained and tortured, to influence or to extract information on their male relatives. Men, too, may suffer reprisals or may be threatened for *failing* to demonstrate their own masculinity and to affirm other men's masculinity by sharing in the control and use of women. Just as men may suffer penalties of ridicule or exclusion for sharing power and daily responsibilities with women equitably in daily life, so men can be penalized or punished for refusing to participate in or to condone violence toward women in contexts of conflict. There are powerful pressures both within men and between men to assert and mutually affirm dominating masculinity.

Specifically Sexual or Reproductive Coercion, Harm, Torture, and Mutilation

Women in some conflict contexts suffer forms of violence similar to those afflicting men, like extrajudicial execution, illegal detention, beatings, and

---

[30] Tina Sideris, "Rape in War and Peace," in *The Aftermath*, Meintjes et al., 146–149.
[31] See Rubio-Marín, *What Happened to the Women?*, for reports on Peru, Guatemala, South Africa, and Timor-Leste.

torture.³² In many cases, however, violence afflicting women includes abuse, torture, terror, and mutilation of women that is specifically sexual in nature, or that targets women's reproductive and sexual parts, not infrequently causing irreparable damage and reproductive disability or inability. In addition to rape and other sexual abuse, reports of sexual mutilation, forced prostitution, sexual slavery, forced pregnancy, forced abortion, forced sterilization, and sexual torture are reported in many contemporary conflict contexts, and rapes include gang rapes, rapes with objects, public rapes, and sometimes men forced to rape women who are related to them.³³ Also reported are tendencies to sexualize the torture of women, raping them, assaulting their breasts, genitals, and reproductive organs, and threatening to do so. From Sierra Leone, Guatemala, and Rwanda come reports of pregnant women's bellies sliced open and fetuses cut out.

Much reported sexual violence surely has instrumental purposes – to terrorize, subjugate, and demoralize women and their communities, and to punish women for political or autonomous activity. In Guatemala, where rape of indigenous women was sometimes "'massive' and/or 'multiple,' performed in public squares or markets, to be seen by the whole community or the victims' families" according to Claudia Paz y Paz Bailey, rape was a form of genocidal violence and was one part of a specific and repeated pattern of massacre and destruction of indigenous communities for which the Guatemalan army trained its soldiers.³⁴ Contemporary patterns of mass rape and sexual mutilation leave no doubt that mass sexual violence is a tool of war, as perhaps historically, in reality, it has always been. Yet the sheer extremity and grotesque cruelty of sexual violence reported in many cases, even if tolerated, encouraged, or required by military, militia, or insurgency authorities, suggests also powerful desires of men to exert total and brutal power over women and engage in sadistic destruction of women's bodies and persons. Postmortem sexual mutilations are not entirely a pragmatic practice, despite their use in terrorizing populations. It seems that under conditions of superior power and extreme violence, just as some combatants will commit other atrocities and massacres out of frustration or with a sense of explosive exhilaration, so too will some men (and, in some cases, women) engage in pointless torture, sexual injury,

---

[32] Guillerot, for example, reports that Peru's Truth and Reconciliation Commission found the crimes most frequently reported by or about female victims were murders and extrajudicial executions (50%), followed by detentions (27%), tortures (23%), kidnappings (17%), disappearances (16%), and rapes (10%); Guillerot, 141–142. Guillerot of course notes the underreporting likely to occur in cases of sexual violence.

[33] See Paz y Paz Bailey, Rombouts, King, and Wandita et al.

[34] See Paz y Paz Bailey, especially 94–101, quote page 97; see also Wandita et al., 290, on strategic uses of sexual violence in Timor-Leste.

and humiliation of women.[35] This fact is perhaps less to be explained than it is to be noted, so that its prevention becomes a priority and the costs of engaging in this kind of violence are made steep, instead of accepted as inevitable or as "collateral damage" to be expected in conflict. In any case, both the coldly planned military and political dimensions, as well as the toleration of excesses, need to be kept in mind.

In some situations, reported sexual violence seems to be almost exclusively directed at women, but no one doubts that sexual violence by men against men occurs and is probably even more underreported than sexual violence toward women.[36] This is a topic that requires further exploration, both in terms of its gendered meaning and impact for and on men, and for its actual occurrence and the conditions under which male-on-male sexual violence occurs. At present, men's sexual violence against women is widely reported and largely predictable; it calls for specific and immediate preventive and deterrent action for that reason.

Targeting Women's Mothering

The vulnerability of women to forms of torment and torture because of their maternal hopes, attachments, and responsibilities deserves separate mention. Diverse forms of reproductive coercion and violation are a part of many contemporary conflicts. Men's ordinary control of women's fertility, through marriage practices and conjugal control, including marital rape and prohibiting or forcing contraception or abortion, is within the category of normative coercion in many societies. Forced pregnancy, forced abortion or sterilization, and forced cohabitation with almost inevitable results of pregnancy are among the forms of reproductive abuse reported in contexts of conflict. These are forms of both physical and psychological violation, with potentially irreversible and dire social consequences, as when women must deal with the stigma of bearing not only children outside marriage, but also children of enemies and those who have engaged in genocide against the women's group, as in the Rwandan and Guatemalan situations. Women's maternal roles and attachments can be exploited to produce anguish and terror; torturers may threaten women's children, and soldiers may abduct or massacre their children as well as raping or sexually mutilating and humiliating the women themselves. Women may

---

[35] On killing frenzy in close combat, see Jonathan Glover, *Humanity: A Moral History of the Twentieth Century* (New Haven: Yale University Press, 2000), 52–57. For some gruesome examples of postmortem sexual mutilation in Guatemala, see Paz y Paz Bailey, 98 and 127, notes 34 and 35.

[36] A recent study is Sivakumaran, "Male/Male Rape."

have to bear the torment of their inability to protect their daughters from abduction and sexual violence and their sons from forced conscription. Population displacements render women unable to care properly for children and frail elders for whom women consider themselves responsible.[37]

The situation of women abducted into domestic and sexual enslavement in which they have given birth presents grave difficulties for the reintegration of both women and their children. A 2002 UNICEF report estimates that although 30% of child soldiers in Sierra Leone were girls, only 8% benefited from the disarmament, demobilization, and reintegration (DDR) program, because the girls were perceived, and perceived themselves, as "sex and domestic slaves." Jamesina King reports the creation in Sierra Leone of a governmental family-tracing program to assist abducted children, but no reparation measures have yet been enacted.[38] The long-term consequences of rape in conflict include disabilities that cause fistula, reproductive injuries, infertility, and the infection of women with AIDS, which not only cause grave suffering but also affect women's social acceptability, marriageability, and childbearing possibilities. Women raped or subjected to sexual slavery have given birth to children for whom they may not be able, or may not wish, to care.[39] Finally, there are cases of fraudulent adoption of infants taken from women murdered or in detention, raising issues of support and search services, as well as the irreparable disruption or loss of familial relationship.[40]

Women and Property

As weighted as gender roles and positions are with symbolism, especially meanings invested in women as sexual beings and as mothers, women also hold and control property and resources and are a major productive force in many local economies. Judith Gardam and Hilary Charlesworth, writing on the protection of women in armed conflict, urge us to take account of women in "the various roles [women] perform in societies and not merely as mothers and sexual objects."[41] Women are a key productive force in the daily survival and reproduction of communities. Yet often women by law, custom,

---

[37] Examples in this category are found in Goldblatt, 54; Paz y Paz Bailey, 97 and 126, note 23; Rombouts, 208; and King, 251.
[38] King, 274.
[39] King, 275–276.
[40] Human Rights Watch, "Argentina: Reluctant Partner: The Argentine Government's Failure to Back Trials of Human Rights Violators," *Human Rights Watch Report* 13, no. 5 (December 2001), Section V, http://www.hrw.org/reports/2001/argentina/index.html, accessed February 26, 2009.
[41] Gardam and Charlesworth, "Protection of Women in Armed Conflict," 166.

and religion do not enjoy control over property and wealth comparable to men of similar class location, and violent upheavals that disrupt and transform traditional divisions of labor, power, and ownership, or that involve relocations, often result in dramatic losses for women economically, or in women's being unable to assert rights to property. Despite a reform of inheritance law adopted in 1999, Rwandan women and girls are still denied equal rights to land under Rwandan customary law in an agrarian society in which survival is determined by access to land.[42] Remaining in or returning to rural villages to coexist with perpetrators of rape and murder are not conditions under which women are likely to assert their rights to land, especially where this means asserting rights to land against men.[43] Official statistics used to define policies of reconstruction may ignore households run de facto by women when husbands are absent or missing.[44] Women may find their land or jobs awarded to demobilized combatants.[45] At the same time, it is virtually always true that women continue to bear responsibility for the care of children, relatives, and elders.

With current, long-delayed, and still not fully effective attention focused on sexual violence toward women in political conflict, there is still the possibility that sexual violence will take so much of the stage that women's losses of livelihood, land, and wealth may be eclipsed by the more shocking facts of mass rape, sexualized torture and mutilation, and sexual enslavement. It would be a terrible irony if women at long last receive adequate recognition of victimization by sexual violence in conflict, only to be *sexualized as victims*, so that their economic and material losses receive little weight. Where women have been abducted and enslaved for sexual use, they also have often been victims of forced labor, a human rights violation and form of exploitation that should be recognized and redressed specifically as such. It should not be assumed, however, that sexual violence and unjust destruction or appropriation of women's property are separate kinds of violence that only circumstantially interact. Whereas men coercively appropriate both daily toil and sex from women, Meredith Turshen effectively argues from the African context that "in civil wars, armies also use rape systematically to strip women of their economic and political assets. Women's assets reside in the first instance in their productive

---

[42] Human Rights Watch, "Struggling to Survive: Barriers to Justice for Rape Victims in Rwanda," *Human Rights Watch Report* 16, no. 10 (September 2004): 11–12. See also Rombouts, 204–205.

[43] Meredeth Turshen, "Women's War Stories," and Clotilde Twagiramariya and Meredeth Turshen, "'Favours' to Give and 'Consenting' Victims: The Sexual Political of Survival in Rwanda," both in *What Women Do in Wartime*, Turshen and Twagiramariya, 8, 109, and 112. See also Rombouts, 231–233.

[44] See Duggan and Abusharaf, "Reparation of Sexual Violence."

[45] Codou Bop, "Women in Conflicts, Their Gains and Losses," in *The Aftermath*, Meintjes et al., 29.

and reproductive labour power and in the second instance in their possessions and their access to valuable assets such as land and livestock."[46] It is imperative that women who suffer violence and harm in conflict be an integral part of processes that define the nature and relative attention to sexual and nonsexual harms, and that these processes anticipate and identify the complex and bidirectional relationships between sexual abuse and material dispossession of women.

Women as/and Social Capital

Social capital accumulates at those points where trust in human connections and networks of communication make cooperation and material resources available to men and women. Social capital is defined as "the rules, norms, obligations, reciprocity and trust embedded in social relations, social structures and a society's institutional arrangements that enable its members to achieve their individual and community objectives."[47] Both men and women are utterly dependent on, and contribute to the production of, social capital embodied in formal institutions and informal networks. Social capital is the human connective tissue that holds households, relationships, localities, and societies together. Women are often seen as symbolizing social capital – the daily order of communal life – but women are in fact concretely indispensable to the maintenance of that order, both materially and socially, through labor as well as maintenance of day-to-day cooperative relationships and informal social networks. This, once again, makes women choice targets for violence in conflict or under repression, where the goal of "the disruption of social arrangements, activities, and institutions that give people a sense of belonging and meaning" is served by targeting women for death, social disgrace, and communal exclusion.[48] Sexual violence is increasingly a strategy for "undermining cultural values and community relationships, destroying the ties that hold society together."[49] Conflict that destroys the infrastructures of electricity, transport, and health care may limit women's mobility; creating rivalry over scarce resources, such as water, can set neighbors against each other; political terror can isolate individuals and households within communities where fear

---

[46] Meredeth Turshen, "The Political Economy of Rape," in *Victims, Perpetrators or Actors?* Moser and Clark, 56.
[47] Moser, "The Gendered Continuum," 43. Moser provides analysis of different forms of social capital and their availability or impact on men and women.
[48] The phrase is from Anu Pillay, "Violence Against Women in the Aftermath," in *The Aftermath*, Meintjes et al., 57.
[49] Human Rights Watch, "We'll Kill You If You Cry," 4. Case studies in Rubio-Marín, *What Happened to the Women?*, include uses of sexual violence for demoralization of communities.

and mutual distrust become survival skills.⁵⁰ All these kinds of conflict and repression inhibit the maintenance of social capital or destroy it. Women's activities and relationships are both generators of social capital and are dependent on its sustainability. The losses that women incur in these dimensions, and the value to women of opportunities to repair and create networks and relationships, are important issues for reparation agendas that seek to address women's wrongful losses. This is also an area in which the creation or reconstruction of collective resources and communal institutions may be relevant in reparations schemes. Heidy Rombouts reports the delicate social ecology of life on the Rwandan hills, and the urgency of considering reparations measures that respect fragile social balances that maintain women's lives.⁵¹ Competition among women, and among and within communities, for scarce resources means that women may not readily sympathize with other women who are victims, and that female victims may not necessarily stand together to seek repair.

Quandaries of Shame and Exclusion

It is important to stress that shame, humiliation, and despair are common reactions of victims of violence, both male and female. Research on traumatic violence, political and criminal, shows that victims experience an intense and overwhelming cluster of emotions after suffering violence or the traumatic loss of loved ones.⁵² Furthermore, victims crave and deserve validation of the fact of their injury and the wrongfulness of what was done to them. When victims are instead shunned, ignored, blamed, or punished, they suffer not only isolation and despair, but a form of normative abandonment, a realization that rules and restraints that might have protected them are not enforced in their case and that they themselves do not matter. Exclusion and abandonment are additional

---

⁵⁰ Moser, 43–46. See also Caroline O. N. Moser and Cathy McIlwaine, "Gender and Social Capital in Contexts of Political Violence: Community Perceptions from Colombia and Guatemala," in *Victims, Perpetrators or Actors?* Moser and Clark.

⁵¹ Rombouts, 231–233.

⁵² Ronnie Janoff-Bulman, *Shattered Assumptions* (New York: The Free Press, 1992), 79–80, notes research that human-induced victimization is apt to be humiliating, having made one helpless or overwhelmed before another person, challenging the victim's "competence and independence." Judith Herman, *Trauma and Recovery: The Aftermath of Violence – From Domestic Abuse to Political Terror* (New York: Basic Books, 1997), 33, also discusses humiliation and grief that result from exposure to "the extremities of helplessness and terror." See also Susan Brison, *Aftermath* (Princeton: Princeton University Press, 2002) on massively altered senses of self and self-control of victims of violence, and Thomas J. Scheff, *Bloody Revenge: Emotions, Nationalism and War* (Lincoln, NE: iUniverse.com, Inc., 2000) on the occurrence of shame in response to violation and the dangers of aggressive rage that arises, or can be induced, as a defensive response to that shame.

emotional, social, psychological, and moral injuries that undermine or destroy trust and hope in those who have already suffered terrible violations.[53]

In the case of women and sexual violence, notoriously, victims may become the target of shaming, blame, and disdain. This is no less true when the sexual violence occurs in political conflict or under repression, both as spontaneous acts of individuals and also, now endemically, as a strategy of genocide, torture, terror, and demoralization of populations. One might hope for communities' solidarity with women who are brutally and ruthlessly used by enemies in the context of conflict, but it appears that this is not usually the case. Every one of the country studies in Ruth Rubio-Marín's *What Happened to the Women?* reports problems of stigmatization, rejection, fear, and shame for raped and sexually abused women, whether the reported incidence of sexual violence is great or less frequent.[54] The shame of women who correctly assume that they will be rejected, scorned, shunned, or driven out by families and communities after suffering sexual violation is well documented. The likelihood of this result is precisely one of the known motivations for those using rape as a strategy to demoralize and break down communities.[55] Even when families are willing to accept and support women who have suffered rape, abduction, and pregnancy due to rape, their larger communities may see these women as stained, unmarriageable, and under suspicion of complicity with the aggressors.[56] The degree to which this is so, however, can vary with the publicity and breadth of sexual violation as well as specific political and cultural contexts.

Even women who do not blame themselves for their violation, and understand that they were raped as a strategy of conflict, may nevertheless experience themselves as "spoiled, worthless, and devalued" because of deep associations between women's dignity and their sexual purity and propriety.[57] Rape and

---

53 Psychologists call this a "second wound." Janoff-Bulman cites Martin Symonds on the "second injury," in *Shattered Assumptions*, 147. On the "second wound" and the "conspiracy of silence," see also Yael Danieli, "Introduction," *International Handbook of Multigenerational Legacies of Trauma* (New York: Plenum Press, 1998), 7. On the complexities of victim response and the importance of validation, see Margaret Urban Walker, "'The Cycle of Violence,'" *Journal of Human Rights* 5 (2006): 81–105.
54 See Goldblatt, 54–55; Paz y Paz Bailey, 100 and 128, note 50; Guillerot, 141 and 146–147; Rombouts, 208–209 and 213; King, 263 and 273; and Wandita et al., 292.
55 Thomas and Ralph, "Rape in War" explains the strategic function of rape that exploits women's "protected status" to shame communities as well as individual victims.
56 Melanie Thernstrom, "Charlotte, Grace, Janet and Caroline Come Home," *The New York Times Magazine*, May 8, 2005, 34–39, reports the situation of four young women who escaped abduction and violent captivity by the Lord's Resistance Army in northern Uganda, where families support them but social reintegration remains tenuous.
57 Sideris, 150, discussing interviews with Mozambican women. See also Human Rights Watch, "We'll Kill You If You Cry," on the profound shame of women even while many are welcomed back by families.

other forms of sexual indignity and atrocity (such as coerced incestuous rape or mutilation of genitals) are often committed publicly to add to the future humiliation of victims under the eyes of their communities. Further, abduction of women and children who are made to serve as combatants or coerced into sexual use and domestic service, and who are commonly "initiated" and subjugated by being forced to kill for and otherwise serve the enemy or insurgent army, has become widespread. Melanie Thernstrom reports of abductees in northern Uganda that "they cannot go back to villages where people recall the night they returned with the rebels and massacred their relatives and neighbors – and sometimes even their own parents."[58] Women may also be ashamed, and may be actively shamed by others, for attempting to get acknowledgment and redress for their injuries and losses, sexual and otherwise, when "there is no comparison to the hardship of battle."[59] In other words, it is the suffering that is paradigmatically that of men in war – or men killed or disappeared in political activity – that deserves attention, and women may be intimidated and shamed for suggesting that their suffering deserves acknowledgment, much less redress. In this way women's own suffering "becomes invisible even to themselves."[60]

As mentioned earlier, the "feminized" position of the victim of sexual violence means that male victims will also bear heavy burdens of shame when they are sexually victimized, although the longer-term social and psychological consequences of being a male victim of sexual violence in conflict, as well as the incidence of sexual violence between men, are unclear in comparison to what we know about women. If the practice of attending to sexual violence toward women in conflict is recent, the practice of recording and investigating sexual violations of men is not clearly established, although there are some pioneering efforts.[61] Proposed reparations in Timor-Leste provide for boys and men who are victims of sexual violence.[62]

---

[58] Thernstrom, 38; Sideris, 148, describes abducted Mozambican women's feeling like "active participants."

[59] Sheila Meintjes, Anu Pillay, and Meredeth Turshen, "There is No Aftermath for Women," in *The Aftermath*, Meintjes et al., 14.

[60] Guillerot, 147. Chillingly, Goldblatt and Meintjes discuss the exposure of women to sexual abuse within their own underground and military organizations. They report from an interview with Thenjiwe Mtintso, a senior member of the South African ANC's army: "She said the men knew that women would not want to talk about having been raped. One of her comrades said to her, 'You know, it's going to get to the point that I am going to rape you. And it's going to be very easy to rape you and I know that there is no way that you are going to stand in front of all these people and say I raped you.'" Goldblatt and Meintjes, "South African Women Demand the Truth," 50.

[61] See Zarkov; see also Sivakumaran.

[62] Wandita, 263.

Women's Insecure Testimonial Positions

Working in the former Yugoslavia, psychologist Ingrid Foeken says, "There was too much shame, and raped women were at risk of being driven out of their community if they were found out," stressing the hesitancy of women to discuss sexual violation even in a therapeutic context, much less to make a public admission or legal complaint.[63] According to Beth Goldblatt and Sheila Meintjes, "Women do not speak about rape out of shame, for fear of loss of status, because they do not want to relive the pain, and because they are often unwilling to subject themselves to cross-examination by the accused person's defense lawyer."[64] Accurate information, accessible processes, a public environment that validates the victim and blames the assailant, and guarantees of confidentiality and security are among the conditions that could increase women's willingness to report and to pursue legal and other redress for sexual violation. Human Rights Watch, for example, describes misunderstandings and lack of protection that have inhibited rape victims from coming forward in Rwanda, and Goldblatt and Meintjes describe women's belief in the South African context that to report sexual abuse to the TRC they had to testify publicly or have their violation revealed.[65] Finally, women often have concrete reason to fear reprisal from men with whom they continue to live in close proximity and who may continue to enjoy social authority in the aftermath of conflict. This is especially true when the likelihood of criminal prosecution is negligible or when amnesty has been given, and it may also affect women's participation in nonjuridical processes like truth commissions or traditional practices like the Rwandan gacacas.[66]

Alongside the burdens of shame and fear women experience in the wake of violence, there is also the commonplace and continuing lack of standing, or uncertain standing, of women to speak publicly or to give testimony in many societies, and there may be additional burdens applied to women in customary and legal practices with regard to sexual assault. Silencing,

---

[63] Ingrid Foeken, "Confusing Realities and Lessons Learned in Wartime: Supporting Women's Projects in the Former Yugoslavia," in *Assault on the Soul*, Sharratt and Kaschak, 93.
[64] Goldblatt and Meintjes, 53. See also Human Rights Watch, "Struggling to Survive," 1–58, on low rates of reporting by women of sexual violence.
[65] Human Rights Watch, "Struggling to Survive," and Goldblatt and Meintjes. See also Debra L. De Laet, "Gender Justice: A Gendered Assessment of Truth-Telling Mechanisms," in *Telling the Truths: Truth Telling and Peace Building in Post-Conflict Societies*, ed. Tristan Anne Borer (Notre Dame: University of Notre Dame Press, 2006).
[66] Meredeth Turshen, "Women's War Stories," in *What Women Do In Wartime*, Turshen and Twagiramariya, 8. See also Human Rights Watch, "Struggling to Survive," and Rombouts, 231–232.

through structural and legal means, as well as direct personal pressure, is an integral part of most oppressive social arrangements, especially where they enable those with superior power to commit violence, and this is definitely true in the subordination of women in many social settings. Truth-telling requires not only the will to do so (raising questions of physical and social security), but also the means, opportunity, and standing to do so. Women have in many societies been assigned "speechless standings" that forbid or disqualify by law or custom their testimony relative to certain matters, that require the permission of men to speak, or that impede women's access to the needed public, legal, and institutional avenues of expression. These are impediments to women being able to enunciate their experiences and report their injuries, and so help render women's injuries invisible.[67] In conflicts involving indigenous communities, vulnerable ethnic groups, or national minorities, women and men who are victims of conflict may be additionally marginalized by the languages they speak, which are usually not the languages of legal and political institutions, a concrete problem of access to reparations mechanisms.[68]

Indeed, when we consider the formidable and continuing barriers – personal, familial, customary, legal, and institutional – to women's speaking publicly and with authority, it helps explain why women who speak about violence tend to do so about the violence inflicted on others, especially others in their families, putting themselves in the service of others' losses and suffering, fearing or ashamed to speak their own. At the same time men are entirely aware of the barriers to women's speaking publicly and appreciate how little recognition and validation women who do manage to speak out are likely to receive. When it comes to sexual violations of women, anticipated impunity and even anticipated invisibility are fully reasonable assumptions for male perpetrators in many social climates, even if they end up on the losing political side in a post-conflict era. In this respect, the surge in attention to sexual violence in the past decade is a mixed blessing in the absence of either effective prosecution or reliable rights to reparation. Lyn Lusi, founder of a clinic for sexual violence victims in the Democratic Republic of Congo, laments, "all that publicity is saying, there's impunity, there's impunity. There's nothing to frighten people... now they know they can do it without paying the consequences."[69]

---

[67] Walker, "Truth and Voice in Women's Rights."
[68] Paz y Paz Bailey, 116–117, reports on multiple barriers for rural Mayan women in Guatemala.
[69] Integrated Regional Information Networks (IRIN) Web Special on violence against women and girls during and after conflict, September 14, 2004, http://www.irinnews.org/webspecials/gbv/gbv-webspecial.pdf, accessed February 26, 2009.

RELEVANT CATEGORIES OF VIOLENCE AND HARM TO WOMEN

It must always be emphasized in considering violence against women in conflict and repression that women in many respects will suffer what men suffer, both as combatants and as civilians. Although war continues to be seen commonly as a male domain, wars of liberation and civil conflicts in Africa and Central America, for example, have involved substantial numbers of women soldiers. Where women fight or engage in combat-support functions, women can be killed, wounded, tortured, coerced into performing atrocities, or detained and punished inhumanely. All forms of acknowledgment, reward, and redress that apply to male combatants and support personnel should routinely go to women on the same bases and to the same extent. A failure of demobilization, peace agreements, or reparation programs to treat women equitably is itself a matter for redress. The categories of violence and harm mentioned below, however, can be visited on women when they are in combatant roles or when they are civilians, and when they are activists or when they are not actively involved in political struggle or resistance. The dualities of combatant/noncombatant and activist/nonactivist should not be intentionally or inadvertently overlaid with a gender division between male and female. In whatever roles or status women inhabit in a context of conflict or repression, they might suffer or be victimized in precisely the same ways that men are, but also in gendered ways reflected in the categories below.

Contemporary warfare undeniably entails huge civilian casualties.[70] The intensity of wars waged within or across borders, close to the ground, primarily with light weaponry, and without sharp boundaries demarcating zones of combat, expose whole populations in any area of conflict to death, injury, and violation and result in large-scale displacement of people from their homes and states.[71] Insofar as women often make up half or a large majority of

---

[70] Cockburn, "The Continuum of Violence," gives a figure of 90% for civilian casualties in contemporary war. Giles and Hyndman, "Introduction," 5 and 35, give a figure of 60% to 80%. I thank Vanessa Farr for pointing out how dubious are comparisons between contemporary wars and earlier ones, given that the sack of cities, the (sometimes genocidal) massacre of populations, and the enslavement of men, women, and children in war seems coextensive with the recorded history of warfare.

[71] On the consequences for civilians of small and light arms in West African conflict, see Corinne Dufka, "Combating War Crimes in Africa," Testimony Before the US House International Relations Committee, Africa Subcommittee, June 25, 2004, http://www.campboiro.org/bibliotheque/hrw/combating_war_crimes.html, accessed February 26, 2009. There is a growing literature on the gendered dimensions of small arms. See Vanessa Farr et al., "Gender Perspectives on Small Arms and Light Weapons: Regional and International Concerns," Bonn International Center for Conversion, Brief 24, http://www.bicc.de/index.php/publications/briefs/brief-24, accessed February 26, 2009.

the populations in most areas, one would expect civilian death, injury, and displacement to afflict women in large numbers, and in some cases (although not necessarily all) women will be disproportionately affected, although sex ratios in refugee or other displaced populations differ in different political situations.[72] Conflict situations that affect particularly large or disproportionate numbers of women need to be tracked and assessed for their impacts – losses, harms, and the burdens of increased vulnerability of several types – the nature and severity of which are likely to be shaped by gender.

The idea of "gender-specific," "gender-linked," or "gender-based" violence naturally appears in discussions of what happens to women in conflict. The terminology of "gender-specific" violation in connection with female victims can carry the misleading implication that some acts of violence, including sexual violence, happen only to women. The idea that violence is "gender-linked" or "gender-based" is usefully broad, but for that reason fairly undiscriminating as to why and how being female or male is a risk-factor for, or an explanation of, certain kinds of violent victimization or the damage that results from certain kinds of violence and harm. The category of gender-based violence applied to women covers every form of violence for which women might be targeted based on their physical vulnerabilities or distinct biology; their economic, sexual, and symbolic values in their own eyes and in the eyes of men and their communities; or their central roles in producing and sustaining children, social structure, and social capital. Beginning from an interest in what (perhaps distinctively) happens to women, I suggest that four broad categories are useful to begin to sort through the different ways that women's physical, sexual, social, economic, political, communal, spiritual, and symbolic positions figure in the violence and harms that befall them in conflict. These categories create a coarse grid but provide an initial basis for understanding different but interacting links between gender, violence, and harm in the case of women.

---

[72] Different figures concerning refugees and internally displaced persons reflect different demographic and political realities. Meintjes reports the 80% figure in Sheila Meintjes, "War and Post-War Shifts in Gender Relations," *The Aftermath*, Meintjes et al., 67. Turshen observes that since women and children account for over 72% of most African populations, "the demographic profile of refugees is little different from that of civilians," in Turshen, "Women's War Stories," 15. Amnesty International counts women and girls as "more than half" of refugees in the world today, in "Rape as a Tool of War: A Fact Sheet," www.amnestyusa.org/women/violence/rapeinwartime.html, accessed February 26, 2009. For exhaustive data disaggregated in multiple ways, see United Nations High Commission on Refugees, The State of the World's Refugees 2006: Human Displacement in the New Millenium, http://www.unhcr.org/publ/PUBL/4444afc50.pdf, accessed February 26, 2009.

1. Gender-Normative Violence and Harm

If masculinity is defined through sexual possession, use, and domination of women, then acts of violence to achieve this are inflicted on women because they are women. If dominance among men and their masculinities is embodied in men's ability to control, exploit, and sexually appropriate "other men's women," then women are targeted precisely because they are women by groups of men who aim to defeat, dishonor, and shame other men. If women are seen as representations of cultural, ethnic, and national identity, as well as repositories of cultural authenticity, communal order, and righteous purity, then women's bodily integrity and purity are attacked and destroyed because they are women and doing so demoralizes and destroys communities and proves their men are inadequate to protect them. If women are both materially and symbolically the guardians of the social and emotional tissue of relations that knit a community, then soiling and shaming women makes them unsuitable or disqualifies them as women for social life and its female functions and offices.

By all reports, sexual violence in current struggles is endemic, and the testimonies of those who survive and are brave enough to tell their tales are heart rending and stomach turning. Amnesty International's 2005 *Report* describes continuing widespread rape and sexual mutilation and humiliation in interstate and intrastate conflicts, with child rape alarmingly common in some areas. Sexual violence is not only the most evident instance of violence that is gender based, but it is a prism that makes visible multiple aspects of female gender that are in play in many societies when women are targets of violence. The key in getting these offenses in proper focus is relentlessly to denormalize and defamiliarize violence against women in every instance, to resist the inertial movement toward seeing the violation and terrorization of women as the way the world is, and toward seeing women's bodies as sexual and reproductive utilities in communities and relationships controlled by men. Additionally, it is important to recognize differences among women with respect to their exposure, their reactions, and the likelihood of their securing attention to gender-normative violence. What is gender normative within a society may differ between social groups; some women's honor and purity may be more highly valued and may be taken more seriously as a representation of national identity than that of others from less-powerful social groups; women of different social groups may bear different burdens of silencing and shame in the wake of violation and abuse. These factors might account for more attention to the injuries of some women, different perceptions of the seriousness of those injuries, or varying needs for confidentiality and prospects of public solidarity among different groups of women.

2. Sex-, Reproductive-, and Care-Specific Violence

Violence toward women, it is abundantly clear, goes very often to their sexuality and reproductive capacity, to their sexual or reproductive parts, and to their role as caregivers responsible for the young and dependent. Though sexual control of women by men is gender normative in many societies, and some forms of specifically sexual violence may be accepted, violent abuse of women that takes a sexual form deserves its own category, for it seems frequently to spill beyond any familiar normative boundary and is often shocking for its gratuitous cruelty and for its potential to mar lives socially, psychologically, and physically. As noted earlier, there are strategic, symbolic, instrumental, and also sadistic aspects to this extremely commonplace form of violence against women. The kind of mistreatment aimed at or exploiting sexuality or gender occurs not only through rape, physical abuse, or mutilation, although the scope and intensity of these forms of violence in conflict seems to be increasing. It occurs also through using women's familial and care-giving roles and responsibilities to terrorize, torture, punish, or degrade women in their own eyes and in the eyes of their families and communities.

Conway Henderson explores through comparative research "an additional pattern of mistreatment" women suffer under political repression.[73] Women in detention, for example, suffer many of the same mistreatments and violations as do men, including beatings, torture, and attacks on psychological integrity. Men too are sometimes sexually abused and humiliated. Even so, there are distinctive and additional forms of cruelty and humiliation that are directed to women's real and perceived vulnerabilities. The gendered specificity of the torture of women in detention, by no means limited to rape, is increasingly documented. Women's sexuality, motherhood, sense of propriety and dignity, and profound sense of obligation for the welfare of their children are levers worked by torturers to inflict unbearable psychological torment on women.[74] In addition, there are forms of humiliation that target women's biologies and social vulnerabilities to disorient women and damage self-respect; these include forced or public nakedness and denials of sanitary provisions for menstruation in detention, rendering women not only uncomfortable but helplessly dirty and ashamed. Latifa Jbabdi reports that women held as political prisoners in Morocco were addressed by men's names and

---

[73] Henderson, "The Political Repression of Women."
[74] Goldblatt and Meintjes, "South African Women Demand the Truth," 37–45, report testimonies of female torture victims in South Africa.

placed in male prisons, not only scorning their womanhood but exposing them to sexual violence as a punishment.[75] Women of differing social positions may be more or less able to join together directly to confront the stigma of sexual violence. Some are likely to be more in need of, or more able to take advantage of, support services or confidentiality. The gender norms and scripts of local cultures will inflect the experience, the expression, and the consequences of surviving these forms of violence. Finally, there is the immense problem of pregnancies resulting from rape and sexual enslavement, a fate only women can suffer and of which the effects are likely to be life-altering.

3. Gender-Skewed Violence and Harm

Losses, harms, and violent injuries need not happen to women directly because of gender-normative assumptions or because women are targeted in ways specific to their sexuality, reproductive capacity, or care responsibilities. Yet in particular situations those who bear the brunt of a certain kind of violence or of certain effects of conflict may turn out to be largely and perhaps disproportionately (in virtue of the demographic of the peacetime population) female. Destruction of home sites, forced displacement, and removal to formal or informal refugee areas seem to be gender-skewed impacts of conflict in many cases. Where internal or external displacement does disproportionately afflict women and children, women may sustain the brunt of the distress, harm, social uprooting, and economic losses these dislocations entail. Displacement due to conflict or persecution constitutes a grave form of harm to those displaced, even if it removes them from the scene of formal conflict. They are no less victims of conflict for being raped, starved, sickened, or stripped of their possessions, documentation, or citizenship once they have become refugees or internally displaced persons.

Contemporary warfare – with either massive bombardment and destruction of infrastructure, or protracted ground war, provisioned by looting, aimed at demoralizing, displacing, or destroying populations – tends to wreak havoc on women, elderly persons, and children in massive numbers. Women who lose their spouses and other male family members to conflict, and who see their children conscripted, abducted, or killed, or who must abandon their homes, suffer what human beings experience as one of the greatest and most enduring

---

[75] Latifa Jbabdi, oral presentation on Morocco, International Center For Transitional Justice Conference on "Gender and Reparations: Opportunities for Transitional Democracies?" July 7–8, 2005, New York.

losses, that of home and family. This happens to women in conflict and because of conflict, so it is indeed a harm of conflict and matter for redress. The prevalence of severe losses and displacements of women noncombatants illustrates the importance of acknowledging grave harms of conflict that are not limited to acts of violence intentionally committed directly on individuals. The design of reparation must consider life-altering losses that result from violence to family and community members, destruction of material and social resources women need to sustain themselves and their dependents, and exposure to illness and violence that befall women under rough or dangerous conditions of displacement or loss of male social protection and status. If these losses are seen as merely collateral, regrettable but not obligatory to compensate, women are likely to be disproportionately and sometimes disastrously disadvantaged in many post-conflict situations. Differences among the situations of urban and rural women, of married and unmarried women, of women with dependent children and elders, and of women who belong to already poor, culturally vulnerable, or indigenous populations are central to accurately reckoning material losses and meaningful forms of material support and compensation.

4. Gender-Multiplied Violence and Harm

Some forms of violent harm or loss precipitate further losses that enlarge the impact of, and may in the end be worse or less manageable than, the original violation or loss itself. When the factors are social or biological ones that cause women to suffer more than their male counterparts would from particular acts of violence, or that render women vulnerable to additional harms as a result of acts of violence or the consequences of such acts, I refer to the harm as "gender multiplied" for women. Multipliers are factors that predictably play roles in causing additional losses or additional exposure to violence. The additional damage may or may not be part of what is intended in the violent act. The absence of intention to cause certain further harms or additional suffering, however, though relevant in a juridical context to assessing the nature of a crime, should not impede recognition of the need for repair of additional harms women suffer as consequences or sequels of violence.

Being the victim of some forms of violence has significant social consequences for females in many societies. The obvious case is sexual violation. It is a fairly recent development in North American and European societies that women are not routinely blamed and despised for having been raped (or at any rate the social presumption has now been shifted at least in formal legal and institutional contexts). In many societies, the onus on the victim of sexual assault remains pervasive, severe, and relatively certain to follow. The victim of sexual violence may be regarded as disgracing family honor, being unclean or contaminated, being a seductress of bad character, or being unmarriageable. Women who are sexually violated, impregnated by rape by enemies, sexually tortured and raped in detention, or kidnapped into sexual and domestic enslavement often are subjected to these socially blighting effects. The original violation is extended, ramified, and augmented in multiple ways that significantly alter the women's physical safety and well-being, social reintegration and status, economic survival, and eligibility for marriage. In addition to social and symbolic multipliers of harm, there is the reality that sexual and sexually directed physical abuse (violation or mutilation of genitals or reproductive parts) of women can produce irreversible and chronic physical disabilities, pain, sterility, or dysfunction. A Human Rights Watch report on Darfur mentions internal bleeding, fistulas, incontinence, and sexually transmitted diseases including HIV/AIDS as results of rape and other sexual abuse.[76] Stephen Lewis, UN ambassador to Africa for AIDS, warned at the 2006 international AIDS meeting that "the violence and the virus go together."[77] Unwanted pregnancies, with significant implications for physical health and social reintegration, are among the consequences.

It is not only victims of sexual violence whose injuries and losses are multiplied. Problems of social stigma and exclusion are not reserved only for women who are noncombatant victims. They can befall women who have been combatants, or who have been placed out of supervision of family or clan or out of traditional roles in ways that are taken to impugn their purity or respectability. Codou Bop describes the demobilization of as many as 12,000 Eritrean women combatants whose military service and involvement in killing left many divorced, "unclean," and unmarriageable, for some a road to urban prostitution.[78] Furthermore, women who lose husbands and children may suffer dramatic losses in economic and social status, and affronts to personal dignity. Meredeth Turshen notes, "War creates widows. In Rwanda it turned independent women into charity cases; women who before the war had access

---

[76] Human Rights Watch, "Sexual Violence and its Consequences among Displaced Persons in Darfur and Chad," Human Rights Watch Briefing Paper, April 12, 2005, 12. See also Rombouts, 208, and King, 251 and 263. A poignant and vivid first-person account of sexual slavery and its physical and emotional consequences is Maria Rosa Henson, *Comfort Woman: A Filipina's Story of Prostitution and Slavery Under the Japanese Military* (Lanham, MD: Rowman and Littlefield, 1999). Mrs. Henson was the first sexually enslaved woman to accept a reparation payment from a privately organized fund.

[77] Lawrence K. Altman, "U.N. Official Assails South Africa on Its Response to AIDS," *The New York Times*, August 19, 2006.

[78] Bop, "Women in Conflicts," 29–30.

to land through their husbands are now destitute and dependent on relatives or social workers. War widows who were raped are stigmatized and find it hard to remarry; widowed rape victims with children are ostracized."[79] Goldblatt and Meintjes report on the South African context, "When women lose their husbands they become doubly repressed by their own community; they become women without standing, almost illegitimate in the present context of South Africa's cultural reality. The son becomes the woman's husband, even if that woman was a very high-powered political activist."[80]

Displacement may also result in loss of access to land and agricultural livelihoods, as well as to trade, either in the place of exile or upon return. The poverty that results may be what stymies possibilities of a stable future that were not precluded by the fact of displacement alone. Women are almost invariably responsible for dependent children's sustenance and welfare, irrespective of external changes in women's abilities to secure food, clothing, and shelter, and to provide for education or other significant needs that may determine their children's future, and by consequence their own future welfare. The pathetic situation of women and children raped and killed because they have to go beyond the protected perimeter of camps to collect firewood for sale or fuel in Darfur has been documented, as have cases of Sudanese women and girls imprisoned for going outside refugee areas in Chad, only to be raped by Chadian inmates while in detention.[81] The UN Security Council has recently condemned sexual abuse and pedophilia among its peacekeeping troops. It now appears that being female (or a child) and part of a civilian population in need of international protection is an additional risk factor for sexual abuse in some areas.[82] Chain reactions of loss, social incapacitation, displacement, poverty, and sexual victimization should be seen as central to

---

[79] Turshen, "Women's War Stories," 16.

[80] Goldblatt and Meintjes, "South African Women Demand the Truth," 35.

[81] Human Rights Watch, "Sexual Violence and its Consequences among Displaced Persons in Darfur and Chad," 8.

[82] "U.N. Council Condemns Sex Abuse by Its Troops," *The New York Times*, June 1, 2005. Save the Children UK reports in 2006 that based on interview studies, Liberian girls as young as eight years old are being sexually exploited by UN peacekeepers, aid workers, camp officials, and teachers; in Sarah Lyall, "Aid Workers Are Said to Abuse Girls," *The New York Times*, May 9, 2006. Economic and social dislocation produced by conflict can press more women into prostitution or make them available to traffickers; reports on trafficking indicate that countries with an influx of international peacekeeping and humanitarian workers attract greater numbers of trafficked women. See Dina Francesca Haynes, "Used, Abused, Arrested and Deported: Extending Immigration Benefits to Protect Victims of Trafficking and to Secure Prosecution of Traffickers," *Human Rights Quarterly* 26 (2004): 221–272. A United Nations policy statement is found in United Nations General Assembly, "A Comprehensive Strategy to Eliminate Future Sexual Exploitation and Abuse in United Nations Peacekeeping Operations," March 24, 2005, A/59/710.

reckoning violence, harm, and loss from the point of view of reparation and social reconstruction.

In addition, since rehabilitation is established in the international standards governing reparation, special attention should be paid to the social, physical, and psychological injuries sustained by women, and care should be taken to find the most productive and culturally attuned interventions. There is no reason to assume, and good reason not to assume, that women's experience and assimilation of harms and losses, or their modes of adaptation and life reconstruction, will be entirely similar to men's. Nor can it be assumed that all women will have a single characteristic experience in a given conflict, or even when they are victims of similar violence in a given conflict. Women of different classes, ethnicities, castes, and religious groups, indigenous women, women who participate in oppositional political movements or are mobilized in combat, urban and rural women, married and unmarried women, women of different age groups and educational levels all need to be addressed as women, as individuals, and as members of groups with particular resources and vulnerabilities. They are likely to face very different challenges, to have access to different kinds of resources, and reasonably to expect very different social responses to their attempts to stabilize and mend their lives. In the case of women, we know that harms can be multiplied in many ways directly linked to gender, but also to gender in the context of race, class, ethnicity, political participation, rural life, or indigenous community.

Finally, there is a widely acknowledged post-conflict effect that afflicts both women who have otherwise suffered violence in or because of conflict as well as those who might have escaped this fate. Several reports affirm that "ordinary" violence against women escalates in post-conflict periods because of men's inability to find positive peacetime roles that restore a sense of masculinity, men's conception of reestablishing the status quo as entailing a return to "traditional" gender relations, or men's desires to reassert control over women who have developed economic and survival skills in wartime that challenge their traditional subordination or that put women in competitive positions with men domestically or occupationally.[83] Women are themselves seen as material assets and may possess material assets that men want to control. In this way conflict itself seems to be a multiplier for women's exposure to "ordinary" violence in the aftermath. But women's antecedent material resources and

---

[83] Meintjes, Pillay, and Turshen, "There is No Aftermath for Women," 4; Sideris, 152; Anja Meulenbelt, "Sympathy for the Devil: Thinking About Victims and Perpetrators after Working in Serbia," in *Assault on the Soul*, Sharratt and Kaschak, 154–155; and Duggan and Abusharaf, "Reparation of Sexual Violence," 627.

social position, and their post-conflict access to local power and larger legal and political structures, are likely to matter profoundly to whether harms multiply. Interventions to neutralize or limit factors that multiply women's losses and suffering cannot be "one size fits all," and women's social power and communal organization or lack thereof may be a factor in containing multiplier effects or in the effectiveness of interventions.

Clearly, these four categories are by no means mutually exclusive in application to women: most sexual violence, for example, is gender normative, sex specific, gender skewed, *and* typically gender multiplied. Sexual mutilation of women is not necessarily gender normative but is sex specific or reproduction specific and may or may not be skewed or multiplied. The destitution women suffer as a result of destruction of physical and social infrastructure is gender skewed in many situations by women's gender-normative economic vulnerability in patriarchal orders, and it is likely to be gender multiplied in distinctive ways, as displacement is likely in some contexts to affect more women and to expose them to gender-normative and gender-multiplied consequences. These categories are a tool both to sort and to link the forms of harms and violence that happen to women "because they are women."

In cases of gender-normative and gender-multiplied violence, women may be reluctant to acknowledge their violation or not inclined to expect or to pursue any form of redress. Having suffered gender-normative and even sexually specific violence, women may be resigned to "what happens to women," or may perceive – sad to say, correctly – that others will view their mistreatment in that way. Where situations of loss are gender skewed, women may themselves perceive their dire situations as a kind of collateral damage, a "secondary" effect for which they in particular are not targeted and no one else in particular is responsible, or as a sort of ill fortune that should not be compared to those who have died or suffered terrible physical injuries. Where this is true, women may focus on the immediate needs of survival assistance and security, or on a longer-term goal of return or resettlement, without expectation of redress. We know that women often tend to focus, and are encouraged to focus, on the harms that befall others to whom they are connected and for whom they are responsible, even to the exclusion of reporting or seeking redress for the violation or loss they themselves have suffered. In addition, women's membership in particular social, economic, and geographical groups is likely to determine what is gender normative for them, what risks of violence and multiplier effects they in particular bear, whether they are likely to report violations, and what potential there is for solidarity among women to secure post-conflict political power and resources. In post-conflict contexts women may be competing for scarce resources and their loyalties may be with family, tribe, clan, or locality, and with the men with whom they share their daily lives and on whom they depend, rather than with other women. Reparations programs must aim at gender justice where women themselves may not see this as a priority. The proposed categories of violence and harm need to be attuned and adjusted to the experience, perceptions, needs, and deserts of particular victims in particular contexts, and these contexts need to be explored directly in every case.

In the interests of gender justice, however, we must also think about men, and about men and women both in comparison and in relationship to understand fully how the violence, harms, and losses of conflict and political repression are structured by gender. Although I have begun with the question "What happens to women?" the categorization I offer can respond to the guiding concern of sensitivity to gender in assessing harms for both women and men. If women suffer kinds of violence and ensuing harm in multiple senses "because they are women," then so do men suffer kinds of violence and ensuing harm "because they are men." The fact that men are usually disproportionately targeted for the gross human rights violations that tend to attract attention in reparations programs (murder, disappearance, kidnapping, illegal detention, and torture) shows that some forms of violence and harm are in many contexts gender skewed and attached to gender-normative masculine roles and activities, like military service and political leadership. The presumably grossly underreported category of sexual violence toward men, especially rape of men by men as well as sexual abuses and mutilation, follows a gender-normative pattern of insult: raped or sexually used men are feminized and "unmanned." Men, too, are targeted for harms and tortures that are directed at their sexual parts and functions.[84] So men experience sex- and reproduction-specific violence, as well as forms of abuse and torture that exploit men's parental and familial love and responsibility. Men are forced to stand by when their parents, spouses, relatives, and children are killed, beaten, raped, or tortured in front of them. Men are coerced or terrorized by threats to their families. Men suffer the trauma of seeing loved ones injured and suffer the shame of their incapacity to exercise culturally valued protective male roles. Men are also subject to grave psychic and physical costs and consequences of participation in combat, and in the atrocities and abuses they witness or commit under the pressures and expectations not only of political ideology and military discipline but of gender norms of manliness and male solidarity. Men, too, may face multiplier

---

[84] See Sivakumaran.

effects when they are victims of violence or loss, and the specific gendered trajectories of men's being disabled, traumatized, displaced, impoverished, or sexually violated require investigation alongside and in comparison to women.

Thus, the categorical framework I propose has potential for multiple and nuanced comparative analyses of the gendered nature and impacts of violence that attends to experiences of both women and men. Within this framework, we can engage in comparative investigation of overall gender-linked differences in the fates of men and women in a particular conflict. We can explore differences in gendered exposure to loss and violence among groups of women or among groups of men differently positioned within the same conflict situation. We might also track and compare overall gendered differences in what happens to men and women in different conflict situations. Or we might explore in depth the fine grain of gender-normative or gender-multiplied harms within or between conflicts. Finally, the same categories might be used or adapted to address the experiences of members of sexual minorities in conflict or under repression where gendered dynamics are apt to play out in distinct ways. These categories offer the potential for a fuller topography of gender and violence, but they are always guided by the question: What distinctive and possibly gendered forms of violence, harm, and suffering must be specifically investigated and addressed in programs designed to deliver effective reparation in the wake of armed conflict or political repression?

CONCLUSION

> Can one actually say it's violence? . . . It's not as serious as my husband being killed in jail. One would say, it's not like me having left my own country going to stay thirty years outside. So that's what I always say to myself, what is this violence? How can one express it to somebody who can actually feel sympathetic? What I'm telling you now is a story. I don't think it will be seen as violence. It's a story that this is how we lived in the past. And this was where it actually crippled me in my mind.
> – Lydia Komape, a black women under South African apartheid, who had to falsify her Bantu identity (a crime), break up her family, and take up domestic labor away from her husband, who risked arrest to see her.[85]

When you hear people like this woman, let's call her Natasha K., who testifies that she has lost 35 people in her family, and then the prosecutor asks her

---

[85] Quoted by Goldblatt and Meintjes, "South African Women Demand the Truth," 33.

to look at photo after photo, and she says this was her husband, this was her uncle, and this was her father-in-law.... You listen to that kind of loss and it's just unbearable.
– Judge Gabrielle Kirk McDonald, former President of the ICTY.[86]

People feel that once we have identified who killed who, we were just about finished. Only then can we address such questions as who raped who, who burned what, and then who stole the cows.
– Patricia Viseur-Sellers, Legal Officer on Gender Issues at the ICTY.[87]

They were so bitter at the state. Their houses were burned, they were raped, their husbands were killed, and their sons were abducted. They feel they lost a lot and must be paid, they must be compensated or the rebels must be arrested and brought to justice.
– A description of the situation of women in war-torn northern Uganda.[88]

The "multi-dimensional nature of their suffering" is a striking theme of investigations of violence toward women and losses experienced by women in conflict and under repression.[89] Looking closely at patterns of violence directed at women and features of women's gendered roles and social expectations is urgent because these patterns have so long been ignored or naturalized as "what happens to women." Specific synergies of loss and suffering must be explored if women are to receive just reparation. In particular, sexual violence in conflict situations very often, perhaps typically, is one aspect of multifaceted episodes of violence and terror in which women are victims of violence to their physical persons, subjected to multiple losses and harms, made instruments of communal intimidation, and made witnesses to other atrocities. A legal advisor to the ICTY reports, "One has to remember that rape is generally not the only crime inflicted against that person on that day. Often in wartime you might have a victim or a witness who has been shot, has seen family members killed before their eyes, been detained, starved or tortured, in addition to the sexual violence inflicted on them."[90] The pattern of multiple and reciprocally magnifying assaults and horrors is common.

---

[86] Sara Sharratt, "Interview with Gabrielle Kirk McDonald, President of the International Criminal Tribunal for the Former Yugoslavia," in *Assault on the Soul*, Sharratt and Kaschak, 26–27.
[87] Sara Sharratt, "Interview with Patricia Viseur-Sellers, Legal Office on Gender Issues," in *Assault on the Soul*, Sharratt and Kaschak, 66.
[88] Quoted by Meredeth Turshen, "Engendering Relations of State to Society in the Aftermath," in *The Aftermath*, Meintjes et al., 95.
[89] Ashnie Padarath, "Women and Violence in KwaZulu/Natal," in *What Women Do in Wartime*, Turshen and Twagiramariya, 68.
[90] Sharratt, "Interview with Patricia Viseur-Sellers," 56.

The many dimensions of harm to women and of women's suffering, and predictable links and devastating synergies among them, present difficult challenges. A central challenge is that recently won attention to sexual violence against women might be at the expense of a fuller and more nuanced understanding of women's losses, injuries, and sufferings. Unbending insistence on the full and accurate recognition and legal and political redress of sexual violence experienced by women is imperative. Even so, sexual offenses against women must not displace or overwhelm recognition of diverse and devastating harms of other types that women suffer, nor of the complex and often brutal causalities that link sexual violence to other kinds of loss, and other kinds of loss to exposure to sexual violence. Needed attention to sexual violence should not sexualize women as victims, duplicating rather than contesting the reduction of women to their sexual and reproductive being. Nor should sexual violence be associated entirely with women, further obscuring what remains largely shrouded in darkness: men are also victims of sexual violence in conflict and under repression. So it is doubly important to resist the conflation of sexual violence with violence against women. Harms suffered by men in conflict, and by men and women who are members of sexual minorities, are also diverse and may also be shaped, aimed, skewed, or multiplied by gender in any of the ways I have outlined. Focusing on women has opened the way for more sensitive, comprehensive, and comparative analysis of how gender shapes violence and harm for both men and women.

Other challenges emerge in identifying harms and their consequences fully and accurately for the purposes of considering and designing reparations. It will not suffice to identify harms to persons in conflict or under state repression only as those intentionally done to them by individual perpetrators, lest many gross harms to women and men fall back into the category of collateral damage. Even the attempt to recognize consequences of violence by incorporating individuals as "secondary" victims, as when a woman is left destitute by the murder of her husband or the abduction of her son, or when a man's wife is made pregnant by rape, for example, can fail to capture adequately the extent of loss and harm that women and men experience. The person whom a perpetrator intends to shoot or beat or rape is typically seen as the "primary" victim, whereas, for example, the wife who witnesses her husband's murder, the father who watches his wife and daughter raped and mutilated, the family that loses the male head of household on whom its economic survival depends, or the spouse who must assume both primary economic and daily care-giving responsibilities for a disabled partner are talked about as "secondary" victims where they are talked about at all. Yet these individuals are primary victims of terror, intimidation, and humiliation often intended to silence them, render them complicit or destitute, or drive them from their property and land; the forms of intimidation and humiliation chosen may follow gendered lines. Even when people are not or not only the direct victims of physical violence, they are the direct victims of intentional acts of terror, intimidation, and coercion that produce grave and life-altering losses that may be further compounded or aggravated in gendered ways.[91] Finally, even when ensuing losses are unintended, and even unforeseen, the losses are no less a product of the violence, and no less devastating for that reason. The typology of victimization remains an imperfect tool in capturing the nature and dimensions of real harm (unintended and intended) that women and men routinely suffer because of armed conflict or political repression.[92]

The 2006 resolution on reparations of the United Nations General Assembly declares that "adequate, effective and prompt reparation is intended to promote justice by redressing gross violations of international human rights law or serious violations of international humanitarian law."[93] Ruth Rubio-Marín adds that helping victims and their families, asserting the commitment to a system of rights, and recreating the conditions of civic trust for victims and others must be conceived together when thinking about reparation.[94] I hope to have shown that appreciating the consequences of violations, grasping their precise and mutually ramifying nature, and creating the ground of trust through adequate acknowledgment of all victims requires close attention to the realities of violence in conflict and, at long last, to its gendered effects

---

[91] Goldblatt and Meintjes say of South Africa's TRC including relatives and dependents as secondary victims, "It is important to see these women as primary not secondary victims, because they themselves have suffered directly," in Goldblatt and Meintjes, "South African Women Demand the Truth," 34. Tristan Anne Borer, "A Taxonomy of Victims and Perpetrators: Human Rights and Reconciliation in South Africa," *Human Rights Quarterly* 25 (2003): 1088–1116, examines the process whereby South Africa's TRC created official victims and perpetrators, and the possibility of sorting "direct victims," "victims once removed," "victims by proxy," and "secondary victims" (1115–1116).

[92] The issue of framing of violation and harm is a central challenge. See Diane Orentlicher, "Promotion and Protection of Human Rights: Impunity: Report of the Independent Expert to Update the Set of Principles to Combat Impunity," E/CN.4/2005/102, 17, where the ideal of "completeness" of reparations is related to "the breadth of the categories of crimes for which the program provides redress." Pablo de Greiff argues for a political, rather than a juridical, perspective for reparations, in Pablo de Greiff, "Justice and Reparations," in *The Handbook of Reparations*. A political perspective might extend as well to the conceptualization of harms and violations in a way less dominated by the legal emphasis on individual perpetrators' intentions (often a defining element of crime) and more attuned to the experience of loss and violations of individuals and communities.

[93] United Nations, "Basic Principles and Guidelines on the Right to a Remedy and Reparation for Victims of Gross Violations of International Human Rights Law and Serious Violations of International Humanitarian Law," March 21, 2008, A/RES/60/147.

[94] Ruth Rubio-Marín, Chapter 2 of this volume.

on women and men. It also demands observation and analysis of how gender creates differences between the experiences of men and women as victims, and how differences among women and among men mean differences in the impacts as well as the injuries they suffer.[95]

---

[95] I wish to thank Ruth Rubio-Marín for insightful editorial direction. Country studies commissioned for the International Center for Transitional Justice project on gender and reparations were published in Rubio-Marín's *What Happened to the Women?* I have benefited greatly from them and from discussion with the authors. Several meetings among authors of the country studies and contributors to the present volume shaped and enhanced this chapter in countless ways. Special thanks to Pablo de Greiff, Director of the Research Unit at the ICTJ, and to the ICTJ staff.

2

The Gender of Reparations in Transitional Societies

Ruth Rubio-Marín

Much has been written, over the last two decades, about the ways gender plays a role in generating, or at least shaping, the forms and the effects of political violence perpetrated under authoritarian regimes and during armed conflict. This literature describes how women suffer as a result of activities that target civilians. It also testifies to the ways women are specifically targeted because of their political agency, their engagement in peace processes, their involvement in communal forms of life, their roles as mothers or family members, and their fight for truth and justice for their loved ones. If some of the reasons for targeting women are gender specific, so are some of the forms of violence women encounter as well as the short- and long-term effects of violence in their lives. Thus, women are more frequently subject to sexual and reproductive violence than men are. They also experience forms of domestic enslavement more often. Finally, women bear the brunt of the consequences of violent actions that target their men, as can be attested to by the many single-headed households after conflict, the vivid expressions of the pain of the mothers of the disappeared, or the overrepresentation of women among the refugees or internally displaced populations in scenarios of conflict. If this is true for women, the gender-specific reasons, forms, and effects of large-scale political violence that disparately impact on men remain to this day largely unexplored.[1]

The recent trend to render women and their experiences of armed conflict and political repression visible has been echoed in UN Security Council

---

[1] Of course, "gender" need not refer to women alone. However, given present conditions, concerns about gender and gender sensitivity – in this and most other contexts in which justice issues arise – refer to the disparities and inequities in access, power, opportunities, and rights experienced by women across a wide spectrum of spheres. I will follow this well-established use of the term "gender" in this article, noting that gender analysis at some point will also have to include a much more serious and systematic treatment of how gender roles may also render men's access to some forms of reparation difficult, something I only start to explore here.

Resolution 1325 on Women, Peace and Security. This trend has not led to any systematic reflection on the bearing that a gendered analysis of violence should have when discussing reparations for victims of mass and systematic abuses of human rights.[2] There may be, however, an incipient current in the practice of reparations that is likely to reverse this. To mention some examples: the Reparations Program recommended in the Final Report of the Commission for Reception, Truth and Reconciliation (CAVR) in Timor-Leste, which was handed down to members of parliament on November 28, 2005, includes gender equity as one of five guiding principles that inspires its overall conception;[3] similarly, Morocco's Equity and Truth Commission (IER) made gender mainstreaming one of the priorities in its reparations policy;[4] and finally, Colombia's recent Commission on Reparations and Reconciliation (CNRR) set up a specific unit with the task of ensuring that all of the policies and recommendations of the Commission take into account the specific needs of women and other marginalized groups.[5]

It has become a commonplace that one of the necessary elements to "engender" reparations is to include sexual violence in the list of crimes that are considered grave violations of human rights and, as such, deserve reparations. This entails departing from tradition, as most reparations efforts in the past have concentrated on violations of a fairly limited and traditionally conceived catalogue of civil and political rights including illegal detention, torture, summary execution, and disappearances. In fact, the one single most organized and well-documented (though still largely unsuccessful) movement for reparations

[2] Filling this gap was one of the goals of the research project that led to this book. The first results it generated were compiled in a previous book, which provides a gendered analysis of reparations discussions, initiatives, and programs in East Timor, Guatemala, Peru, South Africa, Rwanda, and Sierra Leone. See Ruth Rubio-Marín, ed., *What Happened to the Women? Gender and Reparations for Human Rights Violations* (New York: Social Science Research Council, 2006) [*What Happened?* hereafter]. The theory behind this piece and the empirical ground work provided in the country studies have nurtured each other in a relationship of dialectical enrichment for which I am greatly thankful.

[3] See Galuh Wandita, Karen Campbell-Nelson, and Manuela Leong Pereira, "Learning to Engender Reparations in Timor-Leste: Reaching Out to Female Victims," in *What Happened?* 308.

[4] See the final report of the *Instance Equité et Réconciliation* (IER), available in Arabic, French, and Spanish at http://www.ier.ma. (The author of this chapter provided technical advice to the IER on the gender dimensions of reparations.)

[5] Awareness of the importance of reparations for women is also increasing among women's rights global movements. See, for example, the Brussels Call to Action adopted in June 2006 at the International Symposium on Sexual Violence in Conflict and Beyond (calling for reparations for victims of sexual violence), accessed at http://www.unfpa.org/emergencies/symposium06, and the Nairobi Declaration on Women's and Girls' Right to a Remedy and Reparation, March 19–21, 2007, accessed at http://www.womensrightscoalition.org/site/reparation/signature_en.php.

for women is that of the so-called "comfort women," namely, approximately 200,000 women from across Asia who were enslaved by and for the Japanese military during Japan's World-War-II colonial period, some forcefully taken from their homes and homelands to be raped daily by soldiers.[6]

There is, however, a growing sense that including sexual violence among the violations deserving reparations is not all there is at stake, and that concerns with gender justice should somehow be "mainstreamed" in the discussions and design of reparations. The question, then, is what exactly this task entails. This chapter is a contribution to this much-needed conversation. It focuses on large-scale reparations programs rather than on (either national or international) judicially adjudicated reparations because the former are becoming an increasingly common form of handling reparations in the context of massive violations of human rights.[7] Its aim is to flesh out the potential of large-scale reparations

---

[6] See, for example, Yoshiaki Yoshimi, *Comfort Women: Sexual Slavery in the Japanese Military During World War II* (New York: Columbia University Press, 2002), and Margaret Stetz and Bonnie B. C. Oh, eds., *Legacies of Comfort Women During World War II* (New York: ME Sharpe, 2001). Almost nothing was known about these women until the late 1980s. Since then, survivors have come forward to bear witness and mobilize international public opinion, asking for an official apology and reparation from the Japanese government. It was not until 1990, 45 years after the end of World War II, that a Japanese official offered an apology for the acts perpetrated by the military against the comfort women. More recently, the Japanese Diet, although refusing to issue an apology, has allocated money to administer a Fund for Asian Women. Money contributed to the fund is used to aid comfort women in need and support projects addressing contemporary women's issues. In fact, the fund is financed by donations from private individuals and organizations in Japan. Nevertheless, survivors have rejected these gestures as inadequate and reiterate their desire for a formal apology from the Diet and individual compensation through public funds rather than a welfare-type or benevolence-type of assistance based on socioeconomic need. See Karen Parker and Jennifer F. Chew, "Compensation for Japan's World War II War-Rape Victims," *Hastings International and Comparative Law Review* 17 (1994): 498–510.

[7] Clearly, the challenge of avoiding gender bias is just as present when reparations are decided on a case-by-case basis by courts or compensation tribunals. The insight provided in this piece aims to contribute to understanding reparations through the lenses of gender, broadly speaking. This is not to say that it may not be worth discussing whether there are gender-justice-related reasons to prefer legislative and administrative reparations programs over judicial venues to reparations or vice versa. For instance, it has been argued that reparations programs obviate some of the difficulties and costs associated with litigation, including high expenses, the need to gather evidence that in some cases may be unavailable, the pain associated with cross-examination, the lack of trust on the part of victims when the judicial system of the country has remained largely unaffected by the transition in the short run, and so forth. See Pablo de Greiff, "Justice and Reparations," in *The Handbook of Reparations*, ed. Pablo de Greiff (Oxford: Oxford University Press, 2006) [*The Handbook* hereafter], 10; and Heidy Rombouts, Pietro Sardaro, and Stef Vandeginste, "The Right to Reparation for Victims of Gross and Systematic Violations of Human Rights" in *Out of the Ashes: Reparations for Victims of Gross and Systematic Human Rights Violations*, ed. K. De Feyter, S. Parmetier, M. Bossuyt, and P. Lemmens (Antwerpen-Oxford: Intersentia, 2005) [*Out of the Ashes* hereafter], 488. Presumably some of these considerations would weigh in favor of privileging nonjudicial

programs in transitional democracies for recognizing and redressing women victims of human rights abuses. It also provides insight about the transformative potential of reparations, namely, the potential of such reparative efforts to subvert, instead of reinforce, preexisting structural gender inequalities and thereby to contribute, however minimally, to the consolidation of more inclusive democratic regimes.[8] Finally, in an attempt to underscore the need to conceptually broaden the gender and reparations agenda to include men, the chapter contains some incipient insight about how patterns and notions of masculinity might interfere either with the assessment of the harms that men are subject to during times of repression and conflict or with their possibilities for redress.

Section I lays out a normative framework of reparations for massive abuses of human rights that encompasses both individual and societal aims and centers around the notion of due recognition to victims instead of restitution or compensation in strict proportion to harm.[9] I will argue that giving victims due recognition *as citizens* requires all of the following: (1) the recognition of the wrongful violations of victims' rights; (2) the acknowledgment of state responsibility for such violations; (3) the recognition of harms ensuing from the violations; and (4) the attempt to help victims cope with the effects of harms in their lives and to subvert, however minimally, the structures of subordination that might have led to the violations of their rights in the first place. I then elaborate an agenda for "engendering" reparations following each of these four steps (Sections II–V). Broadly speaking, the methodology endorsed in this chapter conceives of "engendering" reparations as a three-fold challenge. First is the challenge of avoiding formal gender discrimination in the design and implementation of such programs. Second is that of looking for ways of ensuring that patriarchal norms and sexist standards and systems of values are not leaked into reparations. Finally, there is the task of exploring ways to optimize the (admittedly modest) transformative potential of reparations programs so that they serve to advance toward the ideal of a society altogether free of gender subordination.

---

venues for reparations for women, both in general but also especially with regards to some crimes, such as those of a sexual nature. This argument is further explored in Ruth Rubio-Marín and Pablo de Greiff, "Women and Reparations," *International Journal for Transitional Justice* 1, no. 3 (2007): 317–337.

[8] For an analysis of these two dimensions of reparations, which I call the *corrective* and the *transformative* dimensions, see Ruth Rubio-Marín, "Gender and Collective Reparations in the Aftermath of Conflict and Political Repression" in *The Politics of Reconciliation in Multicultural Societies*, ed. Will Kymlicka and Bashir Bashir (Oxford: Oxford University Press, 2008). This piece appears in the present volume as Chapter 8.

[9] I borrow (and further elaborate) the normative conception of reparations according to which they have as their immediate goal the recognition of victims and the fostering of civic trust from de Greiff, "Justice and Reparations," 460–464.

I. REPARATIONS PROGRAMS IN TRANSITIONAL SETTINGS: INDIVIDUAL AND SOCIETAL AIMS

In international law, the right of individuals to reparation for the violation of their human rights has been increasingly recognized, although the contours of this right remain unclear. Affirmed initially as a principle of inter-state responsibility linked to the commission of an internationally wrongful act,[10] we can observe a shift of focus to national arenas and away from international disputes. The contours of the obligation to provide reparations to the individual whose rights have been violated remain, however, far from clear. A look at the most relevant international treaties on the protection of human rights provides some textual support but no conclusive evidence.[11]

There are promising signs in the affirmation of the right to reparation. For one thing, the international bodies of human rights adjudication seem to be embracing an increasingly broad interpretation of their remedial powers.[12]

---

[10] See Max du Plessis, "Historical Injustice and International Law: An Exploratory Discussion of Reparation for Slavery," *Human Rights Quarterly* 25 (2003): 631; quoted in Richard Falk, "Reparations, International Law and Global Justice: A New Frontier," in *The Handbook*.

[11] There are not many explicit affirmations in international instruments for the protection of human rights of the principle that international responsibility for human rights violations entails liability to pay damages or, more generally, to offer reparation. Reference to the substantive duty to provide reparation is contemplated only in two very specific cases: unlawful arrest or detention and wrongful conviction; see, for example, Article 9.5 of the International Covenant on Civil and Political Rights (ICCPR) (1966). Thus, the arguments of those who defend the existence of a remedial right to reparation usually call on a seminal norm to be found in all general human rights instruments generically requiring states to establish effective domestic remedies in case the rights recognized are violated (see, for example, Article 8 of the Universal Declaration of Human Rights [1948]; Article 23 [a] of the ICCPR; Article 6 of the International Convention on the Elimination of All Forms of Racial Discrimination [1965]; Article 13 of the European Convention on Human Rights [1950]; Article 25 of the American Convention on Human Rights [1969]; and Article 7 of the African Charter on Human and Peoples' Rights [1981]). Interestingly, the Convention on the Elimination of All Forms of Discrimination Against Women (CEDAW) does not contain an equivalent provision. It has been argued, though, that although CEDAW does not have a specific article on remedies, Articles 2 and 24 apply. The undertaking in Article 2 (b) to adopt "appropriate legislative measures including sanctions where appropriate," and the undertaking in Article 2 (c) "to establish legal protection of the rights of women . . . and to ensure through competent national tribunals and other public institutions the effective protection for women against any act of discrimination," require remedies that ensure the "effectiveness" of the protection. Similarly, Article 24 requires states parties "to adopt all necessary measures at the national level aimed at achieving the full realization of the rights recognized in the present Convention." See Rebecca J. Cook, "State Responsibility for Violations of Women's Human Rights," *Harvard Human Rights Journal* 7 (1994): 127–175.

[12] See Douglas Cassel, "The Expanding Scope and Impact of Reparations Awarded by the Inter-American Court of Human Rights," in *Out of the Ashes*, 191–217; and Arturo Carrillo, "Justice in Context: The Relevance of Inter-American Human Rights Law and Practice to Repairing the Past," in *The Handbook*, 504–538. See also Catalina Díaz, Ruth Rubio-Marín,

Also, since 1989, the UN Human Rights Commission and its Sub-Commission on the Promotion and Protection of Human Rights[13] have been discussing *The Basic Principles and Guidelines on the Right to a Remedy and Reparation for Victims of Gross Violations of International Human Rights Law and Serious Violations of International Humanitarian Law*. These were finally approved in April 2005.[14] The principles present themselves as grounded in the recognition of a right to remedy for victims of violations of international human rights law (found in numerous international instruments) and of international humanitarian law, and emphasize that they do not entail new international or domestic legal obligations but rather identify mechanisms, modalities, procedures, and methods for existing legal obligations. They refer to restitution, compensation, rehabilitation, satisfaction, and guarantees of nonrepetition as forms of reparation for victims of "gross violations of international human rights law" or "serious violations of international humanitarian law."[15] What constitutes either is not defined in the principles themselves.[16]

---

and Clara L. Sandoval Villalba, "Repairing Family Members: Gross Human Rights Violations and Communities of Harm," Chapter 5 in this volume.

[13] Until 1999 the "Sub-Commission on the Prevention of Discrimination and Protection of Minorities."

[14] Resolution 2005/35, E/CN.4/2005/L.48 (henceforth, *UN Principles on Reparations*). For a discussion of the development of these principles, see Dinah Shelton, "The United Nations Draft Principles on Reparations for Human Rights Violations: Context and Contents," in *Out of the Ashes*, 11–31.

[15] According to the *UN Principles on Reparations*, the notion of reparation encompasses several concepts. *Restitution* names those measures to restore the victim to his/her original situation before the violation. These measures include restoration of liberty; enjoyment of human rights, identity, family life, and citizenship; return to one's place of residence; restoration of employment; and return of property. *Compensation* for any economically assessable damage is supposed to be appropriate and proportional to the gravity of the violation, including physical or mental harm; lost opportunities including employment, education, and social benefits; and material and moral damages. Measures of *rehabilitation* include medical and psychological care as well as legal and social services. Measures of *satisfaction* include, among others, the verification of the facts and full and public disclosure of the truth, the search for the whereabouts of the disappeared, public apologies, judicial and administrative sanctions against persons liable for the violations, and commemorations and tributes to the victims. Finally, *guarantees of nonrepetition* include measures to contribute to prevention, such as ensuring effective civilian control of military and security forces, protecting human rights defenders, providing human rights education, and reviewing and reforming laws contributing to or allowing gross violations of international human rights law.

[16] M. Cherif Bassiouni, who together with Theo van Boven was tasked with the study on the right to reparation for victims of human rights violations that eventually led to the *UN Principles on Reparations*, argues that the term "gross and systematic violation" was employed "not to denote a particular category of human right violation per se, but rather to describe situations involving human rights violations by referring to the manner in which the violations may have been committed or to their severity." M. Cherif Bassiouni, *Report of the independent expert on*

Beyond the question of the more-or-less clear confines of the right to reparation for victims of human rights abuses in general, there is something problematic about endorsing a notion of reparation that focuses on (mostly) individual types of remedy aimed at full restitution or compensation of the harmed person to cope with a legacy of massive and gross violations of human rights. The main reason for this inadequacy is that in those scenarios the basic presumption on which the notion of reparation for the violation of a right rests – namely, an overall well-functioning system based on the rule of law and committed to a human rights ethos where violations are the exception rather than the norm – does not apply. The very fact that violations take place on such a massive scale is precisely the result of the state's fundamental lack of commitment to a certain rights order or, at best, its fundamental failure in ensuring the respect of such an order by others.[17]

As Pablo de Greiff has rightly argued, when confronted with this legacy of widespread and systematic violations, governments do best conceptualizing reparations as a (legally grounded, rights-based) political project aimed at the reconstitution of a new political community through the promotion of a minimal degree of both interpersonal trust and trust in the institutions of the new state.[18] Intended as acts of assertion (and not just of validation) of the rights themselves, reparations programs in those scenarios are best conceived as modest acts of creation of the democratic state confirming the basis of legitimacy of a given political order that claims to be grounded in the respect for such rights and the recognition of its citizenry as equal rights holders.

When framed in these terms, the discussion about reparations in post-conflict or post-dictatorship regimes gains a specific gendered dimension. One of the problems of conceptualizing reparations primarily as corrective actions to address every consequence of the breach of a person's rights in

---

the right to restitution, compensation and rehabilitation for victims of grave violations of human rights and fundamental freedoms, UN Doc. E/CN.4/1999/65, Sec. 85, February 8, 1999.

[17] It has been noted that the attempt to provide full restitution or even compensation in strict proportion to harm in the aftermath of episodes of gross and systematic violations of human rights violations would inevitably be doomed to fail for many reasons. These include the incommensurability of some of the harms typically suffered in those scenarios, such as the loss of a loved one; the scarcity of resources and competing needs in societies facing reconstruction; the large number of victims; and the unequal awards and the attendant disaggregation for both victims and reparations efforts that would result from the application of the ideal of full restitution or compensation in strict proportion to harm. See de Greiff, "Justice and Reparations"; Naomi Roht-Arriaza, "Reparations in the Aftermath of Repression and Mass Violence," in *My Neighbor, My Enemy: Justice and Community in the Aftermath of Mass Atrocity*, ed. Eric Stover and Harvey M. Weinstein (Cambridge: Cambridge University Press, 2004), 121–137; and Falk, "Reparations, International Law and Global Justice," 485.

[18] See de Greiff, "Justice and Reparations," 4.

an attempt to revert her to the *status quo ante* (the situation prior to the violation) is that in many societies, even before the outburst of conflict or political repression, women were not treated as equal rights holders but rather were subject to different forms of discrimination and violence. Thus, when reparations are thought of as part of a political project about (re-)constituting a new (more legitimate, democratic, and inclusive) political order – one able to further horizontal and vertical civic trust – a window of opportunity opens up for women. A new space is created that allows for endorsing transformative reparations, which is to say forms of reparations that also aim to unsettle preexisting gender hierarchies that were at the root of women's subordination and account for many of the reasons, forms, and effects of such violence.

In other words, reparations have an individual and a societal dimension and can be seen as bridging the micro- and macro-effects of large-scale violence and political turmoil, linking the recognition of individual rights to a broader political project, namely, one that may require the transformation of a preexisting order when it systemically subordinated certain groups.[19] With this said, it is important when discussing reparations that victims' interests and those of the larger society in the process of political rebirth go hand in hand. Recognizing the experience that victims have undergone and the way it has affected their lives, and helping them and their families cope with the effects of violence, on the one hand, and asserting the broader commitment to a system of rights and recreating the conditions of civic trust on the part of victims and the overall citizenry, on the other, have to be conceived as part of a joint project. The needs of redress, recognition, and compensation to victims must be pondered jointly with the larger political aims of societal healing and national reconciliation. It would not be right to use victims' experiences only as a future-looking pedagogical way of reconstructing the national memory for the purpose of building a more just society, no matter how noble the aim of building a new democratic order may be or how well the process of reconstructing the national memory might serve that purpose. Only when recognizing victims' experiences of oppression and condemning that oppression go hand in hand with helping them cope with some of the consequences of violence in their lives, through palliative and compensatory measures, can reparations be a mechanism for doing some justice to victims and creating a more just political order.

Once we depart from reparations' "aspirational" aims of righting the wrong that has been done and reverting the victim to the situation prior to the violation

---

[19] See Brandon Hamber, "Narrowing the Micro and Macro: A Psychological Perspective on Reparations in Societies in Transition," in *The Handbook*.

and we start to embrace a conception of reparations primarily as acts of due recognition to victims, the question of what the adequate recognition and redress of victims requires becomes of central importance. Although answers to this question may largely depend on contextual factors, I want to defend that, at the very least and at the most abstract level, due recognition of victims, in their common humanity and as equal citizens, should include all of the following:

1. the recognition of the wrongful violation of victims' rights;
2. the acknowledgment of state responsibility for those violations;
3. the recognition of the most serious harms to victims resulting from the violations; and
4. a serious attempt to help victims cope with some of the effects and harms of the violations in their lives and to subvert, however minimally, the structures of subordination that might have led to the violations of their rights in the first place.

Since there are different types of conflicts and transitional processes, it is not surprising that in real-life scenarios, even if consistently guided by all of the above, reparations programs will be different. For the purpose of analysis we can nevertheless think of reparations programs as more or less explicitly structured around a set of common elements including: (1) the definition of "victims"[20] or the selection of a list of violations or crimes for which there will be reparations; (2) the definition of beneficiaries;[21] and (3) the definition of benefits.[22] In the sections to come I want to address the challenge of what "engendering reparations" may entail, following steps 1 through 4, in the process of giving victims due recognition. I will also look specifically at how such aims and their gendered dimensions might be reflected in the process followed to choose a particular reparations package, as well as in the key

---

[20] This definition is generally determined around the selection of certain harms endured or rights violated for which it is decided that there needs to be reparation.
[21] The definition of beneficiary can serve several purposes, including deciding who is to access reparations benefits if the victim is no longer alive; expanding the notion of victim to cover those family members who, other than the victim him/herself, were harmed by a certain violation; or prioritizing some victims over others for the purpose of allocating benefits according to some additional criteria, such as the situation of need or vulnerability of the victim.
[22] The basic distinction of the benefits distributed by reparations programs is between material and symbolic benefits of either an individual or a collective nature. Material reparations can take different forms, including compensation, restitution of material goods, or access to services such as education, health, and other measures for the rehabilitation of victims. Symbolic reparations may include official apologies, the change of names of public spaces, and the establishment of dates and places of commemoration.

substantive and procedural elements in the design of a reparations program including the definition of victims, beneficiaries, and benefits.

II. REPARATIONS AS RECOGNITION OF THE WRONGFUL VIOLATIONS OF VICTIMS' RIGHTS

The very existence of a reparations program implies a degree of recognition of victims. Since reparations programs are articulated around a notion of victim or a listing of violations for which the state takes responsibility and seeks remedy, such programs symbolize the recognition of victims as rights holders. Also, because in most cases victims were victimized and subsequently stigmatized precisely *because* of their political views, ethnicity, race, and so forth, the putting into place of formal governmental mechanisms of redress epitomizes recognition of victims as equal citizens in the community. By allocating material resources, often in the context of general scarcity, reparations programs express the fact that the state takes seriously the rights of victims and the harms ensuing from their abridgment. Moreover, a program may contain specific symbolic measures, such as official apologies, naming of public places after victims, or public monuments, whose aim is precisely to give public visibility to the suffering of victims or to their contribution to the cause of democracy.

More and more, we also find that reparations programs are put in place after countries go through an effort of unveiling the truth about their violent or repressive pasts, typically relying on the work of truth commissions or similar bodies for this purpose. Although the connection between efforts of truth-telling and reparation varies from case to case, the current trend seems to be for truth commissions, under their mandates, to be in charge of framing recommendations on reparations for victims or, more exceptionally, distributing interim/urgent or even final reparations.[23] When this is the case, both truth-telling and reparations can greatly supplement each other in the

---

[23] Both South Africa's Truth and Reconciliation Commission (set up in 1995 and with a mandate that lasted until 1998) and Timor-Leste's Commission for Reception, Truth and Reconciliation (which began its work in 2002 and finished in November 2005) distributed interim/urgent reparations measures. See Beth Goldblatt, "Evaluating the Gender Contents of Reparations: Lessons from South Africa," in *What Happened?*; and Wandita et al., "Learning to Engender Reparations." Both commissions, as well as Sierra Leone's Truth and Reconciliation Commission (which functioned between 2000 and 2004), Chile's National Truth and Reconciliation Commission (1990–1991), Peru's Truth and Reconciliation Commission (2000–2003), and Guatemala's Commission of Historical Clarification (1996–1999), included reparations for victims under the recommendations sections or chapters in their respective final reports. See Jamesina King, "Gender and Reparations in Sierra Leone: The Wounds of War Remain Open," in *What Happened?*; Elizabeth Lira, "The Reparations Policy for Human Rights Violations in Chile," in *The Handbook*; Julie Guillerot, "Linking Gender and Reparations in

task of granting adequate recognition to victims. Indeed, the public visibility and social rehabilitation victims experience is much greater when reparations follow large-scale attempts to unveil the past. Truth commissions elaborate reports that become public historical records of an investigated period, collect the testimony of victims, and often hold public hearings that allow victims and witnesses to present their truth to the public. Also, when a reparations policy is shaped after a truth-finding process, it is likely to be in a better position to identify the variety of violations, the pool of victims and beneficiaries, and the adequacy of proposed reparations measures to redress the harms incurred.

There are several challenges to the recognition of the wrongful violations of women's rights and hence to the possibility of having reparations programs asserting women as equal rights holders. Some of these challenges are epistemic and have to do with what we could summarize as women's lesser opportunities to speak, be listened to, and be believed. Allowing and encouraging women to speak and learning to listen to women are necessary but not sufficient conditions for having reparations programs that duly reflect women's experience of violence. The *selection of violations* for which there will be reparations (as well as the design of concrete reparation measures for each violation) also entails moral and political judgments about the relative gravity and political relevance of the different violations, especially in a context in which such selection inevitably requires an exercise of prioritizing. Given that the definition of the violations of rights around which the notion of victim is structured has clear implications in terms of the recognition dimensions of a reparations program, it is not enough that women be included as possible victims when their rights have been infringed against, something which no reparations program has thus far denied. Rather, one of the most obvious challenges in designing reparations programs that recognize women as equal citizens is to ensure that those violations affecting mostly women or affecting women in a disparate way are not left out of consideration as violations that will trigger access to reparations benefits. This requires at least three things: first, shaping the truth-telling process so as to allow women to speak their truth on their own terms; second, broadening the scope of reparations programs to reflect women's worst experiences of victimization and adapting evidentiary standards accordingly; and third, designing and implementing reparations

---

Peru: A Failed Opportunity," in *What Happened?*; and Claudia Paz y Paz Bailey, "Guatemala: Gender and Reparations for Human Rights Violations," in *What Happened?* Morocco's *Instance d'Equité et Reconciliation* (2004–2005) operated as a truth commission but, in conformity with its mandate, also decided on reparations to victims. See http://www.ier.ma, consulted as of December 2005.

programs that "de-normalize" discrimination on the grounds of sex. Let's take a look at each of these three requirements.

1. Enabling Women to Speak Their Truth

Because of the normalcy of certain forms of violence in women's ordinary lives, even in times of official peace, and because self-sacrifice is an essential component of femaleness and motherhood in patriarchal cultures, women in post-conflict and post-authoritarian regimes have been known to be more active in relation to violations committed against their immediate family members (husbands, brothers, children) than those committed against themselves, which they often consider marginal, private, peripheral, or secondary. It is, for instance, not uncommon to find that women who were harassed, detained, and subject to different forms of violence as family members of political activists almost never talk about their own experiences of victimization. Also, unless asked explicitly, women do not talk much about the impact that violations against family members have had on their own lives. Women with disappeared, murdered, or detained sons, husbands, or brothers are talking about themselves when they refer to the loss of loved ones, but they rarely elaborate on what that loss meant for the development of their life projects. Finally, certain forms of violence, such as sexual violence, can create stigmatizing effects for the victim and her family that can be so large that underreporting is both predictable and inevitable. Collective meanings attached to femininity (which are often at the root of why and how sexual violence against women is perpetrated during the conflict in the first place) are not automatically removed simply because the conflict ends. The same, of course, applies to masculinity. Men too have difficulties addressing publicly sexual violence they are subject to, and thus they experience, through this form of victimization, gender-specific silencing.[24]

It is easy to see, then, that besides ensuring that victims' organizations (often largely composed of and run by women) are adequately consulted in the design of reparations policies, women should be encouraged to think about their own experiences of oppression during the conflict or the period of political turmoil. Also, general public campaigns in opposition to violence against women might be necessary to create an environment that is minimally conducive to the reporting of the sexual violence that occurred in the past. It would seem

---

[24] None of this is to suggest that men are subject to sexual violence to the same extent as women or that the consequences of such experiences are necessarily the same or equally harming.

that the active involvement of women's groups and associations in reparations discussions could encourage both. Ideally, these organizations should not miss the opportunity of shedding light also on the sexual violence men have been subject to. Doing so would probably help show that, in terms of meanings, sexual violence often consists of treating men as "one would treat women." Presumably, it would also show that sexual violence is not only a concern that affects women, even if, admittedly, it affects more women than men and arguably has worse effects on women's lives. All of this could contribute to making both the political dimension and the gendered dimension of sexual violence more obvious.

So have women's groups and associations in the past been active in discussing reparations? Empirical evidence shows that, until very recently, women's groups have not been particularly engaged in dealing with the past in general or in discussing reparations more specifically.[25] Instead, during times of reconstruction or transition, women's associations have often focused on assisting other women with their most urgent needs and coping with the high levels of violence women still experience as part of their normal lives.[26] Establishing the necessary bridges between, on the one hand, victims' groups and human rights groups – the main and most common civil society actors in the fight for reparations – and women's groups, on the other, is therefore a priority. Such groups could also be of assistance in allowing women to come

[25] In the past, women's agency in reparations discussions has been mostly conducted either through their involvement in victims' groups (in which they often participate as family members of the disappeared or killed) or through specific associations representing some sectoral interest (such as widows' associations or associations focusing on the displaced). Relevant examples include women's participation in South Africa through the Khulumani Support Group (formed to assist victims and family members of victims, and 70% of which is made up of women) as well as their involvement through widows' associations in Guatemala (Conavigua), Rwanda (Avega), and Sierra Leone (War Widows Organization). In Guatemala, women, especially indigenous women, mobilized also as a displaced population around issues of land tenure. Only recently can we find instances such as Sierra Leone where women's participation in reparations discussions include the involvement, however limited, of women's groups as such (through the Women's Task Force). In Colombia, this trend has clearly consolidated, women's groups being among the most active in the peace, reconciliation, and reparations discussions. See the case studies on South Africa, Guatemala, and Sierra Leone in *What Happened?*

[26] Some of the reasons accounting for this might have to do with the different social extraction of victims' groups and women's rights groups or with the fact that women's groups are often too busy facing the challenges of the present to care about the past – official peace does not usually mean peace for women, who continue to be subject to many forms of violence after the political turmoil has ended, often in the private sphere. Also, in times of transition women often and understandably put their energy into seizing the window of opportunity for structural and institutional long-term reforms. Finally, female leaders in civil society movements are sometimes co-opted into the new establishment.

forward and participate in truth-telling bodies, something which would also have a bearing on reparations.

As already mentioned, in more and more countries undergoing transitions, truth commissions – which are in charge of taking testimony of victims and investigating past violations of rights in order to document the systematic abuses of the predecessor regime – are also entrusted with granting reparations or, more frequently, making recommendations on reparations programs that the governments are then supposed to implement. Recently there have been signs that these bodies, including the pertinent commissions in South Africa, Peru, Sierra Leone, Timor-Leste, Morocco, and Colombia, have started to internalize the need to incorporate a gender dimension into their work.[27] This is having an impact on the degree to which the experiences of women are rendered visible and politically relevant and on the ability of truth commissions to recommend adequate forms of redress for gender violence (even though, one must say too, unfortunately such recommendations are often insufficiently implemented). Equally important is the contribution that the work of truth

[27] Some examples of this evolution include the holding of truth-commission thematic hearings dedicated to women (as in South Africa, Peru, Sierra Leone, and Timor-Leste), which seem to have offered wonderful opportunities to give women voice but also to ensure that this voice transcends and reaches the public; the formation of special research teams in truth commissions dedicated to women (as in Timor-Leste and Colombia); the consecration of some of the chapters in the commissions' final reports to recording violence against women and the different impact of violence on women's lives (such as in South Africa and Peru) or the explicit attempt to mainstream gender throughout the entire report (as in Timor-Leste). There are other ways to operationalize gender mainstreaming in truth commissions' work. These include ensuring that truth commissions have a gender-balanced composition; that gender justice is explicitly made part of their mandates; that commissioners have adequate gender training; that a balanced gender composition is also sustained in all of the committees that form truth commissions, including, when there is one, the commission in charge of reparations; and that there is adequate coordination and communication between the truth-seeking, investigation, testimony-taking, and recommendation-making tasks inside of truth commissions. Ensuring that there is adequate involvement of victims' groups and women's groups in the process seems also relevant, as is the reliance of the commission on gender-sensitive devices of testimony-taking, including adequate psychological assistance to the victims and creating supportive environments for testifying, especially with regard to crimes of sexual violence. Finally, to give visibility to the fact that the same violations may harm men and women differently, truth commissions' databases should be structured in such a way that they cover not only the violations but also the enabling conditions as well as the most common effects of such violations on victims' lives. On gender and truth commissions, see Debra L. DeLaet, "Gender Justice: A Gendered Assessment of Truth-Telling Mechanisms," in *Telling the Truths: Truth Telling and Peace Building in Post-Conflict Societies*, ed. Tristan Anne Borer (Notre Dame: University of Notre Dame Press, 2006), 151–181; The World Bank, *Gender, Justice, and Truth Commissions* (Washington, DC: The World Bank, June 2006); Vasuki Nesiah et al., "Truth Commissions and Gender: Principles, Policies, and Procedures," ICTJ Gender Justice Series, July 2006; Fionnuala Ni Aoláin and Catherine Turner, "Gender, Truth and Transition," *UCLA Women's Law Journal* 16 (2007): 229–279.

commissions can make to facilitate an environment that helps women talk about their experience of victimization. More creative thinking is required to assess what kinds of environment can help different groups of women (think of girls or ethnic minorities) feel comfortable contributing, if they so wish, with their share of truth, but also what kind of environment would help boys and men render visible they ways in which masculinity models shape their experiences as either perpetrators or victims.

The question of timing is also crucial, especially regarding reparations for crimes of a sexual nature. Since the preconditions for reporting and testifying to sexual abuse are not always present in the aftermath of conflict, reparations programs have to take this into account and not sacrifice adequate accessibility to the otherwise legitimately felt urgency of society to move forward. Although having male and female victims of sexual violence testify in front of truth-telling mechanisms may not only have a reparatory effect for the victims themselves but also contribute to the creation of precisely the type of environment that is conducive to helping others recognize their victimization, linking access to reparations to participation in truth-telling processes (typically by defining victims who qualify for reparations only among those who have come to testify before a truth commission) may run the danger of leaving out the most vulnerable victims, that is, those who may not be in the material or psychological condition to participate in truth commission proceedings. This, for instance, might well have happened in South Africa, where only those who were able or prepared to approach the TRC qualified as victims who could benefit from financial reparations, something which presumably left out poor women in rural areas who lacked the adequate information but also victims of sexual violence who were not able to approach the TRC because of numerous reasons, including fear of stigma or unwillingness to reopen wounds.[28] In this regard, it would be important that the reparations mechanism be endowed with a certain time openness to allow different victims to come forward and claim reparations when they feel psychologically prepared to do so. Aware of this, the truth commission in Timor-Leste recommended that the reparations program consider victims who have come before the commission but that it also allow a two-year period to identify other potential beneficiaries;[29] similarly, in Peru the Truth and Reconciliation Commission decided that although having testified before it could facilitate the reparations process, such testimonies should not be considered as a prerequisite to qualify as beneficiaries.[30]

---

[28] See Goldblatt, "Evaluating the Gender Contents of Reparations," 74.
[29] Wandita, "Learning to Engender Reparations," 309.
[30] Guillerot, "Linking Gender and Reparations," 166.

2. Feminizing Dehumanization

Following situations of political turmoil and large-scale violence, the concept of victim used for reparations purposes will inevitably reflect the particular and most common forms of violence that occurred. However, given the manifold rights that are often violated in such situations, a selection of the worst forms of human rights violations is often necessary. Such selection is also implicit in the notion of "gross" violation of a human right. As mentioned, in the past, most reparations efforts have concentrated on violations of a fairly limited but also traditionally conceived catalogue of civil and political rights including illegal detention, summary execution, and forced disappearances. This has meant that many of the forms of violations more commonly perpetrated against girls and women have until now been excluded as triggers of reparations benefits.

One promising sign of change is the increasingly explicit inclusion of rape and other forms of *sexual violence* among the list of violations for the sake of reparations. Thus, recent (and mostly as of yet unimplemented) reparations programs or laws that have explicitly included some forms of sexual violence among the list of violations include those in Peru, Guatemala, Sierra Leone, and Timor-Leste.[31] In the past, sexual violence was either omitted or covered only implicitly. In view of this, the explicit recognition of sexual violence as a form of human rights violation that triggers reparation is to be celebrated. Nevertheless, it is regrettable that sometimes the category chosen is clearly underinclusive (as when it is defined as including only rape, a notion which all too often is also narrowly defined), leaving out other egregious forms of sexual violence, such as mutilation of sexual organs, sexual slavery, or forced nudity, to mention a few.[32]

Also, although relying on sexual violence as a separate crime/violation category arguably contributes to the breaking of cultural taboos and in most scenarios to the rendering visible of the systematic use of sexual violence, this option also runs certain risks when compared with that of subsuming sexual violence under broader categories such as those of "severe ill treatment" or

---

[31] The category referred to in Peru is "rape victims." In Guatemala it is "victims of rape and sexual violence." The reparations programs recommended by the Sierra Leone TRC referred to victims of "sexual violence" and included women and girls subject to rape, sexual slavery, mutilation of genital parts or breasts, and forced marriage. The urgent reparations delivered by Timor-Leste's CAVR included reparations for victims of sexual violence. The final reparations recommended by the same commission also refer to victims of "sexual violence" in similarly broad terms that include rape, sexual slavery, and forced marriage, among other forms of sexual violence. See *What Happened?* 151, 153, 106, 236, 302, and 309.

[32] As mentioned, Guatemala's national reparations program refers to "rape and sexual violence," but the latter is not interpreted as including sexual slavery, forced union with captors, sexual torture, or amputation and mutilation of sexual organs.

"torture." South Africa provides an interesting example in this regard, for although sexual violence was not explicitly mentioned among the list of violations to be covered, in the end several forms of it were included as falling under the concepts of "torture" and "severe ill treatment" including assault to genitals and breasts, rape, beating leading to miscarriage, and sexual abuse.[33] It is important, in other words, that explicit recognition and the visibility that comes with it are not purchased at the expense of either too narrow definitions or other forms of devaluation of sexual violence, including creating a separate category but then assuming that violations under this category are less serious than others. This was the case in Peru, where violations were ordered on a scale of gravity and rape ended up at the bottom because, allegedly, and implausibly, unlike murder and disappearances, other violations of physical integrity, and imprisonment, it was considered that rape did not end victims' lives, affect their ability to generate income, or interrupt their life projects.[34] Finally, if the circumstances are not given for most victims of sexual violence to "come out" without fear of stigmatization, considering a less explicit modality of inclusion might also be a valuable option.

Including violations perpetrated mostly against women or with a disparate impact on women in the list that will open access to reparations benefits is indeed a sign of progress. But the evidentiary standards to prove the condition of victim or the occurrence of the violation are also worth reflecting on. If, in principle, as administrative procedures reparations programs offer victims the advantage of less burdensome procedures than court proceedings, gender biases may still interfere in such administrative procedures in ways similar to those women have traditionally encountered in front of courts, undermining women's chances to be believed. Ensuring that evidentiary rules concur with women's experiences will mean, for instance, that standards of evidence for cases of sexual violence against women must be adequate to the nature of such crimes. This may require relinquishing the idea that evidence must be based primarily on legal medical examination. Instead, the testimony of the victim, traceable consequences for her mental health, or simply a system of presumptions based on patterns of criminal conduct could be relied on as sufficient sources of evidence.[35]

---

[33] See Goldblatt, "Evaluating the Gender Contents of Reparations," 63.
[34] See Guillerot, "Linking Gender and Reparations," 159.
[35] The Commission on Illegal Detention and Torture in Chile, based on close studies of the *modus operandi* of different detention centers, presumed that whoever was shown to have spent time in certain detention centers in all likelihood had been tortured and therefore deserved compensation accordingly. Sexual violence, of course, calls for equally creative evidentiary procedures. In many cases, there will be a pattern of sexual torture in abuse in detention centers. Other patterns can also be context specific, such as in the example in Guatemala of

Given that fear of stigmatization by society is one of the most difficult hurdles to overcome for victims of sexual violence to come forward and claim reparations, guaranteeing the confidentiality of victims during the entire process is of crucial importance. Allowing women to give testimonies or provide evidence in private, at a distance, through proxy, in the presence of other women, or relying on the help of trained psychological assistance can both protect confidentiality and create a supportive environment. When providing testimonies, women often do not clearly say whether they were raped or subject to other forms of sexual violence, and instead make reference to a rape attempt or threat or to the rape of other women, or simply use vague terminology. Having officials who are adequately trained to listen to and understand this subtle language will thus be equally important. Finally, administrative programs may articulate categories of beneficiaries creatively to cover victims of sexual violence even if they do not come forward as such.[36]

The increasing awareness of the fact that sexual violence is not collateral damage and does count as a grave human rights violation that calls for reparation is indeed a step forward. Unfortunately, it runs the risk of sexualizing women if other equally egregious violations are left out, as is often the case. Many other forms of violence to which women are subject in times of conflict and political turmoil, including, for instance, forced domestic labor, forced "marital" unions, forced impregnations, forced abortions, forced sterilizations, or removal of children, are still commonly left out of reparations programs.[37]

---

the systematic mass rape of women and girls by the army before massacres. See Paz y Paz Bailey, "Guatemala: Gender and Reparations," 98.

[36] See Wandita et al., "Learning to Engender Reparations," 309, providing an example of how this was attempted in East Timor.

[37] Because, as mentioned, the notion of "gross violation of human rights law" is not defined, it will probably help to identify as such those conducts that are typified as international crimes. In some instances this will be adequate to cover the most egregious forms of sexual violence, whereas in others it may not. The Rome Statute creating the International Criminal Court (ICC) includes in the category of *war crimes* the following serious violations of the laws and customs applicable both in international armed conflicts and in armed conflicts not of an international character within the established framework in international law: rape, sexual slavery, enforced prostitution, forced pregnancy (understood as the unlawful confinement of a woman forcibly made pregnant, with the intent of affecting the ethnic composition of any population), carrying out other grave violations of international law (see Article 7 [2] [f]), enforced sterilization, and any other form of sexual violence also constituting a serious violation of Article 3 common to the four Geneva Conventions (which may support interpreting torture or inhuman treatment, willfully causing great suffering, serious injury, and unlawful confinement as covering forms of sexual violence) (see Articles 8 [2] [b] [xxii] and Article 8 [2] [e] [vi]). Also important is the definition of measures intended to prevent births (such as sterilization and forced termination of pregnancy) or the forcible transfer of children of one group to another as *genocide* (see Article 6 [d] and [f]) and the inclusion of rape, sexual slavery, enforced prostitution, forced pregnancy, enforced sterilization, and any other from of sexual

The still shy efforts to include forced displacement among the list of violations triggering reparations, such as those in Peru, Guatemala, and more forcefully in Turkey, are hence commendable given the empirical evidence showing how internally displaced and refugee women and girls are often subjected to further forms of abuse and exploitation.[38]

One of the reasons why this kind of gender bias can take place might have to do with the fact that the hierarchy around which the list of violations in reparations programs is structured is not usually rendered explicit. To give an example, reparations programs have tended to include breaches that affect the right to life (summary executions, disappearances, assassination), presumably on the grounds of the irreplaceable nature of the ensuing loss. Rendering this underlying reason explicit might invite reflection on the kinds of irreplaceable losses women commonly face during conflict. For instance, among the common forms of violence that women are subject to are those practices that intend or result in involuntary pregnancies (such as forced impregnation), miscarriages, or loss of reproductive capacity (such as forced sterilization). Yet violations of women's reproductive rights are not typically included or conceptualized as separate violations, even though they represent harms that are unique and distinct from those that result from other forms of sexual violence.

violence of comparable gravity when committed as part of a widespread or systematic attack against a civilian population and the persecution against any identifiable group or collectivity on several grounds including gender as *crimes against humanity* (see Article 7.1 [g] and [h]). For an example of the impact of relying on categories embraced by international criminal law, see Paz y Paz Bailey, "Gender and Reparations," 106, who explains how in the making of the reparations plan in Guatemala, the definition of gender violence was imported from the Rome Statute, and how this entailed that certain crimes that were not committed during the national conflict were included, whereas others that were committed (such as forced unions with captors, sexual torture, and amputation and mutilation of sexual organs) ended up being left out.

[38] Guatemala's national reparations policies include reparations for victims of forced displacement who should benefit from measures of material restitution, including land restitution, housing, and productive investment. The reparations program proposed by the Peruvian TRC recommended giving both symbolic reparations as well as various services including education and health for the victims of forced displacement. The United Nations Compensation Commission, created in the aftermath of the first Gulf War to provide compensation to victims of the Iraqi invasion of Kuwait, treated being forced to flee from Iraq or Kuwait as a compensable injustice. See Sara L. Zeigler and Gregory Gilbert Gunderson, "The Gendered Dimension of Conflict's Aftermath: A Victim-Centered Approach to Compensation," *Ethics and International Affairs* 20, no. 2 (2006): 185. Turkey has established an ambitious reparations plan that provides benefits to the victims of internal displacement, among others, under Law No. 5233 ("Law on Compensation for Losses Resulting from Terrorism and the Fight against Terrorism," adopted July 17, 2004). See Dilek Kurban, Aye Betül Celik, and Deniz Yükseker, *Overcoming a Legacy of Mistrust: Towards Reconciliation between the State and the Displaced* (Istanbul: Norwegian Refugee Council, Internal Displaced Monitoring Centre, and the Turkish Economic and Social Studies Foundation, 2006).

However, if the criterion for inclusion was the irreplaceable nature of the lost good, one would, for instance, be hard pressed not to include forced sterilization among the list of violations.[39] Many women in general, and more so in societies that define womanhood around motherhood, would clearly experience the loss of their reproductive capacity as irreplaceable and fundamental to the possibility of leading a meaningful existence. If this is so, asking governments to be explicit in the rationale underlying the design of their reparations programs in general, and the inclusion of a list of violations specifically, would allow for an easier identification of possible gender biases.

Rendering the criteria for inclusion of violations explicit would also allow for a productive debate as to whether the selection of such criteria is indeed gender biased. Take the example of forced displacement. Although it is commonly believed that in many conflicts women are disproportionately affected by it, in spite of the exemplary exceptions just referred to, forced displacement has not been included in most implemented reparations programs. In contrast, illegal detention has. If the criteria for this selection had to do with the importance of the affected good, one could make the argument that having to leave everything behind to start a new life and recreate the social tissue and network systems that women so much rely on in their ordinary lives may be much worse than being deprived of freedom, at least if the deprivation is of a short duration. Also, as mentioned, evidence shows that women and girls in refugee camps are extremely vulnerable and often subject to further forms of abuse and exploitation, including sexual exploitation. This brings to the fore the question of whether the fact that some violations of rights create a space of vulnerability inviting further violations should be considered one of the determining criteria, together with the importance or irreplaceable nature of the affected good, in choosing which violations to include.[40]

3. "De-Normalizing" Discrimination on the Grounds of Sex

Broadening the scope of reparations programs to reflect women's worst experiences of victimization means advancing toward the goal of recognizing women as equal rights holders, as it implies that the vision of humanity that such

---

[39] This example also highlights the fact that, given the close ties between the notion of reparation and that of right, it helps when the forms of harm that women experience have first been conceptualized as a matter of right. Otherwise, gender bias in reparations programs may simply result from gender bias in national and international definitions or hierarchical ordering of a certain rights system.

[40] See Margaret Walker, "Gender and Violence in Focus: A Background for Gender Justice in Reparations," Chapter 1 in this volume. Walker's chapter refers to the concept of gender-multiplied violence and harm to describe the forms of harms or loss that precipitate further losses that may in the end be worse or less manageable than the original violation or loss itself.

programs rest on is not exclusively male shaped. However, when conceived as acts of recognition of people's equal citizenship status and as a political project epitomizing the reconstruction of a political order, the notion of reparation poses further specific gendered challenges. Given that many authoritarian regimes also embrace notions of patriarchy that are entrenched in legal systems discriminatory against women, how much can we expect a reparations program to advance in achieving wider structural equality between the sexes? Should, at a minimum, discrimination on the grounds of sex be seen as a grave violation of human rights that in itself calls for reparations in spite of its traditional neglect?

Some feminist scholars have argued that periods of regime change and transition to democracy offer unique historic opportunities for the redefinition of gender roles, not least because those gender roles are too often subverted during such times.[41] One could argue that reparations offer one of the channels for such change in transitional societies. *De jure*, the question is complex, because although the most important human rights treaties do indeed incorporate the prohibition of discrimination on the grounds of sex,[42] those human rights norms that are commonly said to constitute *jus cogens* are the prohibition of genocide, slavery, murder/disappearances, torture, prolonged arbitrary detention, and systematic racial discrimination.[43] The list is not commonly said to include sex-based discrimination.[44] Also, although there seems to be

---

[41] See Sheila Meintjes et al., "There is No Aftermath for Women," in *The Aftermath: Women in Post-Conflict Transformation*, ed. Sheila Meintjes, Anu Pillay, and Meredeth Turshen (London and New York: Zed Books, 2001).

[42] See, for instance, ICCPR, Articles 2.3 and 26; ICESCR, Articles 3 and 7; American Convention on Human Rights, Article 1; African Charter of Human and Peoples' Rights, Articles 2 and 18(3); European Convention on Human Rights, Article 14. See also Anne Bayesfsky, "The Principle of Equality or Non-Discrimination in International Law," *Human Rights Law Journal* 11 (1990): 1.

[43] See Marjorie M. Whiteman, "Jus Cogens in International Law, With a Projected List," *Georgia Journal of International and Comparative Law* 7 (1977): 609. But also see Ian Brownlies, *System of the Law of Nations, State Responsibility*, Part I (Oxford: Clarendon Press, 1983), 81, arguing that the prohibition against sexual discrimination has become customary international law.

[44] In this regard, it is also worth mentioning that Special Rapporteur Stanislav Chernichenko elaborated a "Draft declaration on the recognition of gross and massive human rights perpetrated on the orders of Government or sanctioned by them as an international crime" for the UN Sub-Commission on Prevention of Discrimination and Protection of Minorities. In his working paper, it was proposed that the UN General Assembly would adopt a declaration to the effect that all gross and massive human rights violations ordered or sanctioned by government constituted an international crime. The definition included, among other things, certain forms of discrimination that would qualify as gross and massive violations, such as apartheid and discrimination on racial, national, linguistic, or religious grounds. It did not, however, mention discrimination on the grounds of sex. See Heidy Rombouts et al., "The Right to Reparation," in *Out of the Ashes*, 350–351.

an increasing consensus around the need to embrace some notion of gender justice as a constitutive element of a liberal democratic order based on human rights, there is much less consensus around the question of which concrete rules or practices amount to discrimination on the grounds of sex, as is shown by the wide use of reservations and "interpretive declarations" by many of the states that have ratified the Convention on the Elimination of All Forms of Discrimination against Women.[45]

Needless to say, whether by linking it to a concrete reparations project or otherwise, societies undergoing transitional processes face the challenge of broader institutional reform, and I would argue that removing discrimination on the grounds of sex from the legal system (as well as whatever forms of violence against women such a system may endorse) is an indispensable element in the agenda of establishing a liberal democratic order. I would also argue that, at a minimum, reparations programs should not be designed or implemented so as to embrace sex discrimination or, for that matter, discrimination on any other ground.[46] Indeed, entrenching sex discrimination in reparations programs would be a poor way of presenting reparations as a tool to recognize citizens as equal rights holders.

Going to the other extreme, probably the most ambitious effort in this regard would be to include *de jure* gender-based discrimination, or concrete expressions thereof, in the list of violations in reparations programs. Given the fact that in many transitional societies doing so might turn roughly 50% of the population automatically into victims, this option runs the risk of widening the scope of the program so much that the magnitude of the individual benefits it distributes is altogether sacrificed. Also, given the diffuseness and the multiplicity of the harms that usually result from sex-based discrimination, thinking about ways of providing individual compensation might be a daunting task. Thus, one option might be to limit oneself to those expressions of discrimination that are more aggravating or materially commensurable for the purpose of reparations.[47] Also, since the notion of reparation goes beyond that

---

[45] See Belinda Clark, "The Vienna Convention Reservations Regime and the Convention on the Elimination of All Forms of Discrimination Against Women," *American Journal of International Law* 86 (1990): 643.

[46] It is worth underscoring that the principle of nondiscrimination is also explicitly included in the UN *Principles on Reparations*, under clause XI (nondiscrimination), whereby: "the application and interpretation of these Principles and Guidelines must be consistent with international human rights law and international humanitarian law and be without any discrimination of any kind or ground, without exception."

[47] Spain offers an interesting example. Under Franco's regime women were subject to all kinds of discrimination as, like many other authoritarian regimes, Franco's tried to relegate women to the private domain, which is where they were naturally thought to belong. See Ruth Rubio-Marín, "Women and the Cost of Transition to Democratic Constitutionalism in Spain,"

of restitution or compensation, there may still be an array of meaningful nonmaterial ways of thinking about reparations for discrimination on the grounds of sex. Think of the possibility of granting symbolic reparations along the lines of offering apologies, or incorporating institutional reforms as guarantees of nonrepetition, including measures to remove traces of formal discrimination against women and to facilitate women's equal opportunities. One advantage of linking such institutional reform processes to the reparations debate is that it may give due recognition to the fact that wider patterns of systemic discrimination are often enabling conditions for the severe forms of violence women experience in times of conflict and also account for the seriousness of the resulting harms. As I argue below, it may also provide victims the satisfaction of knowing that their victimization at least is an engine of change that can contribute to the noble cause of gender justice.[48]

III. REPARATIONS AS AN ACKNOWLEDGMENT OF STATE RESPONSIBILITY FOR THE VIOLATION OF VICTIMS' RIGHTS

Reparations initiatives imply the need for the state to devote resources to repairing victims. This in itself expresses the acceptance of some sort of responsibility for their fate. Moreover, as will be discussed, some symbolic forms of reparation, such as official apologies made by the state or by its agents that were more closely responsible for the violations (such as the military or the police), have great potential to underscore the element of acceptance of direct responsibility for the violation of victims' rights.

International Sociology 18, no. 1 (2003): 239–257. With Spain's transition to democracy, equality and nondiscrimination on the grounds of sex were constitutionally enshrined and discriminatory legislation has been reformed. Women who lived under Franco have not thus far received any kind of reparation to compensate for the legal discrimination they were subject to. There is a pending bill in congress to compensate those women who were forcefully deprived of their employment when and because they got married. Until now, it has not gathered sufficient political support to pass.

[48] The South African experience is maybe the most interesting analogy in this respect. Because of the systematic nature of racial discrimination under the apartheid system, the point has been made repeatedly that the definition of "victim" endorsed by the TRC was excessively narrow, leaving out important categories of potential beneficiaries (see de Greiff, "Introduction," in *The Handbook*, 8, citing Mahmood Mamdani, "Reconciliation Without Justice," *Southern African Review of Books* [Nov/Dec 1996]: 3–5). On the other hand, among the reparative measures covered by the TRC's Final Report's Recommended Reparations Program were recommendations on institutional, legislative, and administrative matters that would help prevent the recurrence of the human rights violations that took place under apartheid and promote a human rights culture. See Chris Colvin, "Overview of the Reparations Program in South Africa," in *The Handbook*.

That said, even those states that are in principle not opposed to the idea of offering reparations may end up circumscribing the scope of their responsibility in ways that are dubious and may have a disparate gender impact. Some ways of doing so may include, first, narrowing the relevant violations to only those perpetrated by those actors conceived as state agents, and second, limiting the responsibility to that concerning a certain type of violence narrowly conceived as "political" and, related to this, establishing the limitation on the basis of the location in which the violent actions took place. In other words, the questions of by whom, why, and where the violence was perpetrated can be rendered relevant in ways that have a disparate effect on women. Let's take a look at each of these.

First, then, should it matter who the perpetrators are? There are in principle good reasons to think that state responsibility for the violation of victims' rights varies from case to case in a way that might also influence how reparations are shaped. Relevant to determining the degree of responsibility is not only whether the atrocities were committed by the state, but also whether the state could have taken actions to prevent them from taking place at the hands of others and hence failed in its duty to adequately protect its citizens.[49] Given that in many authoritarian regimes, and more so in situations of large-scale civil strife, the violence perpetrated against women comes often from non-state actors – including members of the guerrillas and civilian self-defense groups – it is of fundamental importance that the concept of victim embraced by a reparations program be in principle adequate to cover such violent acts. This is especially the case when it is these actors, more than the military or other state agents, that are primarily responsible for some of the most egregious and systematic forms of violence against women, as is sometimes the case with forced conscription, domestic and sexual enslavement, or forced abortion or

---

[49] States are responsible for their failures to meet their international obligations even when substantive breaches originate in the conduct of private persons – they therefore have to exercise due diligence to eliminate, reduce, and mitigate the incidence of private discrimination. See Cook, "State Responsibility," 151. In the context of gross human rights violations, the case *Velásquez-Rodríguez* in the Inter-American Court of Human Rights (*Velásquez-Rodríguez Judgment*, Inter-Am. C.H.T., Ser. C, No. 4 [1988]) was paradigmatic in affirming member states' obligation to prevent human rights violations by state *and nonstate* actors. See Dinah Shelton, "Private Violence, Public Wrongs, and the Responsibility of States," *Fordham International Law Journal* 13, no. 4 (1989–1990): 1–34. Tellingly, the UN *Principles on Reparations* cover both relevant state actions and omissions. Thus, the definition of victims entitled to reparations refers to "persons individually or collectively harmed through *acts* or *omissions* that constitute gross violations of international human rights law or serious violations of international humanitarian law" (Principle V) (my emphasis). Moreover, under Principle IX.16, "States should endeavor to establish national programmes for reparation and other assistance to victims in the event the party liable for the harm suffered is unable or unwilling to meet their obligations."

sterilization. Because subversive movements sometimes justify their actions on the need to impose "order and morality" and, in that capacity, enforce sex-specific codes of conduct, women, but also men who are seen as departing from these norms, are often targets of persecution. Colombia's paramilitary groups, for instance, are known to have persecuted prostitutes, gays, and HIV-carriers for the sake of sustaining order and morality in their controlled domains. It is a promising sign, then, for women, but also for those men who in a certain society may not fit prevailing masculinity patterns, that more recent reparations programs, such as those in Peru or Guatemala, are indeed embracing this wide notion of state responsibility by omission.[50] Because these paralegal forces often abuse and exploit boys and girls in gender-specific ways, the promise holds also for them.[51]

In those contexts in which the focus is placed on repairing the human rights violations perpetrated by a repressive and authoritarian state (mostly against political dissidents), or as a result of an armed conflict, a government may choose to make the political connotation of the violation a condition to qualify for reparations. Especially in those cases where the state is willing to accept responsibility by omission, this may be a way of limiting the potential pool of victims by distinguishing political from common criminality. What is crucial for the adequate inclusion of women among reparations beneficiaries, however, is a proper understanding of the way that political agency normally functions within societies organized around patriarchal family structures. It is not uncommon that in those societies "men do politics" while women do other things to sustain "their men." Also, women collaborate and/or are perceived as collaborating politically in gender-specific ways. To avoid the "de-politicization" of women's experience of violence, one has to understand the many ways women are objectified and instrumentalized in political struggles of all kinds that are mostly conducted by men.[52] For instance, in many dictatorial

---

[50] Both in Peru and Guatemala, it was mostly nonstate agents (members of civilian self-defense groups in the first case, and subversive guerrilla groups in the second) who were primarily responsible for certain types of violations against women, including forced abortion, forced contraception, forced marriage, forced labor, and sexual slavery. Although both countries have included victims of state and some nonstate actors in their programs, in Peru this will be of little avail to female victims of subversive groups given that the violations most commonly perpetrated by them have not been included in the catalogue of repairable violations (see Guillerot, "Linking Gender and Reparations" and Paz y Paz Bailey, "Guatemala: Gender and Reparations," in *What Happened?* 108, 153–154).

[51] See Dyan Mazurana and Khristopher Carlson, "Reparations as a Means for Recognizing and Addressing Crimes and Grave Rights Violations against Girls and Boys during Situations of Armed Conflict and under Authoritarian and Dictatorial Regimes," Chapter 4 in this volume.

[52] See Walker, "Gender and Violence in Focus" and Ruth Rubio-Marín, "Gender and Collective Reparations," Chapters 1 and 8 in this volume.

regimes, sisters, daughters, and mothers of political dissidents or activists have been targeted by the police and military forces as a way of punishing or intimidating their male relatives or extracting information about them, or simply because their family ties automatically rendered them collaborators.[53] Women have also been punished for fighting for justice or assisting victims. The violations women are subject to in such settings are essentially political. It is because of the political conflict and, in most cases, because of those women's ties to political activists (and not just as ordinary women) that they were victimized. And this must be acknowledged through reparations.[54]

Finally, it is equally important for women not to be excluded as beneficiaries of reparations because of the locations in which they were victimized. Any narrow interpretation of what constitute spaces of subjection and vulnerability that allow for abuse of power may not adequately reflect the phenomenology of violence against women. After all, much of this violence does not only or commonly take place in detention centers, prisons, or state institutions, but also in people's homes[55] or in women's own homes and neighborhoods, leaving them without the possibility of accessing a safe place.

IV. REPARATIONS AS THE RECOGNITION OF HARMS RESULTING FROM THE VIOLATION OF VICTIMS' RIGHTS

Reparations programs rely on the recognition and assessment of harms in different ways. By linking access to benefits to certain violations of rights, these programs concentrate on what they consider to be the most egregious forms of violations in a context of general violence or systematic repression. This selection requires the implicit or explicit prioritization of those basic

---

[53] Similarly, in the case of widespread civil conflict, Walker (Chapter 1 in this volume) explains how the treatment of women in conflict becomes a place of symbolic exchanges through violence especially among men or between groups. The meanings underlying gender violence include women as moral guardians and representation of purity; effective protection and control of women as an emblem of male strength, authority and masculinity; women's reproductive capacities as the future of a people or nation; women's identification with 'home' and cultural continuity.

[54] Interestingly, in their definition of "victim," the UN *Principles on Reparations* include "persons who have suffered harm in intervening to assist victims in distress or to prevent victimization."

[55] For instance, German reparations to the Jews included compensation for damages to freedom and covered claimants subjected to political or military jail, interrogation custody, correctional custody, concentration camp, ghetto, or *Wehrmacht* punishment entity. It also included forced labor in factories and alike insofar as the persecuted lived under jail-like conditions. Tellingly, though, forced housework was not considered as falling under damages to freedom. See Ariel Colonomos and Andrea Armstrong, "The German Reparations to the Jews after World War Two: A Turning Point in the History of Reparations," in *The Handbook*, 403.

goods and interests that are protected by the selected crimes or rights. In a way, then, arguing for the need to expand the list of violations to include sexual and reproductive violence is a plea for rendering visible the serious and long-term harming effects of such crimes in the lives of women and children.

Beyond this, because the aim of reparations programs is not only to certify that certain violations have occurred but also to assist victims in coping with the effects of such violations through concrete measures, these programs rest on implicit or explicit assumptions about the harm and loss that victims have incurred and about how these can be redressed or compensated for. Notions such as restitution, rehabilitation, or compensation (which can translate into material reparation benefits in the form of services, lump-sum payments, or pensions, as well as into symbolic measures of redress) all assume that a harm has been done and/or a loss has unjustifiably occurred. Defining the concrete remedies inevitably requires, then, an assessment and prioritization of such harms. Such a process can be ridden with gender bias but has also some gender-transformative potential.

As always, there is space for variation. To start with, different programs have placed different degrees of emphasis on the notion of harm and done so in different ways.[56] Sometimes, though rarely so, programs spell out and classify the kinds of harms that have occurred as a result of certain forms of violations in order to determine adequate compensation.[57] More often, we find that programs can allow the notion of harm to play an important role by recognizing that not only the right holder (legally speaking) but also the family members and dependants who are (most directly) affected and harmed by the violation should qualify as beneficiaries. Some programs, such as those

---

[56] There are, of course, also limits to how much a general program can advance in the individual assessment of resulting harms. There is, for one thing, the difficult philosophical question of the incommensurability of certain harms and the issue of the subjectivity around the experience of harm. Beyond this, and contrary to what happens in the individualized assessment of material and moral harms of a traditional torts approach decided by courts on a case-by-case basis, there are obvious inherent limitations as to how much a reparations program for massive violations of human rights can rely on the assessment of resulting harms. Administrative complexity needs to somehow remain manageable. General categories are required in the design of every aspect of a reparations program, including the selection of violations that trigger reparations, the definition of reparations beneficiaries, and the definition of reparation measures.

[57] Germany's Holocaust Reparation Program is a good, though admittedly rather exceptional, example of this. The broad categories used by the German reparations laws include harm to life, body, and health, harm to freedom, harm to possessions and assets, and harm to career and economic advancement. See Colonomos and Armstrong, "The German Reparations to the Jews."

in Chile, Argentina, or Brazil, have also decided who, in case of death or disappearance of the victim, should then be the beneficiary.[58] In doing this, such programs inevitably rely on some preconception of the material and moral damages for other people, mostly close family members, resulting from the victim's illegitimate death.[59]

Among the reparations programs that are most harms-focused, however, are those that have relied on the assessment of harms to prioritize, for the purpose of allocating reparations in the form of material benefits, either those beneficiaries who have endured the most severe forms of harms as a result of the violations or those who are likely to, given their preexisting vulnerable condition. For instance, the reparations program recommended by the Truth and Reconciliation Commission in Sierra Leone does so by reserving physical and mental health care, pensions, and the provision of education, skills training, and microcredit/microprojects for special categories of vulnerable victims such as amputees, other war wounded, children, victims of sexual violence, and war widows.[60] Similarly, the CAVR in Timor-Leste, agreeing to be guided by the principles of feasibility and prioritization based on need, recommended that priority be given to the most vulnerable from those who continue to suffer the consequences of gross human rights violations that took place during the period of conflict, including victims of torture, people with mental and physical disabilities, victims of sexual violence, widows and single-mothers, children affected by the conflict, and communities with a relatively high concentration of victims who suffered large-scale and gross human rights violations.[61]

Elsewhere, I have argued that this mediation of the notion of "right violation" through the notion of "harm," enabled by a definition of victim that is at the same time rights- and harms-based, frames many of the challenges but also

---

[58] In Chile, for instance, pensions were granted to the children, spouse, and parents of the disappeared, educational benefits were granted to the children of the disappeared, and comprehensive health care was granted to family members of the disappeared, executed, returned exiles, and victims of torture (see Elizabeth Lira, "The Reparations Policy for Human Rights Violations in Chile," in *The Handbook*). In Brazil, lump-sum compensation was given to relatives of victims of political assassination and disappearance (see Ignacio Cano and Patricia Galvao Ferreira, "The Reparations Program in Brazil," in *The Handbook*). Finally, Argentina proceeded to give pensions to spouses and children of disappeared persons as well as compensation payments to family members of victims of forced disappearances and assassinations (see María José Guembe, "Economic Reparations for Grave Human Rights Violations: The Argentinean Experience," in *The Handbook*).

[59] On reparations for family members, see Rubio-Marín, Sandoval, and Díaz, "Repairing Family Members," Chapter 5 in this volume.

[60] See King, "Gender and Reparations in Sierra Leone," 266–268.

[61] Wandita et al., "Learning to Engender Reparations," 309–310.

the opportunities that reparations, as a form of redress, present for women.[62] Here, I want to defend that this is so for at least two important reasons. First, looking at the harms produced by violations allows for an understanding of rights violations not only or primordially as an undue dispossession of "assets" but rather as a distortion of relationships and network systems that are sustained by those rights in a way that is especially relevant to women. Second, the compound effect of the (pre-, during-, and post-conflict) violence, discrimination, and exploitation that women and girls are subject to (the so-called "violence continuum") becomes most vivid when we examine the gendered nature of the harms that women endure and the short- and long-term effects on their lives, and this provides a reason for attaching some importance to the notion of harm when addressing reparations. Let us discuss each of these matters separately.

1. Rights Violations and the Interrelatedness of Harms

It is clear, as we have seen, that a gendered understanding of reparations can make a significant difference regarding the type of violations chosen as triggers for benefits. A similarly important question is whether such an understanding will also make it easier to decide whether and, if so, how a reparations program should provide benefits for the (often gender-specific) harms that come about through the disruption of the prevailing organizational structures brought about by human rights violations.

Let us take family first. All of the violations typically committed against men (such as illegal detention or imprisonment, summary executions, etc.) in societies organized around a family structure – virtually all – have a tremendous impact on women's lives. This is only more so when the family structure reflects a patriarchal culture in which women are the primary caretakers of the household. The legacy of widespread violence that targets men is women who are often poorly skilled, trained, and educated, and who end up with the triple challenge of raising and taking care of their own children as well as of a large number of dependants (including the orphans, the sick, the wounded, and the mutilated), finding a livelihood on their own for themselves and their dependants, while at the same time having to deal with state authorities in trying to find their loved ones or their remains or assisting them while in prison.[63] The question then becomes if and how this moral and material

---

[62] See Ruth Rubio-Marin, "The Gender of Reparations: Setting the Agenda," in *What Happened?*, 31–32.

[63] On how political violence shifts the economic burden of caring and sustaining the family further onto women, and how women's plight is exacerbated by a lack of financial means and

damage that is done to women through acts of violence that targeted "their" men and end up disrupting family life can or ought to be recognized and repaired.[64]

In reparations debates, there are at least two ways of reflecting this complexity. One is by embracing an expansive notion of victim that includes both the right holder but also his or her immediate family members and other dependants.[65] This possibility is sometimes phrased as embracing both "primary" and "secondary" or "direct" and "indirect" victims.[66] Alternatively, the notion of victim can be disentangled from that of beneficiary so that the concept of victim is retained for the right holder while family members are

more people to feed and care about, see Sunila Abeysekera, "Maximizing the Achievement of Women's Human Rights in Conflict Transformation: the Case of Sri Lanka," *Columbia Journal of Transnational Law* 41, no. 5 (2003): 523, 531.

[64] This subject is the focus of Rubio-Marín, Sandoval, and Díaz, "Repairing Family Members," Chapter 5 in this volume.

[65] The definition of "victims" of gross violations of international human rights in the UN *Principles on Reparations* provides a relevant example by referring to victims as "persons who individually or collectively suffered harm including physical or mental injury, emotional suffering, economic loss or substantial impairment of their fundamental rights.... Where appropriate, and in accordance with domestic law, the term 'victim' also includes the immediate family or dependants of the direct victim and persons who have suffered harm in intervening to assist victims in distress or to prevent victimization."

[66] Although the act governing the South African TRC defined victims as including relatives or dependants of victims and did not distinguish between primary and secondary victims, the Reparation and Rehabilitation Committee of the TRC did make that distinction (see Goldblatt, "Evaluating the Gender Contents of Reparations," 62). The same terminology was used by Morocco's Equity and Reconciliation Commission when discussing reparations (interview with Latifa Jbabdi, former Commissioner in Morocco's IER, New York, July 2005). The concept of indirect victims was also used by Peru's Truth and Reconciliation Commission and in Peru's reparations program (see Guillerot, "Linking Gender and Reparations," 154, fn. 105). The nominal distinction between "primary" and "secondary" victims has been criticized from a feminist perspective for its potential to symbolically reproduce a gendered hierarchy of harms whereby those endured by men (who are more often victims of those violations that have traditionally been included in reparations programs) are perceived as primary and those ensuing for women as marginal or secondary. The extent to which this objection holds depends on which violations are encompassed by the notion of victim. Ideally, the more progress is made in ensuring that such a notion does not systematically leave out the prevailing forms of violence against women, the less symbolically worrisome is espousing the concepts of primary/secondary victims. So, for instance, as the trend to include sexual violence in the definition of victim is consolidated, we should start spelling out the different kinds of harms that ensue also to the husband, partner, or children of victims of sexual violence and exploring options for their reparation. However, because in patriarchal societies sexual violence against women has traditionally been understood primarily or exclusively as harming men's honor, reputation, and so forth, how to give visibility to the way in which it harms the partner and children of the victim without at the same time reinforcing such stereotypes is a challenging task.

recognized primarily as beneficiaries. Beyond the terminology used, what is crucially at stake here is whether or not the harms experienced by family members are given independent recognition in terms of reparations. In most reparations programs, if the victim has lost his or her life (through execution, murder, or disappearance), the benefit will indeed go to the family. But if the victim is alive he alone will be recognized as a beneficiary, and whether or not he shares reparations benefits with family members will be up to him. The harming effects of violence on the spouse, parents, or descendants of survivors of rape, torture, or illegal imprisonment are thus not duly recognized. Because in many societies combatants or political activists tend to be male, this ends up having a negative disparate effect on women, as it silences their unique experience of moral and material harm linked to the absence or loss of a partner, breadwinner, protector, and status-conferring male figure. Given that the hardship of the violence is borne by both spouses in different ways, it would be more just if both were recognized as victims or at least as beneficiaries. Unfortunately, this is rarely the case, and even those reparations programs that pay lip service to a broad notion of victim (that includes both primary and secondary victims), such as those in South Africa, Peru, and Guatemala, in the end only recognize the latter as beneficiaries in substitution for the former.[67] The injustice that is done when surviving victims, but not their family members, are recognized as the only beneficiaries is rendered most vivid by the experience of many wives in Morocco who spent years raising the family on their own and living with the emotional, physical, and economic strain of an absent husband (whom they also needed to take care of while in prison), only to be repudiated by their husbands when they came out of prison and took new wives. None of them ever touched any reparations awards.[68]

Since scarcity of resources is a real concern in most transitional settings, this insight might find adequate expression in ways other than simply increasing

[67] As mentioned, in South Africa the act governing the TRC defined victims as including relatives or dependants of victims. However, when it came to both the urgent interim reparations and to final reparations payments, relatives became beneficiaries only in the case when the main victim had died (see Goldblatt, "Evaluating the Gender Contents of Reparations," 62). In Peru's proposed reparations program, it is also foreseen that family members will access benefits only when the direct victims are dead or disappeared, even if the former have been theoretically recognized as victims too (see Guillerot, "Linking Gender and Reparations in Peru," 155). The proposed reparations program in Guatemala also embraces a broad concept of victim to cover those who suffered directly or indirectly from the violations, but when it comes to deciding who will be a beneficiary, the program refers to direct family members only in the case of the absence of the direct victim (see Paz y Paz Bailey, "Guatemala: Gender and Reparations," 109).
[68] Interview with Latifa Jbabdi, New York, July 2005.

the overall munificence of reparations programs, as this could compromise their viability.[69] The most obvious way of doing so would be to treat the benefit, if it is material in nature, as an asset that both spouses have "earned" in their marital life and distribute it accordingly. If reparations are service based, family members should also be recognized as independent beneficiaries, especially as regards health services.[70] If, on the other hand, the reparation is mostly symbolic, it is important to make sure it recognizes the specific forms of suffering of both spouses instead of falling into the trap of reproducing only male notions of heroic virtues and sacrifice.

Beyond this, and to the extent that reparations programs try to be sensitive to the ways violence harms the family and its members, there is a broader question regarding the concept of family embraced in reparations programs and whether or not it corresponds to the actual systems of support in different societies and to the way such systems adapt to the needs that present themselves in times of conflict. Polygamous unions, *de facto* unions, same-sex unions, but also more extensive culturally contingent support mechanisms should be adequately represented so as to reflect the real web of dependencies and hence the harms entailed by their disruption. Reparations programs in South Africa, Peru, and Guatemala have all at least made some steps forward in this direction.[71]

On the basis of a concern for gender justice, one should also assess to what extent, on what grounds, and for what purpose the order of access of family members to reparations benefits reproduces or departs from that defined in

---

[69] "Munificence" is the term used by de Greiff to refer to the magnitude of the reparations benefits distributed to individuals. See de Greiff, "Introduction," in *The Handbook*, 12.

[70] The TRC in Sierra Leone has actually recommended including family members of surviving victims among the potential recipients of medical services, including physical healthcare and psychological support. See King, "Gender and Reparations in Sierra Leone," 262–263.

[71] The Regulations Regarding Reparations to Victims in South Africa, by defining "spouse" for the purpose of reparations as "the person married to an identified victim under any law, custom or belief," allow taking into account religious and customary marriages and hence embrace the wide plurality of marital forms that exist in South Africa. It is, however, unfortunate that domestic partners and same-sex partners were not included, which meant that the embraced conception of family still failed to fully reflect the lived reality in the country (see Goldblatt, "Evaluating the Gender Contents of Reparations," 66 and 68). The Peruvian Truth and Reconciliation Commission also recommended that the notion of family be interpreted as broader than the strictly nuclear family so as to reflect the variety of actual family dependency ties under the different customs and traditions of the Peruvian population (see Guillerot, "Linking Gender and Reparations in Peru," 154–155). Similarly, the reparations program in Guatemala embraces a large definition of family as including the spouse or couple living in common-law marriage and simplifies the ordinary procedures to prove the existence of such family arrangements, but no criteria have been thus far established to decide the order of priority in those cases where a missing person was in more than one union (see Paz y Paz Bailey, "Guatemala: Gender and Reparations," 108–109).

the country's inheritance system. For one thing, reproducing the "inheritance paradigm" to allocate reparations benefits may imply reproducing whatever gender bias and capture such a paradigm contains. Moreover, there are deeper and gendered questions about the logic of embracing such a paradigm to designate beneficiaries in the case of death or disappearance of the victim. The inheritance paradigm is one that logically assumes death as a natural end station in life, which means as an event that normally takes place when the previous generation is already gone and the next is self-sufficient. However, the deaths that result from political violence do not fit this paradigm, as, for the most part, they either take place randomly or target the most politically active sector of the population, among which the relatively young are usually overrepresented. This means that for widows of political violence the analogy to "standard widowhood" may be inadequate to capture the particular forms of harms linked to the premature and politically charged loss of their spouses. Being a young widow is quite different from being an older one, as a young widow is more likely to have dependants and a legitimate and prematurely frustrated aspiration to have a long-lasting marital life.

Analogous considerations apply to the possible implications of reproducing/departing from the inheritance paradigm to repair the parents of the victims who will normally be left economically vulnerable but also with the awful emotional distress generated by the premature and violent deaths of their children. Some reparations programs, such as those in Peru and Guatemala, have indeed acknowledged this by including the parents of the victims among the beneficiaries, even if they would not be included in the standard inheritance model, at least not to the same degree.[72] However, how to do this in a way that is also sensitive to the emotional and past and prospective material harms endured by widows, who in most cases are primarily in charge of the household, is a challenging dilemma.

Beyond harming individuals and families, violence typically disrupts entire communities and does so in a way that is likely to have a differential impact on men and women. In charge of reproducing the community's social tissue, providing for its daily existence, and building its support networks, women seem to suffer most when communal resources, infrastructure, and trust are

---

[72] In deciding on the order of access to benefits by family members in the case of death or disappearance of direct victims, the Peruvian Truth and Reconciliation Commission recommended a priority order that departed from Peru's ordinary succession order so as to reflect the pain and the efforts of mothers who had been fighting for truth and justice around their children's destiny for many years (see Guillerot, "Linking Gender and Reparations in Peru," 154). Similarly, Guatemala's reparations program also broadened the definition of inheritors contained in the national legislation in order to include ascendants (see Paz y Paz Bailey, "Guatemala: Gender and Reparations," 108).

undermined as a result of violence in ways that turn daily life into an extraordinary hardship.[73] A reparations policy that focuses too narrowly on repairing individuals whose rights have been violated and at the same time prioritizes violations of civil and political rights over socioeconomic rights can distort reality in terms of the harms people, mostly women, actually suffer in conflict and post-conflict periods.

The notion of collective reparations has been gaining support over time as a way of supplementing (or even replacing) individual reparations. As I have explored elsewhere and discuss in the final chapter of this volume,[74] the term has several competing meanings, and each of them may intersect with gender justice considerations in different ways. Here I would like to underscore the fact that one of those meanings refers to reparations for collective harm, meaning harm to public goods, that is, damage done to the social tissue and infrastructure system in areas that have been especially affected. An example of this is Sierra Leone's recommended reparations program, which includes collective reparations aimed at the reconstruction and rehabilitation of the most war-affected regions.[75] Ghana's proposed measure of reconstruction of local markets could be another example.[76] Collective reparations from this angle may express the belief that individuals who depend on such communal forms of existence and exchanges can find adequate reparation only if redress includes collective remedies to repair such harms. Given that women both are and depend on social capital to such a large extent, whether or not reparations efforts target these diffuse harms done to collectivities and to the resources that enable communal life may affect them particularly. For instance, Jamesina King has noted that the rehabilitation of the worst affected regions in Sierra Leone is most relevant for women because their livelihood will improve if schools, hospitals, and other basic elements of infrastructure are rebuilt, relieving them of the need to migrate to other communities in search of better services and infrastructure.[77] Thus, arguably, other things being equal, a reparations program that includes both individual and collective reparations is more gender sensitive than one that limits itself to individual reparations efforts.[78] A notion of victim or beneficiary that is too narrowly focused on

---

[73] See Walker, "Gender and Violence in Focus."
[74] See Rubio-Marín, "Gender and Collective Reparations."
[75] King, "Gender and Reparations in Sierra Leone," 269.
[76] See *National Reconciliation Commission Final Report* (Accra: National Reconciliation Commission, 2004), vol. 1, ch. 7, "Reparations."
[77] King, "Gender and Reparations in Sierra Leone," 269.
[78] Additionally, in situations of scarce resources, individual reparations may be divisive from a social point of view and, when this is the case, women, who are less used to holding financial

discrete violations of civil and political human rights leaves out of the picture some of the most serious harms ensuing from such violations and does so largely to the detriment of women.

2. Engendering Harm

Along with an understanding of the interrelatedness of harms that result from the political violence inflicted on men and women, introducing a gender perspective into the conceptualization of reparations requires an understanding of how the same violation may harm men and women differently. More broadly, it requires a process of both understanding and measuring harms that is free of gender bias.

To understand why the same violations may translate into different harms for men and women, it is important to bear in mind that prevailing cultural definitions surrounding masculinity or femininity may contribute to the experience of harm itself. The two sexes may also be differently endowed to cope with different forms of violence and their legacies. Several examples come to mind. In more than one country, women who were detained as political prisoners have described their experience as one of double victimization. Women felt they were being punished through physical and verbal abuse not only for contesting the political system, but also for challenging gender norms about the adequacy of female political agency.[79] For these women, holding on to their dignity while in prison was indeed a fight for their political ideology, but it was also, fundamentally, a fight for their right to be respected as political beings, something that was "ordinarily" denied to them. Former political prisoners also complained that once out of prison both stigma (sustained by "ordinary" definitions of femininity) and the fact of being past a certain age diminished their chances of marriage or motherhood, whereas the same was not equally true for their male counterparts. The question then becomes how to recognize in terms of reparation this double victimization of women and whether material and/or symbolic ways of compensating for it are called for. One way to recognize the fact that the same violations generally entail diffuse and more severe forms of harms for women is that recommended by Morocco's Equity and Reconciliation Commission, namely, to systematically

---

assets in their control, may become easy targets of family and communal violence and undue appropriation.

[79] See Walker, "Gender and Violence in Focus," who cites a variety of examples. See also Goldblatt, "Evaluating the Gender Contents of Reparations," 52. In Morocco, prison guards would commonly call female political prisoners by a "male" nickname. Interview with Latifa Jbabdi, herself a former political prisoner, New York, July 2005.

make reparations for female victims (10% to 20%) larger than those granted to their male counterparts for the same type of violation.[80]

Yet another example is whether the moral and material harm endured by widows and widowers (linked to the loss of the spouse) is equivalent when, because of the ordinary socially constructed roles and functions assigned to each of the sexes, women may have more of a difficult time than men remarrying once widowed. The case of mothers and fathers who have lost a child is also a difficult once. We cannot simply assume that biologically mothers love their children more than fathers do, but because in many societies motherhood is conceived as the most fundamental life project for women in a way that finds no parallel in the experience of fatherhood, the loss of a child may indeed entail some additional and gender-specific forms of harm for women, such as harm to a life project. Finally, it is intuitively easy to see why the harms that male and female victims of sexual violence experience are gendered, and this again raises the question as to whether they should be treated differently for reparations purposes. The discussions held in Peru, Guatemala, Timor-Leste, and Sierra Leone concerning whether fathers/mothers, widows/widowers, and male/female victims of sexual violence should all be treated in the same way under their reparations programs reflect a sensitivity towards this question.[81] The gendered meanings around the scarring of bodies or the amputation of body parts provide another interesting area of reflection.

In recognition of the fact that not all victims are equally harmed by the same violations, some reparations programs, such as those in Sierra Leone and Timor-Leste, have opted for endorsing a harms-based approach by granting benefits only to those victims who are the most vulnerable or who have been impacted the most. The broader justification for doing so has often been the

---

[80] See IER report at http://www.ier.ma.

[81] In Peru, although there was a debate as to whether reparations for victims of sexual violence should be reserved for women, as well as about the possibility of providing widows but not widowers with reparations, in the end it was decided to include both male victims of sexual violence and widowers as equal beneficiaries. In Guatemala, it was decided that only female victims of sexual violence would qualify for reparations. Also, although widowers were not in principle excluded from reparations, there is a guideline that establishes priority criteria for individual beneficiaries and refers to the need to pay special attention to widows. In Sierra Leone, the reparations program recommended by the TRC suggested that all victims be granted symbolic reparations but that material reparations in the form of service packages be reserved for those who are in dire need of urgent care, including war widows (but not widowers) and victims of sexual violence (without specification of their sex). Similarly, in Timor-Leste, the reparations program recommended by the Commission on Reception, Truth and Reconciliation states that benefits, also in the form of services, should be kept for the most vulnerable, and explicitly mentions widows and single mothers (but neither widowers nor single fathers). See *What Happened?*, esp. 106–107, 158, 262–263, 309–310.

scarcity of resources. Given the widespread structural discrimination against women in many societies, it is not surprising that women, or some groups of especially vulnerable women (such as widows or victims of sexual violence), have been among the prioritized victims. Children (boys and girls) have been, too.[82] When it comes to compensation, prioritizing victims according to vulnerability can then be a means to advance gender justice through reparations.[83] Alternatively, a reparations program could allocate smaller amounts of equal compensation to all victims, in recognition of their status as equal rights holders, but supplement this with service packages specifically designed to help in the rehabilitation process of the most vulnerable victims, who are likely to be women.

Understanding that the same violations may imply rather different types of harm for male and female victims, and often (though not always) more serious harms for women than for men, is therefore crucial. Similarly, a gender-sensitive conception of harm should warn us against gender bias that may take place in the process of evaluating the harms that result from human rights violations. Take the challenge of reaching an adequate understanding of harms and apply it, for instance, to the case of sexual crimes. As mentioned, including forms of sexual violence in reparations programs has become a recent trend. However, one realizes that even where this is the case, no ample effort is generally made to understand the true and complex nature of the harms that ensue and hence to envision adequate reparations for men or women or, even more so, for different groups of women according to their age, ethnicity, religion, and so forth. It is known that some of the harms typically include trauma, social stigmatization, and ostracism of the victim by her partner, family, or community (with the subsequent emotional distress and

---

[82] Thus, victims of sexual violence, war widows, and children have been included (together with amputees and other war wounded) among the vulnerable groups of victims that should qualify for material reparations in Sierra Leone's recommended reparations program. Victims of sexual violations, widows, children affected by the conflict, and single mothers have also been privileged for the same reasons under Timor-Leste's recommended reparations program. See *What Happened?*, 262–263 and 309–310. See also Mazurana and Carlson, "Reparations as a Means," Chapter 4 of this volume.

[83] Because every situation is different, it is also difficult to generalize about how normatively compelling a specific option may be. In making this kind of decision, other factors would have to be taken into account, including the typology of conflict but also the amount of resources that are available. Since, as conceptualized here, reparations are not designed as a way to compensate victims in proportion to harm but rather to recognize victims as rights holders, what is perceived as a serious attempt by the state to give them adequate recognition is largely a contextual matter. In a situation of terrible scarcity of resources, people may be more ready to understand the logic of prioritizing on the basis of need or vulnerability at least for material, if not symbolic, reparations without feeling that this detracts from their due recognition as victims.

loss of the possibility to marry and gain a stable livelihood and adequate social status). Undesired pregnancies or loss of sexual and/or reproductive capacity may also be at stake. Serious health problems that result from sexual violence, including fistulas and the contraction of life-threatening sexually transmitted diseases such as HIV, must also be mentioned. Focusing on sexual violence exclusively as an affront to the person's physical integrity or dignity, or (worse) to the dignity of her partner, family, or community, according to prevailing gender constructions would amount to entrenching such notions in a way that is unlikely to lead to the identification of adequate reparations measures for women.[84] The same is true of failing to give adequate visibility to the sexual violence that men and boys experience because it perpetuates the notion that only women are "rapable."

Last but not least, gender bias can also occur in the way that the harms ensuing from violations are measured for the purpose of reparations. Loss of income or loss of income potential have often been the default yardstick to measure the harms incurred (especially those that result from bodily harm, amputation, or mutilation) and allocate the corresponding benefits, usually relying on categories drawn from employment disability insurance schemes, which are not necessarily attuned to the specific nature of some of the harms done to women. Moreover, in societies based on the male-breadwinner model, many women do not have equal educational opportunities or paid employment outside the home. They may also perform the lowest-paid jobs, often in the informal sector. In those scenarios, relying exclusively on criteria such as lost opportunities to assess harm would clearly be to the disadvantage of women if the only opportunities that were taken into account (because they are the ones that are valued) are those that are ordinarily reserved for men and those around which the very notion of masculinity is constructed.[85] For instance,

---

[84] Even in a country like Sierra Leone, where a specific effort was made to address the multifaceted nature of the harms that typically result from sexual violence, King regrets the fact that no specific mechanism was designed to allow those mothers whose pregnancies were the result of rape to refuse the responsibility of raising their children (such as giving them to the care and custody of the government). In many other ways, the reparations program recommended by the TRC in Sierra Leone is exemplary and reflects a serious effort to bring the complexity of harms of victims of sexual violence to the fore. One example of this is the variety and adequacy of reparatory measures recommended, including free physical health care – covering specific types of surgery and treatment of STDs – free counseling and psychological support, skills training, and a monthly pension (see King, "Gender and Reparations in Sierra Leone," 266–267).

[85] Sierra Leone's proposed reparations program offers additional illuminating examples. According to it, monthly pensions for victims of sexual violence are to be determined by the implementing body taking the reduction in earning capacity into account, but the mechanisms usually relied on for this purpose – mostly work compensation schemes – generally do not

German reparations to the Jews under the Federal Supplementary Law for the Compensation of Victims of National Socialist Persecution included compensation for health in the form of medical care and an annuity, but for the latter the victim needed to prove a 30% reduction in earning capacity, which was based on the average income of the persecuted for the three years before persecution. Similarly, compensation for damage to career or economic advancement included assistance to make up for missed education, but not compensation for forced sterilization or rape.[86] These examples show that if we do not want to reproduce sexual hierarchies, two things are called for. First, to compensate women not for what they lost but for what they would have lost under a nondiscriminatory system. Second, to measure lost opportunities or income potential also by taking into account the loss of functions that are necessary to do house work, the loss of reproductive capacity, the loss of a husband, and the loss of the possibility to marry (as in many societies), all of which are decisive for women's livelihood and opportunities. One may, of course, hope that these functions become less essential to the definition of femininity in a future and more gender-just society, but until that day comes those are the actual harms that women endure and should therefore embed broad notions such as opportunities, possibilities, or potential whose loss is valued for the purpose of reparations.

V. REPARATIONS AS A GENUINE ATTEMPT TO HELP VICTIMS COPE WITH THE EFFECTS OF VIOLATIONS AND TO SUBVERT PREEXISTING STRUCTURES OF SUBORDINATION

Reparations programs do not simply consist of a thorough attempt to recognize and acknowledge responsibility for rights that have been violated and assess

---

include injuries of a sexual nature. Also, the proposed program has included amputees and war wounded among the beneficiaries. The reduction of earning capacity is the parameter to guide reparations for amputees. Fortunately, though, the idea is that women victims who are amputees will benefit equally as men because "all victims who are amputated will be presumed to have a 50% reduction in their earning capacity irrespective of whether or not they had the capacity to earn before the event." On the other hand, though, the definition of amputees as the loss of upper or lower limbs as a result of conflict is not broad enough to encompass victims of sexual violence whose chances of marriage, and thus in practical terms earning capacity, might have been severely reduced as a result of the stigma and injuries associated with their experience. Similarly, the category of war wounded is defined as victims who have become temporarily or permanently physically disabled either totally or partially, but, again, it is not clear whether the loss of the ability to have children as a consequence of the violation suffered will amount to a total or partial disability under the reparations program (see King, "Gender and Reparations in Sierra Leone," 264–267).

[86] See Colonomos and Armstrong, "The German Reparations to the Jews," 403–404.

how such violations have resulted in individual and collective experiences of harms and loss. Every reparations program also embraces a vision of what could help victims cope with the deleterious effects of violence in their lives. In this way, reparations programs embody a descriptive and normative account not only of the violent past but also of the way in which that violence has irrupted into people's ordinary lives and of what people may require to be brought back to "normalcy." Because in many cases "normalcy" or ordinary life for women meant exposure to multiple forms of discrimination, coercion, subjugation, violence, and exploitation,[87] the idea of redress as repairing the harm done through "extraordinary violence" by reverting to normalcy is at best controversial. At the same time, there is evidence that in times of conflict and political repression women may indeed experience serious harms that are an expression of tremendous and dramatic discontinuities linked to the disruption of preexisting gendered orders. The challenge for gender-sensitive reparations must therefore be one of finding ways of repairing those harms and those orders in ways that help victims reconstruct their lives while contributing as much as possible to the subversion of whatever form of gender subordination the orders might have contained in the first place.[88]

Official apologies, pensions, educational opportunities, access to health services, psychological rehabilitation services, individual payments, and collective projects of reconstruction are some of the many ways in which reparations programs attempt to help victims move forward. The concrete combination of options varies from case to case. Some programs may prioritize individual and material compensation in the form of individual payments, whereas others may place a greater emphasis on access to services and rehabilitation of both individuals and affected communities. Different programs may rely more or less on symbolic and/or collective forms of reparations. Political priorities, but also the number of victims, the amount of resources available,

---

[87] See Walker's concept of gender-normative violence, Chapter 1 of this volume.

[88] In her contribution to this volume, Walker explains how in the literature on violence against women in conflict, the trope of a "violence continuum" is common. She cites, for instance, Amnesty International's 2005 Report, in which violence against women in conflict and post-conflict situations is described as "an extreme manifestation of the discrimination and inequalities women experienced in peacetime." However, she argues (and I agree) that when discussing reparations for women in periods of political reconstruction, it is "victims' experience of catastrophic discontinuity" in those times, and not the notion of continuum, that should hold a central place. Walker writes, "A theoretical explanation that identifies patterns and similarities for purposes of analysis does not necessarily reflect the shattering experience of discontinuity, the sense of enormity and outrage, or the terror, despair, and social ruin of victims in many actual instances of violence in conflict." See also Rubio-Marín, "Gender and Collective Reparations," Chapter 8 of this volume, where I discuss the tensions that may appear between the corrective and the transformative dimensions of reparations and propose a normatively grounded way of addressing such tensions.

as well as the existence of competing needs of the overall population, will inevitably set constraints on the amount of resources ultimately devoted to reparations.

Generalizing about how women, not to mention different groups of girls and women, can be helped to deal with the effects of violence is even more difficult than generalizing about the ways in which women are harmed, if only because the former presupposes the latter. Nevertheless, it may be worth exploring some of the challenges and opportunities that reparations present in helping women in the aftermath of political violence as well as some of the gender-related challenges for redress that men face. I will organize reparations benefits and discuss their gendered dimensions around the goals that they are best suited to achieve, and I will distinguish between four such goals, namely, (1) material restitution and compensation, (2) rehabilitation and reintegration, (3) symbolic recognition, and (4) assurance of nonrepetition.

1. Material Restitution and Compensation

Whether seen as compensating victims in proportion to the harm they have incurred or rather taken as token signs of recognition, some form of material reparation to help victims rebuild their lives is of great importance. Even when, as defended here, the focus of reparations is on recognizing victims' common humanity and equal citizenship status, it is essential that victims perceive the seriousness of this effort. Providing victims with some material compensation, if rightly done, can facilitate such perception. Most reparations programs have indeed distributed lump-sum payments, pensions, or other forms of material compensation. Precisely because victims' perceptions of what a serious effort of material reparation amounts to are inevitably bound to have a subjective dimension, what such an effort should entail, in terms of concrete material benefits, can be the result only of a contextual decision that takes into account both the totality of resources available and the existence of other legitimate needs that any state, especially one in the midst of reconstruction efforts, cannot neglect.

If women, as a group, tend to be overrepresented among the poor, the illiterate, the ill, and those performing low-skill jobs in the informal sector of the economy or providing unpaid labor in the household, it is easy to predict that the disruption of normalcy by large-scale violence or repression will have especially deleterious effects on women's material well-being and that the reconstruction challenge in the aftermath will entail special economic hardship for them. This raises the question of what forms of material reparations would serve female victims best and help them restore their broken lives. Beyond this, there is also the challenge of conceiving reparations programs as opportunities to actively redress, however minimally, the perpetuation of the economic subordination of women.

In view of this, I argue that "engendering" the debate around economic compensation requires at least four steps. First, it is important to hold a gender-focused discussion about the importance that restitution of lost property should have in general and as compared to the resources devoted to compensate victims of rights other than the right to property. Second, engendering economic compensation requires overcoming all forms of formal discrimination on the grounds of sex when designing material compensation benefits. Third, the discussion around gender-sensitive economic compensation should also be one about how to choose, among competing options, those types of material benefits and modes of distribution and administration that may be more autonomy-enhancing for women, as well as more likely to make the money stick to women's hands. Finally, in those reparations programs where the notion of harm is taken into account (in deciding either the form or the quantum of reparations benefits), engendering economic compensation requires bringing to the fore the economic dimension that most violations perpetrated against women have. Let us take a look at each of these.

An important distinction when discussing material reparation is that between restitution or material compensation for the violation of property rights and economic compensation for the violations of other rights (life, freedom, physical integrity, etc.). Although internationally defined restitution measures are not by any means limited to the restitution of property,[89] the concept of restitution is often brought to the fore to endorse the view that reparations must include restitution of lost property. From a gender-justice perspective, this presents a series of challenges. One is that women are often discriminated against in their capacity to hold land or property titles, so that when the focus of a reparations program becomes restitution of (or, in its defect, compensation for) lost property, this may entail a reversion to a system of ownership that excluded women. Vasuki Nesiah describes how in countries such as Sri Lanka initiatives for property restitution and reparations for internally displaced people have often not reached women who should be beneficiaries of such programs because customary practices of holding property in men's

---

[89] In the *UN Principles on Reparations*, restitution refers to measures that "restore the victim to the original situation before the gross violations of international human rights law and serious violations of international humanitarian law occurred." The examples the document cites include return of property but also restoration of liberty, enjoyment of human rights, identity, family life and citizenship, return to one's place of residence, and restoration of employment. See also Rhodri C. Williams, "The Contemporary Right to Property Restitution in the Context of Transitional Justice," ICTJ Occasional Paper Series, May 2007.

name meant that women had few legal protections to buttress their reparations claims.[90] When, on top of this, prioritizing restitution of lost property means using up all (or most) funds available for reparations, this may mean denying women (and property-less men) material reparation for violations of rights not related to property (or reparation at a higher level for the violation of rights not related to property). The importance that should be attached to reparation of property rights therefore requires pondering the relative seriousness of such violations when compared to other types of violations but also taking into account the possibility that in some settings a focus on restitution of property may entail restoring an inequitable system of ownership or a regressive system of land distribution and doing so largely to the detriment of women.[91] Hence, looking at property restitution with a concern for gender justice requires at a minimum correcting outright gender discrimination in property ownership and making sure that the forms of ownership or possession for which there is restitution or compensation cover also informal tenure or ownership of movable goods, livestock, housing, and any other form that might be particularly important to ensure women's livelihood.

Avoiding discrimination on the grounds of sex when designing economic compensation measures is a relevant concern and one that is not limited to property ownership. In many societies, under either national or customary law, women are discriminated against in the inheritance system in a way that has the capacity to make it significantly more difficult for wives and daughters of victims to receive reparations. Reparations programs should not perpetuate such forms of discrimination and must take into account their legacies in devising mechanisms of material compensation that women can truly access. Where the legal system has traditionally discriminated against women in its inheritance regime, it is important that the concept of beneficiary – which determines who can access the benefit if the victim has died or disappeared – does not reproduce such discrimination. The difference that doing so can make is probably best illustrated by Morocco's two recent reparations experiences. Whereas the first reparations commission, the Independent Arbitration Instance (*Instance indépendante d'arbitrage*), which functioned in Morocco from 1999 to 2001, relied on shari'a-based inheritance law to decide on women's access to reparations in case of the death or disappearance of their husband (which, in practical terms, meant that the wife of the victim could receive as little as 8% of the total amount of the compensation), the more recent Equity and Reconciliation Commission (*Instance d'Equite et Reconciliation*)

---

[90] See Nesiah et al., "Truth Commissions and Gender," 31.
[91] See also Zeigler and Gunderson, "The Gendered Dimension of Conflict's Aftermath," 181.

(2002–2005) has corrected and stipulated that spouses will receive 40% of the awards on the basis that reparations are not inheritance but payments in fulfillment of international law-based obligations, which as such require respect for human rights standards.[92]

The transformative project, however, should not be limited to correcting or finding ways of bypassing formal legal discrimination. When designing and implementing reparations programs, one should bear in mind the whole array of possible limitations and impediments that different groups of women ordinarily face in asserting their rights and accessing standard forms of redress. Some of the obstacles that may render women's access to compensation and other forms of reparations difficult include lack of documentation or information, illiteracy, formal and informal pressures (often from family members), mobility constraints, and fear of reprisal, stigma, and communal and family ostracism. Some of these may affect some groups of women disparately. Claudia Paz y Paz Bailey has, for instance, warned that in Guatemala illiteracy and linguistic barriers may affect Mayan-speaking women particularly when trying to access reparations.[93] Whatever implementing body or mechanism is put into place should take all of this into account to ensure that it properly identifies and reaches out to the existing pool of female beneficiaries. One interesting way to make sure that reparations benefits reach women has been recommended by the Commission for Reception, Truth and Reconciliation in Timor-Leste, namely, the setting of a quota of 50% of resources to be earmarked for female beneficiaries, something that may force the implementing body to overcome cultural biases that prioritize the education of boys over girls as well as to find ways to identify widows and single mothers.[94] A gender-balanced composition of the implementation agency and the gender awareness of its members could contribute to thinking about further creative ways of reaching the most marginalized.

These obstacles may have a bearing on women's chances to access all forms of reparation. There may be, however, additional considerations regarding women's access to material compensation measures. For instance, in South Africa, lack of bank accounts or of the necessary documentation to open them proved to be among the most serious obstacles to women's access to monetary reparations.[95] Also, the choice between modalities and forms of reparations including compensation measures might be essential to determine the empowerment of women. It could, for instance, be argued that skill-training

---

[92] Interview with Latifa Jbabdi, New York, July 2005.
[93] See Paz y Paz Bailey, "Guatemala: Gender and Reparations," 116–117.
[94] See Wandita et al., "Learning to Engender Reparations," 308 and 315.
[95] See Goldblatt, "Evaluating the Gender Content of Reparations," 73.

or microcredit programs might be interesting supplements to compensation benefits, such as pensions, that are more assistance based.[96] In Timor-Leste, the CAVR recommended that single mothers, the disabled, widows, and survivors of sexual violence and torture have access to skills training and microcredit for income-generating activities in an effort to choose measures that would empower victims.[97] Though this and similar ideas deserve to be explored in contextualized ways, there is an interesting temporal dimension that should not be overlooked. A reparations program can embody a future-looking vision of what a more gender-just society might look like and of what kind of structural transformations would need to take place for women to enjoy equal opportunities in such a reconstructed society. However, the program should never neglect that its most important immediate goal is to help victims cope with the effects of violence in their present lives. For instance, training women to do things that will not really enable them to have access to a livelihood – if there is currently no market for the goods or services that women are trained for – would be a poor substitute for providing them with the assistance and economic support that they need to make up for the loss of a breadwinner or the increase in family responsibilities. In any event, there remains room to explore other modalities, such as shares in microfinance institutions, which could at the same time trigger transformation and enhance women's economic agency.

The form of distribution matters also. Women's common position within patriarchal family-structure systems and, related to this, women's all-too-frequent greater socioeconomic dependency on the breadwinner should also be kept in mind in order to define material reparations that are adequately empowering. Recognizing the family as the basic support unit and acknowledging women's unique role within it as the main caretakers and facilitators should have a bearing on the choice of the form of distribution of economic compensation measures. In South Africa, the implementing body responsible

---

[96] On reparations and microfinance, see Hans Dieter Seibel and Andrea Armstrong, "Reparations and Microfinance Schemes," in *The Handbook*. On gender, reparations, and microfinance, see Anita Bernstein, "Tort Theory, Microfinance, and Gender Equality Convergent in Pecuniary Reparations," Chapter 6 of this volume. According to Isobel Coleman, although microfinance has been launched for alleviating poverty in a financially sustainable way, its greatest long-term benefit could be its impact on the social status of women. "Women now account for 80 percent of the world's 70 million microborrowers. And studies show that women with microfinancing get more involved in family decision-making, are more mobile and more politically and legally aware, and participate more in public affairs than other women. Female borrowers also suffer less domestic violence – a consequence, perhaps, of their perceived value to the family increasing once they start to generate income of their own." See Isobel Coleman, "The Payoff from Women's Rights," *Foreign Affairs* 83 (May/June 2004): 85.

[97] See Wandita et al., "Learning to Engender Reparations," 310.

for reparations tried, in cases where the money should go to the children of a victim, to give the money to women on the understanding that this money would actually reach the family, whereas men would sometimes misuse it and are less likely to be the actual custodians of children.[98] Also, although distributing material reparations by giving individual grants to victims may in principle be said to have the advantage of enhancing victims' personal autonomy, in societies with a patriarchal family structure that either *de jure* or *de facto* deny women the possibility of being economically self-sufficient while making them primary caretakers of the home and progeny, a reparations program that prioritizes lump-sum one-time payments, such as that in Argentina, over pensions, such as that in Chile, or payments in several installments is likely to be one in which the money ends up in the hands of male figures and is spent in ways that give women little say.

Finally, equally important for the purpose of granting women material reparation is the need to underscore the economic dimension that many of the crimes perpetrated against them or against their men actually have. This is especially important when the notion of material harm is given a bearing on the decision of whether economic reparation is called for and, if so, in what amount. As mentioned above, one interesting challenge in this regard is that of demonstrating the material dimension of the legacy of sexual violence in women's lives. Although some of the intangible assets that are often taken from victims of sexual violence (such as virginity, purity, or social standing) cannot be returned, this should not be an excuse for not thinking about all the tangible assets of which victims of sexual violence are commonly stripped. Communal and family ostracism, abandonment by spouses and partners, or becoming unmarriageable are all too commonly synonyms of material destitution, and the costs of ongoing medical treatment, costs associated with pregnancy and with raising children resulting from rape, are all too real to deny.[99] The fact that in certain cultures accepting money for sexual abuse might be regarded as extremely inappropriate and problematic, or that virtually in every culture victims of sexual violence will need to weigh the costs of denouncing the violations – balancing consideration of material loss (such as loss of property) against the "loss of gendered political assets" (reputation)[100] – does not mean that the question of material reparation for victims of sexual violence should not be taken seriously, but rather that innovative ways of doing so may be necessary. In this line it is worth mentioning that, in its reparations program,

---

[98] See Goldblatt, "Evaluating the Gender Contents of Reparations," 73.
[99] See Zeigler and Gunderson, "The Gendered Dimension of Conflict's Aftermath," 184.
[100] See Colleen Duggan and Adila Abusharaf, "Reparations of Sexual Violence in Democratic Transitions: In Search of Gender Justice," in *The Handbook*.

the CAVR in East Timor recommended providing benefits to *"inan mesak"* (in the Timorese Tetum language literally "mother alone"), a category specifically chosen to include both mothers who were not legally married when their partners were killed or disappeared and victims of sexual violence who bore children out of rape. This was thought to be a way of accommodating the preferences of those women who do not want to "out" their children or "come out" as victims of sexual abuse.[101]

2. Rehabilitation and Reintegration

Because reparations are often discussed in situations of scarce resources, placing the emphasis on rehabilitation services rather than payments may seem a tempting alternative, as it combines development and reparations concerns. Also, when asked directly what material assistance they would like to have to better cope in the aftermath of violence, female victims often seem to think in terms of rehabilitation and reintegration and thus to prioritize their basic needs and those of their family members (including housing, physical and mental health services, employment, and education). The notion of compensation, then, seems to play a lesser role than that of rehabilitation or reintegration. This suggests that the question of what "engendering rehabilitation" requires should start with a conversation about the relative importance of rehabilitation in the overall project of reparations. Besides this, just like with compensation, bringing gender-justice concerns to the discussion of rehabilitation requires exploring the ways in which gender bias and capture may take place when deciding on which rehabilitation measures must be embraced and how to implement them. Finally, some rehabilitation modalities can be more autonomy enhancing and hence more transformative than others for victims in general and for women specifically. This too requires some attention.

To understand what to make of the fact that, when asked, most female victims center their reparations claims around services and basic goods, we have to bear in mind that the kinds of basic goods and services that women ask for are typically those that women are disparately deprived of ordinarily and that women need most in situations in which their family responsibilities increase. Rehabilitation and reintegration, as notions that look to an end-station and promise victims the possibility to enjoy a functional life, are not surprisingly notions that have much more intuitive appeal than those of restitution or compensation (for what has been lost) when victims did not start off from a

---

[101] See Wandita et al., "Learning to Engender Reparations," 309.

promising place anyway. This poses an interesting dilemma. Because many of the goods distributed by reparations programs for the rehabilitation of victims are goods to which citizens ought to be entitled to as citizens, it has been argued that placing too much emphasis on service packages as a form of reparation runs the risk of blurring the conceptual distinction between services that people are entitled to *as citizens* and reparations for victims of violations of human rights *as victims*, thus ultimately diluting the recognition dimension of reparations programs by turning them into general development or assistance programs.[102]

In many real-case scenarios, the dire poverty and destitution of victims implies that those basic services are what victims will inevitably prioritize, especially when they have no good reason, judging by their experience, to expect that they will be able to access them on any other grounds. Yet ideally we would not want to see the state discharge its obligation to compensate victims for their human rights violations simply by fulfilling a different type of responsibility. Drawing a conceptual distinction between the grounds on which victims can expect basic services may not make much practical sense to victims. Keeping the notion of rehabilitation and that of compensation separate, instead of lumped together under the banner of material reparation, may therefore be a helpful reminder of what victims can aspire to, especially for women. On the other hand, underscoring the reality that these women bring to the table, namely, that there cannot be reparation without rehabilitation, is a useful reminder that compensation measures should not eat up all of the resources available. A compromise solution that might work well in many real scenarios would be a combination of smaller individual and periodic payments, as forms of compensation, together with rehabilitation services. A combination

---

[102] See, for example, de Greiff, "Justice and Reparations," 470–471. Granted, this tension could be somewhat eased if violations of socioeconomic human rights were included among those that trigger reparations. Although some reparations programs have included the right to property in the list of violations and have recommended restitution or compensation as a form of reparation for lost property (especially as applied to displaced population), virtually no program has included the generic rights to housing, to health, to nourishment, or to education in the list of violations that should trigger reparations. In many real cases, doing so would turn virtually the entire population into beneficiaries of past and present violations. Rather, there is the sense that development programs should address the general socioeconomic needs of the population and that reparations should be preserved for the most severe violations of civil and political rights and freedoms. Needless to say, this reproduces the hierarchical distinction between political and civil rights, on the one hand, and social, cultural, and economic rights, on the other, which has been so often subject to criticism, not the least by feminist scholars who consider that such a hierarchy disadvantages the most destitute, among whom women are generally overrepresented. However, it may still be worth asking whether in a transitional society a reparations framework is the best one to address issues such as poverty and illiteracy and what would be the likely consequences of doing so.

of small pensions plus medical services and educational opportunities has proven fairly successful in Chile. To the extent possible, the services provided should go beyond those that can duly be asked from the state, as a matter of right. A reparations program that concentrated only on the provision of basic services and tried to limit those to victims as opposed to all citizens would probably risk dividing communities and subjecting beneficiaries, especially women, to strong forms of pressure, as was the case in Rwanda with programs of this sort.[103]

Whatever the importance given to rehabilitation in the larger reparations venture, it is important to discuss the ways in which gender bias can take place when conceptualizing rehabilitation or when designing or implementing rehabilitation mechanisms. It is, for instance, not enough to insist that women be granted the same rehabilitation services that men have access to. Instead, those services should also respond to women's specific needs. Tailoring the services provided in this way requires an effort to overcome whatever gender bias might be entrenched in the existing national service system. One way to overcome such gender bias is to be as explicit and specific as possible in terms of the services to be provided. For instance, rather than simply recommending that victims should have free or privileged access to medical and psychological assistance, reparations programs should spell out the treatments that victims need to be cured or rehabilitated. Because the most common physical and psychological sequels of some of the forms of violence women are most frequently subject to, such as sexual violence, are also fairly easy to classify, this should be a feasible exercise.[104]

It is important to notice that the gendered structure of society does not imply that women will *always* be worse off in terms of capabilities to confront the legacy of a past of mass violence. Often, in their roles as nurturers and caretakers, women are socialized in ways that make them psychologically more fit to articulate and share feelings around emotional loss, an experience that may be essential to their rehabilitation. Also, women may feel less threatened in their self-perception by the need to rely on others for support and thus may be better suited to improvise informal solidarity networks. In fact, many of the women who become actively involved through victims' groups describe the experience and the space that it creates as having a tremendous reparative effect. Also, patterns of male socialization might make men less prone to

---

[103] See Heidy Rombouts, "Women and Reparations in Rwanda: A Long Path to Travel," in *What Happened?*, 228.

[104] There was an attempt to do precisely this in Sierra Leone's recommended reparations program. See King, "Gender and Reparations in Sierra Leone."

rely on self-help groups or civil society beneficence venues to cope with the practical challenge of providing for basic needs in a post-conflict situation or to seek psychological help to deal with emotions around loss. The fact that in many countries mothers seem to have played a much more significant role than fathers in the search for justice for disappeared family members is telling. One feels the urge to ask, "Where are the fathers?" Of course, none of this is to suggest that the state can discharge its obligation to provide rehabilitation to women by claiming that women simply rehabilitate themselves. Rather, the point raised here is that when designing measures of rehabilitation to assist victims, the obstacles that affect men disparately should also be kept in mind.

As with compensation, the modalities of distribution of rehabilitation services may be just as fundamental to ensure that they actually reach women. Other things being equal, family-friendly forms of distribution of the services might reach most women better. One way in which women's roles and predispositions as caretakers can be taken into account to design gender-sensitive ways of distributing reparations measures is by procedurally linking reparations for children to those for their mothers. For instance, in Timor-Leste's recommended reparations program, the scholarship program for children is supposed to be delivered at the same time as services, including medical services, for women. In this way it is hoped that women who would otherwise be reluctant to take time to meet their own needs will now do so motivated by the possibility of getting scholarships for their children.[105] Taking into account women's greater mobility constraints should also be a priority when thinking about adequate delivery mechanisms.

Beyond attending to women's and men's gender-specific needs through adequate services delivered in the proper way, "engendering" rehabilitation and reintegration requires being more aware that the very notions of rehabilitation and reintegration presuppose that of a "healthy" or "functional" life to which the victim is ideally brought. What this entails is both a gendered but also a context-sensitive enterprise, as the adequate notion of "psychosocial" rehabilitation suggests. Issuing death or disappearance certificates for the spouses of the disappeared may be essential to take the wives of the disappeared out of a legal limbo (neither single, nor widowed, nor married) and help them reintegrate in society, as the case of Argentina showed.[106] Helping victims, and

---

[105] See Wandita et al., "Learning to Engender Reparations," 312. Needless to say, whatever mechanism is designed should also take into account that women who do not have children should not be disadvantaged for this reason in their access to reparations.

[106] In Argentina, the widows of the disappeared needed to resolve custody, matrimonial, and succession issues. On the other hand, they were reluctant to ask for a death certificate for their disappeared spouses because this meant accepting that their missing husbands were

especially women, achieve a sense of closure and rehabilitation may require providing them with the truth about their loved ones or helping them perform their duty towards those loved ones through assistance with exhumations and reburial ceremonies or the provision of headstones and tombstones.[107] It may also require punishing the perpetrators. Most likely, creating the conditions for the removal of stigma is also a precondition to societal reintegration, which requires gender-specific attention. Think of the need to remove physical scars from girls and boys who were forcefully recruited and branded as combatants or possessions, or think of the need to adopt measures to help victims of sexual violence recover a communal and family life free of stigma. Ultimately, although rehabilitation, restitution, and satisfaction are conceptualized as different reparations modalities, several restitution and satisfaction measures, including restitution of identity, family life, and citizenship, return to one's place of residence, truth-seeking, the search for the disappeared, the recovery and reburial of remains, and public apologies, may be just as rehabilitative as medical or social services for victims in general, and for women in particular.[108]

Finally, reintegration and rehabilitation may require creating opportunities that were previously denied to victims, often on the grounds of sex. Meaningful employment, education, skill training, and initiatives such as microcredit to motivate economic entrepreneurship are some obvious candidates. Also, because the experience of conflict or political repression leads many women to become publicly and politically active for the first time in their lives, encouraging this agency, say by promoting women's associations or political parties, could also be a way of rehabilitating women in a way that does not revert them exclusively to their forever-changed homes and family lives. In other words, here too there is space for exploring the gender-transformative potential of rehabilitation mechanisms specifically aimed at enhancing victims' agency and autonomy.

---

indeed dead. A creative alternative was found and the government started issuing certificates of "absence by forced disappearance," which allowed surviving spouses, for example, to recover or sell property, remarry, solve custody disputes, and so forth, without generating in them the feeling of betrayal they so frequently reported to be part of a request for a death certificate. See Law 24,321 (1991). See Guembe, "Economic Reparations for Grave Human Rights Violations," 35–36; and Carrillo, "Justice in Context," 507.

[107] Beyond enabling closure, and hence facilitating psychological and social rehabilitation of victims, such measures might also be a precondition to women accessing or even allowing themselves to discuss material reparations without feeling guilt.

[108] See M. Brinton Lykes and Marcie Mersky, "Reparations and Mental Health: Psychosocial Interventions Towards Healing, Human Agency and Rethreading Social Realities," in *The Handbook*, 590.

3. Symbolic Recognition

Measures of symbolic reparation are conceptualized as measures of satisfaction that can also facilitate the process of victims' psychological and social rehabilitation. Their primary aim is to give victims due recognition. In a way, reparations programs, taken as a whole, embody a system of symbols formed around how the violent past, the ensuing disruptions of people's lives, and the needs for reconstruction are conceptualized and prioritized. Beyond this, some reparations programs explicitly include symbolic forms of redress for victims (such as official apologies, commemorative events, renaming of streets and public facilities, establishing a day of remembrance, building monuments, museums, and memorials, etc.). All of these can act as vehicles for the contextualization of other reparations measures. Thinking about symbolic reparations through the lenses of gender offers the opportunity to explore whether men and women are given their share when it comes to symbolic recognition. It also invites a conversation about whether and why men and women and different groups of men and women may require different forms of symbolic redress. Finally, it triggers the question of the transformative potential of symbolic redress and of the possibly gendered meanings that may be captured, reproduced, or transformed through symbolic measures. Let's discuss this by looking first at apologies and then at forms of memorialization.

As the following examples will show, who apologizes, what for, where, and how can all have a gendered relevance. Given the long tradition of conceptualizing violence against women as "private" and blaming female victims for the violence they experience, especially when this violence is sexual in nature, it seems that underscoring the public and political dimensions of the violence women are subject to should be a priority in any reparations attempt that is sensitive to women's specific needs. This is why the push toward expanding the list of violations to cover those violations that target women as such or affect them disparately (such as sexual violence) represents at the same time an expression of the recognition of the political dimension of such forms of violence. It is, however, equally important that reparations programs, in the way they define benefits, refrain from symbolically rendering private those forms of violence that target or affect women disparately. Official apologies by the state and its agents (the military, the police, etc.), and not just fistula surgeries, may be called for to overcome prejudices about the private nature of sexual crimes and to facilitate the psychological rehabilitation of victims. Indeed, this has been recognized in Sierra Leone, where the recommended reparations programs include, among the list of symbolic reparations, the need for the president of the country to acknowledge the harm suffered by women and girls during the conflict and to offer an unequivocal apology to them on behalf of preceding governments of Sierra Leone.[109] Measures of this kind might be a precondition for victims to be able to accept other forms of reparation, including monetary compensation. As the case of the "comfort women" best exemplifies, victims of sexual crimes may not want to receive economic compensation absent an official apology and official recognition of state responsibility.[110]

The modality of apology can be just as relevant. It has been argued that most families of victims experience a need for individualization in symbolic attempts of reparation (such as the inclusion of the names of the deceased family members in a public monument, or the individualization of their remains if they were buried in mass graves).[111] Given women's predisposition to focus on the pain of their beloved ones first and foremost, it would be interesting to devise ways to enhance the symbolic recognition of all their forms of suffering and to underscore the individual dimension of such suffering and resilience. This is something that the functional fusion of womanhood and motherhood and of womanhood and family in most cultures may render extremely difficult even in "normal" times. It is not far-fetched to think that for many women who spend their lives mostly relegated to the private sphere, an official and personalized letter of apology might be one of the first public documents reflecting both their status as citizens and as victims. That the letters reach the homes ensures that women will actually receive the apologies but can also reinforce the idea that it is a private apology that, as such, may not be sufficient to rehabilitate victims socially. Perhaps personal letters of apology can best recognize women if they are at the same time accompanied by public gestures of recognition. At the same time, there are reasons to think that public gestures of recognition that expose individual women are not appropriate until it is certain that such exposure does not lead to their further victimization. This may be best exemplified in the case of victims of sexual violence.

Besides public apologies, public gestures of recognition often consist of measures to represent the conflict, the violence, or the notion of reconstruction that accompanies a reparations and a reconstruction project through the shaping or reshaping of public spaces and objects (monuments, museums, changing of street names and other public spaces). Little reflection has been given to exploring whether there are forms of representation and memorialization that

---

[109] See King, "Gender and Reparations in Sierra Leone," 268–269. Similar measures have been proposed by the truth commission in Ghana.

[110] See Note 6.

[111] See Hamber, "Narrowing the Macro and the Micro."

women might prefer over those that have traditionally been favored by men.[112] There are some incipient ideas about how to commemorate women in public spaces. In South Africa, for example, the women's jail in Johannesburg has been restored and now houses constitutionally created independent bodies including the Commission for Gender Equality. Also, streets and towns have been renamed after famous women.[113] Whichever form or space for commemoration is chosen, an obvious requirement is that women not be silenced or hidden in those spaces (e.g., that the names chosen are not only male names, that the statutes chosen are not only those of men on horses or in combat).

Moreover, it is important that the symbolic ways in which the male and the female are represented in such endeavors be equally empowering to both sexes, something that, once again, requires an adequate balancing of affirmation and transformation. For those monuments and public spaces that are "backward looking" (that try to capture and represent the horror of the past), it seems especially important that the manifold forms of female agency within that past is represented to avoid constructing the female in a way that essentializes women or denies their subjectivity. For those spaces and objects that instead celebrate the future around the notion of reconstruction or reconciliation, it seems especially important not to reduce and romanticize women to stereotypes about their nurturing, forgiving, and self-sacrificial predisposition for the sake of the healed mother nation. Women do suffer as mothers, sisters, and daughters, and this should be recognized, but so should the facts that women also suffer as freedom fighters or simply as civilians randomly targeted and that many of those who suffer in either capacity are far from willing to accept that their suffering was in any way owed to the nation. Because how to best capture the way men or women experience, suffer, contribute, forgive, or remember are all likely to be highly contested notions, it seems especially important that victims and their communities be always consulted on the establishment and placement of appropriate memorials. In this consultation process, female victims and female family members of victims should be given adequate voice and opportunity to participate.

4. Guarantee of Nonrepetition

The guarantee of nonrepetition is a generic category of reparation that, as defined by the UN *Principles on Reparations*, encompasses institutional reform to contribute to prevention by, for example, ensuring effective civilian control

---

[112] See Brandon Hamber and Ingrid Palmary, "Gender, Memorialization, and Symbolic Reparations," Chapter 7 of this volume.
[113] See Goldblatt, "Evaluating the Gender Contents of Reparations," 70.

of military and security forces, protecting human rights defenders, providing human rights education, promoting international human rights standards in public service, law enforcement, the media, and industry, and reviewing and reforming laws contributing to or allowing gross violations of international human rights law. In a way, this is the reparations mechanism that offers the greatest potential for transforming gender relations because, in promising to ensure nonrecurrence, it triggers a conversation about the underlying structural causes of the violence and their gendered manifestation and a discussion about what broader institutional or legal reforms might be called for to ensure nonrepetition. A gender-sensitive reparations program should in principle seize this opportunity to advance, as part of the venture of constructing a new and more inclusive democratic order, a society that overcomes the systemic subordination of women.

Incorporating guarantees of nonrepetition advances general societal goals but can also contribute to victims' reparation in two ways. First, by reducing the chances that victims are exposed to the same or higher degrees of violence in the aftermath and enhancing the effectiveness of the other reparations measures. And, second, by enabling victims to draw a sense of satisfaction and rehabilitation from the fact that their victimization was not totally inconsequential for society, that at least it served as an engine of change for the sake of future generations. Let us look at both of these dimensions.

It has been widely observed that in the aftermath of violent conflict, when "normalcy" is restored and the ordinary family structure recomposed, women not only are left with a disproportionate burden of dealing with the legacy of past violence but also are subject to new and sometimes higher levels of violence. Internalization of violent mechanisms of conflict resolution, accumulated and unresolved feelings of male impotence and frustration, male anxiety around the empowerment of women who have become politically visible during the conflict, or simply the increased vulnerability of women (displaced, widowed, and destitute) may be some of the reasons that make women the targets of rising levels of violence after official peace or democracy has been declared.

Reparations programs that take place at one given point in time (and have an inevitably backward-looking dimension) seem to have inherent limitations as mechanisms to address future violations, even when these are, in part, fairly predictable legacies of a recent violent past. However, here is where the guarantees of nonrepetition, with their future-oriented perspective, can be particularly useful. Such guarantees can ground concrete obligations on the part of the state to take into account the foreseeable short- and medium-term legacies of its violent past for women and, more specifically, adopt measures to avoid the exploitation of women's new forms of vulnerability. The duty to relocate displaced populations or to ameliorate their living conditions could be grounded on this obligation as a form of reparation. Education campaigns targeted at the general population emphasizing women's human rights, providing an adequate understanding of violence against women, or, as recommended in Timor-Leste, raising awareness of the link between past abuses and current violent behavior, including at the workplace and in the home,[114] might also be useful tools to counter the fact that after a period of generalized violence, repression, and terror, women in general, and more so certain groups of women, might be easier targets of old and new forms of violence.[115] Also, as has been rightly noted, the potential healing effect of any one measure "may often depend not only on its congruence with other measures... [but also] with other actions being taken in the society to address the structural problem that gave rise to the conflicts, and especially to end impunity, impart justice and strengthen the rule of law."[116]

Besides breaking cycles of violence fed by the increased vulnerability of women and girls and thereby sparing them from reliving the horror they already lived once, guarantees of nonrepetition, if duly implemented, have the potential to look both further back and forward in time. In doing so, they can detect enabling conditions and long-term legacies of gender violence and can therefore be an adequate platform from which to propose broader structural reforms for the sake of all women, not just victims, and hence for the construction of a more inclusive and gender-just political order. Especially when victims are involved and consulted in the process of their specific formulation, guarantees of nonrepetition can help victims in the process of rehabilitation by giving them the satisfaction of knowing that their experiences were not in vain. Rather, they served as engines of change for the sake of future generations. At the same time, such broader reforms can also be seen as measures of collective reparation for the sake of all women, given the manifold ways in which gender violence harms all women and not just individual victims by reducing their chances of a life free of violence, prejudice, and discrimination.[117] This seems especially apposite for a theory of reparations,

---

[114] See Wandita et al., "Learning to Engender Reparations," 311–312.

[115] A public policy of education for the prevention of violence against women, the training of members of the army and national police on violence against women, and the cleansing of security forces responsible for the violence (including sexual forms of violence) perpetrated against women could also be conceptualized as future-oriented reparations measures covered by the concept of guarantees of nonrepetition.

[116] See Lykes and Mersky, "Reparations and Mental Health," 591.

[117] This point is further elaborated in Rubio-Marín, "Gender and Collective Reparations," Chapter 8 of this volume.

such as the one defended here, that links individual recognition of harm and violence to broader societal processes of democratization through inclusion and transformation.

VI. CONCLUSION

When confronted with a legacy of gross and systematic violations of human rights, reparations should be seen as a modest contribution to democratic state building that gives due recognition to victims and thereby helps the new regime generate trust and assert its overall legitimacy. I have advanced the view that giving due recognition to victims requires the recognition of the wrongful violation of their rights, the acknowledgment of state responsibility, the recognition of the harms to victims, and a serious attempt to help victims cope, however minimally, with some of the effects of violence in their lives and to subvert, however minimally, the structures of subordination that might have led to the violations of their rights in the first place.

Bringing gender-justice considerations to the design and implementation of reparations programs aspiring to achieve the above-mentioned goals requires avoiding sex discrimination and gender bias when conceptualizing reparations schemes but also exploring the possibilities that reparations offer for spelling out the conditions of more gender-inclusive and egalitarian societies. Thus, beyond ensuring that reparations programs do not discriminate among potential beneficiaries on the grounds of sex, I have argued that engendering reparations imposes additional requirements, including making sure that the violations of rights affecting mostly women or women in a disparate way are not left out; that the underlying concept of political violence that reparations try to address not be articulated in such a way as to leave out forms of violence against women that are inextricably linked to the conflict or political repression; and that the harms resulting from the violations of rights be brought to the fore so as to shed light on how their interrelatedness affects women specifically (by damaging also families and communities) and to show the many ways in which the same violations of rights may translate into different and often worse kinds of harms for women both in the short and in the long run.

In allocating material and symbolic resources to help victims move forward, reparations programs that are sensitive to the all-too-common subordinate status of women and to the specific needs that women have in the aftermath of conflict or authoritarian repression should take a wide set of considerations into account. These include the recognition that some material remedies can be more transformative of preexisting forms of women's economic subordination than others, that the material dimension of harms done to women should never be minimized, and that the form of compensation measures and services granted and the way in which they are distributed can have an impact on whether or not they reach female victims. Such programs should consider also that women, girls, and different groups of women may require distinctive forms of material and symbolic redress. A final consideration is that targeting both the individual as well as the family and larger community as units of repair may be more conducive to responding to the multifaceted, interlinked, and diffuse forms of harms that women endure in the aftermath.

Finally, the process of crafting and implementing reparations programs and the timing of reparations must be attuned to women's needs and experiences. Women should (also) own the process leading to reparations. Making sure that women's interests are sufficiently represented by victims' organizations and the other relevant civil society actors seems crucial. The dissemination of information, the identification and registration of victims, and the processing of individual claims should all take into account that women often lack the most basic skills and means to avail themselves of any form of redress (literacy, documentation, mobility, but also bank accounts) and may be subject to all kinds of formal and informal societal pressure, including, of course, that related to the cultural meanings attached to the experience of victimization, especially of sexual violence. For the same reason, the timing of reparations is of utmost importance. Such timing should take into account that victims in general, and victims of sexual violence in particular, may need more time to "come out" as victims and ask for reparations. Also, victims in general, and women in particular, may be hesitant to ask for compensation or even recognition of the harms they have endured before they feel that they have paid their due to those around them and in particular to their family members. Before knowing the fate of their loved ones, recovering their bodies, and giving them proper burial, some victims may not even want to engage in a constructive conversation about additional forms of compensation or redress.

3

Reparation of Sexual and Reproductive Violence: Moving from Codification to Implementation

Colleen Duggan and Ruth Jacobson[1]

INTRODUCTION

The last decade has seen unprecedented progress in the construction of an international legal framework for the criminalization and prosecution of gender crimes perpetrated against women and girls[2] during armed conflict or state repression. The visibility of gender-based violence, especially sexual and reproductive violence (SRV), is now an important part of the legacy of international criminal law. Rape is included in the definitions of a "grave breach" of the Geneva Conventions,[3] of crimes against humanity, and of genocide. Sexual slavery, rape, enforced prostitution, pregnancy and sterilization, and other forms of sexual violence are listed as war crimes and as crimes against humanity in the Rome Statute of the International Criminal Court.[4] Significant changes in the rules and procedures for prosecuting gender crimes in international criminal tribunals and other significant "soft law"

---

[1] We would like to offer our deepest thanks to Ruth Rubio-Marín. Her normative and empirical contributions and her patient and insightful comments on countless drafts have added immensely to our own learning on the issues discussed here.

[2] In this chapter, we use "women" as shorthand to discuss the dilemmas and options for repairing SRV perpetrated against both women and girls. We are aware that SRV has a differentiated impact on girl children, but a full exploration of the differences is beyond the scope of this work. Dyan Mazurana and Khristopher Carlson discuss some of the nuances of reparations for children in Chapter 4 of this volume.

[3] Article 27 of the Fourth Geneva Convention Relative to the Protection of Civilian Persons in Time of War, August 12, 1949, lists rape and enforced prostitution as a violation of a woman's honor.

[4] See *Prosecutor v. Akayesu*, Judgment, No. 96-4-T, International Criminal Tribunal for Rwanda (September 2, 1998). This judgment legally determined that rape committed as a part of the Rwandan conflict constituted a war crime as an instrument of genocide. See also Article 5 of the Rome Statute of the International Criminal Court, A/CONF.183/9*, July 17, 1998, reprinted in 37 I.L.M. 999 (1998). Rome Statute for the International Criminal Court (1998) Elements of crimes against humanity and war crimes are described more fully in note 20.

milestones[5] leave no doubt that we have now reached a watershed moment in galvanizing international attention around the egregious forms of violence that befall women and girls during wartime or periods of mass human rights abuse.[6] As part of this growing commitment, in June 2006 more than 250 representatives of governments, nongovernmental organizations (NGOs), women's organizations, human rights activists, UN agencies, parliaments, the research community, international criminal courts, military, police, and the media met at the International Symposium on Sexual Violence in Conflict and Beyond to exchange strategies for addressing and preventing incidents of SRV in war-affected countries.[7]

Although these developments are encouraging and such landmark events can be characterized only as positive, justice for victims of SRV remains far beyond their reach. In addition, feminists and women's organizations have also voiced the concern that "recently won attention to sexual violence against women might be at the expense of a fuller and more nuanced understanding of women's losses, injuries and sufferings,"[8] which are multiple, multidimensional, and complex.

It would indeed be ironic if, after years of struggle to give adequate recognition to the multiple expressions of gender-based violence that accompany conflict and mass atrocity, women's heavy economic and material losses were to be overshadowed by the more visible realities of mass rape, sexualized torture, mutilation, and sexual enslavement,[9] or if the material effects of sexual violence were to be relatively overlooked. Since this is by no means our intention, we must ask ourselves a number of important questions while contemplating, in this chapter, possibilities for "repairing" what essentially can never be fully repaired. First, if not all violence that happens to women during

---

[5] Security Council Resolution 1820, S/RES/1820 (2008), June 19, 2008, addresses sexual violence in situations of conflict and is the most recent of a string of "soft law" instruments that have been used by nonstate actors, particularly NGOs working for the human rights of women, in their quest to seek greater state responsibility for the failure to eliminate violence against women. A more detailed discussion can be found in Christine Chinkin, "Normative Development in the International Legal System," in *Commitment and Compliance: The Role of Non-Binding Legal Norms in the International Legal System*, ed. Dinah Shelton (Oxford: Oxford University Press, 2000), 31.

[6] For a more detailed discussion of these and other milestones, see "Addressing Impunity: Sexual Violence and International Law," in *The Shame of War: Sexual Violence Against Women and Girls in Conflict* (New York: UN Office for the Coordination of Humanitarian Affairs [OCHA] and Integrated Regional Information Networks [IRIN], 2007).

[7] The symposium produced the Brussels Call to Action (http://www.unfpa.org/emergencies/symposium06), which includes a specific mention of the need for reparation.

[8] Margaret Urban Walker, "Gender and Violence in Focus: A Background for Gender Justice in Reparations," Chapter 1 of this volume.

[9] Ibid.

conflict and political authoritarianism[10] is gendered or sexually linked, are there still valid reasons to put particular emphasis on remedying sexual and reproductive violence? If the answer to this question is "yes," then we must next ask how we can make the best use of the almost singular focus on sexual and reproductive violence adopted by the international community when discussing women's experiences during war and mass violence. We do this with a view to securing for survivors[11] more comprehensive approaches to reparation that include measures for addressing both the immediate and long-term health, social, and economic consequences and impacts of these crimes. Second, if we recognize that sexual and reproductive violence is often an integral part of political violence, then we need also to recognize it as a social and political problem that affects both men and women and thus begin an honest dialogue about its differentiated effects on each.[12]

Though the UN *Basic Principles* on reparation[13] fall squarely within the realm of the juridical, evolving practice suggests that measures for reparation are rooted in a broad interpretation of redress and remedy, spanning multiple fields of intervention that include political citizenship, medical and psychological care, disclosure of the truth and apology, economic compensation, and institutional reform, to mention but a few.[14] Looking through this wide lens, what have we learned from past and current efforts for addressing sexual

[10] Since our discussion aims at a better understanding of reparation during democratic transition, this chapter examines what happens to victims of sexual violence, largely women and girls, during high-intensity armed conflict and also during periods of extreme political authoritarianism, as democratic transition often (although not exclusively) follows both of these. Though there is an important distinction of scale that should be made (armed conflict generally produces more victims than does political authoritarianism), the forms of violence that we discuss can be both systematic and widespread, hence their qualification as crimes against humanity.

[11] In this chapter, we refer interchangeably to those who have been direct victims of sexual and reproductive violence as both "victims" and "survivors." The term "victims" is relevant for fully understanding the panorama of harm, whereas the term "survivor" is used to capture the forward-looking agenda of advocacy for women's rights (including their right to reparation) and the need to promote legal and social change that will enable those affected to move beyond victimhood.

[12] Although this chapter centers on women and girls, it also recognizes that there is an urgent need to broaden this discussion to include men and boys. Viewing SRV through a wider lens may help us begin to understand how men deal with their own compromised masculinity in the face of SRV, a phenomenon that has a direct impact on women's chances for recovery and empowerment. To date, this issue has been neglected in the literature and in practice.

[13] United Nations, *UN Basic Principles and Guidelines on the Right to a Remedy and Reparation for Victims of Gross Violations of International Human Rights Law and Serious Violations of International Humanitarian Law*, A/RES/60/147, March 21, 2006.

[14] See Ruth Rubio-Marín, "The Gender of Reparations in Transitional Societies," Chapter 2 of this volume, for an overview of the UN *Basic Principles*.

and reproductive violence through mass administrative reparations programs? What knowledge and experience can be drawn from other fields of study and practice to inform what else could and should be done? How do we build an effective strategy to reshape the parameters of future efforts for meaningful reparations for the victims whose lives have been tragically shattered by SRV?

With these questions in mind, this chapter will offer a broad discussion of some of the most significant challenges to, and will map out some of the most promising avenues for, conceptualizing and implementing reparations for victims of SRV.[15] We begin by reviewing the most frequent forms of SRV that women and men are subject to during periods of wide state repression or mass violence. We place particular emphasis on understanding both the multifaceted and interconnected detrimental effects of SRV on the lives of survivors and the challenge that the complexities of and interlinkages between different forms of sexual violence present for those working to secure reparations for victims. In the second part of the chapter, we look at the state of empirical practice in implementing reparations programs for victims of SRV in a number of countries and contexts and try to identify relevant positive or negative trends. The final section reflects on additional ways in which the agenda for reparations for SRV during moments of transition could be advanced.

Our analysis is undertaken on the understanding that those who have been victims of sexual and reproductive violence can never be fully compensated for the horrors they have experienced and the grave emotional, spiritual, and material losses they have suffered and continue to endure. However, we contend that well-conceived measures for reparation could achieve three modest yet significant goals. First, reparations could provide some degree of compensation and rehabilitation (albeit imperfect) to victims of SRV. Second, reparations measures could play a significant role in stopping what we call "the domino effect," whereby an act of SRV, especially when perpetrated against women, sets off a chain reaction that precipitates further losses and in many societies prejudices "women's physical safety and well-being, social reintegration and status, economic survival and eligibility for marriage."[16] Third, discussions about state reparations policies could encourage discussions about structural reforms not only for the sake of victims but also for future generations of women and girls, thus contributing to guarantees of nonrepetition.

---

[15] This chapter focuses largely on prospects for redressing sexual and reproductive violence to victims of war or political authoritarianism. However, we also look, when it is appropriate, at established democracies where historical injustice or systemic abuse remains unresolved, thus affecting victims' abilities to exercise their full rights as citizens.

[16] Walker.

SEXUAL AND REPRODUCTIVE VIOLENCE IN THE CONTEXT OF ARMED CONFLICT OR POLITICAL REPRESSION AND ITS IMPACTS

Sexual violence can be defined as "any violence, physical or psychological, carried out through sexual means or by targeting sexuality."[17] For the purposes of this chapter, sexual violence when committed as part of a larger campaign of political violence is understood to include practices such as rape, sexual slavery, enforced prostitution and sexual exploitation, forced marriage, sexual torture or mutilation, and sexual humiliation. Reproductive violence often accompanies and intensifies the effects of sexual violence. It takes place through practices such as forced pregnancy, abortion, or sterilization and includes physical or psychological violence that interferes with men's or women's biological ability to reproduce or effectively parent. International law recognizes the severity of these violations, and core components of most of these crimes are defined within international humanitarian and human rights law, including the Rome Statute for the International Criminal Court, as constituting grave violations, crimes against humanity, and war crimes.[18] These forms of violence have at their root multiple violations of rights, including the right to physical and bodily integrity, the right not to be subject to inhuman and degrading treatment and torture, the right not to be discriminated against on the grounds of sex, the right to health, and the right to control one's sexual and reproductive capacities.

Although the project of incorporating gender into reparations should not involve the creation of "hierarchies of suffering," it is not feasible to design appropriate policies and measures for redress without a more explicit examination of the multiple forms in which sexual and reproductive violence is inflicted on the bodies and minds of women and girls. For our analysis, however, perhaps more useful than a "laundry list" of horrors is some degree of

---

[17] Human Rights Watch, *We'll Kill You If You Cry: Sexual Violence in the Sierra Leone Conflict* (New York: Human Rights Watch, 2003), 2, footnote 1, citing the definition from United Nations, *Contemporary Forms of Slavery: Systematic Rape, Sexual Slavery and Slavery-like Practices during Armed Conflict*, Final Report submitted by Gay J. McDougall, Special Rapporteur, E/CN.4/Sub.2/1998/13, June 22, 1998, 7–8.

[18] The following are the relevant article sections within the Rome Statute for the International Criminal Court's Elements of Crimes pertaining to crimes against humanity and/or war crimes (PCNICC/2000/1/Add.2): rape, Arts. 7(1)(g)-1, 8(2)(b)(xxii)-1, 8(2)(e)(vi)-1, or other grave sexual violence, Arts. 7(1)(g)-6, 8(2)(b)(xxii)-6, 8(2)(e)(vi)-6, including sexual slavery, Arts. 7(1)(g)-2, 8(2)(b)(xxii)-2, 8(2)(e)(vi)-2, enforced prostitution, Arts. 7(1)(g)-3, 8(2)(b)(xxii)-3, 8(2)(e)(vi)-3, and forced pregnancy, Arts. 7(1)(g)-4, 8(2)(b)(xxii)-4, 8(2)(e)(vi)-4; torture, Arts. 7(1)(f), 8(2)(a)(ii)-1, 8(2)(c)(i)-4. Additionally, although forced marriage is not listed as a distinct crime, it could be interpreted as encompassed under the open clauses destined to cover sexual offenses of comparable gravity; see Arts. 7(1)(g)-6, 8(2)(b)(xxii)-6, 8(2)(e)(vi)-6.

reflection on the particular gendered meanings often attached to or mapped onto acts of SRV across different cultures, classes, ethnicities, religions, and social and political groupings. Evidently, it is impossible to capture all of the diverse and devastating impacts that the different forms of SRV can have on survivors in the immediate aftermath of political conflict and over time. Any attempt to do so would risk essentializing victims in general and individual women and girls in particular. Still, lived experiences and the growing literature on women, armed conflict, and humanitarian assistance have enabled us to gain a more nuanced understanding of some of the lesser-known effects and legacies of SRV.[19]

We can distinguish between three main types of harms ensuing from SRV, namely, physical, emotional, and material, all of which are interlinked and reinforce each other. Clearly, the physical traces will vary depending on the form and degree of the aggression inflicted, but it is important to bear in mind that during periods of conflict and authoritarianism the forms of aggression chosen are precisely those that can achieve the maximum terrorization of communities and suffering and humiliation of the victim. For instance, besides being exposed to vaginal penetration, rape victims in these scenarios will also often experience anal rape and the insertion of weapons or broken bottles into the vagina or anus, as well as oral-genital violations. In all contexts, rape is associated with vaginal injury because of the lack of vaginal lubrication. When the rape is of a girl whose vaginal passage is not fully developed and is carried out by groups or over an extended period, it can result in fatal injuries, traumatic fistulas[20] and other long-term medical complications such as uterine prolapse, or other forms of physical injury that may incapacitate the victim.[21] All forms of vaginal injury lead to a higher likelihood of contracting a sexually transmitted disease, including of course HIV. Victims of sexual torture, including those exposed to electric shocks to their genital organs, beatings in the genital area and the womb, or the flooding of fallopian tubes with water, may experience physical and emotional impact that can also be extremely destructive. The

---

[19] Although the literature is vast, two seminal works stand out: Ellen Johnson-Sirleaf and Elizabeth Rehn, eds., *Women, War and Peace: The Independent Experts' Assessment on the Impact of Armed Conflict on Women and Women's Role in Peace-Building* (New York: UNIFEM, 2002); and, more recently, *The Shame of War*.

[20] Physical trauma associated with rape and combined with lack of medical care can lead to a rupture between the bladder and the vagina or between the rectum and the vagina and result in fistulas (abnormal connections or passageways between organs or vessels that normally do not connect). This can leave women incontinent for both urine and faeces, commonly leading to social isolation and increased health problems.

[21] As a result of the systematic and exceptionally violent gang rape of thousands of Congolese women and girls, doctors in the DRC are now classifying vaginal destruction as a crime of combat; see *The Shame of War*.

same may be true of victims of sexual mutilations, such as those of the former Yugoslavia, the Rwandan genocide, the protracted internal conflicts of West Africa and Uganda, and the attacks against indigenous communities in Latin America – conflicts that have all produced instances of mutilation of breasts and female and male genital areas, including castration.[22] In many cases, this mutilation happens immediately after killing the victim; but when the victim of sexual mutilation survives, the physical and emotional effects will be intense and lifelong.[23]

Accounts emerging from many war contexts – but notably the former Yugoslavia, Rwanda, and Sierra Leone – document in significant detail the immense problem of pregnancy and unwanted children as a result of rape, forced impregnation, and forced marriage, a fate that only female victims of SRV can suffer. As in peacetime, in wartime unwanted pregnancies lead to unsafe abortion. Any of these physical traumas can and often do affect the victim's future reproductive capacity (e.g., higher risk of miscarriage and infertility). Women or girls who have been forcibly recruited into fighting forces may come under pressure to end pregnancies since children may be considered a liability for combat functions.[24]

Often, the emotional and psychological consequences of sexual violence will be almost as severe as the physical. Clearly, the emotional damage resulting from rape will be strongly related to the specific constructions of sexuality in the victim's society. That said, across a range of situations of conflict and mass violence there is very widespread evidence of victims' emotional trauma as well as their deep experiences of shame and sometimes guilt, all of which are often also linked to their stigmatization and ostracism. Victims of sexual slavery, often taken captive for sexual and other purposes by state and non-state armed groups during war, may experience particularly acute trauma. In addition to the trauma linked to the original violence, victims of sexual violence often experience shame and guilt when they perceive that they have been "defiled" by having sex before or outside marriage, or that they were themselves

---

[22] M. C. Bassiouni, "Sexual Violence: An Invisible Weapon of War in the Former Yugoslavia," DePaul University International Human Rights Law Institute, Occasional Paper No. 1, 1996.

[23] The impact on the victims' families and communities of witnessing this form of sexual violence and living with its aftermath needs further research.

[24] As has been reported in Colombia by demobilized girl combatants of the Revolutionary Armed Forces of Colombia (FARC). Ironically, the opposite can also be true: research from the UN Population Fund has demonstrated that in Sri Lanka women in zones controlled by the Tamil Tigers have been unable to access child planning services because of a perception that Tamil women should contribute to populating these communities. UN Population Fund, *Global Review of Challenges and Good Practices in Support of Displaced Women in Conflict and Post-Conflict Situations* (New York: UN Population Fund, 2007).

responsible for what happened. For many, such feelings will leave them impaired to have consensual sex in the future or to feel adequately prepared or deserving to become mothers. Male victims of sexual violence also experience deep shame, albeit for different reasons that may be linked to feelings of emasculation. Though there is limited research on the long-term impacts of shame among male victims, there is evidence that experiences of SRV can translate into destructive patterns of behavior (alcoholism, substance abuse, compulsive gambling, domestic violence, incest), intergenerational effects (inability to parent), and early death from a variety of causes, including suicide.[25]

Shame is not a purely internal process. Rather, it is often triggered or accentuated by experiences of stigmatization and ostracism, which could be described as secondary forms of societal violence linked to prevailing cultural norms. In some cases, individual victims may be treated with understanding but still be considered irretrievably "damaged." More commonly, there is a process by which social stigma is transferred from (male) perpetrators to victims. In particular, in some societies women and girls can be stigmatized as "unmarriagable" within their communities.[26] This is emphatically not a phenomenon restricted to any region or culture, but it has particular implications in the context of armed conflict and political repression. Women are frequently deemed culpable through their inappropriate involvement in political activism,[27] for collaboration with "the enemy," for simply having transgressed the gendered distinction between the public/private domain,[28] or on any other grounds that exonerate men. In situations where rape is carried out in "closed" locations, such as barracks, prisons, or secret holding centers, the likelihood is that the

---

[25] Madeleine Dion Stout and Gregory Kipling, *Aboriginal People, Resilience and the Residential School Legacy* (Ottawa: Aboriginal Healing Foundation, 2003), 30–34. Chris Dolan maintains that we need to debunk the existing "hegemonic masculinity" that is constructed and exists in many societies, noting its multiple impacts on men, including high levels of suicide amongst men who cannot attain the masculine norm of marriage, procreation, and protection. Chris Dolan, "Politicising Masculinities: Beyond the Personal," paper presented at an international symposium linking lessons from HIV, sexuality, and reproductive health with other areas for rethinking AIDS, gender, and development, Dakar, October 15–18, 2007, 10. Accessible at http://www.siyanda.org/docs/esplen_greig_masculinities.pdf.

[26] In some indigenous cultures (e.g., in Guatemala), there is an important symbiosis between a woman's gender identity and sexuality/sexual reproduction. Once broken, this linkage can be difficult if not impossible to reestablish within the community. Colleen Duggan, Claudia Paz y Paz Bailey, and Julie Guillerot, "Reparations for Sexual and Reproductive Violence: Prospects for Achieving Gender Justice in Guatemala and Peru," *International Journal of Transitional Justice* 2, no.2 (2008): 13.

[27] As described in Claudia Paz y Paz Bailey, "Guatemala: Gender and Reparations for Human Rights Violations," in *What Happened to the Women?*

[28] Amani El Jack, "Gender and Armed Conflict: Overview Report," Institute for Development Studies, University of Sussex, 2003, 22, cited in Duggan, Paz y Paz Bailey, and Guillerot, 7.

physical and emotional impact will be just as severe. In some situations, it may be feasible for women to avoid being specifically identified as having suffered rape; however, where rape in detention is common knowledge, any victim can experience the same processes of stigmatization and rejection after her release. Stigmatization often leads to rejection and ostracism of raped women who are abandoned by their husband or partner and sometimes the victim's own family or community.[29] Victims of forced marriages may experience the effects of guilt and stigmatization in especially harsh ways. The fact that many victims were forced to bear the children of their captors or bear markings that identify them with a particular fighting force[30] severely undermines their chances for reintegration in the aftermath. Others maintain strong feelings of guilt for atrocities they were forced to commit and fear that they will be unable to reintegrate because of this and other aspects of stigma attached to their association with an armed group.[31]

All the above physical and psychological harms will be intermeshed in patterns that have an immediate material effect on female victims.[32] Victims of rape often remain silent because they ascertain (often correctly) that they will be shunned and will find themselves with limited social and economic options for survival in the aftermath of violence.[33] Access to productive channels of social networking and income generation (such as markets and communal farms) may be denied to ostracized victims.[34] As Dyan Mazurana and Khristopher Carlson recall in Chapter 4 of this volume, in patriarchal societies that value virginity as the paradigmatic female virtue and define a woman's social status around her roles as wife and mother, victims of sexual violence and

---

[29] This sort of rejection has been documented in multiple truth commission reports, including those of Guatemala and Peru. See generally Duggan, Paz y Paz Bailey, and Guillerot.
[30] As has been the case in Sierra Leone.
[31] Mazurana and Carlson.
[32] The physical effects of male anal rape can also be severe and lifelong. For boys, in addition to the risk of contracting HIV, there is the likelihood of emotional trauma impacting on future occasions of consensual sexual intercourse, including male impotence. Although much less is known about SRV against men and boys, in the last decade it has been reported in some 25 armed conflicts across the world (Wynne Russell, "Sexual Violence Against Men and Boys," *Forced Migration Review* 27 [2007]: 22). However, the "conspiracy of silences" surrounding male rape means that male victims are less likely to be stigmatized or rejected, meaning that their material prospects will likely be less affected.
[33] For example, in Colombia indigenous women of the Embera group have reported that women who have been raped by members of any of that country's armed actors have been turned out of their community and forced to live in the jungle. Colleen Duggan and Adila Abusharaf, "Reparation of Sexual Violence in Democratic Transitions: The Search for Gender Justice," in *The Handbook of Reparations*, ed. Pablo de Greiff (Oxford: Oxford University Press, 2006), 634.
[34] Ibid., 635.

mutilation will lose their chances of marriage and hence of reaching the social status given to wives and mothers. Without this status, they also lose access to material goods such as land and property that go with this status. In such circumstances, women and girls can be forced into dangerous situations, such as prostitution or marriage to a less than desirable partner, for example, to a relative (in cultural groupings where tradition dictates that a widow is expected to marry her husband's brother) or a much older man.[35] This also leads to "survival sex" – instances where women and young girls are forced to prostitute themselves for very little payment, typically soap, a plastic sheet, clothing, or some food.[36] Victims of sexual violence resulting in unwanted pregnancies and children are particularly vulnerable to economic destitution. Young mothers who have given birth to unwanted children may themselves reject or abandon their child or give it up for adoption.[37] Those girls and women who instead choose to keep their babies are often stigmatized and cut off from family and social networks. Feeding and raising these children in the absence of education and healthcare services can be exceedingly difficult for young girls who are themselves dealing with trauma and living in precarious conditions of poverty and want.

Clearly, sexual and reproductive violence does not account for all of the different violations and harms that women and girls suffer during conflict and political repression. However, the above analysis sharpens our understanding of why and how SRV produces a domino effect by which the sheer physical and mental brutality of SRV modalities, when coupled with particular ascribed social, cultural, religious, and symbolic meanings, precipitate further losses

---

[35] Such as in Afghanistan, where some families marry girls off early to avoid the risk of rape prior to marriage. In some countries, such as DRC, the fear and stigma that accompany rape may prevent victims from completing their formal education. Young girls may become the second or third "wife" of a married man and enjoy none of the privileges afforded to married women. Marleen Bosmans, "Challenges in Aid to Rape Victims: The Case of the Democratic Republic of Congo," *Essex Human Rights Review* 4, no. 1 (2007): 7.

[36] Incidents of survival sex have been most notoriously documented in the 2002 joint UNHCR/Save the Children UK report on the sexual exploitation of refugee children – some as young as 11 – by aid workers and peacekeepers in West Africa. Cases of similar exploitation by UN peacekeepers in the DRC were again brought to international attention in 2005. Save the Children and UNHCR, "Sexual Violence and Exploitation: The Experience of Refugee Children in Guinea, Liberia and Sierra Leone," Initial Findings and Recommendations from Assessment Mission, October 22-November 30, 2001, cited in Lauren Rumble and Swati B. Mehta, "Assisting Children Born of Sexual Exploitation and Abuse," *Forced Migration Review* 27 (2007): 20.

[37] Recording actual numbers of children born under these conditions has proven difficult. In Rwanda, some sources estimate that there are between 2,000 and 5,000 such children. Heidi Rombouts, "Women and Reparations in Rwanda: A Long Path to Travel," in *What Happened to the Women?* 208, citing Human Rights Watch, *Shattered Lives: Sexual Violence during the Rwandan Genocide and Its Aftermath* (New York: Human Rights Watch, 1996), 3.

and enlarge the impact on victims. As such, what might be understood by many as quintessential gender-normative violence during peacetime (men affirming their male power by controlling women's sexual and reproductive capacities) becomes gender-multiplied during political conflict and its aftermath and results in a downward spiral of harm, loss, and suffering for victims. In the long run, for those women and girls who have survived SRV, the original violation – as terrible as it undoubtedly was – may be but the prelude to additional forms of violence through stigma, abandonment, isolation, and ostracism emanating from their partners, families, villages, and communities. To this we must add the struggles faced by many women for everyday survival in the developing world (poverty, disease, malnutrition, etc.) while dealing with cycles of grief for lost partners or family members and physical and emotional trauma.

SELECTED EXPERIENCES IN ADDRESSING SRV IN STATE REPARATIONS PROGRAMS

We now shift our attention to the question of what we have learned from past (and current) reparations programs. For this part of our analysis, we look mostly to reparations programs that have explicitly included sexual and at times reproductive violence as a category of eligibility for reparations, drawing from the recommendations of truth commissions (or similar bodies) and in some cases the actual implementation of reparations measures. Our analysis focuses on seven countries – South Africa, Guatemala, Peru, Sierra Leone, Timor-Leste, Ghana, and Canada[38] – and is structured to flesh out a number of common challenges that cross-cut these experiences. We hope thereby to gain a better understanding of how these efforts have or have not partially

---

[38] This set of cases is compared using maximum variation sampling, a purposeful sampling strategy that is useful for small samples in that it enables the researcher to quickly identify any common patterns emerging from great variation and captures core experiences and central, shared dimensions of a phenomenon. Michael Quinn Patton, *Qualitative Research and Evaluation Methods*, 3rd ed. (London: Sage Publications, 2002), 240–241. For this discussion, our selection criteria has included geographic diversity, varying degrees of violence or oppression (war, political authoritarianism, and historic violence linked to systemic racism), and different levels of economic development. In most of these countries, the awarding of reparations in general has been limited, is incipient, or has not happened at all. As such, looking at the narrow strand of experience around reparations measures for SRV will also be circumscribed. Unfortunately, prior reparations programs in other countries (for example, Argentina and Chile), some of which have by now been implemented, systematically failed to include victims of SRV.

It should also be noted that these are not the only countries in which dialogue and advocacy around transitional justice are calling for the reparation of sexual violence. Other countries where SRV has or is being discussed as a violation eligible for reparation include Rwanda, Haiti, Morocco, Bosnia and Herzegovina, and Australia. We draw on these cases as appropriate.

addressed the impacts discussed in the previous section. Three key questions guide this analysis:

1. What forms of sexual and reproductive violence have been included in state-sponsored reparations programs or proposed programs?
2. Who is included and who is left out as beneficiaries?
3. What types of measures have been recommended and/or implemented?

But first a preliminary remark. We have decided to purposefully focus on administrative reparations programs instead of judicial avenues for reparation because we believe that the former offer the greatest potential for victims of SRV, especially in the case of large-scale conflict or state repression. The significant underreporting of sexual violence in normal times is explained by the difficulty in many societies for women and men to come out as victims of sexual violence. Women in particular experience difficulties in accessing the criminal justice process, a fact that often results in secondary victimization. Reparations programs can obviate some of the difficulties and costs associated with litigation, including high costs, the need to gather evidence that may not be easily available, the pain and humiliation of cross-examination, and victims' own lack of confidence in the judicial system. However, this is so provided that administrative programs for reparations go out of their way to simplify procedures, lower thresholds of evidence, spare victims the anxiety of cross-examination, and ensure confidentiality.[39]

What Forms of SRV Have Been Included in Reparations Programs?

The various definitions of sexual and reproductive violence offered in a number of truth commission reports and related enabling legislation at the national level reflect multiple and diverse approaches to categorizing harm and violations for the purpose of granting reparations.

In South Africa, one of the earlier cases, a broad definition of sexual violence was adopted by the Truth and Reconciliation Commission (TRC). Instead of a "stand-alone category," rape and other forms of SRV were categorized under torture or inhuman or degrading treatment. Beth Goldblatt suggests that this

---

[39] See Ruth Rubio-Marín and Pablo de Greiff, "Women and Reparations," *International Journal of Transitional Justice* 1, no. 3 (2007). In particular, regarding rules of evidence, it might be that the best way to approach this is by assuming the veracity of victims' testimony and constructing a system of presumptions based on patterns of criminal conduct. As for the need to ensure confidentiality, it would be essential to ensure that victims can give testimony or provide evidence in private, at a distance, or through proxy. Also, the categories of beneficiaries can be crafted in such a way that they cover victims of SRV who are unwilling to come forward as such.

approach allowed the commission to consider a number of harms that were not conceptualized by the drafters of the TRC legislation at the outset, such as forced nakedness.[40]

Certain reparations programs have instead opted for an explicit mention of forms of sexual violence among the list of violations that qualify a victim for reparations. This is the case in Peru (rape victims), Guatemala (victims of rape and sexual violence), Sierra Leone (victims of sexual violence), and Timor-Leste (victims of sexual violence). Besides the explicit reference to sexual violence, one finds increasingly expansive definitions of what is then covered under the notion of sexual violence. In Guatemala, the category of "rape and sexual violence" was not interpreted to include sexual slavery, forced union with captors, sexual torture, or amputation and mutilation of sexual organs.[41] In Peru, several categories of violations were also left out, including forced abortion, forced cohabitation, forced contraception, sexual slavery, and sexual mutilation.[42] More recently, however, Sierra Leone's TRC went out of its way in its effort to be comprehensive, including rape, sexual slavery, mutilation of genital parts or breasts, and forced marriage in its definition of sexual violence.[43] The same was true in Timor-Leste, where sexual violence was interpreted to cover rape, sexual slavery, and forced marriage, among other forms.[44] Interestingly, though, almost no reparations program has thus far distributed benefits explicitly for forms of reproductive violence such as forced impregnation, forced abortion, or forced sterilization as separate categories, even though some of these are now recognized international crimes and though there may be good reasons for doing so.[45]

The shift from using broad categories of violations to more specific definitions of particular types of SRV in reparations discussions, however, has not been universal. In Rwanda's gacaca system,[46] for example, parliamentarians had not originally intended even to classify sexual violence as grave enough

---

[40] Beth Goldblatt and Fiona Ross, *Bearing Witness: Women and the Truth and Reconciliation Commission in South Africa* (London: Pluto Press, 2003).

[41] Paz y Paz Bailey, 106.

[42] See Guillerot, 151, 153.

[43] See King, 262–264.

[44] Wandita, Campbell-Nelson, and Pereira, 302, 309.

[45] See Rubio-Marín, "The Gender of Reparations in Transitional Societies," Chapter 2 of this volume.

[46] Rombouts, 201–203, includes a full account of the different reparations mechanisms that have been discussed or implemented in Rwanda. These include: (1) the International Criminal Tribunal for Rwanda (ICTY), which had no mandate to award reparations but did distribute, through five Rwandan women's organizations, monetary contributions for collective reparations to women; (2) the national courts, which can and have awarded damages; (3) the Assistance Fund for Genocide Survivors (FARG), which has distributed limited resources

to constitute an international crime, and certainly not a constituent part of genocide. Instead, they considered that sexual violence could be adequately dealt with under the existing penal code. It was only criticism from survivor groups that ensured the inclusion of sexual violence in any form. To what extent the gacaca courts may prove to be a path to reparations, however, remains unclear, as attitudes of shame and social rejection of victims of SRV are so strong that such experiences are generally not shared publicly.[47] Other processes in Rwanda involving reparations include the Assistance Fund for Genocide Survivors (FARG), established by the postgenocide government in 1998. Victims of rape, sexual violence, and gender-specific mutilations have not been specifically included as FARG beneficiaries, and the only types of harm indirectly recognized are those experienced by orphans, the handicapped, and widows.[48] These exclusions have acquired a particular relevance in Rwanda because of the emerging patterns of HIV/AIDS associated with the incidence of violent gang rape and repeated forced intercourse during the genocide.[49]

The degree to which an explicit effort is made to spell out different categories of SRV harms and crimes in a reparations program will likely depend on two factors. First, there is the degree of awareness of the scope and seriousness of SRV offences committed during the period covered. Thus, the fact that truth commissions have as of late devoted more energy to investigating the patterns of sexual crimes may in part explain the trend in more recent reparations initiatives shaped after TRC recommendations to delineate more explicitly a wider set of forms of SRV. Second, delineation of the different categories of SRV violations may also depend on the extent to which a reparations program is harm based (meaning that it accords benefits either in proportion to the harm a victim experiences as a result of a violation or at least in a way that is sensitive to the nature of that harm). On this there is significant variation. If a

---

through social-service packages in the areas of education, housing, health, and income generation; (4) the Indemnification Fund (FIND), which exists only as two draft laws that have not been adopted and contemplate the awarding of lump-sum compensation or an equivalent amount in social-service packages; and (5) the gacaca tribunals, which are not mandated to award reparations but are responsible for establishing lists of victims and their damages; until recently, gacaca were not mandated to handle cases of SRV.

[47] At least this has been the experience in the pilot phase of the gacaca; Rombouts, 213, 201–203. In addition, using the gacaca to hear testimonies about sexual and reproductive violence was originally meant only to serve as a forum for gathering evidence on potential cases of SRV for later presentation in the courts, given that sexual violence was considered a Category 1 crime (for treatment by the courts). However, in May 2008 a new law established that gacaca courts would begin handling rape cases in July 2008. Hirondelle News Agency (Lausanne), June 25, 2008, http://allafrica.com/stories/200806260567.html.

[48] Rombouts, 214.

[49] For a detailed account, see Francoise Nduwimana, *The Right to Survive: Sexual Violence, Women and HIV/AIDS* (Montreal: Rights and Democracy, 2004).

reparations program is (at least partly) harm based, then this may encourage thinking about benefits that are more closely tailored to the typologies of harms underlying each specific form of SRV. This was clearly the case in Sierra Leone and Timor-Leste, where both truth commissions decided to prioritize those victims who had endured the most severe forms of harm as a result of violations or of a prior vulnerable condition, including, in both cases, victims of sexual violence. If this is true, then arguably the explicit incorporation of forms of reproductive violence as distinct categories that we are endorsing here would encourage thinking about remedies more attuned to thus-far insufficiently addressed harms such as the loss of a pregnancy, the loss of reproductive capacity, and the imposition of raising unwanted children.

As has been acknowledged, the introduction of more detailed categories of SRV-related harms and violations into truth-telling processes and ensuing policies and programs for reparations can be a double-edged sword.[50] On the one hand, adding separate categories for different forms of SRV may increase the visibility of the gender-specific experiences of victims and open up spaces for more in-depth debate about the "domino effect" of such violence, its long-term impacts, and, in the end, appropriate forms of reparation. For instance, an emphasis on reproductive violence may help draw attention to the loss of reproductive capacity and severe damage to life projects as well as to the grave costs of unwanted pregnancies resulting from rape, costs that accrue not only to the victim but to society as a whole, especially when these children end up on the street.

On the other hand, adopting a more detailed categorization may involve certain trade-offs. For example, as mentioned above, in South Africa the broad conceptualization of sexual violence as inhuman and degrading treatment allowed for the inclusion of practices of humiliation that would probably not have qualified otherwise. Also, a more vague reference to sexual violence might at least in theory allow the inclusion of culturally specific expressions of sexual humiliation (like the cutting of the hair of Mayan women during the conflict in Guatemala), which would otherwise likely be left out. A broad definition has ensured also the inclusion of at least some categories of male experiences of SRV, either specifically or by subsuming them under non–gender-specific terminology.[51] In Rwanda, for instance, the use of the term of "sexual torture" rather than "rape" in the Gacaca Law of 2001 reflected in

---

[50] See Rubio-Marín, "The Gender of Reparations."
[51] Reform of national laws that define rape and other forms of sexual violence will also be important, as in the DRC, where in August 2006 a new law came into force redefining rape to include both males and females. See Claudia Rodriguez, "Sexual Violence in South Kivu, Congo," *Forced Migration Review* 27 (2007): 46.

part the desire to ensure that the experiences of men during the genocide, including sexual mutilation, were not excluded from the law.[52] In addition, the use of broad terms may allow women (and men) to identify themselves as tortured or bodily injured as opposed to sexually abused, thus avoiding social stigma and all of its consequences.

For those programs in which an extension of the list of violations represents an explicit attempt to forge connections with the wide range of harms that victims experience, the question can be asked whether truth commissions and reparations programs can attempt to challenge or reshape gendered social constructions in their definitions of harm. For example, various truth commissions have given appropriate weight to the harms resulting from the rape of young women but have not generally engaged in any interrogation of the culturally and religiously embedded notions of female sexual purity that are associated with the psychoemotional and material outcomes of such violence. There appears to be a dilemma between, on the one hand, acknowledging gendered social constructions around the value of what in patriarchal cultures are taken to be the "primordial female virtues" (sexual purity, capacity to bear children and marry, etc.) and responding to the actual moral, psychological, and material loss and harm experienced by victims deprived of those virtues and, on the other hand, trying to rise above or neutralize "sexist" constructions but failing to compensate current victims adequately.

Who Has Been Included and Who Has Been Left Out?

Truth commissions and other bodies charged with making recommendations about reparations have faced complex issues in the specification of the status of "beneficiary." In some contexts, it has been evident that close family members have been directly affected and therefore have qualified as "indirect" or "secondary" victims. But because in virtually every case where this expansive notion of victim is endorsed it is restricted to instances where the primary victim is absent or dead (disappearances, summary executions, etc.), family members of survivors of SRV tend not to be included. How to assess this fact is a tricky question. Arguably, we can say that, just like family members of victims of other gross violations of human rights, close family members (spouses, children, parents) of victims of SRV may experience moral and sometimes

---

[52] Note however that the inclusion of male-directed SRV in truth commission or tribunal definitions is not sufficient to guarantee greater access to mechanisms for justice. The domestic laws of many countries do not include male victims in their definition of rape, particularly in those cases where homosexuality attracts legal penalties. As Wynne Russell points out, "the human impact of this marginalization and lack of care can only be guessed at." Russell, 22.

material damage (think, for instance, of the spouses of women who have lost their reproductive capacity through physical or emotional trauma). At the same time, though, this interpretation leaves itself open to questions of male control and patriarchy and the dangers of linking women's social and cultural worth to their reproductive capacities alone.[53] One way around this might be to include family members of victims of sexual violence as potential candidates not for compensation but for medical and psychological support, as was recommended by the TRC in Sierra Leone and Timor-Leste.[54]

Those responsible for forming policy on reparations have also had to deal with the "vertical" intergenerational impacts of SRV, noticeably where children born as a result of rape or sexual slavery suffer from social stigma. As Mazurana and Carlson point out, in some African countries young mothers returning to their families with children born as a result of rape have encountered discrimination, with food and clothing being withheld from their offspring.[55] In these instances, those responsible for administering reparations need to consider whether to classify the child as a victim in her or his own right, rather than as a beneficiary by virtue of family membership. Sierra Leone's TRC seems to have used the widest definition of "victim," for example, in its consideration of the implications of SRV for the future lives of female victims and their descendants. It concluded not only that the children of victims of sexual violence should be categorized as "victims," but also that they should have priority status in relation to benefits (along with orphans, children who had suffered forced conscription, and children of amputees). In Peru, the recommendations for reparations also classified as victims children born as a result of rape, noting that they should be entitled to economic compensation up to the age of 18 and should also be eligible for preferential access to education services. In any event, policymakers should not neglect the fact that whatever consideration is given to children of rape, the mothers themselves are also burdened by unwanted offspring regardless of anything else. From this point of view, we can criticize the fact that in Timor-Leste victims of SRV who have given birth as a result of rape can access reparations for the child only on the condition of being a single mother.[56]

The process of being designated as a victim and as a beneficiary for reparations has also varied depending on the context. In this regard, the distinctive feature of the South African process was that it designated only one route to the status of documented victim, which was to testify in front of the TRC. It was

---

[53] Rubio-Marín, "The Gender of Reparations."
[54] King, 262–263.
[55] Mazurana and Carlson.
[56] Wandita, Campbell-Nelson, and Pereira, 309.

envisaged that this essential first stage would open the way to a comprehensive range of reparations, including material assistance and social-service provision, which would have benefited not just individual victims but their families.[57] However, this strategy also circumscribes the timeframe in which victims can give testimony. This can be problematic for victims in general and victims of SRV in particular, who may take months or even years to overcome trauma and stigma before finding the courage to begin seeking reparations. In Timor-Leste, the truth commission tried to overcome this problem by proposing a two-year window for further identification of potential beneficiaries.[58]

Finally, in some countries, including Guatemala and Peru, there was a debate as to whether reparations for victims of sexual violence should be reserved for women only. Whereas in Peru it was decided in the end to include both women and men on equal terms, in Guatemala it was decided that only female victims of sexual violence would qualify. Scarcity of resources and the largely disparate numbers of male and female victims may justify the temptation to limit benefits for women, but doing so reinforces the notion that only women can be subject to such offences, underscoring notions of femininity and masculinity that would actually be worth subverting.

What Types of Measures and Benefits for Victims of SRV?

As mentioned earlier, evolving practice indicates that "reparation" is a broad term under international law, one that allows for a diverse array of reparatory measures. There is a growing practice, especially in massive state-sponsored programs for reparation, of awarding both monetary and nonmonetary reparations measures in both individual and collective form. Since the underlying objective of all reparations measures is to recognize or publicly acknowledge the harm done while reestablishing the victim's dignity and civic identity as a rights holder, nonmonetary measures are of particular significance to the recognition of victims of SRV, whose sense of self-worth and perceived "value" has in many cases decreased significantly in the eyes of their community because of the stigma attached to SRV.[59]

Experiences with Material Reparations

MONETARY COMPENSATION. Experiences with monetary compensation for SRV have been mixed. The idea of compensating survivors of SRV in proportion or at least in relation to the harm endured (as those programs that award

---

[57] See Goldblatt, 62.
[58] Wandita, Campbell-Nelson, and Pereira, 318.
[59] Duggan, Paz y Paz Bailey, and Guillerot, 36.

different compensation amounts for different types of violations do) presents interesting challenges, not least because the value placed on gendered "assets" such as sexual purity would most likely be determined in relation to culture, religion, or tradition, all of which can be deeply imbued with sexist stereotypes. In addition, putting a value on intangibles such as loss of virginity or reproductive capacity seems to reinforce the notion that a woman's value lies mainly in her sexual identity and reproductive capacity. And yet, whereas a refusal to measure this sort of harm because it reinforces patriarchy may help future generations reconstruct a more gender-just political order, it does little to assist victims who are facing poverty and abandonment today.[60] It is important, then, to recognize the material consequences of SRV on victims' lives through monetary compensation, but also to be sure that the way in which the benefits are conceived and delivered ensures that the meanings conveyed will be proper to dignify victims, and that victims who prefer to remain anonymous to avoid secondary harms linked to stigma and ostracism can do so.

Several examples come to mind. Indeed, the oldest and clearest monetary compensation claim for victims of SRV is that of the "comfort women" – women who became sexual laborers for Japanese soldiers during World War II – who, to this day, continue to refuse material reparation unless it comes with an official apology and an official recognition of state responsibility.[61] Guatemala's National Reparation Program (PNR) was established in April 2003, seven years after the signing of the peace agreements, as a result of intense advocacy efforts by human rights groups. The PNR foresees lump-sum compensation payments of US$2,667 for survivors of torture, rape, or other forms of sexual violence. Each beneficiary of the program can also receive up to a maximum of US$5,863 for the loss of more than one family member or for having suffered multiple human rights violations.[62] It would seem that these material awards could represent both state acknowledgment and a serious attempt at compensation, bearing in mind that Guatemala is a low-income country. However, public acknowledgment, though necessary and welcome, needs to be handled in a gender-sensitive manner. In the recent experience of Guatemala, the singling out of rape victims in state-sponsored community ceremonies and the provision of compensation checks that indicate "victim of rape" have identified those who wanted to remain anonymous, serving to

---

[60] Rubio-Marín, "The Gender of Reparations."
[61] An in-depth discussion of the importance of official apologies, especially in the case of the comfort women, can be found in Hamber and Palmary.
[62] The amounts are set out in Act 10–2006 of the *Comisión Nacional de Resarcimiento*, PNR's executive commission.

further stigmatize the women involved.⁶³ In this regard, the Timor-Leste experience offers an interesting counterexample of trying to ensure that access to reparations for victims of SRV does not come at the expense of exposing individuals who would otherwise prefer to remain unidentified. In that case, the idea is that mothers should receive a variety of services, including counseling, peer support, livelihood training, and access to microcredit in the same service delivery organization they would have to visit once a month in order to receive the funds for their children's.⁶⁴ The measure was designed in order to allow victims of SRV to remain anonymous while receiving some form of assistance.⁶⁵

Due recognition of the seriousness of SRV can also fail when the violation is included in the list of selected violations for the purpose of reparation but then "demoted" in the reparations scale or rendered practically impossible to prove.⁶⁶ In Peru, for instance, the Truth and Reconciliation Commission recommended, among other measures, material reparations in the form of life pensions for partial or total disability, whether physical or mental, caused by the gravest category of violations, including rape. It also envisaged that compensation should be paid to rape victims (male or female) and economic support given to children born of rape up to age 18, who would be eligible for a pension until that age, reflecting the higher likelihood that their mothers would experience rejection, abandonment, and destitution.⁶⁷ The recommended amounts were not publicly divulged, but Julie Guillerot states that "violations were classified according to a scale of importance," with rape ending up "at the bottom of the scale" because the commissioners felt it did not have the same impact as death, disappearance, and disability.⁶⁸ Also, as this scholar underscores, it remains to be seen whether evidentiary standards required to prove rape (a medical examination) could be adapted and accepted by public officials, bearing in mind the impossibility of finding physical proof

---

[63] Author's interview with members of Equipo de Estudios Comunitarios y Accion Psicosocial (ECAP Guatemala), a Guatemalan NGO implementing psychosocial programs with survivors of conflict-related SRV, May 8, 2007.

[64] Wandita, Campbell-Nelson, and Pereira., 310.

[65] Although it does raise some questions about women who did not give birth to children but might have suffered rape nonetheless, and women who have given birth to children of rape but are married. Although the CAVR recommendations are to be applauded for their attempt to prioritize the most vulnerable groups, this approach still defines women in terms of their relationships and assumes that married women with children of rape will be living in an environment free of stigma and discrimination.

[66] Rubio-Marín, "The Gender of Reparations."

[67] Guillerot, 159.

[68] Ibid.

so many years after the fact.[69] Because of all of this, although the original recommendations for material provision demonstrated an acknowledgment of responsibility for SRV, actual survivors of SRV are likely to fare worse than other victims of human rights violations when and if implementation takes place.[70]

The provision of material reparation and particularly monetary measures to survivors of SRV involves a series of tensions that merit further discussion. One concerns the way that money itself is perceived. In many societies, awarding money for material and especially moral damages seems to make sense because it is seen to represent something symbolic.[71] The perception of compensation as "blood money," however, especially when it is provided in the absence of genuine recognition and contrition from the state, has been reported in a wide variety of countries including South Africa and Canada. Radically different socially and culturally ascribed meanings of money can be found in both the industrialized north and the developing south. Even within countries, such as Canada, where lump-sum payments are being extended to aboriginal survivors of the government-sanctioned Indian Residential Schools,[72] a wide range of views about money and its meaning can be found among recipients. In Canadian aboriginal communities, money is often viewed by aboriginal people as a collective or *de facto* public good. Large sums of money entering communities – for example, inheritance payments or large gambling or lottery windfalls – are frequently spent out quickly and conspicuously. Resentment and suspicion toward the federal government for the painful legacy of the

---

[69] Ibid., 165.
[70] In Peru, the record on progress on reparations for victims in general, and survivors of SRV in particular, is mixed. The national legal framework required for codifying reparations policy has been established and the institutions necessary for the implementation of this policy have also been set up. Despite these encouraging signs, the actual awarding of reparations has been slow and disappointing. The multiyear budget that had been set up under Alejandro Toledo's administration encountered multiple financial, technical, and administrative difficulties, rendering it all but inoperative. Alan García's administration, which came into power at the beginning of 2007, appears to have revived the multiyear budget, although it is far from being fully implemented. The new government has announced that it will collectively compensate 440 communities through social investment projects that had been previously identified by communities. Duggan, Paz y Paz Bailey, and Guillerot, 39.
[71] Ibid., 49.
[72] As part of its assimilation policy, during the 19th and 20th centuries, the Canadian state sanctioned the forcible removal of aboriginal children from their families so that they could be sent to any one of the 130 church-run industrial schools, boarding schools, and northern hostels for aboriginal children. Many of these children suffered varying degrees of sexual violence and are being offered individual compensation under the 2006 Indian Residential Schools Settlement Agreement.

Residential Schools experience run deep. A recent study on the impact of individual lump-sum payments highlights not only how "ulterior motives and negative consequences are suspected where government money is concerned," but, most importantly, survivors' impression that "the almighty dollar has broken down . . . relationships and community-mindedness."[73]

Though we have limited information about the experiences of survivors of SRV who have received monetary compensation under national programs for reparation, what we do know raises issues of concern. The Indian Residential Schools lump-sum compensation study cited above documents both positive and negative experiences with compensation, but the balance it draws is not particularly positive.[74] The Canadian experience is yet another one in which the experiences of women are relatively underemphasized and, by contrast, a curious focus is placed on men as victims of physical and sexual violence and other types of abuse and as recipients of compensation. In Peru, the debate around "who is in and who is out" of reparations programs is having a divisive effect on communities; it is not uncommon to hear accusations among victims of political manipulation with payments being arranged for influential members of society.[75] In Guatemala, survivors of SRV have reported being pressured by family members to go public with their stories of victimization in order to appear on the registry of victims eligible for reparation. Similarly, some women who have found the courage to claim compensation through the national program are being accused by members of their community of willingly giving sex to the enemy for money.[76]

Another major issue is whether the compensation money is actually used for the economic and psychological benefit of the survivors of SRV. There are few studies that have examined how reparations are spent,[77] but one conducted in South Africa found that single payments given to victims were quickly used up, often to pay off debts that "the family may have quickly re-incurred

---

[73] Madeleine Dion Stout and Rick Harp, *Lump Sum Compensation Payments Research Project: The Circle Rechecks Itself* (Ottawa: Aboriginal Healing Foundation, 2007), v.

[74] See ibid. In fact, this study was commissioned because of past experiences in Canadian First Nation communities with massive and sudden influxes of money into aboriginal communities. Through the 2006 Indian Residential Schools Settlement Agreement, approximately 86,000 survivors stand to receive on average $28,000, with additional payments to those who have suffered sexual violence.

[75] Duggan, Paz y Paz Bailey, and Guillerot, 49.

[76] Duggan, Paz y Paz Bailey, and Guillerot, 49–50, citing interview with ECAP Guatemala staff, May 8, 2007.

[77] Oupa Makhalemele, "Still Not Talking: Government's Exclusive Reparations Policy and the Impact of the 30,000 Financial Reparations on Survivors," Centre for the Study of Violence and Reconciliation Research Report, Johannesburg, 2004; in Stout and Harp's study on Canadian First Nations, Metis and Inuit populations are notable exceptions.

due to the fact that one of the breadwinners was now dead."[78] In the same study, women indicated that they often had little say regarding how the money was spent and that male family members (including partners and sons) often pressured women to hand the payment over to them.[79] Mazurana and Carlson outline some of the problems encountered by girls who have returned to their families after receiving cash benefits through reintegration programs for former combatants, including the money being spent by fathers on alcohol or sexual relations with other women.[80]

These observations are not meant to suggest that reparations programs should not offer compensation to victims of SRV or that survivors should not step forward to claim this right. What we are suggesting is that in situations in which patriarchal structures or complex bureaucracies may undermine chances to exercise agency, instead of giving large lump-sum payments, governments might consider small pensions disbursed over time, place emphasis on rehabilitation services, and explore new measures such as rendering victims shareowners in microfinance institutions.[81] Bosnia has followed this example and become the first post-conflict nation to provide rape survivors with a monthly pension.[82] Experience in aboriginal communities in Canada suggests that governments should look for ways to work in consultation with affected communities to lend support services for financial counseling and planning in order to offset the potential negative affects that the sudden influx of money can have on families and communities, and to protect recipients from fraud or opportunistic business schemes to which recipients have fallen prey in the past.[83]

NONMONETARY MATERIAL REPARATIONS: SERVICES. Public goods in the form of social-service packages (preferential access to health, education, and other

---

[78] Mazurana and Carlson, citing Makhalemele.
[79] Stout and Harp's study on the residential schools compensation payments highlights similar problems related to elder abuse (since many recipients are now senior citizens) and younger generations taking advantage of the elderly who have received payments.
[80] Mazurana and Carlson.
[81] Rubio-Marín, "The Gender of Reparations." As mentioned, South Africa also planned to pay out compensation in six-month installments over six years, but this did not come to pass. Some residential school survivors in Canada also felt that recipients could make better use of the money over time and that it would be less subject to abuse if it was given in small installments. However, they also felt that this idea would be inherently paternalistic and fraught with patronizing assumptions about survivors. Stout and Harp, 71–72. See also Bernstein, and Seibel and Armstrong in *The Handbook*.
[82] Selim Calypkan, "Trauma Response and Prevention: Precondition for Peace and Justice," *Forced Migration Review* 27 (2007): 54.
[83] Stout and Harp, 70–72.

social services such as housing) may also offer some specific advantages for women – at least when granted as a complement to, rather than a substitute for, other forms of reparations. Experience to date indicates that when asked about reparations needs, women often emphasize the provision of basic goods such as health, education, and housing services for themselves and their families. However, governments may need to search for creative mechanisms to deliver reparations to survivors of SRV who, to avoid stigma and shame, choose to remain anonymous.[84] For example, in line with Margaret Walker's assertion that "reparations programs must aim at gender justice where women themselves may not see this as a priority,"[85] in Timor-Leste the designers of the reparations measures proposed by the truth commission "linked reparations to children and women as a way to force the latter to think about themselves."[86] A negative consequence of this is that the women thereby run the risk of exposing their identity as a victim of sexual violence.

Researchers and practitioners of psychosocial approaches to mental health maintain that survivors of sexual and reproductive violence often focus on the immediate needs of survival assistance or on longer-term goals of economic reintegration for themselves and their families.[87] Similarly, the precarious and circumscribed nature of women's pre-conflict economic status in many countries, which has been cited as a contributing factor to their vulnerability to sexual and reproductive violence during conflict[88] and its aftermath, also significantly undermines their chances for mental and emotional recovery. Conflict often destroys electricity and transportation infrastructure, limiting women's mobility, creating competition over scarce resources, pitting neighbor against neighbor, and in general undermining social capital.[89] Reparations agendas that seek to address women's wrongful losses should contemplate how best to repair and recuperate their social networks and relationships.[90] This intention seems to have underpinned the thinking of the National

[84] Rubio-Marín, "The Gender of Reparations."
[85] Walker.
[86] Wandita, Campbell-Nelson, and Pereira, 318.
[87] Patricia Omidan and Kenneth E. Miller, "Addressing the Psychosocial Needs of Women in Afghanistan," *Critical Half. Bi-annual Journal of Women for Women International* 4, no. 1 (Summer 2006): 17.
[88] For example, women often do not have the means to flee either internally or over international borders (as men do) because of their care-related responsibilities; the gendered division of workload can also put women in situations of higher risk, such as in Darfur, where women and girls fall prey to sexual violence when they leave internally-displaced-person (IDP) camps to collect firewood.
[89] Walker.
[90] Ibid.

Reconciliation Commission of Ghana's recommendation that the state rebuild the market in the border town of Namoo.

Social-service packages whose measures focus on communal institutions (schools, healthcare facilities, etc.) could function as enabling conditions for the rehabilitation of victims and thus be understood as a form of reparation when granted as a complement to rather than a substitute for other forms of reparation. Indeed, public goods may offer specific advantages for survivors of SRV, many of whom are not likely to come forward and claim individual measures.[91] The importance of putting in place economic and social conditions for empowering women victims of SRV also appears to have informed recommendations for income-generation and skills-building initiatives made by truth commissions in Sierra Leone and Timor-Leste. As noted in the case of education grants for children in Timor-Leste, the inclusion of training schemes and income-generation activities for survivors of SRV into a larger public-services package could allow for anonymity for victims who fear stigmatization and social rejection. In addition, this "indirect" form of distributing benefits may decrease the risks sometimes faced by women who meet with hostility and open threats when their participation in efforts to pursue justice become known.[92]

An overemphasis on collective measures and social-service reparations may, however, have some serious drawbacks. It is precisely because communal institutions and social-service packages most often provide nonexcludable goods that they do not grant victims the individualized recognition that is a fundamental element of the concept of reparation.[93] The benefits bestowed do not distinguish between victims or perpetrators.[94] Similarly, the motives of governments that place an exclusive focus on public goods may be questioned by victims, who are quick to point out that transitional governments have a responsibility to provide resources for both collective development needs and reparation.[95]

---

[91] Rubio-Marín, "The Gender of Reparations."
[92] As has been the case in Guatemala. Author's interview with ECAP Guatemala, May 2007.
[93] For this and the following argument, see de Greiff, "Justice and Reparations," in *The Handbook*, and OHCHR's document on Reparations part of its Rule of Law Tools for Post Conflict States.
[94] This in itself may not always be a bad thing, especially in situations in which it is difficult to disentangle victims from perpetrators – e.g., in Sierra Leone or northern Uganda, where girls have suffered extreme sexual violence prior to being abducted into fighting forces and have also been forced to commit atrocities in order to survive.
[95] As has been the case in Peru, where the García administration, which came into power in early 2007, announced that it would prioritize the resourcing of 440 social investment projects that had been previously identified in conflict-affected communities. Duggan, Paz y Paz Bailey, and Guillerot, 39.

It is thanks to the work of women's organizations, humanitarian agencies, psychologists, social workers, and health professionals that reparations programs are coming to understand the importance of offering immediate primary medical and mental health assistance to survivors of sexual and reproductive violence. Physical and mental health recovery and well-being, covered under the rehabilitation rubric of reparation, are critical because they provide the foundation needed for victims to exercise other rights, such as restitution of family life or employment and pursuit of prosecution through the courts.

Increasingly, the struggle for reparation for SRV is focusing attention on the need for adequate and functional primary health services for gynecological surgery, including for vaginal and anal fistulas and other complications resulting from traumatic rape. Although agencies such as the UN Population Fund (UNFPA) have been addressing issues of obstetric fistulas through their reproductive health programs for a number of years, the absence of data on traumatic fistulas has hindered a full understanding of the magnitude of the problem.[96] Nevertheless, publicity efforts of humanitarian organizations such as *Médecins Sans Frontières* (MSF) about the tragedy and scale of traumatic fistulas resulting from conflict-related sexual violence has increased awareness and calls for such services, leading to their partial appearance in recommendations for reparations programs such as in Sierra Leone. In many cases, expert surgeons trained in repairing fistulas can mend the damage. According to UNFPA, the average cost of surgery and post-operative care, including trauma counseling, rehabilitation, and physical therapy, is around $300 – a huge sum for most women in the developing world, but a paltry amount in the whole scheme of post-war reconstruction, especially taking into account the enormous immediate impact that such surgeries can have on the life projects and future prospects of victims of SRV.[97] The significance and potential of sexual and reproductive primary health services has been recognized by some of the cases under study here, most notably Sierra Leone's Truth and Reconciliation Commission.[98] Unfortunately, this measure, along with other measures of reparation called for in Sierra Leone, has yet to materialize.

As Walker mentions in Chapter 1 of this volume, there are multiple reasons why women and girls who have suffered gender-normative and gender-multiplied violence may be reluctant to acknowledge their violation and to pursue any form of redress[99] or treatment for their emotional distress. The

---

[96] Arletty Pinel and Lydiah Kemunto Bosire, "Traumatic Fistula: The Case for Reparations," *Forced Migration Review* 27 (2007): 18.
[97] Ibid.
[98] King, 263, citing *Witness to Truth*, vol. 2, 256, para. 140.
[99] Walker.

reality in many situations is that victims of SRV often carry inside them the psychological trauma of what has happened for months or even years. The resulting effects on their mental and physical health can be debilitating and long lasting; survivors may suffer depression, anxiety, nightmares, low self-esteem, cognitive impairment, loss of social competence, and body image concerns, and may engage in inappropriate sexual behavior or substance abuse.[100]

In response to the challenge of providing contextually specific and appropriate interventions for mental health, a growing body of experience has developed in the use of culturally grounded, community-based models and practices for psychosocial well-being. Over the past decade, these experiences have emerged out of a growing unease amongst practitioners – development, humanitarian, medical, and others – with Western, pathologized approaches to mental healthcare, particularly the direct mapping onto diverse cultural and political contexts of Post-Traumatic Stress Disorder (PTSD) constructs that do not accurately reflect survivors' mental conditions or lived experiences since the violation.[101] African researchers such as Alcinda Honwana point out that, with regard to programs aimed at survivors of rape in Africa,

> Western definitions and understandings of distress and trauma, of diagnosis and healing and even of childhood, have often been applied to societies that possess very different ontologies and social-cultural patterns.... Notions of ill-health and healing, and in this particular case of traumatic distress, cannot be "universalised" because the ways in which individuals and groups express, embody and ascribe meaning to traumatic experiences and events is intrinsically related to specific social and cultural contexts.[102]

The work of numerous psychologists, anthropologists, social workers, and other professionals has reflected similar conclusions in a variety of countries and social settings.

Although psychosocial models of community-based mental health interventions are diverse, flexible, and constantly changing and adapting, those that are based on feminist principles should share a number of common goals or desired outcomes. Here we outline three. First, since for a variety of reasons victims of SRV often do not construe what has happened to them as a human

---

[100] Bosmans, 5, citing *Guidelines for Medico-legal Care for Victims of Sexual Violence* (Geneva: World Health Organization, 2003).
[101] For a full account, see M. Brinton Lykes and Marcie Mersky, "Reparations and Mental Health: Psychosocial Interventions Towards Healing, Human Agency, and Rethreading Social Realities," in *The Handbook of Reparations*.
[102] Alcinda Honwana, *Okusiakala ondalo yokalye: Let Us Light a New Fire: Local Knowledge in the Post-War Healing and Reintegration of War-Affected Children in Angola* (Cape Town: University of Cape Town, Department of Social Anthropology, 1998).

rights violation, for which they are not to blame, psychosocial interventions can work with victims to bring greater clarity to past events and to raise consciousness around the victim's right to truth, justice, and reparation. This approach is being used by the international NGO Project Counseling Services (PCS) in partnership with national NGO partners in a number of countries, including Guatemala and Peru.[103] Such efforts are proving to be particularly challenging in small indigenous communities where NGOs working on women's rights to justice and reparation are viewed with suspicion and accused of stirring things up or "waking old ghosts." Building awareness of rights and individual experiences of SRV is considered to be a necessary initial step for achieving a shared understanding and solidarity, first amongst women victims and then between victims and their families and communities. These linkages are particularly difficult to establish in cultures where widows are scorned and looked on with distrust. Widowhood is not typically accompanied by "gender solidarity"; in both Peru and Guatemala, women on their own tend to be perceived as a threat to other women in the community.[104] Similarly, rebuilding bonds between women and their families – who often are unaware that their female relative has been a victim of SRV – is also a painfully slow business.[105] Still, victims in these countries express relief at being able to share their burden with others survivors and to develop a sense of belonging and healing in the knowledge that they are not alone in their experiences. In Guatemala, the PCS project being implemented under the umbrella of a national women's group consortium known as *"Actoras de Cambio"* has achieved some success in improving victims' knowledge of their rights; in one community, after more than three years of group therapy and other collective exercises, 25 women

---

[103] See generally Project Counselling Services, Annual Report 2007. Lima, 2008. Retrievable at http://www.pcslatin.org/english/programs/latinamerica.htm. Accessed 20 September, 2008.

[104] Duggan, Paz y Paz Bailey, and Guillerot, 11.

[105] ECAP Guatemala, "4th Technical Report to IDRC," November 15 to May 15, 2007, project "Procesos generadores de condiciones habilitantes para la exigencia de justicia por parte de mujeres sobrevivientes de violencia sexual durante el conflict armado en Guatemala," Technical Report, November 2006–May 2007 (unpublished), 3. How and when to bring spouses, family members, and the wider community into these discussions is an unresolved tension. Men themselves often feel powerless and ashamed in the aftermath of violence, especially if they have been forced to watch as female family members were raped and feel that they have failed in their role as protector. Without addressing men's masculinity, women may continue to face the intergenerational after-effects of male violent behavior as men seek to reaffirm their dominance, especially in the home. In Canada, female family members of residential schools survivors have commented that they were unaware that their husbands, sons, or fathers had been victims of sexual violence prior to hearing their testimonies in the compensation awarding process (Stout and Harp). They noted that this knowledge helped them put into perspective years of domestic and sometimes sexual abuse at the hands of male family members.

recently decided to break their silence and give their testimonies to officials of the state-sponsored National Reparation Program.[106]

A second broad goal of most psychosocial programs for war-affected women, including survivors of SRV, should be to help the women recover their self-esteem and build resiliency. Though such approaches should not be considered a catch-all for addressing mental well-being and development needs in the aftermath of extreme violence, contextually specific programs can assist survivors to see beyond victimhood and imagine transformative possibilities, especially when coupled with other measures for economic recovery.

A third goal of such programs should be to provide survivors of SRV with specific, culturally grounded tools for processing their experiences in ways that are noninvasive and meaningful, opening the door, if not to closure, then to the possible reestablishment of a daily existence free of guilt, shame, or any of the other emotions that typically torment survivors of SRV. Psychosocial practitioners have devised multiple methods for helping survivors on this journey. The use of life stories or oral testimonies grounded in easily identifiable symbols (such as life being represented by a river) helps put victims at ease and allows them to frame their experiences within larger social and political contexts.[107] So, for example, a victim of SRV can understand her experience not as one of ongoing personal responsibility for something that she did or did not do, but as an incident (or incidents) that fits into a larger and more complex picture of the social and political landscape. Practitioners also point out that narratives of personal experiences can help balance official or gendered discourses around the conflict and better enable planners and policymakers to identify more appropriate ways to respond.[108] The use of participatory video and photography as a tool for psychosocial recovery is also coming to be seen as an important means of raising awareness of and helping to prevent SRV in conflict-affected communities, of assisting survivors to deal with stigma, and of building new technical, interpersonal, and team skills.[109]

Experiences with Nonmaterial Reparations

Nonmaterial reparations such as memorialization, official apologies, and burials are a critical element of reparation and are integrally linked to the notions of

---

[106] ECAP Guatemala, 3.
[107] A description of how some of these approaches have been used in Guatemala can be found in *La vida no tiene precio: Acciones y omisiones de resarcimiento en Guatemala* (Guatemala: United Nations Development Program, 2007).
[108] Siobhan Warrington and Anne-Sophie Lois, "Listening to Individual Voices," *Forced Migration Review* 27 (2007): 73.
[109] Tegan Molony, Zeze Konie, and Lauren Goodsmith, "Through Our Eyes: Participatory Video in West Africa," *Forced Migration Review* 27 (2007): 38.

satisfaction and dignifying victims and to longer-term political aims of societal healing and national reconciliation. The power of nonmaterial or symbolic reparations lies in the recognition of wrong and the acknowledgment of suffering that can be read into such measures when coupled with material forms of redress and compensation.

Experiences with symbolic reparation for victims of SRV are limited, and the very fact that the notion of "symbolic" has multiple meanings – which will in most cases be determined by culture, history, and other variables – makes the crafting of such measures for this type of harm exceedingly complex.[110] For example, it has been suggested that the time has arrived to erect memorials for victims of SRV to "remind the people that such acts of shame must never happen again . . . to portray the women as heroes and survivors of great pain, to honour women rather than to ostracise and blame them, and claim for them a public space to show that respect."[111] This idea, though interesting in principle, may be difficult to implement in practice. For one thing, it may be difficult to visualize what such a monument might look like. If it is too graphic, it may further objectify survivors as sexual beings or revictimize them. On the other hand, if the design is too symbolic, verging on the obscure, then its meaning and desired impact may be lost on some observers.[112] Similarly, it has been suggested that part of the power of monuments lies in the individualization of suffering: victims draw a certain sense of acknowledgment and satisfaction from seeing the name of a loved one written in stone.[113] Because of stigma and ostracism, however, this type of individualization of victims of SRV will likely not be an option.[114] As Brandon Hamber and Ingrid Palmary note in Chapter 7 of this volume, using monuments to capture the complexity of changing gender roles during and after conflict is a difficult undertaking; to this we must add the challenge presented by the almost singular portrayal in the media and literature of women as victims of sexual and reproductive violence, a portrayal

---

[110] For a full discussion of nonmaterial or symbolic forms of reparation, including to victims of SRV, see Hamber and Palmary. We highlight only a few relevant points of discussion here.

[111] Pinel and Bosire, 19.

[112] Hamber and Palmary point out that this may be the case with the National Women's Memorial in Pretoria, South Africa.

[113] Various individuals have commented that this is one of the major strengths of the Vietnam War Memorial in Washington. Brandon Hamber, "Narrowing the Micro and Macro: A Psychological Perspective on Reparations in Societies in Transition," in *The Handbook of Reparations*, 572.

[114] There have also been increased calls from women's organizations for more systematic naming and shaming of individual perpetrators of SRV. These groups note that men seldom admit – until asked – to having committed sexual violence. The argument here is that a more systematic approach to eliciting testimony about SRV would serve in deflecting blame from the victim and focusing it more centrally (and arguably correctly) on the perpetrator.

that could be further manipulated to entrench symbolic reparations for SRV in stereotypes or misplaced and ill-advised images of martyrdom.

Emphasizing the potential of symbolic reparations for social healing through the commemoration of certain sites of human rights violations, such as prisons or locations of massacres, raises further challenges. If the dead victims or survivors of SRV are not specifically included in ceremonies, it reinforces the associations of unalterable shame and stigma and further confines this form of gendered violence to the "private" domain. As already explored, reparation processes should offer spaces to demonstrate that women's existence is not confined to sexual and reproductive capacities. An illustration of this conundrum was played out at an event, funded by the Timor-Leste truth commission's Urgent Reparations Fund in the town of Ainaro, to commemorate local people who had rebelled against the Indonesians in 1982. "Community leaders" read out the names of those to be honored at the site of the violence, but the list failed to contain any of the names of the women who had participated in the resistance or any mention of the hundreds of women who suffered violence in the aftermath. In Ghana, the recommendation of the National Reconciliation Commission that a market be reconstructed in the border town of Namoo could have important symbolic significance. In that case, market women who held particular commercial power in Ghanain society had been targeted for "flogging and other acts of humiliation" (including forced nakedness) by government forces as vengeance for refusing to implement government price controls and for the perception that they were responsible for corruption and hoarding in the country.[115]

The use of official apologies by the state and its agents (such as the military or police) to women, including victims of SRV, such as that recommended by the truth commissions of Sierra Leone, Ghana, and Timor-Leste, merits further reflection.[116] As the reluctance of "comfort women" to access monetary payments without an official apology suggests, such apologies can underscore the public and political dimension of SRV and help overcome prejudices about its private or intimate nature, thus removing stigma from victims themselves.

An increasingly large number of countries in Africa have adopted as part of their transitions a variety of traditional/religious or community-based approaches as measures for symbolic reparation and community reconciliation (other non-African countries, notably Guatemala, Peru, and Timor-Leste, have also adopted some traditional justice mechanisms). These approaches typically include community-level ceremonies and processes that "reconcile"

---

[115] *The National Reconciliation Commission Final Report*, vol. 1, ch. 4.
[116] See King, 268–269.

or "cleanse" the perpetrator and victim and endeavor to restore collective harmony and rebuild broken relationships. These proceedings also often include some form of redress that the perpetrator agrees to pay to the victim. There are undoubtedly potential advantages for survivors of SRV to be able to speak in forums that do not follow the Western, secular, and individualistic model of justice. Similarly, such spaces may be more accessible to women, who often must overcome barriers such as illiteracy and the inability to travel to urban centers because of childcare responsibilities or other restrictions on their movement.

At the same time, however, there is a need to guard against assumptions about the inherent value of "community-based" procedures. Although these mechanisms might be more accessible, they also carry the risk of recreating the structures of control and prejudice that women and other exploited groups are struggling to eliminate. At a general level, this is problematic because most post-conflict societies are highly dynamic places in which values and roles, especially gender roles, have shifted and been transformed. In some contexts, traditional justice practices may not offer women the same guarantees as men. For example, a report by the Liu Institute for Global Issues on possibilities for using traditional justice approaches for women and girl victims of SRV in Acholi-Land in northern Uganda points out that these processes largely exclude women.[117] Traditional justice mechanisms are culturally specific; there may be limited scope for bending or changing culturally ascribed rules in particular circumstances.[118] The biggest weakness of these mechanisms seems to be the ambiguous position that women play in them and the fact that often women's participation is defined as a function of their relationship to men – as wife, widow, or mother.

In addition, there is no reason to believe that a survivor of SRV will be any more eager to discuss what she perceives as essentially a very private experience in the presence of village peers than she would be in front of complete strangers in a truth commission hearing. Local-level conflict resolution approaches may also pose very real dangers to the security of SRV victims when perpetrators are in the direct vicinity.[119] These are only some of the dilemmas

---

[117] Justice and Reconciliation Project, "The Cooling of Hearts: Community Truth-Telling in Acholi-Land," Gulu District NGO Forum and the Liu Institute for Global Issues Special Report, July 2007, 13. Accessible at http://www.northern-uganda.moonfruit.com/.

[118] James Ojera Latigo, "Northern Uganda: Tradition-based Practices in the Acholi Region," in *Traditional Justice and Reconciliation after Violent Conflict: Learning from Experiences*, ed. Luc Huyse and Mark Salter (Stockholm: International IDEA, 2008), 113.

[119] Victims of SRV in Rwanda, Timor-Leste, and Guatemala who have offered testimony in truth commission hearings or have traveled to testify in criminal tribunals have faced (and continue to face) harassment, attack, and in some cases death.

that will inevitably be faced by those endorsing the use of traditional or customary practices aimed at the communal reintegration of perpetrators and victims.

DEALING WITH THE PRESENT, PLANNING FOR THE FUTURE: THE TRANSFORMATIVE POTENTIAL OF REPARATIONS

Comprehensive reparations programs that include individual and collective measures and address the material and nonmaterial dimensions of harm can have both reparative and transformative potential for victims.[120] As Mazurana and Carlson point out, "It is not enough to compensate survivors and send them back into societies that discriminate and are violent to them based on their sex, gender, ethnicity, race, and age. The potential for reparations to play a small, but important role in transformations of societies is clear."[121] Having reviewed both the progress made and some of the obstacles that remain to be faced in the design and implementation of reparations for sexual and reproductive violence, we shift our attention in this final section to the following questions: What else might be done to stop the domino effect of SRV that condemns survivors to continued (and heightened) suffering? How might reparations programs trigger structural reform and contribute to the creation of the transformative environment so vital for the prevention of SRV in the future? In shifting focus in this manner, we realize we are no longer specifically restricting ourselves to reparations in the sense of programs that deliver benefits to victims directly but are rather appealing to the much broader meaning of the term characteristic of its use in international law documents, including the *Basic Principles*, where the term is very closely associated with the much more general category of "'legal remedies."[122] Not being unaware of some of the risks associated with the following proposals, risks that include overburdening programs that typically find it difficult to fulfill their own much more restricted mandates, we nevertheless offer the following arguments, not so much in favor of expanding the agenda of reparations programs (in the narrower sense) but as an invitation to explore synergies and possibilities of coordinating different institutional remedial efforts and initiatives.

---

[120] For a complete discussion of why collective and individual reparations should be bound together, and for the discussion on the notion of reparative and transformative reparations see Rubio-Marín, "The Gender of Reparations" and "Gender and Collective Reparations," Chapters 2 and 8 of this volume.

[121] Mazurana and Carlson.

[122] See de Greiff, "Justice and Reparations," for a clarification of these two uses of the term "reparations."

Reframing Restitution: Victims' Right to Reputation, Family Life, and Citizenship

Discussing restitution for victims of SRV is, in our view, more complex. For most victims of SRV, returning to the *status quo ante* is not wholly desirable given that in many societies, women suffer diverse forms of violence and do not enjoy extensive civil and political rights. Nonetheless, the notion of restitution may still have some potential for survivors of SRV, especially when considering how restitution might be implemented in conjunction with measures for satisfaction aimed at returning dignity to victims. In the aftermath of systemic human rights violations, states can "take steps to provide satisfaction by the execution of acts or works of a public nature or repercussion, which have affects such as... reestablishing (a victim's) reputation."[123] Indeed, practices such as expunging criminal records have been recommended or implemented in some of the countries under study here and are generally viewed by transitional regimes as being fundamental for political citizenship and necessary for restoring a victim's "good name" to his or her community. Restitution can include a wide variety of measures, including the restoration of family life and citizenship.[124] King suggests that in Sierra Leone, "victims of sexual violence whose chances of marriage have been considerably reduced as a result of the stigma and injuries associated with their experience, can be argued to have had a reduction in their earning capacity."[125] If victims' "good name" is a precondition to exercising rights around family life and citizenship, it may suggest that states need to do more to dismantle the social stigma and negative attitudes that plague survivors of SRV. Admittedly, this will be a difficult task. However, efforts to bring taboo subjects into the public domain and change socially and culturally constructed attitudes and practices that are harmful to women are called for and not unheard of. For example, after years of advocacy by the women's movement, and using a variety of strategies adapted for different cultural and religious circumstances, policies to eliminate female genital mutilation and the selective abortion of female fetuses are now being tackled by state authorities in numerous countries in the developing world.

Evidently, the above reading of restitution can also be problematic. In most countries citizenship formation is a highly gendered enterprise. Although it has been suggested that transitional justice needs to be expanded beyond current

---

[123] Carillo, 526.
[124] Basic Principles.
[125] King, 262.

patriarchal notions of what is "political,"[126] the unfortunate reality is that in many societies, women's virtue and "good name" is political currency. This suggests that the above reading of restitution could serve to reinforce gendered social representations and further entrench beliefs that a woman's value is inherently linked to her virginity, marriageability, and reproductive potential. On the other hand, there is an urgent need to find ways to dismantle the social stigma that accompanies SRV and to return to today's survivors a minimum degree of dignity and restored hope for a new life plan.

Guarantees of Nonrepetition: Legal Reforms

The category of guarantees of nonrepetition has consistently been the weak link in strategies for transitional justice in general, and reparations in particular. We perceive the empirical and theoretical literature on gender and transitional justice to be remiss in addressing the transformative potential of guarantees of nonrepetition and in describing in any detail the forms that such measures might take. As argued in Chapter 8 of this volume, a narrow interpretation of the notion of guarantees of nonrepetition seeks to "reassure victims that they will be spared the horror they already lived once, especially if there are concrete circumstances that make reoccurrence likely."[127] A broad interpretation, however, "looks both further back and forward in time to detect enabling conditions and long-term legacies of the gender violence and can therefore be an adequate platform from which to propose broader structural reforms."[128]

We draw on both interpretations to propose a number of concrete measures – in addition to those that have been or are currently being implemented, as discussed in the previous sections – which we believe could be particularly important in reducing multipliers[129] of gendered harm and states of vulnerability, in preventing cycles of violence, and in providing tools of empowerment to survivors of SRV. Undoubtedly, there are a host of measures that can act as building blocks for edifying more equitable and gender-just societies in the aftermath of war and political repression. From this plethora of options, we believe that strategic measures for legal reform represent the one area of intervention that has been systematically underutilized and that stands out

---

[126] Nahla Valji, "Gender Justice and Reconciliation," a study prepared for presentation at the international conference "Building for a Future on Peace and Justice," Nuremburg, June 25–27, 2007, at 13.
[127] Rubio-Marín, "Gender and Collective Reparations."
[128] Ibid.
[129] Understood as "factors that predictably play roles in causing additional losses or additional exposure to violence." See Walker.

for (1) the immediate and dramatic impact it may have in moving the SRV agenda from the international to the national arena, and hopefully from codification to implementation, and (2) addressing the catastrophic effects that sexual and reproductive violence has on the bodies, minds, and life projects of survivors.

It is unquestionable that in any process of democratic transformation, efforts to reform all laws and policies that discriminate against women and measures to facilitate women's equal citizenship opportunities should play a central role. Nonetheless there are three spheres of legal reform that we highlight as having particular relevance for survivors of SRV: laws on abortion, laws on inheritance and property ownership, and laws for addressing violence against women and girls.

As noted earlier, the unwanted pregnancies that often accompany incidents of sexual and reproductive violence can place heavy social, cultural, and economic burdens on victims; these legacies are particularly acute when children are born outside of marriage or when children of rape are perceived as enemies, having been conceived by an enemy combatant engaged in genocidal practices against the mother's group, as in Rwanda, Bosnia, and Guatemala.[130] This raises questions of reproductive rights, particularly around abortion, which have not yet been fully encompassed by in-country debates on reparation or in the literature on gender and reparations. It is a given that all the institutions involved in reparations programs will operate within the boundaries of national law and that they will have to engage with religious and cultural beliefs about abortion. At the same time, women and girls who are pregnant as a result of sexual violence, whether of rape, sexual slavery, or forced marriage, are faced with agonizing choices. In cases where it is both safe and legally available or at least sanctioned, abortion is one option; this was the case in the immediate aftermath of the mass rape of German women by Soviet forces in the last stages of World War II, and it at least reduced some of the impact of the violence on victims' subsequent life courses.[131] In the vast majority of countries in the developing world[132] (and indeed a number in the industrialized world), however, national policies prohibit abortion or are highly restrictive, despite the fact that such policies do not reduce high rates of abortion. Thus, while still dealing with the shock and trauma that accompany sexual violence, victims are often forced to place their lives at further risk in seeking back-street abortions that can result in gynecological complications or death. Campaigns to liberalize abortion laws should be a priority for women's and human rights

---

[130] Walker.
[131] We are indebted to Meredeth Turshen for this point.
[132] Examples include the DRC, Burundi, and until recently Colombia.

organizations, not only in the aftermath of political violence but also, as much as possible, during conflict. Better access to safe and legal abortion could be life-changing for survivors of SRV, as it would immediately allow them to escape the social stigma and economic consequences of giving birth to a child of rape.

As activists for women's rights have found, such efforts need not (and for many could not) wait until the end of political violence. For example, in May 2006 Colombia's Constitutional Court legalized abortion in cases of rape, of endangerment to a woman's health, and where conditions would result in fetal death.[133] The decision will have far-reaching consequences for the women and girls of Colombia who continue to suffer both conflict-related and non–conflict-related rape. Given how time consuming putting into place a reparations program has proven to be in many countries, it is unlikely that an abortion reform triggered through a reparations process will ever come in time to assist most victims of SRV. This is why reparations programs might also consider involving state facilities that will take care of the unwanted children of raped women as well as state services and assistance for those victims of rape who decide to raise the children themselves.

Empirical experience is proving that reforming laws for property ownership and inheritance can be critical for improving women's prospects for recovery and development in the aftermath of political violence. Restitution measures can include restoration of employment and return of property. However, the fact that property and inheritance rights are often not equally recognized for men and women can pose particular challenges in post-conflict moments, when female-headed households are multiplied and women find themselves with no title to property or land.[134] The situation is particularly dire for survivors of SRV, who in the midst of family or community ostracism are left with few (if any) assets. A rights regime that protects the property rights of women may allow female victims of SRV at least to recuperate part if not all of their social position through the standing that is generally attached to land or property ownership in many societies. Holding title to property would also open up the possibility for them to sell what property they own or have inherited and start anew elsewhere, if the conditions that led to ostracism within their local communities proved insuperable.

In post-genocide Rwanda, the government has tried to redress the unequal position of women by reforming the discriminatory inheritance rules under

---

[133] "Colombia High Court Legalizes Exceptions to Abortion Law," *Paperchase Archive*, May 11, 2006, University of Pittsburgh School of Law, http://jurist.law.pitt.edu/paperchase/2006_05_11_indexarch.php.
[134] Rubio-Marín, "The Gender of Reparations."

which women could not inherit. By law, women can now own land.[135] In Guatemala, land-reform measures included in the peace agreements – although not interpreted at the time as a measure for reparation (in the legal sense) – have particular significance for women, particularly Mayan women who continue to face challenges in accessing land through the Land Fund. Guatemala's reparations program specifically lists the awarding of land and the regularization of land-tenure titles as a measure of reparation. Bearing in mind the unequal treatment that women beneficiaries continue to receive from the Land Fund,[136] the National Reparations Program could take special steps to target economically and socially vulnerable women, namely, returnees, widows, single mothers, and victims of SRV.[137]

A third and final area of law reform requiring urgent attention in the aftermath of political violence is that of laws to both prosecute and eliminate all forms of violence against women. Worldwide, there is a growing body of evidence that incidents of violence against women increase in the aftermath of political conflict.[138] This problem is by no means one dimensional. In some cases, men returning from war may have come to view violence as a legitimate means of dealing with conflict and may seek to regain control over family, resources, and women's productive and reproductive rights.[139] In other cases, returning males may be reacting to conflict-related trauma or may be trying to counteract feelings of emasculation, especially if they themselves have been victims of sexual violence[140] or now find themselves unemployed and no longer masters of their domain. Whatever the reason, the weight of

---

[135] Goldblatt, 205. Although Goldblatt also points out that, as with all things legal, the devil is in the details – in this case, the accurate application of the new inheritance law. One of the law's lacunae is that it can be applied only to couples who are legally married – in rural areas many couples do not officially marry. Hence, on the death of a partner, many women are still illegally dispossessed of their land.

[136] As discussed in Byron Garoz and Susana Gauster, "FONTIERRAS: El Modelo de Mercado y el acceso a la tierra en Guatemala. Balance y perspectivas," Coordinación de ONG y Cooperativas, Guatemala, 2003, 93–94.

[137] Duggan, Paz y Paz Bailey, and Guillerot, 18.

[138] For example, the levels of increasing violence against women in post-conflict environments have been documented in Guatemala, South Africa, and Sierra Leone. Valji maintains that this phenomenon is in part due to the false dichotomy of conflict and post-conflict violence and what is considered political or criminal violence. Valji, 13.

[139] Sheila Meintejes et al., "There Is No Aftermath for Women" in *The Aftermath: Women in Conflict Transformation*, Sheila Meintjes, Anu Pillay and Meredith Turshen, eds. (London, New York: Zed Books, 2001), 13, cited in Duggan and Abusharaf, 635.

[140] Men and boys are particularly vulnerable to sexual violence in situations of military conscription or abduction into paramilitary forces. In some places, over 50% of male detainees reportedly experience sexualized torture. Russell, 22.

gender-based violence often shifts from the public back to the private arena, with the result that woman find themselves unsafe in their homes.

If the problem of post-conflict gender-based violence was restricted to the domestic sphere only, the struggle to end such abuses might at least present a manageable advocacy agenda for women and human rights groups; but the problem is even more complex than it would initially appear. There is a growing stream of documented situations in which modus operandi that had been associated with what many analysts understand to be the political motivations of "conflict related sexual violence" – that is the use of sexual violence by groups of the powerful as a means to exert control over the powerless – is moving beyond the boundaries of violence for political gain. In a number of countries, including (but not exclusively) those in Africa, there are increasing reports of civilians participating in rape raids, including attacks on very young girls and babies. In DRC, sexual abuse of young boys by both men and women is also being reported with greater frequency.[141] Although it may be easy to explain away such incidents of what would seem to be randomized violence by the atmosphere of generalized impunity and widespread tolerance of sexual violence that accompanies war, in a number of post-conflict countries levels of "public" acts of sexual and reproductive violence are not dropping during peacetime. In Guatemala, the number of violent homicides suffered by women and the ways in which they were killed (e.g., with visible signs of sexual torture reminiscent of the war) has led many women's and human rights groups to refer to the situation as a "femicide."[142] What is clear is that during moments of transition, violence transmogrifies and merges in complex ways that have a particular impact on vulnerable groups, including women.[143] It is these and other situations that led Noeleen Heyzer, Executive Director of UNIFEM, to declare that "for women living in the midst of their tormentors, justice delayed is more than just justice denied – it is terror continued."[144] The implication is that in the absence of justice for conflict-related crimes and the incarceration of the perpetrators, women run a real risk of further victimization.

---

[141] Bosmans, 8.
[142] See Angelica Chazaro and Jennifer Casey, "Getting Away with Murder: Guatemala's Failure to Protect Women and Rodi Alvarado's Quest for Safety," *Hastings Women's Law Journal* 17 (2006). In March 2008, the Guatemalan government established a national commission on "femicide," composed of officials from the executive branch, the justice sector, congress, and the state statistical agency. In May 2008, the Congress of Guatemala unanimously approved a law establishing penalties of 20 to 50 years' imprisonment for femicide.
[143] Valji, 13.
[144] *The Toronto Star*, August 2, 2007, http://www.thestar.com/comment/article/242217.

There are solid reasons to believe that women and girls who have been victims of SRV in the past are at increased risk of revictimization. As Walker has pointed out, "when victims are . . . shunned, ignored and blamed or punished," it leads to a general acceptance of sexual violence as the norm, leaving victims with "a realization that rules and restraints that might have protected them are not enforced in their case and that they themselves do not matter."[145] Stigmatization of victims suggests that they are somehow less worthy of protection under the law. In extreme circumstances of protracted conflict, the social rejection that follows victims can foster attitudes of cultural obfuscation or male entitlement among generations of youth.[146] A Human Rights Watch report on eastern DRC, for example, concluded that "abusive sexual relationships between men and young girls has become accepted" and that "using the services of girl sex workers is no longer regarded as an act of violence against children, but rather as a favour, providing these girls with a means of surviving."[147]

The struggle to provide reparations to survivors of SRV may provide an occasion for human rights and women's rights groups to come together to advocate for reformed laws that criminalize all forms of gender-based violence against women and children and that set out additional measures to prevent its recurrence.[148] Progress being made in some countries does provide room for cautious optimism. For example, after 14 years of bloody civil war in which sexual and reproductive violence was a daily feature, in December 2005 Liberia passed one of the toughest laws on rape in West Africa and has recently created a special court to deal not only with the rising number of rape cases, but also with other forms of violence against women.[149]

Although it might be argued that reformed laws offer little redress for women and girls who are direct victims of war-related SRV, it is important not to underestimate the reparative effects that such laws can have for survivors who fear not only revictimization of their person but also fear for the future of their

---

[145] Walker.

[146] As evidenced in a focus group conducted by one researcher in DRC who asked a group of youth HIV/AIDS peer educators how they felt about raped girls and was told: "We are boys, and we satisfy our physical (sexual) needs with her"; "There is our culture. One should respect our culture and there is no way she can stay home." Bosmans, 6–7.

[147] Bosmans, 8, citing Human Rights Watch, *The War within the War: Sexual Violence against Women and Girls in Eastern Congo* (New York: Human Rights Watch, 2002).

[148] Women's groups and human rights groups have not traditionally worked together on the issue of reparations. Women's groups have generally focused on legal reform relating to structural changes for women's equality, whereas human rights groups have worked with victims to claim reparations. Ruth Rubio-Marín, "The Gender of Reparations: Setting the Agenda," in *What Happened to the Women?*

[149] "Liberia: Special Court for Sexual Violence Underway," United Nations Office for the Coordination of Humanitarian Affairs, Integrated Regional Information Networks. (IRIN), Monrovia, March 21, 2008, http://www.irinnews.org/report.aspx?ReportId=77406.

children and loved ones. A recent study of women's perceptions of security in three post-conflict countries cited the reform of laws addressing violence against women as a priority for their present and future well-being.[150] A new rape law in DRC that came into force in August 2006 has increased penalties for those successfully prosecuted and has improved some penal procedures, notably prohibiting the settling of cases by "friendly solutions." The prohibition of out-of-court solutions will not come as welcome news to those who favor a market-oriented approach to judicial reform and who ring their hands over weak or inefficient justice systems that are already overburdened, particularly in transitional contexts. However, it will go a long way to prevent instances in which the victims are pressured to marry the perpetrator or to stay in a forced marriage[151] or in which families accept payment from the perpetrator as compensation.

This chapter is subtitled "moving from codification to implementation" mainly because it is here, in the movement from policy formulation to actual policy implementation, that the future well-being of survivors of SRV hangs in the balance. What is striking in our analysis is that, in a number of countries, many of the recommended measures could easily be taken up by those working with governments in international development programming. Our review of past and current efforts to articulate national measures for reparation that address the particular needs of those who have experienced sexual and reproductive violence reveals that, in most cases, the awarding of reparations to victims of sexual and reproductive violence has been uneven and sporadic.

There is inevitably a risk that by widening their definition too broadly to span goals that are both reparative and transformative, reparations could lose some of their normative distinctiveness. Ultimately, acknowledgment and responsibility for harm provide the moral compass required to put the often-invisible victims of SRV on the path to empowerment. What is abundantly clear is that social and economic justice matters immensely in these contexts and that, for the sake of survivors, we need to get much better at bridging legal, humanitarian, and development strategies. There is no convincing reason why, with the careful consultation of victims and the genuine good will of state authorities and international actors, the juridical and ethical power of reparations needs to be lost.

---

[150] Brandon Hamber et al., "Discourses in Transition: Re-imagining Women's Security," *International Relations* 20, no. 4 (2006): 499.

[151] Mazurana and Carlson discuss instances in Mozambique, Angola, Sierra Leone, and Uganda in which formerly abducted girls have been forced or given incentives by local, national, and international actors to stay with their former captors/tormentors.

4

Reparations as a Means for Recognizing and Addressing Crimes and Grave Rights Violations against Girls and Boys during Situations of Armed Conflict and under Authoritarian and Dictatorial Regimes

Dyan Mazurana and Khristopher Carlson[1]

I felt as if my heart had stopped beating, only God gave me the resistance to bear it all. I was very young, but I felt the hardship.... I still dream about Dos Erres and I hear everything I heard then, the shots, the smell, the air, everything.[2]

The violence, abuse, and hardship that girls and boys suffer during armed conflict[3] and political violence under authoritarian and dictatorial regimes ensures that they will never be the same when the war stops or the violent regime ends. Children's experiences of war and political violence – the abuse of their bodies, souls, and minds, the tearing apart of their families and neighborhoods, and the atrocities they witness – shape them and their societies. They experience violations of their civil, political, social, economic, and cultural rights. These include the rights to life, freedom of movement and association, education, health, and knowing and being cared for by their parents.[4]

---

[1] The authors would like to thank Saudamini Siegrist of UNICEF's Innocenti Research Centre, Florence, for her invaluable input and sharing of documents that played a crucial role in shaping the thoughts laid out in this chapter. In addition, Ruth Rubio-Marín provided valuable support, guidance, and patience. Thanks also to Pablo de Greiff, Julie Guillerot, and Jeremy Sarkin for thoughtful reviews. We thank Beth Goldblatt, Julie Guillerot, Elizabeth Lira, Claudia Paz, and Heidy Rombouts for their assistance as we prepared information on children and reparations in South Africa, Peru, Chile, Guatemala, and Rwanda, respectively. We thank and acknowledge Kristen DeRemer for her research assistance.

[2] Commission for Historical Clarification [*Comisión para el Esclarecimiento Histórico*] (CEH), *Guatemala: Memoria del Silencio* (Guatemala: United Nations Office for Projects and Services, 1999) vol. IV, 200.

[3] The term "armed conflict" is used here to describe conflict of varying degrees of intensity. A precise definition of the term is not provided in any treaty body; see United Nations, *Final Report of the Special Rapporteur, Terrorism and Human Rights. UN Sub-Commission on the Promotion and Protection of Human Rights. Final Report of the Special Rapporteur, Kalliopi K. Koufa*, E.CN.4/Sub.2/2004/40, June 25, 2004, 8.

[4] Convention on the Rights of the Child (CRC), CRC/C/113, November 7, 2001.

Their rights to development[5] and to a safe and healthy environment[6] are also violated.

It is not possible to fully repair children after they have experienced such harms. It is not possible to recover the years of lost education, or the time that would have been spent developing emotional and spiritual ties to family, friends, and communities as well as the skills that enable children to take pride in contributing to their households' livelihoods. As a child survivor of the Guatemalan war pointedly asked, "We couldn't go to school, we grew up with a machete, in fear, frightened, worried, poor, instead of growing up with education and tranquility. We spent our whole lives suffering because we were children. How can we recover from that?"[7]

This chapter, which analyzes the experiences, challenges, and possibilities around reparations and children, does so in the spirit of asking what role reparations may be able to play in *partially* addressing the grave human rights violations that children endure during situations of armed conflict and political violence orchestrated by authoritarian and dictatorial regimes. Our approach to reparations draws broadly on an understanding of the concept within international law and reflects on how reparations have been carried out in practice. Hence, we consider both reparations programs designed to distribute direct benefits to the victims themselves – including restitution, compensation, and rehabilitation – as well as other key measures and initiatives within transitional justice that, if crafted with forethought and care, could have reparative effects, namely, rehabilitation, satisfaction, and guarantee of nonrecurrence.[8]

Our chapter focuses on gender and highlights why it matters in reparations for children. Within our gendered analyses of violations, we consider both boys and girls. However, we tend to privilege girls, highlighting how gender matters in their experiences of human rights violations and the aftermath of those violations. We focus on girls not because other work exists on boys and reparations (it does not), but because we have for the last several years been working with girls who have experienced grave violations in situations of

---

[5] Declaration on the Right to Development, adopted by the United Nations General Assembly resolution 41/128 of 4 December 1986.

[6] The right to safe and healthy environment is found in a number of documents, including the Universal Declaration of Human Rights, the International Covenant on Economic, Social and Cultural Rights, the Convention on the Elimination of All Forms of Discrimination Against Women, the Convention on the Elimination of All Forms of Racial Discrimination, the Convention on the Rights of the Child, and the ILO Indigenous and Tribal Peoples Convention (No. 169).

[7] *Memoria del Silencio*, vol. IV, 195.

[8] See Pablo de Greiff, "Justice and Reparations," in *The Handbook of Reparations*, ed. Pablo de Greiff (Oxford: Oxford University Press, 2006), 451–477.

armed conflict. Thus, we have a degree of confidence in thinking about what gender-just reparations for girls might look like. Although we include boys in our analyses to a great extent, we recognize that increased work on this topic for boys, from a gender perspective, is equally necessary and important.

The chapter begins with a concise overview of trends in situations of armed conflict and under authoritarian and dictatorial regimes where children are subjected to systematic forms of grave violence. We then identify and offer a brief analysis of gross and systematic violations against children in these situations. It is critical that such abuses are named and discussed in order to raise awareness of the necessity of including them as part of an integral strategy for reparation and measures that support reparation. As we later demonstrate, there is a significant lack of naming and addressing grave rights violations against children in past reparations programs and efforts, much to the detriment of surviving children.[9] Additionally, we offer the analysis to stress that although truth commissions and reparations programs focus predominantly on the abuse of adults, children are not simply innocent bystanders or unintended casualties; in fact, children are explicitly and specifically targeted and abused. To illustrate, the South African Truth and Reconciliation Commission reported that children and youth, many of them under 18 years of age, were the principal victims in *all* categories of grave rights violations under its consideration.[10] (We recognize that in nearly all the conflicts we discuss, most of the violence is targeted at ethnic or political minorities and the poor, particularly those living in rural locations, and, within Latin America, indigenous populations.) We also concisely review the most pertinent international legal standards' relation to grave human rights violations against children. And finally, we note gendered patterns to these violations.

We then turn our attention to past and present reparations programs that have explicitly included children among those eligible for reparations. We provide an analysis of the results from truth commissions and reparations programs within eight countries in which children are known to have been victims of grave rights violations due to armed conflict and political violence instigated by authoritarian governments. The chapter concludes with ways in

---

[9] Colleen Duggan and Adila Abusharaf make a similar argument in their detailed discussion of sexual violence; see Colleen Duggan and Adila Abusharaf, "Reparation of Sexual Violence in Democratic Transitions: The Search for Gender Justice," in *The Handbook of Reparations*, 623–649.

[10] Truth and Reconciliation Commission, *Report of the Truth and Reconciliation Commission of South Africa* (Cape Town: Juta, 1998), vols. IV and V.

which reparations programs could strengthen reparations for girls and boys who have suffered severe violations of their human rights.

As our focus is on children and reparations, it is useful here to discuss how we conceive of and use the terms "child" and "children." Anthropologists have clearly shown that "child" and "childhood" are culturally and socially inscribed categories that usually do not correspond to set age limitations. Rather, rites of passage such as marriage, child-bearing, ability to perform certain tasks, or specific religious or spiritual rituals mark the transition from childhood to adulthood.[11] These realities are at times in tension with international standards, most notably the Convention on the Rights of the Child (CRC), which defines the child as "below the age of eighteen years unless, under the law applicable to the child, majority is attained earlier."[12] Although it is important to pay attention to age and note patterns reflecting how, why, and if at all it corresponds to young people's experiences and responses, at the same time an artificial age limit for "children" – according to which only a set range of people between certain ages are considered, usually newborns to 15, 18, or 21 years – can hinder efforts to address realities on the ground.

Furthermore, in the reports of bodies that address grave rights violations (such as national and international tribunals or truth commissions), lumping all children between the ages of newborn and 15 or 18 years of age will almost certainly result in the voices, experiences, needs, and priorities of older children or youth overshadowing younger children. It is necessary to understand that young children may have a very different experience of armed conflict and authoritarian regimes than do youth. For example, in a number of countries where children suffered egregious violations, youth were actually a significant portion of those who joined the opposition or government groups that triggered the violence and perpetrated the crimes. Younger children, on the other hand, were more often abducted and forced to participate in hostilities, with little ability to maneuver or negotiate power once in the hands of perpetrators, or to survive on their own if separated from caregivers.[13]

---

[11] See, for example, Jo Boyden and Joanna de Berry, eds., *Children and Youth on the Front Line: Ethnography, Armed Conflict and Displacement* (New York/Oxford: Berghahn Books, 2004).

[12] See CRC, Article 1. However, most international agencies operational in settings where children are experiencing systematic grave violations of their rights, such as UNICEF, Save the Children, International Rescue Committee, Christian Children's Fund, and World Vision, recognize this dual reality and make their programs available to a broader category of youth, inclusive of both children and people aged in their early 30s.

[13] See UNICEF Innocenti Research Centre and International Center for Transitional Justice (ICTJ), *Children and Truth Commissions: Basic Considerations* (Firenze and New York: UNICEF Innocenti Research Centre and ICTJ, forthcoming).

POLITICAL VIOLENCE AND CHILDREN

For the past eight years I have been in the bush. I was totally cut off from the world. It's like being put in a tomb, you are still breathing, but you are in there. In the bush it was always horrible.

I didn't understand at first what they were talking about, you know, someone very old, in his late 50s. You cannot imagine. I thought maybe he was out of his head, not joking, because I have never seen any of them joking. But after that they just have to tie you up and somebody rapes you.

I was always, always afraid they might ask me to kill somebody, I was always, always afraid to do that. One day some girl tried to escape, and they asked us, all 30 of us girls to come. We went there not knowing what was going to happen. They gave us all big sticks and they ordered us to beat her to death. We could not imagine doing this and we refused, we refused. But we were beaten so badly, to the extent that we all had to beat her to death.[14]

As of 2007, there were more than 30 situations of conflict where the rights of children were being systematically and egregiously violated. In the last decade, it is reported that 2 million children have been killed in situations of armed conflict, 6 million children have been permanently disabled or injured, more than 14 million children have been displaced, and more than 1 million have been orphaned and separated from their parents. More than 250,000 children are said to be associated with fighting forces and groups. And every year, 8,000 to 10,000 children are killed or maimed by landmines.[15] The majority of child victims are from ethnic or political minorities and the poor, particularly those in rural locations, and indigenous populations.

The nature and methods of armed conflict mean that the fighting takes place in civilians' communities, villages, fields, and homes, thus sharply increasing children's risk of harm. Although many children are killed by weapons, many more die from the catastrophic impact that the conflict has on their communities' infrastructure (often already weak to begin with) and their families' access to food and health care and ability to maintain their livelihoods. Often the first to die from increased disease and poor sanitation are children under five years of age.[16]

---

[14] Interview with young woman abducted at age 14 by the rebel group the Lord's Resistance Army (LRA) in Uganda; Kampala, Uganda, 2007.
[15] United Nations, *Report of the Special Representative of the Secretary-General for Children and Armed Conflict*, A/60/335, September 7, 2005.
[16] Paul Collier et al., *Breaking the Conflict Trap: Civil War and Development Policy* (Washington, DC: World Bank and Oxford University Press, 2003), 23–24.

Children in war-torn communities who survive are subject to widespread and, at times, systematic forms of crime and resulting human rights violations that have mental, emotional, spiritual, and physical repercussions. Children suffer both from violations directed against themselves as physical, sexual, gendered, and ethnic beings, and from violations that target their parents, siblings, and caregivers. Violations directed toward the child include murder, torture, disappearances, amputation, illegal detention with or without family members, forced recruitment into fighting forces and groups, slavery, abduction and forced removal from families and homes, and a wide range of physical and sexual violations. Children are also greatly affected by what happens to the adults in their lives. As teachers are targeted and killed schools close down; as health care workers are killed or flee, clinics close their doors or provide only rudimentary services. Teachers and health care and social workers are a frontline of defense for protecting children from the ravages of armed conflict; when they are not there, children are increasingly at risk. Perhaps most importantly, the killing, disappearance, death, detention, or flight of parents and caregivers results in the existence of hundreds of thousands of single-parent households and tens of thousands of street children, orphans, and child-headed households, some headed by children as young as eight.[17]

Some of the violations children are subjected to are shaped and carried out with gender in mind – that is, it matters to the attackers that their victim is a boy or a girl and they craft their actions accordingly. Furthermore, because girls and boys are gendered beings living in cultures that ascribe gendered roles and responsibilities, all violations affect girls and boys in ways that have gender-specific consequences. To illustrate, adolescent boys are more commonly subject to voluntary and forceful recruitment by armed forces and groups than are girls, and boys tend to have higher rates of physical injuries due to their participation in fighting. Adolescent girls, though also voluntarily and forcibly recruited, tend to suffer more sexual violations at the hands of members of their own and other fighting forces. At the same time, because captive girls in particular are sexual prizes for commanders and provide the backbone of the labor for maintaining armed opposition groups, they are often the last to be released.[18]

---

[17] The case of an eight-year-old girl heading her own household (which was comprised of her two younger siblings) was reported to the authors during fieldwork in Kitgum, Uganda, by Cornelius Williams, UNICEF, Head of Child Protection, Kitgum and Pader Districts, Kitgum town, Uganda, March 2006.

[18] Dyan Mazurana, Susan McKay, Khristopher Carlson, and Janel Kasper, "Girls in Fighting Forces and Groups: Their Recruitment, Participation, Demobilization, and Reintegration," *Peace and Conflict* 8, no. 2 (2002): 97–123.

As Margaret Walker discusses in Chapter 1 of this volume,[19] the violence and harms suffered by women, and we would add girls and boys, in contexts of armed conflict and political repression are many and are often linked. This can result in exposing children to further future harm that can result in life-altering and life-threatening experiences, even when children are not the primary target of the violence.

Finally, although it is true that children are victimized during armed conflict and under authoritarian and dictatorial regimes, it is incorrect to reduce children only to the role of passive victim. In all conflicts and situations of political violence, children can take – and many choose to take – an active role in supporting or countering the violence. Children make calculated decisions about how to access shelter, food, and medicine, and about the best ways to keep themselves and their family members safe. Sometimes the best way to do this is to support or join various political parties, armed groups, or gangs. So successful are some of these calculated strategies in meeting needs that some young people refer to the height of the violence as "the sweet times" and report finding it much harder to survive in the post-conflict period when the various factions have abandoned them.[20] Beyond the obvious role of children who take up arms to kill and maim, other children come to believe in the logic of violence when confronted with unjust and violent settings. Some may recall lynching and public killings, including burning people alive, as "good solutions" for curbing violence in the community, and they may recommend that those practices be revived in a post-conflict or post-authoritarian period to deal with criminals.[21] Hence, one should not underestimate the potentially pervasive and harmful effects of armed conflict and political violence on children's sense of "security" and "justice" in periods of so-called peace.

At the same time, many more children play a primary role in trying to help maintain the livelihoods and security of their families. At times, such activities put children at great risk and are detrimental to their own education and development. Children also take on additional responsibility to keep themselves, their families, and their families' assets safe. Consequently, children, and especially youth, must be understood and engaged as thoughtful, insightful, and active agents who shape their own lives and the communities in which they live.

---

[19] Margaret Walker, "Gender and Violence in Focus: A Background for Gender Justice in Reparations," Chapter 1 of this volume.
[20] See, for example, Mats Utas, "Fluid Research Fields: Studying Ex-Combatant Youth in the Aftermath of the Liberian Civil War," in *Children and Youth on the Front Line*, 209–236.
[21] Krisjan Rae Olson, "Children in the Grey Spaces Between War and Peace: The Uncertain Truth of Memory Acts," in *Children and Youth on the Front Line*, 145–166.

A BRIEF GENDERED ANALYSIS OF THE WORST FORMS OF DIRECT AND INDIRECT HARM CHILDREN ENDURE DURING SITUATIONS OF ARMED CONFLICT AND UNDER AUTHORITARIAN AND DICTATORIAL REGIMES

They killed them with their machetes, they strangled them and shot them. And they grabbed the children by the feet and beat them against a small tree, and they did this so many times with so many children that they beat against the tree, that the tree died.[22]

All day long the soldiers kept on torturing and massacring children, women and men in different ways. First they took the children away from their mothers. The children stayed huddled together, crying. They smashed in the heads of some of them while they were breast feeding.... When the children saw their parents fall, they fled, and there was a soldier behind a wall with a machete who cut their heads off as they ran by.... I just heard the laments and screams of the children.[23]

All national and international criminal tribunals, truth commissions, and reparations initiatives are faced with making choices about which criminal acts and human rights violations they will address and, within those, which ones they will emphasize for reparation. Before looking at the violations against children that reparations programs have focused on in the past, we offer our own views on which criminal acts and rights violations should, *at a minimum*, be considered by such bodies and initiatives, given their firm prohibition in international law, their severity, and the gravity of their negative (often lifetime-lasting) impact on children.

Significantly, in no way should the crimes and violations we discuss below be seen as an exclusive grouping or in any way suggest that it is only these violations that should be considered or addressed. Nor is it to imply any kind of hierarchy of suffering or horror. Instead, we contend that at a minimum these are the crimes and violations that bodies concerned with reparations, and those that support reparation measures, should consider.

The crimes and grave abuses against girls and boys during situations of armed conflict and, to a lesser extent, under authoritarian and dictatorial regimes encompass, first, those that directly target and affect children. These include: (1) killing or maiming of children; (2) torture and the inhuman

---

[22] Human Rights Office of the Archdiocese of Guatemala (ODHAG), *Informe Proyecto Interdiocesano de Recuperación de la Memoria Histórica (REMHI). Guatemala: Nunca Mas* (Guatemala: ODHAG, 1998), vol. II, 5.
[23] *Memoria del Silencio*, vol. III, 63.

and degrading treatment of children; (3) recruiting, conscripting, or enlisting children in armed forces and groups; (4) abduction of children; (5) rape or other grave sexual violence against girls and boys, which has been found to include sexual slavery, forced pregnancy, enforced prostitution, and sexual exploitation; and (6) forced marriage of girls by armed forces and groups. All of these crimes, with the exception of forced marriage and sexual exploitation, are named as elements of war crimes and crimes against humanity within the Elements of Crimes for the International Criminal Court. Additionally, owing to jurisprudential development within a number of international tribunals, there is an expanding understanding of how these crimes are perpetrated and experienced by victims and survivors. These tribunals have also found that these crimes constitute violations of customary law.

In addition, children experience violations when their parents or caregivers are targeted, in which case both the child and parent or caregiver is affected by the crimes and grave abuses, including: (7) witnessing of grave physical and sexual violence committed against a parent, caregiver, or sibling, including torture and inhuman and degrading treatment; (8) separation from parents who are illegally detained or put in prison, including children who are stolen from their parents; (9) the imprisonment or detention of the child with her or his parents or caregivers, including being born in prison; and (10) loss of parents owing to murder or forced disappearance.

A feminist-gendered analysis is important in understanding the ways girls, boys, men, and women are targeted and experience these violations. To illustrate, let us take the case of girls.[24] In a number of cases, girls are subject to abuses in similar ways to boys, women, and men. But often, because of power imbalances, sexism, and patriarchal control and violence against females, girls are targeted in sexual- and gender-specific ways, particularly so with systematic sexual and reproductive violence. Both Ruth Rubio-Marín and Margaret Walker in this volume discuss the ways women experience violence differently than men, and many of those insights apply to girls as well. At the same time, it cannot (and should not) be assumed that girls always have the same experiences as women. In particular, owing to their age and hoped-for virginity and lower sexual disease rates, girls may be explicitly targeted for sexual violence in ways that women are not. Girls are often specifically targeted for abduction and forced marriage by armed groups, both in patterns (e.g., attacks on girls' schools or girls' dormitories) and numbers (significantly more girls are abducted into fighting forces than are women). Because girls are often more mobile and

---

[24] Because of length limitations, it is not possible in this paper to more fully address the gendered dimensions of these crimes for both boys and girls.

age divisions of labor take them further from the home than women, they are also more likely to encounter attackers, including while moving to and from school, collecting natural resources, and transporting themselves to fields or other places of work. Girls, including very young girls, can also be targeted for extreme forms of sexual violence as perpetrators seek to terrorize and send "messages" to communities, including adult males raping to death girls under the age of four.[25]

In addition, girls are most often even more disadvantaged in laws and customary practices than are women. In patriarchal systems, their virginity and chastity is often the defining feature of their "value" and future status as a wife and mother within the community. Hence, sexual violence, mutilation of their reproductive organs or bodies, or significant visible scaring can almost completely destroy their chances of marriage and hence of reaching the status given to wives and mothers and with it access to social networks and material goods, including land and property. As girls are younger than women, they often lack the social networks, including clan networks through marriage, that women have established and rely on to support themselves. Consequently, girls often face enormous challenges accessing credit, land, property, and forums for customary justice and protection. We also should not automatically assume that older women somehow recognize and empathize with girls' more vulnerable status and hence work to meet their needs; at times, it is older women enforcing patriarchal practices, standards, and violence onto young females.

Girls and boys receive protection from both the general provisions of international humanitarian law[26] applicable to all civilians as well as the indirect benefit of those special provisions protecting pregnant women and mothers of young children. In addition, girls and boys benefit from the specific provisions of international humanitarian law that deal with child protection during armed conflict. State and nonstate responsibilities to protect children's rights as called for within the Optional Protocol to the Convention on the Rights of the Child on the Involvement of Children in Armed Conflict[27] is another area of law affording a number of rights for children in armed conflict.

---

[25] As reported to have occurred in Colombia; see Watchlist on Children and Armed Conflict, "Colombia's War on Children," 2004, http://www.watchlist.org/reports/colombia.php.
[26] Unlike human rights law, international humanitarian law contains no definition of children. Consequently, it is necessary to determine the particular age limitation from the provision in question.
[27] CRC Optional Protocol on the Rights of the Child on the Involvement of Children in Armed Conflict (2000).

Regarding the crimes and rights violations discussed in this paper, international law recognizes the severity of these violations against girls and boys, and core components of most of these crimes[28] are defined within international humanitarian and human rights law, including the Rome Statute for the International Criminal Court, as constituting grave violations, crimes against humanity, and war crimes.[29] Of the ten crimes and grave rights violations that we listed above, most violate children's civil and political rights, including the most fundamental right to life and the right to freedom from torture and inhuman and degrading treatment.[30] Children's rights to not be subject to unlawful or arbitrary arrest and detention, and when held lawfully in detention to be treated with dignity and with all due access to procedures noted in the CRC, are repeatedly undermined by a number of the crimes.[31] Other rights that are violated include freedom of movement and association,[32] particularly relevant for those children forcibly recruited into fighting forces and groups and those illegally detained, and freedom from discrimination of any kind, irrespective of the child's or his or her parent's or legal guardian's race, color, sex, language, religion, political or other opinion, national, ethnic, or social origin, property, disability, birth, or other status.[33] The latter right furthermore includes freedom from all forms of discrimination or punishment on the basis of the status, activities, expressed opinions, or beliefs of the child's parents, legal guardians,

---

[28] Although forced marriage is not yet recognized as a distinct crime under international law, its core components – namely, rape, abduction, sexual enslavement, forced labor, slavery-like conditions, torture, and so forth – are clearly recognized within international law, including the Rome Statute.

[29] The following are the Elements of Crimes pertaining to crimes against humanity and war crimes (PCNICC/2000/1/Add.2) within the Rome Statue for the International Criminal Court (1998): killing of children, Arts. 7(1)(a), 7(1)(b), 8(a)(i), 8(2)(b)(xi), 8(2)(c)(i)-1, 8(2)(e)(ix), or maiming of children, Arts. 8(2)(b)(x)-1, 8(2)(b)(xi), 8(2)(c)(i)-2, 8(2)(e)(ix), 8(2)(e)(xi)-1; using, recruiting, conscripting, or enlisting children in armed forces and groups, Arts. 8(2)(b)(xxvi), 8(2)(e)(vii); attacks against schools or hospitals, Arts. 8(2)(b)(ii), 8(2)(b)(iii), 8(2)(b)(ix), 8(2)(e)(iii), 8(2)(e)(iv); rape, Arts. 7(1)(g)-1, 8(2)(b)(xxii)-1, 8(2)(e)(vi)-1, or other grave sexual violence against children, Arts. 7(1)(g)-6, 8(2)(b)(xxii)-6, 8(2)(e)(vi)-6, including sexual slavery, Arts. 7(1)(g)-2, 8(2)(b)(xxii)-2, 8(2)(e)(vi)-2, enforced prostitution, Arts. 7(1)(g)-3, 8(2)(b)(xxii)-3, 8(2)(e)(vi)-3, and forced pregnancy, Arts. 7(1)(g)-4, 8(2)(b)(xxii)-4, 8(2)(e)(vi)-4; abduction of children, Arts. 7(1)(i), 7(1)(k); forced marriage, Arts. 7(1)(g)-6, 8(2)(b)(xxii)-6, 8(2)(e)(vi)-6; imprisonment or other severe depravation of liberty, Art. 7(1)(e), or unlawful confinement, Art. 8(2)(a)(vii)-2; torture, Arts. 7(1)(f), 8(2)(a)(ii)-1, 8(2)(c)(i)-4.

[30] International Covenant on Civil and Political Rights, A/RES/2200A (XXI), December 16, 1966; Convention against Torture and Other Cruel, Inhuman or Degrading Treatment or Punishment, A/RES/39/46, December 10, 1984; CRC, Article 37.

[31] CRC, Articles 37 and 40.

[32] CRC, Article 15.

[33] CRC, Article 2.

or family members.[34] Children's rights to enjoy the highest attainable standard of health and to facilities for the treatment of illness and rehabilitation of their health are also violated.[35] Children have a right to education on the basis of equal opportunity, which is often violated owing to the harms inflicted by the crimes we discuss below.[36] Children's right to their cultural identity, language, and values is also undermined by these crimes.[37] Their right to remain free from sexual abuse and exploitation is severely undermined,[38] as is their right to remain free from abduction, sale, trafficking,[39] and other forms of exploitation.[40] Children's right not to participate in armed hostilities is undermined in most of the conflicts witnessed to date.[41]

When parents are targeted, killed, disappeared, or unlawfully or arbitrarily detained, children suffer additional violations of their rights. In particular, children's rights to know and be cared for by their parents,[42] to preserve their identity, name, and family relations,[43] to not be separated from their parents against their will,[44] and to have privacy, a family, and a home[45] are violated.

REPARATIONS AND CHILDREN: LESSONS FROM THE PAST TO INFORM THE FUTURE

> Even though you don't want to be, you're marked forever by all of this. Sometimes you try and pretend it never happened. . . . To think that we were twelve brothers and sisters and a family. . . . what I remember of my childhood is that we were a close knit family, that my father had always taught us that, to be close. And all of a sudden there were just four of us left.[46]

We now seek to analyze the experiences, challenges, and possibilities around reparations and children by asking what role reparations may play in *partially* addressing the crimes and grave human rights violations that children endure

---

[34] CRC, Article 3.
[35] CRC, Article 24.
[36] CRC, Articles 28 and 29.
[37] CRC, Articles 8 and 30.
[38] CRC, Article 34.
[39] CRC, Article 35.
[40] CRC, Article 36.
[41] CRC, Article 39; Optional Protocol to the Convention on the Rights of the Child on the Involvement of Children in Armed Conflicts (2000).
[42] CRC, Articles 7 and 19.
[43] CRC, Article 8.
[44] CRC, Article 9.
[45] CRC, Article 16.
[46] *Memoria del Silencio*, vol. IV, 49.

during situations of armed conflict and via political violence orchestrated by authoritarian and dictatorial regimes.

In our discussion, we consider as reparations programs those measures designed to distribute direct benefits to the victims themselves – including restitution, compensation, and rehabilitation – as well as other key measures and initiatives within transitional justice that, if crafted with care, could have reparative effects, namely, rehabilitation, satisfaction, and guarantee of nonrecurrence.[47] Under satisfaction and nonrecurrence, measures include "verification of facts, official apologies and judicial rulings that establish the dignity and reputation of the victim, full public disclosure of the truth, searching for and identifying and turning over the remains of dead and disappeared persons ... application of judicial or administrative sanctions for perpetrators, and institutional reform."[48] Most often associated with compensatory measures, reparations can be in the form of monetary awards and material goods, access to services, symbolic gestures, or remedies through access to justice systems and court services. Reparations should provide a direct benefit to the survivor and can be awarded to individuals or collective groups deemed to have suffered grave violations.[49]

We agree with Pablo de Greiff[50] that reparations programs will achieve their modest goals only if they are linked with other transitional justice measures, and we cannot stress this point strongly enough. Reparations programs that are not linked to additional transitional justice measures, including prosecution, truth-telling and full disclosure, and institutional reform, will be significantly flawed.

Gender-Just Reparations Programs for Children

In reparations programs, it is not enough to compensate survivors and send them back into societies that discriminate against and are violent to them based on their sex, gender, ethnicity, race, class, or age. The need for reparations to play a small but important role in strengthening societies' abilities to uphold the rights of their citizens is clear.

Reparations, at the bare minimum, must not violate international law in the framing or carrying out of programs. In particular, international standards

---

[47] See de Greiff, "Justice and Reparations."
[48] Ibid., 452.
[49] Truth and Reconciliation Commission (TRC) of Sierra Leone, *The Final Report of the Truth and Reconciliation Commission Sierra Leone* (Freetown: TRC, 2007), vol. 2, ch. 4, "Reparations."
[50] See de Greiff, "Justice and Reparations."

for women's, girls,' and boys' rights to inheritance and property ownership, to decide if and when to marry, to freedom from violence, to freedom of expression and association, and to health care and education, among others, should serve as the benchmark for reparations frameworks and programs and should be adhered to and upheld. Where countries have obligated themselves to international laws regarding the rights of women and children, national laws that violate children's and women's rights should be brought into compliance to ensure that individual and community reparations do not replicate discrimination and violations of rights or block access to them. Additionally, they should ensure that survivors are able to receive the full benefits of reparations awarded to them without the negative effects of sex, gender, ethnic, class, or age discrimination. More explicitly, this means that discrimination of this sort in national and customary laws and practices cannot be tolerated, should in no way be replicated in the reparations programs, and should be actively identified and countered. Addressing these forms of discrimination is made even more urgent by the fact that women and girls are often more at risk to both new and old forms of violence in so-called "post-conflict," "peaceful" societies.[51]

In order to learn from the past to inform the present and the future, and to determine and better understand which crimes were considered for benefits and which forms of reparations were most often recommended for or offered to youth and children, we reviewed past reparations programs in eight countries: Argentina, Chile (which has seen two separate commissions and reparations processes),[52] Guatemala, Peru, Rwanda, South Africa, Sierra Leone, and Timor-Leste. It is important to note that, to date, in several of these countries no reparations have yet been awarded. Nonetheless, recommendations for the scope of the reparations programs have been made, and in such cases we drew on this material for our analysis below. In addition, we reviewed the final reports of truth commissions where these reports were available, since within their mandates they are also (increasingly it seems) directed to offer a framework for reparations for victims and survivors.

---

[51] Ruth Rubio-Marín, ed., *What Happened to the Women? Gender and Reparations for Human Rights Violations* (New York: Social Science Research Council, 2006); Emily Bruno, "When Do We Get to Peace? Patterns in Gender-based Violence in Post-Conflict Liberia," thesis prepared for Master of Arts in International Law and Diplomacy, Fletcher School, Tufts University; see also the chapters by Walker and Rubio-Marín in this volume.

[52] Chile has experienced two truth commissions, with the most recent currently ongoing. In this chapter, we provide information on both the first truth commission and the subsequent reparation law that was signed on January 31, 1992 (see also *Report of the Chilean National Commission on Truth and Reconciliation* [Notre Dame, IN: University of Notre Dame Press, 1993]), and on the second, the Commission on Political Imprisonment and Torture, which began in 2004 and is ongoing.

Recognizing and Acknowledging Crimes against Children

Every child in this country has got a story to tell: a heartbreaking one. Unfortunately, only a handful of these stories will be told and made known to the world. But the devastating impact lingers and endures all the time. It continues to linger in the minds and hearts of young people.[53]

Margaret Walker notes that "most victims of violence, whether male or female, adult or child, will suffer their losses – emotional, material, social, moral, and spiritual – without significant attention, much less redress."[54] The fact that in today's conflicts many of the rights violations are committed by nonstate actors means that the mandates of national and international tribunals and truth commissions should consider a broad notion of state responsibility by omission.

As we begin this section on identifying and acknowledging crimes and harms against children, there are two important facts to keep in mind. First, nearly all past truth commissions have failed to consult with child survivors of grave rights violations or with organizations dedicated to children's rights in constructing reparations frameworks and programs, including the determination of which rights violations would be addressed and hence who could benefit. With the notable exceptions of Peru and Sierra Leone, in no other reparations program were child survivors of grave rights violations or child rights organizations systematically consulted to help shape the scope, processes, or outcomes of the programs. In the few cases where there were specific hearings for youth, such as in South Africa, there was little gender analysis or reflection regarding the crimes and harms youth suffered.[55] As a result, child survivors and their advocates played little to no role in shaping the understanding of the commissions and resulting reparations guidelines or programs.

Second, the majority of past truth commissions and fact-finding bodies failed to adequately include gender issues within questionnaires and forms used to collect data and testimonies from survivors. The results of such omissions are often a weakened ability of the commissions and reparations programs to adequately address gender-based and sexually based violations.[56] In addition,

---

[53] Statement by a children's group upon making their submission to the Truth and Reconciliation Commission of Sierra Leone; *The Final Report of the Truth and Reconciliation Commission of Sierra Leone*, vol. 3b, ch. 4, "Children and the Armed Conflict," para. 124.

[54] Walker, "Gender and Violence in Focus," Chapter 1 of this volume.

[55] Beth Goldblatt, "Evaluating the Gender Content of Reparations: Lessons from South Africa," in *What Happened to the Women?* 48–91.

[56] See *What Happened to the Women?* and in particular the case studies by Paz Bailey on Guatemala and Goldblatt on South Africa. See also UNICEF and ICTJ, *Children and Truth Commissions: Basic Considerations*.

the failure to collect age-sensitive data or include children in interviews results in the exclusion of the voices of children and their own understandings and insights into their experiences, needs, and rights.[57] Again, in the light of this poor past record, Sierra Leone stands as an important exception (which we discuss in detail below).

We now turn our attention to the eight countries and their efforts regarding reparations for children victims and survivors of crimes and grave rights violations committed during situations of armed conflict or due to political violence under authoritarian regimes: Argentina, Chile, Guatemala, Peru, Rwanda, Sierra Leone, South Africa, and Timor-Leste.[58] These were selected in part because they represent a range of recent conflict-affected countries where it is widely recognized that children and youth were specifically targeted, and crimes and grave rights violations against children and youth were widespread and systematic. Additionally, in each of the eight countries, tribunals or truth commissions were established, and reparations guidelines were put forward, reparations programs were established, or both. Finally, because they cover a time period ranging from the 1970s to 2007, they provide us with a means to examine developments regarding children and reparations over time. Hence, these eight countries provide a good lens through which to think about children, gender, grave crimes and rights violations, and reparations.

In these eight countries, truth commissions or presidential decrees called for the establishment of reparations programs to address grave rights violations that came about as a result of armed conflict or political violence. To date, reparations programs have been or are being carried out in five of the eight countries (Table 4.1). The remaining countries are split between those in which guidelines were established regarding reparations (and these guidelines vary widely) but in which no reparations have yet been carried out (one country), and those in which reparations were suggested by truth commissions but no reparation programs have been established (two countries).

To date, the majority of national and international tribunals and truth commissions have an uneven and overall poor record of recognizing or addressing

---

[57] See Elizabeth Gibbons, Christian Salazar, Guenay Sari, *Guatemala: Der Krieg und Die Kinder* (German Committee for UNICEF, 2003) (English version: *Between War and Peace: Young Generations on Wings of the Phoenix*, unpublished).

[58] To date, truth commissions or similar fact-finding bodies have been active in 24 countries, some of which also included reparation programs: Argentina, Bolivia, Chad, Chile, Ecuador, El Salvador, Germany, Ghana, Guatemala, Haiti, Nepal, Nigeria, Panama, Peru, Philippines, Serbia and Montenegro (formerly Yugoslavia), Sierra Leone, South Africa, South Korea, Sri Lanka, Timor-Leste, Uganda, Uruguay, and Zimbabwe. In addition to those named, Brazil, Malawi, and the United States have initiated reparation programs for select victims of political violence.

TABLE 4.1. *Countries and reparations programs as of 2008*

Countries where reparations programs were established and reparations carried out	Countries where reparations programs were suggested by commissions but have not yet been adopted by governments
Argentina	Sierra Leone
Chile (both commissions)	Timor-Leste
Guatemala[59]	
Peru[60]	
South Africa[61]	
Rwanda	

the range of grave violations suffered by children. Furthermore, the gender aspect of their experiences – the different ways in which boys and girls were affected by the violence and in the aftermath of violence – has been poorly addressed and largely neglected.

In the final reports of the truth commissions, it is often difficult to identify what happened to children and youth, and even more difficult to comprehend how those experiences were gendered and had gendered outcomes. Often, it is not possible to determine the age of the person whose testimony is given because what is assigned primary importance is the relation of the speaker to the victim (e.g., mother, father, daughter, son, wife, husband, etc.).[62] In several cases, children's experiences are explicitly brought to light in a "youth chapter," which is dedicated to crimes and rights violations against children and youth (Table 4.2). However, within these chapters, with the exception of Sierra Leone, little attention is paid to how girls and boys experienced crimes differently. Additionally, when statistics are offered on the kinds of crimes

---

[59] In Guatemala, individual economic reparations in the form of cash have been received by a number of victims, and reparations to help reestablish the dignity of the survivors, such as exhumation and burial of their dead, have been carried out.

[60] In Peru, no individual reparations have been awarded, and to date collective reparations have occurred only in select regions.

[61] Although several reparation funds have been conceived of, only one national reparation program currently exists in Rwanda, *Fonds d'Assistance aux Rescapés du Génocide* (FARG) (Assistance Fund for Genocide Survivors). For a detailed discussion of the numerous reparation funds that have yet to be enacted, see Heidy Rombouts, "Women and Reparations in Rwanda: A Long Path to Travel," in *What Happened to the Women?* 194–245.

[62] Hence, it is often not possible to determine the age of those speaking, as, for example, testimony could be given by a 40-year-old daughter about her 72-year-old father.

TABLE 4.2. *Final reports of truth commissions (or similar bodies) and chapters on children and youth*

Countries *with* chapters dedicated to the experiences of children and youth	Countries *without* chapters dedicated to the experiences of children and youth	Countries without reports or whose reports are not yet complete
Argentina Guatemala Peru Sierra Leone Timor-Leste	Chile (both commissions) South Africa	Rwanda

children experience, there is no breakdown of crimes experienced by girls or boys; rather, they are all lumped together.[63]

Though incorporating children's experiences throughout final commission reports is necessary, having dedicated chapters is also useful because these make explicit the experiences of children and the crimes and grave violations committed against them. These chapters also help the commission, state institutions, and citizens better understand the experiences of children, which can play an essential role in mobilizing resources (human and material) for addressing the harms suffered and for recovering lost rights. Such chapters play an important role in helping determine which crimes against children are addressed by reparations programs and which children can benefit; inevitably, it is the crimes highlighted in truth commission final reports that make their way into the parameters of reparations programs.[64] Collection of gender-disaggregated data and strong gender analyses would serve to further strengthen these chapters and help in crafting reparations programs that address the crimes girls and boys suffer.

For the eight countries, we compiled a comprehensive list of all the crimes committed directly against children (i.e., where children are the primary victim) and recognized within guidelines provided by the truth commissions for establishing child beneficiaries within reparations programs (Guatemala, Sierra Leone, Timor-Leste). In countries where actual reparations legislation exists (Argentina, Chile, Peru, Rwanda, South Africa), we note which crimes qualified children to benefit from reparations programs (Table 4.3).

[63] For example, in the final truth commission reports for South Africa and Peru, there are no sex-disaggregated data for crimes committed against children or youth.
[64] It should, of course, be noted that not all reparations come as a result of a truth commission, as some reparations may come as the result of a presidential decree or legislation by parliament.

TABLE 4.3. *Crimes where children are the* primary victim *recognized by truth commissions or national legislation that qualify children to benefit from reparations programs or both*

Crime or harm	Argentina	Chile 1990[65]	Chile 2003[66]	Guatemala	Peru	Rwanda	Sierra Leone	South Africa	Timor-Leste
Children absent owing to forced disappearance	X			X	X				
Children abducted					X			X	
Children born owing to rape			X[67]		X		X[68]		
Children born in detention, or children detained with mother	X		X						
Children forced into prostitution				X					
Children forced into sexual slavery							X		X
Children forced into servility				X					
Children forcibly married							X		X
Children illegally removed from their parents				X					
Children killed by individual acts of political violence				X	X			X	
Children who escaped genocidal acts and persecution intended to kill them and who are in need						X			
Children who experienced sexual mutilation of their genitals and breasts				X			X		
Children who were raped				X	X		X	X	X
Children recruited into fighting forces				X	X		X		
Children who suffered psychological damage					X		X		X
Children who suffered sexual violence				X			X	X	X
Children who were tortured			X[69]	X	X			X	
Children with physical injuries, such as amputees and those who were victims of sexual violence					X		X		X
Fraudulently adopted children				X					

[65] See note 61. This column represents only the first truth commission and subsequent reparation law that was signed on January 31, 1992. See also *Report of the Chilean National Commission on Truth and Reconciliation*. The Truth and Reconciliation Commission (1990–1991) identified the disappeared, executed, and victims of political violence, and proposed pensions and other benefits for living relatives of these victims. These reparations were implemented through law No. 19.123 since 1992.

(See footnotes 66, 67, 68, and 69 on page 181)

As Table 4.3 illustrates, most reparations programs consider only a small proportion of the actual crimes, and the grave rights violations that follow such crimes, that girls and boys directly suffered. In particular, crimes that are gender based are often neglected, even though it is acknowledged that they were widespread throughout the armed conflict or political violence by external reports. Another reality illustrated in Table 4.3 is that there is little to no consistency within truth commissions and/or national legislation establishing reparations programs in identifying and acknowledging crimes and grave rights violations against children. Hence, the vast majority of crimes against children are not acknowledged, and most child survivors do not qualify for reparations.

The following table provides a comprehensive listing of crimes committed primarily against close relations of children, most often their father or mother, but that also constitute violations against the children themselves and therefore may qualify them for reparations (Table 4.4). Some truth commissions and reparations programs label such children as "secondary victims," but others contend that primary victims also include the relatives and dependants of those against whom crimes were committed, because their suffering is the direct result of the grave violation.

Table 4.4 illustrates that in regards to violations committed against their parent(s), there is little consistency within truth commissions, national legislation, or both that establish reparations programs in terms of which crimes enable children to qualify for reparations. Important exceptions, for whom there are strong trends in awarding reparations, are children whose parent(s) were (1) forcibly disappeared or (2) killed by wartime violations or as an act of political violence, including executions and torture, undue force, and abuse of power resulting in death. Furthermore, and importantly, only when the parent died because of the crime or disappeared and never returned were children in Peru and South Africa able to qualify for any of the reparations listed in Table 4.4.

It is important to note that in the countries where the largest number of crimes qualified children for access to reparations – Peru, Sierra Leone, and Timor-Leste – to date, no individual reparations have been awarded.[70]

---

[66] The Political Imprisonment and Torture Commission (2003–2005) identified political prisoners, 94% of whom claimed to have been tortured. The Commission proposed several measures of reparations.

[67] Only if the mother was a political prisoner and as part of her torture and abuse was raped during this time and conceived as a result.

[68] Mothers have to be single in order for children to qualify as beneficiaries.

[69] This includes children who were detained as political prisoners with a parent and were subjected to torture.

[70] As of the writing of this manuscript.

TABLE 4.4. *Crimes in which children are victims owing to their status as a relative or dependant of those against whom crimes were committed and who qualify for reparations*

Crime or harm	Argentina	Chile 1990	Chile 2003	Guatemala	Peru	Rwanda	Sierra Leone	South Africa	Timor-Leste
Children of amputees							X		
Children whose mothers were victims of sexual violence									X[71]
Children of victims of sexual violence, including rape, sexual slavery, mutilation of breast or genitals, and forced marriage							X		
Children of war-wounded victims							X		
Children of war widows							X[72]		X
Children who were orphaned by war									X
Children whose parent(s) were forcibly disappeared	X	X	X	X[73]	X[74]				
Children whose parent(s) were killed by wartime violations or as an act of political violence, including executions, killing, torture, severe ill-treatment, undue force and abuse of power resulting in death		X[75]	X	X	X[76]		X	X[77]	X[78]
Children whose parent(s) were killed in massacres deemed to constitute genocide				X					
Children whose parent(s) were raped and died as a result of the crime or other crimes carried out in conjunction with the violation				X	X				

[71] Mother must be single in order for child to qualify as beneficiary.
[72] Mother must be breadwinner of house in order for child to qualify as beneficiary.
[73] The parent(s) must have died as a result of the crime in order for child to qualify as beneficiary.
[74] The parent(s) must have died as a result of the crime in order for child to qualify as beneficiary. However, if the body is still missing but the disappearance is proved, the family should receive reparations.

(See footnotes 75, 76, 77, and 78 on page 183)

There are reasons why in some countries a number of crimes qualify children for reparations and in others very few crimes (and hence children) do. To illustrate, in Sierra Leone, there are several key reasons why we see a more sophisticated and comprehensive approach to crimes and rights violations against children. First, the mandate for the Truth and Reconciliation Commission (TRC) for Sierra Leone was the first to explicitly address and call for investigation into grave rights violations against children committed during the war. Importantly, in this respect, truth commission mandates should include specific reference to crimes against children, and go so far as to name particular kinds of violations that occurred during the armed conflict or political violence, as was done in Sierra Leone, Timor-Leste, and recently in Liberia. Second, as a result of its strong mandate, the TRC's hearings and final report specifically addressed both a range of crimes and rights violations against children, as well as the gendered nature of this violence and its effects on girl and boy survivors in the post-conflict period.

Third, recent international jurisprudence was extremely influential on the mandate and results of the Sierra Leone TRC. The most promising developments in gender-based and sexually based crimes have come in cases before the International Criminal Tribunal for the Former Yugoslavia (ICTY) and, to a much less extent, the International Criminal Tribunal for Rwanda (ICTR), whose rulings are applicable to women and girls and, in some cases, men and boys.[79] Comparatively, however, there has been little development in expanding jurisprudence on crimes against children.[80] In addition, the Elements of Crimes for the Rome Statute provided an important framework in defining and setting broader parameters to understand crimes committed during the

[75] In Chile, five crimes are included here: execution, in any of its forms; use of undue force leading to death; abuse of power resulting in death, if the government has condoned the action or permitted it to go unpunished; torture resulting in death; murder attempts leading to death, committed by private citizens, including acts of terrorism, whether indiscriminate or selective, as well as other kinds of attacks on life. *Report of the Chilean National Commission on Truth and Reconciliation.*
[76] In Peru, four crimes are listed: extrajudicial execution, murder, arbitrary detention, and torture that results in death.
[77] In South Africa, four crimes are noted, including killing, abduction, and torture or severe ill-treatment that results in death.
[78] In Timor-Leste, only children whose parent(s) who have been killed will qualify in this category of crime.
[79] See also Angela M. Banks, "Sexual Violence and International Criminal Law: An Analysis of the Ad Hoc Tribunal's Jurisprudence and the International Criminal Courts Elements of Crimes," prepared for the Women's Initiatives for Gender Justice, The Hague, Netherlands, 2005.
[80] For example, neither the ICTY nor the ICTR has had any specific focus on crimes against children.

conflict in Sierra Leone, including gender-based and sexually based crimes and crimes against children. It was only with the Special Court for Sierra Leone that a tribunal specifically and strongly sought prosecution for violations against children, primarily for forced recruitment and the use of both girls and boys as child soldiers, as well as the widespread abduction and sexual slavery of girls by fighting forces. It would follow that we could rightly expect to see such crimes addressed by the TRC for Sierra Leone.

On this note, we echo Margaret Walker's point in Chapter 1 of this volume that it is important that international jurisprudence continue to expand to recognize the range of *both* sexual and nonsexual forms of violent crimes against girls and boys. For example, the charge of forced marriage raised by the Office of the Prosecutor in the Special Court for Sierra Leone represents an important step, in this respect, in beginning to flesh out the ways both sexual and nonsexual violations against girls and young women have overlapping and cumulative effects that are sex- and gender-specific.[81]

Challenges in Current Definitions of Child Beneficiaries within Reparations Programs

An analysis of the eight countries' reparations guidelines or programs and their treatment of child beneficiaries reveals several important challenges that should be considered in shaping future reparations efforts. Upon closer examination of the crimes that are supposed to qualify children to receive reparations, we find that there are a number of obstacles that prevent many, if not most, child survivors from actually qualifying for or receiving benefits. These appear in the form of children qualifying for reparations only or largely based on violations experienced by their parents; age or time limits regarding qualified children receiving benefits; age-appropriate reparations benefits; requiring multiple harms within crimes and violations experienced by children; selecting crimes and defining them in ways that exclude most child victims and survivors; and failure to consider children as potential victims and hence lack of outreach to child survivors. We identify and discuss each observation and provide specific examples to illustrate our points.

Children as Dependants or "Secondary" Victims

In a number of reparations programs, children appear as rights holders and rights claimants regarding the crimes and violations directed against them

---

[81] Khristopher Carlson and Dyan Mazurana, "Forced Marriage within the Lord's Resistance Army, Uganda," Feinstein International Center, Tufts University, 2008.

TABLE 4.5. *Total number of categories of crimes or harms by which children could qualify for reparations by country*

	Argentina	Chile 1990	Chile 2003	Guatemala	Peru	Rwanda	Sierra Leone	South Africa	Timor-Leste
Total number of crimes that qualify children for inclusion in reparations programs	3	6	5	15	12	1	14	6	10
Number of crimes in which violation directly against child is determining factor	2	0	3	11	9	1	9	5	6
Number of crimes in which child's status as relative or dependant of victim is determining factor	1	6	2	4	3	0	5	1	4

and that they themselves have suffered. In addition, they also appear as rights holders in relation to their parents' lives and the conflict's effects on those adults (Table 4.5).

It is important that children be recognized as rights holders over their own bodies and physical integrity. Failure to acknowledge crimes directly committed against children's bodies and minds may reflect misperceptions regarding children as political actors and agents and rights holders. At the same time, recognition of their victim status owing to the nature of crimes and grave rights violations committed against their parents or caregivers, and hence themselves, is a necessary and important step in ensuring recognition and reparations for children who have suffered these harms.

Age- and Time-Limited Reparations Benefits

Because of the time lapse between the occurrence of violations and the establishment of formal reparation programs, it is likely that many of the potential "child" beneficiaries will be adults when such programs are enacted. In some past reparations programs, such as in South Africa and Argentina, child beneficiaries were able to receive cash reparations, in the form of a pension, only until their 18th or 21st birthday (respectively). As a result, older children do not receive the same amount of cash benefits as younger children. Yet studies comparing the effects of grave crimes and rights violations during armed conflict on youth of different ages find that older child survivors tend to be worse off than younger ones in their physical health, mental well-being, ability to recover opportunities to support themselves economically, and ability to recover lost educational opportunities.[82] Such findings suggest that adolescents who have suffered grave crimes and rights violations are actually a group that needs increased and sustained benefits and assistance, not early cut off.

In other cases, qualified "child" beneficiaries have been denied access to benefits because deadlines expired for receiving benefits owing to inefficient reparations programs. To avoid this injustice, clear guidelines on "grandfathering in" qualified child beneficiaries should be put in place. This could be rather easily addressed as most reparations measures cover a particular time period of a conflict, which should be the determining factor, not the age of the person at the time they apply for reparations.

Age-Appropriate Reparation Benefits

Reparations programs should consider age-appropriate benefits because children's needs range significantly depending on their age and ability. For example, in cases where the beneficiary is nearing adulthood, access to accelerated schooling or assistance with advanced technical training or university education – as was provided in Argentina and by the 2004 commission in Chile – is more appropriate than education benefits that cease upon the completion of secondary school.

Age-appropriate benefits should also take into consideration the responsibilities of the child or adolescent receiving the award. In the case of child-headed households, this is particularly pertinent because eldest girls and boys have to take on numerous adult responsibilities in caring for younger siblings and maintaining the family. Such children nearly always end up curbing their own access to education opportunities and health care. In our work in conflict zones in south, west, and east Africa, we have found that in particular it is the eldest girl who drops out of school, maintains the home, and looks after younger siblings while the child-headed family scrapes together whatever it can to help the eldest boy attend school (in hopes that later he will be able to access a job and maintain the family). In other cases, the eldest boy may migrate for work, sending back remittances to the family. In both cases, the

---

[82] Chris Blattman, Jeanie Annan, and Roger Horton, "The State of Youth and Youth Protection in Northern Uganda: Findings from the Survey for War Affected Youth," report for UNICEF Uganda, September 2006, http://www.sway-uganda.org/SWAY.Phase1.FinalReport.pdf.

majority of the burden of raising the younger siblings falls to the eldest girl in the family.

Requiring Children to Have Experienced Multiple Harms within Human Rights Violations to Qualify for Reparations

There is also a pattern within some past reparations guidelines or programs to make the categories of beneficiaries so multilayered and restricted that few child victims are able to qualify. For example, the Commission for Reception, Truth and Reconciliation (CAVR) of Timor-Leste, set up to deal with rights violations by all armed groups between 1974 and 1999, prioritized victims of grave human rights violations who were thought to have endured the most harm. Children are mentioned within a category called "children affected by the conflict." This is defined as follows:

> Children who suffer from disabilities due to grave human rights violations; children whose parents were killed or disappeared; and children born out of an act of sexual violence whose mother is single; and children who suffer psychological damage. Children will be eligible for reparations if they were 18 years of age or younger on 25 October 1999.[83]

According to this definition, in two cases it is not enough for the child to have suffered the crime – she also must be physically disabled by the crime or suffering psychological damage or both in order to qualify. In a third case, for children born of rape, their mother must be single in order for them to qualify for reparations, thus replicating patriarchal norms that ascribe primary meaning to women's relationships with men, not their own rights or the rights of their child(ren), including the right to reparation.

Selecting Crimes and Defining Them in Ways that Exclude Most Child Victims

Another issue has to do with how categories of children are identified for inclusion in reparations programs. Problematically, the categories exclude many of the most recurrent crimes and grave rights violations that children experience during the conflict. To illustrate, in Guatemala, the PNR regulations identify particular crimes that merit reparations, including "forced recruitment of

---

[83] *Final Report of the Commission for Reception, Truth and Reconciliation in East Timor (CAVR)*, Part 11, "Recommendations," http://www.cavr-timorleste.org or http://www.etan.org/news/2006/cavr.htm.

minors" and "violations against children." Only children who meet the criteria established within these categories of crimes will be eligible for material reparation.

Forced recruitment of minors is defined by the PNR as the incorporation "against their will of minors for undertaking military and paramilitary tasks, exercising any type of pressure on them, violating the principle of non-discrimination for racial, economic, social, ideological or any ground."[84] Within this category of crime, it appears that parameters have been set that would include both boys and girls. It remains to be seen, however, whether there will be sufficient elasticity within the category to ensure inclusion of children associated with fighting forces as defined by the Cape Town Principles[85] and further strengthened by the Paris Principles. Adherence to this broader and more representative definition is particularly necessary to help ensure that girls who have been part of armed forces and groups are able to equally benefit from reparations programs. Girls are often not seen as "real" members of fighting forces and groups because of a gender bias that equates "soldiers" with "males with guns."[86]

Furthermore, within the PNR, violations against children are defined as "illegal removal of children and infants from their parents, enforced prostitution of male and female children and adolescents, fraudulent adoptions, as well as submission to servility; all of these produced within the context of the internal armed conflict."[87] There is no consideration of rape or other forms of sexual enslavement, apart from enforced prostitution, for which the conflict was known. Such narrow definitions of violations against children

---

[84] Article 15 of Governmental Agreement Num. 43–2005, Chapter 1, Article 3, as cited in Claudia Paz y Paz Bailey, "Guatemala: Gender and Reparations for Human Rights Violations," in *What Happened to the Women?*, 107.

[85] According to the Cape Town Principles, a child soldier is "any person under 18 years of age who is part of any kind of regular or irregular armed force in any capacity, including but not limited to cooks, porters, messengers, and those accompanying such groups, other than purely as family members. It includes girls recruited for sexual purposes and forced marriage. It does not, therefore, only refer to a child who is carrying or has carried arms." *Cape Town annotated principles and best practices* (UNICEF, April 30, 1997), 1, adopted by the participants in the Symposium on the Prevention of Recruitment of Children into the Armed Forces and Demobilization and Social Reintegration of Child Soldiers in Africa, organized by UNICEF in cooperation with the NGO subgroup of the NGO Working Group on the Convention on the Rights of the Child, Cape Town, South Africa.

[86] Susan McKay and Dyan Mazurana, *Where Are the Girls? Girls in Fighting Forces in Northern Uganda, Sierra Leone, and Mozambique: Their Lives During and After War* (Montreal: Rights and Democracy, 2004).

[87] Article 17 of Governmental Agreement Num. 43–2005, as cited in Paz Bailey, "Guatemala," 107.

fail to address the systematic, recurrent, and grave human rights violations experienced by children.

Failure to Consider Children as Potential Victims and Hence Lack of Outreach to Child Survivors

Although there are important exceptions, such as in Guatemala, Peru, Sierra Leone, and Timor-Leste, in some countries there was a failure to consider that children had also been subjected to crimes and grave rights violations due to the conflict. This failure resulted in a lack of outreach to child survivors and, we hypothesize, a number of persons who were children when they were affected not being aware of reparations. The recent Chilean Commission on Political Imprisonment and Torture (2003–2005) illustrates this point. In defining the scope of its work, the Commission did not adequately consider, and hence was unaware of, children who may have been victims. As people came to the Commission to speak out, it became clear that some of the victims had been children at the time. A number of children had been imprisoned and tortured for their own social and political activism, and others were kidnapped with their parents, were born in prison, were fetuses at the time their pregnant mothers were tortured, or were born of rape as a form of torture in prison. As these cases came to light, the Commission ensured that such persons could qualify as victims.[88]

Benefits for Child Victims and Survivors of Armed Conflict and Authoritarian and Dictatorial Regimes

Most reparations are distributed either individually or collectively, and appear in material or symbolic forms. Here we offer our thoughts on past benefits for children, and within these discussions we seek to move from learning from the past to further push the envelope of gender-just reparations for children in the future.

Individual Benefits

Individual benefits are those benefits that are intended for and awarded to individuals. Here we discuss cash benefits, access to education and health services, restitution of property, shelter, and services that help offer closure.

---

[88] Elizabeth Lira, personal correspondence with authors, March 13, 2008.

We also discuss some of the challenges associated with these benefits as they relate to girls and boys and their families.

CASH BENEFITS: PENSIONS, LUMP SUM AWARDS, AWARDS IN INSTALLMENTS

One of the most common forms of individual material reparation for children comes in the child's receipt of a percentage of financial reparation for a deceased parent who died from grave human rights violations, or an annual percentage of the deceased parent's pension. These reparations typically end once the child reaches an upper age limit, although in some cases they may continue if the child is impaired or disabled. For example, in Argentina such benefits expired when children turned 21 (later revised to 25) years of age.[89]

The amount of the pension varies among countries. In Argentina, children of disappeared persons received tax-free pensions equivalent to the minimum amount awarded by the pension system for ordinary retirement to workers in the employ of another.[90] In Chile, in the first reparations program, a monthly pension was awarded up to $140,000, plus a percentage equivalent to contributions for health care.[91] Beneficiaries included the victim's wife and biological children under 25 years of age, or disabled children of any age, born legitimate, biological, adopted, or illegitimate.[92]

Where children are entitled to a portion of a deceased parent's cash benefits, it is usually half or less than half of what is awarded to the surviving spouse. For example, in Chile the surviving spouse receives 40% of the pension, the mother of the victim (or father if the mother is dead) receives 30%, the mother or father of the victim's biological children (in the case where this is different than the spouse) receives 15%, and any legitimate, biological, adopted, or illegitimate child of the victim receives 15%. If there is more than one child, all can claim 15% even if the total surpasses the $140,000 limit.[93] In other cases, a flat sum is awarded to the surviving spouse, with no consideration for the number of children. For example, in South Africa the award was a one-time, flat payment of US$3,750 (a sum substantially less than the $2,713 to be paid every six months for six years that the truth commission had recommended),

---

[89] Law 23.466, "Pensions for Relatives of Disappeared Persons," Article 1, reproduced and translated into English in *The Handbook of Reparations*, 702–703.
[90] Ibid.
[91] Ibid., Article 19.
[92] Ibid., Article 20.
[93] Ibid., Article 20 (d).

which did not take into account number of dependants. If no spouse was alive, the money went to the surviving children in equal shares, or to the parents or other relatives of the victim.[94] In Guatemala, the recommendation is for payment over three years (except for those over 50) of US$3,200 to each victim of extrajudicial executions, death in massacre, or forced disappearance, and $2,667 to each victim of torture, rape, or sexual violence. In the case of a deceased victim, the truth commission recommends that the benefit go to the direct family to share equally among spouse or partner, children, mother, and father.

In a number of cases, all children born to the victim, whether within an officially recognized marriage or not, qualify for benefits. This is a necessary recognition that most children are born into and live within families in which the parents may not be officially married. In Peru, for example, the intent of the Truth and Reconciliation Commission in determining who qualified for reparations was to go beyond the notion of the family unit considered by the Peruvian Civil Code, and to recognize the particular nature of the family unit prevailing in the high Andean and jungle communities as well as the impact that violence may have had on those family relations.[95] In fewer cases, as in Rwanda, it appears that children born outside of officially recognized marriages will not be able to qualify for future reparations programs that are currently under design.[96] Obviously, the latter cases represent discrimination against children born out of wedlock, as the majority of rural marriages are traditional marriages or living arrangements that are rarely sanctified by the state. In addition, particularly in Africa, during situations of armed conflict and political violence, women may become responsible for additional children (sometimes called "orphans" even though one parent may still be alive but is unable to care for them). To date, few if any reparations programs we are aware of have taken into account the needs of these children; if they are not born to the victim, most do not qualify for reparations assistance, even if they were completely dependant on the victim.

Less often, children who directly experienced the violation themselves are eligible to receive cash as a form of reparation. For example, in Argentina children born during the deprivation of liberty of their mothers, or who, being minors, were detained with their parents (provided at least one of them was detained or disappeared for political reasons, whether under the control of the National Executive Brand, military tribunals, or both), qualify for cash

[94] See Goldblatt, "Evaluating the Gender Content of Reparations," 66–67.
[95] Julie Guillerot, coordinator of the reparations team of the Truth and Reconciliation Commission for Peru, personal communication with Dyan Mazurana, June 2007.
[96] See Rombouts, "Women and Reparations in Rwanda."

reparations.⁹⁷ The award was a one-time payment of a lump sum of 20 times the monthly remuneration of a high-level civil servant (Level A, Grade 8) with an ability to increase this amount by 50%, 70%, or 100% for very grievous injuries suffered by the child.⁹⁸ As discussed earlier for Guatemala, victims are to be awarded flat sums based on the category of violation.

Either in terms of receiving benefits as dependants or relatives of a victim, or in terms of being identified as victims themselves, in only a few of these cases were provisions made to work with the children on how to manage financial reparations. In the majority of cases, monies awarded to children often end up in the hands of their mother or father. Although ideally one would assume that parents should be the ones to receive the money and would use it in the best interest of the child, the few studies that exist on this matter, as well as our own observations from working with child survivors, suggest the issue is not so clear.⁹⁹

There are few studies that look at how people spend reparations awards,¹⁰⁰ and none have looked in-depth at how children do. A rare study on gender and reparations in South Africa found that when men received cash reparations they tended to spend the money individually, with women in their families having little to no say regarding how it was used. On the other hand, women tended to use their cash awards for the benefits of others.¹⁰¹ When children were paid, practically speaking, the money went to the adult who cared for them, usually a woman. "This was also a positive step for reparation for women,"¹⁰² claims the author; but she goes on to reveal that in interviews with women who received reparations monies, "The single payment, being a small amount, was used up very quickly by most victims, and they did not have the effect of providing for the maintenance of families.... Interviewees described the money as 'peanuts' and 'nothing' and said they had spent all of it on debts."¹⁰³ Such findings lead us to wonder how this money was used to the benefit of the children, who after all were to receive part of those reparations. We wonder how

---

⁹⁷ Law 25.914, "Human Rights," reproduced and translated into English in *The Handbook of Reparations*, 729–731.

⁹⁸ Ibid., 730.

⁹⁹ See Goldblatt, "Evaluating the Gender Content of Reparations." We have also heard from a number of children that when they are awarded compensation or assistance and return home with it, their father or mother may demand the cash or item and then use the cash or sell the item to generate cash to buy goods for themselves or the larger family.

¹⁰⁰ See Goldblatt, "Evaluating the Gender Content of Reparations"; Ereshnee Naidu, "Memorialisation: A Fractured Opportunity," Centre for the Study of Violence and Reconciliation, 2004. This said, numerous studies on poverty and development show that women are more responsible than men with cash and other material benefits.

¹⁰¹ Goldblatt, "Evaluating the Gender Content of Reparations," 66.

¹⁰² Ibid.

¹⁰³ Ibid., 68.

Reparations as a Means for Recognizing and Addressing Crimes 193

these children, who lost out on education, health care, and so on, benefited when all the money was spent paying off debts, which we imagine the family may have quickly reincurred owing to the fact that one of its breadwinners was now dead. Though this study was conducted only in South Africa, it is not hard to imagine similar patterns existing in other countries.

The distribution of cash or financial payments to children survivors presents a number of challenges. Although we know of no studies that look at how children spend reparations monies, there are some that may provide important insights for reparations programs that give children cash. One of the few areas where we do have studies on cash given to children is reintegration programs that seek to assist children who have been part of fighting forces and groups that participated in the armed conflict or political violence. These studies find that giving cash to children leads to a number of negative outcomes.[104] First, when it is known that a cash award is available, children (of all ages) may be pushed by surviving parents, relatives, or abusive authority figures (such as their captors or commanders, who often continue in the post-conflict period to wield power and control over them) to participate in such programs against their wishes, so that the adult can then take the money from the child.[105] In other cases, particularly where there is great stigma attached to the violation, such as those regarding children formerly associated with fighting forces or forced wives, the payment may be seen by some in the community as a "reward" for carrying out or supporting those who carried out atrocities. This can lead to resentment and increased tension and disharmony between the children and their return community.

When the child brings home the money, she and her parents or caregivers may also have conflicting ideas about how it should be spent. This may especially be the case for girls who no longer follow the instructions of their parents or caregivers, thus challenging gender and age roles in the house. For example, some girls in Sierra Leone, given money for their participation in the disarmament, demobilization, and reintegration program, were initially welcomed back by parents who anticipated the girls falling back under their control and turning over the money to their families. The girls, however, had other ideas about how to use the money, and, as a result of increased tensions

---

[104] See, for example, UNICEF, "The Disarmament, Demobilisation and Reintegration of Children Associated with the Fighting Forces: Lessons Learned in Sierra Leone, 1998–2002," New York, 2005.
[105] Ibid.; Dyan Mazurana and Khristopher Carlson, *From Combat to Community: Women and Girls in Sierra Leone* (Washington, DC: Policy Commission of Women Waging Peace, 2004); McKay and Mazurana, *Where Are the Girls?*; UNIFEM, *Getting it Right, Doing it Right: Gender and Disarmament, Demobilization and Reintegration* (New York: UNIFEM, 2004).

over the funds, some actually ended up leaving their homes and families.[106] In other cases, money awarded to girls was used by parents, in particular fathers, to restart their businesses, to rebuild their houses, or on alcohol or sexual relations with other women; the girls themselves were unable to afford their priorities – returning to school, access to health care, and basic clothing.[107] Consequently, giving cash benefits in societies that demand and enforce boys' and, in particular, girls' submission to their families, and in particular to their fathers, can lead to additional problems and stress for children.

Additional challenges in giving children cash awards include the facts that few girls and boys have the skills to properly manage, save, or invest money, and that most have no access to a bank account or private, safe location to keep their money. In many countries, minors are not allowed to open bank accounts. Poor and rural children would be at a significant disadvantage, as potentially are most girls because of lower education and literacy rates.

With this in mind, we do not deny that the awarding of cash can be an important benefit for children, and in particular for girls who might then be able to make certain choices about their future – choices that otherwise might not have been available to them – regarding such things as education and the postponement of early marriage. What is needed, however, is an arrangement in which part or all of the money is held in trust until the child reaches an appropriate age of maturity to make financial decisions. Past studies[108] and anecdotal observations from our own fieldwork suggest that much thought should be put into how fathers in particular are allowed access to children's money – fathers who often are not the real custodians of the children, who may take the money and spend it on themselves, or both. In conjunction with this, courses should be offered to help young people understand money management and accounting, and the money probably should be paid out in smaller amounts over time to the child or young adult. Rural children, poor urban children, and linguistic minority children would likely require additional assistance in setting up and understanding how to manage bank accounts.

RESTITUTION OF PROPERTY

Often during conflict and violence in Africa, Asia, and North, Central, and South America, people's homes and their animals are purposefully destroyed

---

[106] Susan McKay, Mary Burman, Maria Gonsalves, and M. Worthen, "Girls Formerly Associated with Fighting Forces and Their Children: Returned and Neglected," *Child Soldiers Newsletter* (London: Coalition to Stop the Use of Child Soldiers), January 2006.

[107] These observations were made during interviews by the authors with girls formerly associated with fighting forces in Mozambique, Sierra Leone, and Uganda between 2001 and 2007.

[108] Goldblatt, "Evaluating the Gender Content of Reparations," 73–74.

or looted, their possessions taken, and their savings stolen. The loss of livestock is particularly devastating for rural peoples, who rely on their animals as a walking bank (as a means to access education, health care, and medicines, and to perform important ceremonies such as those surrounding marriages, funerals, and births).

It is important that property illegally taken from families be returned to the rightful owners. However, adults who owned the property may have been killed or disappeared during the conflict or political violence. It is thus necessary to find ways for children to have legal ownership of their parent's property, or to be compensated, perhaps in a trust fund, for the appreciated value of the property in cases where restitution is not possible.

In most countries throughout the world, it is not possible for minors to own land or property of substantial value. This is particularly true for girls; in many countries, formal and, most often, customary laws prevent women or girls from owning land. In such situations, reparations programs present an important opportunity to work with other transitional justice measures to ensure that women and girls are able to own and make decisions over property, including land.

In addition, the loss of a parent, particularly an income-generating parent, means that a family's ability to earn and accumulate money is hampered, and thus so is its ability to provide its members with good housing. Access to good housing is something that young people who we have worked with in numerous conflict zones prioritize. For many young people we spoke with, a good house is a safe place where you can rest, be treated well by family members, participate in and play your role within the family, cook, sleep, study, and plan for your future. Youth with no housing or very inadequate housing often told us that they were more tired and less able to go to school or focus on their studies, felt less secure and more susceptible to abuse, and were often worried.[109] Hence, an important form of reparation is not only the restitution of property, but efforts to ensure that the surviving child victims are provided with good housing.

EDUCATION, HEALTH, AND SHELTER SERVICES

Given the rather problematic nature of providing cash benefits to children, we recommend that, in addition, child beneficiaries of reparations should be given access to education and health services, since it is questionable whether awarding money to parents results in children gaining access to these

---

[109] Authors' field notes from Afghanistan, Bosnia, Kenya, Mexico, Mozambique, Sierra Leone, and Uganda.

crucial services. We know of no study that investigates what child survivors of grave rights violations prioritize within the framework of reparations and why. However, from the work of colleagues in the field of children's rights and from our own interviews over several years with hundreds of children (in south, west, and east Africa, the Balkans, and Afghanistan) who have survived grave rights violations (against them and their relatives), we do know that the number one priority for both girls and boys is accessing education, followed by health care for themselves and their families and shelter assistance. Other studies working with child survivors report similar priorities.[110]

Children have a right to education, including free primary education, under the Convention on the Rights of the Child (CRC).[111] This means that educational reparations programs for children would have to go above and beyond what the state is already obligated to provide. As a common form of recommended or offered individual reparations for children, then, educational benefits most often take the form of full access to secondary education or accelerated programs of education. In rare cases, such as in Chile, youth may receive free university education.[112] In the case of Chile, as the stigma surrounding this population of youth has lessened over the years and the political climate has changed, universities now offer particular intake programs for these students to help them succeed at school. We see this as a positive step in helping them realize the fullest advantage of their reparations benefit.[113] In Peru, the educational reparations program recommended by the Truth and Reconciliation Commission is expressly designed for (1) all the individual beneficiaries who,

---

[110] Charli Carpenter, "Forced Maternity, Children's Rights and the Genocide Convention," *Journal of Genocide Research* 2, no. 2 (2000): 213–244; Jean Lieby, "Assessment of the Vulnerabilities and Capacities of Girls, Including Abducted Girls, Who Did Not Go Through DDR in Sierra Leone," UNICEF-Sierra Leone, 2003; Erica Páez, "Girls in the Colombian Armed Groups, a Diagnosis Briefing," Terre Des Hommes, 2001; Save the Children Denmark, "A Study on the Views, Perspectives and Experiences of 'Social Integration' Among Formerly Abducted Girls in Gulu, Northern Uganda," Gulu, Uganda, 2003; Angela Veale, *From Child Soldier to Ex-Fighter: Female Fighters, Demobilization and Reintegration in Ethiopia*, Monograph No. 85 (Pretoria: Institute for Security Studies, 2003); Beth Verhey, *Reaching the Girls*; Women's Commission for Refugee Women and Children, "Against All Odds: Surviving the War on Adolescents, Promoting the Protection and Capacity of Ugandan and Sudanese Adolescents in Northern Uganda," New York, 2001; UNICEF, "Disarmament, Demobilisation and Reintegration of Children Associated with the Fighting Forces"; Women's Commission for Refugee Women and Children, "Precious Resources: Adolescents in the Reconstruction of Sierra Leone," New York, 2002.

[111] CRC, Articles 28 and 29.

[112] Law 19.123, "Establishes the National Corporation for Reparation and Reconciliation and Grants Other Benefits to Persons and Indicated," Title IV, Articles 29, 30, 31, reproduced and translated into English in *The Handbook of Reparations*, 758.

[113] Maria Luisa Sepulveda, Human Rights Advisor to the President of Chile, personal communication with Dyan Mazurana, February 24, 2006, Caux, Switzerland.

as a result of the internal armed conflict, missed the opportunity to receive an adequate education or to complete their studies; (2) children born because of rape; and (3) people who were integrated into a self-defense group as a minor. This program's measures include (i) waiving fees in primary and secondary schools, universities, institutions of higher learning, Occupational Education Centers (COE), and other relevant educational institutions; (ii) competitive scholarship programs (with quotas for regions and certain career tracks) for all types of higher education programs; and (iii) adult educational programs.[114]

A gender-just approach to such educational initiatives could seek to ensure equal participation of girls in primary and secondary schools and university. Studies find that, despite successful efforts to enroll more girls in primary school, girls in many settings are more likely than boys to repeat classes or to drop out altogether. Yet schooling per se will not empower girls unless it goes beyond the current focus on enrollment and gives far more attention to both the quality and content of education and the social structures that reinforce schooling and reward schooled girls.[115]

The school environment for girls often has many negative aspects, such as obsolete and gender-insensitive textbooks that reproduce gender stereotypes. Many girls experience harassment or violence on their way to and from school. The simple threat of harassment violates girls' human rights and keeps many of them out of school, irremediably harming their lifetime opportunities. Even when school enrollment is free of charge, education carries hidden costs that may be borne differently by girls or differently predispose girls' families to reduce their school options. These hidden costs, such as school uniforms, textbooks, and other essentials, as well as transportation to and from school, are often substantial and prevent poor families from sending their children, and in particular their girls, to school.[116]

Education benefits may also include free vocational skills training in such occupations as masonry, carpentry, welding, auto and bicycle repair, tailoring, hair dressing, and so on. Often there is a gendered division of labor, as girls opt for and are encouraged to take up tailoring, hair dressing, and soap making – occupations that will generate little if any income. That said, it is unknown whether boys fair much better given the fact that the quality of the training

---

[114] Law Number 28592, "Law that Creates the Comprehensive Reparations Plan."
[115] Fatuma Chege, "Teacher Identities and Empowerment of Girls against Sexual Violence," expert paper prepared for the United Nations Division for the Advancement of Women in collaboration with the UNICEF Expert Group Meeting on the elimination of all forms of discrimination and violence against the girl child, UNICEF Innocenti Research Centre, Florence, Italy, September 25–28, 2006, EGM/DVGC/2006/EP.13.
[116] Ibid.

they receive (though for potentially higher wage earning) is low and the time duration too short to develop advanced skills; they usually leave with no tools to begin their work and often remain unemployed.[117]

Most vocational skills training programs set up to benefit children who have suffered severe rights violations during armed conflict do not enable the children to provide for themselves or their families. In most cases, the programs are too short in duration (six months to one year) to provide the children with sufficient skills to generate a sustainable livelihood. Additionally, most children graduate from these courses but are given no tools (from carpentry or welding tools to sewing machines) to establish their livelihoods. Thus, although they may have some skills, they lack a means to use them. Furthermore, little to no market analysis is conducted to assess what types of skills and livelihoods may be appropriate and sustainable for young people, and little to no career counseling is offered to assist them in making sustainable choices for the future. As a result, many of these programs fail to provide the young people they are intended to empower with the skills and resources needed to engage in productive and sustainable livelihoods.

A second common form of individual reparations for children is access to health care. Depending on the characteristics of the violence used during the conflict, reparations in the form of health care can include access to drug rehabilitation programming, care for amputees, and care for those mutilated or otherwise disfigured. Only recently have reparations programs begun to be sensitive and responsive to widespread sexual violence used as a weapon against individuals and communities during armed conflict. In such programs, reparations include access to reproductive health care and gynecological services. Importantly, given the levels of sexual violence some girls experience, there is a clear need for health reparations that include surgery or extensive and long-term medical care or both for female survivors; to date, however, this type of benefit has appeared only on paper. Access to mental health care is another provision that is increasingly seen in reparations programs, though we know little about the kinds of mental health care victims and survivors are able to access and the effects of such care. One example of forward-looking recommendations for physical and mental health care comes from the Peruvian Truth and Reconciliation Commission, which proposed that the health reparations program include physical and mental health care through both community and clinical interventions. In addition, it called for a promotion

---

[117] UNICEF, "Disarmament, Demobilisation and Reintegration of Children Associated with the Fighting Forces"; Women's Commission for Refugee Women and Children, "Against All Odds"; Women's Commission for Refugee Women and Children, "Precious Resources."

and prevention component to sensitize people to the physical and psychological effects of the internal armed conflict, including the increase in alcoholism (in men and women, but also adolescents), family violence, infantile and youthful delinquency, learning problems, and suicidal tendencies.[118]

Finally, girl mothers with children born because of rape, in particular, emphasize the need to have their own homes, as they report higher levels of physical, verbal, and mental abuse of their children born of rape by family members and neighbors. Because these girls often have so few resources, and owing to stigma lack much of the necessary social capital needed to survive in poverty-stricken post-conflict areas, they often remain in violent settings.[119] Likewise, in comparison to other similarly aged war-affected males, youth males formerly associated with fighting forces report higher levels of physical abuse at the hands of family members, and at times drift from home to home, looking for a place to live without abuse, harassment, or humiliating treatment.[120]

PSYCHOLOGICAL REHABILITATION

The "Basic Principles and Guidelines on the Right to Remedy and Reparation for Victims of Gross Violations of International Human Rights Law and Serious Violations of International Humanitarian Law" include within their recognition of victims those who have suffered "physical or mental injury, emotional suffering,"[121] and call for attention to mental health needs as part of compensation, which should address "physical or mental harm,"[122] and to rehabilitation, which should include "medical and psychological care as well as legal and social services."[123] Some scholars writing on reparations and mental health contend that, in the end, all reparations are primarily symbolic (given that full restoration is impossible) and thus, whatever form they take, will have at least some psychological impact on victims.

---

[118] Comisión de la Verdad y Reconciliación (CVR), *Informe Final de la Comisión de la Verdad y Reconciliación* (Lima: CVR, 2003); Julie Guillerot, coordinator of the reparations team of the Truth and Reconciliation Commission for Peru, personal communication with Dyan Mazurana, June 2007.

[119] See Khristopher Carlson and Dyan Mazurana, "Forced Marriage within the Lord's Resistance Army"; UNICEF, "Child mothers face stigma of rejection," December 2004, http://www.unicef.org/infobycountry/uganda_24566.html.

[120] Blattman, Annan, and Horton, "The State of Youth and Youth Protection in Northern Uganda."

[121] United Nations, *Basic Principles and Guidelines on the Right to Remedy and Reparation for Victims of Gross Violations of International Human Rights Law and Serious Violations of International Humanitarian Law*, A/RES/60/147, March 21, 2006, para. 8.

[122] Ibid., para. 20 (a).

[123] Ibid., para. 20 (e).

To date, only in Chile has there been the provision of mental health services for large numbers of victims and their families.[124] Although some psychological support was provided for victims who testified in Peru, South Africa, and Sierra Leone, follow-up support was limited. Because this is a new area of study, there is spotty empirical data both on the effects of testifying before truth commissions or courts and the psychological support provided for doing so. Little evidence exists as well on the psychological value of receiving reparations, and often the data that does exist points to contradictory findings.[125] It cannot be stated that reconciliation is the result of truth-telling commissions, fact-finding bodies, or reparations programs, and this is perhaps particularly true in situations in which there is an absence of justice.[126] Indeed,

> continued impunity and the absence of justice greatly limit, or may even annul, the potential for healing in reparatory measures, including material compensation or even well-intended psychological attention.... Reparation without justice is not reparatory and the wider social-political struggles for justice and against impunity and specific psychosocial interventions need to be increasingly consonant and integrated in a unified strategy.[127]

Some very thought-provoking writing is occurring around issues of mental health and reparations that merits attention from those considering children, gender, and reparations. In particular, a more nuanced understanding for the need to pay attention to both individual and collective mental health is evolving. This may include some Western forms of mental health but often goes well beyond this into cultural contexts with specific forms of expressing and experiencing grief, mourning, recognition, and healing.[128] And just as we have advocated above, there is a need for both individual and collective reparation measures, and for careful consideration of the intersection of these approaches. These scholars encourage us to pay attention to and recognize

> each person as fundamentally active in the world and acting on/with others in producing and reproducing themselves and their communities, in nexuses of social relations. This person lives in a particular social context and is

---

[124] Although such mental health services are called for in the reparations programs of Guatemala and Peru, none have been carried out to date.

[125] See, for example, Goldblatt, "Evaluating the Gender Content of Reparations"; M. Brinton Lykes and Marcie Mersky, "Reparations and Mental Health: Psychosocial Interventions Towards Healing, Human Agency, and Rethreading Social Realities," in *The Handbook of Reparations*, 589–622.

[126] See, for example, Lykes and Mersky, "Reparations and Mental Health"; *What Happened to the Women?*; and Shaw, "Rethinking Truth and Reconciliation Commissions."

[127] Lykes and Mersky, "Reparations and Mental Health," 616.

[128] A most excellent example of this work is Lykes and Mersky, "Reparations and Mental Health."

culturally rooted in processes that constrain, facilitate, and give meaning to her or his social subjectivity. [This requires] not only seeking means to address individual suffering, but also understanding that individual and social healing depend in a fundamental way on regenerating, under new terms, the social relations and moral boundaries that were destroyed.[129]

For children, it is important to keep in mind that psychosocial processes are long term and intergenerational. Hence, one of the challenges may be for those planning psychosocial reparations to think well beyond the technical tools used today that are divorced from the larger sociopolitical reality, and instead begin thinking about what inter- or multigenerational processes might look like. Given that widespread crimes and grave human rights violations are at their core attempts to destroy entire communities or peoples by tearing the social fabric sustaining them, psychosocial reparations will need to be shaped closely with the different generations within communities if they are to repair and strengthen this fabric.[130]

We should also be very cautious not to consult only with traditional or religious elders within communities (most often elder males), because very often they cannot speak on behalf of the violations suffered by children, and in particular the girls. What we need to understand is that children's experiences and their responses to events will have an impact beyond the individual or even the community level. These are things that will move a society itself in different directions. Hence, we need to listen carefully to and think hard about the stories that children and their communities tell in order to gain a better understanding of the very new spaces these girls and boys are occupying *and* the ways in which, willingly or not, their societies are forced to move into those spaces with them.[131]

SERVICES THAT OFFER CLOSURE ON VIOLATIONS

Other individual benefits are those that acknowledge and help provide some closure to the violations that occurred. These can include the issuing of death certificates to individual families, exhumation and reburial ceremonies, and

---

[129] Ibid., 600–601. See also David Becker, Elizabeth Lira, Maria Isabel Castilo, Elena Gomez, and Juana Kovllskeys, "Therapy with Victims of Political Repression in Chile: The Challenge of Social Reparation," *Journal of Social Issues* 46, no. 3 (1990): 133–150; M. Brinton Lykes, "Gender and Individualistic vs. Collectivist Bases for Notions About the Self," *Journal of Personality* 53, no. 3 (1996): 356–383.
[130] Lykes and Mersky, "Reparations and Mental Health."
[131] McKay and Mazurana, *Where Are the Girls?*

funds provided for funerals and tombstones.[132] Such benefits may be particularly important for families or individuals with children, siblings, or parents buried in internally-displaced-person (IDP) camps (and not in their villages) or killed in the bush and buried in unmarked graves whose location is known only to government military, militias, or rebel groups.

LIMITATIONS OF INDIVIDUAL BENEFITS

Some of the limitations of individual benefits that we discuss here can be compensated for if they include both individual payments and access to services, in particular health care and education. However, this would depend on the specific needs of child survivors of grave rights violations being explicitly identified and addressed within the context of the larger programs providing basic social services.

It is crucial that reparations beneficiaries are not singled out and treated in ways that further stigmatize them – for example, as "forced wives," "rape victims," "sexual slaves," or "child soldiers" – and mark them as "others" within the communities they are trying to return to and live within. Defining and giving material benefits only to narrow categories of beneficiaries, especially in the case of children formerly associated with fighting forces (who at times are seen as perpetrators and potential enemies), can result in backlash in the community against those child survivors. This does not mean that such children should be excluded from reparations or that all reparations should be collective. Rather, in such cases, creative strategies should be used to ensure that while individual children who have suffered grave rights violations do receive individual reparations, it is done so within larger community-based reparations programs that seek to benefit broader categories of "war-affected children" and help ease the stigmatizing affects of the abuse on the individual beneficiary. Those individuals deemed most vulnerable, which in a number of countries includes orphans, should be prioritized for preferential treatment and assistance.

Collective Benefits

A number of governments in post-conflict periods proceed as if community development programs were synonymous with reparations programs. In many cases, governments prefer collective over individual benefits for war-affected

---

[132] South Africa's reparations program has called these measures symbolic reparations (see Goldblatt, "Evaluating the Gender Content of Reparations"), whereas under Guatemala's reparations program they are identified as measures to dignify victims (see Paz Bailey, "Guatemala").

communities, contending that limited resources are best spent generating services for the greatest numbers of beneficiaries – for example, by building new schools and health clinics, reestablishing infrastructure, and investing in economic development programs. Furthermore, it is typically argued that awarding reparations to some groups of victims and survivors and not others serves only to further divide societies emerging from war and violence. It may also be contended that the identification of victims may actually further stigmatize them and prevent their reintegration and wider societal reconciliation. Thus, the argument goes, it is in everyone's best interest (including the survivors of grave rights violations) that limited available resources be spent on broader, collective, community development initiatives.

We do not believe that it is in the best interests of the survivors, the community, or the nation as a whole to implement development strategies under the auspices of reparation programs. Likewise, reports from South Africa find that "neither women nor men victims generally accepted the argument that the government was responsible for rebuilding the whole society and therefore could not privilege them."[133] Both individuals and groups that suffered severe violations of their human rights should receive the political, societal, and psychological acknowledgment that the acts against them were crimes and that their rights were wrongly violated. In particular, the government and its key institutions that were either by commission or omission responsible for the violations should publicly acknowledge these wrongs and offer redress through material, financial, legal, symbolic, or psychological means. This can be done with *both* individual and collective benefits, and we should resist pressures or discourses that posit these as benefits in opposition to one another. Indeed, reparations programs will be most successful when individual and collective reparations coexist and are mutually reinforcing.

Collective reparations cannot replace and therefore should not be used to try to replace individual benefits, as this would be contrary to the spirit of the right to reparation under international law. At a more practical level, we find it nearly impossible to imagine how agencies that have previously failed to adequately address rights violations against, and support the rights of, numerous categories of high-risk children in conflict zones – such as formerly abducted or recruited youth, girls with children born of rape, and girls subjected to sexual slavery – would somehow suddenly be able to dramatically scale up development programs to address "all" war-affected youth, with such nuanced approaches that these programs could catch within their nets those

---

[133] See Goldblatt, "Evaluating the Gender Content of Reparations," 58.

who have suffered the gravest of rights violations and address their particular needs.

Government leadership and genuine participation are central components of legitimate and successful reparations programs. Unlike general post-conflict recovery efforts, in reparations programs the crimes and harms done to the victims are publicly acknowledged. Additionally, through government involvement, it is recognized that the violations and their effects need to be addressed in order to help restore the citizen-state relationship. If the rights violations in question pertain to children, then the best interests of the child should serve as a primary guiding tool for shaping such acknowledgments (ranging from content to media outlet). The government's leadership and participation in reparations programs is a necessary condition for success, and in best-case scenarios national programs should be established. Government responsibility in this area cannot be ceded or delegated to, or propped up by, any other body, including those of the international community.[134] We argue that this is all the more important in cases involving children and young people, with whom the government must repair the citizen-state relationship in order to stem the recurrence of dissatisfaction due to exclusion, which can lead to further exclusion, continued poverty, and, at times, participation in armed uprisings.

We recognize that the state has an obligation to provide for the education and health of its children. Hence, actions by governments such as (re)building schools and ensuring access to education, (re)constructing and ensuring access to health clinics, and (re)establishing functional justice systems at the subnational level cannot on their own be considered reparations. However, if the government makes the reparative aspect of such work explicit and publicized, then it may be possible for the fulfillment of some of these obligations to constitute collective reparations. For example, the state's education budget could prioritize directing funds toward the immediate rebuilding of schools and providing uniforms, books, paper, and pens to all students – thereby eliminating all fees and hidden costs – in the areas most severely affected by armed conflict or political repression and violence. Such actions should be coupled with explicit national and sub-national decrees and statements from the most (relevant) senior government officials acknowledging that the education of the children in this region is being prioritized in order to ensure their ability to participate equally as citizens with other students throughout the country.

---

[134] de Greiff, "Justice and Reparations."

In some settings, a high proportion of girl and boy survivors of grave human rights violations may need to be reintroduced into schooling or require special adaptations, including internally displaced or refugee children, formerly abducted children, and married girls, who have the same rights to education as other girls but not the same access. All school-going girls and boys have advantages over non-school-goers – even if they enter school late, are not at grade-for-age, or are in poor-quality schools. For girls in particular, school-goers have a better ability to negotiate a later marriage, protect themselves from unwanted sexual relations and pregnancy, and build the social negotiation skills necessary for a decent livelihood.[135]

Likewise, as a measure of collective reparations benefits, ministries of health could prioritize the reconstruction and improvement of health care facilities in the areas most affected by the conflict or political violence. For girls and young women, this would require an emphasis on reproductive health and issues relating to violence against women and girls, including sexual violence. For boys and young men, it could emphasize repairing physical injuries sustained as a result of conflict or political violence, again including sexual violence. Offering such services at no charge to child victims should again be coupled with strong and clear acknowledgment that funds are being prioritized for the purpose of providing these citizens with improved and equal care. In addition, given that many women and girls in the conflict-affected areas may be suffering from physical damage to their reproductive organs due to sexual violence, regionally centralized health-care services should provide the long-term and specialized care they may need, free or at a greatly reduced cost. The cost for this work should be borne by the state as part of its nondiscriminatory collective reparations efforts.

Given the horrific effects of torture, which appear to be more damaging for children than adults,[136] there is a need to establish centers for torture survivors, staffed with personnel with specific training to deal with both child and adult victims of torture, including sexual forms of torture. Given the state's role in torture in a number of countries under consideration here, such centers should be established with government funds but remain independent (under an independent board) to ensure the security and well-being of those seeking assistance.

---

[135] United Nations, *Report of the Secretary-General on the Elimination of All Forms of Discrimination and Violence against the Girl Child*, E/CN.6/2007/2, December 12, 2006.

[136] Ann Maston and John Hubard, "The Effects of Trauma on Children by Age," Center for Survivors of Torture, Minneapolis, 2003, http://www.cvt.org/file.php?ID=5692&PHPSESSID=4b0d4f69399c9dbbfdd9dda96e.

A main criticism of collective reparations is that, in choosing the most affected geographical areas to distribute mostly public or nonexcludable goods, both victims and perpetrators can access them. Thus, they lose their recognition potential and reparative value for victims. Although this is undoubtedly true, in the case of some children, especially those associated with fighting forces, the line between victim and perpetrator is unclear. Therefore, collective reparations for children should not look to define and exclude so-called child perpetrators from accessing important services for their health and well-being. Additionally, children of perpetrators should not be blocked from accessing public goods such as education and health care simply because of the activities of their parents. Again, those groups that are deemed most vulnerable, which in a number of countries include orphans, should be prioritized for preferential treatment and assistance.

Creative Approaches for Collective Reparations Programs for Children

One creative and unique approach that to date has not been adopted by any reparations program, but which we think is well worth considering, is the establishment of girls' and boys' centers or clubs. (The work that has been done on theorizing and setting up such spaces finds that they should be sex-segregated, for the benefit of girls in particular.) Girls and boys have a basic right to a community and spaces that are safe. Personal safety is essential if children are to have meaningful access to the most basic rights to life, shelter, food, and water. Safety in their homes, communities, and schools is the basis for all other efforts at citizenship building and empowerment.

In many communities throughout the world, however, though younger girls may be visible in the street, their sisters approaching puberty are withdrawn because of perceived and real safety concerns. Girls – often in stark contrast to boys – have few opportunities to meet their same-sex peers outside of home, or even in the context of school, in a reliably available and safe place. Perhaps those with the least access to a safe and supportive space are newly married girls – transited from natal homes to marital homes far away, disconnected even from family and the social networks that may have nurtured them. The freedom to move around safely in the public space, to attend school, and to be viewed as an integral part of families and communities is often denied to girls individually and collectively. Physical and sexual abuse is common in many communities, and high proportions of girls report being afraid of the public space, where their reputations and physical integrity are attacked. Harassment and physical attack starkly reduce girls' opportunities, and open violations of rights (such as abduction, marriage, and sexual violence) can significantly impinge on their future rights.[137]

Studies find that girls in all categories seek and enjoy the company of other girls, if given the opportunity. Girls' clubs, when offered, find the ready attendance of girls (provided gate-keeper access has been negotiated). Even girls in extremely difficult circumstances, such as those married as children, can be integrated into communities of support and learning.[138]

Safe, girl-friendly and boy-friendly spaces are thus both essential social platforms through which to deliver programs as well as venues in which girls and boys can develop protective same-sex friendship networks, explore their problems, learn about their rights, develop strategies to protect their safety and their health, practice team building, develop leadership, and play. Social connectedness and affiliation are essential human needs and rights, and a critical and joyful part of childhood and self-realization; such connections contribute to children's long-term capacity to develop a positive self-image, defend their rights, and make responsible and informed decisions on matters affecting their lives.[139] Thus, we encourage national and international actors to consider the establishment of (sex-segregated) girls' and boys' centers as a means of collective reparation.

Challenges for Children's Participation in Individual and Collective Benefits and Redress

Girls and boys face a number of challenges in asserting their rights to reparations. In particular, they lack information, especially information presented in a child-friendly format.[140] Children are not often the target of campaigns to raise awareness about national and international tribunals, truth commissions, or reparations programs. They lack full legal autonomy, and most have little to no understanding of their rights or how to ensure them through local and national state structures. They often do not have necessary documents, including deeds to land or housing or even their own birth certificates and identification, or bank accounts, and usually have little understanding of managing money. Children, especially those now heading their own households

---

[137] This section draws heavily from the ground-breaking work of Judith Bruce on safe spaces for girls, which is represented in *Report of the Secretary-General on the Elimination of All Forms of Discrimination and Violence against the Girl Child.*
[138] Ibid.
[139] Ibid.
[140] UNICEF and ICTJ, *Children and Truth Commissions: Basic Considerations.*

or those who have been forcibly married, may have a great fear of reprisal. Child survivors also face stigma, ostracism, and familial and community violence because of the violations committed against them, such as rape, sexual violence, sexual slavery, forced prostitution, forced marriage, or being part of a fighting force or group, or for being known as a child born of rape.

Thus, girls and boys and national and international organizations dedicated to children's rights and girls' rights should be included in meaningful ways in the process of determining both individual and community benefits and developing programs for awarding those benefits. This will help, in part, highlight and address a number of the challenges noted above and hopefully ensure that children can actually access benefits that are meaningful and useful to them.

Significantly, girls and boys have a right under international law to participate in matters that affect them.[141] Participation is both an individual and collective concept. At the individual level, a girl or boy must feel she or he is able and has a forum in which to express herself or himself. At the collective level, organized channels are needed through which girls and boys – especially the least visible and highest-risk girls and boys – can articulate their needs, which are often different from those of more privileged children. Girls' and boys' participation can be attached to specific projects, such as explicitly engaging them in articulating the issues that affect their lives, in assisting in the design of programs, in implementing simple research and monitoring tasks, and in evaluating the programs' responsiveness to girls' and boys' needs.[142]

Many international, national, and civil society organizations have in recent years taken to "including children's voices" in decision making about their policies and programs. However, it is important that participation of girls and boys – particularly girls and boys from poorer households and in more marginal circumstances – be meaningful and not a mere token gesture. Participation mechanisms must explicitly acknowledge the great diversity of children and seek to ensure the participation of the least privileged and highest-risk children.[143]

Significantly, girls, boys, and their communities can be meaningfully included and rightfully claim compensation only if they are actually aware of the reparations process. This requires making extensive outreach a key priority, including working through radio, newspaper, traditional and religious centers and leaders, parent groups, schools and teachers, and youth and women's groups to reach children and their families. Additionally, linking more closely

---

[141] CRC, Articles 12 and 13.
[142] *Report of the Secretary-General on the Elimination of All Forms of Discrimination and Violence against the Girl Child.*
[143] Ibid.

with women's human rights groups and those working with women victims could be beneficial for child victims, as women victims often report that they prioritize reparations measures in part to help support their children.[144] Follow up to ensure that eligible children actually receive their benefits is also necessary.[145]

SYMBOLIC REPARATIONS AND CHILDREN

Symbolic reparations can never – and should never attempt to – take the place of material reparations. Nonetheless, there is an important role for symbolic reparations. Past symbolic reparations have ranged from the creation of learning centers and museums to the establishment of holidays in commemoration of victims and dedicated to the community as a whole, a number of which highlight the role of child victims and survivors.[146] Based on our own work with survivors, as well as the writings of others, we offer the following thoughts on children and symbolic reparations.

First, where appropriate, symbolic reparations should occur in conjunction with material reparations for the survivors. For example, apologies for the government's failure to prevent the recruitment of children from their schools by armed forces or groups could be issued, collective reparations could prioritize the rebuilding and staffing of schools in the affected areas, and individual reparations could assist children deprived of schooling because of their involvement in the war.

Second, in speaking with children and the parents of children who have survived grave rights violations in conflict situations, we often hear that people want an explicit apology from the government, acknowledging its failure to protect the child victims from harm, and that this should come both as a written letter personally signed by the highest (relevant) official – such as the president, prime minister, or head of the military or police – and through a public ceremony. Such ceremonies or testimonies could be broad in scope or thematic. Victims and survivors should be given assistance (such as bus fare, etc.) to enable their attendance, and there should be strong outreach using radio, newspaper, religious organizations, community gatherings, and so forth to let people know in advance both about the upcoming ceremony and the

---

[144] See, for example, Goldblatt, "Evaluating the Gender Content of Reparations"; Galuh Wandita, Karen Campbell-Nelson, and Manuela Leong Pereira, "Learning to Engender Reparations in Timor-Leste: Reaching Out to Female Victims," in *What Happened to the Women?* 284–335.
[145] UNICEF and ICTJ, *Children and Truth Commissions: Basic Considerations*.
[146] UNICEF and ICTJ, *Children and Truth Commissions: Basic Considerations*.

assistance available for those who wish to attend. These ceremonies should occur with media coverage.

Within public ceremonies regarding past violations, spaces could be created and supported in which perpetrators of violence or state officials are able to safely stand before the communities or individual victims or both and offer their acknowledgment of the harm done and apologize to the survivors. Public acknowledgment of violations and apologies given by the state can play an important role in helping survivors and their communities reduce the stigma associated with the nature of the crimes, in particular gender-based and sexually based crimes, and can be significant in facilitating healing and reintegration. Although we do not recommend or endorse such measures, if child perpetrators wish on their own account (and are not required by traditional, religious, or local leaders) to appear within this space, it should be done in close consultation with persons who have the best interest of the child in mind and in ways that do not put the child at risk within the community or undermine his or her rights under international and national law.

Third, public learning centers, memorials, museums, and monuments can be important forms of symbolic reparations and could, through their words, displays, interactive media, and imagery, acknowledge and apologize to children whose rights were violated. These public forums could also commemorate the actions of children and adults who took risks to speak out against or stop the violations, as well as strongly condemn actions that facilitate or benefit from the abuse of children. In addition, institutions important for the development and well-being of children could be renamed to commemorate the dead, acknowledge a commitment to never let such violations happen again, or distinguish children or adults who worked to stop the violations. The most appropriate of these would include schools, health centers, playgrounds, youth centers, sports stadiums, and religious centers.

Fourth, traditional forms of restoring harmony within the community and asking for forgiveness are often used by communities as a means to redress harm done to child victims and survivors. These may include cleansing ceremonies that are both general and specific to the kinds of harms children have suffered or perpetrated; rituals to promote forgiveness, reconciliation, and reintegration; and ceremonies to restore balance or harmony to members of the community who have suffered particular harms as well as to the war-affected community itself. At times these ceremonies are gender specific, with different actions taken for girls and boys.[147] Significantly, traditional ceremonies and

---

[147] Authors' fieldnotes documenting healing rituals in Mozambique, Sierra Leone, and northern Uganda. In addition, see Alcinda Honwana, "Healing for Peace: Traditional Healers and

rituals should be in keeping with international standards of children's rights, in particular the rights of girls,[148] and should not be endorsed or supported by national or international actors until it is clearly demonstrated that these processes are in the best interest of the child and that measures are in place to ensure that children participating are not put at risk. It should not be assumed that male traditional and religious leaders speak for children, particularly girls, or uphold the rights of girls and boys when conducting or calling for such ceremonies and rituals. Under no circumstance should children be involved in any traditional or community ceremonies or rituals that involve public shaming or confession or any violations of their rights.[149]

Finally, creative and potentially meaningful symbolic reparation could occur through the reworking of school curricula to acknowledge the truths described by a truth commission report, including the explicit recognition of the crimes suffered by children and their families. This should be crafted in a way to help allow children who suffered these violations to recover their dignity and "standing" in front of their peers. Here, a child-friendly version of the final truth commission report could be written and incorporated into the curricula for various age groups. Human rights could be incorporated into the curricula, not to be taught in an abstract form, but grounded in the real experiences of the country itself, as is being experimented with in Peru.[150]

CONCLUSION

> We want to rise up from the ashes of war. We want to become the rebirth of our country. It is a huge task, and we are only children. How can we build a bridge to the future? But, if not us, then who else can do it? It is our country.... The future is our challenge, and we cannot refuse.[151]

In determining which crimes are considered by reparations programs, who qualifies as a beneficiary, and what benefits are offered, we should remember

Post-War Reconstruction in Southern Mozambique," *Peace and Conflict: Journal of Peace Psychology* 3 (1997): 293–305; Alcinda Honwana, "Children of War: Understanding War and War Cleansing in Mozambique and Angola," in *Civilians in War*, ed. Simon Chesterman (Boulder, CO: Lynne Reinner, 2001), 123–142; Rosalind Shaw, "Rethinking Memory in Sierra Leone's Truth and Reconciliation Commission," United States Institute for Peace, Washington, DC, April 2004, http://www.usip.org/fellows/reports/2004/0429_shaw.html.

[148] The CRC is the standard to which we refer.
[149] UNICEF and ICTJ, *Children and Truth Commissions: Basic Considerations*.
[150] Julie Guillerot, coordinator of the reparations team of the Truth and Reconciliation Commission for Peru, personal communication with Dyan Mazurana, February 24, 2006, Caux, Switzerland.
[151] Truth and Reconciliation Commission, *Truth and Reconciliation Report for the Children of Sierra Leone* (Freetown: TRC, 2004), http://www.trcsierraleone.org/pdf/kids.pdf, 52.

that, because the damage done to girls and boys who have suffered grave violations is long lasting (sometimes lifetime lasting), full restoration is impossible. Years of lost access to education and hence skills and livelihood opportunities, returning as a single young parent with children born of rape, and the loss of limbs, friends, and relatives make unattainable the goal of fully restoring the child to his or her former state before the violation.

Because full restoration is impossible, we must move forward in ways that acknowledge the *actual violations* children were subjected to during the conflict or through political violence, not the violations that are most politically expedient and socially acceptable to deal with at the time. If we pay close attention to the violations that girls and boys as gendered beings living in ethnic, racial, and classed societies actually suffered, then we will have a much better idea of the kinds of short-, medium-, and long-term effects they may face, and thus we can design reparations programs that (1) acknowledge those crimes and rights violations, (2) address the heart of those effects, as best as possible, and (3) help identify and dismantle structures and institutions of violence that led to and perpetuated the violations that children experienced.

In this chapter, we have discussed how, during situations of armed conflict and via political acts of violence, girls and boys are specifically targeted for and directly affected by grave rights violations. Consequently, we strongly contend that within reparations programs child survivors of these violations should be seen as rights holders and citizens. They should be actively consulted during the planning and implementation of truth commissions and reparation programs, and their needs and priorities should be given equal weight as those of other survivors and victims.

In theory, child rights groups and women's groups appear to be poised to play a key role in advancing gender justice for girls and boys in transitional periods. However, as Rubio-Marín notes in this collection, and as we have repeatedly seen in conflict situations, many women's associations are focused primarily on assisting women with their most urgent physical and psychological needs, including those resulting from past and current forms of violence. Likewise, we have observed that most efforts for children in transitional periods go toward addressing basic survival needs (immunization, nutrition, and health care) and provision of (often minimal-quality) primary education. Very few groups, including women's and children's groups, are focused on issues of accountability, justice, or access to reparations for girls and boys. Furthermore, we find that, at the national and local levels, women's and children's groups are often not linked to each other and that there is very little exchange or coalition building among them. This often leaves girls in particular with few knowledgeable and committed advocates for justice and remedy for the grave rights violations they have suffered. Consequently, child rights and women's rights groups should begin building alliances and bridges, as the struggle for gender justice in a post-conflict society should be of paramount concern to both.

In order for reparations programs to be meaningful to children, they must resist the impulse in much justice, humanitarian, development, and human rights work to base policy and programs on adults' perceptions of "children," "childhood," and the effects of political violence and armed conflict on children. Because so much of the current discourse couches children as victims, most humanitarian, human rights, and development efforts have systematically failed to treat young people as rights holders who have crucial insights and contributions to make regarding how their rights were violated, the effects this has had on them, their families, and communities, and what they believe will help them move forward to a better future.

As a step toward remedying this, we have presented some of the priorities articulated by children who have suffered grave violations of their human rights during situations of armed conflict. Yet the material presented here should be seen only as a part of initial discussions of what needs to be a much larger and more thorough investigation and debate about reparations among child survivors and those who seek to ensure that their rights are upheld. To date, such discussions have been rare, and perhaps it is only with the case of Sierra Leone that we are beginning to see a coordinated and collective movement in this direction. Adults, therefore, must set aside the resources and make the space to engage in such dialogue, all the time keeping in mind the gendered dimensions of the violence and the spaces in which girls and boys are empowered (or not) to speak, listen, and be heard.

Starting from children's and youth's discussions of challenges and opportunities is an absolutely necessary step toward building reparations programs that actually address young people's lived realities. At the very onset of establishing truth commissions, mandates should be drawn that ensure taking into account rights violations against children, and this includes having commissioners with expertise on children's and women's rights and gender-based and sexual violence. It also includes having courts and hearings that are staffed by persons trained in children's and women's rights. In designing reparations programs, gender- and age-sensitive space must be made for a wide range of young people who have suffered severe human rights violations to present, in a safe and supportive environment, their own analysis of their past experiences, their past troubles, their present problems, and their future goals. Additionally, reparations processes need to allow children to come forward when they are ready and should not exclude those who fail to come forward within the (usually brief) allotted period of time. Support needs to be built into reparations programs to assist girls and boys in coming forward, speaking out, and claiming reparations.[152]

Finally, and perhaps most significantly, persons engaged in reparations and other transitional justice measures must recognize that the violence committed during conflict situations is the result of inequalities among different classes and racial and ethnic groups of women and men and girls and boys that predated the conflict, and that this violence aggravates the discrimination against marginalized groups, and in particular against women and children within these groups. Hence, those involved in reparations programs should be aware of and seek to be part of the transformation of these sociocultural injustices and political and structural inequalities. Customary and religious laws and practices that prevent girls and boys from making and acting on decisions regarding their rights must be confronted. In other words, "reintegration and restitution by themselves are not sufficient goals of reparation, since the origins of violations of women's and girls' human rights predate the conflict situation."[153] Hence, reparation measures must explicitly be based on the principle of nondiscrimination and be in compliance with international and regional standards on the right to remedy and reparation, as well as the human rights of women, girls, and boys.

Girls and boys have a right to a remedy and reparation under international law. They have a right to benefit from reparations programs, in material, symbolic, individual, and collective forms. Reparations for children are not about development programs and they are not about a return to the status quo. They should acknowledge and then go beyond the immediate reasons for and consequences of the crimes and violations in question. Reparations should be part of broader efforts that seek to address the political and structural inequalities and violence that negatively impeded girls' and boys' rights and shaped their lives before, during, and after the conflict or political violence.[154]

---

[152] The Nairobi Declaration on Women's and Girls' Right to Remedy and Reparation, May 15, 2007, http://www.womensrightscoalition.org/site/reparation/signature_en.php.
[153] Ibid., para. 3.
[154] Ibid.

5

Repairing Family Members: Gross Human Rights Violations and Communities of Harm*

Ruth Rubio-Marín, Clara Sandoval,** and Catalina Díaz

I. INTRODUCTION

Many of the forms of violence committed under authoritarian regimes and during large-scale ethnic and civil strife target individuals for reasons such as their political activities, ethnicity, race, and religion. It is individual persons who find their most fundamental human rights violated when subjected to prolonged detention and torture, extrajudicial killings, disappearance, sexual violence, amputation, and forced recruitment and displacement. However, beyond individuals, these violations create communities of harm that include all of those people emotionally tied to the victims or in a relationship of codependency with them.[1] Parents, partners, spouses, children, and siblings are often left both emotionally desolate and economically destitute. In other words, the violence affects not only the targeted individual but also his or her family members. A relevant question becomes, then, whether and how this fact has been or can be acknowledged in reparations initiatives.

Clearly, determining the "family members" who, as such, are entitled to reparations depends on the definition of "victim," and that in turn depends on which violations are considered to be grave or gross violations of human rights that trigger reparations in the first place. Although both national nonjudicial reparations programs and international human rights adjudicatory bodies have

---

* We would like to greatly thank Judge Cecilia Medina, who worked on an initial draft of this chapter and who served as a source of inspiration for parts of this work.
** Clara appreciates the discussions she had with and comments she received from her LLM students Mónica Zwaig, Sergey Golubok, Renata Delgado, Siranuch Sahakyan, and Danai Angeli, from her colleagues Francoise Hampson, Nigel Rodley, Kevin Boyle, from Oscar Javier Parra, and especially from Michael Duttwiler.
[1] On the notion of community of harm, see Fionnuala Ni Aolain, "Sex-based Violence during the Holocaust – A Reevaluation of Harms and Rights in International Law," *Yale Journal of Law and Feminism* 12 (2000): 43–84.

thus far privileged violations of civil and political rights that in many contexts are disparately committed against men (such as disappearances, illegal detention, torture, and extrajudicial killing), many of those who could potentially be included – depending on whether the reparations scheme is sensitive to the impact of violence on the family and to the fact of human interdependency – are in fact women and children.[2] Even if widespread violence targets primarily men, its legacy has profound consequences for women. Women are often left to raise and take care of their own children as well as a large number of dependants (including orphans, the sick, the wounded, and the mutilated). Many of these women are faced with the challenge of finding a livelihood on their own for the first time, one that is sufficient to support them and their dependants, while having to deal with state authorities in trying to find their loved ones or their remains or assisting them while in prison (which is often costly in terms of employment and other opportunities). Often, these women end up experiencing severe poverty, with some of them destined to engage in illegal or exploitive economic activities such as drug dealing and prostitution. The burden of the loss of a male figure, frequently the breadwinner, is most acute in those societies where women lack marketable or income-generating skills, have little education, and may be stigmatized for their involvement in activities outside the home. Women may also be stigmatized when the reputation of one family member affects all other members, such as when one of them is considered to be a terrorist by the state. That stigma follows the rest of the family, generating serious consequences in their day-to-day lives. Finally, family members often have to flee the country or the region as a result of the detention, killing, or disappearance of their beloved ones. In view of these considerations, we can clearly see that when reparations discussions prioritize forms of political violence that target mostly men, it is not obvious how reparations programs under the prevailing individual rights entitlement scheme should deal with family members in general, and women, parents, and children in particular, who endure diffuse, multiple, and often severe harms as a result of the violence.

This chapter addresses the question of whether reparations, determined either by international human rights adjudicatory mechanisms or through national administrative programs, have sufficiently taken heed of relations of dependence in their attempt to redress harms ensuing from violations. The underlying premise of our argument is that, as Fionnuala Ni Aolain has put it,

---

[2] On children and reparations, see Dyan Mazurana and Kristopher Carlson, "Reparations as a Means for Recognizing and Addressing Crimes and Grave Rights Violations against Girls and Boys during Situations of Armed Conflict and under Authoritarian and Dictatorial Regimes," Chapter 4 of this volume.

violations of human rights do "not only destabilize the person(s) toward whom the acts are directly intended but a wider circle whose own autonomous entitlements are precariously in balance with the well-being and safety of others... [producing] a domino effect."[3] The core theoretical questions that ensue are the following: Does the practice of reparations reflect a (harms-based) expansion of the notion of who is a "victim" of a right violation?[4] Can the underlying ontology of the right holder in discussions of gross human rights violations be transformed from that of "unattached autonomous individuals" to that of "persons infinitely connected to their families and communities" in a "relationship of autonomous codependency"?[5] Does the practice of reparations allow for a shift from conceptualizing rights as assets (which stand for the protection of individual interests) to rights as relationships (where the interests protected are also those of the people whose proximity to the victims determines that they too will be deeply affected by and suffer from the violent actions)?

The chapter studies the extent to which, and in what capacity, family members and dependants have been considered to qualify for reparations under both international human rights jurisprudence and large-scale national reparations programs. Since the only international courts adjudicating individual claims of human rights violations with reparations jurisprudence to this day are the European Court of Human Rights (ECtHR) and the Inter-American Court of Human Rights (IACtHR), our jurisprudential analysis will focus on them. More emphasis will be put on the case law of the IACtHR, simply because that court's judgments continue to provide the most wide-reaching remedies afforded in international human rights law in reparations jurisprudence.[6]

The reason for covering both international jurisprudence and national reparations programs is that some of the most sophisticated articulations of the harms that family members endure and the need to repair them do in fact stem from this jurisprudence, in particular from that of the IACtHR. To some extent, this is not surprising, given that judicial reparations procedures operate on a case-by-case basis, which allows them to individualize compensation measures and to tailor them to the harm suffered by each individual victim

---

[3] Ni Aolain, 38–39.
[4] See Ruth Rubio-Marín, ed., *What Happened to the Women? Gender and Reparations for Human Rights Violations* (New York: Social Science Research Council, 2006).
[5] Ni Aolain, 40.
[6] See Dinah Shelton, *Remedies in International Human Rights Law*, 2nd ed. (Oxford: Oxford University Press, 2005), 299; and Arturo J. Carrillo, "Justice in Context: The Relevance of Inter-American Human Rights Law and Practice to Repairing the Past," in *The Handbook of Reparations* [*The Handbook*, hereafter], ed. Pablo de Greiff (Oxford: Oxford University Press, 2006), 507.

and their next of kin. Thus, the legal concepts developed in such international human rights jurisprudence may offer valid normative frameworks for states that have to domestically fulfill their international obligation to provide reparations to victims and their next of kin. In fact, the jurisprudence itself may play a valuable role in catalyzing the willingness of otherwise reticent local governments to establish massive reparations programs.

On the other hand, when reparations are owed to a large universe of victims resulting from widespread and systematic use of violence, administrative (out-of-court) programs are, arguably, better suited to the task,[7] which may explain why governments are increasingly prone to embrace the modality. It is therefore important to see what the trend is, if any, regarding how national reparations programs deal with repairing family members for the harm suffered because of violations perpetrated against their loved ones. After all, this trend may be more indicative of the reality that most family members of victims experience than what is portrayed by the cases that have been resolved by the international courts. This, of course, is not to say that, in their political fight for reparations, family members (who often comprise the majority of victims' associations that mobilize for justice and reparations) do not use the concepts established by international jurisprudence in building their claims. Indeed, the contrary has proven to be true.[8]

To limit the field of analysis, and given the fact that there is no complete consensus as to what and when violations of human rights qualify as gross or systematic, we focus mainly on those violations that have thus far been most frequently treated as such (both by regional courts and by domestic reparations programs), including (arbitrary, illegal, or extrajudicial) killings, torture, disappearance, and arbitrary detention.[9] This is not to say that, space allowing, the study could not be expanded in interesting ways. One of these could be to advance the claim for the inclusion, among the violations considered of utmost gravity, of those that more paradigmatically affect the entire family as a unit, such as forced displacement, in that these violations deprive all family members of things such as home, land, and community, all of which may be essential to family life.

---

[7] See Pablo de Greiff, "Justice and Reparations," in *The Handbook*.
[8] See Carrillo, 508.
[9] Regional human rights courts do not necessarily or consistently refer in their judgments to "gross human rights violations." Nevertheless, it is clear that for these courts there are certain human rights violations, such as the ones just mentioned, which are very serious in nature and which demand special responses from the state and from them. The cases used in this chapter were chosen because their facts were representative of gross violations of human rights taking place in the countries concerned and of their systematic nature.

This chapter aims to provide a comprehensive analysis of how family members have faired in reparations, looking at both international human rights jurisprudence as well as the practice of states that have established large-scale reparations programs. As we advance in presenting a descriptive view of what has been done, we also assess the strengths and weaknesses of the practice thus far and provide insight about ways in which the harms endured by family members could be better addressed in future reparations decisions and programs. The chapter is divided into two parts. The first part (Sections II–IV) covers the experience of the regional human rights bodies. Section II provides an introduction to reparations under both regional human rights systems. Section III describes how family members have been given reparations as successors of the deceased or missing loved ones under both ECtHR and IACtHR jurisprudence. Section IV then analyzes reparations given to family members who are considered either "victims" or "injured parties" with regards to violations committed against their loved ones. The second part of the chapter (Section V) focuses on the practice of granting reparations to family members under national reparations programs, describing the experiences of several countries, including Argentina, Chile, South Africa, Peru, Guatemala, and Sierra Leone.

II. REPARATIONS UNDER THE REGIONAL HUMAN RIGHTS SYSTEMS: THE BASICS

International human rights law establishes the right to an adequate and effective remedy under different treaties.[10] Accordingly, people have the right to equal and effective access to justice and to reparations for harms they suffer when rights incorporated in international treaties or general international law are violated. The implementation of such a right is meant to take place primarily at the domestic level. In cases where a state accepts the jurisdiction of an international court to know of breaches of obligations contained in treaties it has ratified, the court has the right to award reparations for such breaches.

For many years, restrictive interpretations of international human rights law by international lawyers and states' representatives supported the belief that the victim of a gross human rights violation is only the right holder targeted by the violent action – for example, the individual who disappears or is tortured,

---

[10] See Articles 2.3, 9.5, and 14.6 of the International Covenant on Civil and Political Rights, Articles 13, 5.4, 5.5, and 6.1 of the European Convention on Human Rights (ECHR), Articles 1, 2, 8, and 25 of the American Convention on Human Rights (ACHR), and Articles 7, 21, and 26 of the African Charter on Human and Peoples' Rights.

arbitrarily killed, or detained. Since 1990,[11] this belief has been gradually challenged and transformed. The UN Commission on Human Rights and the UN General Assembly supported this shift when they adopted the *Basic Principles and Guidelines on the Right to a Remedy and Reparation for Victims of Gross Violations of International Human Rights Law and Serious Violations of Humanitarian Law*[12] in 2005.[13] According to the *Basic Principles*,

> Victims are persons who individually or collectively suffered harm, including physical or mental injury, emotional suffering, economic loss or substantial impairment of their fundamental rights, through acts or omissions that constitute gross violations of international human rights law, or serious violations of international humanitarian law. *Where appropriate, and in accordance with domestic law, the term "victim" also includes the immediate family or dependants of the direct victim* and persons who have suffered harm in intervening to assist victims in distress or to prevent victimization. [Emphasis added.]

This harms-oriented concept of victim considers the immediate family of the direct victim or his or her dependants as potential victims with one caveat: any possible extension of the term victim to include family members or dependants is subject to domestic laws. The shift toward a harms-based expansion of the notion of victim was already detected in the *Declaration of Basic Principles of Justice for Victims of Crime and Abuse of Power* adopted in 1985[14] and has been confirmed by the recently adopted *UN Convention for the Protection of All Persons from Enforced Disappearances*.[15]

To see whether this nominal harms-based expansion of the notion of a victim of a gross human rights violation has been confirmed by the ECtHR and the IACtHR, we first have to see who is considered a victim under those systems – who, in principle, is entitled to reparations and what are the accepted modalities of reparations.

---

[11] That year the UN Human Rights Committee handed down its decision in the case of *Quinteros v. Uruguay* in which it decided that the mother of the disappeared victim suffered inhuman treatment because of the disappearance of her daughter. Communication No. 107/1981, CCPR/C/OP/2 (1990), 138, para. 14.

[12] http://www.ohchr.org/english/law/remedy.htm.

[13] The *Basic Principles* were approved by the then UN Commission on Human Rights by 40 votes to 0, with 13 abstentions. At the General Assembly, they were adopted without a vote.

[14] Article 2 of the *Declaration* refers to the immediate family members or dependants of the direct victim.

[15] Article 24 of the *Convention* establishes that "victim" means the disappeared person and any individual who has suffered harm as the direct result of an enforced disappearance. See also Heidy Rombouts, Pietro Sardaro, and Stef Vandeginste, "The Right to Reparations for Victims of Gross and Systematic Violations of Human Rights," in *Out of the Ashes: Reparations for Victims of Gross and Systematic Human Rights Violations*, ed. Koen De Feyter et al. (Antwerp: Intersentia, 2005), 360.

1. The European Framework

The notion of family member or dependant, as relevant to defining who is a victim or a reparations beneficiary, is nowhere to be found in the European Convention on Human Rights (ECHR). The concept of "victim" under the ECHR is closely related to that of the applicant in a case. Article 34 of the ECHR establishes that "the Court may receive applications from any person, non-governmental organization or group of individuals claiming to be the victim of a violation by one of the High Contracting Parties of the rights set forth in the Convention or the protocols thereto." Therefore, the basic idea is that the right holder who is claiming to be the victim of a violation is the one who should lodge the complaint before the ECtHR. As this is not always possible (think of a victim of disappearance), the European Commission on Human Rights (ECommHR) and the ECtHR have allowed someone other than the direct victim, mostly a close relative[16] or one of his or her heirs,[17] to appear as an applicant before the court, usually on behalf of that victim when he or she is not in a condition to do so.[18] Accordingly, for example, in right-to-life cases – when a person has allegedly been killed or disappeared – the ECtHR has accepted applications lodged by relatives of the person (including the father, mother, sister, brother, husband or wife, or nephew of the deceased person) on his or her behalf.

Article 41 of the ECHR establishes the legal framework to be followed by the ECtHR when awarding reparations. It states that

> if the Court finds that there has been a violation of the Convention or the protocols thereto, and if the internal law of the High Contracting Party concerned allows only partial reparation to be made, the Court shall, if necessary, afford just satisfaction to the injured party.

Article 41 establishes a subsidiary role in the award of reparation to the ECtHR in relation to ECHR breaches. It is the state that violated the ECHR that should repair domestically the harm produced and identify the means to execute judgments. Only in the absence of such reparation, and if necessary, should the ECtHR order reparations to the victims of violations.[19] According to this

---

[16] ECtHR, *Yasa v. Turkey*, September 2, 1998.
[17] ECtHR, *Deweer v. Belgium*, February 27, 1980, para. 37.
[18] ECtHR, *De Wilde, Ooms and Versyp v. Belgium*, June 18, 1971. More recently, the court again has said that "accepting an application from a 'person' indirectly affected by the alleged violation will be justified only in exceptional circumstances, in particular where it is clearly established that it is impossible for the direct victim to apply to the Court." ECtHR, *Vatan v. Russia*, October 7, 2004, para. 48.
[19] ECtHR, *De Wilde*; and see Shelton, 294.

article, the beneficiary of reparations is the "injured party." In principle, this term should be understood as the equivalent to victim,[20] meaning the person or persons whose rights under the ECHR have been directly breached by the action or inaction of state authorities.[21] Victims or applicants cannot claim reparations for family members who might have arguably experienced moral or material harm but who did not appear in front of the ECtHR claiming to be either victims or successors. Thus, in relation to gross human rights violations, family members may be awarded reparations only under two scenarios. If the victim is dead, the ECtHR recognizes that the next of kin of the victim can receive reparations as successors. The ECtHR has also considered that, under certain circumstances, the next of kin of the direct victim of gross human rights violations can be considered a victim of violations of the ECHR in his or her own right, and as such can be awarded reparations. In any event, reparations for successors and for independent victims for material or moral damages experienced do not exclude each other.

The ECtHR has consistently decided that in awarding reparations, it will always aim for *restitutio in integrum*, meaning that it favors those forms of reparation that are most capable of recreating the situation that "would have existed" before the violation.[22] When going back to the *status quo ante* is not possible, the court will award compensation for pecuniary damages, nonpecuniary or moral damages, and legal costs endured by the victim. Pecuniary damages entail the payment of the material damages that are a direct result of the violation of the right(s) of a person and of its consequences.[23] The ECtHR mainly recognizes material damages for loss of earnings (*damnum emergens*) but also awards reparations for loss of earnings potential (*lucrum cesans*). This means that the court awards reparations for the costs of the damages caused as a result of the violation, such as loss of income, medical expenses, loss of pension rights, loss of enjoyment of property, and replacement of objects destroyed or damaged with the violation.[24] Sometimes, but not always, it also awards reparations for consequential harm, as when the victims lose profits as a result of the violations.[25] Legal costs are awarded by the ECtHR under a separate heading in the judgment and cover the expenses incurred by lawyers

---

[20] ECtHR, *De Wilde*, para. 23.
[21] ECtHR, *Colozza v. Italy*, judgment, February 12, 1985, para. 38.
[22] See Rombouts et al., 395.
[23] ECtHR, *Comingersoll S. A v. Portugal*, April 6, 2000, para. 29.
[24] ECtHR, *Young, James and Webster v. the United Kingdom*, October 18, 1982, paras. 10–11; *Aksoy v. Turkey*, December 18, 1996, paras. 111–113; *Ayder and others v. Turkey*, January 8, 2004, paras. 104 and ss; and *Papamichalopoulos and others v. Greece*, October 31, 1995, paras. 38–39.
[25] ECtHR, *Lingens v. Austria*, July 8, 1986, para. 51. See also Shelton, 301.

in the litigation of the case before the court. The ECtHR awards moral or nonpecuniary damages "for the anxiety, inconvenience and uncertainty caused by the violation."[26] As will be noted in the coming pages, the court does not have quantification systems in place or clear and consistent criteria to award either material or moral damages. In the majority of cases, the court opts to award a lump sum of money based on equity but without explaining how it arrived at such a sum of money.[27]

Although in relation to gross human rights violations the ECtHR has always awarded reparations in the form of compensation for material damages, moral damages, and legal costs, the elements of the awards change from case to case. For the most part, the court has not relied on the other modalities of reparations embraced by international law, such as restitution, rehabilitation, satisfaction measures, and guarantees of nonrepetition.[28] In general, the court considers its judgments to be per se a form of satisfaction.[29]

2. The Inter-American Framework

The IACtHR has a legal framework that allows a better treatment of moral and material damages for family members. The American Convention on Human Rights (ACHR) allows any person, groups of persons, or nongovernmental organization (NGO) recognized in any of the Organization of American States (OAS) member states to lodge a complaint before the Inter-American Commission on Human Rights (IACommHR), so that somebody completely unrelated to the victim may start a procedure.[30] More specifically, the IACtHR Rules of Procedure invite family members to get involved in the process. Thus, Article 23 of the Rules of Procedure establishes that once the IACommHR refers a case to the court and the application is admitted, "the alleged victims, their

---

[26] ECtHR, *Comingersoll S. A*, para. 29.
[27] Shelton, 301.
[28] Recent case law, however, exhibits some willingness to engage with other forms of reparations, such as restitution measures, even if exceptionally. See *Assanidze v. Georgia*, where the court ordered that a detained man in Georgia, who had been granted pardon by the president, be released from prison by state authorities "at the earliest possible date" (April 8, 2004, para. 203). Other cases are *Bromiowski v. Poland*; *Ilascu and other v. Moldova and Russia*; and *Papamichalopoulos v. Greece*.
[29] The reluctance of the court to order states to do things other than give monetary compensation to victims responds in part to the role played by the Committee of Ministers of the Council of Europe, which is charged with monitoring the execution of the decisions rendered by the court and helping states set up preventive measures to avoid human rights violations. There is no equivalent body in the Inter-American system, and this may partly explain why the Inter-American Court has taken some of those tasks upon itself.
[30] Article 44 of the ACHR.

next of kin or their duly accredited representatives may submit their pleadings, motions and evidence, autonomously, throughout the proceedings." Article 2.15 defines the next of kin as "the immediate family, that is, the direct ascendants and descendants, siblings, spouses or permanent companions, or those determined by the court, if applicable." Tellingly, Article 2.15 does not restrict the meaning of family to a rigid or legalistic notion of the term, and explicitly allows the court to go beyond culturally dominant views of the family.

As for reparations, just like the European convention, the ACHR refers to the notion of "injured party" to define a beneficiary of reparations. Indeed, Article 63.1 of the convention establishes that

> if the Court finds that there has been a violation of a right or freedom protected by this Convention, the Court shall rule that the injured party be ensured the enjoyment of his right or freedom that was violated. It shall also rule, if appropriate, that the consequences of the measure or situation that constituted the breach of such right or freedom be remedied and that fair compensation be paid to the injured party.

The term "injured party" in Article 63.1 should be understood, in principle, as equivalent to that of a victim of violations of the ACHR, as is the case in the European system.[31] Nevertheless, the practice of the IACtHR, as we shall discuss, indicates that the term "injured party" has not been limited to those considered victims of a human rights violation under the ACHR. In the American system, family members have accessed reparations as victims (when the violations targeting their loved ones were also considered to amount to violations of their own rights), but also as injured parties or beneficiaries, or dependants morally or materially affected by the violations, even when the court did not recognize them as victims of violations of the ACHR. Additionally, as with the ECtHR, the IACtHR also recognizes the category of successors in right-to-life cases, something that does not preclude the right of people to claim reparations in their own right.

As for the modalities of reparation, the IACtHR has considered that under international customary law the aim of reparations is to produce *restitutio ad integrum* to the injured party of a human rights violation.[32] If it is not possible to return things to the *status quo ante*, the court applies general international law and awards compensation for pecuniary damages, nonpecuniary damages, and legal costs. The court understands as pecuniary or material damage "the loss of or detriment to the victims' income, the expenses incurred as a result

---

[31] Article 2.31 of the Rules of Procedure of the IACtHR defines victim as "the person whose rights have been violated, according to a judgment pronounced by the Court."

[32] IACtHR, *Aloeboetoe v. Suriname*, reparations, September 10, 1993, para. 43.

of the facts, and the monetary consequences that have a causal nexus with the facts of the . . . case."[33] Clearly, pecuniary damages incorporate reparations for loss of earning and loss of earning potential, as happens in the case law of the ECtHR.[34] For the IACtHR, nonpecuniary or immaterial damages "can include the suffering and affliction caused to the direct victims and their relatives, detriment to values that are very significant for individuals, as well as non-monetary alterations in the conditions of existence of the victim or the victim's family."[35] As such damages are difficult to calculate owing to their nature, the court awards them based on equity.

Finally, and unlike its European counterpart, the IACtHR has not shied away from ordering other modalities of reparations, such as measures of satisfaction and rehabilitation and guarantees of nonrepetition, according to the gravity of the violation.

III. REPARATIONS FOR FAMILY MEMBERS AS SUCCESSORS IN THE JURISPRUDENCE OF THE ECtHR AND IACtHR

As we just saw, both the ECtHR and the IACtHR have granted family members reparations as successors of the victim. Let us explore each court's jurisprudence in turn.

1. *The ECtHR and the Payment of Pecuniary and Moral Damages to Successors*

In right-to-life cases, the ECtHR grants pecuniary damages – loss of earnings and earnings potential – to successors if it finds not only a procedural but also a substantive violation of Article 2 of the ECHR (right to life). This requires the court to consider it proved "beyond reasonable doubt" that the state party to the convention failed to investigate the killing or disappearance of the person (procedural violation) and that state agents, or people working under their acquiescence, killed or disappeared the victim (substantive violation). The legal basis for the award of pecuniary reparations is, then, the existence of a "causal link between the damage claimed by the applicant and the violation of the Convention."[36] If the court finds only a procedural violation of Article 2,

---

[33] IACtHR, *Bámaca Velásquez v. Guatemala*, reparations, February 22, 2002, para. 43.
[34] Lost earnings refer to the loss of economic income, past or future. Consequential damages are those expenses incurred by victims and their next of kin in dealing with the effects of the state's violation.
[35] IACtHR, *Bámaca Velásquez*, para. 56.
[36] ECtHR, *Cakici v. Turkey*, judgment, July 8, 1999, para 127.

it does not award material damages, as the direct link between the violation and the damage is absent.

In cases where the ECtHR awards pecuniary damages to successors, its treatment of such damages is very conservative. Firstly, it will not grant pecuniary damages (but only moral damages) to family members as successors unless they present a claim before the court and are able to prove such damages. Secondly, the court is not ready to alleviate the burden or standard of proof as a result of the conditions that surround gross human rights violations, which make it very difficult to prove "beyond reasonable doubt" the damages that took place. It is also very reluctant to rely on presumptions: when it does so to calculate loss of earnings, it is because the claimants so request,[37] and even then not always. Thirdly, the court has typically awarded family members less than what they claimed for pecuniary damage,[38] and only exceptionally has it awarded the applicants what they claimed as successors for material damages.[39] As a result, the court fails to award proper material damages to successors. This has serious consequences for the family in general, and for women in particular, as often the person killed or disappeared was also the breadwinner of the house, which means that women and children are often left without proper redress for these damages.

[37] For instance, in the case of *Akhmadova and Sadulayeva v. Russia*, the mother and the spouse of the disappeared person were the applicants. For them, although the victim did not have a job at the time of his disappearance, he used to work as a butcher in the market, and it "was reasonable to suppose that he would have found a job and earned at least the official minimum wage until 2034, when he would have reached the life expectancy age for men in Russia." The ECtHR accepted the argument and concluded "that it is reasonable to assume that Mr. Akhmadov would eventually have some earnings from which the applicants would have benefited," and awarded 15,000 EUR to them and the children (May 10, 2007, para. 140).

[38] So, for instance, in *Akhmadova and Sedulayeva*, the applicants claimed 44,236 EUR for loss of earning and 1,225 EUR for funeral expenses. The court awarded only 15,000 EUR to both applicants jointly and dismissed the payment of funeral expenses without proper reasoning (paras. 139–143). The main reason for the small award was the lack of evidence to substantiate the claim. Nevertheless, despite the fact that the court found that the son and husband of the applicants, Mr. Akhmadov, was arbitrarily executed by state authorities and that his body was found more than a month after his disappearance, it did not award compensation for the funerary expenses (para. 92).

[39] Shelton, 304. This was the case in *Cakici v. Turkey*, where the court awarded 11,534.29 GBP for loss of earnings, as claimed by the applicants, based on "the detailed submissions by the applicant concerning the actuarial basis of calculation of the appropriate capital sum to reflect the loss of income due to Ahmet Çakici's death" (para. 127). See also *Salman v. Turkey*, judgment, June 27, 2000, para. 137. In cases such as *Cakici* and other Turkish ones, the lawyers of the applicants used the UK "Ogden tables" to calculate such losses. Such tables indicate different multipliers to bring to present value the future income that the victim would have had. See UK Government's Actuary Department, Actuarial Tables with Explanatory Notes for Use in Personal Injury and Fatal Accident Cases, 6th edition, http://www.gad.gov.uk/Publications/docs/Ogden_Tables_6th_edition.pdf.

Regarding compensation for moral damages, the basic principle applied by the ECtHR is that the more serious the violation, the higher the award.[40] As already said, this is another area where the ECtHR lacks systematic calculation rules. The only rule applied by the court indicates that it will award reparations for moral damages to the successors on behalf of the deceased only when it has been proven that the victim was arbitrarily detained or tortured before being killed or disappeared.[41] This is in striking contrast to the IACtHR, which, as we will see below, always awards moral damages to the successors of a disappeared or killed person. The ECtHR also has an inconsistent approach to the award of moral damages to successors. In some cases the court will grant them and in others not. It is not possible to identify an underlying explanation for this approach. One of the determining factors seems to be whether or not the applicants ask for moral damages on behalf of the victim, which is not always the case.[42]

As for the rules of distribution of reparations awards (both for material and moral damages) to successors on behalf of the deceased if the disappeared or killed person was married or had a companion and children, the ECtHR will recognize the spouse or companion (without differentiating among them) and the children of the disappeared or killed person as heirs.[43] If the person was not married and had no descendants, the court will award pecuniary damages to the father and mother of the victim if both are alive, or to one of them if the other is dead. Nevertheless, the court is not interested in identifying each one of the possible successors. If the applicants do not indicate the successors, the court does not make any substantial efforts to try to identify them. Indeed, in the majority of decisions, the court indicates that the pecuniary and nonpecuniary damages of the deceased should be paid to the wife and children without giving any further details. Thus, despite the court's recognition of the categories of successors and heirs, it has not established a working principle to be applied across cases to identify who these people are. Further, the court has not indicated the way money should be distributed between successors.

---

[40] ECtHR, *Mentes and others v. Turkey*, judgment, July 24, 1998, para. 20.

[41] ECtHR, *Timurtas v. Turkey*, June 13, 2000, para. 127.

[42] So, for instance, in *Akhamadova*, each applicant requested 20,000 EUR as victims, and not as successors. Similarly, in *Imakayeva v. Russia*, where the son and the husband of the applicant were disappeared, she claimed 70,000 EUR on her own behalf (judgment, November 9, 2006, paras. 214–216). In contrast to this, in the case of *Celikbilekv v. Turkey*, the brother of the deceased requested 40,000 GBP on behalf of the deceased, and the ECtHR awarded 20,000 GBP to be held by the brother for the widow and children of the deceased as successors (judgment, May 31, 2005, para. 122).

[43] In *Celikbilekv*, the wife and children of the deceased were awarded pecuniary damages. In the case of *Tanis et al. v. Turkey*, the ECtHR awarded pecuniary damages to both the wife of one of the disappeared persons and to his companion jointly (judgment, August 2, 2005, para. 232).

The case law of the system fluctuates between the distribution of equal shares among successors[44] and the distribution of pecuniary damages according to what the successors decide.[45]

2. The IACtHR and the Payment of Pecuniary and Moral Damages to Successors

The IACtHR has established clearer principles and presumptions regulating the award of reparations to successors. The basic rule is that "the right to compensation for damages suffered by the victims up to the time of their death is transmitted to their heirs by succession."[46] In cases where the beneficiaries are minors, the court tends to decree the establishment of a trust.[47] The court calculates lost earnings of a killed or disappeared person by calculating the income that, had the violation not taken place, would have entered the victim's patrimony "based upon the income the victim would have received ... up to the time of his (or her) possible natural death."[48] It also takes into account the age of the person at the time of the events, the life expectancy in the country, and the particular facts of the case.

Moreover, the IACtHR is willing to rely on certain presumptions. Thus, if the IACommHR or the petitioner or both are unable to prove the salary earned by the deceased including bonuses, the court will presume with respect to loss of earnings that a person would have had a job earning at least the minimum wage in the country at the time of the violation, and will adjust that wage according to inflation until the moment the person would have died at the age of life expectancy in the country. The court will, in principle, deduct 25% of that total amount of money on the presumption that the deceased would have used that money to cover personal expenses and spent most of the rest on the family.[49] It will never award less than the minimum wage, even if the victim earned less than that, as happened in the cases of *El Amparo v. Venezuela* and *Street Children v. Guatemala*.[50] Since this translates into a

---

[44] In *Akhmadova*, the mother, wife, and children jointly received compensation for loss of earnings.
[45] ECtHR, *Celikbilekv*, paras. 119 and 122.
[46] IACtHR, *Garrido and Baigorria v. Argentina*, reparations, August 27, 1998, para. 50.
[47] Carrillo, 525.
[48] IACtHR, *Velásquez Rodríguez v. Honduras*, reparations, July 21, 1989, para. 46.
[49] IACtHR, *Castillo Paez v. Peru*, reparations, November 27, 1998, para. 75, and *Caracazo v. Venezuela*, reparations, August 29, 2002, para. 88. Such a reduction is not applied when the victim of the violation is a disabled person who presumably depended almost entirely on the care of others. See IACtHR, *Caracazo*, para. 89a.
[50] In the *Street Children* case, the court awarded loss of earnings to the deceased street children based on the minimum wage for nonagricultural activities in Guatemala. IACtHR, *Street*

presumption that a person would have always earned at least the minimum wage (which is not always the case), it has the effect of compensating for structural inequalities to the advantage of those in a more precarious situation in society. This is to be valued, since most of the time those who will have access to the loss of earnings are women and children as successors. Indeed, the IACtHR goes even further: in situations of gross and systematic human rights violations where there are multiple victims and where evidence to prove material damages is more difficult to gather, the court is ready to award loss of earnings to the successors based simply on equity.[51]

The IACtHR has also recognized the right of successors to inherit the award for moral damages made to the victim of a right-to-life violation. The court has established in different cases that "anyone subjected to aggression and abuse will experience moral suffering"[52] (whether he or she survives the violation) so that no proof is required other than the finding that the violation – execution, disappearance, torture, or other serious abuse attributable to state agents – occurred. As a rule, moral harm (mental anguish, emotional distress, pain and suffering) will be presumed with respect to the victim but also, as we will see, to the victim's close relatives. The court has also presumed that nonpecuniary damage is more severe when children are the victims.[53] In other words, any

---

Children v. Guatemala, reparations, May 25, 2001, para. 79. See also *El Amparo v. Venezuela*, reparations, paras. 28–29. Additionally, the court is ready to repair lost opportunities when the killing or disappearance of a child or of a young adult is at stake. Accordingly, it will award loss of potential earnings to the successors of the deceased based on sufficient evidence that the child or young adult would have followed a particular profession. If the court is unable to establish the profession with certainty, it will still award loss of such earnings to the successors (the parents) based on equity, as happened in the case of *Bulacio v. Argentina* with the child who was killed and in the case of *Castillo Páez* with the 22-year-old disappeared man. See *Castillo Paez*, para. 74, and *Bulacio v. Argentina*, judgment, September 18, 2003, para. 84.

[51] This was the case in *Castro Castro Prison v. Peru*, where the court awarded US $10,000 to the successors of each of the 41 inmates who were killed during "the operative transfer I" (organized by Alberto Fujimori at the high security prison in May 1992), for the work they could have carried out in the future. IACtHR, *Castro Castro Prison v. Peru*, judgment, November 25, 2006, para. 424. Equally, in *Pueblo Bello v. Colombia*, the court relied mostly on equity (but also on presumptions around life expectancy in the country or the economic activity the person would have continued to do) to calculate the material damages of each one of the 37 disappeared and six killed persons by paramilitary groups in Colombia, awarding each one of them between US $40,000 and $85,000. The court acknowledged that, because of the particular facts of this case, family members were displaced without being able to take with them receipts or other relevant information to prove material damages (judgment, January 31, 2006, paras. 247–251).

[52] IACtHR, *Garrido and Baigorria*, para. 49, and *Loayza Tamayo v. Perú*, reparations, November 27, 1998, para. 138.

[53] In the *Street Children* case, for instance, it awarded high moral damages (between US $23,000 to $30,000) to the five victims – three of whom were children and two of whom were 18 and 19 years old at the time of their killings – explicitly taking into account their age and condition (para. 90). Such awards were given, in full, to four of the mothers and one grandmother

person who is a victim of a gross human rights violation under the ACHR is by definition entitled to moral damages. This, as noted before, contrasts with the more restrictive approach of the ECtHR.

As for who is recognized as successor, the IACtHR has decided that, in principle, it will be the children and the spouse or companion of the direct victim.[54] Companions and spouses are treated equally by the court, as are other persons with whom the victim might have had a similarly strong emotional bond.[55] If the victims did not have children, then the court will generally award more or less the same percentage of money to the parents and to the spouse or companion of the victim. In the absence of children and spouse or companion, the parents and siblings of the victim are considered as heirs.[56]

Concerning the distribution of pecuniary as well as moral damages among the potential successors, the IACtHR does not apply only one rule, as it prefers to take into account the specifics of each particular case.[57] In doing so, it will take into account, among other things, domestic succession law (not necessarily following it), the harm experienced by different family members, their involvement in the case, and the degree of closeness and dependency between the deceased and the family member.[58] This said, in its last decisions the court has predominantly distributed pecuniary and nonpecuniary damages

---

of the deceased as successors. In the case of *Pueblo Bello v. Colombia*, where 37 persons were disappeared and six were killed, the court awarded each of them US $30,000 for moral damages, except for the three persons who were children at the time of the events who received $35,000 (para. 258). See also *Ituango v. Colombia*, judgment, July 1, 2006, para. 390.

[54] In cases such as *Bámaca Velásquez* or *Aloeboetoe*, the court explicitly indicated that although in most jurisdictions the children are to be considered as heirs, in some jurisdictions in the Americas the wife is also an heir. When she is not, she also has access to the inheritance as she has rights over the matrimonial assets. In the latter case, she is not really considered a successor, as the court is simply recognizing her rights as a result of being married, rights she would also have in case of divorce. What is important for our purposes is that the court recognizes the rights of wives and companions over the reparations awarded to their deceased partner. *Bámaca Velásquez*, para. 32, and *Aloeboetoe*, para. 62.

[55] In *Pueblo Bello*, for instance, the court recognized that the two partners of four different victims had the right to inherit their reparations (para. 240). In *Street Children*, a grandmother was treated as a mother and received reparations as such (para. 83). In *Caracazo*, two aunts of two of the deceased who lived under the same roof as their nephews were also treated as mothers with rights as successors over the awards made by the court (para. 91). In *Mapiripán v. Colombia*, the stepdaughters and sons of one of the deceased were treated as his heirs (judgment, September 15, 2005, para. 259).

[56] IACtHR, *Aloeboetoe*, para. 54.

[57] IACtHR, *Velásquez Rodriguez*, para. 48.

[58] In the *Street Children* case, all the awards given for material and immaterial damages to the five street children went to four mothers and one grandmother because the children had grown up with single mothers and/or without their fathers (para. 83). In *El Caracazo*, the court allotted half of the compensation for lost earnings in equal parts to the victim's children; a quarter to his or her spouse or permanent companion; and a quarter to the parents (para. 91).

according to the following rule: 50% will be given to the children of the deceased in equal parts and 50% to the spouses or companions of the deceased. If the deceased had more than one spouse or companion, the court distributes the 50% in equal shares. If the deceased was not married or did not have children, 50% will be given to the parents in equal parts. If one of the parents is dead, the surviving one will receive 50%, and the remaining 50% will be given to the siblings of the deceased to be distributed in equal shares. If some members of the family do not exist in the categories just mentioned, the money awarded to other members of the family will increase proportionately.[59]

Worth underscoring is the effort the IACtHR has made to reflect culturally diverse family notions in the reparations domain. As early as 1993, in the case of *Aloeboetoe v. Suriname*, the court used domestic law, traditional Saramaka custom, and the ACHR to grant reparations to successors. Domestic law concepts such as direct ascendant, descendant, and spouse were important, but the court interpreted them taking into account traditional Saramaka customs, which recognize, for instance, polygamy. Yet at the same time, the IACtHR clearly established that "in referring to 'ascendants,' the Court shall make no distinction as to sex, even if that might be contrary to Saramaka custom."[60] This last approach aimed to balance respect for cultural differences with the right of women not to be discriminated against on the grounds of their sex. A similar sensitivity was shown by the court in *Bámaca Velásquez v. Guatemala*, the case of a guerrilla member who was subjected to forced disappearance in Guatemala while in combat. His wife and the IACommHR requested the court to apply Mam customs in the distribution of material and moral damages among the next of kin so as to incorporate not only the victim's wife but also his father and sisters, reflecting a Mam tradition whereby the eldest son contributes to the expenses of his parents and siblings. The court granted this request based on the need to respect Mam culture.[61]

IV. REPARATIONS TO FAMILY MEMBERS AS VICTIMS AND INJURED PARTIES

The concepts of direct and indirect victims are sometimes used by legal operators. The usage of these terms is so common that even the *Basic Principles on Reparations* refer to "direct victims." These terms, however, are not proper

---

[59] IACtHR, *Cantoral Huamaní and García-Santa Cruz v. Peru*, judgment, July 10, 2007, para. 161; *Zambrano Vélez v. Ecuador*, judgment, July 4, 2007, para. 136; *La Rochela v. Colombia*, May 11, 2007, para. 137; and *Castro Castro Prison*, para. 421.
[60] IACtHR, *Aloeboetoe*, para. 62.
[61] IACtHR, *Bámaca Velásquez*, para. 52.

legal terms. Nor are they part of the repertoire of legal concepts deployed by regional courts in a systematic manner, even though sporadic reference to such terminology can be found in the case law.[62] In popular parlance, a *direct victim* of a violation is often referred to as the person who suffers, first in time and physically, a human rights violation (for instance, the person who is disappeared or tortured). An *indirect victim* is any person who (a) can be considered a separate victim of violations of rights as a result of one and the same action that violated the rights of the direct victim (say, the disappearance of a person may cause great suffering to his parents and this may in itself be considered to amount to a violation of their own rights) or (b) can be considered a victim of violations in his or her own right not because of the primary act but owing to subsequent (though strictly related) actions that violated his or her rights (as when a wife is denied justice by the domestic system when trying to clarify the whereabouts of her disappeared husband).

Whatever we may think of this construct[63] for the purpose of this chapter, the terminology remains too limited when analyzing the jurisprudence of the IACtHR, which has recognized that people other than those who can be technically considered victims of violations of their rights under the ACHR may nevertheless be considered beneficiaries of reparations as either "injured parties" or "dependants." Because what interests us is to understand when family members become beneficiaries of reparations, the analysis that follows will be comprehensive. This is why the following pages will cover all modalities that have turned family members into reparations beneficiaries on their own (as opposed to in their status as the victims' successors), whether or not they are themselves technically conceptualized as victims of gross human rights violations by the courts.

1. The Approach of the ECtHR to Family Members as Victims of Gross Human Rights Violations in Their Own Right

In the reparations context, the ECtHR has afforded a restrictive meaning to the word "injured party." For a next of kin of a victim to have access to reparations in his or her own name (and not as a successor), the person must claim that he or she is an autonomous victim of a violation of some of the rights included in the ECHR. The person could, for instance, claim that she has been subject to inhuman treatment (Article 3 of the convention prohibits torture and inhuman

---

[62] Judge Cançado Trindade used this terminology in his separate opinion in the *Street Children* case. The ECtHR has also referred to indirect victims in the case of *Cakici*, paras. 94–97.

[63] For instance, the distinction between the two concepts can be criticized for being artificial and having the potential to create improper hierarchies of suffering between categories of people.

treatment) or deprived of a right to an effective remedy (as recognized under Article 13).[64] In fact, these are some of the most common allegations of family members of disappeared or extrajudicially executed persons. Further, as we will see, the court has recognized different members of the family as victims in those situations,[65] but the case law appears to indicate that mothers and fathers tend to be the only ones recognized as such by the court.[66]

The ECtHR has established a narrow understanding of what amounts to a violation of Article 3 in relation to the next of kin of a person. As a general rule, the court may find such a violation in relation to disappearances only if certain factors additional to the violation itself are present in the case. The ECtHR first addressed this question in the case of *Kurt v. Turkey*, where it recognized that the mother of the disappeared had suffered inhuman treatment because the disappearance of her son and the complacency of the authorities in relation to her distress caused her great anguish.[67] Although in this case the court placed most of the emphasis on the bond tying the victim and her mother and on the suffering of the latter, soon the court changed its understanding to one in which special factors and not just the primary violation per se were required. Among these the state authorities' reaction to the situation stood out, becoming henceforth a necessary condition for a violation of the family member's right not to be subject to inhuman treatment under Article 3. In the words of the court in *Cakici v. Turkey*:

> Whether a *family member is such a victim* will depend on the existence of *special factors* which gives the suffering of the applicant a dimension and character distinct from the emotional distress which may be regarded as inevitably caused to relatives of a victim of a serious human rights violation. Relevant elements will include the proximity of the family tie – in that context, a certain weight will attach to the parent-child bond – the particular circumstances of the relationship, the extent to which the family member witnessed the events in question, the involvement of the family member in the attempts to obtain information about the disappeared person and the way in which the authorities responded to those enquiries. *The Court would further emphasise that the essence of such a violation does not so much lie in the fact of the "disappearance" of the family member but rather concerns*

---

[64] See Article 13 of the ECHR at http://www.echr.coe.int/NR/rdonlyres/D5CC24A7-DC13-4318-B457-5C9014916D7A/0/EnglishAnglais.pdf.

[65] In the case of *Tanis and others v. Turkey*, the court considered as autonomous victims of violations of the ECHR the father, the brother, and the wives of the two disappeared persons (judgment, August 2, 2005, paras. 221 and 235).

[66] ECtHR, *Kurt v. Turkey*, judgment, May 25, 1998, paras. 130–134; *Timurtas v. Turkey*, paras. 125–128; and *Imakayeva v. Russia*, para. 213.

[67] ECtHR, *Kurt v. Turkey*.

the authorities' reactions and attitudes to the situation when it is brought to their attention. It is especially in respect of the latter that a relative *may claim directly to be a victim* of the authorities' conduct.[68] [Emphasis added.]

Thus, the ECtHR distinguished between two kinds of harm. On the one hand, there is the natural emotional distress caused to the next of kin of a disappeared person, which the court does not consider to amount to a violation of Article 3 prohibition of inhuman treatment. On the other hand, there is the harm primarily determined by the response family members receive from national authorities as well as by other special circumstances, which may provide the court with grounds to find a violation of Article 3. This approach, which the court applies to date, is based primarily on the idea that the next of kin are not victims because of the act that violated the rights of their beloved ones, but only as a result of further acts of state authorities that violated their rights autonomously.

In practice, what this means is that the court will check for the existence of some or several of the *Cakici* factors together with the inaction of state authorities. Otherwise, it will not consider that a violation of Article 3 took place in relation to the next of kin of the disappeared person.[69] It is not clear, though, how many of the *Cakici* factors (beyond the passivity of the state) must be present in a case for the court to find a violation of the right not to be subject to inhuman treatment. However, in all cases after *Cakici*, the special factors have been taken into consideration. It is fortunate that the court has sometimes been willing to give a contextualized interpretation of these factors.[70]

It is important to notice, though, that the ECtHR will find that there has been a violation of Article 3 (or any other right in the ECHR) only in relation to the applicant(s), and not in relation to other members of the family who do not act as applicants in the case and who do not claim to be victims. The case of *Cakici* illustrates this point. Mr. Cakici, brother of a disappeared person, claimed to be a victim of Article 3 together with his brother's wife and children.

---

[68] ECtHR, *Cakici*, para. 98.

[69] See *Seker v. Turkey*, where the court rejected the claims of a father whose son disappeared in Bismil on the grounds that "nothing in the content of the tone of the authorities' replies to the enquiries made by the applicant could be described as inhuman or degrading treatment" (judgment, February 21, 2006, paras. 83–84). See also *Tekdag v. Turkey*, judgment, January 15, 2004, paras. 83–84; *Neisbe Haran v. Turkey*, judgment, October 6, 2005, paras. 82–84; and *Koku v. Turkey*, judgment, May 31, 2005, paras. 171–172.

[70] In the case of *Akhmadova and Sadulayeva*, the wife of the disappeared, who was also one of the two applicants in the case, despite participating in some of the search for information about the whereabouts of her husband, had to stay at home most of the time to take care of her five children. Therefore, most of the requests to national authorities were made by her mother-in-law (the other applicant). The court did not penalize this behavior and, sensitive to the circumstances, awarded the same amount of money to both applicants (para. 15).

TABLE 5.1. *Disappearance cases: Reparations for moral damages to the next of kin of the disappeared as autonomous victims of violations of article 3 of the ECHR*

Case	Moral damages to family members (as victims – violation of Article 3)
Kurt v. Turkey (1998)	10,000 GBP[71] to the mother of the disappeared
Timurtas v. Turkey (2000)	10,000 GBP[72] to the father of the disappeared
Tanis and others v. Turkey (2005)	20,000 GBP[73] each to the father, the two brothers, and the wife of the two disappeared
Imakayeva v. Russia (2006)	70,000 EUR[74] to the applicant, mother, and wife of a disappeared son and a disappeared husband
Akhmadova and Sadulayeva (2007)	20,000 GBP[75] each to the mother and wife of the disappeared man

But the court considered that it could not look at the claim in relation to people who did not appear as victims or applicants before the ECommHR, as was the case with the wife and children of the disappeared victim.[76]

When the court finds that the applicant in a disappearance case is indeed an autonomous victim of Article 3, it will award relatively high moral damages. Examples can be seen in Table 5.1.

The table shows that the court has over time increased the amount of money given to family members for moral damages, and that it tends to award the same amount of money to the different family members who act as applicants. The only time the court awarded more money than usual to an applicant was the case of *Imakayeva*, where the son and the husband of the applicant were both disappeared in Chechnya. The large award was given in recognition of the anguish and distress that the applicant suffered as a result of the facts of the case and the destruction of her family.[77]

---

[71] 10,000 GBP was equivalent to US $16,300 on the date of the judgment according to http://www.oanda.com/convert/classic.
[72] 10,000 GBP was equivalent to US $15,128 on the date of the judgment.
[73] 20,000 GBP was equivalent to US $35,370 on the date of the judgment.
[74] 70,000 EUR was equivalent to 47,000 GBP and to US $89,444 on the date of the award.
[75] 20,000 GBP was equivalent to US $39,843 on the date of the award.
[76] ECtHR, *Cakici*, para. 97.
[77] Thus, although in principle she ought to have received around 20,000 GBP for her spouse and for her son (adding up to 40,000 GBP) for moral damages, she received 7,000 GBP more. This award is easily explained if it is taken into account that besides the violations found by the court of the rights of her husband and son, it also found breaches of the rights of Ms. Imakayeva to humane treatment (Article 3) and to private and family life (Article 8) (paras. 161–167, 183, 214–216).

The ECtHR has been reluctant to consider family members as victims in their own right in cases other than disappearances. A recent case, *Bitiyeva and X v. Russia*,[78] shows the inconsistencies of this rule. In the case, the first applicant first came to the court claiming to have been arbitrarily detained in Chernokozovo and subjected to inhuman and degrading treatment by Russian authorities in Chechnya in 2000. In 2003, the first applicant was killed in her house together with three other members of her family. Her daughter X decided to continue with the case at the ECtHR and brought new claims, one of which was that she was a victim of inhuman treatment because of her suffering as a result of the extrajudicial killing of four members of her family. The court considered that "while [it] does not doubt that the death of her family members caused the second applicant profound suffering, it nevertheless finds no basis for finding a violation of Article 3 in this context" as it is not a disappearance case.[79] This decision had two dissenting opinions by judges Loukis Loucaides and Dean Spielmann. They believed the daughter to be a victim of inhuman treatment because of the seriousness of the case and the fact that she had lost her mother. Both judges considered that had the *Cakici* factors been applied to the case, the applicant would have been found to be a victim of inhuman treatment under Article 3. Judge Spielmann explicitly stated that he found "somewhat artificial that a finding of a violation of Article 3 of the Convention should be limited to cases of 'disappeared persons.'"[80] In fact, the court could have seized this opportunity to overturn its doctrine, departing from its precedent, as it had already done in two exceptional cases decided before *Bitiyeva*, namely, *Akpinar and Altun v. Turkey* and *Akkun and others v. Turkey*.[81] What the ECtHR has recognized, though, is that applicants in arbitrary killing cases (as well as in disappearance cases) can claim to be victims of a violation of the right to effective remedies often under Article 13 of the ECHR.[82]

---

[78] ECtHR, *Bitiyeva and X v. Russia*, judgment, June 21, 2007.
[79] Ibid., para. 153.
[80] Ibid., para. 11 of Spielman dissenting opinion.
[81] In these cases, different family members (the sister and the father of the killed person in the first, and the father of the killed person in the second) were considered autonomous victims of violations of Article 3 as they were exposed to the mutilated bodies of their loved ones (whose ears were cut). The court considered that such treatment of the bodies, for religious reasons among others, produced extraordinary anguish for the family members. It is not clear what precedential value these cases will have, especially after *Bittiyeva*. Nevertheless, they clearly questioned the view that takes into account only the nature of the violation (a disappearance or an arbitrary killing) rather than the pain and suffering experienced by family members in relation to these or other human rights violations. ECtHR, *Akpinar and Altun v. Turkey*, February 27, 2007, paras. 84–87, and *Akkun and others v. Turkey*, March 24, 2005, para. 259. Contrast also with *Musayev v. Russia*, judgment, July 26, 2007, paras. 167–170.
[82] This article refers to the obligation that states parties to the ECHR have to provide people with effective remedies within their jurisdiction to protect the rights of the convention.

TABLE 5.2. *Disappearances and extrajudicial killings cases: Reparations for moral damages to next of kin as victims of violations of article 13*

Case	Moral damages to next of kin (as victims – Article 13)
Cakici v. Turkey (1999)	2,500 GBP[83] awarded to the brother of the disappeared
Celikbilekv (2005)	3,500 EUR[84] awarded to the brother of the deceased
Semsi Onen (2002)	16,000 EUR[85] to each of the two sisters who saw the killings and 13,000 EUR to each of the other 9 siblings of the killed person[86]
Bitiyeva and X v. Russia (2007)	75,000 EUR[87] to the surviving applicant, who was also the daughter of the first applicant in the case

In most cases where the court does not find the applicant to be a victim of inhuman treatment for the disappearance or illegal killing of a person, it will find that the applicant did not have access to effective (not necessarily judicial) domestic remedies to protect his or her rights under the ECHR and to redress in relation to an arguable claim that such violation(s) had or were taking place. In disappearance and arbitrary killing cases, for instance, the court usually finds that Article 13 has been violated (a) because the authorities failed to carry out an effective and thorough investigation into the alleged disappearance or arbitrary killing, failing to identify and punish those responsible for such acts, (b) as a result of the lack of access to the procedures given to the complainant, or (c) as a result of lack of reparation for the harms done.[88] In such cases, the applicant is equally a victim, but the award for moral damages is notoriously lower than the one awarded when the court finds a violation of Article 3, with the exception of *Bitiyeva and X v. Russia*. A look at Table 5.2 will confirm this to be the case.

[83] 2,500 GBP was equivalent to US $3,894 on the date of the judgment.
[84] 3,500 EUR was equivalent to US $4,365 and to 2,395 GBP on the date of the judgment.
[85] 16,000 EUR was equivalent to US $14,587 and to 10,015 GBP on the date of the award, and 13,000 EUR was equivalent to US $11,852 and to 8,137 GBP on the date of the award.
[86] A possible explanation for the large award in this case is the fact that the parents and a brother of the applicants were killed in front of two of them, and that the authorities failed to investigate the facts of the case, causing grave distress to all the siblings. See *Semsi*, paras. 110–112.
[87] 75,000 EUR was equivalent to US $100,696 and to 50,589 GBP on the date of the award. An explanation of the award is that, although the court did not find a violation of Article 3 in relation to the daughter, it still recognized that her suffering was severe and awarded her what it would have awarded if it had found such a violation. Compare this case with that of *Imakayeva*.
[88] *Cakici v. Turkey*, paras. 108–114; *Celikbilek v. Turkey*, paras. 100–111; *Semsi Onen v. Turkey*, May 14, 2002, paras. 96–100; and *Bitiyeva v. Russia*, paras. 154–159.

So far we have dealt only with moral damages. How has the ECtHR addressed material or pecuniary damages to the next of kin of disappeared and arbitrarily killed persons? In spite of the well-known evidence of the lost opportunities and income as well as costs (including funerary, medical, and legal expenses) that family members often experience when their lives are affected by the violent death or disappearance of a loved one, the court does not always award pecuniary damages to applicants, and when it does, it usually requires thorough substantiation and evidence of the claims. As we already indicated, on most occasions when the court awards such damages, it will calculate them based on equity. Most of the time, the court refuses even claims for the reimbursement of funeral expenses[89] or the expenses incurred for the education of the children of a disappeared person.[90] Since the court has also been unwilling to provide other forms of reparation such as rehabilitation measures (e.g., psychological or medical services), its shyness in this respect can only be regretted. Because in many scenarios it is mothers and wives as well as children whose lives are most changed by such drastic events, this jurisprudential gap is likely to have a negative impact on them.

The treatment by the ECtHR of the next of kin of victims of arbitrary detention or torture who are still alive is even more restrictive. Indeed, the court has never recognized them as autonomous victims of Article 3 violations.[91] In the research conducted for this chapter, no cases were found where an allegation had been made and then denied by the court that the next of kin of a person who was arbitrarily detained or tortured was the victim of an Article 3 violation. Nevertheless, it is possible to infer from the court's treatment of the next of kin in cases of disappearances and arbitrary killings that it would not be likely to consider as a victim the next of kin of an arbitrarily detained or tortured person because of the rigidity of the *Cakici* factors and the nature of the violation(s). A possible explanation of why the court has not even been asked to decide on the matter might be that the majority of these cases are brought by the direct victims of the violations, who fail to indicate other possible victims (such as the next of kin) to the court.[92]

---

[89] ECtHR, *Akhamadova and Sadulayeva*, para. 141. Interestingly, funeral expenses have been granted in other cases by the ECtHR but in relation to nongross violations of the ECHR. See the case of *öneryildiz v. Turkey*, November 30, 2004.

[90] ECtHR, *Celikbilekv*, para. 115, and *Aktas v. Turkey*, judgment, April 24, 2004, para. 356.

[91] This is not to say that the next of kin will be unable to claim to be victims of other rights violations under the ECHR such as Article 13.

[92] In *Aydin v. Turkey*, the applicant was the same victim of arbitrary detention and rape, Mrs. Şükran Aydin. Equally, in *Chitayev and Chitayev v. Russia*, the two applicants and victims were the two brothers, who were arbitrarily detained and tortured while in detention and later released. *Aydin v. Turkey*, judgment, September 25, 1997, and *Chitayev and Chitayev v. Russia*, judgment, January 18, 2007.

Yet the court has been asked to award reparations for loss of earnings to the next of kin of a tortured victim. In the case of *Mikheyev v. Russia*, the applicant/victim claimed to have been arbitrarily detained for a crime he did not commit and to have been subjected to torture, as a result of which he threw himself through a window to avoid further ill-treatment. He was left permanently disabled as he broke his spine.[93] The applicant requested the court to award loss of earnings to his mother as she had had to stop working in order to look after him because they did not have the money to pay for the special care he needed. He asked for 10,000 GBP[94] for his mother's lost income, but the claim was denied without an explanation by the court.[95] Given that in many families the role of caretaker to the disabled, sick, or wounded falls disproportionately on the women, this jurisprudential line is to be deeply regretted.

In summary, the jurisprudence of the ECtHR does not give proper weight to the emotional and the material harm experienced by close family members of victims of gross human rights violations such as disappearances, arbitrary killings, torture, or arbitrary detention. Certainly the court reads in narrow terms the concept of inhuman treatment under Article 3 of the ECHR, denying its application to cases other than disappearances and requiring even in those cases special factors, other than the disappearance itself, to consider that the violation took place. Further, the court does not even presume the existence of funeral expenses in cases of killings and is reluctant to compensate in an adequate manner the family members of killed or disappeared persons for the material damages they experience. Finally, the court has not given independent recognition to the moral and material harm experienced by family members of arbitrary detention or torture survivors, as victims or as beneficiaries, either in terms of compensation, rehabilitation, or otherwise. As a consequence, families are not properly redressed for all they have to undergo, not only in terms of suffering, but also in terms of expenses, lost opportunities, and physical and psychological harm due to the loss and the suffering of their beloved ones.

2. *The Approach of the IACtHR to the Next of Kin of Victims of Gross Human Rights Violations as Victims or as Injured Parties*

The IACtHR has gone further than the ECtHR in the treatment granted to the next of kin of victims of gross human rights violations, both as victims and

---

[93] ECtHR, *Mikheyev v. Russia*, judgment, January 26, 2006.
[94] 10,000 GBP would have been US $17,859 on the date of the judgment.
[95] Nevertheless, the ECtHR awarded him pecuniary and nonpecuniary damages because of his need for permanent medical treatment and the fact that he also "lost his mobility and sexual and pelvic function [being] unable to work or have children." The court awarded him 250,000 EUR. See paras. 162–163.

as injured parties. Indeed, the harm caused to the family unit or to family members in these situations seems to be of utmost importance to the IACtHR, and it is sometimes explicitly discussed in the hearings to deal with reparations that invite the testimony of experts in the area.[96] Occasionally, the court has explicitly incorporated such expert views into its judgments. In the case of *Molina Theissen v. Guatemala*, for instance, the IACtHR stated that "Marco Antonio Molina Theissen's forced disappearance has caused suffering and fear among the members of the family who, in turn, were harassed and persecuted; this forced them into exile and broke their family ties. Furthermore, their search for Marco Antonio has been fruitless, and this has caused them anguish and grief."[97]

This sensitivity toward the pain and loss experienced by family members has shaped many of the features of the court's jurisprudence that stand out in contrast to the European jurisprudence. These include the fact that a wider range of family members have been considered beneficiaries of reparations, including members of the extended family of the victim such as grandparents, aunts, and cousins, both as victims of violations and as injured parties. The court has also relied on a set of rules and presumptions that help the victims and their next of kin advance their claims. It has also considered the next of kin of victims of gross human rights violations as victims of violations of the right to humane treatment not only in disappearance cases but also in cases of arbitrary killings and arbitrary detention and inhuman treatment. The court has also been much more generous when awarding reparations both for moral and material damages to family members, going as far as to include damages to family assets. All of this, plus the fact that it has often ordered nonmonetary reparations measures that are essential to the well-being of family members of the detained, killed, and disappeared (such as rehabilitation, satisfaction measures, or guarantees of nonrepetition), allows us to conclude that the IACtHR has responded better to the reality of a community of harm in cases of gross human rights violations.

The first thing to bear in mind is that the concept of next of kin for the IACtHR is not reduced to the members of the nuclear family of the victim, that is, to those who have rights as heirs or successors. Instead, the IACtHR recognizes as autonomous victims or as injured parties other members of the extended family, such as siblings, aunts, grandmothers, and cousins. The key factor for the court is the existence of a close kinship with the victim of the

---

[96] See, for example, IACtHR, *Paniagua Morales v. Guatemala*, reparations, May 25, 2001, expert Graciela Guilis, para. 66, and *Street Children*, expert Ana Deusch, para. 56.

[97] *Molina Theissen v. Guatemala*, reparations, July 3, 2004, para. 37.10. See the separate opinion by Judge Cançado Trindade in the *Street Children* case, para. 2.

violation.⁹⁸ In fact, the court has also theoretically embraced the possibility that other people, tied to the victim in a relationship of dependency, be considered reparations beneficiaries even if they had no blood ties to the victim.⁹⁹ Although no case thus far has applied this option, it confirms the court's willingness to bring to the fore the notion of harm. Also, the court has not relied on a legalistic reading of the notion of next of kin; it has, for instance, systematically treated spouses and companions in the same way for reparations purposes and even made up for contrary state practice.¹⁰⁰

The first decisions handed down by the IACtHR in relation to disappearances, arbitrary killings, and arbitrary detention and torture did not treat the next of kin of the victims as autonomous victims of violations of the ACHR, even if they were treated as injured parties for the purposes of reparations.¹⁰¹ With time, though, the court has been more and more prone to qualify some

---

⁹⁸ *Loayza Tamayo*, paras. 90–92.

⁹⁹ In *Aloeboetoe*, the IACommHR requested the court to award reparations to dependants, that is to say, to people who "received financial support from the victims, whether in cash, in kind, or through contributions of personal work." The IACtHR did not award such reparations because the evidence provided to support the claim was insufficient to prove the link. However, the court recognized the possibility of awarding reparations on those grounds but conditioned such reparation to the following requirements: "First, the payment sought must be based on payments actually made by the victim to the claimant, regardless of whether or not they constituted a legal obligation to pay support. Such payments cannot be simply a series of sporadic contributions; they must be regular, periodic payments either in cash, in kind, or in services. What is important here is the effectiveness and regularity of the contributions. Second, the nature of the relationship between the victim and the claimant should be such that it provides some basis for the assumption that the payments would have continued had the victim not been killed. Lastly, the claimant must have experienced a financial need that was periodically met by the contributions made by the victim. This does not necessarily mean that the person should be indigent, but only that it be somebody for whom the payment represented a benefit that, had it not been for the victim's attitude, it would not have been able to obtain on his or her own" (paras. 68–69).

¹⁰⁰ In *La Rochela*, the court considered that the domestic rule in Colombia, according to which moral damages to the companion of a deceased person are to be 20% less than those awarded to wives, was incompatible with the court's equal treatment of wives and companions, and it awarded further reparations to the companions in the case (para. 268).

¹⁰¹ In *Velásquez Rodriguez v. Honduras*, the first disappearance case it decided, the court treated the next of kin of the disappeared only as successors. Nevertheless, in other cases after *Velásquez Rodriguez*, the court began to treat the next of kin of victims of gross human rights violations in a different form. For instance, in *Aloeboetoe*, the court awarded moral damages to the parents of some of the deceased as injured parties because of the suffering they experienced as a result of the killing and suffering of their sons, even though it did not find them to be victims of violations of the ACHR, and they did not qualify as successors for the purposes of reparations; the court also awarded nonmonetary reparations that benefited the community in the same case. The court has, however, never justified in a principled way the distinction between victims and injured parties (paras. 74–78). Equally, see *Neira Alegria v. Peru*, judgment, September 19, 1996, paras. 40–42.

of the next of kin of victims of gross human rights violations as victims of violations of the ACHR in their own right in cases of disappearances, extrajudicial killings, and illegal detention and inhuman treatment.

The court first treated the next of kin of a disappeared person as a victim in the case of *Blake v. Guatemala* in 1998. The IACommHR alleged before the court that Mr. Blake's parents and two brothers were autonomous victims of the violations of the right to humane treatment (Article 5),[102] the right to fair trial (Article 8),[103] and the right to judicial guarantees (Article 25)[104] of the ACHR. The court considered that Article 8.1 had indeed been violated because no effective investigation, prosecution, punishment, and reparation had taken place in Guatemala as a result of the disappearance of Mr. Blake.[105] Equally, the IACtHR found a violation of the right to humane treatment (Article 5), as "the circumstances of such disappearances generate suffering and anguish [in the family], in addition to a sense of insecurity, frustration and impotence in the face of the public authorities' failure to investigate," all of which was accentuated by the burning of the mortal remains of Mr. Blake.[106] The IACtHR did not find a violation of Article 25, as the relatives of Mr. Blake never made use of any judicial remedy, such as the habeas corpus.[107] But since this case, the court has as a general rule found violations of all these rights, including Article 25, in relation to the next of kin of a disappeared victim.[108]

As for arbitrary killings, the IACtHR considered the next of kin of the victims as victims of violations of their rights under Articles 5, 8, and 25 for the first time in the *Street Children* case in 1999. The IACommHR indicated to the

---

[102] See Article 5 of the ACHR, the right to humane treatment, available at http://www.corteidh.or.cr/sistemas.cfm?id=2.

[103] See Article 8 of the ACHR, the right to a fair trial, available at http://www.corteidh.or.cr/sistemas.cfm?id=2.

[104] See Article 25 of the ACHR, the right to judicial protection, available at http://www.corteidh.or.cr/sistemas.cfm?id=2. The first case where the IACtHR found a violation of Article 25 in relation to the next of kin of a disappeared person was *Castillo Páez*. The court, however, did not find the next of kin to be victims of other rights under the ACHR. This case was decided by the court almost two months before *Blake*. IACtHR, *Castillo Páez v. Peru*, judgment, November 3, 1997, paras. 80–84.

[105] IACtHR, *Blake v. Guatemala*, judgment, January 24, 1998, para. 9.7. This deprivation of judicial truth is what the Inter-American system has understood as the right to know the truth. The next of kin of the victim are the real right holders of this right. See Douglass Cassel, "The Inter-American Court of Human Rights," in *Victims Unsilenced: The Inter-American Human Rights System and Transitional Justice in Latin America* (Washington, DC: Due Process of Law Foundation, 2007), 151–166, at 159.

[106] *Blake v. Guatemala*, para. 115.

[107] Ibid., para. 104.

[108] IACtHR, *Bámaca Velásquez v. Guatemala*, judgment, November 25, 2000, paras. 159–166; *Serrano Cruz Sisters v. El Salvador*, judgment, March 1, 2005, paras. 111–114; *Goiburú et al, v. Paraguay*, judgment, September 22, 2006, paras. 95–104.

court that the circumstances of the death of the victims together with the lack of action by the State had caused the victims' next of kin "anxiety and also considerable fear," which amounted to a violation of Article 5 of the ACHR. The court considered that the mothers of four street children and the grandmother of one of them had indeed suffered inhuman treatment, as well as violations of their rights in Articles 8.1 and 25 of the ACHR. The court has confirmed this jurisprudence in later cases,[109] stating clearly that the "violation of the right to psychological and moral integrity of the next of kin [as encompassed by the right to humane treatment under Article 5 in the convention] is a direct consequence of the unlawful and arbitrary detention... of the maltreatment and torture... and of the death,"[110] whether or not the inaction of state authorities aggravate it.

As already mentioned, the court has also accepted the possibility of considering family members of victims of inhuman treatment and arbitrary detention to be victims in their own right even when the original victims are still alive. The next of kin, for example, can claim a violation of their right to humane treatment under Article 5 of the ACHR.[111] The court was asked to adjudicate on this issue for the first time in *Cantoral Benavides v. Perú* in 2000, where Mr. Cantoral, a young man, had been arbitrarily detained and tortured. Despite acknowledging the suffering of the mother and brothers of Mr. Cantoral, the court decided to treat them as "injured parties" and to make them beneficiaries of reparations, but did not consider them to be victims.[112] This approach, however, has changed in recent years. Indeed, in cases such as *Tibi v. Ecuador* and *De la Cruz Flores v. Perú* in 2004, the IACtHR has found violations of the right to humane treatment in relation to the next of kin of those who were arbitrarily detained and subjected to torture or inhuman treatment.[113]

---

[109] IACtHR, *Gómez Paquiyauri v. Peru*, judgment, July 8, 2004, paras. 118–119.

[110] Ibid., para. 118.

[111] IACtHR, *De la Cruz Flores v. Peru*, judgment, November 18, 2004, paras. 119 and 136.

[112] IACtHR, *Cantoral Benavides v. Peru*, judgment, August 18, 2000, para. 105, and reparations, December 3, 2001, para. 38. Something similar happened in the case of *Maritza Urrutia v. Guatemala*, November 27, 2003, para. 97.

[113] IACtHR, *Tibi v. Ecuador*, judgment, September 7, 2004, paras. 160–163, and *De la Cruz Flores*, paras. 135–136. In the case of *De la Cruz Flores*, a woman who worked as a pediatrician in a hospital in Lima (Peru) was detained for over eight years and subjected to inhumane treatment for, allegedly, supporting an armed strike by the Shining Path (para. 73.8). The IACtHR considered that "the detention of Mrs. De La Cruz Flores, and the conditions in which this occurred, resulted in the rupture of her family structure, so that her children grew up without their mother and had to abandon their personal plans." The court specifically recalled that Mrs. De La Cruz Flores indicated in the statement made before notary public that her next of kin "suffered as if they had been in prison with me." Moreover, the detention conditions caused her next of kin "severe mental anguish" (para. 135). Based on this, the

We should note that when the court deals with violations of Article 5 in relation to the next of kin of a victim of gross human rights violations, the crucial factor has always been the harm produced by the violation to family members rather than the lack of adequate behavior of national authorities in relation to their requests. This allows us to conclude that although the ECtHR and the IACtHR take into account similar factors when addressing possible violations of Article 3 of the ECHR or Article 5 of the ACHR, the weight given to the factors is different in the two systems. For the ECtHR, it is necessary that the reactions and attitudes of state authorities toward the next of kin have been inadequate, whereas for the IACtHR, this is just one factor that explains the gravity of the suffering. Indeed, the IACtHR has considered that in disappearance cases "the violation of the right to mental and moral integrity of the victims' next of kin is a *direct result*, precisely, of this phenomenon, which causes them severe anguish owing to the act itself, which is increased, among other factors, by the constant refusal of the State authorities to provide information on the whereabouts of the victim or to open an effective investigation to clarify what occurred" (emphasis added).[114] This is not to say, however, that the IACtHR will not take into account other factors to assess the seriousness of the suffering of the next of kin, including the disregard and disrespectful treatment they might have received from national authorities. In fact, it will do so to decide on the exact reparations award.[115]

Despite the significance of this jurisprudential development for international human rights law, the IACtHR missed the only opportunity it has had to date to apply such standards to a case where it considered sexual violence as torture. Indeed, with *Castro Castro Prison v. Perú*, the IACtHR dealt with a case concerning the killing and ambush in two pavilions of a high-security facility where men and women were detained or imprisoned for the crimes of terrorism and treason. The court addressed allegations, among others, of sexual violence against one inmate who claimed to have been subjected to a vaginal inspection and six other inmates who were forced to remain naked in front of male security officers for several days and unable to do their physiological needs in private. The court considered that a vaginal inspection constitutes rape, which is a form of torture, and regarded the other acts as serious inhuman treatment. To be consistent with its dictum in *Tibi* and *De la Cruz Flores*, the

IACtHR found a violation of Article 5 of the ACHR in relation to the daughter, son, mother, and siblings of Mrs. De la Cruz Flores (para. 136).
[114] IACtHR, *Goiburú*, para. 97.
[115] The level of detail the court gets into is illustrated by its treatment of the suffering of the next of kin of the disappeared persons in the case of *Goiburú*. See ibid.

court should have awarded reparations to the next of kin of the woman who was subjected to rape/torture, or at least it should have explained the reasons for deciding otherwise. The court did neither.

In summary, the IACtHR has found that the next of kin can be considered victims or injured parties in cases of extrajudicial killings, detention, torture, and disappearances of their loved ones and has been willing to award reparations both for their moral and their material damages. Because of the rich jurisprudence of the court, we will analyze these in turn.

a) The IACtHR and Moral Damages for Victims and Injured Parties

The IACtHR refers to moral damages as nonpecuniary damages. It awards them to repair the "pain and suffering caused to the direct victims and to their loved ones, [for the] discredit to things that are very important for persons, [for] other adverse consequences that cannot be measured in monetary terms, and [for the] disruption of the lifestyle of the victim or his family."[116] In cases of gross or systematic human rights violations that involve the responsibility of the state in an aggravated manner,[117] reparations measures for moral damages, according to the court, include the judgment of the court, an award of money decided in equity, and all other nonmonetary measures necessary to produce full reparation for the harm done, including rehabilitation and other satisfaction and nonrepetition measures.[118]

Regardless of whether it considers the next of kin as victims or injured parties, the IACtHR has applied certain presumptions to calculate moral damages to the next of kin in cases of gross human rights violations. Firstly, it is

---

[116] IACtHR, *Cantoral Benavides*, reparations, para. 53.
[117] The IACtHR developed the concept of aggravated state responsibility to refer to breaches of the ACHR that amount to violations of peremptory norms of international law as a result of the "State's intention (act or omission), or tolerance, acquiescence, negligence or omission in relation to grave violations of human rights and international humanitarian law perpetrated by its State agents, even in the name of a State policy" that is systematic in nature and is concealed and in relation to which there is impunity. This concept was first introduced by Judge Cançado Trindade but is now part of the court's jurisprudence. See, for instance, *Plan de Sanchez*, judgment, April 29, 2004, para. 35; *Myrna Mack v. Guatemala*, judgment, November 25, 2003, paras. 139, 151, 261, and Reasoned Opinion by Judge Cançado Trindade; *Goiburú*, judgment, September 22, 2006, but also the separate opinion by Judge Sergio García and the one by Judge Cançado Trindade.
[118] The court usually deals with satisfaction and nonrepetition measures under a separate heading of the judgment. Nevertheless, the court clearly indicates that they are awarded to repair the nonpecuniary damage caused. See *La Rochela*, paras. 275–276.

presumed that the parents, the children, and the siblings of a victim of disappearance and extrajudicial execution suffer moral damages as a result of their relative's torment. This presumption was first applied to the pain suffered by the mother, father, kids, and the companion or spouse of the victim.[119] For some years, the court was of the view that siblings were not covered by this presumption unless they could provide "credible or convincing evidence demonstrating an affective relationship with the disappeared person that goes beyond simple consanguinity."[120] However, this changed in the case of *Paniagua Morales v. Guatemala*, where the court extended the presumption to cover siblings as well.[121] The court has continued to apply this presumption in later cases such as *Pueblo Bello v. Colombia*[122] and *Goiburú et al v. Paraguay*.[123]

We should bear in mind that as the court began to consider the next of kin of the victim as victims of violations of the ACHR (such as of Article 5), the need to rely on this presumption became less significant at the reparations stage, because a victim – a person whose rights under the ACHR have been violated – is entitled to reparations in his or her own right.[124]

Nevertheless, this presumption is also used by the court at the merits stage when considering violations of Article 5 of the ACHR, and here a recent and regrettable change took place that has an adverse effect on reparations. In the case of *La Cantuta v. Peru*,[125] where 10 persons were abducted and then disappeared, the court considered that the siblings of the disappeared had to prove their suffering to be considered victims of violations of Article 5.[126] As a result of this judgment, the representatives of the victims requested an interpretation of the judgment. The court was asked for an explanation of the reasons why two of the siblings of two of the disappeared persons were not considered as victims of Articles 5, 8, or 25 of the ACHR and not awarded any reparation, despite the fact that they were acknowledged as siblings of the disappeared. The court responded that to be considered a victim of a violation

---

[119] IACtHR, *Caracazo*, para. 51.
[120] IACtHR, *Garrido and Baigorria*, para. 64.
[121] IACtHR, *Paniagua Morales*, para. 110, and particularly the separate opinion by Judge Carlos Vicente de Roux.
[122] IACtHR, *Pueblo Bello*, para. 257.
[123] IACtHR, *Goiburú*, para. 159.
[124] A careful look at the cases decided by the court where it has found the next of kin of the victim of serious human rights violations to be victims shows that the court has not used the presumption when awarding nonpecuniary damages, but has awarded reparations based on the fact that the next of kin are victims. See *Cantoral Huamaní*, paras. 178–180, and *Escué Zapata v. Colombia*, judgment, July 4, 2007, paras. 147–155.
[125] IACtHR, *La Cantuta v. Peru*, judgment, November 29, 2006.
[126] Ibid., para. 128.

of Article 5, it is not enough to prove the blood relationship with the victim. Instead, evidence of the emotional bond is required. As this was not proved in the case, siblings were not awarded reparations on the grounds that "the injured party is made up by those people that have been declared victims in the judgment."[127] Judge Cançado Trindade wrote a concurring opinion to the interpretation of the judgment in which he fiercely criticized the IACtHR. For him, this new standard in relation to siblings is a move backward that contradicts the experience of the court over many years dealing with the suffering of the next of kin of victims, and that also disregards the close family bonds that exist in the continent.[128]

Therefore, although the court is ready to use presumptions to award moral damages to the next of kin of direct victims of gross human rights violations, its views in *La Cantuta* suggest that it is currently reconsidering how far it is ready to go to acknowledge different members of the family as victims and, as a consequence, as recipients of reparations. Its current position in relation to siblings is to be regretted, especially if it means that the court is also departing from an elastic concept of injured party that allowed both victims and injured parties to receive reparations.

The award of monetary reparations for nonpecuniary damages will vary to some extent depending on whether the cases deal with disappearances, detention and torture, or arbitrary killings. Although the court has considered the seriousness of all these violations, it has awarded greater amounts for moral damages in cases of disappearances and arbitrary killings than in torture cases. Several examples will illustrate this.

We should bear in mind here that neither the ECtHR nor the IACtHR awards reparations for each one of the violations it finds; rather, they both award reparations treating the situation as a whole (including all different violations), not distinguishing the grounds of the award in terms of breached rights. Nevertheless, we can still make a comparative analysis of the treatment given by these courts to gross human rights violations, as it is still possible to identify patterns in the case law. If we analyze Tables 5.3 and 5.4 regarding a disappearance case decided in 2005 (*Gómez Palomino v. Peru*), we can see that the IACtHR awarded US $20,000 more for moral damages to the disappeared person than it did in *De la Cruz Flores* to Ms. De la Cruz for her arbitrary detention and inhuman treatment. Equally, the mother, the daughter, and the siblings all received in *Gómez Palomino* twice or more what the court awarded the next of kin as victims in the case of *De la Cruz Flores*.

---

[127] IACtHR, *La Cantuta v. Peru*, Interpretation of the Judgment, November 30, 2007, para. 31.
[128] Ibid., paras. 40–58.

TABLE 5.3. *Forced disappearance cases: Reparations for nonpecuniary damages to the victim and next of kin*

	Victim/next of kin	Reparations for nonpecuniary damages
Mr. Gómez Palomino	Disappeared person	US $100,000
Victoria Palomino	Mother	US $80,000
Ana María Gómez	Daughter	US $80,000
Six siblings	Siblings	US $30,000 to each of the siblings
Esmila Conislla	Companion	US $10,000

Cases of arbitrary killings are treated in similar ways to those of disappearances. For instance, in the case of the brothers *Gómez Paquiyauri*, the court awarded US $100,000 in moral damages to each of the killed victims, exactly what it awards in cases of disappearances. As for the rest of the next of kin, the court tends to award a bit less in monetary reparations for moral damages than in disappearance cases.

It should to be noted that the approach of the court to the award of monetary reparations for nonpecuniary damages changes when there are multiple victims of disappearances, arbitrary killings, or torture. In such cases, the court tends both to award less in monetary reparations for nonpecuniary damages and at the same time to diversify the modality of reparations measures. The cases of *Pueblo Bello* and *la Cantuta* illustrate this approach, as shown in Tables 5.6 and 5.7. In *Pueblo Bello* there were 37 disappeared persons and 6 killed, and in *la Cantuta* there were 10 disappeared persons.

TABLE 5.4. *Detention and torture case: Reparations for nonpecuniary damages to the victim and next of kin*

	Victim/next of kin	Reparations for nonpecuniary damages
Mrs. De La Cruz Flores	Victim of arbitrary detention and inhuman treatment	US $80,000
Widow de la Cruz	Mother	US $40,000
Ana Teresa	Daughter	US $30,000
Danilo	Son	US $30,000
Alcira I de la Cruz	Sister	US $30,000
	Other siblings	US $15,000 each

TABLE 5.5. *Arbitrary killings case: Reparations for nonpecuniary damages to the victim and next of kin*

	Victims/next of kin	Reparations for nonpecuniary damages
Rafael Samuel and Emilio Moisés Gómez Paquiyauri	2 Killed victims (siblings)	US $100,000 each
Ricardo Samuel Gómez Quispe	Father	US $200,000 for the entire family. The money was given to the parents to be distributed among members of the family at their discretion
Marcelina Paquiyauri Illanes de Gómez	Mother	
	Five other siblings of Rafael Samuel and Emilio Moisés	
Jacinta Peralta Allccarima	Girlfriend of Rafael Samuel[129]	US $40,000
Nora Emely Gómez Peralta	Daughter of Rafael Samuel	US $60,000

Within the same or similar types of violations, there are some variations as to the awards given to victims and their next of kin because of the facts of each particular case. Take, for instance, the following three cases of arbitrary detention and inhuman treatment.

In the case of *Loayza Tamayo*, the court considered that Maria Helena, the person who had been arbitrarily detained and subjected to inhuman treatment, was the only victim. Although she argued that "her children and other next of kin were directly affected by the abuse she suffered and were socially stigmatized," the court considered her parents, two children, and siblings as injured parties, not victims, and awarded them moral damages.[130] It considered that the daughter, son, and parents of Maria Helena suffered similar pain and anguish and awarded all of them the same amount of money.

---

[129] She was the girlfriend of one of the victims but they did not live together. She was two weeks pregnant when her boyfriend was killed, and she had to raise their daughter on her own and with the help of his family. She was equally recognized as a victim of Articles 5 and 11 of the ACHR. All of this explains why, despite not living together with the victim and being only the girlfriend, she was considered as a victim and awarded reparations. *Gómez Paquiyauri*, paras. 119, 197, and 211–222.

[130] IACtHR, *Loayza Tamayo*, paras. 134–143.

TABLE 5.6. *Multiple disappearances and extrajudicial killings case: Reparations for nonpecuniary damages to the victim and next of kin – pueblo bello*

Victim/next of kin	Reparations for nonpecuniary damages
Each of the 37 disappeared persons and the six arbitrarily killed	Average US $30,000 each
Fathers and mothers	Average US $10,000 each
Spouses or companions	Average US $10,000 each
Daughters or sons	Average US $10,000 each
Siblings	US $500 each

TABLE 5.7. *Multiple disappearances case – la cantuta*

Victim/next of kin	Reparations for nonpecuniary damages
10 disappeared persons	The court did not award damages as the state had already paid their successors compensation for this harm at the domestic level
Wife	US $50,000
Daughters or sons	Between US $50,000 and $58,000 each
Fathers or mothers	Average of US $50,000 each
Uncles or aunts	Average of US $50,000 each as they are assimilated to parents
Siblings	Average of US $20,000 each

TABLE 5.8. *Arbitrary detention and ill-treatment case: Reparations for nonpecuniary damages to the victim and next of kin considered injured parties*

	Victim and next of kin (considered as injured parties)	Reparations for nonpecuniary damages
Maria Helena Loayza	Direct victim	US $50,000
Gissele	Daughter	US $10,000
Paul Abelardo	Son	US $10,000
Julio and Adelina	Father and mother	US $10,000 each parent
	Siblings	US $3,000 each sibling

TABLE 5.9. *Arbitrary detention and torture case: Reparations for nonpecuniary damages to the victim and next of kin considered injured parties*

	Victim and next of kin (considered injured party)	Reparations for nonpecuniary damages
Luis Alberto Cantoral	Direct victim	US $60,000
Gladyz Benavides	Mother	US $40,000
Luis Fernando Cantoral	Twin brother	US $20,000
Isaac Alonso Cantoral	Brother	US $5,000
Jose Antonio Cantoral	Brother	US $3,000

The case of *Cantoral Benavides* is another one where the court did not consider the next of kin of the victim of arbitrary detention and torture as victims but as injured parties. Table 5.9 indicates the monetary reparations for nonpecuniary damages awarded by the court.

Special factors were taken into account by the court when awarding moral damages to the next of kin of Mr. Cantoral. His mother suffered tremendously with his detention and torture, and was also subject to inhuman treatment when "humiliated, harassed and intimidated" by state authorities in having to undergo vaginal inspection when visiting her son. Also, she was not allowed proper physical contact with her son.[131] Moreover, her family "broke apart" as her three other sons had to leave the country. In the case of his brothers, Luis Fernando was the twin of Mr. Cantoral and was also detained, suffering first hand what his brother was going through. There was also a very close bond between the two of them. The other two brothers also suffered moral damages, but the court considered them to be less intense than that of the mother and twin brother, even though they were also intimidated and harassed and had to leave the country.[132]

Finally, in the case of *De la Cruz Flores*, the court considered the next of kin of the victim of arbitrary detention and inhuman treatment to be a victim of Article 5 of the ACHR. This case and others such as *Tibi* represent a change in the jurisprudence of the IACtHR, which had until then considered that the next of kin of a victim of arbitrary detention and inhuman treatment could be treated only as injured parties of reparations but not as victims. Table 5.10 shows the monetary reparations for nonpecuniary damages awarded to the victims.

[131] IACtHR, *Cantoral Benavides*, para. 61.a.
[132] Ibid., paras. 61b–61d.

TABLE 5.10. *Arbitrary detention and inhuman treatment case: Reparations for nonpecuniary damages to the victim and next of kin considered victims*

	Victims and next of kin (also considered victims)	Reparations for nonpecuniary damages
Mrs. De La Cruz Flores	Victim	US $80,000
Vida de la Cruz	Mother	US $40,000
Ana Teresa	Daughter	US $30,000
Danilo	Son	US $30,000
Alcira Isabel de la Cruz	Sister	US $30,000
	Other siblings	US $15,000 each

Looking at Tables 5.8, 5.9, and 5.10, we draw the conclusion that the conceptualization of the next of kin as injured party or as victim has no significant bearing on the reparations amounts. Thus, taking into account the differences in the value of money between the years when the decisions were taken by the court (1998, 2001, and 2004) and the difference in the nature of the violations,[133] the tables show only a small difference in the treatment of the next of kin, whereby an injured party would tend to receive slightly less in monetary reparations for nonpecuniary damages, as happened to the next of kin of Maria Helena. Nevertheless, the mothers of Luis Alberto and De la Cruz Flores, the former an injured party and the latter a victim, received the same award of money regardless of the category under which the award took place. Only in the case of the siblings do the economic awards seem substantially better if they are considered victims of violations of the ACHR, as seen in the case of *De la Cruz Flores*.[134]

The most striking differences in the awards seem to result from the effort of the IACtHR to ponder the different circumstances in each case and how such circumstances have a bearing on the degree of suffering of victims and their

---

[133] The violations found by the court refer, in their majority, to the same rights of the ACHR, but each of those rights is analyzed by the court in the light of the facts of each case. So, for instance, the court found that the right to humane treatment of both Maria Helena and Luis Alberto was violated, but in the latter case the court considered that there was torture besides ill-treatment, whereas in the former it found only ill-treatment. Equally, in the cases of *Cantoral Benavides* and *De la Cruz Flores*, the court also found violations of Article 9 of the ACHR (freedom from ex post facto laws).

[134] It has to be said that since the court has more recently opted to treat the next of kin of direct victims of disappearances, arbitrary killings, arbitrary detention, and torture as autonomous victims, the distinction between injured party and victim is likely to become less relevant. The distinction might still be useful to deal with people who are not next of kin and could still claim to be injured parties.

next of kin. The court's desire to treat each case according to its own merits allows it to take into account different factors – such as the relationship of each member of the family to the direct victim, their degree of closeness, and their behavior with regards to the violation since it took place. Doing so allows it to respond in more appropriate terms to the multiple harms that different family members experience as a result of such gross violations. This flexible approach characterizes the reasoning of the court in the area of reparations. For instance, one of the brothers of Cantoral Benavides and one of the sisters of De la Cruz Flores received higher reparations than the rest of their siblings because the court recognized their special suffering or their efforts to release their siblings from detention.[135] This was so despite the fact that the court seems to presume that the pain of siblings is far less than that suffered by parents or by offspring, and tends to award the same amount of money to each one of them, as seen in the case of *Loayza Tamayo*.[136]

This willingness of the IACtHR to take into account all particular information in each case and its commitment to afford just and adequate reparation to the next of kin has the potential to be apposite to repair the damage done to children (who often suffer more) and women (who are often subject to additional sex-specific forms of abuse as family members). In *Goiburú*, for instance, where four different persons were disappeared, the court awarded moral damages to the next of kin taking into account particular circumstances. Each next of kin of the victims (parents, daughters and sons, and wives or companions) was awarded US $25,000, but the court awarded US $5,000 more to those who were less than 18 years old at the time of the facts on the assumption that, as minors, their suffering was greater.[137] The wife of one of the disappeared, who was also detained with him at the time of the facts and whose months-old baby was taken away from her without indication of where it was being taken, was awarded an additional US $10,000. Another US $8,000 was also awarded to the sister of one of the disappeared because she was also detained for being a sister and gave birth in a police station and then suffered house arrest.[138] This said, it is worth emphasizing that although the court has relied on the presumption

---

[135] IACtHR, *De la Cruz Flores*, para. 162.
[136] See also *la Cantuta*, *Pueblo Bello*, and *Goiburú*.
[137] IACtHR, *Goiburú*, paras. 16–161. See also *la Cantuta*, para. 219.
[138] IACtHR, *Goiburú*, para. 160. See also *Suarez Rosero v. Ecuador*, reparations, May 29, 1999, paras. 65–67. The case concerns the arbitrary and incommunicado detention of Mr. Suarez Rosero for issues concerning trafficking of drugs. His wife gave birth to their baby in a cell at the prison and had to raise their daughter on her own while her husband was in prison. This also affected the child. The IACtHR took this situation into account and awarded US $20,000 as moral damages to Mr. Rosero and to his wife because of the gravity of the situation. The daughter was awarded US $10,000.

that children suffer more, it has not similarly presumed that female victims or female family members are often subject to additional and sex-specific grievances; it has only pondered this on a case-by-case basis.

The final feature of the IACtHR's jurisprudence that has proven essential to the reparation of the nonpecuniary damages experienced by family members has been the fact that, together with monetary compensation awards, the court has been willing to grant other types of reparations such as measures of satisfaction, rehabilitation, and nonrepetition. The award of these reparations varies depending on the gross human rights violation and the degree of impunity that exists in the country under scrutiny. They can consist, however, of ordering the state to provide victims, family members, and sometimes also communities with things that are essential for their redress, including access to medical and psychological services; treatment and medicines; apologies and other forms of symbolic redress;[139] the investigation, prosecution, and punishment of the perpetrators of the crimes (both material and intellectual); and finding the bodies of the disappeared and giving them proper burial according to the traditions chosen by the family.[140] Table 5.11 indicates the kinds of measures, other than monetary compensation measures, that the court may grant in disappearance cases.

In each case, the court details the meaning of these measures, often adjusting them to the specific needs of family members. In some cases, the court has shown itself to be particularly sensitive to the long-term and intergenerational effects of the violations.[141]

---

[139] The court has used different symbolic reparations such as a public apology admitting responsibility; naming of a street or a square or an educational establishment in honor of the victim or the victims; and covering the expenses for the maintenance of a chapel in which the survivors pay tribute to the victims of the massacre. See, for example, *Cantoral Benavides*, para. 81; *Myrna Mack*; *Street Children*, para. 103; and *Massacre of Plan de Sánchez*, para. 104.

[140] The court has always acknowledged that establishing the whereabouts of a victim's mortal remains and returning them to the next of kin constitute "an act of reparation as it leads to restore the dignity of the victims, to honor the value of their memory to those who were their beloved ones, and to allow them to adequately bury them." *El Caracazo Case*, para. 123; *Velásquez v. Rodriguez*, para. 181.

[141] In *Gómez Palomino v. Perú* (a disappearance case), the court included an education program as a form of reparation to compensate for the fact that the three youngest siblings of Mr. Gómez had to stop studying because of their state of depression and to lack of resources – Mr. Gómez had been the breadwinner in the household. According to the decision, if the siblings wished to resume their studies, the state should facilitate and pay for their primary and secondary adult education, during the night shift if they so wished to make it compatible with their jobs. Nevertheless, the court asserted that serious human rights violations, such as that experienced by Mr. Gómez, harm not just the victims and their next of kin in the long term but also "future generations." Thus, the court considered that if the siblings of Mr. Gómez did not want to take this opportunity to study, they could pass on the benefit to their sons and daughters by way of

TABLE 5.11. *Forced disappearance cases: Nonpecuniary reparations measures to next of kin*

Reparations measures for next of kin	La Cantuta	Pueblo Bello	Goiburú
Obligation of the state to investigate, prosecute, and punish those responsible for the violations (right to the truth)	X	X	X
Finding, exhuming, identifying, and burying the bodies of the disappeared. The state has to assume the cost of these expenses	X	X	X
Adequate medical and psychological care to the next of kin of the victim, free of charge, including access to medicines	X	X	X
Guarantees of security to the next of kin of the victims who wish to return to the village, including the implementation of a housing plan for the next of kin who return to the place		X	
Public apology and acknowledgment of international responsibility	X	X	X
Construction of a public monument in the place of the events		X	X
Publication of the pertinent parts of the judgment	X	X	X
Training in international human rights law for the intelligence services, the military, and the police	X		X
Reform of domestic legislation			X

As Table 5.12 shows, although the IACtHR has also awarded nonmonetary reparations measures in cases of arbitrary detention and torture, it does so to a lesser extent and with most of such measures addressing the needs of the survivor rather than of their next of kin (as either victims or injured parties). The court has, nevertheless, awarded sums of money as pecuniary damages in some cases, such as *Cantoral Benavides*, to cover present and future medical expenses of some of the next of kin of the victim who require medical and

> a primary and secondary school scholarship in a public school. Further, the court ordered a similar scholarship, including university studies, for the daughter of Mr. Gómez (judgment, November 22, 2005, paras. 144–148).

TABLE 5.12. *Arbitrary detention and inhuman treatment cases: Nonpecuniary reparations measures to the victim*

Reparation measures granted only to the victim (not the next of kin)	Cantoral Benavides	De la Cruz Flores
Public apology and to admit responsibility in the case	X	
Obligation to investigate, prosecute, and punish those responsible for the violation (right to the truth)	X	
The state should nullify the decision convicting the victim and expunge any criminal records	X	
Fellowship for advanced university studies as a reparation to the life plan of the victim	X	
Rehabilitation and medical services for the victim		X
Restitution of the job the person had before the violation, including actualization of the profession		X
To release the person from detention		X
Publication of relevant parts of the decision by the IACtHR		X

psychological treatment.[142] In a more recent case, *Gutiérrez Soler v. Colombia*, the court also awarded medical and psychological assistance to the main victim of arbitrary detention and torture as well as to his next of kin (who were also considered as victims) as a nonpecuniary reparation measure. The differences in the treatment of these cases can be explained, in our view, by two factors, among others. Firstly, in cases such as *Cantoral Benavides*, the court did not recognize the next of kin of the victim as autonomous victims but as injured parties or beneficiaries of reparations, whereas in the case of *Gutiérrez Soler* they were victims.[143] Secondly, the court takes into account the particular facts of the case. The decisions in cases such as *Cantoral Benavides* fall below desired standards, as his next of kin (mainly his mother and brother) suffered intense

---

[142] See also *El Caracazo*, where the court awarded compensation for "expenses incurred or to be incurred for medical treatment" required by the survivors of a massacre and the numerous next of kin of the deceased victims (paras. 86–87).

[143] A further difference may lie in the fact that *Cantoral Benavides* is one of the first cases where the court recognized the next of kin of a victim of torture and arbitrary detention as an injured party. This may account for the fact that it was more prudent when awarding reparations.

pain, and the payment of money for medical expenses was not enough to deal appropriately with their harm. More could have been done in this sense. Still, the court ordered Peru to make a public apology and to admit responsibility in the case, a measure that is of outmost importance to the family.

b) The IACtHR and Material Damages for Next of Kin as Victims and Injured Parties

In cases of disappearances, arbitrary killings, and arbitrary detention and inhuman treatment, the IACtHR has recognized that indirect victims and injured parties can also suffer material damages. The court will compensate for actual expenses when these are proven or when they could be presumed to have been incurred. For instance, the court will typically reimburse for medical costs assumed by the next of kin in dealing with the aftermath of the violation.[144] However, it is also willing to rely on some presumptions regarding costs that the next of kin commonly incur. In cases of disappearances and arbitrary killings, for instance, the court relies on certain presumptions regarding funerary expenses. If the body of the disappeared or killed person was recovered before its decision, the court presumes that the next of kin of the victim would have paid the funerary expenses. Therefore, if such costs cannot be proven, the court will award a sum of money based on fairness, as happened in *el Caracazo*, where it awarded each one of the next of kin of the killed persons the sum of US $600.[145]

In disappearance cases, the court applies another important presumption. It will presume that the next of kin incurred costs in trying to find out the whereabouts of their beloved one; if they are unable to provide evidence of such costs, the court will award a sum of money based on equity. What is essential for this presumption to work is that the costs presumed to have been incurred or claimed have a causal relationship with the violation. Although in *Velásquez Rodriguez* the court refused to cover such expenses, in many disappearance cases after *Velásquez Rodriguez* it has been willing to award a lump sum of money to the next of kin of the victim or to the family to cover various expenses, such as travel expenses, medical expenses, visits to jails and hospitals, and communications.[146] In later jurisprudence, the court has refined

---

[144] As happened in *Blake*, *Street Children*, and *Bámaca Velásquez*.
[145] IACtHR, *Caracazo*, para. 85.
[146] The court did not award such costs in *Velásquez Rodriguez* because "they were not pleaded or proven opportunely," but it recognized that such expenses are part of material damages (para. 42). The treatment has been different in other disappearance cases. In *Paniagua Morales*, for instance, the court awarded US $10,000, and in *Castillo Páez*, it awarded $25,000 to the family to cover such costs.

TABLE 5.13. *Disappearance cases: Reparations for material damages of next of kin*

Source of the expenses	Material damages
The mother, the aunt, the wife, and the sister of four of the ten disappeared persons had to abandon their jobs to try to find the truth	Two of them were awarded US $20,000 and the other two were awarded $25,000[147]
Expenses incurred by eight other next of kin in their search for the truth. They were the brother and sister, the father, the mother and father, the father, and the father and the mother of five of the ten disappeared persons	The eight next of kin were awarded US $5,000 each

this approach and currently awards reparations for material damages spelled out under different headings, which now include not only costs but also loss of earnings.[148] For example, Table 5.13 shows what expenses were recognized and awarded by the court in the case of *La Cantuta*.

As Table 5.14 shows, in cases of arbitrary detention and inhuman treatment, such as *De la Cruz Flores*, the court also recognizes the existence of expenses of indirect victims that have a direct connection with the violations found by the court, such as those resulting from transport to visit the victim at the place of detention or to give clothing, food, and medicines to the victim. This has been the position of the court in similar cases, even if in those cases the court refers to those damages under different headings, such as *damnum emergens*, damage to the patrimony of the family, and consequential damage.[149]

---

[147] Although the court does not explicitly explain why it awards US $5,000 more to two of them, it can be inferred that this was because two of them had better jobs/occupations. Although the ones who received $20,000 worked washing clothes and at the market, the situation of the other two was different: one was a primary teacher and the other had to stop her university studies. *La Cantuta*, para. 214.

[148] In *Bámaca Velásquez*, the victim was a guerrilla captured in combat by the Guatemalan army who had been disappeared since then. The court awarded his wife, Jennifer Harbury, US $80,000 for her lost income as a result of her intensive dedication to the case, as well as $25,000 for her medical treatment, and another $20,000 for other expenses related to pursuing the case. These large awards respond to the fact that Jennifer was a lawyer who had to stop earning a high salary in the United States when her husband disappeared. Equally, she undertook several hunger strikes in Guatemala and the United States. She also carried out a detailed investigation into the facts of the case. See her books, *Searching for Everardo* (New York: Warner Books, 2000) and *Torture, Truth and the American Way* (Boston: Beacon Press, 2005), in which she describes in detail her experience in the case pursuing justice both in the United States and in Guatemala and shows the complicity of the US government in the disappearance of her husband.

[149] For instance, *Tibi*, para. 234; *De la Cruz Flores*, paras. 153–154; and *Gutiérrez Soler v. Colombia*, judgment, September 12, 2005, paras. 77–78.

TABLE 5.14. *Arbitrary detention and inhuman treatment cases: Reparations for material damages of next of kin*

Source of the expenses	Material damages
Expenses incurred by the mother of the detained woman to buy the sanitary items, clothes, and medicines of the latter	US $5,000
The sister of the detained woman was awarded reparations as she had to leave her studies in Brazil to become a second mother for the kids of her sister and to help in her defence	US $5,000

The majority of these costs have been granted by the court based on equity, as applicants do not tend to keep receipts of all the expenses they incur. Nevertheless, the court has not been creative in dealing with material damages of the next of kin of victims of arbitrary detention and inhuman treatment who are still alive. It usually awards them a small sum of money based on equity; it could try to calculate, however, in more realistic terms the material damages they – most of them women – suffered.

The following example illustrates this lack of creativity and the challenge ahead. In *De la Cruz Flores* the court awarded only US $5,000 to compensate the victim's sister for stopping her university studies in Brazil and taking care of the victim's children, whereas in *la Cantuta* the sister of one of the disappeared persons received US $25,000 for having to leave her university studies. One of the problems comparing these two cases is the lack of reasoning found in the judgments as to how the court quantified the damages. Clearly, it used the equity principle, but it does not make explicit the fundamental grounds for the five-fold difference in the awards besides the fact that one case deals with a disappearance and the other with arbitrary detention and inhuman treatment. One may think that the different treatment had to do with the fact that in one case, but not the other, the person returns and resumes her responsibilities, therefore relieving those who had taken over. But we do not know whether this is actually the case. In any event, situations such as this one require an approach by the court that takes into account the many ways in which the day-to-day life of the next of kin of victims is dramatically altered from an economic point of view.

Finally, an interesting peculiarity is that the IACtHR has sometimes taken the family as a unit to assess the resulting economic harm. This was the case, for instance, in *Gutiérrez Soler v. Colombia*, where the court awarded US $75,000 as reparations for material damages suffered by the patrimony of the family, to be distributed among the victims as indicated in the judgment of the court.[150] The court has not systematically awarded reparations to the family as a unit for material damages, but it has done so in different cases related to disappearances, arbitrary killings, and arbitrary detention and inhuman treatment.[151] According to the court, such an award is given when there is a substantial change in the conditions and quality of life of the victims as a result of exile or relocation, suspended studies, expenditures to find a new job, loss of valuables, as well as damages to the physical and emotional health of the family.[152] The court began to award material damages to the family as a unit because of the request of the victims themselves and of the IACommHR. In fact, in the cases of *Castillo Paez* and *Molina Theissen*, it was the next of kin of the victim who asked the court to order a payment for the material damage suffered by the family. In other cases, such as *Paniagua Morales*, the court awarded payment *motu proprio*, probably as a result of the decision it had just made in the case of *Castillo Páez*.

In ordering damages for the family as a unity, the IACtHR is not doing anything other than putting together under one heading reparations for material damages it would have awarded in any case for the material harm caused to the victims in the case. But, the court seems to be tempted to award damages in this way especially in cases where the harm produced had a clear devastating impact on the family of the direct victim. Thus, it seems to use this heading to symbolically acknowledge that the suffering took place in individual persons but that such harm also affected the family unit. Despite this symbolism, we should note that the court quantifies reparations considering the family as a unit but awards the reparations individually. Indeed, the court indicates how the money should be distributed across family members. For example, in *Molina Theissen*, it awarded US $80,000 to be divided between the mother and the deceased father of the disappeared, and $60,000 to be distributed in equal shares between the three sisters of the boy.[153] Equally, in

---

[150] These large awards are explained by the fact that most members of the family had to leave the country as a result of the threats they received, the bombs that were placed in the house of the parents of the victim and inside an envelope delivered to the brother, and the attempt to kidnap the son of the main victim in the case. *Gutiérrez Soler*, paras. 101–103 and 77–78.

[151] In the case of *Castillo Páez*, a disappearance case, the family requested US $200,000 as compensation for the nuclear family's patrimonial damages constituted by the bankruptcy of the business of the victim's father, the sale of the home occupied by the family at a reduced cost, and family expenses occasioned by their current residence. The court awarded $25,000 based on equity (para. 76). See also IACtHR, *Paniagua Morales*; *Baldeón Garcia v. Perú*, judgment, April 6, 2006; *Molina Theissen*; and *Gutiérrez Soler*.

[152] IACtHR, *Baldeón Garcia v. Perú*, paras. 186–187.

[153] In this case, nevertheless, the court awarded pecuniary reparations for expenses incurred by the next of kin to provide themselves with psychological treatment under the heading of consequential damage (para. 58).

Baldeón Garcia v. Peru, the court awarded US $20,000 to one of the sons of the victim, and US $10,000 each to the wife and the other sons and daughters of the deceased.[154]

To conclude, the IACtHR awards pecuniary damages to the next of kin as victims or injured parties but is more restrictive in its approach than when it awards moral damages. Still, we should remember that most next of kin in cases of arbitrary killings and disappearances are also successors, which means that the court also recognizes their losses by way of awarding them the pecuniary and nonpecuniary damages that would have otherwise corresponded to their beloved ones. Further, in cases of arbitrary detention and inhuman treatment as well as arbitrary killings and disappearances, the court also awards other reparations measures. Maybe the most regrettable doctrine remains the court's lack of sensitivity when awarding material damages to the next of kin of the victims in cases of arbitrary detention and inhuman treatment where the victim survives, as it fails to adequately recognize the way the life plan of family members can be severely damaged by such events.[155]

It should be noted that the recipients of such pecuniary damages are usually women, unless the award is made to the family unit as such, in which case the court indicates the recipient and the quantity of the award. Still, overall the IACtHR has specifically advanced the protection of the family and acknowledged its suffering by way of both pecuniary and nonpecuniary measures. In the meantime, the ECtHR remains reluctant to change its approach to reparations for gross human rights violations. In particular, it has largely failed thus far to reflect in a significant way the moral and material loss the family members experience or to duly recognize their efforts in achieving justice for their loved ones.

---

[154] IACtHR, *Baldeón*, para. 187.
[155] Among the various headings of damage, the court has referred in different cases to the notion of damage to the life plan. This was recognized for the first time in *Loayza Tamayo*, where the court described the concept as encompassing all those elements, possibilities, and options that concur to ensure the realization of "personal fulfillment" and "self-actualization," which in turn are based on the freedom of individuals to lead their own life in accordance with what in *Loayza* the court identified as the victims "calling in life, her particular circumstances, her potentialities and her ambitions [which would have permitted] her to set for herself, in a reasonable manner, specific goals and to attain those goals." In *Loayza*, as well as in other cases, the court has refrained from awarding compensation under this heading because it believes that the awards granted in each case already repair the damage to the life plan. However, the court should consider other notions such as "family plan" to try to capture the unique and additional way in which many women are harmed when their families are destroyed in those situations where having a family was the crucial element in their life project. See *Loayza Tamayo*, paras. 147–148.

V. FAMILY MEMBERS UNDER REPARATIONS PROGRAMS

In contexts of massive human rights violations, and often pressed by victims' movements, inquiries or truth commissions, the donor community, and international or domestic judicial decisions, governments have adopted administrative reparations measures for victims of state and nonstate violence. Recognizing that neither international legal remedies nor the domestic judicial system are capable of coping with thousands – hundreds of thousands, in certain cases – of potential claimants, parliaments and governments have passed extraordinary legislation awarding certain reparations benefits to various categories of victims. Let us take a look at some of these measures and assess how they have treated family members for purposes of reparations.

The Argentinean reparations measures for the victims of the military dictatorship (1976–1983) are contained in more than eight different laws and presidential decrees adopted between 1984 and 1997.[156] The first laws[157] were intended to redress the harm done to public servants who were dismissed by the dictatorship. The laws proceeded to reincorporate some of them into the public service while recognizing their status for pension and retirement benefits. Subsequent legislation[158] awarded lifetime pensions to the family members of the persons subjected to forced disappearance. Next came legislation[159] awarding economic compensation benefits to those persons who were arbitrarily detained and imprisoned – graduating the sums according to the time of detention and taking into consideration whether the person suffered from severe injuries during detention – and to their family members, but only when the victims were dead or missing. Finally, in 1994 Law 24.411 was passed, granting lump-sum awards for successors of those assassinated and disappeared.[160]

In Chile, reparations for the victims of the military dictatorship (1973–1990) are also comprised of a series of successive measures adopted during

---

[156] For a comprehensive and detailed analysis of reparations for victims of state terrorism and political repression in Argentina, see María José Guembe, "Economic Reparations for Grave Human Rights Violations: The Argentinean Experience," in *The Handbook*. An updated version of the original text in Spanish was published as "La Experiencia Argentina de Reparación Económica de Graves Violaciones a los Derechos Humanos," in *Reparaciones para las Víctimas de la Violencia Política*, ed. Catalina Díaz (Bogotá: International Center for Transitional Justice, 2008).

[157] Law 23.053 of February 1984; Law 23.117 of September 1984; Law 23.238 of September 1985; Law 23.523 of June 1988.

[158] Law 23.466 of October 1986.

[159] Decree No. 70/91 and Law 24.043/91.

[160] This law was amended in 1997 by Law 24.832, which introduced critical provisions finally making the implementation of the lump-sum awards possible.

the early 1990s and then updated and modified in 2004.[161] Following the recommendations by the National Truth and Reconciliation Commission, the government proposed a draft bill awarding pensions, lump sums, and other reparations measures (such as educational and health services) to the families of the disappeared and assassinated, which was finally approved by parliament in February 1992.[162] The program of comprehensive healthcare for victims of human rights violations (PRAIS) began its work in 1991, offering physical and psychological healthcare to former political prisoners, family members of the executed and disappeared, those dismissed from their jobs for political reasons, the returning exilees and their families, and every person who had suffered human rights violations of any kind during the military regime. The situation of those victims who were subjected to torture and arbitrary imprisonment, however, was fully addressed only ten years later with the creation of the Ethical Commission against Torture and the subsequent Commission on Political Imprisonment and Torture, which issued its final report in 2003. Reparations measures for tortured victims, including pensions and educational benefits, were implemented in only 2004.[163]

In Brazil, the human rights violations committed by the military dictatorship (1964–1985) were far fewer in number than those perpetrated by its Argentinean and Chilean counterparts. Nevertheless, several attempts by family members, victims' and human rights organizations, and various initiatives supported by committed members of congress led to the passage in 1995 of Law 9,140. The law officially recognized the deaths of 136 persons who participated or were accused of participating in political activities, were arrested by public agents, and then disappeared between 1961 and 1979.[164] This law also stipulated that efforts should be made to locate the remains of the victims, and it awarded lump-sum payments to the family members of the disappeared and executed. The law provided for the creation of a special commission ascribed to the ministry of justice that would recognize the disappearance or execution of other victims who were not included in the original list. The commission

---

[161] For a comprehensive and detailed analysis of reparations for victims of the military dictatorship in Chile, see Elizabeth Lira, "The Reparations Policy for Human Rights Violations in Chile," in *The Handbook*. The original Spanish version of the chapter was reprinted as "La Política de Reparación por Violaciones a los Derechos Humanos en Chile," in *Reparaciones para las Víctimas de la Violencia Política*.

[162] Law 19.123.

[163] This was done through the approval of Law 19.992.

[164] For a comprehensive and detailed analysis of the Brazilian reparations for victims of political repression, see Ignacio Cano and Patrícia Salvao Fereira, "The Reparations Program in Brazil," in *The Handbook*.

would also consider reparations petitions and would try, as much as possible, to locate the corpses of the missing. Carefully examining individual petitions, the special commission acknowledged the execution and disappearance of 148 victims – in addition to those who were initially included in the official list – and in total granted reparations to the family members of 280 victims. Several states also passed regional legislation establishing local inquiry commissions and creating local programs directed toward the compensation of victims of torture, arrest, and banishment.

The Committee on Reparations and Rehabilitation (CRR) of the South African Truth and Reconciliation Commission (TRC) made recommendations for Urgent Interim Reparations (UIR) and for final reparations aimed at victims of apartheid.[165] UIR comprised financial assistance in the form of lump-sum payments intended to ensure access to or pay for services or both, as well as a services referral policy, including social welfare counseling and healthcare. Those considered by the CRR to be in urgent need included "victims or their relatives and dependants who have urgent medical, emotional, educational, material and/or symbolic needs." The UIR payments were calculated according both to need and to the number of dependants the victim supported, ranging from US $250 to $713. UIR were directly implemented by the CRR between July 1998 – as the TRC was winding down its work – and April 2001. In total, US $5.5 million was paid to approximately 14,000 victims. The TRC submitted its final report in 1998, including a chapter recommending final material and symbolic reparations. Material reparations included community rehabilitation and yearly grants – for six years – based on the median annual household income in 1997 for a family of five in South Africa ($2713). Symbolic reparation measures and institutional reform were also recommended. In April 2003, the government agreed to a one-time payment of US $3,750, a considerably smaller amount than that proposed by the TRC; the great majority of reparations payouts were distributed between November 2003 and April 2004.

The Peruvian Truth and Reconciliation Commission (CVR) submitted its final report in August 2003, giving an official account of the internal armed conflict and state repression experienced by the country between 1980 and 2000.[166]

---

[165] For a comprehensive and detailed analysis of reparations in South Africa, see Christopher J. Colvin, "Overview of the Reparations Program in South Africa," in *The Handbook*. See also Beth Goldblatt, "Evaluating the Gender Content of Reparations: Lessons from South Africa," in *What Happened to the Women?*

[166] For the most up-to-date comprehensive description of the Peruvian reparations program and its implementation, see Julie Guillerot. "Reparaciones en la Transición Peruana: ¿Dónde Estamos y Hacia Donde Vamos?" in *Reparaciones para las Víctimas de la Violencia Política*. See also Julie Guillerot and Lisa Magarrell, *Reparaciones en la Transición Peruana: Memorias de un*

The report included a quite detailed proposal of a Comprehensive Reparations Plan (PIR) incorporating six different programs: (1) the symbolic reparations program; (2) the health reparations program; (3) the educational reparations program; (4) the citizens rights restoration program; (5) the economic reparations program; and (6) the collective reparations program. In February 2004, the President of the Republic created a multi-institutional commission (CMAN) – with participation of different civil society sectors – responsible for monitoring the implementation of the CVR recommendations.[167] The PIR was given a legal basis in 2005.[168] The law assigned the CMAN the function of designing the different programs incorporated into PIR. The CMAN is also responsible for establishing a reparations council in charge of the creation of a unified victims' registry, as recommended by the CVR. During the year 2007, 440 communities were identified as priority beneficiaries of the program, and 463 more were added to the priority list in 2008[169]; the reparations council has, in turn, identified and registered 15.276 individuals and 3,610 affected communities that qualify as beneficiaries of the reparations program. Each community has to define a project of no more than US $30,000 to be implemented by the respective municipality. By July 2008, 416 projects were approved and 40 had been completed. No other material reparations measures have been implemented thus far.

The Guatemalan Commission for Historical Clarification (CEH), which sought to redress the victims of the internal armed conflict and state repression in the country from 1960 to 1996, recommended in its final report (1999) a national reparations program and called for the creation of an executive body to implement it.[170] After various attempts, in May 2003 the government approved by executive decree the creation of the National Reparations Program (PNR), the official agency in charge of designing and implementing

---

Proceso Inacabado (Lima: ICTJ/Asociación Pro Derechos Humanos [APRODEH]/OXFAM, 2006); and Julie Guillerot, "Linking Gender and Reparations in Peru: A Failed Opportunity," in *What Happened to the Women?*

[167] Guillerot and Magarrell, 62.

[168] This was done through Law 28592.

[169] Interview with Julie Guillerot, former member of the working group assigned to the design of the Integral Reparations Plan (PIR) at the Peruvian CVR, August 2007. For a detailed discussion on the implementation of the collective reparations program, see APRODEH and ICTJ, *Escuchando las Voces de las Comunidades. Un Estudio Sobre la Implementación de las Reparaciones Colectivas en el Perú* (Lima: APRODEH/ICTJ, 2008).

[170] For a comprehensive description and up-to-date analysis of the implementation of the Guatemalan reparations program, see Programa Nacional de Resarcimiento, *La Vida no Tiene Precio. Acciones y Omisiones de Resarcimiento en Guatemala* (Guatemala: Programa Nacional de Resarcimiento, 2007). See also Claudia Paz y Paz Bailey, "Guatemala: Gender and Reparations for Human Rights Violations," in *What Happened to the Women?*

a national reparations policy. In July 2004, it established the National Commission for Reparations (CNR), the highest political instance of the PNR. The PNR and the CNR have elaborated various policy documents to implement CEH recommendations – the last of them, *Criterios Básicos para la Aplicación de Medidas de Resarcimiento* (Basic Criteria for the Implementation of Reparations Measures), issued in January 2007, updated and revised during 2008. These policy documents contain the basic elements of the reparations program, which include material restitution (land restitution, housing benefits, productive investment), economic compensation (lump-sum payments, educational stipends, physical and mental health services), as well as cultural and symbolic reparation measures. A wide range of individual and collective beneficiaries are eligible for the various measures. The actual distribution of reparations in Guatemala has begun with the payout of lump-sum awards. As officially reported by the PNR, from 2005 to 2007, 13,014 beneficiaries received reparations checks ranging from US \$2,660 to \$3,200.[171] For the year 2008, the goal was to distribute economic compensation to 8,000 beneficiaries, which was successfully met.[172] The PNR estimates that since the establishment of the program, more than 38,000 petitions have been submitted.

Finally, the Truth and Reconciliation Commission (TRC) in Sierra Leone presented its final report in October 2004, addressing the 11-year civil war in the country (1991–2002).[173] The commission elaborated in a detailed manner the fundamental components of a reparations program.[174] Amputees, other war wounded, victims of sexual violence, children affected by the war, and war widows are the categories of beneficiaries identified by the TRC as those eligible for reparations. Reparations benefits include physical and mental healthcare, pensions, education benefits, skills training, microcredit schemes, and symbolic and collective reparations. Following the TRC recommendation, in September 2006 the National Commission for Social Action (NaCSA) was

---

[171] Information provided by Rafael Herrarte, former executive secretary of the National Reparations Program, February 2009.

[172] Presentation given by the former executive secretary of the National Reparations Program, Rafael Herrarte, at the conference "Reparación Integral Desde un Enfoque de Derechos," Bogotá, Colombia, October 22–23, 2008, co-organized by ICTJ, Alto Comisionado de Naciones Unidas para los Refugiados (ACNUR), Norwegian Refugee Council (NRC), and Centre on Housing and Evictions (COHRE). On file with authors.

[173] For a comprehensive and detailed analysis of the reparations program, see Jamesina King, "Gender and Reparations in Sierra Leone: The Wounds of War Remain Open," in *What Happened to the Women?*

[174] Chapter 4 of Volume 2 of the report contains guiding principles, definitions of beneficiaries and benefits, and recommendations of how to implement effectively the reparations program. Accessible at http://trcsierraleone.org/drwebsite/publish/v2c4.shtml?page=1.

Repairing Family Members 267

formally designated by the government as the official agency to implement a comprehensive reparations program. The Steering Committee of the UN Peace Building Fund approved in July 2008 a US $3 million project aimed at establishing a Reparations Unit within NaCSA that will make operational the implementation of the reparations program. Expected specific outputs of the project are the establishment of the special fund for war victims and a database of victims' profiles.[175]

Although the described programs are clearly at different stages of implementation, it is our purpose here to assess whether they have been sensitive to the reality of the impact of violence on family life and family members, and whether any evolution can be identified in this respect. In doing this, we will ask ourselves

1. whether family members are considered victims in their own right,
2. whether family members are considered beneficiaries and in what capacity,
3. and whether benefits and their modality of distribution are shaped to reflect the needs or harms of different family members.

1. Defining Victims: From Family Members as Heirs and Dependants to Victims in Their Own Right

Just like the above examined jurisprudence of regional human rights systems, administrative reparations programs have come to recognize family members not only as heirs or dependants but also as victims in their own right. Whereas what might be identified as first generation reparations programs[176] – Argentina, Chile, and Brazil – considered family members mainly as heirs and *assignees*[177] of the victims of forced disappearance and extrajudicial execution, second generation reparations programs[178] have gone beyond that notion by including family members in the category of victims.

Political repression under military dictatorships in Argentina (1976–1983), Chile (1973–1990), and Brazil (1964–1985) had common traits, and so do reparations measures adopted by the democratic governments succeeding the

---

[175] See www.unpbf.org/docs/projects/.
[176] We call first generation reparations programs those that consist in a series of successive legislative and administrative reparations measures.
[177] *Causahabiente* as referred to by Argentinean legislation.
[178] We call second generation reparations programs those that have been articulated as comprehensive programs (often following up truth commission recommendations) that include various types of material and symbolic – individual and collective – reparations benefits for wide ranges of beneficiaries.

military regimes. In all three cases, special legislation was passed that awarded economic compensation to the family members of the forcibly disappeared and those assassinated for political reasons. In all three cases, mothers, fathers, spouses and partners, children, and siblings were considered as heirs or *assignees* of the disappeared and assassinated. Family members were not considered as victims in their own right. Express legal language as well as the way in which the economic benefits were conceived sent the message that compensation was awarded for the lost loved one, rather than as a means for alleviating the surviving family members' *own* suffering and harm.[179]

In contrast, second generation reparations programs proposed by truth commissions in South Africa, Guatemala, Sierra Leone, and Peru expressly included certain family members in the category of victims. The programs defined as persons eligible for reparations victims of human rights and humanitarian law violations – or acts associated with a political objective for which amnesty had been granted in South Africa – *and their family members and dependants*.

Awarding economic compensation to family members in their status of *assignees* or heirs of their disappeared or executed loved ones can foster anguish, rage, and guilt among family members entitled to compensation benefits. This can be illustrated with the example of Argentina. Argentine Law 24.411 (1994) granted economic reparation – in the form of national public debt bonds – to persons who at the time of the law's enactment were disappeared – a sum that would be received by those persons' *assignees*.[180] The person whose forced disappearance had been judicially declared would receive the pecuniary compensation through his or her successors, who had to validate their status before a court.[181] Although ironically this inheritance mechanism resonated with the express request by the victims that "any money paid by the State be given in the victim's name and not in the name of his or her legal successors," economic compensation benefits were controversial among a sector of victims' groups in the country. These groups feared that the state was offering money for silence about what happened and impunity for those responsible.[182]

---

[179] In fact, using traditional civil law language, Chilean Law 19.123 (1992) expressly states that the "source" of the reparations is to be found in those persons subjected to forced disappearance and political assassination.

[180] Guembe, 39.

[181] Ibid.

[182] Ibid., 35.

The same was true, though to a lesser extent, in Brazil.[183] Tellingly, the sector of victims' groups which objected to Law 24.411 in Argentina had not objected to the pensions awarded by the Argentine State to the spouses and children of the disappeared in 1986, as part of the first reparations measures by the democratic government. The pensions had been understood as fulfilling the State's duty to provide help to those who were in a precarious situation because of forced disappearance.[184]

2. Defining Beneficiaries: Going Beyond Terminology

The definition of the crimes that trigger reparations and the scope of beneficiaries respond to the particularities of repression and war, to the status and power of different stakeholders within society – including groups of victims, former oppressors, the human rights community and, as of recent, the feminist movement – and to policy considerations of resource availability. Truth commissions and other bodies designing reparations programs have been challenged to subvert social stereotypes about hierarchies of suffering that place at the bottom of the list crimes considered not to be as serious as those compromising the value of life. The same happens with regard to the coverage of family members: social preconceptions and financial considerations have usually placed family members of surviving victims off the list of beneficiaries.

Ironically, although what we have called second generation reparations programs have nominally recognized family members as victims following developments in international law, family members are not always included as beneficiaries of reparations measures. Additionally, as will be discussed in the next section, benefit structures and prioritizing and distribution mechanisms are still based on an heir/dependant logic.

Although the list of crimes subject to reparations has grown as international law has developed, incorporating demands from different social movements (as has been the case, for example, regarding sexual violence), this has not brought with it extensive coverage of family members as beneficiaries. Compare Charts 5.I and 5.II. Chart 5.I shows the types of violations included in the reparations programs examined in this study, whereas Chart 5.II shows the violations included in these reparations programs that enable family members to receive reparations measures.

---

[183] Cano and Ferreira, 139.
[184] Guembe, 25.

CHART 5.1. *Human rights and humanitarian law violations entitling victims and beneficiaries to reparations*

	Argentina	Chile	Brazil	South Africa[185]	Peru	Guatemala	Sierra Leone
Forced disappearance	X	X	X	X	X	X	X
Extrajudicial execution/political assassination	X	X	X	X	X	X	X
Torture	X	X	–	X	X	X	X (Amputees and other war wounded)
Rape and other forms of sexual violence	–	X (In connection with illegal imprisonment and torture)	–	X	X	X	X
Arbitrary detention/ illegal imprisonment	X	X	–	X	X	–	–
Internal forced displacement	–	X[186]	–	X	X	X	–
Forced recruitment	–	–	–	–	X	X	X
Exile	–	X	–	–	–	–	–

Looking at the charts, above and on page 272, it seems that a first necessary distinction is between the family members of nonsurviving victims and those of surviving victims. Family members of the dead and disappeared are almost automatically considered as beneficiaries of reparations measures, as is the case in all programs examined in this study. In contrast, family members of surviving victims – tortured, illegally imprisoned, raped, or sexually abused – are rarely recognized as beneficiaries of reparations measures. In the South African case, family members of nonfatal victims become beneficiaries only with the subsequent death of the victim: family members are not entitled to reparations benefits in their own right; only when the tortured, illegally imprisoned, or raped victim dies do his or her family members receive the benefit. This might well be evidence of a still-dominant – though tacit – inheritance paradigm, since the source of the right to receive the reparations benefit is not the autonomous harm or suffering experienced by the family member as a result

[185] We are referring here to final reparations as proposed by the Truth and Reconciliation Commission and later on implemented by the government.

[186] Peasants expelled from their land, as well as *Relegados*, people who were forced to live in a confined region and subject to periodic control by the police instead of being imprisoned.

of the violation of a right (definitions of victimhood notwithstanding) but the death of the primary beneficiary. In other words, reparations programs for the most part still do not recognize the harms suffered independently by women whose sons and husbands were imprisoned, tortured, or suffered severe ill-treatment, nor by the victims' children, even though accounts of such suffering are common in truth commission reports.

The South African and Chilean examples are particularly telling. Although the South African TRC explicitly accepted that the distinction between victims and relatives or dependants should not be based on the notion that relatives or dependants suffered less, the Reparation and Rehabilitation Committee determined that, as "secondary victims," relatives or dependants were entitled to grants only when and if the "primary victim" had died.[187] The Chilean Commission on Political Imprisonment and Torture (2003) gathered systematic evidence on the harm suffered by the children of the imprisoned and tortured, including their inability to complete their education because of the impact of the violations on their parents' employment.[188] Based on what had been repeatedly expressed by the victims in their testimonies about their own ideas for reparations, the commission proposed to grant tuition waivers and other educational benefits to the children of the victims of imprisonment and torture. But the government and subsequently the congress rejected the proposal.[189]

Marking an important difference with the other reparations programs examined here, the Sierra Leone Truth and Reconciliation Commission recommended that immediate family members (wives, male spouses in certain cases, and children under 18) of amputees, of other war wounded, and of victims of sexual violence should be included as beneficiaries of healthcare reparations measures. Similarly, Chile has also made medical services available to family members of victims of torture.

3. *Whether Benefits and Their Modality of Distribution are Shaped to Reflect the Needs or Harms of Family Members*

As shown in Chart 5.II, following, family members have commonly been recognized as beneficiaries of various reparations measures in the cases of the extrajudicial execution or political assassination and the forced disappearance of their loved ones. Indeed, with the exception of Sierra Leone, all the reparations

---

[187] Goldblatt, 62.
[188] Commission on Political Imprisonment and Torture, Final Report, 2004, 525.
[189] Interview with Cristián Correa, former executive secretary at the Commission on Political Imprisonment and Torture, August 2007.

CHART 5.11. *Reparations measures for family members of those who suffered human rights and humanitarian law violations*

Beneficiaries: Family members of those who suffered	Argentina	Chile	Brazil	South Africa[190]	Peru	Guatemala	Sierra Leone
Forced disappearance	Health Services, Pensions, Lump Sums	Health Services, Education, Pensions, Lump Sums	Lump Sums	Lump Sums, Collective Rep. Measures	Health Services, Education, Pensions, Lump Sums, Collective Rep. Measures, Housing Assistance, Employment Assistance	Health Services, Lump Sums, Collective Rep. Measures	Assist organizations that provide skills training (war widows) Education (orphans)
Extrajudicial execution/ political assassination	Lump Sums	Health Services, Education, Pensions, Lump Sums	Lump Sums	Lump Sums, Collective Rep. Measures	Health Services, Education, Pension/Lump Sums, Collective Rep. Measures, Housing Assistance, Employment Assistance	Health Services, Lump Sums, Collective Rep. Measures	Assist organizations that provide skills training (war widows) Education (orphans)

Violation					
Torture	Only when the primary victim was dead or missing, Lump Sums	Health Services	—	Only when the primary victim was dead, Lump Sums	—	Health Services, (Family members of amputees; wives and children of other war wounded) Education (children of amputees)
Arbitrary detention/ illegal imprisonment	Only when the primary victim was dead or missing, Lump Sums	Health Services	—	Only when the primary victim was dead, Lump Sums	—	—
Rape and other forms of sexual violence	—	—	—	Only when the primary victim was dead, Lump Sums	Only children of rape, Education, Pensions	Health Services (children and spouses or companions as long as the direct beneficiary continues to be eligible for the benefit) Children of rape if mothers are single (Health Services, Education)

[190] We are referring here to final reparations as proposed by the Truth and Reconciliation Commission and later on implemented by the government.

programs examined have distributed – or plan to distribute – economic compensation benefits among family members of the dead and disappeared. This renders the analysis of reparations benefits granted to widows and widowers, orphans, and parents of the dead and disappeared particularly suitable for determining how sensitive reparations programs have been to the harms suffered by family members. In particular, as we will see, the nature and distribution mechanisms of benefits can have a significant impact on the level of recognition given to different family members. Crucial also will be the extent to which economic compensation benefits are combined with social services benefits that must necessarily be harms tailored.

Chart 5.III describes the beneficiaries under different reparations schemes in cases of forced disappearance and extrajudicial execution or political assassination and the benefits to which the beneficiaries are entitled. Taking a look at this chart with a view to assessing whether benefits and their modality of distribution have been shaped to reflect the needs and harms of different family members, we can establish interesting comparisons by looking at

a) The treatment of different family members,
b) Distribution mechanisms,
c) The complexity of benefits.

a) The Treatment of Different Family Members

SPOUSES, PARTNERS, AND COMPANIONS AS BENEFICIARIES. In general terms, it appears that reparations programs have recognized the various forms of union prevalent in each country context, going beyond legalistic marital definitions to include common-law partners and those united under different rites and traditions.[191] There are nevertheless still some traces of the conservative understandings of marriage and family. The Chilean and Brazilian examples are two cases in point.

The Chilean Statute 19.123 (February 1992) – the first piece of legislation establishing reparations measures for the family members of those subjected to forced disappearance and political assassinations – placed unmarried companions in a clearly inferior situation. Common-law partners were considered beneficiaries of the reparations benefits awarded to "legitimate" spouses only in their capacity as "mother" or "father" of the victim's offspring, and even so to a lesser extent than married partners. Thus, the mother or father of a victim's out-of-wedlock offspring was awarded a substantially smaller pension

---
[191] Vasuki Nesiah, *Truth Commissions and Gender: Principles, Policies and Procedures* (New York: ICTJ, 2006).

CHART 5.III. *Beneficiaries and benefits awarded to family members of those who were subjected to forced disappearance, extrajudicial execution and political assassination*

Beneficiaries	Argentina — Forced disappearance	Argentina — Extrajudicial execution	Chile	Brazil	South Africa	Perú	Guatemala	Sierra Leone
Spouses, partners, companions	Lump sum award US$224,000(1) Distributed according to a priority order: 1. Descendants 2. Spouse (including common-law marriages, as long as the couple had been together for two years, immediately preceding the disappearance) 3. Ancestors 4. Relatives to the fourth degree **Spouses (married or who had lived with the victim for five years minimum, immediately preceding the disappearance)**: Life time pension minimum ordinary amount received by a retired public servant Healthcare	Lump sum award US$224,000(2) Distributed according to a priority order: 1. Descendants 2. Spouse (including common-law marriages, as long as the couple had been together for two years, immediately preceding the disappearance) 3. Ancestors 4. Relatives to the fourth degree	**Spouses(3), mother or father of a victim's out-of wedlock offspring**; Life time pension 40%(4) of the total amount of US$537(5) Lump sum award equivalent to 12 months of pension payments Healthcare	Lump sum award equivalent to a sum (US$3,000[6]) for every year of live lost (difference between the age at death and the life expectancy), distributed according to a priority order: 1. Spouse 2. Common-law spouse 3. Descendants 4. Ancestors 5. Collateral relatives up to fourth kin	Lump sum award of USD 3,750(7) distributed according to a priority order: 1. Spouses (the person married to the victim under any law, custom or belief) 2. Children 3. Parents 4. Other relatives	**Spouses/partners (civil, religious or de facto unions)**: Pension 50% of the minimum legal wage (when they are over 50 years old at the time of the benefit distribution) Lump sum award 2/5 of the total amount of US$10,000(8) Healthcare Preferential access to state-funded housing and employment program	**Spouses/ partners**: Lump sum award of US$3,200(9) distributed according to a priority order: 1. Spouse or partner 2. Children 3. Parents 4. Siblings Healthcare Property restitution	**War widows**: The government should assist organizations that provide skills training

(continued)

CHART 5.III (*continued*)

Beneficiaries	Argentina		Chile	Brazil	South Africa	Perú	Guatemala	Sierra Leone
	Forced disappearance	Extrajudicial execution						
Children	**Children (until 25 or when receive university degree):** Pension of minimum ordinary amount received by retired public servant Healthcare		**Children (until the age of 25):** Pension 15% of the total amount each, of US$537 Lump sum award equivalent to 12 months of pension payment Educational benefits up to 35 years of age Tuition and other fees waivers and monthly stipend in certain cases Healthcare			Pension (until 18) Lump sum award 2/5 of the total amount, of US$10,000, to be distributed among all the children Healthcare Educational benefits	Healthcare	Educational benefits

| Parents | Disabled parents (who do not have other source of income): Pension minimum ordinary amount received by a retired public servant
Healthcare | Mother or in her absence (due to death, renunciation, or simple absence) father: Life time pension 30% of the total amount of US$537
Lump sum award equivalent to 12 months of pension payments
Healthcare | **Parents**: Pension when they are over 50 years old at the time of the benefit distribution
Lump sum award 1/5 of the total amount of US$10,000
Healthcare
Preferential access to state-funded housing and employment programs | **Parents**
Healthcare |

(continued)

CHART 5.III (continued)

	Argentina		Chile	Brazil	South Africa	Perú	Guatemala	Sierra Leone
Beneficiaries	Forced disappearance	Extrajudicial execution						
Siblings	Disabled siblings (who do not have other source of income) and orphan siblings under age (who had lived regularly with the victim): Pension minimum ordinary amount received by a retired public servant Healthcare		Healthcare					

Notes:

(1) At the time of its enactment, US$ 1 = 1 Argentinean Peso. In September 2007, US$1 = 3.13 Argentinean Pesos. Equivalent to the monthly earnings of employees at level A of the roster of civil servants of the National Public Administrator, multiplied by a coefficient of 100. Paid in Bounds of Consolidation of the National Public Debt.

(2) Idem.

(3) Law 19,123 of February 8, 1992 – through which the reparations pensions, the healthcare, and educational benefits were established – recognized the surviving spouses as beneficiaries, excluding the unmarried companions. This was modified in a certain way by Law 19,980 of October 29, 2004, enabling the president of the Republic to grant a maximum of 200 "grace pensions" to those family members who were excluded by the original Law (Law 19,123), among them companions who had lived with the victim for "a long period of time" and who "economically depended on the victim."

(4) Under Law 19,123 of February 8, 1992, the amount awarded to the mother or father of a victim's out-of-wedlock offspring corresponded to 15% of the reference sum. Law 19,980 of October 29, 2004 equaled the sum to that awarded to the spouses.

(5) The figure corresponded to an approximate average of medium class family earnings in 1992. Law 19,980 of October 29, 2004 increased by 50% the amount of all the monthly pensions being awarded to the different beneficiaries, as defined by Law 19,123 and modified by Law 19,980.

(6) It is not clear how this figure was originated, according to Cano y Salvao Ferreira. However, some of the interviewed Commissioners expressed that the figure was established according to other civil compensations. *The Handbook*, 114.

(7) In its final report the TRC recommended an annual grant of US$2,713 for six years. The figure corresponded to the median annual household income in 1997 for a family of five in South Africa. In April 2003, the government agreed to a one-time payment of US$3,750, without any indication about the basis for the new amount. Goldblatt, 67.

(8) This figure corresponds to the maximum indemnification award provided for demobilized members of self-defense committes by Supreme Decree No. 068-98-De-S/G of September 27, 1998. Interview with Julie Guillerot, September 2007.

(9) This figure results from acute debates among PNR members, taking into considerations justice, equity, and resorce availability. Early estimations took into consideration minimum legal wage. Interview with Licenciado Matín Arévalo, Executive Secretary PNR, September 2007.

sum than the "legitimate" spouses: whereas spouses were to receive a sum corresponding to 40% of the reference amount (US $537), mothers or fathers of a victim's out-of-wedlock offspring were awarded a sum corresponding to only 15%. Only more than 10 years later, on a presidential initiative, did the Chilean congress address the issue. The discriminatory dispositions were, however, not fully overcome by the amendments introduced by Statute 19.980 (October 2004). The statute authorized the president to award 200 "grace pensions" to those family members who were excluded from the reparations program as designed under Law 19.123, explicitly mentioning companions who did not have children with the victim but who lived with the victim for a long period of time and were economically dependent. Thus, the discrimination against unmarried partners persists in the Chilean reparations program. According to the language in Statute 19.980, the qualifying criterion for the reparation pension seems to be the economic dependency bond more than the pain and suffering that the execution or disappearance of a partner might have caused. This is not the case for spouses, who are not required to prove any type of economic dependency bond.

In the Brazilian case, common-law partners are situated in the second level of the priority order, after spouses. This means that the lump-sum award goes to the spouse and only in his or her absence to the common-law partner, which clearly amounts to discrimination against common-law partners.

CHILDREN AS BENEFICIARIES. Like adults, children have been considered as beneficiaries of reparations programs both as victims of gross human rights violations and as family members of others considered victims.[192] With the exception of the Brazilian and South African programs, all of the reparations programs studied here have distributed or planned to distribute reparations benefits among children – in certain cases until they are 25 or 35. In fact, in comparative terms, the reparations packages designed for children are quite complete, including pensions and lump-sum awards and healthcare and educational benefits.

With the exception of Argentina and Chile, reparations programs recognize as child-beneficiaries those persons under 18 years of age. Considering the periods of time between the commission of the violations against their parents or other adults in charge of them and the actual distribution of reparations benefits, those children who were affected are often likely to be adults at the time benefits are awarded. These children (now adults) might be left off the list of beneficiaries. For instance, a child whose education was truncated by

---

[192] On children and reparations, see Mazurana and Carlson, Chapter 4 of this volume.

the assassination of her father and by her mother's need to have her work to help support the family, and who at the time of the implementation of the reparations programs is already 20 or 21, would not qualify as a beneficiary for either a pension or educational benefits. This seems to be manifestly unjust, since the young adult might well be experiencing – in addition to pain and moral distress – the consequences of having an incomplete basic education.

The Chilean and Argentinean cases demonstrate that it is possible to better recognize the harm done to children whose parents were assassinated or disappeared. In both cases, a reparation pension is awarded to children until the age of 25. The Argentinean pension for the children of the disappeared is maintained even beyond the age of 25, until the person receives his or her university degree. The Chilean educational benefits (tuition waiver and other fees, and a monthly stipend in certain cases) are awarded until the age of 35.

PARENTS AS BENEFICIARIES. The parents of those persons subjected to forced disappearance and extrajudicial execution or politically motivated assassination have also been considered as beneficiaries by some of the reparations programs examined. As can be seen in Chart 5.III, however, parents are not a top priority in most reparations programs. In those cases where economic compensation is distributed according to a priority order (such as Argentina, Brazil, South Africa, and Guatemala), parents are placed third, after spouses or partners and children. This may express the conviction that parents are left in a less vulnerable position by a victim's disappearance than the children and the spouse.

In fact, in some cases, such as Argentina and Peru, parents are included as beneficiaries explicitly attending vulnerability or economic dependence criteria. For instance, the Argentinean program awards a lifetime pension to disabled parents (of the forcibly disappeared) who do not have other sources of income. The disabled parents are also included as beneficiaries of special healthcare benefits. When this is the case, it is important that the notion of vulnerability is defined in a way that is adequate to capture the reality of women. For instance, under the Peruvian scheme, in addition to lump-sum awards, parents are eligible for a pension when they are over 50 years old at the time of the implementation of the benefit. According to Julie Guillerot, the pension scheme is based on the assumption that women under 50 are capable of generating enough income to make up for that of the dead or disappeared men. She explains that the objective of the pension "is to compensate for the economic difficulties caused by the absence of a family member and to provide support in those times when needs are generally most acute, that is, when children are still going to school and when adults are too old to provide for themselves."[193] However, as pointed out by Guillerot, because people in the targeted communities get into unions at a very young age, a high percentage of women will not qualify for the pension. Interestingly, however, the Peruvian reparations scheme for parents includes, in addition to the pension, a lump-sum award that does not allow the moral harm suffered by the parents to remain unacknowledged.

Other programs, such as in Peru, and in Chile with respect to the mother, rely on apportioning to recognize the harm suffered by the parents, awarding them a certain percentage of the reparations benefit. For instance, whereas the Chilean program distributes pensions among all beneficiaries and assigns the mother 30% of the total reference amount, the Peruvian scheme allocates a smaller share (20%) of the lump-sum award to the parents and distributes the other 80% among the spouse or partner and the children in equal shares (40% to each group).

Exceptionally, the Chilean program favors the mother over the father of the executed or disappeared victim. The reparations benefits – lifetime pension, lump-sum award, and healthcare – are assigned primarily to the mother, and only in her absence to the father. Law 19,980 (October 2004) stipulates that the father *inherits* the benefits with the death or renunciation of the mother. The preference given to the mothers responds to the fact that the overwhelming majority of those who undertook the search for the disappeared and the struggle for truth and justice were the mothers. The vulnerability and poverty experienced by women – and older women particularly – might be an additional explanatory criterion.[194]

SIBLINGS AS BENEFICIARIES. As evidenced in Chart 5.III, siblings have not generally been included in reparations programs. In general terms, siblings have not been considered as beneficiaries of economic compensation or service packages. Exceptionally, the Chilean health reparations program PRAIS includes siblings as beneficiaries, and the Argentinean scheme takes particularly vulnerable siblings into account: disabled siblings who lack other sources of income and orphan siblings under age who lived regularly with the victim are beneficiaries of lifetime pensions and healthcare benefits.

---

[193] Guillerot, "Linking Gender and Reparations in Peru" 160.
[194] Interview with Cristián Correa, former executive secretary at the Commission on Political Imprisonment and Torture, August 2007.

b) Distribution Mechanisms: Priority Orders among Family Members Versus Apportioning

Various reparations programs – Argentina, Brazil, South Africa, and Guatemala – have distributed economic compensation according to priority orders among different family members, whereas other programs have relied on a system of apportioning to distribute the awards and pensions among different family members.

Those programs that have relied on a priority order system have used different systems of ordering. Whereas the Argentine program places descendants first and spouses second, the Guatemalan, Brazilian, and South African final reparations programs use exactly the opposite order: spouses first and children second. All four schemes leave parents in third place. The Argentinean priority order reproduces domestic inheritance rules.

In the Argentinean case, the civil code inheritance regulations were strictly reproduced in the reparations order system only with the distinction of incorporating unmarried partners as beneficiaries.[195] In the Guatemalan design, domestic inheritance rules were first abandoned and then taken up again, in a certain sense, by the National Reparations Program (PNR). Initially, an apportioning system was proposed, according to which the lump-sum award would be distributed among qualifying family members (spouse or partners, children, and parents) in equal shares. In January 2007, a new comprehensive set of criteria for the implementation of the reparations measures was adopted by PNR, and the new policy instrument devised a priority order that places spouses first, children second, and then parents third. The explanation for this change was that distributing the lump sum in equal shares among the three groups of beneficiaries would end up *fragmenting* the economic compensation sum into too many portions, lowering the amount corresponding to each beneficiary, particularly given the large numbers of children in Mayan families.[196] According to former PNR's executive secretary, the potential negative effects of the priority order distribution mechanism are thwarted with the supplement of education stipends and health benefits for children.[197]

Both reproducing inheritance rules and relying on a system of priority order seem to be flawed in several respects.[198] A system of apportioning, however,

---

[195] Interview with María José Guembe, September 2007.
[196] Interview with Martín Arévalo de Leon, PNR's executive secretary until December 2007, September 2007.
[197] Ibid.
[198] See Ruth Rubio-Marín, "The Gender of Reparations in Transitional Societies," Chapter 2 of this volume.

sends the message that the harm suffered by all is to be taken into account. Apportioning also avoids relying on presumptions about whether some family members are more or less likely to spend the money on others, including, for instance, the presumption that the surviving spouse or partner will distribute the benefits among the children.[199] Leaving out close members of the family altogether may also trigger conflict within families.[200]

Economic compensation designs in Chile and Peru have followed an apportioning approach. Spouses or partners, children, and parents are designated as autonomous beneficiaries of lump-sum awards and, in certain cases, pensions. Spouses or partners are entitled to 40% of the total amount of the monthly pension in Chile and the lump-sum payment in Peru. The percentages corresponding to children and parents vary slightly from one program to the other. Whereas the Chilean scheme assigns to the mother of the victim – and only in her absence to the father – 30% of the lifetime pension, the Peruvian one reserves 20% of the lump-sum award for the parents of the victim. As for children, the Peruvian scheme assigns them 40% of the lump sum, whereas the Chilean one provides 15% of the reference sum of the lifetime pension to each child. Moving away from domestic inheritance rules, both the Chilean and Peruvian reparations programs include the parents as beneficiaries, concurrently with spouses and children, thus recognizing their anguish and the crucial role of mothers in the struggle for truth and justice.[201]

As to how economic compensation is distributed among members of each category (spouses and partners, children, and parents), we find that in some cases, such as Peru, the fixed amount (40% of the lump-sum award) is assigned

---

[199] Based in part on Goldblatt's research in South Africa and on their own field research in Sierra Leone, Mazurana and Carlson (Chapter 4 of this volume) question the extent to which children actually benefit from economic compensation awarded to their parents. On the one hand, there is evidence that when men received cash reparations, they tend to spend the money individually, whereas women tend to use their cash awards for the benefit of others. But, as demonstrated in the South African context, the payments, being rather small amounts, often do not have the effect of providing for the maintenance of families. Considering that families that have lost a breadwinner might have pressing obligations (debts, rent, taxes), in order to guarantee that children's needs will be covered it seems more adequate to award them independent economic compensation. On the other hand, one should take into account the precarious situation of parents (and especially mothers) in single-headed households, who are primarily responsible for the well-being of children in deciding the adequate apportioning rules.

[200] The South African case is particularly telling about the negative effects of distributing economic compensation according to priority orders. According to Goldblatt, "the designation of the person who went to the TRC (e.g. the mother of a man killed) as the main relative/dependent beneficiary, rather than some other relative/dependent (e.g., his wife), has caused conflict in some families." The situation is aggravated by the poverty faced by most victims and their families. Goldblatt, 69.

[201] Interview with Julie Guillerot, September 2007.

to all the children, to be distributed among the number of given children in equal parts. The amount does not vary according to the number of child beneficiaries. This does not have to be the case. The Chilean case shows that it is possible to be more sensitive to the needs of the family by taking into account its size, allocating monthly pensions amounting to 15% of a reference sum (US $537) to each of the children. In both the Peruvian and Chilean schemes, pensions are an element of a more complex reparations package that includes education and healthcare benefits.

c) Complexity of Reparations Programs: The Relevance of Combining Economic Compensation with Social Services

Administrative reparations programs tend to distribute a diverse set of reparations benefits.[202] The programs discussed here have distributed economic compensation in various forms, including monthly, bi-annual, and yearly pensions, lump-sum awards, or a combination of the two; social services in the form of free, special, or priority healthcare; education benefits; housing benefits; skills-training programs; microcredit; and collective reparations measures. Reparations programs have also included symbolic reparations measures in the form of official and nonofficial memorialization initiatives, official private and public recognition, statements and apologies, and public ceremonies of commemoration and presentation of findings about the violence and repression. Satisfaction and nonrepetition measures have also been recommended.

As evidenced in the various examples discussed below, victims and beneficiaries have expressly demanded and particularly valued that certain social services be included in reparations programs. Healthcare services and education benefits have great potential as reparations measures that take into consideration family members' needs. Social services can be tailored according to specific needs caused by the impact of the death, disappearance, torture, or imprisonment of loved ones. Psychological and psychosocial services specially oriented toward human rights violations related trauma and physical healthcare services explicitly connected the violations can have a significant reparative effect among victims. Education packages – including tuition waivers and other fees and maintenance stipends – can also adequately address the negative impact of the death, disappearance, torture, or imprisonment of a breadwinner on the educational opportunities of the children and young adults in the family. Skills-training programs could, interestingly, deal with

---

[202] See the notion of *complexity* of a reparations program in de Greiff, "Justice and Reparations."

the negative impact of the absence or impairment of the breadwinner on the labor and professional development of the partner or spouse. Several examples can illustrate the importance of including services of different kinds among reparations benefits aiming to reach different family members.

The Chilean case confirms that combining economic compensation with health and education benefits can positively impact family members' reparations experience, even though formally in Chile family members were not considered as victims in their own right either. In addition to monthly pensions, family members were entitled to comprehensive physical and psychological healthcare; children of the disappeared were granted tuition waivers at the institutions of their choice at any level until the age of 35, and those attending primary school or enrolled in technical or higher education additionally received maintenance stipends.[203] Such well-designed health and education benefits for family members likely sent a message of recognition of their particular needs and a commitment by the state to contribute to their fulfilment. Indeed, the comprehensive physical and mental health program PRAIS in Chile has been so highly valued by its beneficiaries that they formed a national organization in 1998 to defend the original conception of the program as a component of the reparations policy, and they succeeded in securing the permanence of the program by sanctioning it through a law.[204] Subsequently, the victims of torture and arbitrary imprisonment and their family members who gave testimony before the Valech Commission also widely expressed their desire to secure education benefits for the children of the direct victims as reparations measures. However, despite the negative impact that torture and imprisonment had on the possibility for educational development of the children of affected families, and despite the recommendations of the Valech Commission, the government and congress dismissed the proposal, partly on resource-availability grounds.

In Peru, the education reparations program was added to the CVR's first reparations draft proposal after a series of consultation meetings in which victims and surviving family members made a strong demand for the inclusion of education benefits in the program. The CVR recognized that the internal armed conflict resulted in the loss of educational opportunities for children and youth, who had to abandon school because of the death or disappearance of their parents, because of forced displacement, because they had to

---

[203] Lira, 61.
[204] Law 19.980, enacted in 2004. See Lira, 71.

play an active role in defending their communities, or simply because of the destruction of infrastructure.[205]

The reaction of South African victims to the lack of implementation of the social services referral policy is also indicative of the importance that surviving family members gave to access to those services.[206] As reported by Beth Goldblatt, South African victims felt strongly that "they should have been put at the front of the queue" for government services such as housing.[207] In a study referred to by the author looking at how victims have spent lump-sum awards and what they still ask for, "the common desires were for housing, jobs, health care, education for children and counselling services."[208] Social services claims – such as support for their families, education for their children, and housing – were often related to the caring role that women play in South African society.

Now, it is important to note that in the contexts where victims have positively valued social services as reparations measures, those benefits are a component of a broader reparations package, including pensions or lump-sum awards. This might be indicative of the noninterchangeable nature of the two: both might be necessary to address the negative impact of human rights violations on the life of family members, the pain and moral distress inherent to the violent loss of a loved one, and the need for symbolic recognition. More research needs to be done in contexts such as Sierra Leone, where certain beneficiaries will be eligible only for healthcare services – and not for economic compensation in the form of lump-sum awards or pensions. Be that as it may, the reparative effect of economic compensation is strictly linked to the coherence[209] – or lack thereof – with other justice measures, such as acknowledgment of responsibility, truth-telling and commemoration, institutional reforms to guarantee the nonrepetition of the violations, and criminal punishment.

VI. CONCLUSIONS

Albeit slowly, international law has begun to reflect a finer understanding of the connections and codependency that constitute the family unit and the way it is affected by gross violations of human rights. This is confirmed by developments in international law ascribing the status of victim to family members of those

---

[205] CVR, *Final Report of the Truth and Reconciliation Commission* (Lima: CVR, 2003), Annex 1, 21.
[206] Goldblatt, 67 and 69.
[207] Ibid., 71.
[208] Ibid., 69.
[209] On *external coherence*, see de Greiff, "Justice and Reparations."

persons subjected to gross human rights violations. Good evidence is provided by the UN *Basic Principles on Reparations* and the UN Convention for the Protection of all Persons from Enforced Disappearances (not yet in force), both of which acknowledge that family members of victims can also qualify as victims and receive reparations. These relevant instruments are complemented by the practice of regional human rights courts, especially the IACtHR, and by the important state practice developed through reparations programs studied in this chapter. Yet this framework is far from being a consolidated and coherent one. The next of kin's harm has been acknowledged, but serious questions still need to be addressed. For instance, what amounts to adequate reparation for this harm? And, what are the criteria to qualify as a beneficiary as a next of kin? The answers to these questions vary largely and no consistent set of practices can be drawn from the regional courts and domestic reparations programs.

Of the two regional human rights courts, the IACtHR stands out for its important contributions to the treatment that should be given to the next of kin of victims of disappearances, arbitrary killings, inhuman treatment, and arbitrary detention. One of this court's major contributions has been its broad interpretation of the concept of "injured party" under Article 63.1, which has allowed it to cover both victims of violations of the ACHR and persons who, in spite of not qualifying as victims, are acknowledged by the court as having suffered harm and deserving reparations.

The interpretation of the notion of "next of kin" has a great impact on the determination of who can be awarded reparations. In this respect, the practice of the IACtHR contrasts with that of the ECtHR. The former court does not limit reparations to the nuclear family of a direct victim. It has recognized that members of the extended family, such as aunts, uncles, stepmothers or stepfathers, stepsons, and even girlfriends, can also be injured parties/beneficiaries or victims. In this sense, it is important to remember that the IACtHR has moved toward recognizing the next of kin of direct victims of gross human rights violations as victims and not only as injured parties. More importantly, the next of kin of direct victims of disappearances, arbitrary killings, inhuman treatment, and detention can claim to be victims of different rights under the ACHR. This is to be applauded, especially in relation to violations of the right to humane treatment. The court acknowledges the suffering of the next of kin of victims of gross human rights violations, including that experienced by the next of kin of a person subjected to arbitrary detention and inhuman treatment who is still alive, and it awards reparations on this ground. Finally, the court has also been sensitive to different cultural understandings of the next of kin.

In contrast, the ECtHR has accepted only that some members of the nuclear family of a victim can access reparations, and only if they qualify as autonomous victims or as successors. Also, this court has not shown any sensitivity toward different cultural understanding of the concept of family. Moreover, it establishes a hierarchy of gross human rights violations and suffering in relation to the next of kin that should be challenged. For the court, only the next of kin of a disappeared person can claim to be victims of violations of the right to humane treatment, and only if they show that they have suffered harm beyond the "normal" harm ensuing from the disappearance of the family member as a result of the misconduct of public authorities. In other words, the moral and material harm caused by the disappearances itself or by other gross human rights violations to the next of kin is not taken into account by the ECtHR.

The reparations awards given by the two regional courts are in sharp contrast as well. Whereas the IACtHR is ready to award reparations for pecuniary and nonpecuniary damages suffered by the next of kin in their own right, the ECtHR, if at all, will typically award moral damages to the next of kin in disappearance and killing cases, but not always pecuniary damages. When it does, it generally awards substantially smaller amounts than those claimed, and it requires a thorough substantiation and evidence of the claims. For the IACtHR, one area, among others, that requires urgent thought is reparations for material damages, as these remain very low compared to the awards of the court for moral damages. Although the IACtHR treats each case on its own merits, it is important that the court has been willing to rely on a wide set of cross-cutting principles, such as the principle of equity, to quantify the damages. Finally, unlike the ECtHR, the IACtHR has not limited itself to the award of economic compensation. Instead, it has ordered more complex reparations packages that include rehabilitation and satisfaction measures such as truth and justice.

The contrast between the two courts also extends to their treatment of the burden and standard of proof to be applied for reparations purposes. The IACtHR, very conscious of the terrible effects of gross human rights violations and of the evidentiary problems they create, has established a solid framework to alleviate the burden and standard of proof, and it often relies on important presumptions to assume that damage has taken place and to quantify it. The ECtHR does completely the opposite. Regardless of the nature of the violation at stake, it requires evidence beyond reasonable doubt, which works to the detriment of victims of gross human rights violations. It thus forgets the fact that procedural aspects should always be consistent with the nature of the violations in question and with the aims of justice.

The increasing acknowledgment of the devastating consequences of violence on familial fabrics has also inspired the evolution of administrative reparations programs. Indeed, the more recent reparations programs have adopted broad definitions of victim, expressly including family members. Unfortunately, however, progress in terminology has not necessarily meant entitlement to reparations benefits.

There is a huge gap between the treatment reparations programs give to family members of nonsurviving victims and to those of surviving ones. Family members of the disappeared and killed are effectively recognized in their victim status. In fact, even before the adoption of international principles expanding the notion of victim, restored democracies in Argentina and Chile distributed lifetime reparations pensions and healthcare and education benefits among family members of the disappeared and executed. The moral and material harm that the family members of the surviving victims experience, however, has not been adequately recognized by administrative reparations efforts. Reparations programs tend to include the victims of torture and arbitrary detention, and increasingly the victims of sexual violence and forced recruitment, as beneficiaries of reparations measures. Their partners, children, and parents, however, tend to be left without economic compensation of any sort. This exclusion occurs despite detailed accounts of the consequences of torture, arbitrary imprisonment, sexual violence, and forced recruitment on those who bear care-giving roles within the family and on those who affectively and economically depend on the victim. Resource availability arguments are quite dominant in the debate. Efforts to include family members of the tortured and arbitrarily imprisoned as beneficiaries of healthcare services, such as the Chilean PRAIS, are therefore significant. Vulnerability and harm-based approaches such as the one adopted by the Sierra Leonean TRC also facilitated the inclusion of family members of the amputees, other war wounded, and the victims of sexual violence among the beneficiaries of healthcare services and education benefits in the case of the children of amputees. Entitling children born out of rape to pensions and education benefits, as proposed by the Peruvian TRC, is also a step forward in the recognition of the domino harming effect of human rights violations.

This said, there are valid feasibility concerns when reparations beneficiaries are greatly multiplied. The concern is only more grounded given the trend in reparations programs to increasingly aim at comprehensiveness by expanding the typology of serious human rights violations that qualify for reparations (including, for instance, sexual violence, forced exile, and forced displacement, among others). On the other hand, freed from the strictures of the notion of *restitutio in integrum* and restoration to the *status quo ante* (and the obligation to calculate loss of earnings and opportunities), administrative reparations programs can come up with creative ways of meeting the actual needs and expectations of victims and their family members with reparations measures, providing them an adequate degree of recognition and some assistance with achieving a better quality of life. This is especially so if the programs have the desired degree of complexity and include material and symbolic as well as individual and collective forms of redress, and if they rely, as they increasingly seem to do, on the rule of apportioning among different family members.

6

Tort Theory, Microfinance, and Gender Equality Convergent in Pecuniary Reparations

Anita Bernstein

INTRODUCTION

In numerous possible contexts, national governments can start reparations programs. This chapter focuses on reparations for the effects of a crisis that ravaged a whole nation – for example civil war, genocide, dictatorship, apartheid – rather than a single, discrete deviation from the norms of a functioning democracy. Isolated incidents can generate urgent needs of repair,[1] but the reparations under discussion in this chapter presume a more fundamental ambition: a declaration of the nation's past as broken, and its future in need of mending.

Precedents for this undertaking provide models for the subcategory of interest here, pecuniary reparations – that is, programs that seek to identify and compensate individual citizen-claimants in recognition of human rights violations that they suffered during the recent past. Such recognition can take monetary form in transfer payments to individuals. Argentina, which through legislation in 1994 appropriated reparations for victims of forced disappearances and detentions that took place from 1975 to 1983, paid in the form of bonds;[2] Chile, which in 1992 appropriated pension funds for the victims of human rights violations that took place from 1973 to 1990;[3] and South

---

[1] I remark on the problematic nature of "isolated incidents" in Anita Bernstein, "Treating Sexual Harassment with Respect," *Harvard Law Review* 111 (1997): 445, 499 n. 331. This reservation noted, I mean to exclude for this purpose reparations contexts such as the internment of Japanese citizens in the United States during World War II, or the "stolen generation" of aboriginal children forcibly separated from their parents during the twentieth century in Australia, focusing instead on comprehensive national schemes.

[2] María José Guembe, "Economic Reparations for Grave Human Rights Violations: The Argentinian Experience," in *The Handbook of Reparations*, ed. Pablo de Greiff (New York: Oxford University Press, 2006), 29–31.

[3] Elizabeth Lira, "The Reparations Policy for Human Rights Violations in Chile," in *The Handbook*, 83–85.

Africa, which disbursed cash payments totaling US $5.5 million to approximately 14,000 apartheid-era victims[4] – these are among the countries that have distributed pecuniary reparations following national crises. In less wealthy nations, including Peru, Rwanda, Haiti, Sierra Leone, and Guatemala, units of government have expressed approval of providing monetary compensation to citizen-victims in the wake of national crises, suggesting that pecuniary reparations can hold appeal as policy in nations hard-pressed to finance a new round of transfer payments.

By opting for pecuniary reparations, a national government necessarily rejects the arguments that the endeavor of reparation is futile, that money in particular cannot effect meaningful reparation, and that payments to individuals waste money compared to collective payments. Consistent with Pablo de Greiff's "Justice and Reparations,"[5] such a government implicitly deems insufficient two significant constituents of transitional justice: nonmaterial reparations (such as an apology)[6] and disbursements that pursue a collective goal (such as economic development) and make individuals better off only indirectly.[7]

Economic development is part of the context within which reparations are considered. Because reparations programs are frequently established in situations characterized by disarray and vulnerability, they likely coexist with fragile national economies, shaky financial institutions, uncertain or erratic regulation of these institutions and related commercial practices, patchy telephony, and technological underdevelopment generally. Systemic human rights violations for which states have acknowledged responsibility usually are part of a larger devastation that damaged the rule of law and had harmful effects on both the safety and protection of investment capital and the physical safety of civilian citizens.[8] A government certain of its plan to make transfer

---

[4] Christopher J. Colvin, "Overview of the Reparations Program in South Africa," in *The Handbook*, 188–189.

[5] Pablo de Greiff, "Justice and Reparations," in *The Handbook*, 451.

[6] In 1991, for example, Pope John Paul II proclaimed an apology for the injuries done to Africa by Christian Europe.

[7] After World War II, for example, Japan invested in the economies of Burma, the Philippines, Indonesia, and Vietnam pursuant to treaties whose names included the word "reparations."

[8] "In a total crisis, the state virtually ceases to exist, national economies disintegrate, and social and political structures melt away. A significant number of people are exposed to a day-to-day struggle for survival, often separated from their homes and deprived of their usual sources of livelihood. In particular, total crisis means that national governmental and civil society organizations have been destroyed; the production and market distribution of goods and services has been disrupted; institutional capacity for policy decision and planning at [the] national level has been eliminated or curtailed ... [and] large numbers of individuals have been physically and socially displaced and were subject to traumatizing experiences of

payments to victims could decide to wait for some marker of stability to arrive before forming its plan. But the wait might be too long, especially for a government that wants to capitalize on some of the advantages of economic reparations. If (contrary to rhetoric heard from some transitional governments), far from having to choose between reparations programs and development programs, one could design a reparations program in a way that serves developmental goals, the advantages of moving forward immediately become plain.

One mechanism for potentially realizing this prospect of achieving both reparation and development is "microcredit" or "microfinance." Many observers continue to believe that gains rooted in small banking transactions change the world. Indeed, the 2006 Nobel Peace Prize went jointly to an economist and the high-yield bank he founded, which had about $564,000,000 on deposit at the time of the award.[9] "Lasting peace can not be achieved unless large groups find ways to break out of poverty," the Norwegian Nobel Committee said in its announcement of the prize. "Micro-credit is one such means. Development from below also serves to advance democracy and human rights." Tellingly for this volume, the Committee added that microcredit was "an important liberating force in societies where women in particular have to struggle against repressive social and economic conditions."[10]

This chapter examines pecuniary reparations for human rights violations as a point of convergence of three different concepts: tort theory, microfinance, and gender equality. It begins, in the first section, with a discussion of economic compensation for individuals, emphasizing what a torts perspective can bring to the design of this kind of reparations program. The next section advocates for the payment of compensation in the form of shares in a microfinance institution, highlighting the benefits of this form over cash transfers. The final section builds on this proposal by linking microfinance with both tort theory and gender equality. As other contributors establish elsewhere in this volume, the effort to achieve reparation following national crisis is at least hobbled, if not defeated, by conceptions of agency, identity, and recognition that take inadequate note of women's experiences and consciousness.

---

violence." Hans Dieter Seibel, *From Recipients of Reparation Payments to Shareholders of Microfinance Institutions: A Study of the Possible Relations Between Reparations for Victims of Human Rights Abuses and Microfinance*, presented October 15–18, 2003, http://www.uni-koeln.de/ew-fak/aef/08-2005/2003-6%20ICTJ%20Microfinance.pdf (hereinafter Seibel, *Reparations Shareholders*).

[9] http://www.grameen-info.org/bank/GBGlance.htm.

[10] Press release, Norwegian Nobel Committee, The Nobel Peace Prize for 2006, October 13, 2006, http://nobelprize.org/nobel_prizes/peace/laureates/2006/press.html.

ECONOMIC COMPENSATION FOR INDIVIDUALS POST-CRISIS: A TORTS PERSPECTIVE

International law creates at least a basis if not a mandate for reparations that can take a pecuniary form. Numerous legal instruments[11] declare a right to redress for human rights violations,[12] and, broadly understood, reparations constitute one form of such a legal remedy. The law continues intertwined with reparations at every stage, from the early design of each program to its conclusion: legislation creates reparations schemes;[13] national laws decree what the government may do and which individuals will participate in processes; and judges, advocates, and administrative lawyers play leadership roles in the implementation of reparations measures. Even when laws and lawyers are absent from a particular locus of reparations, a discourse associated with law — words such as rights and justice — will likely be present, and reparations themselves serve as instruments to rebuild or install the rule of law.

Although these iterations of law in reparations emphasize "public" law — especially international law, human rights law, and criminal law — the identification of individual victims also invokes a field of "private" law, the law of personal injuries. Tort law provides for compensation to persons injured by wrongful conduct. Within law, it contains its own jurisprudence — a perspective on law-based responsibility that, although compatible with the public law governing states, crimes, and assertions of human rights violations, brings its own concerns to the assignment of entitlements and responsibilities. This jurisprudence provides for torts-focused views on particular choices that face reparations planners, which this section of the paper will examine.

Compensation as a Constituent of Doing Justice

International law recognizes a variety of means, not just money, to effect repair following violations of human rights. In 2006, the UN General Assembly adopted a report of the High Commissioner for Human Rights declaring that reparations to, or in respect of, victims encompass "restitution, compensation,

---

[11] The Universal Declaration of Human Rights; the International Convention on the Elimination of All Forms of Racial Discrimination; the International Covenant on Civil and Political Rights; the Convention Against Torture and Other Cruel, Inhuman or Degrading Treatment; the Convention on the Rights of the Child; the European Convention for the Protection of Human Rights and Fundamental Freedoms; the American Convention on Human Rights; and the African Charter on Human and Peoples' Rights.

[12] Human Rights and Equal Opportunity Commission [Australia], Social Justice Report 2000, ch. 5, "Reparations" http://www.hreoc.gov.au/social_justice/sj_report/chap5.html#ch5_international_law.

[13] *The Handbook* contains almost three hundred pages of primary documents and legislation.

Tort Theory, Microfinance, and Gender Equality Convergent 295

rehabilitation, satisfaction and guarantees of non-repetition."[14] The last two are particularly broad categories that include a range of measures: verification of facts and disclosure of truth, searches for corpses, public apologies, tributes to victims, civilian control of the military, an independent judiciary, and the installation of codes of conduct and ethical norms.[15]

A torts perspective on reparations casts no slight on these ambitious ends by focusing on a discrete portion of them. The torts vantage point shares de Greiff's view that the word reparations "refer[s] to measures that provide benefits to victims directly."[16] It emphasizes compensation more than restitution, while acknowledging overlap between these two categories.[17] Most fundamentally, it emphasizes the need for money (or its close equivalent) to change hands. An entity accepting responsibility for past wrongs – probably a government – disburses money, and victims or their heirs receive it.

The monetary nexus is integral to torts. In its use of the term "damages" for "the monetary award for legally recognized harm,"[18] tort law aspires to integrate wrongs and rights through the disbursement and receipt of money. This implicit unity appears more explicitly in the American compendium *Restatement (Second) of Torts*, which defines damages as "the sum of money awarded to a person injured by the tort of another"[19] and declares that this money is awarded to vindicate the ideals of tort law generally.

> The rules for determining the measure of damages in tort are based upon the purposes for which actions of tort are maintainable. These purposes are:
>
> (a) to give compensation, indemnity or restitution for harms;
> (b) to determine rights;
> (c) to punish wrongdoers and deter wrongful conduct; and
> (d) to vindicate parties and deter retaliation or violent and unlawful self-help.[20]

---

[14] UN General Assembly, Sixtieth Session, Agenda item 71(a), *Basic Principles and Guidelines on the Right to a Remedy and Reparation for Victims of Gross Human Rights Violations of International Human Rights Law and Serious Violations of International Humanitarian Law*, A/RES/60/147, 2006, 18.

[15] Ibid., 22–23.

[16] de Greiff, "Justice and Reparations," 453.

[17] *Restatement (Second) of Torts* (Philadelphia: American Law Institute, 1977), sec. 901(a) (asserting that the first principle of tort actions is "to give compensation, indemnity or restitution for harms"). On the ranking of compensation ahead of restitution, see ibid., cmt. *a* (noting that tort law, unlike the law of unjust enrichment, does not focus on the benefit that the defendant received: "This first purpose of tort law leads to compensatory damages"). See also John C.P. Goldberg, "Two Conceptions of Tort Damages: Fair v. Full Compensation," *De Paul Law Review* 55 (2006): 435 (parsing distinctions between compensation and indemnification, which parallel distinctions between full and fair compensation).

[18] Dan B. Dobbs, *The Law of Torts* (St. Paul: West Publishing Co., 2000), 1047.

[19] *Restatement (Second) of Torts*, sec. 902.

[20] Ibid., sec. 901.

Several writers have pointed out the shortcomings of, and dangers associated with, monetary compensation as a means of reparation following a national crisis. Taking the perspective of a victim, they question the reparative effect of receiving cash from a distant government.[21] Taking the perspective of a payor-planner or observer, they doubt that disbursements to individuals constitute a priority for a nation as it emerges from chaos and crisis.[22]

A torts-centered response to these criticisms would agree that money is indeed never sufficient to repair serious violations of human rights, but insist that it is necessary. Truth commissions, apologies, forward-looking rhetoric, newly elected democratic governments committed to change, and other non-pecuniary measures are crucial to the rebuilding of societies in transition; but the currency of torts redress is literally found in currency. Moreover, because human rights violations trammel on persons as individuals, the currency of reparations must go to them directly and personally: collective payments and programs, though undoubtedly salubrious, do not discharge this obligation.

Torts perspectives focus on a crucial half of a balance that otherwise might be overlooked. According to de Greiff, reparations payments without truth-telling can look to victims like "blood money," whereas without payments truth-telling can look like "cheap talk."[23] Truth-telling ceases to be cheap talk when it includes the receipt and the disbursement of reparations monies. The value of receipt is at one level obvious: for most people, to have more of it is better than to have less. The rare recipient who disagrees and deems money odious may repudiate or give away her payment. (Exploring another level, I take up the question of how to refine the payment of money to enhance its gains in "Choosing Among Means to Convey Pecuniary Reparations through Microfinance" later.)

---

[21] Women are prominent among the money-skeptics. Roman David and Susanne Choi Yuk-Ping, "Victims on Transitional Justice: Lessons from the Reparation of Human Rights Abuses in the Czech Republic," *Human Rights Quarterly* 27 (2005): 392, 403 (noting that some mothers of disappeared sons in Argentina refused financial compensation on the ground that it would reduce their quest for "truth and justice"); Martha Minow, *Between Vengeance and Forgiveness: Facing History after Genocide and Mass Violence* (Boston: Beacon Press, 1998), 103 (arguing that "reparations fall short of repairing victims or social relationships after violence" and questioning "whether the most obvious need of victims is for compensation"); ibid., 110 ("Social and religious meanings rather than economic values lie at the heart of reparations"). See also Tom Tyler and Hulda Thorisdottir, "A Psychological Perspective on Compensation for Harm: Examining the September 11 Compensation Fund," *De Paul Law Review* 55 (2003): 355, 361 (emphasizing that from a victim's point of view, monetary compensation can never be adequate: only "moral accountability" can satisfy).

[22] Minow, *Between Vengeance and Forgiveness*, 93; Maryam Kamali, "Accountability for Human Rights Violations: A Comparison of Transitional Justice in East Germany and South Africa," *Columbia Journal of Transnational Law* 40 (2001): 79, 129 n.173.

[23] de Greiff, "Justice and Reparations," 461.

Disbursement yields its own benefits to the society and its government. Instrumentalists may note that by declaring a financial obligation that a successor regime owes to victims, these payments open the possibility of deterrence: even though primary wrongdoers are likely not available to share in the obligation, a pecuniary program of reparations establishes ledgers that can be used in the future should wrongdoer-controlled assets become accessible. Technological innovation having made recordkeeping cheaper and hidden wealth easier to uncover, the establishment of these ledgers declares that this government has not only the machinery but the will to find, catalogue, and reallocate the wealth that human rights violators wrongly hold. For noninstrumentalists and instrumentalists alike, ledgers affirm an ideal of governmental responsibility – not only to apologize and tell the truth, but to pay for its own misdeeds as measured in wrongs and rights. The endeavor of determining a monetary amount to be paid, both in the aggregate and to each recipient, makes the reality of past wrong concrete and visible even before any funds are transferred.[24]

Not Just Money: Torts as Recognition

Monetary compensation and truth-telling in the view above are incomplete halves, each needing the other to effect real reparation. How do the two come together? The annals of reparations present several possibilities, to which the tort-focused approach of this chapter adds its own perspective. For this purpose, torts emphatically does not reduce to the payment of damages. It concerns itself at least as much with the agency of the victim, and the generation of recognition for an affront to her agency, as with her pecuniary state.

Mere compensation has never accounted for all of what tort law and policy seek to accomplish. Any law-based scheme that purports to compensate without recognition of the individual behind a claim – a person who holds rights and freedoms – is abjuring torts for something else.[25] Tort law endeavors to speak for victims by supporting them as they speak for themselves. Complaint-initiated engagement of the legal system is a hallmark of tort – in

---

[24] Cf. Christian Sundquist, "Critical Praxis, Spirit Healing, and Community Activism: Preserving a Subversive Dialogue on Reparations," *New York University Annual Survey of American Law* 58 (2003): 659, 697 (arguing that reparations for African Americans ought to take pecuniary form in order to highlight the economic privileges of white Americans, to "foster community activism," and to emphasize the need among recipients for economic self-sufficiency).

[25] For discussion of alternative routes to the ends associated with torts, especially compensation and deterrence, see Stephen D. Sugarman, *Doing Away with Personal Injury Law: New Compensation Mechanisms for Victims, Consumers, and Business* (New York: Quorum Books, 1989).

sharp contrast to criminal prosecutions, administrative regulations, and social welfare spending, which all alter the status quo only after government takes some initiative.[26]

Reparations planners start their work familiar with the protest that the central tort equation – approximately: wrongs = damages = money – does not align with injury as victims have experienced it. But it is a mistake to think that a tort approach would reduce reparations to cash transfers. An article from a bygone era is instructive on the point. The American civil procedure scholar Maurice Rosenberg once contended that government had a role to play as facilitator and supporter of personal injury claims.[27] The notion sounds jarring today, at least in the United States.[28] Rosenberg in 1971 nevertheless envisioned government as intervening to assert the interests of injured citizens. He proposed a new ministry, named the Department of Economic Justice, that would pay out cash in response to reports of injury and also be empowered to go after the wrongdoers it identified as responsible, taking "legal action appropriate to the situation, including wholesale (and hence, economically worthwhile) suits to recover amounts it had already paid out administratively, along with costs, interest, and other economic sanctions."[29]

Anyone inclined to deem this suggestion a naive, idle dream about benevolence in support of other persons' injury claims should remember that the principle of vicarious liability is heeded in daily practice throughout the developed world.[30] An entity that did not participate directly or personally in wrongdoing may in some circumstances nevertheless be required, without a finding of its own "fault," to compensate victims who suffered at the hands of individual wrongdoers. The best-known example of vicarious liability is *respondeat superior* (according to which a principal is responsible for its agent), a form of strict liability prevalent worldwide. In the United States, business entities can also take on vicarious liability by succession: they might, through the purchase of corporate assets, gain ownership of a business's liabilities too.[31] After being

---

[26] Anita Bernstein, "Complaints," *McGeorge Law Review* 32 (2000): 37.

[27] Maurice Rosenberg, "Devising Procedures that are Civil to Promote Justice that is Civilized," *Michigan Law Review* 69 (1971): 797.

[28] In contemporary American debates, liberals defend tort law as practiced, and associate proposals to reform it with business interests. Stephen D. Sugarman, "Ideological Flip-Flop: American Liberals are Now the Primary Supporters of Tort Law," UC Berkeley Public Law Paper No. 925244, January 17, 2005, http://papers.ssrn.com/sol3/papers.cfm?abstract_id=925244.

[29] Rosenberg, 814.

[30] Thanks to Mark Geistfeld for clarifying this point, and to John Owen Haley for his insights into the relation between subrogation and torts-thinking about reparations, which inform these paragraphs.

[31] See generally Symposium, "Multinational Corporations and Cross Border Conflicts: Nationality, Veil Piercing, and Cross Border Liability," *Florida Journal of International Law* 10 (1995): 221, 272 (discussing divergence between US and UK law).

compelled to pay damages pursuant to vicarious liability, an entity has the prerogative to seek indemnification from the person responsible for having committed the more fundamental, primary wrong.[32] In this light it becomes plausible to envision a unit within a national government taking on the role of a successor government, empowered to recoup plundered national assets from notorious wrongdoers.

Such persons by hypothesis may have lost their power to inflict harm on their fellow citizens but also may own property sufficient to pay for some of their past harms. Examples abound. The rumor that Augusto Pinochet had stashed nine tons of gold in a Hong Kong bank vault proved to be untrue, but the estimate of $28 million deposited in foreign accounts was well founded;[33] this sum could have made an impact on Chile's reparations program.[34] One human rights group has tried to force a reckoning of the gains amassed by the multinational corporations that did business in South Africa and were supportive of the apartheid regime, the subject of another reparations program.[35] Haile Mengistu Meriam, under whose rule an estimated half-million civilians were killed in Ethiopia, took up residence in Zimbabwe endowed with "a free apartment and a fleet of luxury cars" that could have been liquidated to pay reparations to families of these civilians, a group that includes political dissidents killed by his military junta in the 1970s.[36] Too poor to effect its limited reparations scheme that had budgeted about US $3,500,000,[37] Haiti could certainly use some of the money that the Duvalier family embezzled

---

[32] On the common law entitlement of an entity defendant to recover against an individual wrongdoer for monies that the entity paid to a third party as compensation for physical injuries, see *Lister v. Romford Ice, etc. Co. Ltd.*, [1957] A.C. 555; *Saranillo v. Silva*, 889 P.2d 685 (Haw. 1995); *Jackson v. Associated Dry Goods Corp.*, 192 N.E. 2d 167 (N.Y. 1963).

[33] Eva Vergara and Patrick J. McDonnell, "No Pinochet Gold Hoard, Bank Says," *Los Angeles Times*, October 27, 2006, A7.

[34] See Lira, "Reparations Policy," 55.

[35] "Jubilee South Africa has pointed out that the multinational corporations that helped to finance the apartheid government in its final, most repressive years removed roughly R3 billion (US $375,000,000) a year between 1985 and 1993 from the country. Jubilee argues that if 1.5 percent of these profits was returned every year for six years, financial reparations at the level of the original TRC recommendations could be paid." Colvin, "Overview," 176, 199. Jubilee also supported a lawsuit in the United States against several of these corporations, arguing that they violated international law by exploiting cheap labor and collaborating with armed enforcers of the apartheid government. In *re South African Apartheid Litigation*, 346 F. Supp. 2d 538, 544–45 (S.D.N.Y. 2004) (dismissing the action on the ground that plaintiffs did not demonstrate a violation of international law).

[36] Victor T. LeVine, "Taylor Case Only a Start: Leaders Seldom Answer for Abuses, But That May Be Changing," *St. Louis Post-Dispatch*, April 9, 2006, B4.

[37] Alexander Segovia, "The Reparations Proposals of the Truth Commissions in El Salvador and Haiti: A History of Noncompliance," in *The Handbook*, 154, 164. Segovia does not attribute Haiti's failure to implement a program simply to scarcity of resources, but the nation's poverty played an undisputed role.

before fleeing, even if the astounding estimate of "up to US $900 million"[38] overstates what it stole.

In this torts-influenced reckoning, victims of human rights violations would assert their claims and receive reparations payments from governments to compensate for discrete wrongdoing, with human malefactors borne in mind. The government would accept responsibility on its own behalf – either for having done wrong itself or for not having fulfilled its duty to protect citizens from active wrongdoers[39] – and also as a quasi-insurer making payments for the wrongs of others, pursuant to its obligation. It would pay reparations to citizen-victims without condescension, valuing its right of indemnification against the persons and entities that bear primary responsibility for harm.

Conveying payments for wrongful violations of human agency would thus signal not only an acknowledgment of responsibility but a tacit pledge to pursue, or at least care about, the reclamation of this money from primary offenders. The tacit pledge, implying that the giver values its payment, expresses recognition of a particular historical event and the claim of right that derives from a wrong. When the primary offenders gained the holdings in question through theft, extortion, or wrongful seizure, the reclamation effort also links the pathology of rights-violation with the pathology of plundering a nation's wealth – a connection that stands up for fiscal law and order along with human rights, and thus could enhance the reparations program in the eyes of foreign investors.

Honoring Both (and Mediating between) Security and Freedom through Reparations

Reparations planners who have decided to pay monetary compensation to victims might consider the purposes of transfer payments that are made as compensation for injury in ordinary litigation: security and freedom. Tort-thinking pursues security and freedom for both sides of the litigation caption. A tort claim by a plaintiff complains of an invasion that may be seen as a breach of security; but defendants, for their part, are entitled to shelter from the danger of an arbitrary official conclusion that they caused injuries for which they must pay. For defendants, security takes form in procedural justice. Tortious conduct impinged on the freedom of persons who were hurt by it; at

---

[38] Paul Hamel, "Preventing Democracy in Haiti: Turning the Light Off at the End of the Tunnel," *Peace Magazine*, January 1, 2005, 14.
[39] Ruth Rubio-Marín, "The Gender of Reparations in Transitional Societies," Chapter 2 of this volume.

the same time, too much tort liability – condemnation out of proportion to the magnitude of real injuries and risks – unduly impinges on freedom of action.

Divergent perspectives on torts share these two priorities even while unaligned on other questions. For example, "security" speaks as pertinently to various problems of economic efficiency in torts as it does to corrective-justice attention to the nature of the wrong that a victim suffered;[40] human freedom is as integral to the jurisprudential concept of "fairness" as to the prerogative to engage in profitable activity that occupies the center of "welfare."[41] The paired ends of "compensation" and "deterrence" mediate between security and freedom while honoring them both.[42]

Enhancing Security

Although security applies to both sides of the litigation caption, it functions more fundamentally on the plaintiff side. After defendants are deemed responsible for injury following a procedure that is faithful to the rule of law, security in tort law addresses mainly the safety or settled equilibrium that these defendants disturbed. Wrongfully inflicted injury is a breach of the peace whose consequences extend into a victim's future. Any national-scale repair of this disruption, then, must consider the period of time ahead that ought to be made secure.

In this reparations context, consider violence that agents of government initiated or condoned, followed by post-traumatic stress disorder and related anxieties. Tort-thinking reminds policymakers that the repair of this injury cannot succeed without acknowledging its future effects. Every wrong amenable to legal redress, not just trauma, protrudes forward in time. Some of the protrusion into the future may be juridical rather than inherent in the wrong itself – that is, kept alive by the preparation of testimony, narration in public venues (such as truth commissions), or the tendency of adjudication to look backward – but victims feel its effects all the same. Inflictors of injury know, or should know, that what they commit will undermine a victim's security even after they stop acting.

---

[40] Among numerous examples: insecurity as a transaction cost impedes bargaining; the right to hold property is integral to participation in civil liability system as well as to one's status as an economic actor; threats to physical security absent tort liability would be guarded against by wasteful precautions.

[41] Notwithstanding the contention in one widely cited work that fairness and welfare are opposites, Louis Kaplow and Steven Shavell, *Fairness Versus Welfare* (Cambridge, MA: Harvard University Press, 2002).

[42] In principle, deterrence can be severed from compensation, as long as a system forces actors to internalize the costs of their activities by some other means such as fines; but welfare analysts prefer to empower compensation-seeking victims as enforcers of this obligation, at least in settings like the United States where these alternative sources of cost internalization are weak.

A quest for monetary compensation in court for noncontractual wrongs necessarily complains about a violation of security; at the same time the resistance that a defendant mounts is a plea to keep the tranquility of the status quo, casting the plaintiff as disruptor. Private-law adjudication sets out in binary fashion to determine who of the two is the troublemaker, the putative wrongdoer or the complainant,[43] and then, if the plaintiff wins, to fashion a remedy to restore equanimity and civil peace.[44] Part of the work of recompense is to give the victim more security in the future. Money damages paradigmatically do this job.

Enhancing Freedom
Perpetrators of wrongdoing found obliged under tort law to pay victims for recompense – in contemporary practice, such perpetrators could be nation-states or business entities, not just individuals – overindulged in their own freedom, hurting other people at least along the way, if not on purpose. Their freedom to commit an act of violence, or to not care about the foreseeable consequences of their inattention, or recklessly to neglect the basic safety of their citizenry, should have ended before the other person was hurt, but did not. They wrongly felt free to cross a boundary. "Our autonomy is limited," writes torts scholar and philosopher Jules Coleman, "only insofar as we are not free to cross the borders that define the protective moral spheres of our neighbors. Boundary crossings are violations, and should harm ensue, compensation is owed."[45] Whether taking a trivial form, such as a minor automobile collision, or a serious one, such as a massacre, every wrongfully inflicted injury calls out for repair of what it inflicted on its victim. Too much prerogative – insufficiently checked and inhibited – has violated the rights of a human being.

Pecuniary recompense for wrongdoing reminds the recipient that freedom exists for her or him too. After legal proceedings have concluded, the recipient will ordinarily enjoy more choice than before. If a monetary transfer succeeds in enhancing security for victims, then that increase in security will foster a sense of power over their environment. Receiving money adds

---

[43] Anita Bernstein, "Reciprocity, Utility, and the Law of Aggression," *Vanderbilt Law Review* 54 (2001): 1.

[44] Even in an idealized version of this restoration, nominal winners often fail to get what they really want. American tort plaintiffs, for instance, often seek medical monitoring following the exposure to toxic substances, but almost never receive it. The focus of law (as contrasted to "equity") on monetary damages forecloses creative remedies. See also Stephen G. Gilles, "The Judgment-Proof Society," *Washington and Lee Law Review* 63 (2006): 603 (noting the difficulty of collecting judgments).

[45] Jules L. Coleman, "Legal Theory and Practice," *Georgetown Law Journal* 83 (1995): 2579, 2615.

a layer of freedom to this minimum where the best revenge, so to speak, is not actual vengeance against perpetrators nor withdrawal from civil society but a superior exercise of one's human prerogatives: doing what one wants in a way that, unlike the actions of the wrongdoer, violate the rights of no one else.

Again, money makes for an effective instrument. Tortfeasors found liable in the legal systems of developed nations provide money that victims can spend as they choose. Measures of compensation that reparations programs might use should also foster choice, and thus freedom, as well.

MICROFINANCE AS A DEVICE FOR REPARATIONS

Reparations planners willing to consider the medium of pecuniary compensation face the question of which means of payment to use. This section of the paper outlines a proposal to convey payment in the form of shares in a microfinance institution. To assess and defend the suggestion, it begins with "microfinance" in contradistinction to the more familiar term "microcredit." It next explores alternative structures for microfinance programs, and considers what microfinance has to offer that simple cash transfer payments do not. The following section – "Microfinance Payments as Sources of Gender Fairness and Welfare" – builds on this case by linking microfinance with the normative ambitions of tort theory and the enhancement of gender equality.

Nomenclature: "Microfinance"

Coinage of the neologisms "microcredit" and "microfinance" added a contemporary gloss to ancient practices: small-time financial transactions are as old as commerce itself. Lack of clarity about what "microcredit" in particular means, however, has sown confusion.[46] Today, decades after it entered into development discourse in the mid-1970s, "microcredit" might refer to many kinds of small-time lending and borrowing: "agricultural credit, or rural credit, or cooperative credit, or consumer credit, credit from the savings and loan associations, or from credit unions, or from money lenders."[47] The younger word "microfinance" was coined by the German development scholar Hans Dieter

---

[46] "The word has been imputed to mean everything to everybody," wrote Muhammad Yunus, the banking pioneer who went on to Nobel acclaim; "we really don't know who is talking about what." Muhammad Yunus, *What is Microcredit?*, January 2003, http://www.grameen-info.org/mcredit.

[47] Ibid.

Seibel in 1990.[48] Year of Microcredit 2005, a nonprofit corporation registered in the United States, suggests that "microcredit" is a subset of "microfinance":

> Microcredit is a small amount of money loaned to a client by a bank or other institution. Microfinance refers to loans, savings, insurance, transfer services, microcredit loans and other financial products targeted at low-income clients.[49]

Respecting the distinction between these two terms, this chapter examines the virtues and limitations of distributing reparations benefits in the form of microfinance: that is, by giving beneficiaries new opportunities for savings and credit rather than loans.[50]

The appeal to microfinance instruments rather than microcredit is consistent with a crucial characteristic of reparations: as complete or perfect transfers, they come with no obligation to be returned. Loans, credits, and exhortations to the poor to cultivate their inner entrepreneur are different from the transfer of wealth. Identified victims of serious human rights violations hold no responsibility for earning and paying for their own reparations.[51]

Choosing among Means to Convey Pecuniary Reparations through Microfinance

Continuing the theme of going beyond credit to include an array of financial activities, the general plan offered here, derived from work by the development economist Hans Dieter Seibel and others, would establish recipients of reparations payments as shareholders in microfinance institutions. The transfer

---

[48] Hans Dieter Seibel, "Does History Matter? The Old and the New World of Microfinance in Europe and Asia," University of Cologne Development Research Center, October 2005, 1 n.1, http://www.uni-koeln.de/ew-fak/aef/10-2005/2005-10%20The%20Old%20and%20the%20New%20World%20in%20Europe%20and%20Asia.pdf.

[49] http://www.yearofmicrocredit.org/pages/whyayear/whyayear_aboutmicrofinance.asp. The definition reserves "low-income clients" for microfinance only, leaving open the possibility that high-income clients might partake of microcredit. In common parlance, however, they do not: high-income borrowers do not need small loans. See also Micro Capital Institute, The Social Impact of Commercial Microfinance, http://microcapital.org/downloads/whitepapers/Social.pdf, 4 (noting that loan size "can be used as a proxy for the social aspects of microfinance").

[50] This section sweeps past an extensive bitter political battle over the two words. The United Nations "year," for instance, is of microcredit rather than microfinance, despite lobbying for "microfinance" by nongovernmental organizations. Connie Bruck, "Millions for Millions," The New Yorker, October 30, 2006. For a victory of "microfinance" over "microcredit," see Stephanie Strom, "What's Wrong with Profit?" The New York Times, November 13, 2006, Giving Section, 1, 12 (noting $100 million donation of Pierre Omidyar to Tufts University as earmarked for "developing microfinance").

[51] References to "microcredit" arise occasionally in this chapter, however, because the development literature often uses this term when it intends the wider menu of microfinance.

payment from government to citizen-victims would take the form of shares. For this purpose, a microfinance institution is an entity that provides financial services – at least credit and savings, possibly others – to customers who would normally be considered too poor for a bank to profit from serving them.[52]

Microfinance institutions can be, in Seibel's helpful tripartite scheme, either "formal," "semiformal," or "informal." The first category of "formal" institutions includes, or resembles, banking in the developed world: an institution (typically a bank or finance company) functions under regulation and supervision by a governmental authority. "Semiformal" institutions are registered but not regulated as financial entities. They include savings and loan cooperatives and nongovernmental organizations (NGOs) that provide credit.[53] "Informal" institutions, including low-level moneylenders and self-help groups, are neither regulated nor registered, although their activities may fall within customary law.[54] Governments going the "informal" route would make reparations payments in the form of shares in existing unregulated, unregistered local institutions.[55]

Accountability, transparency, and protection of the rights and interests of shareholders and those who deal with them commend a preference for formal or semiformal entities as reparations vehicles, unless only informal institutions are available during the nation's transition. Absent a minimal degree of economic development and stability, informal institutions could join the plan with the understanding that their connection to a government program demands a degree of extra oversight. Engagement with national reparations would necessarily push the institution upward toward the semiformal category.

One common starting place for a reparations program, feasible in most countries that have begun to emerge from crisis and falling under the "semiformal" category of microfinance institution, is the credit NGO. A credit NGO typically offers small loans, often along with other interventions (education, counseling, health care), to its low-income clientele.[56] Capitalized by external donor agencies, this entity would have been at work inside the strife-torn country before the government starts to disburse its reparations payments. A reparations program could partner with a credit NGO in a transitional relationship aimed ultimately at forming a freestanding financial institution that

---

[52] Seibel, *Reparations Shareholders*, 1–2.
[53] The Grameen Bank started out as a credit NGO, funded first by "soft loans and grants" before becoming more self-sustaining. Bruck, "Millions."
[54] Seibel, *Reparations Shareholders*, 1 n.2.
[55] See generally Douglas Snow, *Microcredit: An Institutional Development Opportunity*, http://spaef.com/IJED_PUB/v1n1_snow.html ("Sustainable microcredit programs must be embedded in the network of existing local institutions").
[56] Seibel, *Reparations Shareholders*, 8–9.

citizen-recipients would own collectively.⁵⁷ The NGO would deliver financial services to this clientele, along with practical means of help (such as office space for its operations) on terms of cooperative ownership, until the membership of shareholders achieves the capacity to govern itself.⁵⁸ Working with an existing credit NGO offers this reparations plan an established connection between funders and poor people, as well as the flexibility to take on new projects quickly;⁵⁹ these advantages might outweigh the difficulties presented by shared governance.

Reparations planners could alternatively pursue a type of partnership with a different mix of advantages and disadvantages for the program. Governments might bypass (or be unable to engage) a credit NGO and instead link up with informal – unregulated and unregistered – local institutions that function only as microfinancers.⁶⁰ Recipients of reparations would acquire shares in existing entities that might have been formed as associations, cooperatives, or foundations. Their government-disbursed payments would join capital already held by the informal institution. Such an arrangement would on one hand lack the access to capital and established routes to reach the poor that a credit NGO would likely have, but on the other hand could pay undivided attention to microfinance and enjoy freedom to veer from the mandate of a foreign entity.

A third possibility for reparations-through-microfinance is the formation of a new microfinance institution from the ground. When choosing this approach, the government would make reparations payments in the form of shares in new institutions. Experience suggests that planners of this new entity should strongly consider building a revenue base consisting of more than government-directed transfer payments – adding the "savings of other people, no matter how small" would make the institution more likely to succeed in its community.⁶¹ The Arab *sanadiq* (a plural noun) present a model for this approach. *Sanadiq*, financed by "a mixture of member-equity and external equity contributions,"⁶²

---

⁵⁷ In Rwanda, for example, a nation that has tried to use microcredit as a constituent of reparations, an NGO called AVEGA extends microcredit to genocide widows. See Global Youth Connect, *Rwanda Program Report*, May 21–June 19, 2006, http://www.globalyouthconnect.org. An existing relation like this one could form the base of microfinance in contrast to microcredit.

⁵⁸ Seibel, *Reparations Shareholders*, 12 (noting NGOs will resist); Bruck, "Millions" (quoting one founder of a credit NGO: "If you give them a loan and don't see that their other needs are met, perhaps they are worse off. They have a debt to pay, but still they have no sanitation, no health care, no education").

⁵⁹ Seibel, *Reparations Shareholders*, 9.

⁶⁰ Ibid., 12.

⁶¹ Ibid., 16.

⁶² Ibid., 18.

have succeeded in Syria[63] and offer a model for reparations someday in Iraq.[64]

In every form that a national reparations program might pick to convey reparations payments, the microfinance institution deployed would establish recipients who suffered violations of their human rights as owner-decisionmakers, thereby enhancing their agency in the process of rehabilitation. Victims of abuses would receive their reparations payments in the form of shares in an enterprise that offers them savings and the prospect of credit. Pooled capital would become their shared portfolio, amenable to diversification and oriented toward pecuniary returns for its owners.[65] Restrictions on how to trade or otherwise alienate shares in the microfinance institution would necessarily vary from country to country in response to existing corporate law and the reparations goal of maximizing the autonomy, agency, and welfare of shareholder-recipients.

Simple Transfer Payments Contrasted

Although microcredit is an extraordinarily popular tool in the development kit, even its admirers like to call it "no panacea"[66] and counsel caution in its application. The lexical move from "microcredit" to the broader (and, of course, debt-free, at least before the institution starts making loans)

---

[63] Markus Buerli and Aden Aw-Hassan, "Assessing the Impact of Village Credit and Savings Associations on the Rural Poor in Low Rainfall Areas in Syria," *Deutscher Tropentag*, October 5–7, 2004, http://www.tropentag.de/2004/abstracts/links/Buerli_fHJgUS4i.pdf.

[64] Seibel, *Reparations Shareholders*, 18.

[65] The government would need to resolve, preferably by transparent means, the contentious question of how much freedom these shareholders should have to govern their institution. At present, a consensus in the development literature advocates the frank pursuit of profit by microfinance institutions: shelter from the market results in the squandering of opportunity, in this view. A national government supportive of this stance would encourage recipients of reparations payments to become small capitalists. As shareholders of their institutions, they could extend credit at uncapped (even usurious) interest rates, foreclose on loans no matter how poignant the defaulting debtors; in general they would live by a free-to-fail market ideology. This development-literature consensus could shift in the future to favor more regulation and less owner-manager prerogative.

[66] For example, Nan Dawkins Scully, "Micro-Credit No Panacea for Poor Women," http://www.gdrc.org/icm/wind/micro.html (conceding that "microenterprise development has, in some circumstances, contributed positively to women's empowerment"); Lisa Avery, "Microcredit Extension in the Wake of Conflict: Rebuilding the Lives and Livelihoods of Women and Children Affected by War," *Georgetown Journal of Poverty Law and Policy* 12 (2005): 205, 228 ("Microcredit is Not a Panacea"); Yunus, *What Is Microcredit?* (recommending more clarity in the definition of terms); Celia W. Taylor, "Microcredit as Model: A Critique of State/NGO Relations," *Syracuse Journal of International Law and Commerce* 29 (2003): 303, 320–335 (contending that the effects of microcredit on international law warrant more attention).

"microfinance" may ease some worries, but it does not eliminate all controversy in the recommendation. Scarcity, for example, tends to unite those who might otherwise disagree on reparations policy: microeconomic understandings of what choosers gain and lose, the macroeconomic theories that underlie development intervention, and national governments making policy decisions all would call on an advocate of microfinance in reparations to say why this particular expenditure makes sense as a means to effect a reparative goal when this choice would necessarily conflict with other means. The most straightforward alternative to microfinance is a simple cash transfer payment.[67] The cash transfer alternative, however, though attractive in its simplicity, is inferior to microfinance in several ways.[68]

The first advantage of microfinance over cash transfers is a practical one, as well as a reminder of the central role of security in reparations: functioning in the role of shareholders in a microfinance institution gives recipients a safe place to store their monetary property, which includes not only reparations payments but also their savings. Given the near certainty that poverty will accompany a reparations program, planners who seek to make pecuniary distributions need to address the question of whether a recipient can hold on safely to the money she receives. Around the world, poor people – who never own absolutely nothing – suffer from this lack of basic security. They struggle to find substitutes for the insured and well-guarded bank accounts that wealthy people take for granted.[69]

Second, microfinance opens the possibility of expanding credit to the poor who would otherwise be regarded as ineligible to borrow money. The microfinance institution funded by the government scheme would go on to lend out portions of its capital, probably offering small loans to borrowers in its community who would otherwise have little or no access to credit. By this move, a significant share of reparations money makes a transition through microfinance into microcredit, and shares in microcredit's considerable success.

[67] Another, and to many observers a more attractive, alternative to both microfinance and simple cash transfer payments would be "collective payments" or social welfare spending, for the good of the entire public rather than to benefit individuals identified as victims of wrongdoing. A government might establish new health clinics, for example, or implement programs that reduce or eliminate school fees. Such spending would in many cases do more good for the country than pecuniary reparations for individuals. One would hope that governments recognize the public good of expenditures on the needs of citizens. This chapter omits study of this alternative, however, in the belief that social welfare spending is not reparations.
[68] Seibel, *Reparations Shareholders*; Hans Dieter Seibel with Andrea Armstrong, "Reparations and Microfinance Schemes," in *The Handbook*, 676, 678.
[69] "With no safe place to store whatever money they have, the poor bury it, or buy livestock that may die, or invest in jewellery that may be stolen and can be hard to sell." Tom Easton, "The Hidden Wealth of the Poor," *The Economist*, November 3, 2005.

For reparations purposes, the curative effect of expanded credit reaches fundamentally into a victim's well-being. The word "victim," the source of her entitlement to become a shareholder, loses its hold as she moves to bankability, becoming more autonomous, and more likely to enjoy both self-respect and the respect of others, than a person shut out of both borrowing and lending. As they become investors, reconstructors, and rebuilders of the social tissue, these shareholders gain in relative social status, and by their work and risk-taking they earn this gain.[70]

Third, through their investment decisions and eventual extraction of income from the microfinance institution, recipients gain routes to the social services that some deem at least as central to compensation for the human rights violations they experienced[71] (planners think first of medical clinics, but counseling, adult education, and vocational and agricultural training are also among the possibilities). A recipient who gains a cash transfer payment can obtain social services by spending the transfer on them; a recipient who obtains shares in a microfinance institution can obtain social services by turning her shares into cash and by directing investment into for-profit vehicles that make social services likely to emerge and flourish faster than they would from the injection of more money into the local economy – by elevating per capita income, engaging women as adult civic participants, and strengthening networks. Microfinance thus comes closer than cash payments to the social-investment alternative expenditure that some observers would prefer. Indeed, over time microfinance delivers these other two types of recompense, cash and (for those recipients who want them) social services.

The fourth advantage of microfinance moves from individuals to societies: in action, microfinance moves beyond savings and credit as pursued and deployed by citizens to social effects. As a means of reparation, it enlists recipients into a common pursuit of institution-building and the relationships that follow the rise of stable institutions. Any national repair following a total crisis requires both sustainable income-generating activities and sustainable local entities that can extend capital to finance them.[72] Neither of these two conditions

---

[70] Thanks to Ruth Rubio-Marín for underscoring this point.
[71] Reparations in Guatemala, for example, emphasize the need for social supports and direct relatively little funding to what the program calls "economic indemnification." Claudia Paz y Paz Bailey, "Guatemala: Gender and Reparations for Human Rights Violations," in *What Happened to the Women? Gender and Reparations for Human Rights Violations*, ed. Ruth Rubio-Marín (New York: Social Science Research Council, 2006): 92, 110. One alderman in Chicago has issued a call for slavery reparations in the United States that would eschew transfer payments in favor of social supports. Fran Spielman, "Slavery Reparations Leaders Rip Bank's Scholarship Offer," *Chicago Sun-Times*, January 23, 2005, 10.
[72] Seibel, *Reparations Shareholders*, 1.

will endure without the other; both call on citizens to participate in collective undertakings. The establishment of microfinance institutions for reparations supports both conditions. New capital makes sustainable income-generating activities more likely to occur, and extending shareholder ownership to victims of human rights abuses engages these individuals in civic repair. Seibel has gone further, noting that new loci of economic power pull wealth away from a government that has been at best unreliable in the past: microfinance "creates alternative nongovernmental sources of power," and thus "is a potential impediment to future abuses by the central government."[73]

To this four-item virtues list — safe savings for the poor, enhancement of agency, expansion of services, and civic repair through the building of financial institutions — one might add a pecuniary fifth that builds on the second, third, and fourth points: reparations programs that feature microcredit would share in extraordinary worldwide enthusiasm for this measure,[74] and thus might become simply more likely to happen.[75] An international donor disinclined to finance a cash-transfer or social-supports reparations program, on the ground that mending a nation following crisis is a task for government rather than foreign benefactors, may hold a different view of a program patterned in part on long-standing development initiatives.[76]

---

[73] Seibel with Armstrong, *Reparations Schemes*, 679.

[74] Avery, "Microcredit Extension," 207–209 (summarizing acclaim); Press Release, cited above, n. 10 (recognizing microcredit in the awarding of the Nobel Peace Prize).

[75] It would be irresponsible not to acknowledge, in a work on reparations, that some reparations plans fail.

[76] Many who laud this form of development have added hard capital of their own, not just words of praise, to the microfinance endeavor. One admirer, who in the early 1980s asked Muhammad Yunus for advice on how to apply the small-loan methods of the Grameen Bank to alleviate poverty in the low-income US state of which he was governor, declared two decades later a Clinton Global Initiative that placed $30 million in microcredit funds in NGOs around the world. *Commitment Announcement 2005*, http://www.clintonglobalinitiative .org/home.nsf/cmt/c0ACDB3018B91004B8852570B4006723EE. Other American politicians admire microcredit too. American legislation identified microcredit as a measure to address women under conditions of transitional justice with the Women and Children in Conflict Protection Act, introduced in the United States Senate in 2003. S. 1001, 108th Cong. Focused on acute humanitarian needs, this bill also addresses longer-term problems of sustainability and includes provisions for microcredit as a source of enhanced economic security for women as household providers. Ibid., Title III, Sec. 306(b). The story of the $27 loan that Dr. Yunus made out of his own pocket to Bangladeshi basket weavers in 1976 joined the folklore of a multibillion-dollar business in which some of the world's largest financial institutions – including Citibank, Deutsche Bank, and the Dutch giant ABN AMRO – have become players. Mark Sappenfield and Mark Trumbull, "Big Banks Find Little Loans a Nobel Winner, Too," *Christian Science Monitor*, October 16, 2006, World Section, 1. Microcredit also appeals to big businesses beyond big banks: as one industrialist remarked at a microcredit summit, success in microlending would mean new prospective customers for his own company. Remarks of Hugh Grant, Chief Operating Officer, Monsanto Company, *Microcredit E-News*, March 2003, http://www.microcreditsummit.org/enews/2003-03_sp_grant.html.

"Microcredit" as a buzzword still enjoys continuing popularity with numerous and varied sources of development funding. No jargon will stay eternally in fashion. By any name, however, microcredit as macro-prescription will continue to appeal to sources of capital located outside the boundaries of the nation that builds a reparations scheme.[77] This sector of foreign supporters reliably prefers entrepreneurship to mere "handout[s],"[78] or what Seibel has called "one-off payments."[79] Another virtue that might remain central after the figurative Year of Microcredit ends is that whereas this technique flatters neoliberalism and the politicians who promote markets in the West, microcredit also can be practiced in harmony with Islam.[80] Partnerships between national reparations-through-microfinance plans and foreign sources of capital could thus arise in Muslim contexts with relatively little worry about provoking militant disruption – an unusual advantage for a device that gets praised as feminist and for serving as a force for more secularization in the Muslim nation of Bangladesh.[81]

---

[77] For a more cynical expression of this point, see Walden Bello, "Microcredit, Macro Issues," *The Nation*, October 14, 2006, http://www.thenation.com/doc/20061030/bello (arguing that microcredit holds strong appeal within "establishment circles" because "it is a market-based mechanism that has enjoyed some success where other market-based programs have crashed. Structural-adjustment programs promoting trade liberalization, deregulation and privatization have brought greater poverty and inequality to most parts of the developing world over the last quarter century, and have made economic stagnation a permanent condition").

[78] On the contrast between the two as seen by a microcredit leader, see "Can Technology Eliminate Poverty?" *Business Week Online*, December 16, 2005, http://www.businessweek.com (quoting Dr. Yunus: "I get very upset when people say [the poorest] people don't have the entrepreneurial ability, initiative, and skills to use loans, so they need some other kind of intervention like subsidy, handout, or charity"); Evelyn Iritani, "Tiny Loans Seen as Big Way to Invest in Developing Nations' Poor," *Los Angeles Times*, July 28, 2006, C1 (reporting the strong interest that successful high-tech entrepreneurs have in microcredit and its "hand-up, not a handout" approach to poverty).

[79] Seibel, *Reparations Shareholders*, 1 (noting that, in contrast to microfinance, the benefits of such payments "tend to be short-lived and unsustainable").

[80] Zofeen Ebrahim, "Pakistan: Islamic Teachings Inspire Loans to Poorest of Poor," *Inter Press Service*, February 5, 2006 (reporting that one microcredit lender in Pakistan espouses the religious tenet of *Qarze-e-Hasna*, or "helping someone in need with interest-free loans, which are preferred over charity"). The question of interest on the loans would play a part in Muslim opinions of microcredit schemes but poses no insurmountable hurdle: enterprises do transact financial business in the Muslim world while respecting its disapproval of interest. Jerry Useem, "Banking on Allah," *Fortune*, June 10, 2002, 154 (describing solutions to the problem within Islamic doctrine, including *murabaha*, a method of profiting on a transaction that resembles interest but differs from it, and *darura*, the excuse of "overriding necessity"). Going beyond microcredit to microfinance, http://www.islamic-microfinance.com features a range of materials of interest to planners.

[81] Celia W. Dugger, "Peace Prize to Pioneer of Loans for Those Too Poor to Borrow," *The New York Times*, October 14, 2006, 1 ("In the overwhelmingly Muslim nation of Bangladesh, Mr. Yunus's approach also offered hope and ideas to compete with the allure of fundamentalist

MICROFINANCE PAYMENTS AS SOURCES OF GENDER FAIRNESS AND WELFARE

According to the many admirers of microfinance, this innovation, particularly its variant of "microcredit," permits women to flourish. The citation for the Nobel Prize awarded to Muhammad Yunus and the Grameen Bank mentioned women's liberation as one of the effects of microcredit. Conventional wisdom holds that women who receive microloans work hard, repay debts faithfully, encourage fellow borrowers to comply with loan terms, and, perhaps, manifest ideals of community and team-player solidarity from which a male-dominated model of commercial banking could learn.[82] In response, critics have called microcredit a false cure for female poverty and powerlessness.[83] This critical literature prompts a useful reminder of the difference between "microcredit" and "microfinance" for reparations purposes: because it regards reparations payments as conveyed outright, rather than loaned to recipients, the microfinance scheme advocated here does not create the burden of new debt, and so even if critics are correct to worry about the imposition of loan repayment obligations on women who may not be able to control the money they borrow, that concern does not pertain to such a reparations plan.

This reservation noted, microfinance and what one World Bank report calls gender equality – a term defined there to include "equality under the law, equality of opportunity (including equality of rewards for work and equality in access to human capital and other productive resources that enable opportunity), and equality of voice (the ability to influence and contribute to the development process)"[84] – have common elements. Both have to do, at least

---

Islamic causes. 'It's a very secular movement,' Professor [Amartya] Sen said, 'very egalitarian, market friendly and socially radical'").

[82] Avery, "Microcredit Extension;" Fundacíon Adelante, *What We Do: Our Loan Program*, http://www.adelantefoundation.org/sub/our_loan_program.php (attributing a better than 95% repayment rate to "character-based lending" to poor female borrowers in Honduras, in contrast to traditional "collateral-based lending").

[83] Anne Marie Goetz and Rina San Gupta, "Who Takes the Credit? Gender, Power, and Control Over Loan Use in Rural Credit Programs in Bangladesh," *World Development* 24 (1996): 45 (noting that male relatives control much of the loaned capital that women are obliged to repay); Gina Neff, "Microcredit, Microresults," *Left Business Observer*, October 1996, http://www.leftbusinessobserver.com/Micro.html (criticizing Yunus and the Grameen Bank for failing to lift most borrowers out of poverty; using entrepreneurship rhetoric to divert women from wage labor that would pay better; and restricting women borrowers to low-yield work that men do not want to do).

[84] World Bank, *Engendering Development Through Gender Equality in Rights, Resources, and Voice*, http://www-wds.worldbank.org/external/default/main?pagePK=64193027&piPK=64187937&theSitePK=523679&menuPK=64187510&searchMenuPK=64187283&siteName=WDS&entityID=000094946_01020805393496 2–3.

in part, with the distribution of material goods.[85] Both are secular phenomena. Both are at least consistent with, if not committed to, the seizure of new opportunity by historically oppressed persons. As practiced around the world, microfinance puts money in the hands of women, an outcome that advocates of gender equality pursue.

To add tort theory to the mix of gender and microfinance, consider the quest for security and freedom that underlies tort actions as prosecuted in the courts. Tort principles emerge with reference to the purposes and functions of civil liability as policy. Its doctrine compels wrongdoers to pay damages to their victims not only to enhance the freedom and security of individuals in the correct balance but also, at a societal and conceptual plane, to achieve fairness and welfare. Fairness (associated with corrective justice) looks backward, to redress injury attributed to wrongdoing; in this perspective, leaving the injury unrectified is wrong. Some observers of tort law regard fairness as central; others deem it peripheral and subordinate to its rival, welfare, which looks forward to increase the wealth of persons in the aggregate. Reparations through microfinance comports with both fairness and welfare.

Reparations through Microfinance as a Source of Fairness for Women

Ameliorating the Additional Injustice of Having Been Deprived of a Fair Measure of Control Over Money

The endeavor of planning reparations for recent human rights violations coexists with a less vivid, but older and more deeply rooted, wrong: throughout human history, and continuing to this moment, women have not enjoyed equality with men with respect to the possession of and control over wealth. Laws and norms have taken money out of their hands as if women were moral children and money something too dangerous for them to hold. A generation ago, the United Nations made a famed announcement on point: women do two-thirds of the world's work (as measured in hours), earn one-tenth of the world's income, and own less than one-hundredth of the world's property.[86]

Although the UN has not updated this notorious global statistic, local studies continue to find that big disparities remain. For example, the UN Millennium Task Force reported in 2005 that women produce 80% of the food in Africa and the Caribbean,[87] and that women in Zambia devote an extraordinary

---

[85] Some strands of "feminism" do not share this inclination: "gender equality," by contrast, cannot escape the material world.

[86] Catharine A. MacKinnon, *Are Women Human?* (Cambridge, MA: Belknap Press of Harvard University Press, 2006), 21 (quoting United Nations, *The State of the World's Women* 1979).

[87] UN Millennium Project, *Taking Action*, 77.

800 hours a year to gathering food and firewood.[88] Yet ownership of land – a time-honored means for individuals to accrete economic strength – is less available to women than men, particularly in developing countries. The World Bank reports that many national laws still place women under the guardianship of husbands and recognize "no independent right to manage property."[89] Several African countries deny married women the right to own land,[90] and take land ownership away from women who become widowed or divorced.[91] Studies of cultivated-land ownership in Asia and Latin America as well as Africa show that women possess smaller parcels, inferior land, and less farming equipment than men.[92]

These conditions – more toil, less income, and much less property for women – persist and appear more benevolent than they are with the help of ideology. Patriarchy posits a male provider who heads his household and meets the needs of the women and children inside. It further asserts that the women inside are better off than they would be under conditions of gender parity.[93] The male-headed household protects women from their various infirmities regarding money and property. Women, it is said, are too naive to manage money, too swayed by emotion to retain it, too busy with child-making and -minding to have time for it, too petty-minded to leverage it, or too pure to want it. Unequal educational opportunity for girls and young women, a dire pattern in much of the world, is both a symptom and a cause of these beliefs.

Payments in the form of shares in a microfinance institution can serve to repair this unfairness more effectively than other forms of pecuniary reparations. No matter the level of formality of the microfinance,[94] these shares can

---

[88] Ibid., 7.
[89] World Bank, *Engendering Development*, 37.
[90] Ibid.
[91] Ibid., 51.
[92] Ibid., 51–52; see also ibid., 120–21 (reporting that much land reform of the 1990s in Latin American and Africa has failed to alleviate these conditions).
[93] One expression of this ideology argues that it benefits women. "The women of every society save our own have understood that the male's nature is such that he must be given a special position in the family if he is to peacefully take his place in it.... Women have realized that men will not even attempt to suppress [their socially disruptive] tendencies if they are offered no distinctive and respected position in the family, a position that can act as counterpoise to both the limits marriage sets on male behavior and the centrality that the woman's unique physiological and psychological bond to the infant automatically gives her. In response to the refusal to grant them their traditional role men will tend to either a) disrupt the family as they attain through aggression that which they were once granted, or b) channel their energies into sexual conquest outside the family. Women will find that they are raising their children either on a battlefield or alone, wondering why loudmouthed Rambos have replaced strong, silent defenders of justice and protectors of women." Steven Goldberg, "Can Women Beat Men at Their Own Game?" *National Review*, December 27, 1993, 30.
[94] Seibel, *Reparations Shareholders*, 4 (sketching three levels of formality).

work to rectify historical gender-injustice. Formal institutions offer women recipients access to technologies and services that had been closed off to most of them in the past. The category of semiformal institutions available for reparations through microfinance is dominated by nongovernmental organizations, which can offer women recipients a range of supports as well as a place to hold their reparations shares. Informal institutions can advance women's interests by honoring compatible local traditions and promoting ideals of self-help.[95]

The simultaneous creation of a savings account and a modicum of power over the economic lives of other people bestows property on women whose value exceeds that of the sum transferred. Shares in microfinance institutions give all women recipients at least de facto savings accounts (which might previously have been out of their reach) and for some fraction of recipients will create real opportunities to govern the institution. Because virtually every microfinance institution makes loans, these women shareholders have a voice in capital investment decisions affecting their communities. A reparations payment with the name of a woman on it links these small savings accounts and shares in a business with the rectification of injustice. If microfinance can generate even a portion of the wealth that its admirers believe it can create, then a reparations scheme that transfers shares of a microfinance institution to women as recipients and owners will contribute to improving the statistic that half the world's population owns less than a hundredth of its property.

Shares in a microfinance institution for women thus take a stand against both the injustice of human rights violations and the unjust effects of patriarchy within a national economy. Patriarchy had instructed women to abjure any desire for overt power in the hope of gaining security in return. Microfinance teaches just the opposite, that the security one receives from holding money takes form not in a barrier from public life but in decisions, choices, and investment. Shareholders effect their own wishes and respond to the material consequences of what they express. Even if they participate in microfinance unable to forget even for a moment the human rights violations for which they received monetary compensation, or, at the other extreme, feel determined never to think about their past and only look forward as investors, they can reclaim what was theirs all along: recognition and agency.

In standing up against both acute crisis and quotidian patriarchy, this measure of reparation emphasizes what the two wrongs have in common. The stated transformation of wrongdoing and suffering into shares for holders who may have had no prior experience with financial instruments reminds participants and observers of the connection between, on one hand, the episode of

---

[95] Ibid., 14–15 (describing informal microfinance institutions).

oppression that gave rise to a reparations scheme, and, on the other, the duller background condition of women disabled from full rights to own property. To name these two wrongs in the same sentence is not to equate them. The first is not only more vivid but worse. Linking a historical antecedent with a facet of everyday life does not deny any portion of the horror inherent in a particular national crisis, however. On the contrary, catastrophes become both more intense and more poignant when one becomes aware of an infrastructure that amplifies their harm. To put the point more optimistically, a reparative project that enables women to hold and spend their own money installs an architecture that can help achieve other repairs, should a subsequent crisis ensue. An architecture that puts money in all its facets – saving, spending, diverting, withholding, encouraging, investing – in the hands of women also makes civil society stronger.

Fairness through Shareholding rather than the Receipt of Quick Cash
As we have seen, one reason for policymakers to choose shares in microfinance institutions as the means of effecting pecuniary reparations is to augment "security," in the sense of allowing a recipient to safely keep her payment rather than have to hide it in her home or convert it into none-too-safe chattels that could be destroyed or taken from her.[96] Reparations-through-microfinance offers security in other senses, including the prospect of leveraging one's payment into additional income that can buy more shelter from various dangers – cleaner food and water, safer housing, respite from exhausting or dangerous labor – and the fostering of sustainable income-generating activities. There remains for brief treatment here one more crucial "security" theme, present in any plan for pecuniary reparations: the danger that (male) relatives or intimate partners could seize money nominally distributed to (female) recipients.

Layers of complication challenge the delivery of security- and freedom-enhancing increments to women through any pecuniary reparations program, not just the microfinance variant advocated here. Some women recipients might, in particular, wish to share or relinquish what they receive – and believe they enjoy more freedom or more security as a consequence. At least some, if not most, women who receive reparations money would without hesitation try to share it with their children, certainly spending part of it on education, health care, and food for their young overriding such choices by women, or making them difficult to effect, could undermine the ambitions of compensation. The large feminist literature on choice and agency cautions against accusing women of "false consciousness" for manifesting decisions that

[96] See earlier, "Simple Transfer Payments Contrasted."

appear self-negating,[97] but it offers little guidance on how to make reparations money stay with the women who receive it. Here, thinking about security and freedom becomes helpful after the fact, as a way to understand what might otherwise look like squandering. The point of the endeavor had been to enhance the security and freedom of recipients. Recipients' diverting their money to men and children might have been consistent with this goal.

That said, however, it would be a facile error to condone any and every distribution of reparations payments as always enhancing the security and freedom of their female recipients. Reparations programs owe to recipients not only the rendering of a designated payment but the safeguards that protect it from intentional or unintentional disappearance. Like commercial creditors, investors, and mortgagees, women recipients of reparations are entitled to enjoy whatever the rule of law can provide to safeguard their property. Accordingly, the design of a program must anticipate foreseeable obstacles to delivery and receipt of the transfer of wealth.

When recipients are women, one key obstacle worthy of attention is the belief that women ought not have the power to spend money on their own, or for themselves. One can envision women who simply do not feel entitled to make spending decisions that enrich themselves directly until they know that their families' needs have been satisfied first. A reparations planner probably cannot thwart such an inclination, but each payment should at least have a chance to get to each individual woman first, rather than to her men or dependent children; and shares in an institution achieve this result better than any other rendering of money. These shares have women's names on them. They implicitly contain protection against theft and loss. They state plainly that recipients include individual women (or men), and shares are not paid only to households, families, or communities.

These specifics might provoke an objection, familiar from the gender controversies surrounding microcredit in the Grameen mode, that recognizing women as individuals with competence in worldly realms and who hold personal identities separate from household and tribe offends the cultural norms of a particular country, and thus that such a reparations scheme would be unsustainable in that venue. And, indeed, perhaps there are places where cultural predilection and commercial backwardness intersect to destroy basic safeguards that would otherwise protect property transferred to women. As the experience of microcredit around the world demonstrates, however, women even in backward economic settings have held this property successfully. The

---

[97] For example, Kathryn Abrams, "Sex Wars Redux: Agency and Coercion in Feminist Legal Theory," *Columbia Law Review* 95 (1995): 304, 324–350; Nadine Strossen, "A Feminist Critique of 'The' Feminist Critique of Pornography," *Virginia Law Review* 79 (1993): 1099, 1139–1140.

limited successes of microcredit would be enhanced by shareholding in contrast to the receipt of quick cash, which nonrecipients could grab and squander. Shares in a financial institution, in sum, can offer the best prospects for fairness in the delivery of pecuniary reparations.

Reparations through Microfinance as a Source of Gender-Egalitarian Welfare

In contrast to the fairness perspective, welfare analysis looks forward, striving to increase wealth for persons in the aggregate. It seeks incentives. In the context of personal injury law, the welfare perspective encourages legal systems to force injury-inflictors to pay for the injuries they cause, when the internalization of these costs of harm-causing activities would enhance social wealth.[98] Recognizing that human activity produces prosperity along with losses, welfare analysis seeks to foster optimal rather than unbounded investments in safety; and so it requires those who inflict injury to pay for not having taken only cost-justified measures, rather than every possible measure, to avoid causing injury.[99]

Welfare analysis of injury law may appear to deviate slightly from the scope of this chapter because, first, it is normally used to study accidental harm, not the intentional or reckless injuries that reparations programs address; and, second, in principle, welfare analysis does not pursue the compensation of victims, but rather the imposition of monetary sanctions. As long as the injurer pays – and as long as potential injurers as a group have to take into account their obligations to pay should they injure someone – it matters not to welfare analysis whether any injured person collects anything. These deviations do not limit the value of the exercise, however. Nothing in welfare analysis precludes applying it to intentionally or recklessly inflicted harms,[100] and efficiency-minded scholars have recognized that because fines and other public sanctions are typically underused and too cheap, empowering the victim as recipient can help ensure that wrongdoers pay at the optimal level.[101]

---

[98] Steven Shavell, *Economic Analysis of Accident Law* (Cambridge, MA: Harvard University Press, 1987).

[99] In other words, if a precaution would have cost more money than it would have saved, the inflictor should not have to pay for the resultant loss. This possibility lies outside the scope of this chapter.

[100] Indeed one prominent practitioner, Richard Posner, applied this analysis to rape. Richard A. Posner, *Sex and Reason* (Cambridge, MA: Harvard University Press, 1992), 384–385.

[101] Writings on this point from the law and economics camp include Jennifer H. Arlen, "Compensation Systems and Efficient Deterrence," *Maryland Law Review* 52 (1993): 1093, 1114 (emphasizing that civil actions may be more likely than criminal actions to be prosecuted);

Though other variables will complicate their assessment of a reparations program, in general the awarding of monetary reparations to individual victims in the form of microfinance will make sense to welfare analysts. Even though reparations planners may feel confident that the nation has turned a corner and thus that traumas to citizens will not recur, a project of reparation does not supersede the quest of deterrence through incentives. Although many individual wrongdoers will now be out of power, awarding money to victims from the government deemed responsible teaches prospective wrongdoers about this particular aspect of the new rule of law. Furthermore, among the different ways to distribute pecuniary reparations, microfinance in the post-crisis context is particularly attractive to welfare analysts because of the connection between microfinance and sustainable economic development.[102]

With the welfare effects of a reparations-through-microfinance scheme noted, government planners can pay heed to the distributive effects of this reparations policy. This is where gender enters the picture. Welfare analysis aggregates people into groups, and so one may generalize about "men" and "women," individual exceptions notwithstanding. In this framework, placing value on the interests and experiences of women citizen-recipients is a good idea if it would make societies better off, a bad one if it would make societies worse off. Because this extra attention to women would have the effect of transferring money into women's hands, the question becomes whether societies are better off or worse off when, other things being equal, women gain control over more money.[103]

Ronen Perry and Yehuda Adar, "Wrongful Abortion: A Wrong in Search of a Remedy," *Yale Journal of Health Policy and Ethics* 5 (2005): 507, 585 (arguing that "wrongful abortion" warrants more deterrence than either tort or criminal liability can deliver, and proposing that courts make available "an extra-compensatory civil fine" to be divided between plaintiffs and the state). See generally Richard Craswell, "Instrumental Theories of Compensation: A Survey," *San Diego Law Review* 40 (2003): 1135 (arguing that whether requiring the payment of compensation accords with the goal of efficiency is a complex question whose answer depends on variables). Another prominent economic analyst argues that mandating compensation to victims is *more* necessary in the case of intentional torts as compared with "ordinary" or accidental torts, so as to eliminate inefficient expenditures in self-protection that victims make. William M. Landes, "Optimal Sanctions for Antitrust Violations," *University of Chicago Law Review* 50 (1983): 652, 673.

[102] See generally Seibel, *Reparations Shareholders*, 7.

[103] Other welfare effects relating to reparations for women, though beyond the scope of this chapter, warrant brief note here. Researchers have estimated that violence against women cost the national economy of Nicaragua 1.6% of its GDP ($29.5 million) in 1999, and 2% of the GDP of Chile ($1.56 billion) in 1996. Andrew R. Morrison and Maria Beatriz Orlando, "Social and Economic Costs of Domestic Violence: Chile and Nicaragua," in *Too Close to Home: Domestic Violence in Latin America*, ed. Andrew R. Morrison and Maria Loreto Biehl (Washington, DC: Inter-American Development Bank, 1999), 51. To the extent that reparations payments promote stability through civic engagement (see Rubio-Marín's "Gender of Reparations," Chapter 2

Evidence indicates that societies will indeed be better off if they transfer money to women (and if they use microfinance rather than simple cash payments to effect this transfer) because male and female adults – the majority of whom in every country have children – provide for their children unequally. Money in the hands of a woman is more likely to buy "goods that benefit children and enhance their capacities." Around the world, men devote more money to pleasures for themselves – cigarettes, alcoholic beverages, leisure activities such as sports, sexual conquests – than do women. By contrast, "studies conducted on five continents have found that children are distinctly better off" when their mothers have more money to spend.[104]

In Kenya, for example, the more income controlled by women in sugar-cane farmer households, the greater the household caloric intake. In Jamaica, female-headed households spend more on food and less on alcohol. Data from the Ivory Coast suggest that doubling the proportion of income controlled by women would cause a 26% reduction in amounts spent on alcohol and a 14% reduction in money spent on cigarettes. "In Brazil, $1 in the hands of a Brazilian woman has the same effect on child survival as $18 in the hands of a man," Crittenden reports.[105] In richer countries, where calorie counts are a less reliable proxy for well-being, one finds other indicators – for example, affluent divorced fathers in the United States are less likely than their (somewhat less) affluent ex-wives to cooperate with paying for their children's college education.[106] Around the world, female legislators introduce and promote more child-friendly government expenditures,[107] suggesting a secondary

---

of this volume), and thereby diminish violence against women, national economies can look forward to becoming more prosperous. Another example is the correlation between GNP and the enrollment of girls at school. UN Millennium Project Task Force on Education and Gender Equality, *Taking Action: Achieving Gender Equality and Empowering Women* (London: UN Millennium Project, 2005), 47.

[104] Ann Crittenden, *The Price of Motherhood: Why the Most Important Job in the World Is Still the Least Valued* (New York: Metropolitan Books, 2001), 120.

[105] Ibid., 120–122.

[106] Ibid., 122.

[107] Matthew M. Davis and Amy P. Upston, "State Legislator Gender and Other Characteristics Associated With Sponsorship of Child Health Bills," *Ambulatory Pediatrics* 4 (2004): 295 (reporting study of American state legislatures); Crittenden, *Price of Motherhood*, 126 (noting the same pattern in Scandinavia). The voting rights activist Carrie Chapman Catt, working for suffrage in the United States, looked at several other countries where women had the vote in 1915 – including Australia, New Zealand, Norway, and Finland – to conclude that "wherever women, the traditional housekeepers of the world, have been given a voice in the government, public housekeeping has been materially improved by an increased attention to questions of pure food, pure water supply, sanitation, housing, public health and morals, child welfare and education." Carrie Chapman Catt, *Do You Know?* (1915), http://douglassarchives.org/catt_a07.htm.

welfare effect: the more women can avail themselves of education and other sources of access to civic life, the better off children will be.[108]

Experts on economic intervention, having for more than a decade recognized that development-related expenditures that benefit women yield payoffs to societies, share this assessment.[109] "This claim has now achieved 'motherhood' status, in virtue of the accumulating evidence confirming what has long been available at an intuitive level, which is that 'investing in women,' especially in the areas of health and education, is likely to generate payoffs or 'positive externalities' for the well-being of children, the household, and the economy as a whole."[110] One microcredit leader accordingly decided early in his banking career to take gender into account in his lending decisions, believing that the children of low-income parents would profit more from loans to their mothers.[111]

Differences between microcredit and microfinance are pertinent to this welfare perspective. Microcredit has won both praise for making poor women wealthier and blame for forcing them to toil in repayment efforts. A harried woman struggling to repay her loan might feel compelled to draft her children into her struggling business; under this pressure, a daughter would probably look more valuable to her mother as a housekeeper and child-minder than a student continuing her education. The form of microfinance proposed here – that is, shares in a financial institution that carry no repayment obligation – does not generate new pressure to turn children into laborers, however. True, it does not eliminate the deleterious effects on society of financial hardship,

---

[108] Some criticisms of the Crittenden thesis may be noted briefly. Crittenden writes that men in governments, especially American governments, dislike making transfer payments to mothers because they believe – correctly, it turns out – that money helps women abandon their unsatisfactory relationships with men. It may thus be prudent to anticipate on our welfare ledger an increase in divorce and the severance of informal unions (although it appears equally likely that the receipt of reparations payments would enhance peace and stability in a household). Children are probably still better off. See Crittenden, *Price of Motherhood*, 126 (arguing that poor children are best off when no man has familial input on how money is spent). Another possible criticism: nations could use excise taxes to pursue the same welfare gains that redistribution in favor of women would achieve. Thus, "sin" taxation of liquor, cigarettes, motorcycles, brothels, and so on could in theory generate enough revenue for governments to enhance child welfare through public programs. Such an agenda would burden a transitional democracy trying to repair its recent failure to uphold the human rights of its citizens, however. It would be better, probably, to pursue welfare by putting money into the hands of mothers.

[109] See generally World Bank, *Engendering Development*, ch. 5, and sources cited therein.

[110] Kerry Rittich, "Engendering Development/Marketing Equality," *Albany Law Review* 67 (2003): 575, 580.

[111] Bruck, "Millions" (referring to the policies of Mohammad Yunus and the Grameen Bank).

but neither does any other mode of reparation; and even though becoming a shareholder in a financial institution can disrupt a woman's life, the disruptions of microfinance payments that beget no new debt are much gentler than the disruption of money-lending among the poor.

The scenario of an engaged, decision-making, money-spending, policy-directing female citizenry, then, becomes attainable – even likely to develop – and conducive to the good of all persons in the nation implementing reparations. Wealth in the hands of women enhances welfare not only for children, as recipients of expenditures, but also for mothers, as determiners of these expenditures. Developmental economics regards microfinance as an especially effective means to maximize the value of an initial investment. Thus for purposes of enhancing welfare, the combination of female recipients and microfinance presents an exceptionally high-potential yield for a reparations plan.

CONCLUSION

Standing alone, pecuniary reparations leave the effects of serious human rights violations unrepaired. They do not take recipients back to an idyllic past where they were safe from large-scale horrific wrongdoing. They cannot be rendered in proportion to the harm suffered. Of themselves they provide no truth-telling, nor guarantees of nonrecurrence, nor the kind of government and civil society that fend off wrong before it arises.

These infirmities of pecuniary reparations do not obscure a quality necessary to effect recognition of wrongs and an ambition to change current conditions: governments and individuals who engage in reparation cannot deny the microeconomic tenet of scarcity. The phrase "cheap talk" adverts to the infinite supply of words available to the disingenuous or distracted, who can denounce past wrongdoing endlessly without having to surrender anything they value enough to hold.[112] A recipient of pecuniary reparations, by contrast, knows that the payor has parted with something scarce in order to affirm the truth of what happened to her. This monetary acknowledgment does not of itself correct the wrong but it honors her experience, augments her agency, holds potential to increase her security and her freedom, and invites her concretely, as a holder of power, into the emergent civil society.

Once identified as integral to the nation's larger reparative endeavor, pecuniary reparations ought to take the form that best advances the agency, recognition, security, and freedom of injured citizens. This ideal form will seldom

---

[112] de Greiff, "Justice and Reparations," 461.

be simple cash transfer payments, which are too easy for a recipient to forfeit, alienate, and lose. The alternative presented here – establishing each recipient as shareholder of a financial institution – conveys money to her in commemoration of the nation's past, where she suffered a wrong, and its future, which her choices and prerogatives will shape.

7

Gender, Memorialization, and Symbolic Reparations

Brandon Hamber and Ingrid Palmary[1]

The reified essence of evil in the very being of their bodies, these figures of the Jew, the black, the Indian, and the woman herself, are clearly objects of cultural construction, the leaden keel of evil and of mystery stabilising the ship and course that is Western history.[2]

Reparations are the things done or given as an attempt to deal with the consequences of political violence. In line with the approach taken in this volume,[3] and drawing on previous work,[4] we understand reparations in the narrow sense, that is, to refer to "the attempts to provide benefits directly to the victims of certain types of crimes."[5] This narrow definition of reparations does not include broader strategies such as institutional reform or truth-telling,[6] but it fits neatly with the understanding of reparations as acts or objects, as things done or given. This chapter is concerned mainly with what are termed symbolic reparations insofar as they are granted under the auspices of a massive reparations program. Symbolic reparations may include, for instance, official apologies, the change of names of public spaces, the establishment of days of commemoration, and the creation of museums and parks dedicated to the memory of victims, among others.[7] Naomi Roht-Arriaza refers to these as

---

[1] Our thanks to Ruth Rubio-Marín, Claire Hackett, and Roberta Bacic for comments on earlier drafts of this chapter.
[2] Michael Taussig, "Culture of Terror – Space of Death. Roger Casement's Putumayo Report and the Explanation of Torture," *Comparative Studies in Society and History* 26 (1984).
[3] Ruth Rubio-Marín, "The Gender of Reparations in Transitional Societies," Chapter 2 of this volume.
[4] Brandon Hamber, "Narrowing the Micro and Macro: A Psychological Perspective on Reparations in Societies in Transition," in *The Handbook of Reparations*, ed. Pablo de Greiff (Oxford: Oxford University Press, 2006).
[5] Pablo de Greiff, "Justice and Reparations," in *The Handbook of Reparations*, 453.
[6] Ibid.; Rubio-Marín, "Gender of Reparations."
[7] Ibid.

moral reparations and would include, in addition to the above, assistance in reburials and appropriate rituals, finding missing bodies, and converting of repressive sites into museums.[8]

Symbolic reparations are, of course, only one component of a comprehensive reparations program. When thinking about mass atrocity and conflict and dealing with the consequences, one has to acknowledge that different societies and different interest groups will want, or have, different resources to implement symbolic reparations. This inevitably involves a discussion about prioritizing symbolic reparations relative to other types of reparations. Although this chapter focuses on symbolic reparations, it does not argue that these should be privileged over other types, but rather that they should be viewed as *one* of the components of a holistic reparations program. Some forms of symbolic reparations are not particularly resource intensive, such as apologies or creating a day of remembrance (with limited public sponsored activity), which makes them fairly easy to implement but becomes problematic when it means they are prioritized simply on this basis or to offset investing in compensation or a more broad-based reparations program. In spite of this, and as discussed below in the section "Overview of Symbolic Reparations," certain truth commissions, such as those in Chile and Ghana, have noted the centrality of symbolic reparations to the overall ethos and process of making amends. In short, a balance is needed, and later sections of this chapter discuss the issue of how material and symbolic processes of addressing the legacy of violence might work in tandem or in an integrated way.

In addition, from an individual perspective it is important to remember that reparations for human rights violations are always trying to repair the irreparable.[9] From the perspective of direct victims of political violence, and even from a collective perspective, acknowledgment, apology, recognition, and even substantial material assistance do not "bring back the dead," nor are they guaranteed to converge with, or ameliorate, all the levels of pain suffered. No matter what the motive, all reparations strategies face this intractable problem. All reparations, whether financial or in the form of an object, are nominal in nature.[10] It is impossible to completely close the gap between an individual's personal needs and what society can offer at a social and political level.

Degrees of dealing with the consequences of extreme political violence and trauma are, nevertheless, achievable. It is possible to reach a situation where a

---

[8] Naomi Roht-Arriaza, "Reparations Decisions and Dilemmas," *Hastings International and Comparative Law Review* 27, no. 2 (2004).
[9] Brandon Hamber, "Repairing the Irreparable: Dealing with the Double-Binds of Making Reparations for Crimes of the Past," *Ethnicity and Health* 5, no. 3–4 (2000).
[10] Hamber, "Narrowing the Micro and Macro."

substantial degree of personal resolution takes place, that is, where the trauma is no longer seen as unfinished business requiring, for instance, a compulsion to take revenge. Grief and loss no longer plague the individual consciously or unconsciously, and the loss is to a large extent accepted and incorporated into the functioning of everyday life.[11]

Yet it is often interventions at the level of society that may, in fact, have a greater impact on a person's resolution of trauma than those at the individual level.[12] It has been argued that the trauma of war or of living in a repressive state must be read and responded to within its cultural, social, and political meanings over time rather than locating or addressing it exclusively within affected individuals.[13] This indicates both the extent to which the division between individual trauma and social trauma is an artificial one[14] and the importance of considering how different groups of victims may engage with symbolic reparations, which generally take place at the level of the social.

Having said this, and given that what has been lost can never be fully replaced, we affirm that the type of reparation that symbolic reparations can contribute to individual victims can at best be psychologically "good enough,"[15] that is, the victim feels subjectively satisfied that sufficient actions have been taken to make amends for her suffering, and a psychological state is achieved in which some sort of resolution concerning past trauma is reached. Admittedly, this is a less than conclusive way of thinking about the issue, especially for policymakers. However, this more modest approach to thinking about the impact of symbolic reparations is important. It guards against the possibility of symbolic reparations, or any other type of reparations for that matter, being used as a way to try and dampen victims' other concerns such as alternative forms of justice, socioeconomic development, and equality.

---

[11] Brandon Hamber and Richard Wilson, "Symbolic Closure through Memory, Reparation and Revenge in Post-Conflict Societies," in *The Role of Memory in Ethnic Conflict*, ed. Ed Cairns and Michael Roe (New York: Palgrave/Macmillan, 2003).

[12] Patrick J. Bracken and Celia Petty, eds., *Rethinking the Trauma of War* (London: Free Association Books, 1998).

[13] M. Brinton Lykes and Marcie Mersky, "Reparations and Mental Health: Psychosocial Interventions Towards Healing, Human Agency, and Rethreading Social Realities," in *The Handbook of Reparations*.

[14] Bracken and Petty, *Rethinking the Trauma of War*.

[15] The concept of "good enough" is loosely borrowed from psychoanalyst D.W. Winnicott. He uses the concept in relation to parenting, arguing that parents need not be perfect but simply "good enough" and that the mother needs to treat the child with a "primary maternal preoccupation" [sic] and create a "holding environment." We think the broad notion of this concept is a fitting way to think of reparations, which can never be perfect from an individual perspective, but can be "good enough." The environment in which they are delivered is also essential.

With these provisos in mind, this chapter focuses on the gendered dimensions of symbolic reparations. It is concerned partly with how female victims of political violence might engage with or benefit from symbolic reparations. This entails, according to Ruth Rubio-Marín, understanding the different ways women experience conflict and authoritarianism, the different needs and priorities that diverse groups of women have, the different obstacles they may face in dealing with a legacy of mass political violence and repression, and how the broader normative aims underlying reparations in transitional settings are defined.[16] The chapter considers also symbolic reparations from a wider perspective, that is, how they can be used to challenge dominant femininities and masculinities that are produced in times of armed conflict and in its aftermath.

The chapter begins by briefly outlining how some truth commissions have approached the issue of symbolic reparations and the kinds of reparations that have been recommended. Thereafter, we highlight some of the challenges facing the notion of granting symbolic reparations from a gendered perspective, drawing on the field of commemoration and memorialization more broadly. These broader examples are used to make general observations about how women and men are remembered, and how their experience and activity in conflict are symbolically recognized afterwards. Examples of specific symbolic measures flowing from reparations programs are discussed, although the implementation of these has been limited in most contexts. The chapter then suggests how symbolic reparations could both be more gender sensitive as well as make a more substantial contribution to promoting gender justice by incorporating sufficiently complex and rich notions of masculinity and femininity.

OVERVIEW OF SYMBOLIC REPARATIONS

As noted above, the remit of what constitutes symbolic reparations can be fairly wide. Most truth commissions have in their recommendations for reparations made specific mention of symbolic reparations, and some have seen symbolic measures as critical to the entire ethos of the process. For example, the Chilean truth commission report notes that "more than ever our country needs gestures and symbols of reparation so as to cultivate new values that may draw us together and unveil to us common perspectives on democracy and development."[17] In a similar vein, the Ghanaian commission notes that

---

[16] Ruth Rubio-Marín, "Gender of Reparations."
[17] The National Commission for Truth and Reconciliation, established in 1990 by then-president Patricio Aylwin, reported in February 1991. Its mandate was to investigate death or disappearance between September 11, 1973 and March 11, 1990.

because no reparations, monetary or otherwise, can restore victims (direct or indirect) to the *status quo ante*, symbolic reparations are probably the most significant of all forms of reparations.[18] It is often, nonetheless, the financial components of reparations programs that receive the most public, and certainly policy, scrutiny. In addition, the limited implementation of symbolic reparations in most contexts testifies to the complexity of actually using symbolic reparations for the ends that they are intended.

The types of symbolic reparations that have been recommended between 1990 and 2006 in truth commission reports, and by wider commissions that have looked at human rights violations, typically include:

- Commemorative monuments to all victims of human rights abuses, or a national memorial or process of memorialization (Chile, El Salvador,[19] Ghana, Peru,[20] Sierra Leone,[21] Timor-Leste,[22] Guatemala[23])
- Erecting plaques and tombstones, building new cemeteries, renaming streets and public buildings, developing education facilities (Chile, Peru, South Africa, Guatemala)
- Apologies (Ghana, Peru, Sierra Leone, Japan, Chile)
- Building public parks in memory of those who lost their lives (Chile, Guatemala)

---

[18] National Reconciliation Commission, *The National Reconciliation Commission Report* (2004), vol. 3, ch. 2, 2.3.1.6, published online by the Government of the Republic of Ghana, http://www.ghana.gov.gh/NRC/index.php (accessed January 10, 2007).

[19] See Commission on the Truth for El Salvador, *From Madness to Hope: The 12-Year War in El Salvador: Report of the Commission on the Truth for El Salvador* (1993), published online by the United States Institute for Peace, http://www.usip.org/library/tc/doc/reports/el_salvador/tc_es_03151993_toc.html (accessed January 10, 2007), especially ch. V. Recommendations.

[20] Comisión de la Verdad y Reconciliación (CVR), *Final Report of Truth and Reconciliation Commission* (in Spanish) (2003), published online by the CVR, http://www.cverdad.org.pe/ingles/ifinal/index.php (accessed January 8, 2007).

[21] See Sierra Leone Truth and Reconciliation Commission, *Final Report of the Truth and Reconciliation Commission of Sierra Leone* (2004), published online by the Sierra Leone Truth and Reconciliation Commission, http://www.trcsierraleone.org/drwebsite/publish/index.shtml (accessed January 5, 2007), especially vol. 2, ch. 4, which focuses on reparations.

[22] See Commission for Reception, Truth and Reconciliation in East Timor (CAVR), *Final Report of the Commission for Reception, Truth and Reconciliation in East Timor* (2006), published online by the International Center for Transitional Justice, http://www.ictj.org/en/news/features/846.html (accessed December 28, 2006), especially Part 11 Recommendations, sec. 12.

[23] See Guatemalan Commission for Historical Clarification (CEH), *Guatemala: Memory of Silence. Report of the Commission for Historical Clarification* (1999), published online by the American Association for the Advancement of Science (AAAS), http://shr.aaas.org/guatemala/ceh/ (accessed November 28, 2005).

- Creating national days of remembrance, thanksgiving, or reconciliation (Chile, El Salvador, Ghana, Peru, Sierra Leone, South Africa, Guatemala)
- Organizing campaigns and cultural celebrations that promote reconciliation (Chile)
- Making available national reconciliation memorabilia, stamps, coins, and badges (Ghana)
- Closing prisons and military institutions (Peru) or converting them into sites of remembrance (South Africa, Chile)
- Reburials, exhumations, commemorative services, and marking and honoring mass graves (Chile, Sierra Leone, South Africa, Timor-Leste, Guatemala)
- Certificates or declarations of death in the case of people who have disappeared, and expunging criminal records (South Africa)

Interestingly, most of the recommendations made to date concerning symbolic reparations have two broad characteristics. First, they generally do not delineate which symbolic acts should take place; and second, the specific mention of gender is largely, although not exclusively, absent.

Some truth commission reports, however, do contain limited specificities. For example, the Sierra Leone report recommends that January 18 – the day in 2002 that President Ahmad Tejan Kabbah declared the conflict over – be commemorated as National Reconciliation Day. The Ghanaian report of the National Reconciliation Commission[24] recommends a National Memorial be located in Accra. Some reports call for apologies, often to be given by the army or head of state. However, when it comes to symbolic reparations, a list of possible options and proposals, rather than specific recommendations, are usually made. This is necessary on one level as more recent truth commissions have recognized the need for consultation in the development of symbolic measures (Timor-Leste), and for symbolic reparations to be tailored to meet the different needs of different communities. However, at the same time, this highlights how symbolic reparations remain a fairly open policy area that is still developing. Recommendations concerning compensation, for example, which has for some time been the focus of legal and international policy discussion, are generally much more specific.

Although some truth commission reports, especially more recent ones, have highlighted the gendered dynamics of conflict, gender is almost a nonexistent

---

[24] The commission was appointed in May 2002 to investigate past human rights abuses in the country. It released its report in April 2005.

component of symbolic reparations recommendations. It could be argued that the mentioning, detailing, and acknowledging of gender-based and sexual crimes in truth commission reports is, to date, the most symbolic act associated with truth commissions and other official processes that have looked at human rights violations. In other words, actual forms of symbolic reparations targeted at women (such as apologies and memorials) have been limited, but the recognition given to the gendered nature of political violence in public and official reports, as has occurred more recently in truth commissions (e.g., Peru, South Africa, Ghana), could be seen as a limited form of symbolic reparations, or at least recognition of the suffering of women. It has been argued in Guatemala, for example, as is discussed in more detail later in "Reconnecting Women Victims with Society and the State," that the only measure taken that is aimed at dignifying female victims of sexual violence and rape following the Commission for Historical Clarification was the publicity of its final report.[25] Although this form of acknowledgment is important, especially in a context where acknowledgement is often nonexistent, it hardly constitutes a significant component of a symbolic reparations program.

One exceptional case is the Ghanaian one. The Ghanaian truth commission has been by far the most specific in making recommendations for symbolic reparations with a gendered component. Specifically, the report recommends (1) a special apology from the president to the Ghanaian woman for the indignities and the atrocities she has endured; and (2) a monument to be erected in honor of the Ghanaian woman. This is an advancement, and in fact the Ghanaian reparations recommendations are arguably the most comprehensive and specific to date. That said, at the time of writing, there had been little development in implementing any of these symbolic measures in Ghana, although it has been announced that those "deserving compensation" will begin receiving ¢2 million (US$215) to ¢30 million (US$3220)[26] per person (totalling about ¢13.5 billion), depending on the extent of abuse or violation.[27] Another rare example is that of the reparations program recommended by the truth and reconciliation commission in Sierra Leone, which states the need for the president to acknowledge the harm suffered by women and girls during the conflict and to offer an

---

[25] Claudia Paz y Paz Bailey, "Guatemala: Gender and Reparations for Human Rights Violations," in *What Happened to the Women? Gender and Reparations for Human Rights Violations*, ed. Ruth Rubio-Marín (New York: Social Science Research Council, 2006).

[26] Figures at the exchange rate of approximately ¢9215 to the US$1 on January 15, 2007.

[27] Lucy Adoma Yeboah, "Aftermath of National Reconciliation, ¢13.5bn Allocated for Victims," *Graphic Ghana* 2006, http://www.graphicghana.info/article.asp?artid=13731.

unequivocal apology to them on behalf of proceeding governments of Sierra Leone.[28]

SYMBOLIC REPARATIONS: GENDERED LIMITATIONS

Drawing on the framework developed by Rubio-Marín,[29] a number of key issues concerning gender and reparations that are relevant to this chapter can be extracted. These are summarized as follows:

1. Violence against men in reparations programs – and specifically certain types of violence – is generally privileged, and violence against women is silenced, or at least depoliticized;
2. Reparations programs can struggle to represent women in ways that recognize their agency;
3. A tension exists between targeting reparations at individuals and massive reparations programs seeking more collective forms of redress, a tension that has unacknowledged gender dimensions; and
4. Women are often excluded from consultation and discussion in the development of reparations programs.

When considering symbolic reparations, the question, however, is whether the concerns outlined above apply as equally to symbolic reparations processes as they do to other forms of reparations such as material reparations. Our contention is that symbolic reparations developed to date do in fact share some of the common characteristics and problems identified by Rubio-Marín. In the following sections we discuss in turn each of the four points summarized above. We consider how symbolic reparations – and symbolic processes that attempt to deal with the legacy of conflict more generally, even if not tied to reparations programs directly – have been limited and challenged in how they deal with the question of gender.

1. *Violations and the Politics of "Privilege"*

In considering the impact of political violence in societies coming out of conflict, certain types of violations are often "privileged." Notwithstanding the fact that many women have been direct victims of torture and abuse during

---
[28] Jamesina King, "Gender and Reparations in Sierra Leone: The Wounds of War Remain Open," in *What Happened to the Women? Gender and Reparations for Human Rights Violations*, ed. Ruth Rubio-Marín (New York: Social Science Research Council, 2006, 269).
[29] Rubio-Marín, "Gender of Reparations."

conflict,[30] it is mainly violations against men – which tend to be more direct and result in death, especially in combat-related situations – that are seen as "primary" human rights violations.[31] There have been many critiques of the assumption that women are not involved in conflict, alongside an increasing awareness of how conflict impacts on women. In spite of this, however, the *belief* that women are not involved in armed conflict remains implicit in reparations programs. Similarly, and perhaps as a result, women themselves speak often not of human rights violations committed against them, but rather of the violations against their husbands and sons.[32] For example, an analysis of the South African Truth and Reconciliation Commission reveals that although many women and girls were detained by the apartheid state in the 1980s, most women testified regarding the experiences of their male relatives.[33] The tendency to downplay women's own roles was present even among the most prominent women in the South African struggle, such as Albertina Sisulu, who commented that she felt "more able to talk about her husband and children's experiences than her own."[34] The range of popular assumptions about what women are and what they do in times of conflict downplays women's political engagement to that of a male relative. This then directly impacts on who gets remembered and how we remember individuals after the war.

In addition to recognizing women's political activism, a gender-sensitive approach to reparations requires us to challenge the very notion of what

---

[30] For example, gender-specific forms of torture such as assault and electric shocks on pregnant women; inadequate medical care leading to miscarriages; rape; flooding of fallopian tubes with water, sometimes leading to infertility; see Beth Goldblatt, "Evaluating the Gender Content of Reparations: Lessons from South Africa," in *What Happened to the Women?*

[31] For a discussion of the limitations of this perspective see Rubio-Marín's "Gender of Reparations" in this volume, and see Vasuki Nesiah et al., "Truth Commissions and Gender: Principle, Policies and Procedures," Gender Justice Series, ICTJ, July 2006.

[32] Margaret Walker, "Gender and Violence in Focus: A Background for Gender Justice in Reparations," Chapter 1 of this volume, calls this "women's insecure testimonial positions."

[33] Pumla Gobodo-Madikizela (with contributions by Fiona Ross and Elizabeth Mills), *Women's Contributions to South Africa's Truth and Reconciliation Commission: Truth and Reconciliation in South Africa: How Women Contributed* (Cambridge and Washington, DC: Women Waging Peace, 2005); Beth Goldblatt and Sheila Meintjies, "Gender and the Truth and Reconciliation Commission – A Submission to the Truth and Reconciliation Commission," Johannesburg, 1997. Goldblatt and Meintjies blame this in part on the structure of the TRC, stating that "in the first week of the Truth Commission's hearings in the Eastern Cape, the widows of the 'Cradock Four' came to speak about their murdered husbands. They themselves had been harassed and arrested, yet their stories were not probed and were treated as incidental. Our society constantly diminishes women's role and women themselves then see their experiences as unimportant." Cited in Beth Goldblatt and Sheila Meintjies, "South African Women Demand the Truth," in *What Women Do in Wartime: Gender and Conflict in Africa*, ed. Meredith Turshen and Clothilde Twagiramariya (London: Zed Books, 1998), 37.

[34] Goldblatt and Meintjies, "South African Women Demand the Truth," 37.

constitutes political activity and recognize that activities that take place within the private sphere, such as women's resistance to taking primary responsibility for childcare, are themselves political. Georgina Waylen takes this further in her claim that "women use their socially prescribed roles to act politically" and argues that women's challenges to the ways in which their bodies and sexuality are controlled (for example, through anti-abortion laws) should be recognized as political acts.[35] Excluding these kinds of acts from the realm of the political reproduces the notion that conflict and politics do not enter the family and, as such, risks creating the impression that woman are not involved in conflict. Consider, for example, the consumer boycotts that took place in South Africa in protest against apartheid. These are acts that took place within families and in which women, given their central role in the family, played a central part. Similarly, Ingrid Palmary,[36] researching women from Rwanda and the Democratic Republic of the Congo (DRC), found that they most commonly described three situations: the attempts by military groups to take their property, including cars, houses, and land; attacks for hiding people who were being targeted (most commonly Rwandans or Tutsis); and being forced to provide food or sex or to expose people to be killed by these groups. The descriptions indicate the ways in which the conflict permeated everyday life and involved a number of acts not typically thought of as political violence. As Aili Mari Tripp states, "many of the national level struggles over access to resources and power are played out at the household level. In spite of their different level and scope, household conflicts are every bit as 'political' as the struggles that 'engage' the state, but with the consequences of differing scope."[37] However, these are often not remembered as acts of heroism or political engagement and are generally overlooked in reparations programs.

Furthermore, it is necessary to recognize that for many women the family is the basic support unit and sphere of influence.[38] To this end, it is important, as Rubio-Marín argues, to acknowledge women's unique role within the family unit as the main caretakers and facilitators of daily life.[39] But in line with the general argument presented in this chapter, the family too is a

---

35 Georgina Waylen, *Gender in Third World Politics* (Buckingham: Open University Press, 1996), 17.
36 Ingrid Palmary, "Engendering Wartime Conflict: Women and War Trauma" (Johannesburg: Centre for the Study of Violence and Reconciliation, 2005).
37 Aili Mari Tripp, "Expanding 'Civil Society': Women and Political Space in Contemporary Uganda.," in *Civil Society and Democracy in Africa. Critical Perspectives*, ed. Nelson Kasfir (London: Frank Cass, 1998), 87.
38 Rubio-Marín, "Gender of Reparations."
39 Ibid.

contested political space in spite of not always being seen as part of the politics of war, repression, and conflict. This discussion has implications for how we think about symbolic reparations, in particular post-conflict reparations projects such as oral history or representation through museums. Although such mechanisms are increasingly documenting the varied experiences of women, they still often ignore the political nature of women's lives and the resistance that takes place outside of formal military engagements.

It is important to acknowledge that women have often used informal structures (that is, structures other than dominant systems of political representation) in order to organize politically, and that they have often mobilized according to traditionally defined feminine roles. For example, in Peru, women in victims' and relatives' organizations were prone to seek truth and justice for relatives as mothers, sisters, daughters, and wives.[40] In Rwanda after the genocide, one of the main victims groups to emerge has been the Association of Widows of the Genocide (AVEGA). In Northern Ireland one of the victims groups first to emerge was of similar ilk, entitled Widows Against Violence (WAVE). And similarly, the largest victims group to emerge in South Africa, the Khulumani Victims Support Group, began largely, although not exclusively, through the impetus of women, a fact used to define its character at times.[41]

Each of these groups draws on their gendered social position to mobilize and draw attention to the large numbers of men who were killed and the consequences of this for women in the aftermath of conflict. This gendered social position can be instrumental in the lobbying for certain types of reparations. For example, in 2004, the former minister of law and order in South Africa, Adriaan Vlok, met with the Mamelodi Mothers of the Disappeared and apologized for the disappearance and killing of their sons and husbands, for which the mothers were reportedly grateful.[42] Their request for apology as "bereaved mothers" had a strong emotional pull, which no doubt played a part in ensuring this action took place. In Rwanda, AVEGA promoted a monetary approach to reparations and argued for reparations for both "legitimate" and "illegitimate" widows and wives.[43]

---

[40] Julie Guillerot, "Evaluating the Gender Content of Reparations: Lessons from South Africa," in *What Happened to the Women?*
[41] Brandon Hamber et al., "Speaking Out: The Role of the Khulumani Victim Support Group in Dealing with the Past in South Africa," paper presented at the "Psychosocial Programs after War and Dictatorship" Conference, Frankfurt, Germany, June 17–21, 2000.
[42] Khulumani Victim Support Group, "Press Release: International Day of the Disappeared Event: August 30, 2006," http://www.khulumani.net/content/view/1582/110/.
[43] Heidy Rombouts, "Women and Reparations in Rwanda: A Long Path to Travel," in *What Happened to the Women?*

The idea that women are active only in their "traditional" gender roles, however, risks disregarding or stigmatizing women who do step outside of such roles. Women who transgress their socially assigned meanings provoke forms of repression and violence.[44] Lorraine Dowler has commented on how women soldiers are, in contrast to men, not heroes but tainted.[45] Similarly, women who were active in *Mkhonto we Sizwe* (MK)[46] in South Africa have been referred to as "flowers of the revolution," a title that, though acknowledging that women were active in the armed forces, represents them in such a way that the essential male/female, active/passive division is not undermined.[47] This is unsurprising if we accept that the emphasis on masculinity in war and the celebration of the heroic deeds of young men draw greater power from their juxtaposition with images of femininity that conform to gender stereotypes.

In addition, Nira Yuval-Davis among others shows how violence against women in times of armed conflict is mediated by their role as biological reproducers of the members of national groups.[48] To this end, women's sexuality and reproduction has often been actively manipulated. Examples include the unauthorized sterilization of black women in South Africa during apartheid, the anti-abortion laws in many countries, and the opposition of the Catholic Church to contraception. Similarly, Carol Summers described the central role played by early reproductive and parenting programs in Uganda for the project of colonial governance.[49] This is linked to women's socially defined role as reproducers of the nation, where the control of women's sexual behavior is required to maintain boundaries of group membership. Equally, restrictions on sexual or marital relations, of which the South African Mixed Marriages Act (no. 55 of 1949) under apartheid is an example, often serve to maintain an artificial boundary between those who belong to a "race" group and those who do not. Similarly, Louise Ryan describes the symbolic cutting of women's hair in the Anglo-Irish war by the British military as an act of humiliation.[50] Thus, women's primary representation as mothers and guardians of the family often shapes the forms that violence against them takes.

---

[44] Walker, "Gender and Violence in Focus."

[45] Lorraine Dowler, "And They Think I'm Just a Nice Old Lady: Women and War in Belfast, Northern Ireland," *Gender, Place and Culture* 5, no. 2 (1998).

[46] *Mkhonto we Sizwe* (MK) was the armed wing of the African National Congress during the South African war against apartheid.

[47] Personal communication, MK veteran.

[48] Nira Yuval-Davis and Floya Anthias, *Women-Nation-State* (London: Macmillan, 1989).

[49] Carol Summers, "Intimate Colonialism: The Imperial Production of Reproduction in Uganda, 1907–1925," *Signs: Journal of Women in Culture and Society* 16, no. 4 (1991).

[50] Louise Ryan, "Drunken Tans: Representations of Sex and Violence in the Anglo-Irish War (1919–21)," *Feminist Review* 66 (2000).

This point is further illustrated when considering the Rwandan genocide. Many authors[51] have noted that Rwanda is a patrilineal society and that women and children generally take on the ethnic identity of the husband. This would arguably work to ensure that every person held an uncontested ethnic identity. In spite of this, during the genocide Tutsi women married to Hutu men were targeted and killed as Tutsis. This targeting took a particular gendered form, and male Hutus were encouraged to kill their Tutsi wives as a testament to their commitment to Hutu nationalism. Reflecting the discussion thus far, much Hutu nationalist propaganda during the genocide was focused on women (both Hutu and Tutsi) in their roles as wives and mothers. Equally, reducing the number of marriages and sexual relationships across ethnic groups was a central concern of the wartime propaganda. For example, of the widely promoted Hutu Ten Commandments published in a December 2000 issue of the newspaper *Kangura*,[52] four regulated marriage and sexual relationships across ethnic divisions. They stated that

> every Hutu should know that a Tutsi woman, wherever she is, works for the interest of her Tutsi ethnic group. As a result, we shall consider a traitor any Hutu who: marries a Tutsi woman; befriends a Tutsi woman; employs a Tutsi woman as a secretary or concubine. Every Hutu should know that our Hutu daughters are more suitable and conscientious in their role as woman, wife and mother of the family. Are they not beautiful, good secretaries and more honest? Hutu woman, be vigilant and try to bring your husbands, brothers and sons back to reason; The Rwandese Armed Forces should be exclusively Hutu. The experience of the October [1990] war has taught us a lesson. No member of the military shall marry a Tutsi.[53]

Similarly, anti-Tutsi propaganda showed Tutsi women as manipulative and emphasized how they used their beauty to lure Hutu men, and images of the war propaganda showed Tutsi women in sexual positions with UN peacekeepers. According to Llezlie Green,[54] Tutsi women were socially positioned at the permeable boundary between the two ethnic groups, which accounts for the particular focus on them. This in turn can have consequences for reparations. For example, Tutsi women married to Hutu men were often denied

---

[51] Mahmood Mamdani, *When Victims Become Killers: Colonialism, Nativism and the Genocide in Rwanda* (Princeton: Princeton University Press, 2001).

[52] The media has been viewed as a central tool of the Rwandan genocide and this newspaper was actively used to promote anti-Tutsi propaganda. See Llezlie Green, "Propaganda and Sexual Violence in the Rwandan Genocide: An Argument for Intersectionality in International Law," *Columbia Human Rights Law Review* 33 (2002).

[53] Ibid., 733–755.

[54] Ibid.

reparations benefits under the 1998 FARG (Assistance Fund for Genocide Survivors) Law because of the presumption that they enjoyed protection and hence were not persecuted.[55] However, this presumption is challenged if we consider that violence within families of mixed ethnicity is equally political.

These examples illustrate how important women's sexuality becomes in times of conflict and repression, and why rape might be a particularly effective form of torture. Yet there has been ambivalent attention to rape as a form of political violence, which has implications for symbolic reparations. It is now well established that rape is and can be used as a weapon and strategy of war;[56] there is a growing recognition of it as a specific and direct war crime, and as intrinsically political. As a result, there is increasing inclusion of rape and other forms of sexual violence among the list of violations eligible for reparations.[57] However, coercion of and violence against women are normative.[58] The "normal" violence perpetrated against women, which can include "multiple forms of coercion, subjugation, violence and exploitation,"[59] seldom receives attention in reparations programs and society more generally.

This complexity of women's involvement in and victimization during conflict is often eclipsed in the design of symbolic reparations, which frequently draw on the assumption that women are not involved in conflict and privilege men's actions. Jacklyn Cock, for example, relates how Afrikaner national identity in apartheid South Africa relied on the construction of the passive female suffering in the British concentration camps of the South African Anglo-Boer War of 1899–1902 in order to mobilize men for the conflict.[60] At a symbolic level, this is precisely captured in the National Women's Memorial in South Africa, built (and designed and established by men) in 1913 by the Afrikaner nationalist government. One of the central features of the monument is a sculpture, the messages and meanings conveyed by which are captured by Sabine Marschall when she writes:

> The pathos of the entire monument is condensed and epitomized in Anton van Wouw's emotionally charged central sculptural group. Formally modelled on a conflation of the Christian iconographic traditions of Anna Selbdritt and the Pietà, the group consists of a seated woman with bare feet and a look of sadness, despair, and exhaustion on her face. She is holding a dead

---

[55] Rombouts, "Women and Reparations in Rwanda."
[56] Roy L. Brooks, "Reflections on Reparations," in *Politics and the Past: On Repairing Historical Injustices*, ed. John Torpey (Oxford: Rowman and Littlefield, 2003).
[57] Rubio-Marín, "Gender of Reparations."
[58] Walker, "Gender and Violence in Focus."
[59] Ibid.
[60] Jacklyn Cock, *Women and War in South Africa* (Cleveland: The Pilgrim Press, 1993).

South African Women's Memorial, 1913.

child in her lap, clearly evoking the lamenting Mary holding the deceased Son of God.... It was during the early 20th century that the Afrikaner ideology of the volksmoeder emerged, and – as Liese van der Watt contends – van Wouw's sculpture can be considered one of the earliest examples of visually representing this tradition. The discourse of the volksmoeder associates women with the domestic sphere and particularly with child-rearing – not only as mother of a private household, but as mother of the nation or the volk.[61]

The work of these authors suggests that women are remembered in post-conflict contexts. However, the form of this remembrance conforms to the belief that women do not actively participate in politics or conflict. Women have not so much been left out of symbolic representations of war as selectively remembered in a way that continues to legitimate violence in defense of the defenseless – a tension that Cynthia Cockburn refers to as the "present-absence" of women in representations of armed conflict.[62] Moreover,

---

[61] Sabine Marschall, "Serving Male Agendas: Two National Women's Monuments in South Africa," *Women's Studies* 33 (2004): 1014.

[62] Cynthia Cockburn, *The Space between Us: Negotiating Gender and National Identities in Conflict* (London: Zed Books, 1998).

representations of masculinity in war are framed with reference to women and draw strength from representations of femininity.⁶³ Such masculinization of the protection of the national territory relies on the assumption that women are naturally vulnerable, and on emphasizing their role as reproducers and carers.⁶⁴ This is equally seen in the recent US invasion of Afghanistan, where war was justified because of the oppression of Afghan women by Afghan men.

2. *Representing Women's Agency*

The above debates about how women's varied activities during violent conflict are remembered raises another related problem, that is, that most reparations initiatives have represented women as lacking in agency. In many such programs, women's actual role in conflict or combat is ignored, or they are generally painted as passive, disengaged victims.

In terms of the role of women in conflict or combat, it is important to note that, whereas the activities of men – mostly those that are a part of formal armed forces – have been privileged, women in the armed forced have not been awarded equal attention. In fact, there has been a reluctance to consider the role of women in the armed forces, particularly on the African continent, where women (and children) have been active in armies and militia groups. In part this is likely because to do so would challenge the notion that women are outside the conflict and its victims rather than actively engaged in it. It is, therefore, not surprising that many women themselves are resistant to creating tributes to women in armed forces. Women who are perpetrators of violence are met with horror because of the assumption that women are not naturally violent. Being seen to be involved in conflict (particularly as an activist or perpetrator) can carry with it a stigma for having transgressed gender norms. Again, this represents difficulties for reparations programs that want to challenge dominant representations of women in war, as they risk stigmatizing women for their active role. This is particularly the case in conflicts where the distinction between victim and perpetrator cannot be neatly drawn. As a result, many reparations programs in Africa fail to adequately capture the blurred divisions between civilian/soldier and victim/perpetrator.

Instead, reparations programs are often designed around the presumption of rigid boundaries between victim and perpetrator. Trying to incorporate an understanding of gender, as articulated above, into symbolic reparations projects so that they do not fall into these overly simplistic and stereotyped

⁶³ Ryan, "Drunken Tans."
⁶⁴ Sarah A. Radcliff, "Gendered Nations: Nostalgia, Development and Territory in Ecuador," *Gender, Place and Culture* 4, no. 6 (1996).

representations is demanding. Equally, however, some symbolic reparations offer a unique opportunity because, unlike legal questions concerning, say, compensation where more clear delineations are needed, symbolic measures, such as memorials or museum projects, can offer abstract and complex representations of conflict.

In a similar vein, Jacklyn Cock considers the extent to which the military in apartheid South Africa drew on a representation of women as disengaged from the conflict, which reinforced an artificial division between protectors and protected. This was rooted in an insistence on an essential femininity that, although it required expansion to incorporate women's support of the armed forces, retained the strict division between men's and women's roles.[65] This representation often functions to justify violence within the public realm of politics and war and exists precisely because of an assumption that women are "agentless" and require men's protection. Of course, images of femininity conjured up in times of conflict are shaped by other relations of structural oppression, such as class and race.[66] That said, our aim in drawing out these more general trends is not to imply that conflicts mobilize gender in the same ways across all contexts, but rather that reparations, if they are to meet the needs of women, require analysis across a range of different contexts.

Notions of women as outside of the conflict, and as passive in the face of it, have been central to achieving the belief that it is women who keep "normal" (conflict-free, gendered) life going in times of war.[67] Although this representation has been challenged, its central consequence for this chapter, and for how we conceptualize symbolic reparations from a gendered perspective, is that images of domesticity and gendered "normal life" that exist outside of the war render family relationships apolitical while simultaneously identifying the protection of the family as the legitimating force for war. The carefully drawn lines between public and private, and their mapping onto masculine and feminine, become central in times of war because representations of femininity as outside of the public, political realm of war have been mobilized to justify war in the name of protecting the "women and children."[68] The complexity of this, however, when thinking about making symbolic reparations, can be extensive. Take, for example, the oft-made recommendation for a day of remembrance

---

[65] Jacklyn Cock, "Manpower and Militarisation: Women and the Sadf," in *War and Society: The Militarisation of South Africa*, ed. Jacklyn Cock and Laurie Nathan (Cape Town: David Phillip, 1989).

[66] For example, Cock shows how constructions of Afrikaner women represented them as tougher than English women. Cited in Cock, *Women and War in South Africa*.

[67] Angela K. Martin, "The Practice of Identity and an Irish Sense of Place," *Gender Place and Culture* 4, no. 1 (1997).

[68] Nira Yuval-Davis, "Gender and Nation," in *Space, Gender, Knowledge: Feminist Readings*, ed. Linda McDowell and Joanne P. Sharp (London: Arnold, 1990).

or commemoration. These too can suffer from the tendency to see women as outside of conflict and typically rooted in the private sphere. A clear illustration of this is the way that Women's Day in South Africa has been celebrated. Women's Day (August 9) marks the anniversary of a 1956 march by women to the Union Buildings in Pretoria to protest against the extension of pass laws to black women. Each year the way that this day has been remembered has tended to reinforce two of the forms of gendered remembering that have been critiqued.

First, the descriptions of the march have reinforced the notion that women typically were not part of the "mainstream" struggle. The march is presented as a response to something that is considered a "women's issue," namely, that they too may be subject to the same repressive pass laws as their male counterparts. The discussions around Women's Day tend to create the impression that participation in the struggle was not the norm for women but rather was an indication of how severe the situation had become, because even the women were part of protests. In this way, remembering women's political action does not challenge the assumptions that women are not a part of armed conflict. It also ignores the everyday level on which the struggle was fought, and which affected men as much as women as in the previous example of consumer boycotts.

Second, the explanation given for women's participation in the march is justified and explained as being in the interests of the family and, particularly, children. At the time, one of the reasons that women demanded that the pass laws not be extended to them was that it would be detrimental to the welfare of children, who may be separated from their mothers as a result (i.e., women being arrested for not having a "pass" to enter certain areas). This continues to be remembered as a moment where women defied gender norms by participating in public protest, but this participation is rendered more palatable by its being framed as an act in the interests of the children and the family (which is at best only partly true). It could be argued that framing women's participation in the protest in this way makes it more socially acceptable in a context where women's participation in conflict is generally deemed unacceptable. To this end, we can see that symbolic reparations processes, such as days of commemoration or remembrance, are not straightforward matters if one looks at them with a gendered lens. The core discourse surrounding them can be critical in how they perpetuate or challenge gendered narratives of conflict. Furthermore, as much as the day may have been originally anticipated to present a particular representation of women, this representation can and will evolve over time.

Similar processes can be seen in memorialization. For example, it is interesting, if not disturbing, to note that a memorial to the horses that died in the South African War of 1899–1902 was built in 1905 in Port Elizabeth

World War II Women's Memorial in London.

(a site itself of one of the British concentration camps that resulted in the death of thousands of women and children)[69] nearly a decade before the Afrikaner Memorial to Women was built in 1913. Notwithstanding the fact that the 1913 memorial was designed entirely by men and represented women in an extremely passive way,[70] such processes of seeing the achievements of women as secondary and as in need of protection and aggressive defense (therefore justifying war) continue to the present day. Similar criticism can be leveled against the UK memorial to commemorate the role of women during World War II, which was built only in July 2005.

The role monuments and memorials play in valorizing certain actions of men, and generally hiding women from the public space, is almost universal. For example, Sabine Marschall notes that in post-apartheid South Africa, although there has been the establishment of the new National Women's

[69] British concentration camps during the South African War of 1899–1902 resulted in the deaths, mainly from starvation and disease, of 27,000 Boer women and children; 22,000 of these deaths were children under the age of 16. It is also vitally important to acknowledge that some 14,000 Black Africans died in these camps too, although it is likely this is an underestimate. These deaths have been almost written out of history, although they are gaining more prominence in post-apartheid South Africa.

[70] Marschall, "Serving Male Agendas."

Monument at the Union Buildings in Pretoria, the erection of statues and portrait busts has almost exclusively been of men.[71] These have included Nelson Mandela, Mahatma Gandhi, Oliver Tambo, Albert Luthuli, Braam Fischer, and Steve Biko.[72] Her research reveals only one statue to a woman set up since 1994 – a life-size bronze in Durban Harbor of the "Lady in White" or Perla Siedle Gibson, an international soprano who sang to the crews of incoming ships during World War II to improve their morale.[73] Even post-apartheid film has been criticized for focusing mainly on the stories of male activists.[74] Marschall concludes that the most marginalized voice in South Africa remains that of black women.[75]

This is not to say that memorials of women are nonexistent. There are certainly many memorials to women in the armed forces in the United States, for example, and a selected number of memorials to famous women across the globe, such as, among others, Marie Curie (Belfast), Amelia Earhart (Hollywood and Derry), Florence Nightingale (London), Emmaline Pankhurst (London), Annie Oakley (Ohio), and Pocahontas (Virginia).[76] Furthermore, notwithstanding the way women are portrayed, there are some monuments to women in war situations, such as those highlighted on the website "Monuments and Memorials to Women Warriors in the US."[77] Despite its title, however, most of the memorials on this site concern women as "carers," such as the monument to Jane Delano and all of the military nurses who died during World War I, or women as "auxiliary helpers," such as the monument in Ohio to Elizabeth Zane, who fetched gunpowder outside of a fort in 1792 during an attack from Native Americans. There are some memorials, certainly in the US, that are dedicated to women in active combat; for example, a statue in Sharon, Massachusetts, of Deborah Samson, who fought disguised as Robert Shirtliffe in the Continental Army, serving for three years and receiving a military pension.

That said, representations of women in times of political struggle – say, through a symbolic reparations program – that do not reinforce the notion of women as passive victims (and occasional helpers in armed conflict) are difficult to create. The issue of rape in war provides a challenging example.

---

[71] Ibid.
[72] Ibid.
[73] Ibid.
[74] Ibid.
[75] "Hour of the Thug," *The Guardian Unlimited*, March 10, 2006 (cited March 21, 2006), http://film.guardian.co.uk/features/featurepages/0,1727356,00.html.
[76] See "Women on Pedestals" at http://www.factmonster.com/ipka/A0768462.html, for a list of some individual statues of famous women.
[77] See http://userpages.aug.com/captbarb/monuments.html.

Although rape may be a strategy of war, and as mentioned above gains have been made insofar as rape and other forms of sexual violence are increasingly being considered for reparations in many countries,[78] <u>the view that rape is a sexual apolitical crime still dominates most societies</u>. Rape is still seen as literally inevitable in war,[79] perversely demonstrated through the issue of "comfort women" (discussed later in "Increasing the Gendered Impact of Symbolic Reparations," Subsection 2b) by the fact that "one of the official aims of the comfort system was to prevent soldiers from randomly raping the women of occupied territories."[80]

The failure to eradicate this view, and the tendency to blame the victim, are factors that continue to leave rape survivors isolated, ostracized, and feeling shameful.[81] Such feelings remain the hallmarks of being a victim of a crime that is still seen as private and apolitical. This is evidenced in a number of countries. For example, in Sierra Leone, one of the biggest problems that women who were raped during the conflict have to endure is familial and communal ostracism.[82] In Bosnia, Muslim rape victims are considered soiled and unmarriageable, with some even believing exile or death is the only way to cleanse men and families of the shame.[83] This can have direct implications for reparations programs. For example, in Rwanda, as mentioned earlier, some victim groups lobbied for monetary reparations for "legitimate" and "illegitimate" widows and wives,[84] but there was less organization and lobbying around reparations for gender-based or sexual violence.[85]

An important issue here is how to represent and deal with crimes such as rape in the public domain, generally the sphere in which many symbolic forms of reparations operate. Most reparations programs to date have failed to do this at all. A specific question facing a symbolic reparations program would be how to represent physically (e.g., through memorials, or interactive educational displays in museums), or publicly acknowledge, crimes such as rape. This also belies a bigger question: how to memorialize and remember (say, through a day of remembrance) such crimes in a context where the (mythical) public/private

---

[78] Rubio-Marín, "Gender of Reparations."
[79] Brooks, "Reflections on Reparations."
[80] Chunghee Sarah Soh, "Japan's Responsibility toward Comfort Women Survivors," Encinitas: Japan Policy Research Institute, 2001, cited at http://www.icasinc.org/lectures/soh3.html, sec. on "National Interest Versus Healing Truth," para. 3.
[81] Walker, "Gender and Violence in Focus," also discusses this issue.
[82] Jamesina King, "Gender and Reparations in Sierra Leone: The Wounds of War Remain Open," in *What Happened to the Women?*
[83] Brooks, "Reflections on Reparations."
[84] Rombouts, "Women and Reparations in Rwanda."
[85] Ibid.

dichotomy and apolitical view of women in conflict remains, not to mention ongoing patriarchy and negative perceptions about women on the whole. In societies where problematic attitudes to women remain, such as Sierra Leone, it has been argued that focusing various components of the reparations program specifically at victims of sexual violence (e.g., education programs, healthcare, skills training) could acknowledge the harms women suffered and help victims overcome the familial and communal ostracism they sometimes endure as victims of sexual violence.[86] But there are risks with such programs. Simply making such issues public, and memorializing, remembering, and discussing them, could fuel prejudice rather than ameliorate it. For example, it is questionable the degree to which the public controversy about the "comfort women" has changed Japanese attitudes or reinforced them. A 1997 opinion survey found that only 50.7% of contemporary Japan felt there should be an apology, and a survey in 1998 and 1999 found that two-thirds of Japanese military veterans felt that there was no need for an apology or compensation because the women had been paid.[87] Research in South Africa has also found that some men, because of a growing public emphasis on women's issues, feel that women have gained disproportionately from the transition relative to men, despite this being statistically incorrect.[88]

We are, of course, not making an argument that such issues should not be discussed publicly. On the contrary, we are inquiring into how such processes can be used not only to break silences about past abuses but also to challenge dominant narratives. This is not a straightforward issue in societies where the public/private dichotomy and apolitical view of women in conflict exists. It raises the specific question: How do you adequately provide recognition and visibility to women's experience when the context of interpretation for such experience is provided by collective meanings that are difficult and slow to change? Bringing issues such as rape and its systematic use in war to the public might be essential both to stir the transformation and to challenge narratives (for the sake of a better future), but it might not always assist current victims. This issue is explored further in the final section of this chapter.

---

[86] King, "Gender and Reparations in Sierra Leone."
[87] Soh, "Japan's Responsibility toward Comfort Women Survivors."
[88] Brandon Hamber "Masculinity and Transitional Justice: An Exploratory Essay," *International Journal of Transitional Justice* 1(3), (2007), 375–390. Also see Brandon Hamber, "'We Must Be Very Careful How We Emancipate Our Women': Shifting Masculinities in Post-Apartheid South Africa," paper presented at the "Re-Imagining Women's Security: a Comparative Study of South Africa, Northern Ireland and Lebanon Round Table," New York, October 12–13, 2006. For more details on this project, see http://www.incore.ulst.ac.uk/research/projects/rwsst/.

3. Individual and Collective Representations and Actions

The act of trying to balance the individual versus collective focus of reparations is difficult and complex, and it has a gendered dimension. Individual victims might be central to a reparations process, but their experience and attempts at redress cannot be divorced from the wider political aims of the program or the context of the violations. Massive reparations programs by their nature contain a collective element, but equally they need to attempt to meet the needs of individuals. For example, monuments and memorials as reparations must have something "sacred" about them to have an interpersonal (individual) and social (collective) meaning simultaneously.[89] The individual political trauma needs to be placed within a context for healing to occur.[90] The public recognition of suffering gives it meaning, coherence, and historical significance for the individual.[91] But, at the same time, whose trauma is remembered and the degree to which private trauma can ever overlap with collective attempts (and agendas) to recognize it are complex questions because the relationship between the individual and the context, with its multiple systems, is multifaceted. As indicated earlier, this may be particularly difficult in some cases, such as those involving victims of sexual violence, precisely because the public recognition of suffering and of overcoming private trauma, and the interconnection between them, raises unique temporal challenges.

Nevertheless, the importance of acknowledging women's experiences is being recognized – for example, in truth commission processes – but exactly how to do so is still a difficult issue to resolve. Women's hearings, such as what took place in South Africa and Sierra Leone, can be important in acknowledging the role of women in conflict and the specific violations they suffered, but at the same time they can feed into the notion of women's experiences as separate from formal politics. Equally, trying to represent women within the mainstream hearings or separate chapters in truth commission reports can

---

[89] Hamber, "Narrowing the Micro and Macro." In essence, in this work it is argued that memorials, for example, the Vietnam War Memorial, which have an individual element (individual names) but appeal to and locate the individual in a larger collective (the entirety of the wall), have the most resonance for families and victims linked with such memorials.

[90] David Becker, "Confronting the Truth of the Erinyes: The Illusion of Harmony in the Healing of Trauma," in *Telling the Truths: Truth Telling and Peace Building in Post-Conflict Societies*, ed. Tristan Anne Borer (Indiana: Notre Dame Press, 2006); David Becker, "Dealing with the Consequences of Organized Violence," in *Berghof Handbook for Conflict Transformation* (Berlin: Berghof Research Center for Constructive Conflict Management, 2001); Hamber, "Narrowing the Micro and Macro"; Lykes and Mersky, "Reparations and Mental Health."

[91] Michael Humphrey, *The Politics of Atrocity and Reconciliation: From Terror to Trauma* (London: Routledge, 2002).

leave women victims' experiences being subsumed into male narratives (as mentioned earlier in relation to women talking of violations against men).

This is true for some symbolic forms of reparations. Should violations against women and women's role in conflict be remembered in separate processes or as part of the dominant conflict narrative? Should individuals or the collective plight of women be highlighted? Such dilemmas play themselves out within the debate concerning memorials or monuments dedicated specifically to women as opposed to thinking of how these types of symbolic reparations could incorporate a gendered perspective (e.g., in a national memorial to all victims of a conflict). There is a growing tendency toward remembering with dedicated memorials and monuments focused on women. Although not flowing from reparations programs, examples include the new "National Women's Monument" in South Africa, the "Women in Military Service for America Memorial" in Arlington Cemetery in Washington, DC,[92] and the "Vietnam Women's Memorial," also in Washington, DC. As was mentioned, the Ghanaian truth commission recommended a monument to be erected in honor of the Ghanaian woman. These could, on one level, be considered to constitute an advancement in gendering memorialization; but equally there is the risk that such separate processes could leave male narratives and symbols that dominate the public space unchallenged, and at times reinforced.

Traditionally, where women are depicted in memorials it is generally in stereotypical ways, that is, as passive, in need of assistance, or as caregivers. Marina Warner, in her book *Monuments and Maidens: The Allegory of the Female Form*, notes that

> although the absence of female symbols and a preponderance of male in a society frequently indicates a corresponding depreciation of women as a group and as individuals, the presence of female symbolism does not guarantee the opposite, as we can see from classical Athenian culture, with its subtly psychologized pantheon of goddesses and its secluded, unenfranchised women; or contemporary Catholic culture, with its pervasive and loving celebration of the Madonna coexisting alongside deep anxieties and disapproval of female emancipation.[93]

Take, for example, the Vietnam Women's Memorial, unveiled in 1993, which consists of three uniformed women (at least one is a nurse) and a wounded male

---

[92] This large memorial is very difficult to describe because of its size, but suffice to say it is a large granite structure fitting in with many of Washington DC's larger memorials. For more details visit http://www.womensmemorial.org/.

[93] Marina Warner, *Monuments and Maidens: The Allegory of the Female Form* (London: Vintage, 1996), xx.

Vietnam War Women's Memorial, Washington, DC.

soldier.[94] One woman is nursing the male soldier, one is on her knees possibly praying, and another looks upwards as if for a rescue helicopter. Although this to some degree reflects the formal role of women in the war (11,500 American women served in Vietnam, 90% of whom were medical personnel), the choice of imagery uncannily reinforces stereotypes of women as carers, comforters, and in need of rescue. In many senses, the memorial fits the description given by Rubio-Marín of monuments that "romanticize women to stereotypes about their nurturing, forgiving, and self-sacrificial predisposition for the sake of the healed mother nation."[95]

The UK memorial to women who served in World War II (p. 342) moves beyond this to a limited extent, with the bronze sculpture showing the uniforms of women in the forces next to the working clothes of women factory workers and medical staff; but gender stereotypes still abound. Again, women are reflected to some degree as passive, and in this case their bodies are completely

[94] The process of getting the broader role of women recognized is another issue altogether (the eight women who died in Vietnam are named on the Vietnam War Memorial). It took considerable campaigning to get the Women's Memorial set up. It was unveiled on Veterans Day, November 11, 1993.
[95] Rubio-Marín, Chapter 2 of this volume.

missing, and only their clothes are present. The monument tackles the issue of roles in both the public and private spheres, which certainly moves the debate forward, but at the same time reinforces these spheres, at least to a degree, as separate worlds.[96] On the other side of the coin are the soldiers depicted in the Korean War Memorial in Washington, DC, as armed, active, and on patrol, which equally perpetuates the stereotypes of men.[97] Arguably, it is not merely the more limited portrayal of women in symbolic processes that perpetuates damaging perceptions of women, but rather the consistent display of imagery that reproduces masculinity and hyper-machismo that is of an even greater concern.

We can see, then, that when it comes to memorialization – as one component of a potential symbolic reparations program – considering how to represent a collective experience of women can be challenging. By focusing on the collective, there has been the tendency to draw heavily on gender stereotypes in ways that further marginalize the varied wartime experiences of women. There are problems equally, however, with a more individual approach. Given the way the whole family or community was often drawn into conflict in societies such as Rwanda and Sierra Leone, where family members were called up or partook in killing relatives, community harms cannot be easily addressed through individual reparation processes, such as grants.[98] A further problem is that the process of memorialization (unlike other forms of symbolic reparations such as a day of remembrance) is generally dominated by an individual (hero-driven) ethos. Although some memorials focus on the collective, there still is a propensity to memorialize in a highly individual or event-driven way, generally with strong gendered overtones.

Examples of monuments and memorials of this type abound. Take, for example, Monument Avenue in Richmond, Virginia, which features statues of the Confederate Civil War heroes Jefferson Davis, Robert E. Lee, Stonewall Jackson, and J.E.B. Stuart, and oceanographer Matthew Fontaine Maury. Most are on horseback and in military uniform. It is only the statue of Arthur Ashe,

---

[96] This does not mean, however, that there is only one way to interpret this monument. Another view could be that the purpose of the sculpture is disembodiment. To this end, the monument represents a clash between the clothes (and the roles that they represent) and the female body (an inherent contradiction), therefore the only way to recognize a women's role in war is to convey the message that these women are disembodied, and these are not female bodies.

[97] Gender issues do not only concern women, and, of course, we also need to think about issues concerning masculinity in reparations processes. This chapter focuses largely on women, and work remains to be done on the issue of masculinity and symbolic reparations. For example, this chapter unpacks how women are represented in monuments, but the same could be done for men's role in conflict, aiming to represent this in alternative, more challenging and complicated ways. This subject requires a focus in itself.

[98] Roht-Arriaza, "Reparations Decisions and Dilemmas."

Arthur Ashe Memorial in Richmond, VA.

renowned black tennis star, that stands out.[99] Abraham Lincoln and Ulysses S. Grant are obviously missing, but statues of them are ubiquitous in other parts of the United States. Of course, Lincoln is most prominent, again larger than life and foreboding, at the top of Washington Mall. The mall in Washington, DC, is a contested memorial space among many groups,[100] but scattered around

---

[99] There was much dispute about the Arthur Ashe monument because of the incongruous nature of the memorial relative to the military monuments around it. Some argued that this, and that Ashe was a black man from Richmond, was why it was particularly important. Nonetheless, the monument remains controversial for a number of reasons: racial tensions in the city, the fact that the Ashe statue is considerably smaller than those of the generals, and the fact that its actual design (i.e., of Ashe with a raised tennis racket and children at his feet) makes it look from a distance as if he is trying to hit the children.

[100] Andrew M. Shanken, "Planning Memory: Living Memorials in the United States During World War II," *The Art Bulletin* LXXXIV, no. 1 (2002).

the complex are the Korean War Memorial and the Vietnam Memorial, both including statues of soldiers in combat gear and armed.

James Loewen highlights, somewhat sarcastically, the nature of much of the memorialization in a city such as Washington, DC. He writes,

> Civil War statues also exemplify a problem in how our public history portrays women. Across the country, women rarely get statues, partly because they have rarely been governors or generals, partly because the landscape is biased against them. In almost every traffic circle in Washington stands a Union general on his horse. Some of these horses were mares, who performed exactly the same functions as their male counterparts. General Winfield Scott's favourite was a mare, which he rides today in Scott Circle, but Scott's grandchildren thought this wasn't manly, so they got the sculptor to add 'stallion attributes.'[101]

This type of memorialization glorifies the role of individuals and hides the experience of the collective. Furthermore, it makes a clear point about what acts are seen as "heroic" and what acts are not – that is, active combat is privileged over, for example, women's "heroic" fulfilment of daily tasks around survival and their importance in nurturing and sustaining the collective. The result is that women's collective experience and their role within the collective are largely ignored in memorialization and other so-called post-war remembering processes.

In a study across a number of African countries – including Namibia, Zimbabwe, South Africa, Malawi, and Mozambique – memorialization processes in all countries, including memorials, monuments, days of remembrance, and naming of streets, found it hard to move away from this kind of "heroic" imagery,[102] a problem that of course is not confined to Africa. Symbolic processes in these societies are integrally linked with national projects and are largely about bolstering nationalist and political ideals of ruling elites. The result is that most nongovernmental organizations in Namibia, Zimbabwe, Malawi, and Mozambique (with South Africa to a much lesser degree) see the memorialization processes in their countries fairly negatively. According to the study, "a few monuments and national holidays – and the little that is, serve only one party political end, namely, the justification of the powers that be."[103] In post-apartheid South Africa, it has been argued that similar processes are

---

[101] James Loewen, "The Sociology of Selected Monuments in Washington, DC, or Stories Behind the Stones," *Footnotes* (April 2000), http://www.asanet.org/footnotes/apr00/stones.html.

[102] Southern African Reconciliation Project and Centre for the Study of Violence and Reconciliation, "Memorialisation and Reconciliation in Transitional Southern African Societies," Centre for the Study Violence and Reconciliation, Johannesburg, 2005.

[103] Ibid.

at work. There has been, writes Ereshnee Naidu, a concentration on memorializing individuals and events, which has inadvertently distracted the nation from remembering regular activists and the South African collective that were victims of injustices and human rights violations.[104] These have been characterized as "massacre memorials" or "heroes monuments."[105] In the former victims are both men and women, but generally remain unnamed, and in the latter the notion of hero is generally limited to a militaristic definition linked with those armed combatants fighting to end apartheid, limiting references to women.[106]

It remains to be seen how this issue will be dealt with by the new Freedom Park memorial site just outside Tshwane (formerly Pretoria) in South Africa. This is a massive development that will not be completed until 2009 and is reported to be linked with the South African Truth and Reconciliation Commission's recommendations for symbolic reparations.[107] The 52-hectare site includes a memorial with the names of all those killed in the various wars in South Africa and will ultimately include a museum, an array of sculptures, and various water features within botanic and reflective gardens. The development appears to be driven by the "hero" ethos to a degree, with the main memorial being divided into three sections to reveal the important contributions made by leaders throughout the world to freedom. These include, among many others, South African leaders such as Oliver Tambo, continental leaders such as Julius Nyerere, and international leaders such as "Che" Guevara. Although women are present in these lists, they are, given the traditional political focus, inevitably outnumbered drastically. It is likely, however, that the site, which is laden with symbolism, will acknowledge the contribution of women, even if nominally, and does have some collective elements within it. For example, the garden of remembrance, which has a strong African traditional feel, has and will be

---

[104] Ereshnee Naidu, "Memorialisation: A Fractured Opportunity," Centre for the Study of Violence and Reconciliation, Johannesburg, 2004. Naidu also adds: "The phenomenon of memorialising events and heroes in the South African liberation struggle is not limited to national government projects. Local and provincial governments are responsible for initiating community memorialisation projects, however, as in the case of Sharpeville and the Alexandra projects, focus is still being given to heroes and events (albeit in more creative ways). Scholars and those working within the field of public memory viewed this as a result of memorial sites being linked to economic and tourist 'spin offs' where sites are focused more on meeting the needs of the foreign visitor rather than that of the community."

[105] For example, the Langa Massacre Memorial in Uitenhage, the Bisho Massacre Memorial, the Hector Pieterson Memorial in Soweto, or the Sharpeville Memorial; also see Marschall, "Serving Male Agendas."

[106] Ibid.

[107] See the Freedom Park website, http://www.freedompark.org.za/theproject.php, where this point is made.

used for collective healing and cleansing rituals. The trustees claim to have consulted with women, as well as youth, traditional leaders, artists, religious organizations, war veterans, and even Afrikaans cultural organizations, in its development.

As a rule, however, writes Esther Levinger, war memorials commemorate the heroism of men in defense of their country and its values.[108] The creation and design of monuments and memorials (and museums and days of remembrance) are also largely, although certainly not exclusively, established and designed by men, and thus represent their interests. Although no systematic analysis exists, it is safe to say that the vast majority of monuments across the globe are dedicated to men (mainly soldiers) and display the imagery of men generally in bold, larger-than-life, and masculine poses. Women are largely nonexistent, and men are represented as active, powerful, and in control. Where women are represented, the monuments generally reproduce the private/public dichotomy discussed earlier, depoliticizing women and expropriating their "bodies" for wider (gendered) political ends.

With this in mind, one has to question whether the difficulties of individual and collective representations are consistent across all types of symbolic reparations. Monuments and memorials pose a specific problem with regard to how collective experiences might be conveyed, and how individuals (if this is deemed appropriate) might also be commemorated. It is questionable whether reparations programs, which essentially have a collective aim at their core, should ever engage in the creation of individual-orientated memorialization. Instead, highlighting individuals *within a collective structure* (such as names on a monument) might be more appropriate for a mass-based reparations program. Also, other forms of symbolic reparations that are necessarily less individualized, such as a day of commemoration, can be important. At the same time, it is also worth considering whether more individual monuments and memorials to women are needed to offset the current proclivity for cities to be littered with individual memorials of men – although this may in turn merely perpetuate the practice of individualization. This issue will be revisited later in the chapter.

The issue of apologies also poses some unique challenges in the individual and collective reparations debate. Blanket apologies, as with collective memorials, could serve some psychological and socially reparative function. The recommendation by the Ghanaian truth commission for a collective apology to women who suffered indignities would fall into this category. Again, however, a balance in any reparations process between meeting individual and

---

[108] Esther Levinger, "Women and War Memorials in Israel," *Woman's Art Journal* 16, no. 1 (1995).

collective needs might be necessary. In Chile, for example, the apology by President Patricio Aylwin for the violations of the Pinochet regime was seen by some as symbolically meaningful and healing to a degree. At the same time, so too was the delivery of the truth commission report to the house of each victim, with a card from the president of the Republic attached; for some this was even more significant.[109]

Just as street names being changed to commemorate individual women, or collective memorials having the names of men and women on them, or important buildings being named after women could be part of a symbolic reparations program, so too could apology be both individual and collective. Along these lines, Rubio-Marín highlights the importance of individualized letters of apology in the case of some women. She argues that because many women are generally relegated to the private sphere and rarely experience or perceive themselves as citizens, an official and personalized letter of apology might be able to provide both recognition of their individual experience and acknowledge their role in the wider social and political collective.[110]

4. Consultation and Voice

A lack of consultation with regard to the development of symbolic ways of dealing with a legacy of conflict is common. It is a frequent complaint about the establishment of almost all memorials, museums, and days of remembrance and commemoration, regardless of their focus. For example, research has found a general lack of representativeness and consultation and the marginalization of local communities in several state processes to set up memorials in post-apartheid South Africa.[111] An analysis by the Healing Through Remembering project in Northern Ireland of some 15 days of remembrance and commemoration around the world found that lack of consultation was a widespread grievance.[112] Where such consultation does take place, there is generally a gender bias.[113] Women's organizations are less likely to be consulted,[114] and processes often target some community leaders or so-called representatives who are not closely connected to local communities. Women are often excluded from consultation and discussion in the development of reparations programs

---

[109] Roberta Bacic, personal communication, September 6, 2006.
[110] Rubio-Marín, "Gender and Reparations."
[111] Ereshnee Naidu, "A Community-Centred Approach to Memorialisation: A Living Memory Intervention Process," Centre for the Study of Violence and Reconciliation, Johannesburg, 2004; Naidu, "Memorialisation: A Fractured Opportunity."
[112] Healing Through Remembering, "International Experiences of Days of Reflection & Remembrance," Belfast, 2006.
[113] Naidu, "Memorialisation: A Fractured Opportunity."
[114] Rubio-Marín, "Gender and Reparations."

and even more so from actually taking part in building them. For example, of the 1,000 memorials in Israel, only 30 were erected by women, with only 12 women artists involved out of 300.[115]

This, of course, is not to assert that the reproduction of images of women is solely a male business, or that memorials and monuments to women do not exist, but they certainly represent a minority of the public space in most countries. The public representation of women, though largely shaped by men, is influenced by women in some cases. A closer analysis of the establishment of the Horse Memorial in South Africa reveals that, although it was a long time ago, women played a central role in lobbying for the memorial to be set up.[116] The new Women's Monument in South Africa (discussed later) was a process essentially developed and run by women, and some famous memorials (e.g., the Vietnam War Memorial and the Vietnam Women's Memorial) were designed by women. One cannot assume, however, that memorials designed by women will be any more effective in challenging the representations of women in war and conflict. Indeed, women often have as great an investment in the representations of women in war as men do, at least in part because of the potential stigma associated with alternative representations.

Furthermore, in terms of being part of developing reparations policies, the role of women has largely been limited, such as in Timor-Leste where there was not a wide-ranging process of consultation in establishing the parameters of the reparations program.[117] There are, however, exceptions to the rule; for example, in Peru the development of the reparations policy following the truth commission was participatory and part of a national consultative process.[118] And, in fairness to the Timor-Leste process, though consultation in establishing the reparations program was limited, the commission did argue for consultation with victims groups during the implementation phase[119] – although the gender components of this consultation, though present, have

---

[115] Levinger, "Women and War Memorials in Israel."

[116] The main lobbying for the memorial came through a "ladies committee" formed by Mrs. Harriet Meyer. In his speech unveiling the memorial the mayor at the time noted: "The unveiling of this monument marks the completion of what has been an arduous undertaking on the part of those ladies with whom the idea of raising a monument to the horses originated." Quoted in the Eastern Province Herald, February, 1905 available at http://stgeorgespark.nmmu.ac.za/content/thepark/displayarticle.asp?artid=thepark_010.

[117] Galuh Wandita, Karen Campbell-Nelson, and Manuela Leong Pereira, "Learning to Engender Reparations in Timor-Leste: Reaching out to Female Victims," in *What Happened to the Women?*

[118] Guillerot, "Evaluating the Gender Content of Reparations."

[119] According to Wandita, Campbell-Nelson, and Leong Pereira, in "Learning to Engender Reparations in Timor-Leste," the CAVR omitted to mention specifically the consultation with women's victims' groups, but since the proposed programs specifically address women victims, their involvement in the further design of the program is logical.

Vietnam War Memorial, Washington, DC.

been criticized for being fairly minimal and not integrated throughout.[120] In fact, no major symbolic reparations process that has a gendered perspective has flowed from a truth commission to date.

INCREASING THE GENDERED IMPACT OF SYMBOLIC REPARATIONS

Having identified some of the difficulties with symbolic reparations, and symbolic reparations processes, this section highlights some steps that can be taken at a social and political level to potentially increase the impact of symbolic reparations on women victims of political violence, and on society more broadly. Elsewhere[121] it has been argued that all objects or acts of reparations have a symbolic meaning to individuals – they are never merely acts or objects. This symbolism *to individuals* operates at two levels:

1. Reparations generally symbolize something to individuals; that is, in form, quality, shape, or image they represent or indirectly express something abstract or invisible such as the memory of a loved one. Such acts

[120] Guillerot, "Evaluating the Gender Content of Reparations."
[121] Hamber, "Narrowing the Micro and Macro."

and objects can be profoundly meaningful to victims or survivors on a psychological level.

2. Reparations also represent or indirectly express something abstract or invisible to victims about those giving or granting the reparations; for example, an admission of guilt, benevolence, care for citizens by society, or a willingness to pay back what has been lost.[122]

However, when thinking about reparations from a feminist perspective, a third level needs to be added, that is, the degree to which symbolic reparations can either challenge or reinforce dominant gender discourses, social hierarchies, and gendered social representations. Given the gendered nature of social relationships, and the way women remain discriminated against and socially excluded in many post-conflict societies, it is important not just to seek reparations measures that have individual meaning and significance to individual female victims of political violence, but also to look for ways in which symbolic reparations can contribute, however minimally, to subverting gender hierarchies.

If we accept that, as Rubio-Marín argues, reparations are not only an "expression of recognition to the victims, an admission of past and/or future responsibility for certain type of conducts or omissions," but also "a symbolic expression of the deontological code of the new political order," then – and particularly from an activist-driven gender perspective – more is needed in terms shaping the new political order. Thus, a third level can be added and summarized.

3. Reparations *at a collective level* also represent or indirectly express how a society understands and represents gender relations; that is, the relationship between and roles of men and women; the place (public, private, political) of women in society; and the value and significance of women's social, political, and cultural contribution to society, and hence their potential to de/reconstruct gender roles, however minimally.

Each of the three levels is important, and the question is, how can a symbolic reparations program be designed, promoted, and implemented in a way that addresses all three levels from a more gendered perspective? In terms of the first, how does one create a reparations program that can, through the objects and acts that it gives or does, embody meaning and significance to individual female victims? The second level highlights the importance of the gendered messages conveyed by a reparations program to victims, particularly by the state or the community, and goes to the core of the question of the extent to which the notion of democracy requires that public authorities address

[122] Ibid.

women as full and equal citizens. The final level stresses the importance of the collective social (gendered) messages a reparations program conveys, more broadly speaking. In particular, it stresses how the program projects a more gender-balanced picture of social and political relations and the role of women within this picture, as well as how it shapes wider societal attitudes and behaviors toward women and relates to other processes to deliver gender justice.

The issues embodied in the three levels are addressed in the final two sections of the chapter. Before exploring these, however, it is important to note that the three levels can stand in tension with one another. For example, an individual act or object might convey meaning to a specific woman (say, acknowledging her role as a nurse in a conflict) but at the same time might serve to reinforce a gendered stereotype that, on its own, will not challenge representations of gender relations. Equally, however, it would not be accurate to ignore such experiences. As such, the challenge becomes how to represent and acknowledge multiple and complex roles over time.

1. *Embodying Individual Meaning and Significance*

In the design of massive reparations programs, greater attention can be paid to the nature and type of reparations offered and to their psychological meaning to women. Reparations encompassing both acts and objects have a greater likelihood of being considered meaningful, and of being of value to recipients, if they have a direct and personalized reference to the issue or form of suffering they are trying to deal with.[123] Reparations objects too need to embody a good mix of individual, political, and social symbolism. To this end, we need to ask: Do men and women require different forms of symbolic redress?[124]

One of the debates at the core of this issue, albeit a fairly old one, is between the idea of "living" and "dead" memorialization. Andrew Shanken dates this argument back to post-World War I and contends that there was a shift in North American public opinion between the two world wars about how to commemorate[125] – from considering more traditional, "dead" forms of memorials such as statues, obelisks, triumphal arches, and other commemorative structures, which are built essentially with a memorial purpose in mind, to the concept of "living" memorial.[126] Examples of the latter include useful projects

---

[123] Ibid. This work outlines in great deal why reparations work best symbolically if they have an individual and collective dimension.
[124] Rubio-Marín, "Gender and Reparations."
[125] Shanken, " Planning Memory."
[126] Ibid.

such as community centers, libraries, forests, peace gardens, and even roads and highways, normally marked with some form of plaque.[127] The result of this shift has been to permeate the symbolic reparations debate with recommendations for replacing large, purposeless granite objects with a focus on education, public sensitization, days of remembrance, museums, and apologies. Some truth commissions have recommended the establishment of a national war memorial (e.g., Sierra Leone), but most opt for more localized processes. In Timor-Leste, the development of popular literature, music, and art for remembrance was recommended.[128]

Broadly speaking, there seems to be a common perception that "traditional" forms of representation (that is, through large monuments) are the domain of men. Arguably, many memorialization processes appeal directly to some of the qualities associated with masculinity. As Lynn Lovdal notes, "The unwritten rules governing the traditional activities of men and women are sharply but subtly defined. Women's work has traditionally been repetitive and ongoing, and its end result short-lived and impermanent. In contrast, the activities of men are traditionally long-lived, durable, or permanent."[129] In this context, it is no wonder that men are more readily represented in monuments, and that memorials themselves are built very often (by men) with the idea of longevity, durability, and permanence in mind.

As early as 1945, articles can be found in popular magazines, including *Good Housekeeping*, arguing that women prefer "living" and practical forms of memorialization more than men.[130] More recently, others have argued that "traditional" forms of memorialization intersect with a masculine conceptualization of permanence and dominance,[131] and that some memorials designed by men are considered typically phallocentric.[132] It is hard to resist such psychoanalytic (perhaps bordering on pop psychological) perceptions of many imposing phallocentric monuments, such as the Washington Memorial or the statue to Yuri Gagarin at Ploshad Lenina in Moscow, a 70-meter-tall,

---

[127] Ibid.
[128] Wandita, Campbell-Nelson, and Leong Pereira, "Learning to Engender Reparations in Timor-Leste."
[129] "Monuments are for Men, Waffles are for Women: Gender, Permanence and Impermanence," film produced by Lynn Lovdal (USA, 2000). Quotation taken from website about the film, see http://www.berkeleymedia.com/catalog/berkeleymedia/films/american_studies/monuments_are_for_men_waffles_are_for_women_gender_permanence_and_impermanence.
[130] Shanken, "Planning Memory."
[131] "Monuments Are for Men, Waffles Are for Women." Quotation taken from website about the film.
[132] Referring to the Afrikaner National Women's Monument of 1913 in South Africa, which Cloete has called "the transcendental signifier of a phallocentric volks-metaphysic." Cited in Marschall, "Serving Male Agendas."

Yuri Gagarin Memorial in Moscow.

shining metal pillar topped with a robot-looking and muscular "Yuri" blasting into space.

Although somewhat essentialist, Esther Levinger feels that when it comes to designing memorials, women prefer more natural materials such as stone rather than concrete and steel, which she sees as a male preoccupation.[133] The case of the new National Women's Memorial in South Africa, unveiled at the Union Buildings in Pretoria in 2000, provides a good example. Entitled "Strike the Woman Strike the Rock – *Wathint' Abafazi Wathint' Imbokodo*," the memorial commemorates the 1956 women's march mentioned earlier in the chapter. The monument was established through a transparent and participative process in which women's groups were extensively consulted.[134]

[133] Levinger, "Women and War Memorials in Israel."
[134] Marschall, "Serving Male Agendas."

The winning design[135] (by a male architect and a female designer) focuses primarily on resistance and triumph over oppression but seeks to do this in a way that is not Eurocentric and appeals to the ordinariness of the actors involved.[136] The monument consists of a grinding stone, or *imbokodo*, placed in one of the vestibules of the Union Buildings and includes a soundtrack of the phrase "Strike the Woman Strike the Rock" being chanted over and over again in the 11 official languages of South Africa. The stone and audio track is meant to chime with the slogan of the march (as in the monument's title). On the whole, the monument is meant to be antiheroic, anti-elitist, accessible, and reflect an icon of African culture, that is, the maize grinding stone.[137]

Marschall, however, is highly critical of the monument. She questions how inclusive the imagery is; for example, the grinding stone represents only a sect of black-African (largely rural) culture and fails to recognize the modernization of many African women, and, in addition, it does not represent the true racial diversity of the march.[138] The problem with the above statements about women's preferences for particular types of monuments, then, according to this criticism, is that they do not account for the diversity among women. In addition, Marschall feels that "the monument ultimately strikes the unassuming viewer as overly academic, rational, dry and 'belabored' in its eagerness to be different."[139] She argues that in a context such as South Africa where "heroic" (largely male) memorialization is the order of the day, the new monument conveniently obliterates the need to commemorate women and their contributions elsewhere, and negates to a degree the extensive contribution of women in terms of political activism of many types.[140] Evidently, in a context where the wider society expects grander monuments, this one does not command attention and in fact is not even recognized by some passers-by as a monument, inviting in its unassuming nature "usage as an ashtray or rubbish bin."[141] In terms of physical access, it is interesting to note that the Women's

---

[135] Marschall also interestingly notes that most of the entries emphasized triumph over an adversary; she thinks these were reminiscent of the tradition of official socialist art, i.e., representations of the dynamic, heroic female – the generic superwoman. Cited in Marschall, "Serving Male Agendas."

[136] Ibid.

[137] Ibid. Marschall also compares the new Women's Monument to the old 1913 Afrikaner monument, noting that the new one is a female symbol, i.e., it is a receptacle and vaginal, whereas the old monument was an obelisk and essentially phallic.

[138] Ibid.

[139] Ibid.

[140] Ibid.

[141] Ibid, 1028.

Memorial is no longer accessible to the public and is behind the security of the Union Buildings.[142]

Clearly, Marschall would have preferred what she describes as a more democratic process of symbolizing the significance of the march. She points to an entry in the design competition by Andrew Lindsey, noting that he envisaged working with as many women as possible from rural and marginalized constituencies and asking them to interpret the event in any medium (including mosaic, poetry, and sculpture).[143] Thereafter, the best works would be installed in the park at the front of the Union Buildings,[144] the result of a more authentic and accessible process.

As Marschall acknowledges, the South African experiment does at least attempt to alter perceptions of how memorialization takes place. At the same time, it highlights the complexities of thinking about the nature and type of symbolic reparations that might flow from a massive reparations program. The issues of accessibility, capturing multiple voices, reflecting the complexity of roles during conflict, and including the most marginalized voices make any reparations process incredibly challenging. The South African effort also highlights the importance of thinking beyond representing the role of women (or men for that matter) in conflict in the stock bronze body in sculpture, which arguably can never adequately capture the complexity of the experience of conflict and its gendered nature. In addition, it highlights the importance of integrating symbolic measures with other activities more suited to representing complex histories, such as oral history and some museum-related practices. At the same time, however, it leaves one wondering whether abstract representation is sufficient, especially in contexts where large structure-driven or statue-rich memorialization is the order of the day. There is no easy resolution to this debate, and it indicates that, at a bare minimum, conceptualizing symbolic reparations requires rigorous public discussion and the involvement of victims themselves. It also requires a process of changing (feminizing the male form of) or shifting away from traditional memorialization practices toward new and alternative attempts such as the new South African Women's Memorial (despite its flaws).

This can apply to other forms of symbolic reparations too. For example, although it may be more contemporary to consider developing open, usable spaces as forms of symbolic reparations, such as community centers, parks,

---

[142] A visit to the memorial by one of the authors in April 2007 and the other in 2008 revealed that the monument is now inside the security zone around the building. The author was told that "national security clearance" was needed to visit the memorial.

[143] Marschall, "Serving Male Agendas."

[144] Ibid.

or forests, more traditional practices, such as changing street names, erecting memorials to individual women, or naming buildings after individual women victims or those who have contributed to peace, should not be completely dismissed. Although these may traditionally be "male" practices, women need to be represented in this way too if conventional gender practices are to be challenged within both old and new paradigms.

An integrated, multiple-axis gender analysis of symbolic reparations is needed, however. So although it may be necessary to develop new symbolic practice and transform traditional practice simultaneously, it may be as important to consider "who" leads the symbolic practice as what it consists of or where it takes place.[145] For example, reparations policy might result in streets being renamed or new public buildings, but if the unveiling of these is continually done by men in powerful positions, who in doing so continue to speak of women in a patronizing manner or to reinforce private/public divisions, this can undermine the gains made by the development of a more gendered approach to the granting of reparations. It may also be important regarding apologies to consider who is making the apologies and to whom they are directed. The symbolic weight, for example, of the former apartheid minister of law and order recently washing the feet of Reverend Frank Chikane[146] (director-general in the presidency who survived assassination attempts by the apartheid government), as an act of contrition, is significant. The symbolic power in this case comes from the direct relationship, albeit previously fraught, between the men; other symbolic markers are also important here, such as Vlok being white and Chikane being black. In the same vein, if Vlok had carried out his act of contrition with a black woman and perhaps someone not holding office, it would have been even more powerful, and certainly would have challenged dominant gender narratives. In spite of the power of this act, the recent decision by the National Prosecuting Authority to prosecute Vlok for his role in apartheid atrocities has been criticized by some members of the Afrikaans community who held that Chikane's forgiveness meant that Vlok should not be prosecuted.[147] On the opposite end of the spectrum, many black South Africans remain unconvinced by Vlok's actions and see it as a cynical move.[148]

Apologies from those not directly involved in atrocities can also be powerful. The most well-known cases are probably those of President Aylwin of Chile apologizing for the Pinochet regime and German Chancellor Willy Brandt's

---

[145] See Rubio-Marín, "Gender and Reparations."
[146] "Feet Washed in Apartheid Apology," *BBC Website*, August 28, 2006.
[147] "I forgive but I can't protect Vlok," *Independent Online*, 9 August 2007.
[148] Qwelane, John, "Vlok Apology Means Nothing," *News 24*, September 4, 2006.

kneeling at a death camp in Poland. Both had the effect of dissociating the state from previous atrocities while acknowledging continuity and the need to address the past in the present, even if those delivering the apologies themselves were not responsible for the atrocities.[149] Considering the power of such acts through a gendered lens (e.g., a powerful man apologizing to women for atrocities) offers a new insight into the potential power of symbolic reparations, not only for what they might mean to victims themselves, but also how they might challenge gendered narratives.

2. Reconnecting Women Victims with Society and the State

The issue of recognition of suffering cannot be underestimated when trying to understand how victims interpret or react to reparations. Reparations are laden with value judgments for victims. For many victims of direct political violence, it is the denial of their victim status, the social and political silence about their victimization, or the untruths told through official sources about the reason for their victimization that are most difficult to bear. From their perspective, these are often the fundamental injustices they wish to see set right, at least to some degree, through symbolic reparations.

In terms of the second level of symbolism discussed earlier, that is, what the granting of reparations represents to victims about those giving or granting them, a few points are also worth making. First, the establishment of a massive reparations program can represent to victims a societal or community willingness to both deal and part with the past. This can assist victims to feel a greater level of integration, recognition, and acceptance into society. Reparations, writes Roht-Arriaza, are the embodiment of society's recognition, remorse, and atonement of harms inflicted.[150] At the same time, they can combat feelings of isolation and silence, both common consequences of political violence. In Guatemala, for example, it has been argued that apologies from a range of groupings, including the state and military, are essential to combating the stigmatization, isolation, and shaming suffered by Guatemalan women who were raped during the civil war.[151] It is also possible that reparations can lead, at the individual level, to greater feelings of recognition by the state and increased levels of civic trust.[152] If victims feel their hurt is recognized and adequately acknowledged, it is completely plausible that this will contribute to a sense of citizenship and social belonging for the recipients. At a minimum,

---

[149] Michael Ignatieff, "Articles of Faith," *Index on Censorship* 25, no. 5 (1996).
[150] Roht-Arriaza, "Reparations Decisions and Dilemmas."
[151] Paz y Paz Bailey, "Guatemala: Gender and Reparations for Human Rights Violations."
[152] de Greiff, "Justice and Reparations."

victims should perceive the seriousness of the effort.[153] This can be vital in terms of healing insofar as reconnecting an individual with her society is a crucial dimension of dealing with trauma.[154]

But genuine reparation and the process of healing – and reconnecting women victims with their society and state – do not occur only or mainly through the delivery of an object or an act of reparation, but also through the process that takes place around the object or act.[155] The task, then, is to create an environment conducive to this process unfolding in such a way that the dilemmas that arise when making reparations are verbalized, dealt with, and appreciated as important components of any massive reparations program. Three main factors surrounding delivery need to be given as much attention as debates about what will ultimately be delivered.[156] These concern (a) the process that surrounds the granting of reparations, (b) the messages conveyed by the program to individuals, and (c) how the program fits within a broader social context, in this case how it relates to wider attempts to deliver gender justice. These factors are examined next.

(a) Process

In order for reparations to have a powerful impact, an adequate context needs to be fostered. Such an environment would be one where the attempts to address the needs of those harmed are acted on in a timely fashion, and reparations are in some objective sense considered to be substantial relative to other social priorities (not to mention the program being internally and externally coherent, as Pablo de Greiff suggests[157]). An important part of this context is the reparations process itself. Although in some objective sense adequate acts of reparations may have taken place in a society, the process by which they were granted may have been unsatisfactory to many of those concerned. Conversely, although reparations may be interpreted as being insufficient at the individual level, the process of granting reparations can be a mediating variable.

It is helpful here to refer back to Marschall's criticisms of the new South African Women's Monument. Her conclusions are instructive: it would have been better to let people affected by the conflict construct symbolic reparations

---

[153] Rubio-Marín, "Gender and Reparations."
[154] Becker, "Dealing with the Consequences of Organized Violence"; Lykes and Mersky, "Reparations and Mental Health."
[155] Hamber, "Narrowing the Micro and Macro."
[156] Ibid.
[157] de Greiff, "Justice and Reparations."

themselves rather than commission an artist to render them. On the whole, if victims are part of the process of creating the meaning and symbolism of an object such as a memorial or influencing the text of an apology (as in the case of the "comfort women"), and the symbol relates personally to them and their suffering,[158] it is more likely to have increased "inner" significance to them.[159] This is certainly true with rituals, for example, especially those carried out by local communities after the location of the bodies of the "disappeared."[160] The ability of symbolic measures to speak to the individual and link with the collective is a vital issue to consider in designing massive reparations programs – doubly significant if one considers the fact that women are generally marginalized from such processes.

In addition, since activities carried out by women are often rendered private, part of the reparations process might be to bring these into the public sphere and give them new political significance. A good example of this would be the Aids Quilt, which turns the private (largely female) activity of sewing into a public political statement. A conflict-related example, which uses the same principle, is the quilt produced by the Association Kuyanakuy, a group of women from Ayachuco in Peru. This quilt depicts community life before and after the political conflict, and the women used it as their "testimony" to the Peruvian truth commission, first presenting it in private on May 1, 2002. In June of that year they then displayed the quilt as part of a 24-hour vigil outside the Court of Justice, demanding truth and accountability.[161] It is also interesting to note that this quilt, unlike the Aids Quilt, displays community life rather than individual squares, perhaps highlighting the more community-orientated perception of life in rural Peru.

Individual and culturally appropriate commemoration may be best served when women themselves construct reparative symbols or processes, as

---

[158] Elsewhere it has been argued that symbolic processes that have the ability to have highly individual components while being part of a collective work best, such as the Aids Quilt; for a detailed discussion on this see Hamber, "Narrowing the Micro and Macro."

[159] This is not always the case, as sometimes memorials can in themselves take on significance after they have been created, despite opposition during the process of their development. The Vietnam War Memorial in Washington, DC, is a case in point. Many veterans and members of the public were opposed to Maya Lin's proposed design, but once the memorial was built "the debate about aesthetics and remembrance surrounding its design simply disappeared.... The experience of viewing Lin's work was so powerful for the general public that criticism of its design vanished." Cited in Jenny Edkins, *Trauma and the Memory of Politics* (New York: Cambridge University Press, 2003).

[160] See, for example, Shari Eppel, "Healing the Dead: Exhumation and Reburial as Truth-Telling and Peace-Building Activities in Rural Zimbabwe," in *Telling the Truths*.

[161] The quilt was recently displayed at the West Belfast Festival 2006 on loan from Gaby Franger and Rainer Huhle; see http://www.menschenrechte.org/. Our thanks to Roberta Bacic for also informing us of this process.

Marschall suggests. But, in order for reparations to be effective, they generally also have to be official and linked with guarantees of nonrepetition. The state needs to have a hand in their creation (to a limited degree) if reparations, as Sharon Lean argues, are to demonstrate that state's interest in, and acceptance of responsibility for, the well-being of its citizens.[162] In the Peruvian example above, this might mean the state reacting to the women's quilt "testimony" by addressing questions of truth or providing additional reparations concerning land.

In the final instance, it may be the process of developing symbolic reparations, and the inclusion of those affected in shaping its content, that will determine a program's success, at least to those directly concerned. If symbolic reparations are delivered, the individual generally (but not always) needs to feel that her suffering, or her relative's suffering, is adequately reflected in these measures. Adequate reparations, symbolic or otherwise, cannot be guaranteed without the adequate participation and public involvement of key stakeholders in their development and conceptualization. Victims and their organizations need to be part of this process, but so too do the larger community[163] and the state.

(b) Discourse

Symbolic reparation measures are primarily about the recognition of suffering. The language that surrounds the development and delivery of reparations has an important symbolic component and can be one of the primary vehicles for conveying how the suffering of recipients is understood and recognized by the state and society more broadly.[164] This can happen in two ways: first through how recognition is conveyed by the symbolic actions of others; and second, through what is publicly said about the different types of symbolic reparations.

In terms of thinking about the symbolic value of the actions of others, apologies are probably the most common form of symbolic reparations. Space does not permit a detailed discussion of the symbolic value of apologies,[165] but it is

---

[162] Sharon Lean, "Is Truth Enough? Reparations and Reconciliation in Latin America," in *Politics and the Past*.
[163] Roht-Arriaza, "Reparations Decisions and Dilemmas."
[164] Hamber, "Narrowing the Micro and Macro."
[165] See, amongst others, Hilary K. Josephs, "The Remedy of Apology in Comparative and International Law: Self-Healing and Reconciliation," *Emory International Law Review* 18 (2004); Nicolas Tavuchis, *Mea Culpa: A Sociology of Apology and Reconciliation* (Stanford, CA: Stanford University Press, 1991); Hiroshi Wagatsuma and Arthur Rosett, "The Implications of Apology: Law and Culture in Japan and the United States," *Law and Society Review* 20, no. 4 (1986). See also Trudy Govier and Wilhelm Verwoerd, "Taking Wrongs Seriously: A Qualified

striking that currently there is no research that focuses directly on the gendered nature of giving and accepting apologies, that is, what the importance of apology is to women, and whether factors such as where, how, and by whom the apology is made impact on its reparative value for women. Some have argued that women are more likely than men to offer apologies in the workplace,[166] but a genuine study of the gender politics of apology at a macropolitical level, and following political transition, remains to be done. Before looking at the issue of apology, however, it is important to note that there are other symbolic actions that can form part of the repertoire of symbolic reparations.

For example, it was noted earlier that in Sierra Leone and Bosnia the ostracism of women who were raped in war is commonplace. Such situations require a social response first and foremost (e.g., support groups, working with local communities, carrying out local rituals of integration), but they could, arguably, benefit from other "symbolic" actions. To this end, the role of influential political and social figures in recognizing ostracism, breaking silences about it, and challenging it by educating people about its impact, apologizing for it, or by example (e.g., a prominent figure talking about how a loved one was raped and has been accepted back into the family) cannot be underestimated.

At the more active level in terms of symbolic reparations, the society too needs to be seen to help create the social space in which victims of crimes such as rape are allowed to commemorate. For example, in Bosnia, Muslim women raped in a sports center used by Bosnian Serb soldiers in Foca in 1992 wanted to put a plaque outside to remember the atrocities and victims. The power of this sort of symbolism is evidenced by the fact that the Women Victims of War Association, which wanted to erect the plaque, was driven away by members of the Serb Republic's Association of Wartime Camp Inmates, who objected because they were not allowed to erect similar memorial signs in Sarajevo or Tuzla.[167] Intervening at a governmental level to facilitate a resolution to

Defence of Public Apology," *Saskatchewan Law Review* 65, no. Winter (2002); Trudy Govier and Wilhelm Verwoerd, "The Promise and Pitfalls of Apology," *Journal of Social Philosophy* 33, no. 1 (2002); Paul Davis, "On Apologies," *Journal of Applied Philosophy* 19, no. 2 (2002); Nicolaus Mills, "The New Culture of Apology," *Dissent*, no. 113–116 (Fall 2001); Kathleen Gill, "The Moral Functions of an Apology," *Philosophical Forum* 31, no. 1 (2000); Aaron Lazare, "Go Ahead, Say You're Sorry," *Psychology Today* 28, no. 1 (1995); Jana Thompson, "The Apology Paradox," *Philosophical Quarterly* 55, no. 201 (2000); Jean Harvey, "The Emerging Practice of Institutional Apologies," *The International Journal of Applied Philosophy* 9, no. 2 (1995); Aviva Orenstein, "Apology Expected: Incorporating a Feminist Analysis into Evidence Policy Where You Would Least Expect It," *Southwestern University Law Review* 28 (1999).

[166] Deborah Tannen, *Talking from 9 to 5: Women and Men at Work* (New York: Harper, 1995).
[167] "Bosnian Serbs Reject Rape Plaque" BBC, October 1, 2004 (cited May 5, 2006), http://news.bbc.co.uk/2/hi/europe/3706554.stm.

such conflicts, publicly acknowledging the wrongs committed, and ensuring that such victims are given public space is vital. Again, a core function of such actions is to render what is considered "private" into the public and acknowledging its political and social significance.

Opening up social space to discuss the violations of the past can be made easier when there is some recognition of the importance of doing so by reparations programs and truth commissions. The Peruvian truth commission's recommendations on reparations are helpful here. Although none of its proposed reparation measures are exclusively designed for women, and especially victims of rape, the commission makes recommendations focused on the importance of public gestures.[168] Its report says that all public gestures should "devote significant time to explain the facts and abuses that occurred in homes or communities, at army barracks or prisons, which were a direct outrage against the sexuality, honor and dignity of women."[169]

In terms of thinking about symbolic reparations from the perspective of what is publicly said and how such discourse can influence the impact of reparations on victims, the case of the so-called "comfort women"[170] is illustrative. Between September 1972 and August 2005, we have identified 40 official apologies by the Japanese government, either as statements, letters between officials or to victims, or part of official speeches. Most of these deal with acts of aggression by the Japanese military and focus particularly on the treatment of the citizens of other Asian countries in World War II, such as China and the Republic of Korea, and the atrocities then committed. Some focus on the treatment of prisoners of war. Eight of the forty apologies identified focus on the "comfort women" and were issued between 1992 and 2001.

On the surface this could be considered a fairly high percentage of the official apologies, if you consider the vast number of atrocities and acts of aggression committed by the Japanese during World War II. However, on closer inspection, we note that the apologies very seldom mention the exact

---

[168] Guillerot, "Evaluating the Gender Content of Reparations."
[169] CVR, *Final Report of the Truth and Reconciliation Commission*, vol. IX, 169, cited in ibid.
[170] "Comfort women" is "the Japanese euphemism, *jugun ianfu* (military comfort women), categorically refers to women of various ethnic and national backgrounds and social circumstances who became sexual laborers for the Japanese troops before and during the Second World War. Countless women had to labor as comfort women in the military brothels found throughout the vast Asia Pacific region occupied by the Japanese forces. There is no way to determine precisely how many women were forced to serve as comfort women. The estimate ranges between 80,000 and 200,000, about 80% of whom, it is believed, were Korean. Japanese women and women of other occupied territories (such as Taiwan, the Philippines, Indonesia, Burma and the Pacific islands) were also used as comfort women." Cited in Chunghee Sarah Soh, The Comfort Women Project website, http://online.sfsu.edu/~soh/comfortwomen.html.

nature of the violations committed against the women forced to work as sex slaves in military brothels across a number of Japanese-occupied territories. In fact, the statements in their anodyne content partly reinforce the euphemism of "comfort women."

Clearly, on reading the apologies, there is a substantial attempt to show remorse. The issue is spoken about in several of the apologies as "seriously heartbreaking" and "entirely inexcusable," and it is acknowledged that women "suffered indescribable hardship," "immeasurable pain," and "unbearable suffering and sorrow" as a result of being sexual slaves to Japanese troops. The apologies themselves are said to be "sincere" and "heartfelt." However, throughout the decade in which various statements and apologies were made, there is remarkable consistency of language. For example, several stressed the issue of honor and dignity:

> "... that severely injured the honor and dignity of many women"
> (Chief Cabinet Secretary Yohei Kono, August 4, 1993);

> "... seriously stained the honor and dignity of many women"
> (Prime Minister Tomiichi Murayama, August 31, 1994);

> "[quoting a comfort woman] ... nothing injured the honor and dignity of women more than this"
> (Prime Minister Ryutaro Hashimoto, June 23, 1996);

> "... a grave affront to the honor and dignity of large numbers of women"
> (Prime Minister Ryutaro Hashimoto, July 15, 1998).

And several made references to the psychological and physical damage to women in a fairly standard way:

> "... who suffered immeasurable pain and incurable physical and psychological wounds"
> (Chief Cabinet Secretary Yohei Kono, August 4, 1993);

> "... underwent immeasurable and painful experiences and suffered incurable physical and psychological wounds as comfort women"
> (Prime Minister Ryutaro Hashimoto, July 15, 1998);

> "... women who underwent immeasurable and painful experiences and suffered incurable physical and psychological wounds as comfort women 2001"
> (Prime Minister Junichiro Koizumi, 2001).

The consistency of the language highlights two issues. First, the issue of "honor and dignity," which comes up routinely, may well be consistent with the demands of the women to have their dignity "repaired," which might have significant cultural resonance. What is interesting in the apologies, however, is the marked absence of providing detail about the atrocities and of naming such violations for what they were, that is, sexual slavery and rape, which beyond harming women's dignity presumably also undermined their health and psychological well-being. In this sense, the apologies are to a degree acontextual and generic; that is, by not talking about what happened specifically (or at least naming it as sexual slavery), because presumably it is "shameful," the lives of women affected are rendered shameful too. Drawing on the Peruvian truth commission recommendation outlined earlier, we can say that the apologies certainly do not, as public gestures, devote significant time to explaining the facts and abuses that occurred.[171] At a deeper level, this raises a further problem, namely, that harm (i.e., against honor and dignity) is measured relative to a definition of the worth of women that is contingent on their virginity, sexual availability, sexual purity, and so forth. What this suggests is that it is the underlying systems of meaning in which violations are explored, and not just the ways in which such violations are explained, that should be challenged.

Second, the consistency of language suggests an official government line and position on the issue, which is probably linked with the various legal concerns raised around compensation. This belies a wider issue, that is, whether the Japanese government should pay compensation directly. Compensation has been offered through the Asian Women's Fund, a private institution, which has, despite the apologies, failed to satisfy the demands of many "comfort women."[172] The Japanese government set up the Fund with the intention of raising funds (from donations) to improve the conditions of all women, rather than pay individual reparation.[173] Some have criticized the system for being a welfare approach that fails to recognize the moral issues at stake and allows the government to continue to avoid taking responsibility,[174] further highlighting the tension between individual and collective forms of reparation. What is needed, it is argued, is "not redress in the form of reparations; atonement

---

[171] Of course, the statement made by the Peruvian commission cannot simply be assumed as relevant in all cultures. This point should not be read as implying that all details of the events should be made public in a gratuitous way, but rather that a culturally relevant approach should be developed that moves beyond the acontextual and the generic, as the rest of this section argues.

[172] John Torpey, "Introduction: Politics of the Past," in *Politics and the Past*.

[173] Stef Vandeginste, "Reparation," in *Reconciliation after Violent Conflict: A Handbook*, ed. David Bloomfield, Teresa Barnes, and Luc Huyse (Stockholm, Sweden: International Institute for Democracy and Electoral Assistance, 2003).

[174] Ibid.

can only be achieved through money paid by the government in the form of personal compensation, along with a formal apology from the Diet."[175] This is presumably important to the women because they see the state, and the Diet (Japan's legislature) in particular, as previously condoning the violations committed against them. The legislature itself, as the embodiment of the nation, thus needs to make corporate amends to build "civic trust." Again, as discussed earlier, the women want to be individually recognized through individual apology letters at the same time as collective action takes place.

An official apology was issued and now accompanies the compensation from the Asian Women's Fund. But, again, closer analysis is revealing. C. Sarah Soh carried out an examination of the official letter of apology[176] and concludes that although the letter mentions "honor and dignity" and "remorse," it fails to reference the war of aggression or colonial domination,[177] again highlighting its acontextual nature. She also notes that activists for state compensation also found fault with the phrase "my personal feelings" in the prime minister's original letter, as it could convey individual rather than corporate or state responsibility.[178] From 1998 onward, after Keizo Obuchi replaced Hashimoto as prime minister, the term "personal" was taken out.[179] On the positive side, Sarah Soh also notes that Obuchi's letter contains the word *sajoe* in the official Korean translation, which implies admission of a crime, rather than just a mistake.

This example raises the issue of what sort of apologies work and, more specifically, the importance of who does the apology and what this conveys

---

[175] Roy Brooks, *When Sorry Isn't Enough: The Controversy over Apologies and Reparations for Human Injustice* (New York: New York University Press, 1999), 89, cited in Vandeginste, "Reparation," 40–41.

[176] Letter from Prime Minister to the former comfort women, since 1996: "Dear Madam, On the occasion that the Asian Women's Fund, in cooperation with the Government and the people of Japan, offers atonement from the Japanese people to the former wartime comfort women, I wish to express my feelings as well. The issue of comfort women, with an involvement of the Japanese military authorities at that time, was a grave affront to the honor and dignity of large numbers of women. As Prime Minister of Japan, I thus extend anew my most sincere apologies and remorse to all the women who underwent immeasurable and painful experiences and suffered incurable physical and psychological wounds as comfort women. We must not evade the weight of the past, nor should we evade our responsibilities for the future. I believe that our country, painfully aware of its moral responsibilities, with feelings of apology and remorse, should face up squarely to its past history and accurately convey it to future generations. Furthermore, Japan also should take an active part in dealing with violence and other forms of injustice to the honor and dignity of women. Finally, I pray from the bottom of my heart that each of you will find peace for the rest of your lives. Respectfully yours, Ryutaro Hashimoto, Prime Minister of Japan" (Subsequent prime ministers who signed the letter are: Keizo Obuchi, Yoshiro Mori, and Junichiro Koizumi.).

[177] Soh, "Japan's Responsibility toward Comfort Women Survivors."

[178] Ibid.

[179] Ibid.

both about the apology itself and about how the harm is conceived. The issue is vitally important when it comes to questions of sexual violence, which in order to be moved away from the "private" and "apolitical" must be public and official. Michael Ziesing argues that a strong apology is appropriate only in the context of responsibility and intentionality.[180] Hiroshi Wagatsuma and Arthur Rosett[181] argue that a "meaningful apology" must acknowledge that: "(1) the hurtful act happened, caused injury, and was wrongful; (2) the apologizer was at fault and regrets participating in the act; (3) the apologizer will compensate the injured party; (4) the act will not happen again; and (5) the apologizer intends to work for good relations in the future."[182] Applying these five points to the "comfort women" case, it is primarily the third one concerning compensation that undermines the many apologies made to date. There were also, however, concerns about the way the apology was made and the degree to which the state, along with the direct perpetrators, was at fault.

The same framework can be applied to other apologies, although those directed at women are few and far between. But take, for example, Pope John II's apology to women: "Women's dignity has often been unacknowledged and their prerogatives misrepresented; they have often been relegated to the margins of society and even reduced to servitude.... And if objective blame, especially in particular historical contexts, has belonged to not just a few members of the Church, for this I am truly sorry. May this regret be transformed, on the part of the whole Church, into a renewed commitment of fidelity to the Gospel vision. When it comes to setting women free from every kind of exploitation and domination..."[183] Again, issues concerning compensation are not present (although whether they should be attached to such a broad apology is arguable), but, more importantly in this case, given the continued exclusion of women in the Catholic Church, the idea of "the act" not happening again feels misdirected and improbable.

---

[180] Michael Ziesing, "I'm Sorry: A Cross-Cultural Exploration of Apologizing," *PASAA* 30 (December 2000), also available at http://www.ajarnmichael.com/ImSorry.html.

[181] Wagatsuma and Rosett, "The Implications of Apology."

[182] This is similar to what Ziesing believes makes a good apology: "(1) a willingness to accept the negative consequences of the deed; (2) a desire to make reparations of some kind; (3) an admission of weakness of some kind: egotism, sinfulness or something of that nature; and (4) humility in the face of such weakness, such that one may, for example, 'beg for' forgiveness." Cited in Ziesing, "I'm Sorry." In terms of the "comfort women," the question of appropriate reparations, or at least who they come from (in this case the desire is to get reparations directly from government), is one of the factors undermining the apology. It is also interesting to consider the last two of Ziesing's points more broadly. They are perhaps most tied to questions concerning negative masculinity, i.e., lack of humility, egotism, etc., which could constrain the "ability" of many men to make such apologies.

[183] Letter of John Paul II to Women, June 29, 1995. Available at www.vatican.va/holy_father/john_paul_ii/letters/documents/hf_jp-ii_let_29061995_women_en.html.

Of course, apologies are not a "magic bullet" for solving all issues.[184] And a gendered analysis of apology, as mentioned earlier, still needs to be done. Furthermore, some question whether apologies at the individual level work the same at the collective level[185] because an "authentic apology cannot be delegated, consigned, exacted, or assumed by the principals, without totally altering its meaning and vitiating moral force."[186] That said, however, they can have a powerful role in symbolic reparations processes (the "comfort women" campaign started with a demand for an apology). They are also useful in distinguishing a settlement from a genuine attempt at reparation,[187] with the latter normally being accompanied by an apology.[188] Apologies are important both in terms of their relationship to other more material processes (in this case compensation), but, as has been emphasized here, they also highlight the symbolic value of the actual words used. These are both factors that would need to be considered if apologies – or any other measure that includes public gestures and statements – were to form part of a wider symbolic reparations process.

(c) Context

Any reparations process, symbolic or otherwise, is delivered and mediated through a political and social context. This context can be one characterized by extreme economic and social deprivation, which means that symbolic reparations need to be linked with concrete social change. According to a study of reparations in several African countries,

> What they [victims of abuse] want and demand, in their majority, is very concrete: recognition of their suffering through reparations, as replacement of personal material losses, as local infra-structural improvements, or as acknowledgement of guilt by the perpetrators where reparation by replacement is not possible, as in the case of murdered relatives – ideally all this in combination. If public memorialization – national days of remembrance, shrines, monuments, etc. – does not take place against such a background, it is declared a sham, inadequate, and not suited to lead toward reconciliation. In other words, it is the *context* of memorialization that determines whether it is a genuine undertaking.[189]

[184] Wagatsuma and Rosett, "The Implications of Apology."
[185] Torpey, "Introduction: Politics of the Past."
[186] Ibid., 23.
[187] See Hamber, "Narrowing the Micro and Macro," for a discussion of the difference between reparations (plural) and the aim of reparations, i.e., to attempt to achieve reparation (singular).
[188] Brooks, "Reflections on Reparations."
[189] Southern African Reconciliation Project and Centre for the Study of Violence and Reconciliation, "Memorialisation and Reconciliation in Transitional Southern African Societies."

In Peru it has been found that demands for reparations are also fairly concrete and material, with women's particular demands including measures related to their own physical or mental health, their children's education, jobs for themselves and their children, and compensation.[190]

Structural inequality and ongoing oppression are two of the most destructive factors that undermine a conducive context for granting reparations.[191] Symbolic reparations need to be keyed into and part of socioeconomic change processes, as well as a broader, multifaceted approach to post-conflict justice and social reconstruction.[192] If, for example, symbolic reparations stand in isolation to other processes that deliver truth and justice, they can appear hollow and as an attempt to silence historical grievances rather than address them. Furthermore, the complex interplay between past conflict-related violence and violence perpetuated against women in societies coming out of political violence is an additional element of the context of symbolic reparations. A debate exists as to whether so-called political violence is "on a continuum" with the nature of everyday violence against women in posttransition periods.[193] The implications of this are beyond the scope of this chapter, but, nevertheless, ongoing violence against women can be a factor that undermines the conducive environment in which reparations, symbolic or otherwise, might be granted.

The symbolic power of various reparations processes, then, can be fully realized only if at the same time gender justice, the prevention of violence against women, and material change in women's lives are being effected. To this end, it is useful to consider guarantees of nonrepetition and institutional reform, which are vital to creating a context conducive to the granting of symbolic reparations, as well as the practical link between symbolic processes and real social change.

One way of achieving this symbolic and material change might be to develop symbols that have a functional impact, such as schools, libraries, or community centers. However, it is not enough to simply develop symbolic reparations that have a functional purpose and are grounded in consultation and participation. If we take context seriously, we also have to ask how this would work in a context where patriarchy and discrimination against women continues. Earlier in this chapter, reference was made to a case where Bosnian women were prevented from installing a plaque to remember the violations committed against them. Even if this plaque had been erected, however, we have to ask what it means to remember victims, and particularly rape victims in this case, within a

---

[190] Guillerot, "Evaluating the Gender Content of Reparations."
[191] Hamber, "Narrowing the Micro and Macro."
[192] Roht-Arriaza, "Reparations Decisions and Dilemmas."
[193] See Walker, "Gender and Violence in Focus."

context where negative views about such victims continue to exist. In this sense, and if one takes the quest for gender justice seriously, a memorial or remembrance day to rape victims is not enough – such measures also need to challenge or be accompanied by processes that challenge dominant discourses. Memorializing acontextually can perpetuate misperceptions, leave dominant gendered narratives untouched, or even potentially ghettoize victims further. If such measures flow from reparations programs, they need to be linked with other processes such as education campaigns, advocacy, museum education, and school programs. At a broad level, this means linking symbolic measures to institutional reform processes, which not only affects change, but also allows victims to feel that their suffering is an engine for change.[194]

CONCLUSIONS AND POLICY RECOMMENDATIONS

There is a growing propensity for truth commissions to incorporate a gender dimension into their reparations recommendations.[195] That said, there is a long way to go, and symbolic reparations are probably one of the least developed areas of reparations processes, especially when it comes to thinking about the gender dimensions thereof. Very few, if any, reparations processes to date flowing from a truth commission have integrated a gendered perspective into the symbolic reparations recommended. To genuinely attempt to do this would be, as this chapter has shown, a complex endeavor. This is partly because the representation of women during and after conflict and war is generally seen as domestically rooted, and their activities as politically disengaged. The inevitable result is that women's complex and varied engagement with war, as well as their support of and resistance to it, not to mention the range of identities prescribed by it, are written out of society's transition from dictatorial regime or from conflict or war.[196] For example, women writers have been quick to notice that in times of armed conflict women have often moved out of their traditional gender roles. Meredith Turshen notes how women who previously led almost no public life have become community leaders, activists, and economic providers.[197] Similarly, Tovi Fenster observes how Ethiopian women, integrated into Israeli society, made far more rapid advances in employment than had been initially planned for,[198] a development that

---

[194] Rubio-Marín, "Gender and Reparations."
[195] See *What Happened to the Women?*
[196] Ryan, "Drunken Tans."
[197] See *What Women Do in Wartime.*
[198] Tovi Fenster, "Ethnicity, Citizenship, Planning and Gender: The Case of Ethiopian Immigrant Women in Israel," *Gender Place and Culture* 5, no. 2 (1998).

tested the patriarchal form of the family as increasingly unemployed men retreated into the private sphere and increasingly economically active women took up roles in the public sphere. And while some feminist writing has tried to rewrite women into wartime representations,[199] there has, however, been less focus on the post-conflict period.

We should not automatically celebrate the effects of armed conflict as disorganizing patriarchal social relations. In many instances,[200] women's involvement in the public sphere has been temporary and is often met with increasingly repressive ideologies issuing severe penalties once war is officially over. Indeed, one of the primary functions of some post-war reconstruction efforts may be to return to a previously gendered lifestyle.[201] In many cases, women have also argued for reinforcing their role in the private sphere.[202]

The process of thinking about symbolic reparations and their delivery as mechanisms to remember victims and suffering generally takes place within

[199] For example, Cock, "Manpower and Militarisation," notes how, in the South African war, many "white" women actively contributed to the militarization of South African society through support organizations and the provision of material and ideological backing for the soldiers in the South African Defence Force. In addition, they were active in commando units in rural areas and were trained in the "civil defence program" – a process that required both a restructuring and expansion of traditional notions of femininity. Similarly, Margaret Ward considers the role that Northern Irish women played in the conflict and how the very nature of the violence, which was fought at a community level, challenged the carefully drawn lines between military and civilian. Margaret Ward, *In Their Own Voice: Women and Irish Nationalism* (Dublin: Attic, 1995), cited in Ryan, "Drunken Tans." These two interventions produce different readings of women's activities through local contexts and indicate the diverse ways in which women engage with armed conflict at different political moments.

[200] Denise Riley, *Am I That Name? Feminism and the Category 'Women' in History* (Basingstoke: Macmillan, 1988).

[201] This is evident in the South African "moral regeneration" program, which focuses very centrally on the "reconstruction" of the family. The (then) deputy president Jacob Zuma, who led the campaign, stated in his address at the moral regeneration movement rally in 2002, "Almost all breakaway groups in the Moral Regeneration Summit in Pretoria stressed the importance of strengthening the institution of the family; which is a cornerstone in the foundation of our communities and the whole of society. We need to commit ourselves to working harder to build stronger family units." The interests that this moral regeneration serves and the nature of the (pre-war) family that is being invoked clearly need to be critically assessed for their potential to disadvantage women. Cited in Jacob Zuma, "Address to the Moral Regeneration Movement Rally," paper presented at the Moral Regeneration Summit, Pretoria, 2002.

[202] Cock, *Women and War in South Africa*, notes that in South Africa the damage done to African families by apartheid, especially by the migrant labor system, resulted in both men and women mobilizing in defense of a very conservative notion of the family. Similarly, "black" African women's mobilization against the extension of the pass laws to women was largely framed in terms of the impact it would have on their roles as mothers and wives; see, for example, Elizabeth Schmidt, "Now You Have Touched the Women: African Women's Resistance to the Pass Laws in South Africa 1950–1960," *Kalamu: The Pen of African History Magazine* (1983). This highlights the importance of understanding intersections of gender and "race" in the postcolonial context.

this context. Michael Humphrey writes that "legacies of war persist in private memory as trauma, physical scars and gross bodily deformities, and are selectively turned into collective memories through commemoration in war memorials, war memoirs, literature, family biography and archived testimony,"[203] but at the same time he notes that the process of remembering is (as are symbolic reparations processes to date) highly selective. To be commemorated, injury and suffering experienced by the victim, he argues,[204] need to be seen as blameless. On the flipside, to be remembered as someone who contributed to change, one's action typically has to be seen as courageous and heroic. This polemic is deeply gendered, as we have argued. The depoliticization of women's engagements with the conflict, and the drive to keep the public and private spheres separate, means that remembering women – and conceptualizing and implementing symbolic reparations – is about remembering in a contested and reified space. The role of symbolic reparations in this space cannot be underestimated because symbols themselves are key to the way gender is constructed. To this end, great care needs to be taken to ensure that symbolic reparations measures do not reinforce existing patriarchal social relations and damaging gendered narratives. This is a challenge, as this chapter has shown, but it also offers significant opportunities for representing and remembering war and conflict, and their gendered nature, differently.

To this end, some broad policy conclusions and principles, extracted from the chapter, are worth considering in the development of a symbolic reparations program:

1. A balance is needed between offering material and symbolic processes of addressing the legacy of violence. Consideration should be given to how these might work in tandem with each other or be integrated. Symbolic reparations are only *one* of the components of a massive reparations program. The symbolic power of various reparations processes can be fully realized only if gender discrimination, gender justice, the prevention of violence against women, and material change in women's lives are being effected simultaneously. Questions of truth, justice, and guarantees of nonrepetition for past violations are also integral to this.
2. Drawing on the Peruvian truth commission's recommendations, all public gestures such as apologies, unveiling of monuments, speeches concerning redress, public commemorations, museum displays, the way days of commemoration or remembrance might be framed, and the like, should devote significant time to explaining the facts and abuses

[203] Humphrey, *The Politics of Atrocity and Reconciliation*.
[204] Ibid.

that occurred across society and that affected women specifically, and how this manifests both privately and publicly. The socioeconomic, political, and structural factors contributing to such facts and abuses in the past and present should be explained. This means that narratives of conflict should be retold, reexamined, and challenged for the ways in which women and gender are neglected, (selectively) remembered, and represented. Sufficiently complex and rich notions of masculinity and femininity should be incorporated into all symbolic reparations processes.

3. It should be recognized that some symbolic reparations offer a unique opportunity to produce complex narratives because, unlike legal questions concerning, say, compensation where more clear delineations are needed between victims and perpetrators, symbolic measures, such as memorials, apologies, public acknowledgments, or museum projects, can offer abstract and complex representations of conflict. Advantage should be taken of this in designing massive reparations programs.

4. As a principle, it is not enough simply to seek to find reparations measures that have individual meaning and significance to female victims of political violence; it is also necessary to look for ways in which symbolic reparations can contribute, however minimally, to subverting dominant gender hierarchies.

5. As a rule, symbolic reparations processes, or a massive reparations program as a whole, should seek ways to meet both individual and collective needs simultaneously. For example, apologies could be made by a state at a collective level and victims could be written to individually, or collective memorialization could include individual elements such as names.

6. Symbolic reparations such as apologies, memorials, monuments, and museums should seek ways at all times to render the so-called "private" and "apolitical" lives of women in conflict as public and political, as well as to reinforce the agency of women and their multiple roles in conflict and afterwards. Bringing issues such as rape and its systematic use in war to the public might be essential both to spark transformation and to challenge narratives (for the sake of a better future). Of course, this might not always assist current victims – the moral dilemmas it creates and the importance of bringing such crimes into the public domain should be considered.

7. Memorialization and commemoration may require a process of shifting away from traditional practice toward new and alternative measures such as abstract representation, visual or creative arts, or the use of living

memorialization. At the same time, a process of changing (feminizing the male form of) traditional memorialization practice might need to take place. In other words, abstract symbolism and living memorials may be needed, but statues and public representations (whether through memorialization, commemoration, historicization, apologies, or public discourse) of *women and men* as equally capable of fulfilling roles as carers, heroes, fighters, and physically and emotionally affected by conflict may also be needed.

8. An integrated multiple-axis gender analysis of symbolic reparations is needed. So although it may be necessary to develop new symbolic practice and transform traditional practice simultaneously, it is also important to consider the gender dimensions of who performs the practice or where the practice takes place. For example, as was mentioned earlier, reparations policy might result in streets being renamed or new public buildings, but if the unveiling of these is continually done by men in powerful positions, who in doing so continue to speak of women in a patronizing manner or to reinforce private/public divisions, this can undermine gains made by the development of a more gendered approach to the granting of reparations.

9. Consultation and participation are critical to symbolic reparations processes, and vital when considering the needs of women who are most often excluded from such processes. Adequate reparations, symbolic or otherwise, cannot be guaranteed without adequate participation and public involvement of key stakeholders in their development and conceptualization. This is of greater importance when considering symbolic reparations, because such reparations will realize their maximum symbolic power only if they resonate with those they intend to assist or offer redress to.

8

Gender and Collective Reparations in the Aftermath of Conflict and Political Repression*

Ruth Rubio-Marín

When the rebels attacked Kingtom, we ran into hiding but unfortunately, someone told the rebels that we were in the mosque.... They located us, killed six people, chopped off my sister's head, raped me, tied me up and amputated my foot... for four days I was there alone and maggots started coming from my foot.... Later I was rescued by some ECOMOG soldiers who took me to the hospital where I learnt I had become pregnant and had to do an abortion.[1]

Ideas of "reconciliation" and "transitional justice" have rapidly diffused around the world in the past two decades, intended to help post-authoritarian or post-conflict societies deal with the legacy of gross human rights violations. Much of the debate to date has focused on the status and treatment of the offenders, and in particular whether they should be prosecuted for their actions or accorded some form of amnesty or forgiveness in the name of national healing and reconciliation. However, there are equally important developments regarding the status and treatment of the victims, and in particular whether they should receive some form of reparations.

Indeed, reparations for victims of gross human rights violations are becoming an increasingly common feature of transitional processes. We can see this trend in the recommendations of various truth commissions and in the

---

* This article was first published in *The Politics of Reconciliation in Multicultural Societies*, ed. Will Kymlicka and Bashir Bashir (Oxford: Oxford University Press, 2008), 192–214. I want to express my thanks to the editors of that volume for insightful and useful input that helped shape the article.

[1] A 15-year-old girl testifying to the Truth and Reconciliation Commission of Sierra Leone during closed hearings in Freetown, *The Final Report of the Truth and Reconciliation Commission of Sierra Leone*, Volume B: Chapter 4: Children and the Armed Conflict in Sierra Leone, para. 120. Cited in Dyan Mazurana and Khristopher Carlson, "Reparations as a Means for Recognizing and Addressing Crimes and Grave Rights Violations against Girls and Boys during Situations of Armed Conflict and under Authoritarian and Dictatorial Regimes," Chapter 4 of this volume.

emerging jurisprudence of national and international human rights adjudication bodies,[2] and it has recently been endorsed by the UN in its *UN Basic Principles and Guidelines on the Right to a Remedy and Reparation for Victims of Gross Violations of International Human Rights Law and Serious Violations of International Humanitarian Law* (2005).[3] Transitional justice mechanisms have been supplemented with reparations initiatives and programs for victims in South Africa, Germany, Chile, Brazil, and Argentina.[4]

These reparations programs serve a dual function. Looking backward, they are intended to repair a past wrong. Reparations programs are typically structured around the definition of "victims" or the selection of a list of violations or crimes that took place in a certain predetermined period of the past, and they seek, as a general inspirational aim, to "repair" the wrong that has been done. But they also have a forward-looking goal of helping rebuild society. In allocating benefits, both material and symbolic, reparations programs rest on future-oriented notions of rehabilitation, satisfaction, and reintegration, tracing an end-station through which victims will be dignified. More importantly, at least in those scenarios self-reflectively identified as "transitional," discussions about reparations tend to coincide with broader structural, political, legal, and institutional reforms seen as foundational to a "new democratic order." The needs of redress, recognition, and compensation to victims are therefore pondered jointly with the larger political aims of societal healing and national reconciliation.

This dual function of reparations has implications for the kinds of reparations that are adopted. A purely backward-looking focus would presumably aim to provide remedies to individuals in strict proportion to the harm they have suffered. Case-by-case remedies in strict proportion to harm might be best decided by courts. But the enormous range of violations, the number of victims, and the fact that societies that emerge from conflict or long periods of authoritarian rule are often faced with a wide set of competing reconstruction and development needs, make the idea of compensation in strict proportion to harm illusory.[5] Moreover, such an exclusively backward-looking focus

---

[2] This includes the European and the Inter-American Courts of Human Rights.

[3] Resolution 2005/35, E/CN.4/2005/L.48. The UN principles refer to restitution, compensation, rehabilitation, satisfaction, and guarantees of nonrepetition as categories of reparations measures.

[4] See Pablo de Greiff, ed., *The Handbook of Reparations* (Oxford: Oxford University Press, 2006) [*The Handbook*, hereafter].

[5] See Pablo de Greiff, "Justice and Reparations," in *The Handbook*, 451–477; Naomi Roht-Arriaza, "Reparations in the Aftermath of Repression and Mass Violence," in *My Neighbor, My Enemy: Justice and Community in the Aftermath of Mass Atrocity*, ed. Eric Stover and Harvey M. Weinstein (Cambridge: Cambridge University Press, 2004), 121–137; Richard Falk, "Reparations, International Law and Global Justice: A New Frontier," in *The Handbook*, 478–503.

ignores the contribution reparations can make to building a new democratic order.

In both the theory and practice of reparations, therefore, the idea that reparations should not only or primarily be seen as means to provide individual remedy to the victims (so as to restore them to the situation prior to the violations) has been gaining support.[6] When confronted with a legacy of mass and grave violations, acts of reparation should be thought of not only as means to provide remedy but also as an expression of commitment to a system of rights and, thus, as acts of affirmation and (re-)creation of the democratic state. Granting adequate recognition to victims as equal right holders by turning them into reparations beneficiaries serves this wider purpose of contributing to the creation of the new democratic order.[7]

Conceived in this way, the goal of reparations is not to address every consequence of the breach of a person's rights and try to restore her to the *status quo ante* (the situation prior to the violation). Rather, reparations become a measure that promotes both interpersonal trust and trust in the institutions of the "new state" as well as in its overall legitimacy and efficacy. Reparations become an expression of the recognition of victims as human beings and as equal citizens in the new political order, an admission of past or future responsibility for certain types of conduct, and, at the same time, a symbolic expression of the deontological code of the new political system. In this lies their potential, however modest, for contributing to democratic state building.

The shift from judicial reparations directed at individual victims to broader reparations programs is therefore not just a concession to practical considerations. It also reflects a broadening of the underlying normative goals and ideals of reparations, supplementing the traditional goals of restitution and compensation with broader ideals of affirming equal citizenship and strengthening a more democratic and inclusive political order.

One dimension or implication of this shift has been the increased use of *collective* reparations. Again, this is partly a matter of administrative convenience, given the scarcity of resources and the urgent need for development and reconstruction measures, and the difficulty of making individual-level judgments about harm. However, the increasing interest in collective reparations may also reflect a modest but growing recognition of the group-based nature of past rights violations, and it may in fact be useful in contesting the inherited stigmas and hierarchies that often underpin those rights violations in order to build a new democratic order. Sensitivity to the group-based nature of violence and the group-differentiated impact of violations is also reflected in

---

[6] de Greiff, "Justice and Reparations."
[7] Ibid.

the increasing trend to recognize that reparations must be gender sensitive and that they must address the specific needs and concerns of women, indigenous peoples, and other marginalized populations.[8]

I believe that these shifts toward broader reparations programs, including the use of collective reparations, are potentially important contributions to the (re-)building of democratic societies. However, these shifts also raise a number of dilemmas, since the different functions or justifications of reparations may pull in different directions. In particular, there is a potential conflict between what I will call the *corrective* dimension of reparations (namely, giving adequate redress to victims) and the *transformative* dimension of reparations (advancing the consolidation of a more inclusive democratic system).

These tensions remain largely unaddressed, in part because the notion of collective reparations has not yet been systematically explored in the transitional justice literature. In this chapter, I will explore the corrective and transformative dimensions of reparations and the tensions that are likely to appear between them. To do so, I will focus in particular on women and gender-based reparations. The multifaceted group-based harms done to women during conflict and under authoritarianism can give rise to claims for collective reparations. It is important, therefore, to consider the possibilities for a project of reparations that seeks both (corrective) redress for victims and (transformative) progress in dismantling patriarchy. As we will see, however, combining the corrective and transformative dimensions of collective reparations in the context of gender is not easy. Policies of compensation, restitution, or rehabilitation of victims can be used to help transform inherited gender-based stigmas and hierarchies that predated the conflict, but they can also affirm and reproduce those stigmas and hierarchies.

I begin by exploring the notion of collective reparations as reparations to encapsulate group-based harm (Section I). I then consider violence against

---

[8] Examples of this trend include the Reparations Program recommended in the Final Report of the Truth, Reception and Reconciliation Commission in East Timor, handed down to Parliament in November of 2005, which includes gender equity as one of five guiding principles that inspires its overall conception (see Galuh Wandita, Karen Campbell-Nelson, and Manuela Leong Pereira, "Learning to Engender Reparations in Timor-Leste: Reaching Out to Female Victims," in *What Happened to the Women? Gender and Reparations for Human Rights Violations*, ed. Ruth Rubio-Marín (New York: Social Science Research Council, 2006) [*What Happened?* hereafter], 308). Similarly, Morocco's Equity and Truth Commission (IER), set up in 2004 and with a mandate that lasted until December 2005, made gender mainstreaming one of the priorities in its reparations policy (see the final report of the *Instance Equité et Réconciliation* [IER], available in Arabic, French, and Spanish at http://www.ier.ma). Finally, Colombia's current Commission on Reparations and Reconciliation (CNRR) has established a specific unit with the task of ensuring that all of the policies and recommendations of the Commission take into account the specific needs of women and other marginalized groups.

women as an important example of the sort of group-based harm that collective reparations might remedy (Section II), and I identify some of the dilemmas between the corrective and transformative dimensions of gender-based reparations (Section III). I conclude with some reflections that draw links between this discussion and the wider debate on the relationship between democracy and reparations politics (Section IV).

I. COLLECTIVE REPARATIONS AND GROUP-BASED HARM

What, then, are collective reparations? In the reparations literature in the transitional justice domain it has become a commonplace to distinguish between symbolic and material reparations, on the one hand, and between individual and collective reparations, on the other. In spite of this, there is little conceptual clarity as to what exactly collective reparations are about.

Sometimes it seems that the narrative of collective reparations is deployed to deny the need for reparations altogether. For example, it is sometimes said that in the aftermath of conflict or widespread repression, it makes better sense to preserve scarce resources for development and general reconstruction to the benefit of the entire society. At other times, it seems that collective reparations are endorsed not as a substitute for reparations but as a *modality of distribution*, collective here meaning that instead of being given to each victim individually, the benefit is given to a "group" or to certain "groups" of victims. A third use of the expression is that which reflects the nature of the benefit when what is given as a form of reparation is a *public* or *nonexcludable* good, in the sense that, once put in place, it benefits not only victims but a wider population. On some other occasions, the idea of collective reparations is used to describe the option of concentrating reparative efforts on certain *geographical regions*, generally those most severely affected by a conflict and hence with a larger number of victims. Finally, there is a growing but still diffuse sense that when the violence inflicted on individuals is tied to their *group membership* (such as the violence inflicted on indigenous people or ethnic groups), this results in harms that are collective in nature and therefore need collective forms of redress.[9] This last notion of collective reparations is the one that I will explore here.

Collective reparations can indeed be a response to group-based violence. Group-based violence is the violence victims experience when it is linked to

---

[9] An example of this is Guatemala's National Reparations Program, which includes cultural reparations measures seeking to promote the revitalization of the cultures affected by the internal armed conflict, mainly the Mayan culture (see Claudia Paz y Paz Bailey, "Guatemala: Gender and Reparations for Human Rights Violations," in *What Happened?* 113).

their belonging to certain groups or collectivities (along the lines of gender, sexual orientation, race, ethnicity, religious beliefs, language, etc.). In particular, group membership might be connected to either the rationale for or the form of expression of the violence. Think of genocidal violence where people are persecuted *because* of their ethnicity and the way such violence can contribute to shaping ethnic identities and social perceptions thereof. Think also of gender-specific forms of violence that happen to women *because* they are women in times of conflict and repression; these are the kind that we will explore in the sections that follow. Collective reparations in this sense would refer to the need to redress the harm to the identity and social status of the targeted individuals as well as the diffuse harms ensuing to the entire group. Reparations benefits could include public goods for the entire group. Measures of redress would be inspired by the need to reshape social meanings and allow present and future members of those groups to preserve their identity, status, culture, and sense of self-worth, thereby reducing the chances of exposure to ongoing widespread societal discrimination and violence.

One paradigmatic example of collective reparations in this sense would be reparations for the violation of collective or group-based rights, meaning those rights specifically recognized to certain groups as such. A useful illustration drawn from the jurisprudence of the Inter-American Court of Human Rights is the granting of reparations for the destruction of and displacement from villages occupied by indigenous populations.[10] However, this category of collective reparation is not exhausted by the notion of remedy for the infringement of

[10] The Inter-American Court of Human Rights has embraced an evolutionary interpretation of the right to property under article 21 of the American Convention as including communal property. This has allowed it to decide the need for collective reparations for collective harm experienced by native communities who are forced out of their village and suffer cultural harm, including the disarticulation of their local structures of power, the impossibility to perform death rituals for their deceased loved ones, and the transmission of culture across generations. See, for instance, *Moiwana Village v. Suriname* (June 2005) and *Yakye Axa Indigenous Community v. Paraguay* (June 2005). The Court has also interpreted the right to cultural and religious freedom as having a collective dimension. Thus, in *Plan de Sanchez Massacre v. Guatemala* (April 2004, Reparations decision November 2004), the Court found that the massacre of 268 members of various Mayan Achí communities by Guatemalan armed forces during the internal armed conflict in the country violated both the individual right to life of those killed and the collective right of the Maya Achí community to cultural and religious freedom. This latter finding was based on the facts that survivors were forced to abandon the area for years and were unable to bury the dead or practice other religious or cultural rites and that the death of women and the elderly foreclose the possibility of passing on the Maya Achí culture to the next generations. The Court ordered the payment of pecuniary damages for individual survivors as well as collective measures such as community development in affected areas, the funding of the study and dissemination of the Maya Achí culture in the affected communities, and the publication of the decision in the relevant indigenous language.

collective or groups-based rights. This is so for three reasons. First, as a matter of law, many groups or collectivities are not accorded any form of group rights and yet are specifically targeted in some conflicts. Second, group-based harm may result from the violation of individual rights and not only from those more traditionally conceptualized as group rights or collective rights.[11] Finally, the notion of group-based harm includes harms done to people who are not commonly recognized as the sorts of collectivities that might be entitled to group-rights, such as women or sexual minorities, even though it often is the case that belonging to such groups is in fact related to either the rationale for or form of violence they experience.

Here I want to argue that a conception of reparations that places the focus on giving victims recognition as *equal* citizens, thereby contributing to the creation or affirmation of a more inclusive and democratic political ethos, must capture the group-based dimension of violence and hence include collective reparations. This is so because in those cases victims can be recognized as equal citizens only if they feel that they are not being penalized for belonging to certain groups or collectivities, which requires that these be treated with equal respect instead of oppressed, systematically marginalized, or structurally subordinated. Without the latter, the former is not conceivable. People killed, maimed, tortured, or raped because of their religion, race, or ethnicity are being denied the status of equal citizens not only because their inalienable rights to life and physical and moral integrity are infringed, but also because they are being persecuted on the grounds of their race, ethnicity, or religion. The violence they experience sends a message to them, and to other members of the group and to the wider society, about the lack of worthiness of their identity or condition.

II. THE GENDERED MEANINGS OF VIOLENCE AGAINST WOMEN AND THE VIOLENCE CONTINUUM

In the light of this meaning of collective reparations, we can now ask whether it makes sense to consider women as their potential beneficiaries. Are women appropriately identified as a distinct category of victims to whom collective reparations are owed? And, if so, what form of reparations would serve both

---

[11] This was recognized in *Yatama v. Nicaragua* (June 2005), a case in which the Inter-American Court, having found that Nicaragua did not adopt the necessary measures to ensure the individual rights of the Yatama people to run for candidates in local elections without discrimination and that this generated collective harm, ordered collective reparations both monetary and nonmonetary.

to correct (to right the wrong) and to transform (to build a more inclusive democratic order)?

From a structural perspective, leaving the group dimension of large-scale violence and political repression unaddressed, and presenting the violent period as a sum of separate violations of individual rights, is an insufficient response. It misses a historic opportunity to spell out true guarantees of nonrepetition for victims, to engage in a conversation about what forms of institutional reform might be called for to accommodate minority or oppressed groups in the "new" democratic order, and to discuss which of the possible democratic models best ensures its inclusiveness. The promise of a common set of individual rights that will not be violated in the future is important for the recognition of victims as equal citizens, but it is also likely to leave unaddressed ingrained prejudices, misperceptions, and structural imbalances that were among the root causes of the group-specific violence. When the structural causes of the violence remain unaddressed, the real chances that in the new democracy those citizens will in fact enjoy equal rights and freedoms without sacrificing their identity and unique forms of cultural and communal life are reduced. Collective reparations, then, from this perspective, are measures specifically targeted to capture and redress the group-based harm both to individual victims as well as the entire group they belong to.

To explore this question, we need to consider in more depth the nature of the group-based harms that women suffer in war or under authoritarian regimes. There is an increasingly rich literature on women under authoritarian regimes and women in war describing the manifold forms of victimization of women.[12] Women, of course, suffer from operations that randomly target the civilian population. Like men, they are detained, imprisoned, extrajudicially executed, and subject to torture or inhuman and degrading treatment for fighting in resistance movements. Women are also frequently punished for their family or communal links. They are harassed, sexually assaulted, and

---

[12] See, for instance, Meredeth Turshen and Clotilde Twagiramariya, eds., *What Women Do in Wartime: Gender and Conflict in Africa* (London: Zed Books, 1998); Sheila Meintjes, Anu Pillay, and Meredeth Turshen, eds., *The Aftermath: Women in Post-Conflict Transformation* (London: Zed Books, 2001); Susie Jacobs, Ruth Jacobson, and Jennifer Marchbank, eds., *State of Conflict: Gender, Violence and Resistance* (London: Zed Books, 2000). See also Margaret Randolph Higonnet, Jane Jenson, Sonya Michel, and Margaret Collins Weitz, eds., *Behind the Lines: Gender and the Two World Wars* (New Haven: Yale University Press, 1987). On women under Apartheid, see Diana E. H. Russel, *Lives of Courage: Women for a New South Africa* (New York: Basic Books, 1989). On women under the Pinochet dictatorship in Chile, see Marjorie Agosin, *Scraps of Life: Chilean Women and the Pinochet Dictatorship*, Cola Franzen (trans.) (Trenton, NJ: The Red Sea Press, 1987). On women under fascism, see Victoria de Grazia, *How Fascism Ruled Women: Italy 1922–1945* (Berkeley: University of California Press, 1992).

held in prison for being family members of men involved in the conflict or simply for belonging or being perceived as belonging to and sustaining communities suspected of collaboration. Women are also persecuted, raped, forcefully impregnated, sterilized, or killed because of their ethnicity, race, nationality, or religion. By oppressing women in times of political turmoil, the state, subversive groups, and civilian self-defense groups rely on forms of violence that are common to men and women as well as on other forms much more specifically tailored for women, such as sexual and reproductive violence or domestic and sexual exploitation. Boys and girls are included among the pool of victims, and some of the violence they experience is also gendered in that either the reason for or the modality of the violence is conditioned by their gender.

A systematic analysis of the most common rationales and modalities of violence against women shows that, beyond killing, maiming, traumatizing, and exploiting human beings, such violence harms women *as women* because it rests on and exacerbates social meanings that feed the construction of gender relations as a system of dominance. In reinforcing sexual hierarchies, this type of gender-specific violence undermines women's chances to live a life with self-respect and free of prejudice and subordination.

There are at least four different but interrelated meanings underlying either the "why" or the "how" of violence against women *as such*.[13] They are neither mutually exclusive nor exhaustive: there are undoubtedly other factors explaining why women are targets of violence in scenarios of mass atrocity or systematic political repression. However, these four meanings do capture the group dimension of the harm done to women in these situations and therefore allow us to lay the ground for the quest for collective forms of redress.

First, much of the violence women encounter in these contexts is essentially an *assertion of female subordination*. Men are the speakers, women the audience. Women are subject to sex-specific and sexual forms of violence that target both the physical and moral attributes of the female condition more than other less sex-specific forms of violence, the act of violence being at the same time an opportunity for the affirmation of sexual hierarchies. Common examples include sexual forms of torture and violence; the amputation of female attributes; and the infliction of pain by making women feel that they fail in their primordial roles as mothers (as when their children are removed from them while in prison, or when women are threatened with the infliction

---

[13] Walker develops a slightly different typology from the one sustained here, which has, nevertheless, largely benefited from the former. Margaret Urban Walker, "Gender and Violence in Focus: A Background for Gender Justice in Reparations," Chapter 1 of this volume.

of pain on their children or forced to witness such pain). The speech that this type of violence expresses is directed by the perpetrator not only at the individual victim, but at the female condition. Indeed, this explains its systematic use, such as when women are systematically raped before being massacred. That the meaning conveyed transcends the individual women sacrificed is rendered vivid by the fact that some of the most abhorrent sex-specific practices are performed on women after they have been killed, such as the opening of assassinated women's wombs to extract and destroy their fetuses.

Related to such violence, but with a different audience in mind, is the violence that women and girls endure as a means for men to assert or show their masculinity and, often and related to it, to *assert their absolute or relative male power*. Compared with the previous form, one could say that women here are "downgraded" in an act of ruthless reification: from despised and subordinated interlocutors to mere instruments of assertion of male power in front of themselves and in relation to other men. Whereas on some occasions violence against women simply constitutes an opportunity for male bonding ("this is what we men do"), more frequently violence against women is a form of expression of relative social power: "this is what we do to (your) women to show our power over you." Killing and raping the women of the enemy men, often in their presence, is a way of emasculation that consists of humiliating these men by showing them that they have failed in their manly role to protect women as honor, property, or reputation.

Much of the violence that women and girls are subject to can be understood as sheer acts of *appropriation and exploitation that rest on women's prior reification*. Indeed, women and girls are often treated as objects for male sexual satisfaction or as labor at men's disposal. When taken from others, then, their labor and bodies become stolen "property" and the act of theft possibly also a form of male affirmation. When taken as a price for conquest, they become war booty. The abduction of girls and women, their forced recruitment, their sexual or domestic enslavement and exploitation, as well as the practice of forced prostitution, are all-too-common examples of gender violence as a form of appropriation.

Finally, because women are often perceived and defined primordially as engines of social, cultural, and biological reproduction, certain forms of violence against women are commonly intended as forms of *biological and cultural engineering*. Forced displacement, massacres, mass rape, forced pregnancies, abortion, and sterilization are all tools to destroy morale as well as the actual chances of a community to reproduce itself. "Ethnic contamination," cultural humiliation, or extinction of the community may be behind the efforts to control women's reproductive capacity or to spoil them as repositories of tradition, culture, and collective honor. Both this and the previous meaning of gender violence share the construct of women as subordinate and functional. In the first case, women are primordially there to serve and be used by men. In the second, they serve their communities. They can be sacrificed to either.

So now we know better why and how women and girls become targets of violence in times of political repression and widespread conflict. But what distinguishes this from the forms or meanings of violence that women are *ordinarily* subject to? This question has given rise to what is known as the *violence continuum thesis*. It is widely accepted in the gender and conflict literature that the distinction between "ordinary" and "extraordinary" violence, as applied to women, constitutes a misrepresentation of what women and girls endure before, during, and after times of conflict or political repression. According to the violence continuum thesis, violence against women is better understood as a continuum stretching from "the gender violence of everyday life, through the structural violence of economic systems that sustain inequalities and the repressive policing of dictatorial regimes, to the armed conflict of open warfare."[14] This assertion rests on the fact that, as Margaret Walker puts it, violence against women is still *normative*, by which she means that men's aspiration to control women's lives – including their productive, sexual, and reproductive activities and capacities, as well as their speech and self-expression – remain, to a greater or lesser extent, a rather undisputed fact in human societies.[15]

Having said this, Walker herself warns that the violence continuum thesis might not be the right paradigm to capture "the sense of enormity and outrage, or the terror, despair, and social ruin" that many victims experience in actual instances of violence in conflict.[16] According to her, the key is remembering that "normative social behaviors and positions, by their nature, constitute an *order*, and that order is in many and profound ways suspended, deformed, or destroyed in conflict situations."[17] The idea that violence against women is normative, then, does not imply that all forms of subordination, exploitation, and oppression of women are more or less familiar or expected for women. Some forms of violence clearly imply the breakdown of an order, and hence the suspension of the limits and whatever protection the old order used to offer. This is why, seen from the victims' perspective, their experiences may well be

---

[14] Cynthia Cockburn, "The Continuum of Violence: A Gender Perspective on War and Peace," in *Sites of Violence: Gender and Conflict Zones*, ed. Wenona Giles and Jennifer Hyndman (Berkeley: University of California Press, 2004), 19.
[15] Walker, "Gender and Violence in Focus."
[16] Ibid.
[17] Ibid.

one of extreme and traumatic "discontinuities" and why, from that perspective, it may still be relevant to distinguish the ordinary from the extraordinary.[18]

Identifying continuities of violence for purposes of analysis and theoretical reflection may not be adequate to capture victims' experiences of rupture. Instead, the theoretical construct of a continuum is a reminder that violence against women "is primarily about control, where controlling women – either one's own or those of other men – is emblematic of masculine power. This factor predicts features of pre-conflict, conflict, and post-conflict situations for women as targets of violence."[19] This includes the retrenchment of masculine and feminine roles with men as leaders before the conflict, the escalation beyond normative bounds during conflict of the forms of coercion that are common in everyday life, and the increase in violence against women after the conflict, when men may find themselves with the "need to reassert control over women ... [or] to reestablish their place in masculine groups and hierarchies."[20]

Although the idea of a violence continuum has a role to play in explaining the sequence and forms of violence women are subject to, it accounts for victims' experiences only imperfectly. This becomes even clearer when we focus on the collective dimension of the experience. Moving beyond the individual victims, and thinking in terms of harm to the group linked to the extraordinary forms of domination and violence that women are subject to during conflict and authoritarianism, we can identify two main forms of such harms. On the one hand, in many ways the extraordinary is simply an exacerbation of the ordinary, and so the gendered meanings underpinning ordinary violence inflicted on women are reasserted in times of conflict and political repression. On the other hand, the new experiences of violence also represent a disruption of a gendered order – an order that sanctions female subordination but also contains its forms and modalities of expression defining what is "normal" for women to expect but also what is *not*. This new experience of unbound violence and domination disrupts the ordinary by further dehumanizing women, broadening the imagination as to what women are for, who women belong to, what can be done to women, what causes women can be sacrificed for and what is a woman's proper place in society. Moreover, all of this works to the detriment of women's overall social status *as women*, and often, as women belonging to certain religious, ethnic, or racial groups also. If this is so, then increased violence against women in the

---

[18] Ibid.
[19] Ibid.
[20] Ibid.

aftermath of a conflict in which women have experienced extraordinary forms of violence may be not only collateral damage in the process of reconstructing a system of a gendered social order, but also the expression of new forms and degrees of violence that have been normalized and hence become less "unthinkable" in a post-conflict society.

This double dimension of "extraordinary" violence against women (as both affirmation and subversion of preexisting meanings and orders) makes the project of reparations for survivors one that is inevitably ridden with tensions. On the one hand, the disruption of a preexisting order may be the source of corrective claims of victims to have it reestablished and affirmed (going back to "normal"). On the other, victims and women in general may also have legitimate expectations to push a transformative agenda when asking for reparations so as to question sexual hierarchies that were embedded in the "ordinary" accounting for many of the forms of violence they experienced in their normal lives. This possibility of advancing a transformative agenda is likely to present itself only when the wider societal conditions allow for a fruitful dialogue between the process of historical clarification and rectification, on the one hand, and, on the other, the ongoing challenge of strengthening and deepening democracy by making the contestation of inherited gender stigmas and hierarchies a paradigmatic expression of democratic progress.

III. GENDER-BASED VIOLENCE AND COLLECTIVE REPARATIONS: FROM VICTIMS TO AGENTS OF CHANGE

We now have a better sense of the tensions that may surface in a project of reparations that tries to address both the individual and collective effects of gender violence. Because reparations for women have not figured prominently in the reparations agenda of most countries, these underlying tensions have received little attention to date.

It is widely acknowledged that women play an essential role during periods of violence and its aftermath, working to sustain and reconstitute families and communities, demanding justice for their loved ones, and trying to revert life back to normalcy. Nonetheless, reparations programs in transitional societies have, for the most part, not been explicitly designed with a gender dimension in mind. The inroads of feminism in international law, especially since the 1990s, coupled with the trend of more participatory processes of reparations, has raised awareness that something "has to be done about the women." However, all too often this has meant more meetings in which women meet other women, but not many of the decision makers, who continue largely to be male. Until very recently feminist organizations and women's rights organizations tended to be largely absent from the discussions of reparations, even in those cases where they had been actively involved in discussing the conflict and fighting for peace. This is partly due to the fact that women's groups are often of a different social, cultural, or ethnic background than victims. Also, the energies of women's groups in times of transition often go toward seizing the window of opportunity for structural and institutional future-looking and long-term reforms, which are often more inspired by global feminist movements than by women's extraordinary suffering in the past, even fairly recent suffering.

Thus, it is not surprising that although there is an increasing interest in exploring collective forms of reparation, there is virtually no discussion of how this interest and that of "engendering" reparations may intersect in ways that are conducive to pushing forward the agenda of "engendering" democracy. Can collective reparations (such as those for group-based harm to women) serve to promote a more democratic order (including a more gender-inclusive democracy)? As discussed earlier, the notion of collective reparations is used to refer to a variety of things, and it is unlikely that there will be one single answer to this question. Here I would like to focus on the one meaning of collective reparations that I have explored and defended above – namely, collective reparations as those measures that address and attempt to *redress the harm to identity and status resulting from group-based violence*, in this case from gender-based violence.

We saw above that the violence women experience during times of "extraordinary" conflict and authoritarian repression asserts gender meanings in ways that both confirm and expand those underlying "ordinary" violence against women. It was argued that, as a result, structural oppression and subordination of women is reaffirmed to the detriment not only of individual victims but of women in general and of those belonging to certain ethnic, religious, or racial groups in particular. I would now like to argue that addressing the broad implications of gender-based violence allows us to connect the "backward-looking" reparations agenda to the "forward-looking" institutional and legal reform agenda. This potential connection is greatest precisely in those moments that tend to be identified as moments of "democratic state building," and I believe that the notion of collective reparations can be especially apposite for drawing this connection. At the same time, though, I will show that the case of gender-based collective reparations reveals the complexities involved in trying to combine the corrective and transformative dimensions of a reparations project.

So what could be some forms of collective reparations for women? How could women's past experience of violence (and the analysis of its underlying and enabling structural conditions) contribute to reforms aimed at ensuring women equal citizenship in more inclusive democracies? Answers to such questions must be context specific and will probably be determined both by the specific history and forms of female subordination and by the prevailing conception of democracy in each society. Short- and long-term measures of collective reparations could include things as diverse as sensitization campaigns regarding women's human rights or violence against women; training of the army and police forces on these matters; vetting of the public-order forces that engaged in the worst forms of gender violence; gender-sensitive school programs; symbolic reparations (such as a collective apology to the women); and reforms of the constitutional and legal systems to remove traces of formal discrimination against women as well as to facilitate women's equal opportunities. Gender quotas or political parity measures to ensure women's effective political representation would also count. Other legal reforms and structural measures to address women's economic subordination (such as reform of patriarchal land tenure, ownership, or inheritance rules) or their reduced chances of a life free of violence and sexual abuse are also relevant examples. These would all have to be supplemented with measures designed to address the harm in status and identity resulting from those violent actions that targeted women both as women and as members of certain national, ethnic, or religious minorities.

If defined with the participation of victims, and if meaningfully implemented, these measures of cultural, social, institutional, and legal reform could connect collective and individual reparations processes. Thus they could bring up the status of women in general, and of those belonging to minority groups in particular, enhancing their chances to live a life with self-respect and free of prejudice and subordination. They would also reduce the odds of repetition for victims by helping stop cycles of violence and vulnerability.[21] Finally, the adoption of such reforms could also give victims, especially those involved in the process of defining reparations, a sense of satisfaction in that it would recognize them as agents of social change, something that could facilitate their rehabilitation process. Indeed, contributing to the creation of a better, more just society in which their children and the generations to come will be spared the injustice they had to experience can be a source of meaning, especially in the case of lives otherwise dramatically truncated by the disruption of violence.

---

[21] In fact the Inter-American Court of Human Rights (the international human rights adjudicatory body that has thus far gone the furthest in articulating the right to monetary and nonmonetary reparations for victims of human rights violations) has on several occasions ordered states to engage in certain legislative or institutional reforms or to adopt certain policies for the sake of nonrepetition. For concrete examples, see Arturo J. Carrillo, "Justice in Context: The Relevance of Inter-American Human Rights Law and Practice to Repairing the Past," in *The Handbook*, 527.

At the same time, though, it is important to keep actual victims' legitimate claims, including those of restitution and compensation, in the picture. Using victims' experiences of unspeakable pain and anguish only or primarily as material for pedagogical future-looking nation building or political re-foundation, without doing anything concrete to help victims out of their devastation, would be perceived at best as a purely instrumental use of victims and at worst as an exercise of empty rhetoric. It is only when the two processes go hand in hand that victims may gain a sense of satisfaction from the fact that their pain was not in vain and their lives were not entirely wasted. But the two goals may not always be easy to reconcile, as some of the expectations of victims to have their broken lives restored may entail the affirmation (rather than transformation) of preexisting gender hierarchies.

Several examples can illustrate the complexity. Within reparations parlance, *restitution* measures seek to restore the victim to the original situation before the violation and may include restoration of employment and return of property. One common problem is that often employment opportunities and property rights were not equally recognized to men and women to start with (precisely because women were seen as subordinate to men or as male extensions rather than as citizens and full subjects of rights). What to do, then, with the all-too-common post-conflict scenario where female-headed households are suddenly multiplied? Here "meaningful" restitution can only be transformative. Men can't be brought back to life. To the extent that restitution is embraced, it must mean "transformative restitution," bringing the victim not to where she was but to where she ought to have been. Restoring a discriminatory system of property and employment would be of little avail to females who suddenly find themselves alone in heading households (often with more dependants than before), or to women more generally. This is an example of how, under certain circumstances, the transformative solution may be to the advantage of both victims and the wider group of women.

Think of *compensation* measures now. Compensation is often provided as a form of reparation. It can simply involve a token recognition of the fact of a rights violation, or it can aim at redress in proportion to harm or, if not in strict proportion to harm, at least aim to be sensitive to the seriousness of the violation and attuned to the affected good, the ensuing harms, and the lost opportunities. The idea of compensating women for the violation of rights or in proportion to harm presents interesting challenges not only, as the previous example shows, because women are often simply denied some rights, but also because what something is "worth" is often the result of external sources of evaluation. Take the example of women who are subject to sexual and reproductive violence and, as a result, lose their virginity or their capacity to bear children. On the one hand, assessing the harm done to victims of sexual and reproductive violence in terms of loss of virginity or loss of reproductive capacity, far from being transformative, reinforces the notion that women are primarily to be valued for their sexual purity or as reproductive vessels. On the other, women and girls who have lost virginity or the capacity to conceive children, or who have been forced to marry the enemy or bear their children, do find their chances of marrying significantly reduced. They also commonly experience family and communal ostracism. And all of this means that their opportunities to achieve equal status, protection, and income are severely undermined. Measuring this harm in terms of lost opportunities seems to convey and perpetuate the "wrong gender meanings," and refusing to measure compensation in this way may seem like an act full of promise for future generations of women. Yet such a transformative stance would do little to help actual victims avoid dire material destitution. Where restitution through reconstructive surgeries may not be a sufficient solution, pensions might be a good way to address the "disability" that women are left with in societies whose patriarchal cultures can't be changed all at once.

Let us take an example drawn from another modality of reparation: <u>rehabilitation</u>. To some extent rehabilitation may actually require a degree of social and cultural transformation. The best example may again be that of victims of sexual violence, because in most scenarios the violence these victims endure at the hands of their perpetrators is only the prelude to additional forms of violence through stigma, abandonment, isolation, and ostracism coming from their partners, families, villages, and communities. Healing, then, can come only from a transformed society that stops the process of holding victims themselves (partly) responsible for their own victimization. The fact that such transformation can take place only at a certain pace represents one of the most daunting challenges for the full psychosocial rehabilitation of women who have been sexually abused and exploited.

On the other hand, rehabilitation may also require a certain measure of corrective reparation, whatever its shortcomings for advancing a transformative agenda. Indeed, to the extent that its goal is reinserting women back into their societies and allowing them to recover a functional life, rehabilitation must be attuned to victims' felt experiences of trauma, and these often involve the sense of a prior order being disrupted. The area of symbolic reparations illustrates this. Brandon Hamber and Ingrid Palmary explore the role of apologies and memorials as forms of symbolic reparation and recognition in helping rehabilitate victims and give them a sense of satisfaction.[22] These scholars have pointed out the fact that women's manifold forms of agency

---

[22] See Brandon Hamber and Ingrid Palmary, "Gender, Memorialization, and Symbolic Reparations," Chapter 7 of this volume.

during times of conflict are rarely recognized in memorials, and that, when portrayed as victims, the focus is on women's suffering as mothers and wives. This can be criticized for reproducing sexual stereotypes that "depoliticize" women's lives and life within the family. Indeed, memorials and statues that emphasize women's experiences *only* as mothers and wives during times of political turmoil send out wider messages about proper male and female roles that are likely to reinforce patriarchy. However, it is also true that people's experiences of loss, pain, and trauma are partly shaped through social meanings that must be acknowledged if we want victims to *feel* duly recognized. We can and maybe should insist that in the aftermath women reclaim more space to analyze the ways in which they both participated and suffered beyond their roles as mothers and wives. But this cannot mean silencing women's articulated pain and sense of loss as mothers or wives by judging it primarily as an expression of false consciousness or indoctrination.[23]

In short, restitution, compensation, rehabilitation, and satisfaction measures must help victims connect past and future and enable them to move on with their lives. Keeping in mind victims' experiences and the societies and cultures that act as vehicles for the meanings through which those experiences are interpreted is crucial. A policy of reparations that takes place at a given point in time cannot entirely and immediately reconstruct victims' experiences or their societies from scratch in the light of transformative conceptions of gender relations. A balance must be drawn. Focusing only on "restoring" victims to a place as close to the one where they were before "the events" is clearly insufficient, for several reasons. It fails to address the cumulative effects of the (often-intertwined) ordinary and extraordinary forms of subordination women experience; it does not pay due attention to the fact that gender violence results in harms to all women and not just victims of certain atrocities; and it misses the importance of conceptualizing gender subordination as fundamentally incompatible with the promise of inclusive democracy. Reparations must, therefore, include transformative as well as restorative dimensions. On the other hand, optimizing only the transformative dimension of reparations (by privileging those concrete reparations benefits that would best suit the new conception of a more emancipated woman in a more egalitarian society) is equally inadequate. It betrays victims to the extent that the system of meanings

---

[23] See also Fionnuala Ni Aolain, "Sex-based Violence during the Holocaust – A Reevaluation of Harms and Rights in International Law," *Yale Journal of Law and Feminism* 12 (2000): 19–20, arguing that refusing to address the harm of maternal separation under the Holocaust as a genuine harm to women for fear of essentializing the female as mother shows the dangers of creating "totalizing theories of harm that fail to account the specific and lived experiences of the victims... shunning the concrete in pursuit of universal truth."

underlying gender-normative violence is unlikely to change fast enough and in ways that are concrete enough to allow victims to make sense of their past and future lives. In some respects, then, the most that can be asked from victims is that they take an active role, if they so wish, to act as facilitators of change for the benefit of future generations. Procedurally, this can be done only when reparations are shaped through a deliberative process that includes victims' voices and visions of a better society.

IV. CONCLUDING REFLECTIONS: ON REPARATIONS AND DEMOCRACY

All of the above suggests that reparations should not be seen as an attempt at closure aimed at settling once and for all the debts of the past, tracing a rigid line that historically divides the "evil past" from the "redeemed present and future." Rather, the struggle for reparations can be seen as an ongoing struggle for recognition aimed at achieving ever-more inclusive democratic orders. After all, the political life of reparations is often fluid. In many countries, including Chile and Argentina, reparations policies have evolved in a piecemeal way rather than as part of an encompassing plan decided once and for all. And although we have focused in this article on scenarios self-reflectively defined as "transitional" because of their recent departure from authoritarianism or armed conflict, many of the countries that pride themselves on being consolidated democratic regimes are also addressing reparations claims as part of larger efforts to tackle long-standing forms of exclusion (e.g., in Australia, the United States, Canada).

The ongoing struggle to redefine the "demos" in a way that allows for the contesting of hegemonic discourses and patterns of exclusion requires meaningful recognition and redress of a past characterized by the systematic denial of equal citizenship linked to group membership. After all, many of the countries in which transitional justice practitioners work are not only societies coming to terms with past massive human rights violations – they are also societies coming to terms with ethnic, religious, or linguistic divisions and patriarchal orders that may have been at the root of the violations themselves. As Pablo de Greiff argues compellingly, we have a duty to remember collectively what we cannot reasonably expect our peer citizens to forget.[24] And this includes the fact that certain groups among us have been systematically oppressed and marginalized and the concrete ways in which such oppression has deeply affected their lives and those of their descendants. Such a recognition might be essential to reconstructing a shared political memory that enables a renewed political

---

[24] See Pablo de Greiff, "The Duty to Remember," unpublished manuscript, forthcoming.

"we" as well as to triggering social change and transformation to ensure the overcoming of domination and hierarchy.

This reconstructed "we" would not necessarily rest on the possibility of the "healing of a preexisting people," on the prospects for reconciliation as an inner spiritual process, or, for that matter, on the chances to achieve a new *common* identity through the act of reconciliation. Rather, reparations are (more modest) acts of recognition of people as equal citizens and rightholders that, paraphrasing Andrew Schaap, will facilitate the recognition of the other as "sharing a space for politics within which citizens divided by memories of past wrongs could debate and contest the terms of their political association."[25] Women, sexual minorities, religious minorities, racial or ethnic minorities, and indigenous peoples can use the banner of reparations to contest the terms of their political association if they do not limit themselves to pressing claims to have a certain order of things restored but instead push to have that order transformed in ways that are identified by multicultural and deliberative theories of democracy. In this sense, reparations politics and multicultural and deliberative theories of democracy can be seen as potentially supplementing each other in their joint, never-ending search for ever-more inclusive and egalitarian political systems. More specifically, reparations struggles remind us of the need to explore continuities between past and present patterns of exclusion, a need which is too often ignored under the uplifting but delusional effects of the promise of a clean slate epitomized by gender-, race-, sex-, language-, and religion-neutral rights and institutions of the liberal state.[26] At the same there is growing awareness that the potential healing effects of reparations measures cannot be achieved unless society is taking measures to address the structural problems that gave rise to the conflict.

Reparations can also contribute to a more inclusive deliberative process. Reparations debates are discursive instruments that can give voice to the

---

[25] Andrew Schaap, "Political Reconciliation as Struggles for Recognition?" *Social and Legal Studies* 13, no. 4 (2004): 538.

[26] See also Bashir Bashir, "Accommodating Historically Oppressed Social Groups: Deliberative Democracy and the Politics of Reconciliation," in *The Politics of Reconciliation in Multicultural Societies*, ed. Will Kymlicka and Bashir Bashir (Oxford: Oxford University Press, 2008), 48–70; Paul Muldoon, "Reconciliation and Political Legitimacy: The Old Australia and the New South Africa," *Australian Journal of Politics and History* 49, no. 2 (2003): 195–196, for whom reconciliation should also be viewed as a conversation forum for public deliberation about the past and its links to the present; and Lawrie Balfour, "Reparations *After* Identity Politics," *Political Theory* 33, no. 6 (2005): 802, arguing, in the context of the struggle for slavery and Jim Crow in the United States, that reparations politics provides "a critical discourse that serves as a counterweigh to race-blind language and incorporates acknowledgment of the past into present practices."

historically oppressed, who often find mainstream institutions particularly inaccessible. Such debates give groups a say on what it is that they need in order to feel that their past has been adequately recognized, thereby allowing them to move forward and be reconciled as members of a shared political space.[27] The increasing awareness within transitional justice initiatives about the need to guarantee victims' participation in the process that leads to reparations coincides with the claims of participatory models of democracy, which argue that, in general, it is not enough that citizens in liberal democracies are bearers of rights entitlements. There is a need to adopt measures that will enable citizens also to be participants in the democratic dialogue.[28] Clearly, victims of historical injustices (or reparations commissions claiming to articulate their views, or courts claiming to defend their rights) do not have the unilateral right to define or implement on their own broader structural, institutional, or legal reforms that will shape not just the future of victims but also that of the entire society. But giving victims a voice in the process of defining measures of redress and nonrecurrence can enhance the inclusiveness of the democratic process, whose long-term legacies of systemic discrimination against historically oppressed and silenced groups cannot be erased in a single moment. Indeed, most victims experience the possibility of expressing and voicing their grievances "officially" as having in itself a reparative dimension, from which they draw a renewed sense of dignity.[29]

In summary, debates about reparations should not be seen as expressing an inherent flaw or insufficiency of democracy in a "post-political" era but can rather be interpreted as opportunities to discuss our democratic hopes. In post-conflict or post-authoritarian situations, they provide a forum to discuss what it is that democracy requires in a period self-identified as "transitional"; in consolidated democracies, they provide a forum to discuss whether the democratic aspirations once embraced have in fact delivered the promise of equal citizenship. In particular, reparations discussions offer the possibility to address historical injustices against groups that have been adequately recognized thus

---

[27] This is of course not to deny the obvious fact that admission of responsibility for historical injustices requires a relative political strength on the part of victims to start with. Rather, it is to suggest that such power should also take the form of agency. See Elazar Barkan, "Restitution and Amending Historical Injustices in International Morality," in *Politics and the Past: On Repairing Historical Injustice*, ed. John Torpey (Lanham, MD: Rowman and Littlefield, 2003), 93.

[28] Jürgen Habermas, *Between Facts and Norms: Contributions to a Discourse Theory of Law and Democracy*, William Rehg (trans.) (Cambridge: Polity Press, 1996), ch. 9, esp.

[29] Martha Minow, *Between Vengeance and Forgiveness: Facing History after Genocide and Mass Violence* (Boston: Beacon Press, 1998), 93, 99.

far, and to draw lessons about the measures needed to prevent discrimination and ensure intergroup equality (including group rights).[30] The conclusions and deficits identified in each national conversation stirred up by reparations claims will vary, in part because there are competing and changing conceptions of what equal citizenship means. These variations show how, although inspired by a universalist ethos, democracy remains a historically grounded and shaped venture, always open for revisitation with an eye both to the past and the future.

This becomes even more obvious when we underscore the fluid boundaries between the "ordinary" and "extraordinary" forms of violence, marginalization, and exclusion signaling the "before" and the "after" of a certain historical episode collectively understood as "the dark ages." Rather than taking place at one single point in time with final closure as a necessary end station, the struggle for reparations can recur whenever sufficient progress in either democratic conviction or practice has been made to "signal" a foundational break with the past, enabling a collective reinterpretation of the meaning and relevance of both past and present forms of exclusion. For women, who have thus far rarely been the protagonists of discussions about historical injustices and reparations,[31] this opens up the possibility that, in time, all of the gender-based forms of systemic discrimination, violence, and subordination will come to be judged as "extraordinary" and, hence, as essentially antithetical to the democratic promise, triggering, among other things, a call for reparations.

---

[30] In fact claims of reparations and restitution have been crucial to push indigenous people's agenda for broader recognition of group rights including self-government rights. See Barkan, 94–97.

[31] According to John Torpey, it is primarily the "Holocaust analogy" that has allowed race and ethnicity to have a greater intuitive appeal as criteria for determining membership in a victim group and therefore accounts for the predominance of ethnicity and race-based reparations movements over those which have or could have focused on different criteria of victimization, including gender or class (John Torpey, "'Making Whole What has Been Smashed': Reflections on Reparations," *The Journal of Modern History* 73, no. 2 [2001]: 351–352). It seems to me that an insufficient analysis of the gendered dimensions of episodes predominantly portrayed as "religion, race or ethnicity-based," including the Holocaust, suggests that the root causes for the historical neglect of gender based violence may be only partially explained by the lack of a Holocaust-type analogy. On gender and the Holocaust, see Leonore J. Weitzman and Dalia Ofer, eds., *Women in the Holocaust* (New Haven, CT: Yale University Press, 1998).

Index

Abortion
  forced (*See* Sexual and reproductive violence)
  reform of laws, 156–157
Administrative reparations, 132, 218, 284, 288–290
Afghanistan
  oppression of women in, 338–339
Agency of women, representing, 339–345
AIDS Quilt, 366
Amnesty International, 28–29, 49
Anglo-Boer War, 337–338, 341–342
Apologies
  children as victims, 209–210
  gender and, 367–368
  generally, 114–115, 369–371, 372–374
  individual *versus* collective reparations, 353–354
  persons not directly involved in violence, by, 363–364
  stigmatization, overcoming, 364–365
Appropriation, violence as, 390
Arbitrary detention and inhuman treatment, 242–243, 249–252
Argentina
  children as victims in
    analysis of reparations, 177, 179
    monetary compensation, 190, 191–192
    reparations, 185–186
  defining beneficiaries in, 89–90
  evolution of reparations in, 399
  families as victims in
    children as beneficiaries, 279–280
    defining victims, 267–268
    distribution of reparations, 282
    parents as beneficiaries, 280–281

  reparations, 262
  surviving victims *versus* non-surviving victims, 289
  monetary compensation in, 107–108, 291–292
  rehabilitation and reintegration in, 112–113
  transitional justice in, 381–382
Ashe, Arthur, 349–351
Ata Turk, 35
Australia, 399
Aylwin, Patricio, 353–354, 363–364

Bangladesh
  microcredit in, 310–311
Basic services. *See* Non-monetary services
Bernstein, Anita, 9–10, 17
Biko, Steve, 342–343
Biological engineering, violence as, 390–391
"Blood money," 141–142, 296
Bop, Codou, 53–54
Bosnia
  caregivers, targeting of, 156–157
  monetary compensation in, 143
  sexual and reproductive violence in, 344, 368–369
  Women Victims of War Association, 368–369
Brandt, Willy, 363–364
Brazil
  defining beneficiaries in, 89–90
  families as victims in
    children as beneficiaries, 279
    defining victims, 267–268
    distribution of reparations, 282

Brazil (*cont.*)
    parents as beneficiaries, 280
    reparations, 263–264
    spouses, partners and companions as beneficiaries, 279
    transitional justice in, 381–382
    welfare analysis in, 320–321

Canada
    Indian Residential Schools, 141–142
    monetary compensation in, 141–142, 143
Cape Town Principles, 188
Caregivers as victims
    children, harm to, 170
    mothering, targeting of, 38–39
    rehabilitation and reintegration, relevance to, 111–112
Carlson, Khristopher, 8–9, 13–14, 129–130, 137, 142–143, 153
Categories of violence
    framework, 58
    gender-multiplied violence, 52–56
    gender-skewed violence, 51–52
    generally, 23, 47–48
    normative violence (*See* Normative violence)
    overlapping of, 56
    sexual and reproductive violence (*See* Sexual and reproductive violence)
Catholic Church, 373
Chad, 54–55
Charlesworth, Hilary, 39–40
"Cheap talk," 296, 322
Chechnya
    families as victims in, 235–237
Chikane, Frank, 363
Children as victims
    active role of children, 168
    actual violations, focus on, 212
    age and time limitations on benefits, 185–186
    age-appropriate benefits, 186–187
    anti-discrimination principle in responding to, 214
    child rights organizations, role of, 212–213
    collective reparations, 202–209
        challenges to participation, 207–209
        creative approaches, 206–207
        generally, 202–206
        girls' and boys' clubs, 206–207
    deaths, 166
    defining children
        challenges in, 184
        generally, 165
        problems with perception of, 213
    dependents, as, 184–185
    educational services for, 196–198
    enumeration of crimes, 169–170
    exclusion from reparations, 187–189
    forced recruitment of, 188
    gendered analysis of, 169–173
    gender-just reparations for, 174–175
    gender-specific violence, 167–168
    generally, 162–165
    health services for
    impossibility of full restoration, 211–212
    memorialization, 201–202, 210
    mental health services for, 199–201
    monetary compensation, 190–194
        amount of, 190–191
        distribution of, 193–194
        eligibility for, 191–192
        financial management skills, 192–193, 194
        importance of, 194
        limitations on, 202
    multiple harm requirement for benefits, 187
    nation-by-nation analysis, 176–184
        tables, 178–185
    nonmonetary services, 195–199
    outreach to, 189, 213–214
    psychological rehabilitation, 199–201
    reparations
        age and time limitations, 185–186
        age-appropriate benefits, 186–187
        collective reparations, 202–209
        exclusion from, 187–189
        gender-just reparations, 174–175
        generally, 173–174, 189, 214
        monetary compensation, 190–194
        multiple harm requirement, 187
        nonmonetary services, 195–199
        psychological rehabilitation, 199–201
        restitution of property, 194–195
        symbolic reparations, 209–211
        tables, 178–185
    restitution of property, 194–195
    secondary harms, 167
    secondary victims, as, 184–185
    sexual and reproductive violence, 171
    statistics, 166
    symbolic reparations, 209–211
        apologies, 209–210
        combination with monetary compensation, 209
        education and, 211
        generally, 209

memorialization, 201–202, 210
public gestures, 210
traditional forms, 210–211
targeting of, 212
women's organizations, role of, 212–213
Chile
apologies in, 353–354
children as victims in
analysis of reparations, 177, 179
monetary compensation, 190–191
outreach to, 189
psychological rehabilitation, 200
reparations, 186
Commission on Political Imprisonment and Torture, 189, 262–263, 271
defining beneficiaries in, 89–90
embezzlement in, 299–300
Ethical Commission against Torture, 262–263
evolution of reparations in, 399
families as victims in
children as beneficiaries, 279–280
defining beneficiaries, 271
defining victims, 267–268
distribution of reparations, 283–284
non-monetary services for, 285
parents as beneficiaries, 281
reparations, 262–263
siblings as beneficiaries, 281
spouses, partners and companions as beneficiaries, 274–279
surviving victims *versus* non-surviving victims, 289
monetary compensation in, 107–108, 291–292
National Truth and Reconciliation Commission, 262–263
rehabilitation and reintegration in, 110–111
symbolic reparations in, 325, 327–328
transitional justice in, 381–382
Valech Commission, 285
Citizenship, right to, 154–155
Cock, Jacklyn, 337–338, 340
Cockburn, Cynthia, 28–29, 33–34, 338–339
Coherence of reparations, 14–15
Coleman, Jules, 302
Collective reparations
children, for, 202–209
challenges to participation, 207–209
creative approaches, 206–207
generally, 202–206
girls' and boys' clubs, 206–207
continuum of violence and, 391–393

democracy and, 399–402
democratic state-building and, 394
equality and, 387
extraordinary violence and, 392–393
forms of, 394–395
gender and, 388–393
generally, 96–97, 381–385
geographical focus, 385
group-based harm and, 385–388
individual reparations and
connection with, 395
preservation of, 395–396
institutional reforms, 394
legal reforms, 394
membership in group, focus on, 385
modality of distribution, as, 385
monetary compensation, 396–397
public goods, as, 385
redress of harm through, 394
rehabilitation, 397–398
restitution, 396
satisfaction, 397–398
sexual and reproductive violence, for, 396–397
transformative dimension of, 398–399
Colombia
abortion laws in, 157
Commission on Reparations and Reconciliation, 63–64
focus on women, 76–77
sexuality and violence in, 86–87
"Comfort women," 13–14, 64–65, 139–140, 344–345, 369–373
Common elements of reparations, 71–72
Communities as victims, 95–96
Compensation. *See* Monetary compensation
Complexity of reparations, 13–14
Congo. *See* Democratic Republic of Congo
Continuum of violence
collective reparations and, 391–393
destruction of normal life order, 29–31
generally, 28–29
necessity of confronting, 32–33
predictive value of, 31–32
sexual and reproductive violence and, 30–31
theoretical framework, 29
Contrition, 363
Convention on the Elimination of All Forms of Discrimination against Women, 83–84
Convention on the Rights of the Child (CRC), 165, 171–173, 196–197
Credit NGOs, 305–306

Crittenden, Ann, 320–321
Cultural engineering, violence as, 390–391
Curie, Marie, 343

Damages
 moral damages (*See* Moral damages)
 reparations as, 295
Darfur
 displacement in, 54–55
 sexual and reproductive violence in, 52–53
Davis, Jefferson, 349–351
de Greiff, Pablo
 children and, 174
 collective reparations and, 399–400
 reparations and, 69
 symbolic reparations and, 365
 taxonomy of, 11–12
 tort theory and, 292, 295, 296
Delano, Jane, 343
Democracy and reparations, 399–402
Democratic Republic of Congo
 household level, violence at, 332–333
 prosecution of violence in, 159–160
 rape laws in, 160–161
 sexual and reproductive violence in, 46
Denormalization of discrimination, 82–85
Dependents, 232
Destructive synergies, 20–21, 59
Díaz, Catalina, 9
Direct victims, 231–232
Disappearances, 233–235, 239–240, 242, 246–247, 248, 257–258
Displacement, 54–55, 80–81
Dowler, Lorraine, 334–335
Dual function of reparations, 382–383
Duggan, Colleen, 7–8
Duvalier family, 299–300

Earhart, Amelia, 343
East Timor. *See* Timor-Leste
Educational services
 children, for, 196–198
 families, for, 284–285
Egeland, Jan, 30–31
Emphasis on women, 4
Empowerment of men through violence, 25–26
Enabling women to speak truth
 normative violence, effect of, 74
 public campaigns, role of, 74–75
 truth and reconciliation commissions, role of, 76–77
 women's organizations, role of, 75–76
Engendering harm
 cultural definitions and, 97–98
 degree of harm, relevance of, 98–99
 gender bias, effect of, 100–101
 generally, 97
 type of harm, relevance of, 99–100
 widows and widowers, 98
Ethiopia
 embezzlement in, 299–300
European Court of Human Rights (ECHR)
 Article 2, 225–226
 Article 3, 232–239
 Article 13, 232–233, 235–237
 Article 41, 221–222
 burden of proof in, 288
 defining victims, 221
 disappearances, 233–235
 flexibility of reparations, 223
 generally, 217
 injured parties, family members as, 232–239
  monetary compensation, 238
  moral damages, 235
  next of kin, 287–288
 monetary compensation in
  generally, 288
  injured parties, family members as, 238
  successors, family members as, 226
 moral damages in
  injured parties, family members as, 235
  successors, family members as, 226–227
  tables, 235–237
 procedures for obtaining reparations, 221–222
 restitutio in integrum principle, 222–223
 successors, family members as, 225–228
  distribution of reparations, 227–228
  monetary compensation, 226
  moral damages, 226–227
  torture, 238–239
Exploitation, violence as, 390
Extrajudicial killings, 242–243, 247–248
Extraordinary violence against women, 392–393

Families as victims
 administrative reparations, 288–290
 benefits tailored to needs of, 271–274
 children as beneficiaries, 279–280
 defining beneficiaries, 269–271
 defining victims, 215–216, 268
 disappearances and, 233–235, 248
 distribution of reparations, 282–284
 ECHR, reparations in
  injured parties, family members as, 232–239

successors, family members as, 225–228
educational services, 284–285
feasibility of reparations, 289–290
generally, 91–92, 215–219
health services, 284–285
IACHR, reparations in
  family treated as unit, 259–261
  injured parties, family members as, 239–261
  monetary compensation, 257–261
  moral damages, 245–257
  successors, family members as, 228–231
inheritance rights and, 94–95
injured parties, family members as
  ECHR, reparations in, 232–239
  IACHR, reparations in, 239–261
mental health services, 284–285
monetary compensation
  ECHR, in, 226, 238, 288
  IACHR, in, 257–258
moral damages
  ECHR, in, 226–227, 235
  IACHR, in, 245–248
nontraditional families, 94
parent and child, 95, 137
parents as beneficiaries, 280–281
regional human rights systems, reparations under, 219–220
scarcity of resources and, 93–94
secondary victims, 92–93
sexual and reproductive violence, 136–137, 244–245
siblings as beneficiaries, 281
spouses, partners and companions as beneficiaries, 274–279
successors, family members as
  ECHR, reparations in, 225–228
  IACHR, reparations in, 228–231
surviving victims *versus* non-surviving victims, 269–271, 289
torture and, 238–239
training programs, 284–285
Family life, right to, 154–155
Female subordination, violence as assertion of, 389–390
Feminism, 393–394
Feminizing dehumanization
  gender bias, effect of, 79, 81–82
  generally, 78
  sexual and reproductive violence
    inclusion in reparations considerations, 78–79
    overshadowing of other forms of violence, 80–81
    stigmatization from, 80
Fenster, Tovi, 376–377
Finality of reparations, 15
Fischer, Braam, 342–343
Foeken, Ingrid, 45
Forced abortion. *See* Sexual and reproductive violence
Forced disappearances, 233–235, 239–240, 242, 246–247, 248, 257–258
Forced displacement, 54–55, 80–81

Gagarin, Yuri, 359–360
Gandhi, Mahatma, 342–343
Gardam, Judith, 39–40
Gender-multiplied violence, 52–56
Gender-neutral reparations, 2–3
Gender-skewed violence, 51–52
Geneva Conventions, 121–122
Germany
  Federal Supplementary Law for the Compensation of Victims of National Socialist Persecution, 100–101
  transitional justice in, 381–382
Ghana
  apologies in, 353–354
  collective reparations in, 96–97
  memorialization in, 347
  National Reconciliation Commission, 144–145, 151, 329
  nonmonetary services in, 144–145
  symbolic reparations in, 151, 325, 327–328, 329–330
Gibson, Perla Siedle, 342–343
Goldblatt, Beth, 45, 53–54, 132–133, 286
Grameen Bank, 312
Grant, Ulysses S., 349–351
Green, Llezlie, 335–337
Growth in reparations, 1–2
Guarantee of nonrepetition of violence
  generally, 116–119
  reform of laws, 155–161
  sexual and reproductive violence, 155–161
Guatemala
  apologies in, 364–365
  caregivers, targeting of, 156–157
  children as victims in
    analysis of reparations, 177, 179
    exclusion from reparations, 187–189
    harm to, 163
    monetary compensation, 190–192
    outreach to, 189
  Commission for Historical Clarification, 265–266, 329–330
  engendering harm in, 98

Guatemala (*cont.*)
  families as victims in
    defining victims, 268
    disappearances and, 239–240, 242
    distribution of reparations, 282
    non-traditional families, 94, 231
    parents as beneficiaries, 95, 280
    reparations, 265–266
    secondary victims, 92–93
  forced displacement in, 80–81
  homicide in, 159
  inheritance laws in, 157–158
  Land Fund, 157–158
  monetary compensation in, 106, 139–140, 142, 291–292
  mothering, targeting of, 38–39
  National Commission for Reparations, 265–266
  National Reparation Program, 139–140, 147–149, 157–158, 187–189, 265–266, 282
  nonmonetary services in, 147–149
  punishment of gender transgression in, 36
  sexual and reproductive violence in, 36–38, 78, 133, 135–136, 138
  sexuality and violence in, 86–87
  symbolic reparations in, 151–152, 329–330
Guevara, "Che," 352–353
Guillerot, Julie, 140–141, 280–281

Haiti
  embezzlement in, 299–300
  monetary compensation in, 291–292
Hamber, Brandon, 10–11, 13–14, 397–398
Hashimoto, Ryutaro, 372
Health services
  children, for
  families, for, 284–285
  sexual and reproductive violence, for, 146
Henderson, Conway, 50–51
Heyzer, Noeleen, 159
Honwana, Alcinda, 147
Human Rights Watch, 18–19, 29, 45, 52–53, 160
Humphrey, Michael, 377–378

Importance of reparations, 23–24, 61–62
Indirect victims, 231–232
Individual *versus* societal aims of reparations, 67–72
Inheritance
  distribution of reparations and, 282–284
  reform of laws, 157–158
  right of, 94–95

Injured parties, family members as
  ECHR, in, 232–239
    monetary compensation, 238
    moral damages, 235
    next of kin, 287–288
  IACHR, in, 239–261
    extended family members, 240–241
    next of kin, 241–245, 287
Instrumentalism, 296–297
Integrity of reparations, 14–15
Inter-American Court of Human Rights (IACHR)
  arbitrary detention and inhuman treatment, 242–243, 249–252, 258–259
  Article 2.15, 223–224
  Article 5, 242–244, 246–247
  Article 8, 242–243, 246–247
  Article 8.1, 242–243
  Article 25, 242–243, 246–247
  Article 63.1, 224, 287
  burden of proof in, 288
  collective reparations in, 386–387
  complaints in, 223–224
  defining victims, 224
  dependents, family members as, 232
  disappearances, 239–240, 242–243, 248, 257–258
  extrajudicial killings, 242–243, 247–248
  families as victims
    family treated as unit, 259–261
    injured parties, family members as, 239–261
    monetary compensation, 257–261
    moral damages, 245–257
    successors, family members as, 228–231
  flexibility of reparations, 225
  generally, 217–218, 287
  injured parties, family members as, 239–261
    extended family members, 240–241
    next of kin, 241–245, 287
  monetary compensation in, 257–261
    arbitrary detention and inhuman treatment, for, 258–259
    disappearances of family members, for, 257–258
    generally, 288
    presumptions, 257–258
    tables, 258
  moral damages in, 245–257
    case-by-case basis, 252–254
    multiple victims, effect of, 248
    presumptions, 245–247
    tables, 248

type of crime, effect of, 247–248, 249–252
  variations in, 247–248, 249–252
restitutio in integrum principle, 224–225
Rules of Procedure, 223–224
successors, family members as, 228–231
  defining victims, 230
  distribution of reparations, 230–231
  moral damages, 229–230
  non-traditional families, 231
  presumptions, 228–229
symbolic reparations in, 254–257
torture, 243
International Center for Transitional Justice (ICTJ), 3, 32–33
International Criminal Court (ICC), 18–19, 121–122, 125, 169–170, 172–173, 183–184
International Criminal Tribunal for Rwanda (ICTR), 18–19, 183–184
International Criminal Tribunal for the Former Yugoslavia (ICTY), 18–19, 183–184
International Symposium on Sexual Violence in Conflict and Beyond, 121–122
Iraq
  microfinance in, 306–307
Israel
  memorialization in, 354–355
  women and work in, 376–377
Ivory Coast
  welfare analysis in, 320–321

Jackson, "Stonewall," 349–351
Jacobson, Ruth, 7–8
Jamaica
  welfare analysis in, 320–321
Japan
  apologies in, 369–371, 372–373
  Asian Women's Fund, 371–372
  "comfort women" and, 13–14, 64–65, 139–140, 344–345, 369–373
  monetary compensation in, 371–372
John Paul II, 373
Judicial reparations, 4–5

Kabbah, Ahmad Tejan, 329
Kenya
  welfare analysis in, 320–321
King, Jamesina, 39, 96–97, 154

Lean, Sharon, 366–367
Lee, Robert E., 349–351
Levinger, Esther, 353, 360–361
Lewis, Stephen, 52–53

Liberia
  children as victims in, 183
  rape laws in, 160
Lincoln, Abraham, 349–351
Lindsey, Andrew, 362
Liu Institute for Global Issues, 152
Loewen, James, 351
Louciades, Loukis, 235–237
Lovdal, Lynn, 359
Lusi, Lyn, 46
Luthuli, Albert, 342–343

Malawi
  memorialization in, 351–352
Male exchanges, 33–35
Male power, violence as assertion of, 390
Male solidarity through violence, 28, 33–34
Mandela, Nelson, 342–343
Marginalization of violence, 26–27
Marschall, Sabine, 337–338, 342–343, 361–362, 365–367
Masculinity contests, 27–28
Material reparations. *See* Monetary compensation
Maury, Matthew Fontaine, 349–351
Mazurana, Dyan, 8–9, 13–14, 129–130, 137, 142–143, 153
Médecins Sans Frontières, 146
Meintjes, Sheila, 45, 53–54
Memorialization
  design considerations, 360–362
  effect of, 210
  embodying individual meaning in, 358–364
  gender differences in, 358–364
  generally, 201–202
  individual *versus* collective representation, 346–354
  "living" *versus* "dead" memorialization, 358–360
  use of space, 362–363
  women and, 341–343
Men, violence against, 57–58, 127–128
Mengistu Meriam, Haile, 299–300
Mental health services
  children, for, 199–201
  families, for, 284–285
Microcredit, 303–304, 310–311
Microfinance
  advantages over transfer payments, 307–311
  credit NGOs, 305–306
  defined, 303–304
  expansion of credit, possibility of, 308–309
  formal institutions, 305

Microfinance (cont.)
  gender and
    generally, 312–313
    lack of control over money, addressing, 313–316
    shareholding, 316–318
    welfare analysis, 318–322
  generally, 303
  global enthusiasm for, 310
  informal institutions, 305
  microcredit distinguished, 303–304
  new institutions, 306–307
  partnership with existing institutions, 306
  security of, 308
  semiformal institutions, 305
  services, access to, 309
  shareholding
    gender and, 316–318
    generally, 304–305
    pooling of capital, 307
  social effects of, 309–310
  welfare analysis, 318–322
Monetary compensation
  avoiding discrimination in, 105–106
  benefits of, 296–297
  "blood money," 141–142, 296
  children, for (See Children as victims)
  collective reparations, 396–397
  damages, as, 296
  distribution of, 107–108
  ECHR, in
    generally, 288
    injured parties, family members as, 238
    successors, family members as, 226
  economic dimension of violence, 108–109
  engendering of compensation, 104
  families, for
    ECHR, in, 226, 238, 288
    IACHR, in, 257–258
  forms of, 103–104
  generally, 322–323
  IACHR, in, 257–261
    arbitrary detention and inhuman treatment, for, 258–259
    disappearances of family members, for, 257–258
    generally, 288
    presumptions, 257–258
    tables, 258
  justice and, 294–297
  microfinance (See Microfinance)
  moral damages (See Moral damages)
  necessity of, 296
  obstacles to, 106–107
  property or economic rights versus other rights, 104–105
  purposes, 103
  recognition of violations and, 297–300
  restitution
    children, for, 194–195
    collective reparations, 396
    sexual and reproductive violence, for, 138–143
  shortcomings of, 296
Moral damages
  ECHR, in
    injured parties, family members as, 235
    successors, family members as, 226–227
    tables, 235–237
  families, for
    ECHR, in, 226–227, 235
    IACHR, in, 245–248
  IACHR, in, 245–257
    case-by-case basis, 252–254
    multiple victims, effect of, 248
    presumptions, 245–247
    tables, 248
    type of crime, effect of, 247–248, 249–252
    variations in, 247–248, 249–252
Morocco
  Arbitration Commission, 17
  Equity and Truth Commission, 17, 63–64, 97–98, 105–106
  focus on women in, 76–77
  gendered nature of violence in, 50–51
  Independent Arbitration Instance, 105–106
  monetary compensation in, 105–106
Mothering, targeting of, 38–39
Mozambique
  memorialization in, 351–352
Multidimensional nature of violence, 59
Munificence of reparations, 15–16
Mutilation. See Sexual and reproductive violence

Naidu, Ereshnee, 351–352
Namibia
  memorialization in, 351–352
Nesiah, Vasuki, 104–105
Ni Aolain, Fionnuala, 216–217
Nightingale, Florence, 343
Nonmaterial reparations
  rehabilitation and reintegration (See Rehabilitation and reintegration)
  symbolic reparations (See Symbolic reparations)
Nonmonetary services

children, for, 195–199
educational services
  children, for, 196–198
  families, for, 284–285
health services
  children, for
  families, for, 284–285
  sexual and reproductive violence, for, 146
mental health services
  children, for, 199–201
  families, for, 284–285
sexual and reproductive violence, for
  health services, 146
  non-monetary services, 143–149
  psychosocial services, 146–149
Northern Ireland
  Healing Through Remembering, 354–355
  Widows Against Violence, 334
Norwegian Nobel Committee, 293
Nyerere, Julius, 352–353

Oakley, Annie, 343
Obuchi, Keizo, 372
Official apologies. *See* Apologies
Openness of reparations, 16–17
Ostracism, 344, 368–369
Overview, 5–11

Palmary, Ingrid, 10–11, 13–14, 332–333, 397–398
Pankhurst, Emmaline, 343
Paris Principles, 188
Patriarchy, 314, 315–316
Paz y Paz Bailey, Claudia, 37–38, 106
Pecuniary compensation. *See* Monetary compensation
Peru
  Association Kuyanakuy, 366
  children as victims in
    analysis of reparations, 177, 179, 181
    consultation with, 176
    monetary compensation, 191
    non-monetary services, 196–197, 198–199
    outreach to, 189
    psychological rehabilitation, 200
    symbolic reparations, 211
  Comprehensive Reparations Plan, 264–265
  consultation with women, 355–356
  demands for reparations in, 375
  engendering harm in, 98
  families as victims in
    defining victims, 268
    distribution of reparations, 283–284
    nonmonetary services for, 285–286

  nontraditional families, 94
  parents as beneficiaries, 95, 280–281
  reparations, 264–265
  secondary victims, 92–93
  sexual and reproductive violence in, 244–245
  torture and, 243
  focus on women in, 76–77
  forced displacement in, 80–81
  monetary compensation in, 140–141, 142, 291–292
  non-monetary services in, 147–149
  public gestures in, 369
  punishment of gender transgression in, 36
  sexual and reproductive violence in, 78–79, 133, 137, 138
  sexuality and violence in, 86–87
  symbolic reparations in, 151–152, 329–330
  Truth and Reconciliation Commission, 140–141, 191, 196–197, 198–199, 264–265, 285–286, 289
  victims' groups in, 334
Peterson, V. Spike, 35–36
Pinochet, Augusto, 299–300, 353–354, 363–364
Pocahontas, 343
Polygamy, 94, 231
Post-traumatic stress disorder, 147
Preexisting structures of subordination, attempts at subverting, 101–103
Privilege and violence, 331–339
Project Counseling Services (PCS), 147–149
Property
  reform of laws, 157–158
  women and, 39–41
Prosecution of violence, 158–160
Prostitution. *See* Sexual and reproductive violence
Psychosocial rehabilitation, 112–113
Public gestures, 115–116, 210, 369
Public goods, 385
Punishment of gender transgression, 35–36
Punitive damages. *See* Moral damages

Questions regarding violence, 21–22

Rape. *See* Sexual and reproductive violence
Recognition of violations
  basic principles, 70–71
  generally, 119–120
  monetary compensation, 297–300
  state responsibility, acknowledgment of
    generally, 85
    identification of perpetrators, 86–87

Recognition of violations (*cont.*)
  location of violence, relevance of, 88
  means of avoiding, 86
  politicization of violence, 87–88
  symbolic reparations (*See* Symbolic reparations)
  tort theory and, 297–300
  victims, 72–74, 88–91
Regional human rights systems, 219–220
Rehabilitation and reintegration
  advantages over monetary compensation, 109–110
  caregiver role, relevance of, 111–112
  children, psychological rehabilitation, 199–201
  collective reparations, 397–398
  combination with monetary compensation, 110–111
  distribution of, 112
  economic opportunity, creating, 113
  engendering rehabilitation, 109
  gender bias, effect of, 111
  non-monetary services and, 110–111
  psychosocial rehabilitation, 112–113
Reintegration. *See* Rehabilitation and reintegration
Reluctance to acknowledge violence, 56–57
Reparations. *See specific topic*
Reproductive violence. *See* Sexual and reproductive violence
Reputation, right to, 154–155
Restatement (Second) of Torts, 295
Restitutio in integrum principle, 222–223, 224–225
Restitution
  children, for, 194–195
  collective reparations, 396
Roht-Arriaza, Naomi, 324–325, 364–365
Rombouts, Heidy, 41–42
Rome Statute, 121–122, 125, 172–173
Rosenberg, Maurice, 298
Rosett, Arthur, 372–373
Rubio-Marín, Ruth
  children and, 170–171, 212–213
  generally, 6–7, 9
  reparations and, 61–62
  sexual and reproductive violence and, 43
  symbolic reparations and, 326–327, 331, 333–334, 347–348, 354, 357
Runyan, Anne Sisson, 35–36
Rwanda
  Assistance Fund for Genocide Survivors, 133–134, 335–337
  Association of Widows of the Genocide, 334
  caregivers, targeting of, 156–157
  children as victims in, 177, 179
  gacaca, 133–134, 135–136
  household level, violence at, 332–333
  Hutus in, 335–337
  ICTR, 18–19, 183–184
  inheritance laws in, 157–158
  inheritance rights in, 39–40
  memorialization in, 349
  monetary compensation in, 291–292
  mothering, targeting of, 38–39
  rehabilitation and reintegration in, 110–111
  sexual and reproductive violence in, 36–37, 45, 127, 133–134, 135–136, 344
  social capital, women as, 41–42
  Tutsis in, 335–337
  widows in, 53–54
Ryan, Louise, 335

Same-sex marriage, 94
Samson, Deborah, 343
Sandoval, Clara, 9
Schaap, Andrew, 400
Scope of reparations, 12
Scope of violence, 19–20
Scott, Winfield, 351
Secondary victims
  children as, 184–185
  families as, 92–93
  generally, 60–61
  sexual and reproductive violence, 136–137
Second generation reparations programs, 268, 269
Seibel, Hans Dieter, 303–305, 310–311
Serbia
  Association of Wartime Camp Inmates, 368–369
Services. *See* Nonmonetary services
Sexual and reproductive violence
  administrative reparations, 132
  armed conflict, in, 343–345
  categorization of, 50–51
  children, against, 171
  collective reparations for, 396–397
  defined, 125
  destruction of normal life order, 30–31
  emotional harm from, 127–129
  families as victims, 136–137, 244–245
  forms of, 132–136
    generally, 125–126, 130–131
    specificity, 134–136
  generally, 121–124
  guarantee of non-repetition, 155–161
  health services, 146

inclusion in reparations considerations, 64–66, 78–79
material harm from, 129–130
men, against, 57–58, 127–128
monetary compensation, 138–143
nonmonetary services, 143–149
ostracism for, 344, 368–369
overshadowing of other forms of violence, 60, 80–81, 122–123
persons included and excluded as victims, 136–138
physical harm from, 126–127
psychosocial services, 146–149
reparations
  generally, 138
  health services, 146
  monetary compensation, 138–143
  nonmonetary services, 143–149
  psychosocial services, 146–149
  symbolic reparations, 149–153
secondary victims, 136–137
selected experiences, 131–132
shame and exclusion due to, 128–129
significance of, 36–38
stigmatization due to, 80, 128–129, 364–365
symbolic reparations, 149–153
Sexuality and violence, 335–337
Shame and exclusion
  generally, 42–44
  sexual and reproductive violence, due to, 128–129
Shanken, Andrew, 358–359
Shareholding
  gender and, 316–318
  generally, 304–305
  pooling of capital, 307
Sierra Leone
  children as victims in
    analysis of reparations, 176–177, 179, 181–184
    focus on, 178–179
    generally, 213
    monetary compensation, 193–194
    outreach to, 189
    psychological rehabilitation, 200
  collective reparations in, 96–97
  economic harm in, 154
  engendering harm in, 98–99
  families as victims in
    benefits tailored to needs of, 271–274
    defining beneficiaries, 271
    defining victims, 268
    nonmonetary services for, 286
    reparations, 266–267
  focus on women in, 76–77
  memorialization in, 349, 358–359
  monetary compensation in, 291–292
  National Commission for Social Action, 266–267
  nonmonetary services in, 145, 146
  prioritizing reparations in, 15–16
  sexual and reproductive violence in, 29, 36–37, 78, 127, 133, 134–135, 136–137, 344–345, 368
  slavery in, 39
  Special Court for Sierra Leone, 183–184
  symbolic reparations in, 114–115, 151, 329
  Truth and Reconciliation Commission, 90, 133, 146, 266–267, 271, 289
  women's hearings in, 346–347
Sisulu, Albertina, 331–332
Slavery. *See* Sexual and reproductive violence
Social capital, women as, 41–42
Social services. *See* Nonmonetary services
Soh, C. Sarah, 372
South Africa
  Afrikaner Memorial to Women, 337–338, 341–342
  Anglo-Boer War, 337–338, 341–342
  boycotts regarding, 332–333
  children as victims in
    analysis of reparations, 177, 179, 181
    consultation with, 176
    generally, 164
    monetary compensation, 190–191, 192–193
    psychological rehabilitation, 200
    reparations, 185–186
  Commission for Gender Equality, 115–116
  Committee on Reparations and Rehabilitation, 264
  disengagement of women from armed conflict in, 340
  downplaying of women as victims in, 331–332
  families as victims in
    children as beneficiaries, 279
    defining beneficiaries, 269–271
    defining victims, 268
    distribution of reparations, 282
    nonmonetary services for, 286
    nontraditional families, 94
    parents as beneficiaries, 280
    reparations, 264
    secondary victims, 92–93
  focus on women in, 76–77
  Freedom Park, 352–353

South Africa (cont.)
  Horse Memorial, 355
  Khulumani Victims Support Group, 334
  Mamelodi Mothers of the Disappeared, 334
  memorialization in, 351–352, 354–355
  Mixed Marriages Act, 335
  Mkhonto we Sizwe, 334–335
  monetary compensation in, 106–108, 141–143, 291–292
  National Women's Monument, 347
  public attitudes toward women's issues, 344–345
  punishment of gender transgression in, 36
  Reparation and Rehabilitation Committee, 271
  sexual and reproductive violence in, 45, 132–133, 135–136, 137–138
  symbolic reparations in, 115–116, 329–330
  transitional justice in, 381–382
  Truth and Reconciliation Commission, 18–19, 132–133, 164, 264, 271, 331–332, 352–353
  Urgent Interim Reparations, 264
  widows in, 53–54
  Women's Day, 340–341
  women's hearings in, 346–347
  Women's Monument, 342–343, 355, 360–362, 365–366
Spielmann, Dean, 235–237
Sri Lanka
  reparations in, 104–105
SRV. *See* Sexual and reproductive violence
State responsibility, acknowledgment of
  generally, 85
  identification of perpetrators, 86–87
  location of violence, relevance of, 88
  means of avoiding, 86
  politicization of violence, 87–88
Stigmatization
  sexual and reproductive violence, due to, 80, 128–129, 364–365
Stuart, J.E.B., 349–351
Successors, family members as
  ECHR, in, 225–228
    distribution of reparations, 227–228
    monetary compensation, 226
    moral damages, 226–227
  IACHR, in, 228–231
    defining victims, 230
    distribution of reparations, 230–231
    moral damages, 229–230
    nontraditional families, 231
    presumptions, 228–229
Sudan (Darfur)
  displacement in, 54–55
  sexual and reproductive violence in, 52–53
Summers, Carol, 335
Suriname
  families as victims in, 231
Symbolic reparations
  agency of women, representing, 339–345
  apologies (*See* Apologies)
  children, for (*See* Children as victims)
  consultation with women, 354–356
  contrition, 363
  discourse regarding, 367–374
  embodying individual meaning in, 358–364
  empowering nature of, 116
  family role of women and, 332–334
  gender differences in, 358–364
  gendered limitations, 331
  generally, 114, 324–327, 376–378
  IACHR, in, 254–257
  importance of, 325–326
  increasing gendered impact of, 356–358
  individual *versus* collective representation, 346–354
  limitations of, 325
  memorialization (*See* Memorialization)
  political and social context, 374–376
  prioritizing, 325
  process regarding, 365–367
  psychological effects of, 326
  public gestures, 115–116, 210, 369
  recommendations regarding, 378–380
  reconnecting victims with society and state, 364–365
  sexual and reproductive violence, for, 149–153
  variations in, 327–331
  victims' groups, role of, 334–335
Symbolism of gender, 35–36
Syria
  microfinance in, 306–307

Tambo, Oliver, 342–343, 352–353
Testimonial position of women, insecurity of, 45–46
Thernstrom, Melanie, 43–44
Timor-Leste
  children as victims in
    analysis of reparations, 177, 179, 181–183
    outreach to, 189
    reparations, 186
    sexual and reproductive violence in, 44
  Commission for Reception, Truth and Reconciliation, 13, 63–64, 90, 106–107, 108–109, 187

consultation with women, 355–356
emphasis on gender in, 13
engendering harm in, 98–99
focus on women in, 76–77
guarantee of nonrepetition of violence in, 117–118
memorialization in, 358–359
monetary compensation in, 106–107, 108–109, 139–140
nonmonetary services in, 143–144, 145
prioritizing reparations in, 15–16
punishment of gender transgression in, 36
rehabilitation and reintegration in, 112
sexual and reproductive violence in, 44, 78, 133, 134–135, 136–138
symbolic reparations in, 151, 329
Urgent Reparations Fund, 151
Tort theory
   benefits of monetary compensation, 296–297
   damages, reparations as, 295
   freedom, enhancing, 300–301, 302–303
   generally, 291–293, 322–323
   justice and, 294–297
   legal perspective, 294
   microfinance (See Microfinance)
   necessity of monetary compensation, 296
   recognition of violations and, 297–300
   security, enhancing, 300–302
   shortcomings of monetary compensation, 296
   vicarious liability, 298–299
Torture, 238–239, 243
Transformative potential of reparations, 17, 153, 384, 398–399
Trindade, Cançado, 246–247
Tripp, Aili Mari, 332–333
Turkey
   families as victims in, 233–235
   forced displacement in, 80–81
   unveiling of women in, 35
Turshen, Meredith, 40–41, 53–54, 376–377

Uganda
   sexual and reproductive violence in, 43–44
   symbolic reparations in, 152
UNICEF, 39
United Kingdom
   memorialization in, 341–342, 343, 348–349
United Nations

Basic Principles on Reparations, 1–2, 116–117, 123–124, 153, 199, 219–220, 231–232, 286–287, 381–382
Convention for the Protection of All Persons from Enforced Disappearances, 219–220, 286–287
Declaration of Basic Principles of Justice for Victims of Crime and Abuse of Power, 219–220
High Commissioner for Human Rights, 1–2, 294–295
Human Rights Commission, 67–68
Millennium Task Force, 313–314
Peace Building Fund, 266–267
Population Fund, 146
Security Council Resolution 1325, 1, 20–21, 63–64
Sub-Commission on the Promotion and Protection of Human Rights, 67–68
United States
   exclusion in, 399
   Korean War Memorial, 348–351, 355
   memorialization in, 343, 349–351
   Vietnam War Memorial, 349–351, 355
   Vietnam Women's Memorial, 347–348
   Washington Memorial, 359–360
   welfare analysis in, 320–321

Victims. See also specific reparations
   caregivers as
      children, harm to, 170
      mothering, targeting of, 38–39
      rehabilitation and reintegration, relevance to, 111–112
   children as (See Children as victims)
   collective reparations and, 96–97
   communities as, 95–96
   direct victims, 231–232
   public campaigns, role of, 74–75
   truth and reconciliation commissions, role of, 76–77
   women's organizations, role of, 75–76
   cultural definitions and, 97–98
   degree of harm, relevance of, 98–99
   gender bias, effect of, 100–101
   generally, 97
   type of harm, relevance of, 99–100
   widows and widowers, 98
   families as (See Families as victims)
   feminizing dehumanization
      gender bias, effect of, 79, 81–82
      generally, 78

Victims (*cont.*)
  sexual and reproductive
    violence; inclusion in reparations
    considerations, 78–79; overshadowing
    of other forms of violence,
    80–81; stigmatization from, 80
  indirect victims (*See* secondary victims)
    231–232
  role of victims' groups in reparations,
    334–335
  secondary victims (*See* indirect victims)
    children as, 184–185
    families as, 92–93
    generally, 60–61
    sexual and reproductive violence,
    136–137
Violence. *See specific topic*
Vlok, Adriaan, 334, 363

Wagatsuma, Hiroshi, 372–373
Walker, Margaret
  children and, 168, 170–171, 176, 184
  collective reparations and, 391–392
  generally, 5–6, 11
  sexual and reproductive violence and,
    143–144, 160
Warner, Marina, 347–348
Waylen, Georgina, 332–333
Welfare analysis, 318–322
Widows, 53–54
World Bank, 312–314
World War II, 156–157

Yugoslavia
  ICTY, 18–19, 183–184
  sexual and reproductive violence in, 45,
    127
Yunus, Muhammad, 312
Yuval-Davis, Nira, 35, 335

Zambia
  women and work in, 313–314
Zane, Elizabeth, 343
Ziesing, Michael, 372–373
Zimbabwe
  memorialization in, 351–352